INTERCULTURAL BUSINESS COMMUNICATION

Fourth
Edition

INTERCULTURAL
BUSINESS
COMMUNICATION

Lillian H. Chaney
The University of Memphis

Jeanette S. Martin
The University of Mississippi

PEARSON
Prentice
Hall

UPPER SADDLE RIVER, NEW JERSEY 07458

Library of Congress Cataloging-in-Publication Data

Chaney, Lillian H.
   Intercultural business communication / Lillian H. Chaney, Jeanette S.
Martin. —4th ed.
      p. cm.
   Includes bibliographical references and index.
   1. Business etiquette. 2. Corporate culture. 3. Business communication.
4. Intercultural communication.
I. Martin, Jeanette S. II. Title.
HF5389.C47 2005
395.5'2—dc22   2005026163

VP/Editorial Director: Jeff Shelstad
Senior Acquisitions Editor: Jennifer Simon
Assistant Editor: Rich Gomes
Editorial Assistant: Denise Vaughn
Marketing Manager: Anne Howard
Associate Director: Judy Leale
Managing Editor: Renata Butera
Production Editor: Suzanne Grappi
Permissions Coordinator: Charles Morris
Manufacturing Buyer: Indira Gutierrez
Production Manager, Manufacturing: Arnold Vila
Cover Design Manager: Jayne Conte
Composition/Full-Service Project Management: Interactive Composition Corporation
Printer/Binder: Courier Stoughton
Typeface: Times Ten Roman 10/12

Credits and acknowledgments borrowed from other sources and reproduced, with permission, in this textbook
appear on appropriate pages within text.

Pearson Education, LTD.   Pearson Education Australia PTY, Limited
Pearson Education Singapore, Pte. Ltd.   Pearson Education North Asia Ltd
Pearson Education, Canada, Ltd   Pearson Educación de Mexico, S.A. de C.V.
Pearson Education—Japan   Pearson Education Malaysia, Pte. Ltd

10 9 8 7 6 5 4 3 2
ISBN 0-13-186009-7

Contents

Foreword

With the globalization of the world economy, it is imperative that managers, both present and future, be sensitive to differences in intercultural communication. Professors Lillian H. Chaney and Jeanette S. Martin have done an admirable job in addressing a broad range of issues and skills that are crucial to effective intercultural encounters. In the book, the most significant issues pertaining to cross-cultural interaction are covered: culture, intercultural (both verbal and nonverbal) communication, and cultural shock. In addition, the book contains practical guidelines and information on how to conduct negotiations across countries and write business letters in different societies as well as other general dos and don'ts in international business. College students and businesspeople new to the international business scene can certainly benefit from such practical advice.

This book can also sensitize readers to the dynamics of international diversity. With the increasing multiethnic composition of the North American labor force and the growing participation of women in the professional and managerial ranks of organizations, it is equally important that students, the managers of the future, be attuned to the issues associated with managing and valuing diversity within a domestic context. The book addresses the issues of gender differences and how these impact communication styles and patterns.

While recognizing the significant differences that can exist across cultures and subcultures, it is important to acknowledge the existence of individual differences within any given society. Just as it is naive to assume that all cultures are similar, it is equally fallacious to fall into the trap of "cultural stereotyping." To quote Lao Tzu, the famous Chinese philosopher who is usually considered to be the spiritual leader of Taoism, "The one becomes the many." Although people in a given society may share certain common values and characteristics, there can be important differences in how these are applied and exhibited in specific situations. In addition, these intranational differences can be exacerbated by religious influences, exposure to Western philosophies and ideas through education at universities abroad, overseas travel, and social and business contacts with peoples from other cultures. Furthermore, it is significant to note that cultural values and norms do evolve over time, however slowly. Some of the cultural characteristics alluded to in this book may be changing or have changed. A cursory review of the dramatic upheavals that have taken and are still taking place in virtually all aspects of societal and organizational functionings in many socialist and former socialist countries will attest to the fact that culture is not static; rather, it evolves over time.

Judicious application of the principles and techniques introduced in this book will enable readers to develop a proficiency in managing diversity, both cross-nationally and internationally.

Rosalie L. Tung
The Ming and Stella Wong Professor
of International Business
Simon Fraser University
Canada

Preface

PURPOSE

With the increasing number of intercultural corporations and the internationalization of the economy, intercultural business communication continues to become more important. Government leaders, educators, and businesspersons agree that internationalizing the curriculum is important to maintaining the competitive position of the United States in the world economy. Because all international activity involves communication, students need knowledge of intercultural business communication to prepare them for upward mobility and promotion in tomorrow's culturally diverse domestic and international environments.

CONTENTS

Topics selected for *Intercultural Business Communication* were those considered important or essential by three Delphi panels of experts: international employees of multinational corporations, college professors who teach intercultural communication, and members of the Academy of International Business.* We know of no other book on intercultural communication that has used research involving experts' perceptions of the importance of topics to be covered as a basis of content selection.

The topics include

- The nature of intercultural communication
- Universal systems
- Contrasting cultural values
- Cultural shock
- Language
- Oral and nonverbal communication patterns
- Written communication patterns
- Global etiquette
- Business and social customs
- Intercultural negotiation process
- Intercultural negotiation components
- Laws affecting international business and travel

---

*Martin, J. S. (1991). *Experts' Consensus Concerning the Content for an Intercultural Business Communication Course.* Unpublished doctoral dissertation, The University of Memphis. Major professor, L. H. Chaney.

Each chapter contains objectives, terms, questions and cases for discussion, and activities. Also provided are exercises to be used for self-evaluation of material covered and illustrations to depict various aspects of the content.

Both authors have traveled or worked in a number of countries or multinational corporations and, therefore, have firsthand knowledge of many of the topics covered.

CHANGES TO THE FOURTH EDITION OF THIS BOOK INCLUDE

- Updated all information presented in the third edition to reflect changes that have taken place in the various countries identified. More recent editions of books cited in the third edition were used as well as more recent journal articles.
- Made extensive revisions to Chapters 10 and 11 on intercultural negotiation; made changes in Chapter 12 to update laws and trade agreements.
- Expanded country-specific information in all chapters so that students have a broader knowledge of life in specific cultures. Countries highlighted are those with which the United States conducts the majority of its international trade.
- Added cases to selected chapters to provide additional topics for class discussion.
- Revised the Instructor's Manual, Test Bank, and PowerPoint slides as needed to include content changes.

PROPOSED USE

Intercultural Business Communication is designed to be used as a text for a college-level course in intercultural business communication or to augment courses in which intercultural communication is a major component.

About the Authors

Lillian H. Chaney is a Professor of Management and Distinguished Professor of Office Management at The University of Memphis. She received both the M.S. and the Ed.D. from the University of Tennessee. She is coauthor of textbooks on business communication and office management and has published numerous articles on these topics in professional journals. Dr. Chaney teaches graduate and undergraduate courses in business communication, executive communication, and international business communication and negotiation. She has teaching experience at a South American university and has conducted training programs on communication, corporate etiquette, and business ethics for international corporations, educational institutions, and government agencies.

Jeanette S. Martin is an Associate Professor at the University of Mississippi. She received her B.A. from Michigan State University, M.B.A. from the University of Chicago, and her Ed.D. from The University of Memphis. She has considerable corporate experience in both U.S. multinational corporations and foreign multinational corporations. Dr. Martin has published several articles involving intercultural business communication, education, and management information systems. Her current research and consulting interests include NAFTA and the effects intercultural communication has on such international agreements, as well as emotional intelligence and how it is affected by culture.

1

THE NATURE OF INTERCULTURAL COMMUNICATION

Objectives

Upon completion of this chapter, you will

- understand such terms as intercultural, international, intracultural, multicultural, and ethnocentric.

- recognize how communication barriers affect intercultural communication.

- understand the differences between norms, rules, roles, and networks.

- distinguish between subcultures and subgroups.

- understand the concept of business globalization.

- differentiate between ethnocentric, polycentric, regiocentric, and geocentric management orientations.

The number of North Americans who work for foreign employers and the number of foreign companies who have built plants in the United States is increasing. Evidence that the world is becoming more cosmopolitan can be seen in the number of international businesses, such as Coca-Cola, McDonald's, Sony, and Honda, which are common around the world. The new economic bonanza is apparent in the universal appreciation of food such as sushi, fashion such as jeans, and music such as U.S. jazz and rock. Because of the global boom, more and more business will involve international activities, which require the ability to communicate across cultures.

Because communication is an element of culture, it has often been said that communication and culture are inseparable. As Alfred G. Smith (1966) wrote in his preface to *Communication and Culture,* "Culture is a code we learn and share, and learning and sharing require communication. Communication requires coding and symbols that must be learned and shared. Godwin C. Chu (1977) observed that every cultural pattern and every single act of social behavior involves communication. To be understood, the two must be studied together. Culture cannot be known with a study of communication, and communication can only be understood with an understanding of the culture it supports." (Jandt, 2000, p. 22)

To gain a better understanding of the field of intercultural communication, knowledge of frequently used terms is important. Such terms as intercultural, international, and multicultural are often used interchangeably; however, certain distinctions should be made.

Edward T. Hall first used the term intercultural communication in 1959. Hall was one of the first researchers to differentiate cultures on the basis of how communications are sent and received. Hall defined **intercultural communication** as communication between persons of different cultures.

Intercultural business communication is a relatively new term in the business world and is defined as communication within and between businesses that involves people from more than one culture. Although we generally think of the United States as one culture, a great deal of cultural diversity exists. For example, more than 35% of residents of New York City are foreign born, Miami is almost three-fourths Latin American, and San Francisco is one-third Asian. In fact, African Americans, Asians, and Latin Americans make up 30% of the U.S. population. An increase in the Asian and Latin American populations is expected during the next decade. Many U.S. citizens communicate interculturally almost daily because communication occurs between people of different cultural backgrounds (U.S. Census Bureau, 2003).

Susumu Yoshida, Managing Director of Sumitomo Chemical Asia Pte Ltd., in his address to a group of international business executives in Kyoto, Japan, June 19, 2002, said: "We are on the threshold of globalization. The world economy is 'borderless' and markets are becoming essentially one. Corporations are looking at the free flow of goods and services, capital, and human resources, as well as information, as the pathway to growth. Hence, the corporate strategy of going global is no longer a choice but rather a 'must' for survival. . . . A lack of effective intercultural communication skills often causes misunderstandings. This leads to irritation and even distrust between the parties concerned. More often than not, problems arise from differences in communication styles." (2002, pp. 708, 710)

As contact occurs between cultures, diffusion takes place. **Diffusion** is the process by which the two cultures learn and adapt materials and adopt practices from each other. This practice is exemplified by how Columbus joined the Old and New Worlds. The Old World gave the New World horses, cows, sheep, chickens, honeybees, coffee, wheat, cabbage, lettuce, bananas, olives, tulips, and daisies. The New World gave the Old World turkeys, sugarcane, corn, sweet potatoes, tomatoes, pumpkins, pineapples, petunias, poinsettias, and daily baths (Jandt, 2000).

With the increased globalization of the economy and interaction of different cultures, the concept of a world culture has emerged. A **world culture** is the idea that as traditional barriers among people of differing cultures break down, emphasizing the commonality of human needs, one culture will emerge, a new culture to which all people will adhere. So why study intercultural business communication? Because it addresses procedural, substantive, and informational global problems, intercultural business communication allows you to work on the procedural issues of country-to-country contacts, diplomacy, and legal contexts. You can then become involved with the substantive, cultural level and become sensitized to differences. You can also gather information to make decisions when you are in an intercultural environment (Rohrlich, 1998).

The United States continues to welcome a large number of immigrants each year and has been referred to as a melting-pot society. **Melting pot** means a sociocultural assimilation of people of differing backgrounds and nationalities; the term implies losing ethnic differences and forming one large society or **macroculture.** Although the idea of everyone's being the same may sound ideal, the problem with this concept is that many U.S. citizens want to maintain their ethnic-cultural heritage. Rather than being one melting-pot society, therefore, the reality is that many U.S. cities are made up of neighborhoods of people with a common heritage who strive to retain their original culture and language. In San Francisco, a visit to Chinatown with its signs in Chinese and people speaking Chinese verifies this reality. Many street signs in other U.S. cities, such as New York, Miami, or Honolulu, are in another language in addition to English. The result has not been the melding of various cultures into one cultural group as idealists believed would happen. Because cultures exist within cultures (**microcultures**), communication problems often result. In reality, the United States is a salad bowl of cultures rather than a melting pot. Although some choose assimilation, others choose separation. Thus, the assumption that America is a cultural melting pot, which assumes assimilation, is no longer valid (Differences, 1996).

Intracultural communication is defined as communication between and among members of the same culture. Generally, people who are of the same race, political persuasion, and religion or who share the same interests communicate intraculturally. Having the same beliefs, values, and constructs facilitates communication and defines a particular culture (Gudykunst & Ting-Toomey, 1988). However, because of distance, cultural differences may exist within a culture, such as differences in the pace of life and regional speech patterns between residents of New York City and Jackson, Mississippi. Distance is also a factor in the differences in the dialects of the people of other cultures, such as in northern and southern Japan.

The terms intercultural communication and international communication should not be used interchangeably. Intercultural communication, as stated previously, involves communication between people of different cultures. **International communication** takes place between nations and governments rather than individuals; it is formal and ritualized. The dialogue at the United Nations, for example, is international communication.

Because all international business activity involves communication, knowledge of intercultural communication and international business communication is important to prepare you to compete successfully in international environments. In fact, upward mobility and promotion in tomorrow's corporate world may depend on your knowledge of intercultural business communication.

GLOBALIZATION

Although globalization has come to the world, most of the world's businesses are not globalized. Business **globalization** is the capability of a corporation to take a product and market it in the entire civilized world. International firms have subsidiaries or components in other countries; however, control of the foreign operations is maintained at the home country headquarters. Multinational firms allow their foreign operations to exist as domestic organizations. Most firms are international, either sourcing, producing, or exporting. Many times, the product may also be partially or completely manufactured somewhere other than the United States. In the past, some U.S. corporations have been largely insulated from globalization because of a strong domestic market and an absence of foreign competitors. However, this trend is changing as foreign corporations enter the U.S. market.

The personnel of an organization must have a global mindset for the firm to succeed in the international marketplace. Laurent (1986), in a study of multinational corporations, found that successful multinational corporations do not submerge the individuality of different cultures completely in the corporate culture, that intercultural contact can promote a determination not to adjust to other cultures, and that new management theory and practice can be presented only to individuals who are culturally able and willing to accept it. Rhinesmith (1996) states, "The corporate culture contains the values, norms of behavior, systems, policies, and procedures through which the organization adapts to the complexity of the global arena" (p. 14). Successful corporations have found that the values, beliefs, and behaviors of the parent corporation do not need to be the beliefs, values, and behaviors of the offices in other cultures. Hofstede's (2004) study of IBM determined that managers had to adjust the corporate management philosophy to fit the beliefs, values, and behaviors of the country in which they were working. Companies with franchises abroad have had to make certain adjustments to accommodate the tastes and preferences of individual countries; for example, Tex-Mex cuisine is prepared kosher in Israel. According to Rhinesmith (1996), "Diversity—both domestic and international—will be the engine that drives the creative energy of the corporation of the twenty-first century. Successful global managers will be those who are able to manage this diversity for the innovative and competitive edge of their corporations" (p. 5). Evans, Doz, and Laurent (1990) state that the five elements critical to building a successful corporate culture are 1) a clear and simple mission statement, 2) the vision of the chief executive officer, 3) company-controlled management education, 4) project-oriented management training programs, and 5) emphasis on the processes of global corporate culture (p. 118).

> Lopez-Vasquez, director of multicultural affairs at the Oregon Health Sciences University and a consultant with IEC Enterprises, Decatur, Georgia, believes that well-meaning managers who become supervisors of Hispanic workers often make the mistake of attempting to adopt a "color-blind" approach. "The cultural disparities are obvious," he says.
>
> Lopez-Vasquez argues for what he calls "essential treatment" for Hispanic employees. "I suggest that companies recognize that today it's essential to take steps to recruit and retain Hispanics, because Hispanics in the United States represent a fast-growing market and because Central and South America are key areas for success in international markets," he says. (Staa, 1998, p. 8)

Although the United States depends on foreign economic opportunities, the multinational firms have had problems with U.S. citizens working in foreign assignments. The failures to adapt included differences in lifestyle, language, and business philosophy as well as problems with finances, government, cultural shock, housing, food, gender, and family. Ruch (1989) found that the ability to blend with the host culture and explain one's own culture is more important than product, price, or quality advantages. Although many of the people sent on foreign assignments know their U.S. market, they are unable to accept another culture on that culture's terms even for short periods.

CULTURE

Whereas communication is a process, **culture** is the structure through which the communication is formulated and interpreted. Culture deals with the way people live. When cultures interact, adaptation must take place for the cultures to communicate effectively. With intercultural business communication, being aware of each culture's symbols, how they are the same, and how they are different is important.

Dimensions of Culture

To communicate effectively in the intercultural business environment, knowing all the cultural factors that affect the situation is essential. The graphical representation of culture in Figure 1-1 has three primary dimensions—languages, physical, and psychological (Borden, 1991, p. 171).

The language, physical, and psychological dimensions of culture are interdependent. As we are born into a society, no one dimension is more important than the others. The individual dimensions develop in harmony with each other.

First, the language dimension is used to communicate with other people who have similar values and beliefs. Second, the physical dimension relates to the physical reality of our environment and the cultural activities of the people. The physical dimension is measured objectively. Third, the psychological dimension relates to our knowledge, beliefs, and mental activities. The psychological dimension is measured subjectively.

FIGURE 1-1   Dimensions of Culture

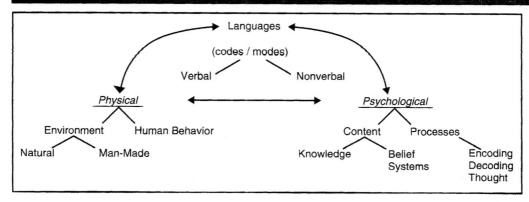

Although we can alter these characteristics and our way of communicating with others, we must first understand our own personal dimensions and understand why we are the way we are.

Culture is learned through perception. Perceptions are formed in various ways: where we are born and raised, the language we learn, the people and environment with which we live, and the psychological stimuli we encounter. No two individuals view the external world the same because no two individuals receive exactly the same stimuli or share the same physical sensory receptors. Because we know only what we have personally perceived and cannot know for sure what someone else has perceived, intercultural communication involving different cultures becomes particularly difficult (Singer, 1998).

Glen's (1981) cognitive approach to studying culture suggests that different cultures structure knowledge differently and that these differences determine aspects of behavior and communication such as information that is accepted as proof for an opinion or argument, the syntax of the information, and the topics that are considered appropriate to discuss.

If you find that a particular cultural attitude is constant across cultures, then you do not have to be concerned about that particular cultural trait. However, if you find that a particular cultural attitude varies for specific cultures, you should consider the effect it will have on communications with cultures that possess this attitude. A **cultural symbol** is a word or object that represents something in the culture. Cultural symbol variability may be included in social cognitive processes such as information processing, persuasive strategy selection, conflict management styles, personality, social relations, and self-perceptions as well as habits, norms, rules, roles, networks, language, and environment. All the factors interact and influence each other. To communicate effectively in the intercultural business environment, it is important to know all the cultural factors that affect the situation.

Stereotypes of U.S. Culture

Stereotypes, perceptions about certain groups of people or nationalities, exist with U.S. persons and those of other cultures. Although stereotyping is a guide to a national culture, it does not work well with individuals, particularly those who have worked in international business or who have lived or studied abroad. Individuals generally have differences from their national culture (Lewis, 2000).

In *American Ways*, Althen (2003) describes typical U.S. businesspersons as people who tend to do the following:

- Be informal in their relationships.
- Be rather formal in their business attire (suits for men and dresses or suits for women); however, many firms are becoming more relaxed in their dress codes or have a casual day when employees can dress less formally.
- Be workaholics because they spend more time working than they do with their families or social engagements; U.S. executives tend to put in long hours at the office.
- Embarrass foreign businesspeople by doing manual labor (e.g., mowing their own lawns) or tasks that would be done by the lower class or servants in their country.

- Be overly concerned with time, money, and appointments; people of other cultures interpret the need of U.S. businesspeople to begin meetings on time and start business discussions immediately as an indication that they are unfriendly, impersonal, and cold.
- Make decisions on hard, objective facts rather than on personal feelings, social relationships, or political advantage.
- Consider contracts and the written word as very important and to be taken very seriously.
- Be aware of the status differences within the organization; however, generally no display of superiority or inferiority is made, which tends to make rank-conscious foreigners very uneasy.
- Be mobile; they rarely work for one company all their lives, which is very different from many countries in the world.
- Convey superiority in their actions because they feel the United States is a superior nation.*

Axtell (1994) agreed with Althen (2003) regarding the stereotype that U.S. persons are workaholics; he added these stereotypes of persons in the United States: arrogant, loud, friendly, impatient, generous, and monolingual. These descriptions, admittedly, are stereotypes.

Stereotypes of Persons in Other Cultures

Axtell (1994, pp. 83–84) asked people in the United States who conduct business with persons outside the United States to give one-word descriptors of their impression of people of other nationalities. Some of these stereotypes follow:

Culture	*Image*
English	conservative, reserved, polite, proper, formal
French	arrogant, rude, chauvinistic, romantic, gourmet, cultural, artistic
Italians	demonstrative, talkative, emotional, romantic, bold, artistic
Latin Americans	*mañana* attitude, macho, music loving, touching
Asians	inscrutable, intelligent, xenophobic (fear/hatred of strangers/ foreigners), golfers, group-oriented, polite, soft spoken

By recognizing differences as well as similarities, businesspersons can adjust their mode of communication to fit the individual culture with which they are communicating.

ENCULTURATION

Enculturation is the socialization process you go through to adapt to your society. When you grow up in one culture, you learn one way of classifying, coding, prioritizing, and justifying reality. Cultural information that you are willing to share with outsiders is considered **frontstage culture,** while cultural information that is concealed

---

*Adapted from *American Ways,* (2nd ed.) by Gary Althen, 2003, Yarmouth, ME: Intercultural Press, Inc. Used by permission.

from outsiders is considered **backstage culture.** An example of frontstage culture is a sales representative who loudly announces, "We got the Hunter Fan account." This information is readily shared. An example of backstage culture is the sales representative who conceals the fact that his child is mentally retarded. Frontstage and backstage culture vary by culture and by individuals within the culture because some people are inherently more open than others. As a representative of your company, you need to learn what the culture with which you are working considers acceptable frontstage information that can be shared and what is considered backstage information that is not to be shared with others.

Datan, Rodeheaver, and Hughes (1987) use the concept of scripts to explain the cognitive imprinting that happens during enculturation:

> Individuals experience events in their lives as "scenes"—organized wholes combining people, places, time, actions, and in particular, affects that amplify these experiences and provide a sense of urgency about understanding them. Out of early scenes, the individual develops sets of rules for interpreting, evaluating, producing, predicting, or controlling future scenes. These rules— "scripts"—are initially innate but are supplemented and replaced by learned scripts. Higher-order scripts are created when scenes are combined and instilled with fresh affect—"psychological magnification.". . . The order in personality development, then, derives from the individual's need to impose order—the script—on the critical events, or scenes, in life. And, finally, scripts that initially arise from scenes begin to give rise to scenes instead, as the individual's construction of experience affects experience itself. (p. 164)

Examples of such scripts are the inability of the Japanese to say the word "no" directly but instead to say that "it would be difficult," and the difficulty for someone of a strong Christian background to lie to save face when lying is never condoned for a Christian.

ACCULTURATION

People do not want to abandon their past; therefore, they acculturate new ideas into their existing culture. **Acculturation** is the process of adjusting and adapting to a new and different culture (Hazuda, Stern, & Hoffner, 1988). If people of two different cultures absorb a significant number of each others' cultural differences and have a number of similarities, **cultural synergy** takes place with the two cultures merging to form a stronger overriding culture. Corporate cultures are examples of the synergy of diverse cultures.

A manager, to be productive and creative, must make his or her workers realize that the corporation is more important than individual differences. Differences are not to be suppressed but instead managed to maximize the group's productivity and creativity (Weaver, 1998). Hofstede's (2004) work shows that what motivates a worker in one country may or may not be important to a worker in another country. For corporations to get the most from their people, they must have managers who can work effectively with many cultural groups.

People who learn more than one culture are **multicultural** and can move between two cultures very comfortably. An example of multicultural persons is the royal Grimaldi family of Monaco. Princess Grace was a U.S. citizen and married Prince Ranier of Monaco. The Grimaldi children were raised in Monaco; however, because of the time they spent in the United States, they were acculturated to this country. Although acculturation increases the interconnectedness of cultures, differences are sources of potential problems. All differences will probably not be absorbed by either culture.

Acculturation has four dimensions: integration, separation, assimilation, and deculturation. When a minority moves into a majority culture, he or she will choose one of these modes either consciously or subconsciously. Although as a majority culture we may feel that assimilation is the correct acculturation process, the individual may not feel that this fits his or her needs. Assimilation takes place when individuals are absorbed into their new culture and withdraw from their old culture. Integration takes place when individuals become an integral part of the new culture while maintaining their cultural integrity. Separation happens when individuals keep their culture and stay independent of the new culture. Deculturation occurs when individuals lose their original culture and do not accept the new culture, leading to confusion and anxiety (Alkhazraji, 1997). The acculturation mode that an individual chooses is governed by the individual's views and desired ways of life.

ETHNOCENTRISM

Ethnocentrism is the belief that your own cultural background, including ways of analyzing problems, values, beliefs, language, and verbal and nonverbal communication, is correct. Ethnocentrists believe that their culture is the central culture and that other cultures are incorrect, defective, or quaint. When we evaluate others, we do it through our self-reference criterion because it is what we know. Fisher (1997) in his research refers to ethnocentrism as mindsets.

Mindsets are ways of being that allow us to see, perceive, and reason through our own cultural awareness. Mindsets are learned by growing up in a particular culture. We learn to be open or closed to others and their way of living; however, these mindsets can be altered. Mindsets include the psychological and cultural factors that make us individuals and make us different or similar. We are predisposed because of enculturation to perceive and reason according to our cultural upbringing. Our reactions to situations are preprogrammed until we decide to change. Every culture in the world has a different mindset, and every individual within that culture has a variance to that mindset (Chaney & Martin, 2005).

The U.S. mindset includes the concept that the American way is best. ("American" as used in the United States is an example of ethnocentrism because the term "American" actually refers to all the people in North, South, and Central American countries.) Although this is mainly a U.S. concept, people who are born in smaller countries feel the same about their own country—that *it* is the best place to live. The belief that one's own culture is best is a natural phenomenon common to all cultures. Although it is natural to be ethnocentric and have a particular mindset, we need to look at other mindsets from the perspective of the people who hold them before we judge them as good or bad. However, we must be careful about generalizing about other cultures or making assumptions about how they view the United States.

The term "Ugly American" was derived from the behavior of U.S. travelers observed by persons in other cultures who judged them inconsiderate of the culture they were visiting. This term came from the 1958 book by William Lederer and Eugene Burdick and the subsequent 1963 movie by the same name. The book and movie depict an incompetent, ignorant U.S. ambassador in a fictional Southeast Asian country. The term quickly caught on to describe rude, self-centered people who have no sensitivity for those who are different from themselves. In reality, most U.S. Americans, when traveling to other countries, do not fit this stereotype of the Ugly American. They want to understand people of other cultures but are simply uninformed (Bosrock, 1995).

NORMS, RULES, ROLES, AND NETWORKS

Norms, rules, roles, and networks are situational factors that influence encoding and decoding of both verbal and nonverbal messages within a culture. They are unwritten guidelines people within the cultural group follow. **Norms** are culturally ingrained principles of correct and incorrect behaviors that, if broken, carry a form of overt or covert penalty. **Rules** are formed to clarify cloudy areas of norms. The U.S. Supreme Court is an excellent example of an organization that looks at the intent of a rule and determines how strongly or loosely it should be followed. A **role** includes the behavioral expectations of a position within a culture and is affected by norms and rules. **Networks** are formed with personal ties and involve an exchange of assistance. Networks and the need to belong are the basis of friendships and subgroups (Chaney & Martin, 2005). An example of a political network is the exchange of votes between U.S. legislators needed to support their projects. When the United States decided to help the people of Kuwait defend themselves against Iraq in 1992, the U.S. ambassador to the United Nations called in the other ambassadors within his network for their concurrence. The ability to develop networks in intercultural situations can enable you to do business more effectively in multicultural environments. In some cultures such as the Arab, Spanish, and Japanese, networking is essential because they prefer to conduct business with people they know or with associates of people they know (Gudykunst & Ting-Toomey, 1988).

SUBCULTURES AND SUBGROUPS

Subcultures are groups of people possessing characteristic traits that set apart and distinguish them from others within a larger society or macroculture. The U.S. macroculture, which comprises 69% of the population, is white. The largest U.S. subcultures include Hispanics (or Latinos) (13.5%), African Americans (13%), Asians and Pacific Islanders (4%), and Native Americans (1%) (*CultureGrams*, 2004). In addition to ethnicity and race, subcultures in the United States may be categorized by age, religion, and sexual preferences. Examples of subcultures (or microcultures) in the United States include teenagers, baby boomers, African Americans, Catholics, disabled individuals, and trade associations. All these groups have similarities to the macroculture but also have some differences. To meet the definition of a subculture, these three criteria should be met:

- The group members are self-identifiable; that is, group members want to be considered a part of the group.
- Group members exhibit behavior that is characteristic of the group.
- The macroculture recognizes the group as a subculture and has given it a name; for example, senior citizens (Klopf, 1997). A term used more recently for subcultures is "cocultures," because of the possible implication that members of "subcultures" or "nondominant groups" are perhaps inferior (Samovar & Porter, 2004).

Intercultural business communication necessitates working with subcultures. The subcultures form a diversity of ethnic identities with which managers must learn to work harmoniously. Women are one such subculture. As Adler (1993) states, "Although women represent over 50% of the world's population, in no country do women represent half, or even close to half, of the corporate managers"(p. 3). In some Middle East, Far East, and South American countries, business is male oriented. Because North American women have progressed in the business world faster than their counterparts in most other countries of the world, they may expect to automatically be accepted by men who would be offended by women in business in their own culture. Although men in some countries are still apprehensive about conducting business with women, Bosrock (1995) states that "regardless of the attitude toward women in a given country, most women are treated politely. Much of the resistance to women in business is directed at local women, not Westerners" (p. 109). Even in Asian and South American cultures where women are traditionally seen as nurturers of the family, attitudes are changing. Many employers now are less concerned with gender than performance (Bosrock, 1994, 1997). Women sent abroad have a very high success rate. A self-report showed that 97% of the female expatriate managers were successful, a much higher percentage than reported by male expatriates (Adler, 1993).

Subgroups, although also part of the macroculture, are groups with which the macroculture does not agree and with which it has problems communicating. Members of these groups often engage in communication behavior that is distinctively different from that of the dominant culture. Examples of subgroups include youth gangs, prostitutes, saboteurs, embezzlers, and other groups that have unique experiences or not and/or characteristics not sanctioned by the macroculture (Dodd, 1997). The vocabularies of subgroup members make it difficult for members of the macroculture and subcultures to understand the intended meanings of the words used by subgroup members (Samovar & Porter, 2004).

CULTURAL INTELLIGENCE

Cultural intelligence, according to Peterson (2004), is the ability to exhibit certain behaviors, including skills and qualities, which are culturally tuned to the attitudes and values of others. Cultural intelligence involves the areas of linguistic intelligence, spatial intelligence, intrapersonal intelligence, and interpersonal intelligence. Although speaking a second language is not essential to **linguistic intelligence,** it is helpful to learn about the customer's native language when conducting business internationally. In addition, using international business English can increase effectiveness when communicating with persons of other cultures. **Spatial intelligence** is an important aspect of cultural intelligence; it involves the way space is used during greetings and introductions, as well as during meetings and other encounters. **Intrapersonal intelligence** involves an awareness of one's own cultural style in order to make behavioral adjustments to international counterparts. **Interpersonal intelligence** includes the ability to understand other people and their motivations. Peterson (2004) recognized psychologist Howard Gardner's theory of multiple intelligences and summarized succinctly the preceding four categories of cultural intelligence: "To interact well with people from other cultures, it helps to (a) speak a bit of their language, (b) know how closely to stand (and other nonverbal behavior), (c) know about your own cultural style, and (d) know how your cultural style meshes with those of others" (p. 95).

COMMUNICATION BARRIERS

When encountering someone from another culture, communication barriers are often created when the behavior of the other person differs from our own. **Communication barriers** are obstacles to effective communication. An example of such a barrier is the head nod. The nod indicates understanding in the United States, but in Japan it means only that the person is listening. By understanding intercultural communication, we can break down barriers and pave the way for mutual understanding and respect.

The following are barriers to communication:

- **Physical**—time, environment, comfort and needs, and physical medium (e.g., telephone, letter).
- **Cultural**—ethnic, religious, and social differences.
- **Perceptual**—viewing what is said from your own mindset.
- **Motivational**—the listener's mental inertia.
- **Experiential**—lack of similar life happenings.
- **Emotional**—personal feelings of the listener.
- **Linguistic**—different languages spoken by the speaker and listener or use of a vocabulary beyond the comprehension of the listener.
- **Nonverbal**—nonword messages.
- **Competition**—the listener's ability to do other things rather than hear the communication.

Several cultural iceberg models exist. What you do not see culturally can be a barrier to your ability to communicate effectively and complete your agenda. As shown in Figure 1-2, the values that are below the "waterline" represent those on which behaviors are based; however, we respond to the surface values that we can sense. To truly understand a culture, we must explore the behaviors below the waterline. The common elements of trust, sincerity, and integrity are necessary to

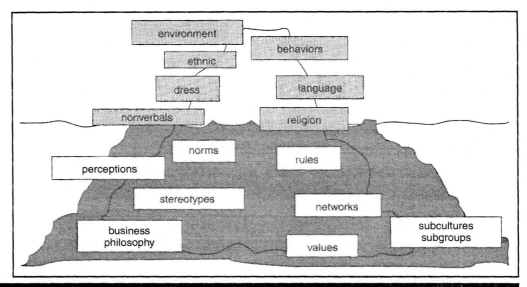

FIGURE 1-2   Cultural Iceberg

building successful business relationships when cultural differences exist (Funakawa, 1997).

INTERCULTURAL CONSTRUCTS

Borden (1991) lists seven constructs that individuals must possess if they are going to succeed interculturally. The degree to which we can understand intercultural communication depends on the degree to which the following are true:

- We are aware that our intent to communicate, either as communicator or communicatee, may result in only expressive behavior or information gathering, respectively.
- Our cybernetic (self-concept) in one culture can operate independently of our cybernetic in another culture.
- We are competent in the languages of other cultures.
- We are able to work within the constraints (personal, situational, and cultural) of the human communication system established by the communication from other cultures.
- We are culturally literate in our own and other cultures.
- We know the position of our culture and other cultures on the four universal dimensions of values and their interaction with the cultural orientation model.
- We know the cultural orientation of our culture and other cultures on the associative-abstractive, particularistic-universalistic, and closed-minded/open-minded dimensions and can use it as the first approximation of the cognitive style of the communicants (pp. 210–213).

The components of Borden's constructs are discussed in later chapters.

MULTINATIONAL MANAGEMENT ORIENTATIONS

To compete successfully in a global economy, a knowledge of management styles used by international corporations is also important. With the emergence of the concept of world culture has come a heightened awareness of the interdependence of nations and the need to break cultural barriers and find ways to work harmoniously with people of all cultures.

Multinational firms, those located in more than one nation, generally will follow either an ethnocentric, polycentric, geocentric, or regiocentric form of management. Multinational firms such as Sony, Quaker Oats, ExxonMobil, Robert Bosch, and Nissan may follow a single management style at all global locations or may use various styles of management to increase productivity while maintaining worker morale. All multinational or global corporations are **transnational,** which means they cross the borders of countries in conducting their business (Moran & Stripp, 1991).

Not all these management styles consider the diversity of cultures working within them, nor are they managed to take advantage of the surprises that surface in multinational management. As Rhinesmith (1996) has stated, global managers have a mindset that allows them to take advantage of and manage the complexity, adaptability, teams, uncertainty, and learning that the global organization requires. Because people are the most critical factor for an organization to succeed globally, people are also the restraining factor in the firm's capability to survive and grow. Human resource development personnel must be involved in the education and changing of the mindsets. The global mindset differs from the domestic mindset, as illustrated in Table 1-1 (Rhinesmith, 1996, p. 27).

The person who can manage a domestic operation does not necessarily have the competencies to manage a global operation. People who have a global mindset tend to live life in many ways that may be physically, intellectually, emotionally, or spiritually different, depending on the culture with which they are interacting.

When a firm is located in one country and all its sales are in the same country, **ethnocentric management** practices are employed. Ethnocentric management does not account for cultural differences in the workforce. All workers will be treated the same. Many times the management practices employed rely on one person's views of how the organization should be run. Some domestic corporations financed from abroad that purchase goods from abroad for resale at home or buy technology abroad,

TABLE 1-1 Comparison of Domestic and Global Mindsets	
Domestic Mindset	*Global Mindset*
Functional expertise	Bigger, broader picture
Prioritization	Balance of contradictions
Structure	Process
Individual responsibility	Teamwork and diversity
No surprises	Change as opportunity
Trained against surprises	Openness to surprises

Source: From *A Manager's Guide to Globalization* (p. 27), by S. H. Rhinesmith, 1996, Homewood. IL: Richard D. Irwin. Inc. Used with publisher's permission.

still need to think globally because of their international activities (Moran & Stripp, 1991). For example, U.S. car manufacturers complained that their cars were not selling in Japan. These manufacturers, however, had not changed the position of the steering wheel from the left to the right for driving on the opposite side of the road from the United States, and they had not downsized their cars in consideration of the limited space available to park cars in Japan. When a company expands internationally, it must consider the consumers who are targeted to buy its products.

> Werner G. Hennecker (Pegasus Gold): "We run our business on a certain set of standards, regardless of whether we're in the United States or Kazakhstan. Our in-house environmental policy is much more stringent than that required by any of the areas in which we operate, but it's inviolate. It's been interesting getting people in some parts of the world that haven't worried much about environmental issues to focus on them. Our solution was to base a large part of our bonus program on employees' avoidance of environmental incidents." (Donlon, 1996, p. 3)

Polycentric management practices consider the culture of the country in which the firm is located. The people in charge consider the cultural needs of the workers in the area in which the firm is located. A melting-pot effect may seem to exist because the majority's culture is considered in management decisions. In the United States, you see this particularly in small firms. Leaving the polycentric management practices behind is part of the problem employees have when they move to a foreign country to work because they were comfortable with the old management style (Moran & Stripp, 1991).

Regiocentric management considers the region rather than the country in which the firm is located, realizing that countries can and often do have many different cultural backgrounds. The regional theory acknowledges that in the United States all areas are not the same. For example, different management strategies are required for running a production facility in Michigan with high unionization and a facility in Mississippi with low unionization and different ethnic bases. Management strategies consider the diversity of the workforce (Moran & Stripp, 1991). Unions tend to keep the workers from interacting directly with management. Many firms now want to use Total Quality Management (TQM), which utilizes interaction between workers and management. Saturn automotive built their plant in Springfield, Tennessee, because they could start the plant without a union and implement TQM. Although Saturn now has a workforce that is unionized, the union works with management; and the quality and sales of the Saturn automobile have been better than any other General Motors' product.

> Shepard: "We've also developed a program called Aegon University, in which we put managers in their 30s and 40s from different countries into a dormitory setting and bring in international executives to speak to them. Even more important, this gives them the opportunity to network individually. They are building an e-mail system among the graduates of Aegon University that lets them share practices they think might work across borders in addition to potential customers that operate globally in the pension business." (Donlon, 1996, p. 4)

Geocentric management requires a common framework with enough freedom for individual locations to operate regionally to meet the cultural needs of the workers. Geocentric refers to the synergy of ideas from different countries of operation. The most successful multinational corporations use integrated geocentric management. Corporations have common control practices that the individual locations are free to modify. Recognizing the management style used is helpful to competing successfully in a global economy (Moran & Stripp, 1991).

> Claude I. Taylor (Air Canada): "When we first started to go international, we had Canadians everywhere. We found that didn't work, because they weren't accepted and they didn't understand the local culture. That meant we had two levels of labor problems: We had a management problem and a contract problem.
>
> Today, we're expanding rapidly in the United States, and we have the odd Canadian in there part-time. But our philosophy for outside markets is to bring foreigners—from France, Germany, Hong Kong, and South Korea, for example—into Canada for six months, indoctrinate them about what we do, and then send them back." (Donlon, 1996, p. 3)

The ability of different cultures to communicate successfully in a business environment, to assimilate their cultures and conduct business, and to do this either within the United States or abroad is the emphasis of intercultural business communication. Different cultures do present communication problems; differing business practices and negotiation strategies pose additional problems. Intercultural business communication involves a knowledge and understanding of other cultures, including their subcultures, subgroups, and standards of behavior. With the emergence of the concept of a world culture has come a heightened awareness of the interdependence of nations and the need to break the cultural barriers to find ways to work harmoniously with people of all cultures.

Bosrock (1995) offers the following "Ten Commandments for Going International":

1. Be well prepared.
2. Ask questions, be observant, and listen.
3. Make an effort; trying and making a mistake is better than not trying at all.
4. When problems develop, assume the main cause is miscommunication.
5. Be patient; accomplishing your goals in another country/culture usually requires more time and effort.
6. Assume the best about people; most people act on the basis of their learned values and traditions.
7. Be sincere.
8. Maintain a sense of humor.
9. Make an effort to be likable; when people like you, they will forgive your mistakes.
10. Smile.

Because the emphasis of this book is intercultural **business** communication, countries selected for examples from various cultures focus on those countries with which the United States conducts most of its international business. According to the report of U.S. Exports to Individual Countries for 2003, the top 10 countries (in order of high to low) are Canada, Mexico, Japan, United Kingdom, Germany, China, South Korea, the Netherlands, Taiwan, and France. Examples from other countries are included within chapters to illustrate cultural variations in business communication.

Terms

- Acculturation
- Backstage culture
- Communication barriers
- Cultural intelligence
- Cultural symbol
- Cultural synergy
- Culture
- Diffusion
- Enculturation
- Ethnocentric management
- Ethnocentrism
- Frontstage culture
- Geocentric management
- Globalization
- Intercultural business communication
- Intercultural communication
- Interpersonal intelligence
- International communication
- Intracultural communication
- Intrapersonal intelligence
- Macroculture
- Melting pot
- Microculture
- Mindsets
- Multicultural
- Multinational firm
- Networks
- Norms
- Polycentric management
- Regiocentric management
- Roles
- Rules
- Spatial intelligence
- Stereotypes
- Subculture
- Subgroup
- Transnational
- World culture

Exercise 1.1

Instructions: Match the following terms with their definition.

1. Belief that your own culture is superior
2. The socialization process we go through to learn a culture
3. A sociocultural assimilation
4. Cultural information concealed from outsiders
5. Absorption of new ideas into existing culture
6. Between members of same culture
7. Between persons of different cultures
8. Between nations and governments
9. Groups having traits differing from the macroculture
10. Culturally ingrained principles of correct/incorrect behavior

A. Acculturation
B. Backstage culture
C. Enculturation
D. Ethnocentrism
E. Frontstage culture
F. Intercultural
G. International
H. Intracultural
I. Melting pot
J. Norms
K. Subcultures

Questions and Cases for Discussion

1. The United States has long been called a melting pot. What does this term mean?
2. What does it mean for a firm to be global?
3. Give examples of how products have been globalized.
4. Explain the differences between norms, roles, rules, and networks.
5. Define a subculture and give examples of U.S. subcultures.
6. What is cultural synergy?
7. Distinguish between intercultural communication and intracultural communication.
8. Identify the dimensions of culture.
9. Identify types of barriers to communication.
10. Are business cultures necessarily aligned to national cultures?

Cases

The following procedure is recommended for analyzing the cases: (a) read the case carefully, paying attention to details; (b) read the questions at the end of the case; (c) reread the case, taking notes on or highlighting the details needed for answering the questions; (d) identify relevant facts, underlying assumptions, and critical issues of the case; (e) list possible answers to the questions; and (f) select the most logical response to the question. Your professor may ask that you submit answers to the case questions in writing.

Case 1

At a reception for a U.S. political candidate, the guests appear to be divided into groups. People in some groups are all African American, others are Latin American, and others are Asian. Explain the cultural phenomena that are operating at this political gathering.

Case 2

The U.S. automotive manufacturers have complained about Japanese automotive imports and that the U.S. car firms are locked out of the Japanese market. The Japanese have countered that the U.S. firms have not done their homework; they offer cars that are too big or are not fuel-efficient. Although U.S. car sales have decreased in the United States, Japanese car sales have increased. Japanese manufacturers have begun to assemble cars in the United States; many U.S. firms are moving part of their operations to Mexico. Discuss the implications to these firms as they globalize.

Case 3

In 1979, the shah of Iran was admitted to the United States for medical reasons. The Iranians reacted by holding all the diplomatic personnel hostage in the embassy in Iran. The secretary of state was Henry Kissinger, and the president was Jimmy Carter. The United States took the position that the Iranians should not be upset with the shah's being allowed into the United States for the humanitarian reason of medical need. The shah had been a friend to the United States and the United States to the shah; therefore, the U.S. government felt a certain obligation to the shah. The revolution in Iran was based on Islamic religious assumptions. Give two position statements, one using the mindset of the United States and the second using the mindset of Iran to show how and why each viewed its position as correct. Is objectivity difficult to maintain when writing the Iran position statement?

Case 4

The United States has globalized faster than it has paid attention to mindsets that differ from the U.S. mindset. The world is connected by news satellites that allowed the Persian Gulf War to be viewed as it unfolded—the world literally watched the war happen. Explain how the world and public opinion has been affected by mass media. Include how world negotiations have changed for governments, diplomats, politicians, and businesses.

Activities

1. Clip a story from the local newspaper that is related to some aspect of intercultural communication, such as problems encountered by persons of other cultures in the acculturation process or problems between subgroups; give a short report to the class.
2. Ask a member of the class who is from another culture to discuss how cultural norms and rules in his or her culture differ from those in the United States.
3. Invite a member of the business community who conducts business globally to address problems encountered when dealing with representatives of other cultures whose form of management (ethnocentric, polycentric, geocentric, or regiocentric) may be different from that in the United States.
4. Interview a foreign student on roles of women and children in his or her culture. In a report to the class, make comparisons between these roles and those in the United States.
5. Write a one-page proposal for improving relationships between U.S. students and students from other cultures in your school.
6. Analyze a multinational corporation's annual report and determine where it is producing and selling goods and what the profit margins of those goods are compared to other multinational firms.

References

Adler, N. J. (1993). Competitive frontiers: Women managers in triad. *International Studies of Management and Organization, 23*(2), 3–23.

Alkhazraji, K. M. (1997). *Immigrants and cultural adaptation in the American workplace.* New York: Garland.

Althen, G. (2003). *American ways* (2nd ed.). Yarmouth, ME: Intercultural Press.

Axtell, R. E. (1994). *The do's and taboos of international trade.* New York: John Wiley.

Borden, G. A. (1991). *Cultural orientation: An approach to understanding intercultural communication.* Upper Saddle River, NJ: Prentice Hall.

Bosrock, M. M. (1994). *Put your best foot forward: Asia.* St. Paul, MN: International Education Systems.

Bosrock, M. M. (1995). *Put your best foot forward: Europe.* St. Paul, MN: International Education Systems.

Bosrock, M. M. (1997). *Put your best foot forward: South America.* St. Paul, MN: International Education Systems.

Chaney, L. H., & Martin, J. S. (2005). Intercultural communication: Bridging cultural differences. In S. O'Brien (Ed.), *Communication for a global society, 2005 NBEA Yearbook* (pp. 100–114). Reston, VA: National Business Education Association.

CultureGrams 2005, USA. (2004). Lindon, UT: ProQuest Information and Learning.

Datan, N., Rodeheaver, D., & Hughes, F. (1987). Adult development and aging. In M. R. Rosenzweig & L. W. Porter (Eds.), *Annual Review of Psychology, 38,* 153–180.

Differences between sexes are shrinking. (1996). *USA Today, 124*(2608), 10.

Dodd, C. H. (1997). *Dynamics of intercultural communication* (5th ed.). New York: McGraw-Hill.

Donlon, J. P. (1996, September). Managing across borders. *Chief Executive, 117,* 58–68.

Evans, P., Doz, Y., & Laurent, A. (Eds.). (1990). *Human resource management in international firms: Change, globalization, innovation.* New York: St. Martin's.

Fisher, G. (1997). *Mindsets* (2nd ed.). Yarmouth, ME: Intercultural Press.

Funakawa, A. (1997). *Transcultural management: A new approach for global organizations.* San Francisco: Jossey-Bass.

Glen, E. S. (1981). *Man and mankind.* Norwood, NJ: Ablex.

Gudykunst, W. B., & Ting-Toomey, S. (1988). *Culture and interpersonal communication.* Newbury Park, CA: Sage.

Hazuda, H. P., Stern, M. P., & Hoffner, S. M. (1988). Acculturation and assimilation among Mexican Americans: Sales and population-based data. *Social Science Quarterly, 69,* 687–706.

Hofstede, G. (2004). *Cultures and organizations* (2nd ed.). London: McGraw-Hill.

Jandt, F. E. (2000). *Introduction to intercultural communication* (3rd ed.). Thousand Oaks, CA: Sage.

Klopf, D. W. (1997). *Intercultural encounters* (3rd ed.). Englewood, CO: Morton.

Laurent, A. (1986). The cross-cultural puzzle of human resource management. *Human Resource Management, 25*(1), 91–102.

Lewis, R. D. (2000). *When cultures collide: Managing successfully across cultures.* London: Nicholas Brealey.

Moran, R. T., & Stripp, W. G. (1991). *Dynamics of successful international business negotiations.* Houston: Gulf.

Peterson, B. (2004). *Cultural intelligence: A guide to working with people from other cultures.* Yarmouth, ME: Intercultural Press.

Rhinesmith, S. H. (1996). *A manager's guide to globalization: Six skills for success in a changing world.* New York: McGraw-Hill.

Rohrlich, P. E. (1998). Why do we study intercultural communication? In G. R. Weaver (Ed.), *Culture, communication, and conflict: Readings in intercultural relations.* New York: Simon & Schuster.

Ruch, W. V. (1989). *International handbook of corporate communication.* Jefferson: McFarland.

Samovar, L. A., & Porter, R. E. (2004). *Communication between cultures* (5th ed.). Belmont, CA: Wadsworth/Thomson Learning.

Singer, M. R. (1998). The role of culture and perception in communication. In G. R. Weaver (Ed.), *Culture, communication, and conflict: Readings in intercultural relations.* New York: Simon & Schuster.

Staa, D. (1998). No need for inter-American cultural clash. *Management Review, 87*(1), 8.

U.S. Census Bureau. (2003). American Community Survey. Retrieved September 24, 2004, http://factfinder.census.gov

Weaver, G. R. (Ed.). (1998). *Culture, communication, and conflict: Readings in intercultural relations.* New York: Simon & Schuster.

Yoshida, S. (2002). Globalization and issues of intercultural communications, *Vital Speeches of the Day, 68*(22), 708–712.

CHAPTER

2

UNIVERSAL SYSTEMS

Objectives

Upon completion of this chapter, you will

- increase your understanding of systems that are universal to all cultural groups and their relationship to communicating and negotiating in a global setting.

- understand the role that economic and political systems play in communicating interculturally in business settings.

- see the relationship between educational systems and global communication.

- gain insight into social systems and hierarchies that affect effective intercultural business communication.

Cultural systems have an impact on multicultural communication. **Cultural universals** are formed out of the common problems of all cultures. The following systems are found in all cultures: economic systems, political systems, educational systems, marriage and family systems, and social hierarchies and interaction. Knowing how cultural systems in the United States differ from those of other cultures can enhance communication effectiveness when conducting business with persons of other cultures. Although these systems are universal to all cultures, different cultures may deal with an issue in a significantly different way. In communicating interculturally, the variabilities are equally as important as the similarities.

ECONOMIC SYSTEMS

A culture develops an economic system to meet the material needs of its people. The way in which the products that meet the material needs of the people are produced, distributed, and consumed is referred to as the **economic system.** All societies not only work out ways of producing or procuring goods but must also determine the procedure for distributing them.

The different economic systems in the world today include capitalism, socialism, agrarianism, and barter. The United States and Japan are capitalistic, Sweden and China are socialistic, Belize and Cambodia are agrarian, and Laos and the Marshall Islands barter. The relationship between the public and private sectors and which sector dominates may make some economic systems a blend of the first three systems. No single correct economic system exists. The U.S. method of distributing goods is based on the capacity to pay, although such countries as Cuba distribute goods according to need.

ECONOMIC "-ISMS"

- **Socialism**—You have two cows. The government takes one and gives it to your neighbor.
- **Communism**—You have two cows. The government takes both of them and gives you part of the milk.
- **Nazism**—You have two cows. The government takes both your cows and then shoots you.
- **Capitalism**—You have two cows. You sell one of them and buy a bull.
- **Fascism**—You have two cows. The government takes both cows and sells you the milk.
- **Bureaucracy**—You have two cows. The government takes both of them, shoots one, milks the other, and then pours the milk down the drain.
- **Democracy**—Everyone has two cows. A vote is taken, the loser cries discrimination, the lawyers sue (on a contingency basis), and the government takes at least 39% (Axtell, 1999, pp. 209–210).

In addition to identifying the type of economic system a country follows, it is also important to understand other aspects of the country's economy, including **imports** (goods brought into the country) and **exports** (goods sent out of the country). This knowledge may prove useful in the negotiation process (see chapter 10). The top 10 countries to which the United States exports (according to the U.S. Census Bureau, 2004) are Canada, Mexico, Japan, United Kingdom, Germany, China, South Korea, the Netherlands, Taiwan, and France. The only African nation making the top 50 trading partners of the United States is South Africa. The Scandinavian countries and their positions as U.S. trading partners are Sweden, 30; Norway, 51; Finland, 46; Denmark, 48; and Iceland, 86. Latin American countries that are in the top 50 U.S. trading partners are Brazil, 15; Venezuela, 32; Colombia, 27; Dominican Republic, 26; Costa Rica, 29; Chile, 35; Honduras, 33; Argentina, 40; Guatemala, 41; El Salvador, 44; Jamaica, 50; Panama, 42; and Peru, 47.

A brief description of the economic systems of the United States and 16 countries with which the United States conducts international business follows. Also included are other details of the economies of these countries (*CultureGrams,* 2004; *CIA Factbook,* 2004; *U.S. Trade in Goods,* 2004; *Human Development Reports,* 2004; U.S. Census Bureau, 2004). The GDP per capita figures are given as the purchasing price parity to the United States dollar. The unemployment numbers are 2004 estimates.

United States

The U.S. economic system is capitalistic with socialistic overtones. Free-market principles tempered by government regulations operate the economy. In addition, the United States is a financial center with an economy that affects the world. The U.S. capitalistic system is affected by inflation (brought about by the change from an industrially oriented economy to a service and technical economy), unemployment, and the economy of other countries as many U.S. corporations have become multinational. The 2003 trade deficit was $496.5 billion. Direct foreign investments by other countries into the United States was $29.8 billion; direct foreign investments by the United States abroad was $151.8 billion in 2003 (*U.S. Trade in Goods,* 2004).

The economy in the United States is the largest and most technically advanced in the world with an average real gross domestic product (GDP) per capita in 2002 of $35,750. (GDP is the value of goods and services earned per capita.) Unemployment in the United States in November 2004 was 5.4%. The U.S. exports include capital goods, cars, consumer goods, food, and machinery. Tourism is important to many state economies. U.S. citizens believe that materialism is an important aspect of life. This materialism encourages replacement of possessions. Much of this purchasing is done with credit cards, and credit card debt is very high. The United Nations *Human Development Reports* (HDI) ranks the United States 8 out of the 177 countries ranked. HDI measures poverty, literacy, education, life expectancy, and other such factors.

The United States is part of the North American Free Trade Agreement (NAFTA), which is expanding markets, services, and manufacturing between the United States, Canada, and Mexico. (NAFTA is discussed in greater detail in chapter 11.) The unit of currency is the U.S. dollar.

Australia

Vast mineral deposit exports and beef and sheep production keep Australia strong. The GDP for Australia is $28,260, and the unemployment rate is 6%. Australia is third in the HDI rankings. Australia is the United States' 14th largest trading partner. The currency is the Australian dollar (AUD).

Canada

Canada's economy is very strong worldwide. The economy is capitalistic with socialistic controls in the areas of health care and the retirement system. Manufacturing, mining, fishing, farming, and food processing drive the economy. Canada's real GDP per capita as of 2002 was $29,480. (Dollars in text are U.S. dollars unless otherwise specified.) Unemployment was 7.6% as of August, 2004. The HDI rank for Canada is 4 out of 177 countries. Canada is a world leader in the production of gold, uranium, silver, oil, natural gas, agriculture, wood pulp, timber, and copper. Canada exports wheat, barley, oats, and other agricultural products. Tourism is an important source of revenue in recent years. Canada exports more products to the United States than it imports.

In 1993, Canada joined Mexico and the United States in signing NAFTA which provides expanded markets for goods. The unit of currency is the Canadian dollar, also called the loonie by Canadians. Canada was the largest trading partner of the United States in 2003.

China

The Chinese government is supporting the growth of the private sector. Half of China's population is employed in agriculture. China leads the world in the production of rice, tobacco, corn, barley, soybeans, and peanuts. It produces manufactured goods, oil, minerals, coal, and steel. The real GDP is $4,580; the Special Administrative Region of Hong Kong's GDP is $26,910. China's HDI ranking is 94 of 177 countries, but the Special Administrative Region of Hong Kong is ranked 23 out of 177 countries.

The unemployment rate in urban areas was 9.8% in 2003, while unemployment overall was 20%. The economy has grown quickly since the 1990s. China is the sixth largest trading partner of the United States. A large deficit budget threatens the social security systems that are in place. The currency is the renminbi; the standard unit is the yuan (¥).

England

England is located in the British Isles on the island of Great Britain and has one of the largest economies in Europe. England's economy is based on capitalism; however, many sectors of the economy were nationalized or socialized between 1945 and 1980. Since the 1980s, some of the sectors have been privatized, and less industry regulation has been encouraged. England is still a major industrial power in the world. England does most of its trading with the European Union. The average annual real GDP per capita is $26,150. Unemployment was about 5.1% for 2003. Exports include manufactured goods, crude oil, and consumer goods. England's natural resources include oil, natural gas, iron ore, and salt. The United Kingdom is 12 out of 177 countries in the HDI rankings. The pound sterling (£) is the unit of currency. England is the fourth largest trading partner of the United States.

France

The French economy, which is the world's fourth largest, is a free-market system and one of the most highly developed in the world. Also, France is the tenth largest trading partner of the United States. The French standard of living is high with an average annual real GDP per capita of $26,920. Unemployment is usually high. The HDI ranking for France is 16 out of 177 countries. France is a major producer of such products as wine, milk, butter, cheese, barley, and wheat. The principal exports are machinery and transport equipment, steel products, and agricultural goods. The euro (€) is the unit of currency.

Germany

Germany is one of the largest economies in Europe and in the world, behind the United States and Japan. The German economy is based on principles of free enterprise and private ownership; however, government and business work together closely. The former communist system of East Germany is now being changed; emphasis is now on deciding what is best for the economy of the unified Germany. Germany has an average annual real GDP per capita of $27,100. The HDI ranking for Germany is 19 out of 177 countries. Germany's main exports are cars, steel, aluminum, televisions, and other manufactured goods, making it one of the largest exporters in the world. Germany is the United States' fifth largest trading partner. Germany's unemployment rate is 10.6%. The euro (€) is the unit of currency.

India

India's economy includes farming, handicrafts, modern industries, and support services. India has a large number of well-educated people skilled in the English language who are being used by software services companies. The World Bank is still concerned about the public-sector budget deficit, which is approximately 60% of GDP. GDP in India is $2,670, and the unemployment rate was 9.5% in 2004. India is ranked 127 out of 177 countries in the HDI rankings. India is the 24th largest trading partner of the United States. The *rupee* (INR) is the unit of currency.

Iraq

Iraq's economy is dominated by oil. The U.S.-led coalition in March/April 2003 resulted in major changes in the economy. Currently the rebuilding of oil, electricity, and other production is proceeding with foreign support and despite the continuation of severe internal strife. A joint UN and World Bank report released in the fall of 2003 estimated that Iraq's key reconstruction needs through 2007 would cost $55 billion. Many nations to whom monies were owed by the old regime have forgiven Iraq those debts. Iraq's GDP is approximately $1,500; the unemployment rate is undeterminable due to the war. The HDI ranking is also not available. The currency is the New Iraq Dollar (NID).

Japan

Japan's economy is a capitalistic/free-market one based on manufacturing, fishing, and exporting. Except for fish, Japan must import more than half of its food supply. Japan must also import most of its raw materials for manufacturing, and more than 95% of exports are manufactured goods. The 1990s recession and near collapse of the yen caused businesses to lay off or retire employees early.

Japan is one of the world's most productive nations. The average annual real GDP per capita is $26,940. The HDI rank for Japan is 9 out of 177 countries. Machinery, electronics, engineering, textiles, and chemicals are major industries in Japan. Japan exports much more to the United States than it imports; this trade imbalance is a source of friction between Japan and the United States. Japan is the third largest trading partner of the United States. The yen (¥) is Japan's currency.

Mexico

In Mexico, the oil industry, agriculture, tourism, and *maquiladoras* (Mexican assembly facilities often near a major U.S. market) employ most of the working people. The government is attracting foreign investments, privatizing state-owned companies, and deregulating trade to combat unemployment, high inflation, and debt.

U.S. companies such as General Motors, Sam's Wholesale Clubs, Hunter Fan, and Blockbuster Video have shown their faith in Mexico's economic stability by investing billions of dollars there. Export industries have been growing since 1993 with the passage of NAFTA with the United States and Canada. NAFTA resulted in lowered trade barriers and led to an increase in *maquiladoras*. By 1996, Mexico's unemployment rate had dropped to 6%. However, 10% of the population lacks education and economic opportunities. Mexico is the second-largest trading partner of the United States. Mexico's HDI ranking is 53 of 177 countries. Mining and petroleum are the two most important industries, but tourism is a source of employment for many people. Mexico exports oil, coffee, agricultural products, and engines. Mexico is also a major supplier of marijuana despite costly efforts to curb the drug trade. Real GDP per capita is $8,970. The unit of currency is the Mexican peso (MXN).

The Netherlands

The Netherlands has an open economy dependent on foreign trade. The economy has stable industrial relations and is a major European transportation hub. Industries include food processing, chemicals, petroleum refining, and electrical machinery. The country continues to lead European nations in attracting foreign direct investment.

The GDP for the Netherlands is $29,100, and unemployment is 5.3%. The Netherlands is the United States' eighth largest trading partner. The Netherlands is ranked 5 out of 177 on the HDI rankings. The Netherlands uses the Euro (€) as its currency.

New Zealand
New Zealand is an industrialized, free-market economy that competes globally. GDP in New Zealand is $21,740, and unemployment is 4.7%. New Zealand imports a lot of agricultural products. New Zealand is 18 out of 177 in the HDI rankings. New Zealand is the 43rd largest trading partner of the United States. Australia and New Zealand have a free trade agreement called Closer Economic Relations (CER). The currency is the New Zealand dollar (NZD).

Saudi Arabia
With the largest oil reserves in the world, 90% of the Saudi Arabian economy is accounted for through oil export earnings. The real GDP is $12,650 per capita; unemployment is high. The private sector is small. The HDI for Saudi Arabia is 77 out of 177 countries. The average individual has not shared in Saudi Arabia's oil prosperity, although the living conditions have improved. Saudi Arabia is the United States' 25th largest trading partner. The currency of Saudi Arabia is the *riyal* (R).

Singapore
Although Singapore is the smallest country in Southeast Asia, it has a highly developed and successful free-market economy. Singapore's GDP in 2002 was $24,040. Singapore ranks 25 out of 177 in the HDI rankings. The unemployment rate in 2004 was 4.8%. Electronics and manufacturing are the main source of exports. The recession from 2001 to 2003 caused a slump in the technology sector. Singapore is Southeast Asia's financial and high-tech hub. Singapore is the United States' 11th largest trading partner. The currency is the Singapore dollar (SGD).

South Korea
The late 1990s proved detrimental to the South Korean economy. Strikes, a large budget deficit, political scandals, bankruptcies, and competition from other countries and corporations affected the economy. The South Korean economy is very dependent on international trade. The real GDP is $16,950 per capita. The HDI for South Korea is 28 of 177 countries. South Korea is the United States' seventh largest trading partner. The currency of South Korea is the *won* (W).

Taiwan
Taiwan is a major exporter of textiles, electronics, machinery, metals, timber products, and high-technology items. Taiwan has a large middle class and a highly skilled labor force. Unemployment is currently at 5%. The real GDP is $23,400 per capita. Taiwan is the United States' ninth largest trading partner. China is Taiwan's largest trading partner. The currency is the New Taiwan dollar (NT$).

POLITICAL SYSTEMS

The **political system** is the governing system of the country, which can be based on dictatorship, inherited rights, elected procedures, consensus, or conquest. A person's age, economic expertise, or marital status may be considered when selecting people for political positions in some countries. In other countries, oratory skills and the ability to sway public opinion may be factors. Group members may even select a political leader because they believe the person to have supernatural powers. A description of a few political systems follows (*CultureGrams,* 2004).

United States

The U.S. political system is a democratic federal government with individual states having designated rights. The president is elected by the Electoral College, and other positions are voted on by the people. Congress, which is dominated by the Democratic and Republican parties, has two houses: the 435-seat House of Representatives and the 100-seat Senate. U.S. citizens tend to be very proud of their political system yet may not be well informed about politics. However, U.S. citizens do not like their system to be criticized. The voting age is 18.

> U.S. Americans tend to embody what to many is a curious combination of admiration for their political system in general and disdain for its particular operations. They criticize their leaders but do not want foreigners to do so. They think about politics as a separable aspect of life, one they can choose to ignore. Since 9/11, there has been a strong resurgence of patriotism in the United States. This resurgence has again raised the question of separation of church and state in the country.

The United States has a separate judicial branch of government. Lobbyists are very influential groups in regard to government policies.

Australia

Australia, which is a federal parliamentary state, has six federated states, the Australian Capital Territory, and the Northern Territory. Queen of England is head of state, but she is represented by an Australian governor-general. The prime minister and federal Parliament (76 Senators, 148 House of Representatives) are elected by those over 18 years of age. Failure to vote in federal and state elections may result in a fine. The major parties are the Labour Party, the Liberal Party, and the National Party.

Canada

Canada is officially a confederation with a parliamentary democracy, a system partially patterned after that of Great Britain and the United States. The Parliament includes up to 104 senators, who are appointed, as well as 301 members of the House of Commons, who are elected. The people elect the prime minister, who is the leader of the dominant political party in the House of Commons. The central government has power in the areas of national health insurance, trade, the military, and development.

The country is divided into provinces; each province controls its region. The Queen of England is represented by a governor general. The voting age is 18.

China

The national policies of the People's Republic of China are determined by a 20-member Politboro and a 7-member Standing Committee. The only legal party is the Chinese Communist Party (CCP). The president of the country is the general secretary of the CCP. The National People's Congress has 2,979 locally elected members.

Hong Kong is a self-governing region of China. The Hong Kong's chief executive is advised by 15 Executive Councilors and 60 Legislative Councilors. Hong Kong has 36 representatives to China's national legislature.

England

The United Kingdom (of which England is a part) is ruled by a constitutional monarchy with a parliament. Although the monarch (Queen Elizabeth II) is head of state, elected officials govern through Parliament. England has no written constitution. The main legislative body is the 659-member House of Commons, 529 of whom are from England, elected by citizens over the age of 18. The party with the most members in Parliament governs; that party's leader becomes the prime minister, who, along with the cabinet, governs as the executive body. The 1,200-member House of Lords makes up Parliament's upper chamber; two-thirds are hereditary members, and one-third is made up of appointed life members.

France

The French Republic has 22 regions divided into 96 departments. The president serves as head of state and as the executive head of the government for a seven-year term. The president from the majority party in the National Assembly appoints the prime minister. The National Assembly has 577 members who are elected for five-year terms. The Senate has 321 members who serve nine-year terms and have staggered elections every three years by 130,000 local councilors. The voting age is 18.

Germany

Germany's president is elected by members of the federal and state legislatures for up to two five-year terms. The chancellor is head of the government and is elected by the lower house of Parliament, the Federal Assembly. The legislature has two houses, the Federal Council (*Bundesrat*) and the Federal Assembly (*Bundestag*). There are 16 states in the country, and each has its own legislature and autonomy in many matters. State governments elect 69 members to the *Bundesrat*, and 598 members of the *Bundestag* are elected by popular vote. The voting age is 18.

India

India is a democratic republic that has 26 states and 6 union territories. India has a president, prime minister, and the parliament. The parliament has two houses: the *Rajya Sabha* (the Council of States) and the *Lok Sabha* (the House of the People). The *Rajya Sabha* has 250 members, and the *Lok Sabha* has 543 elected members. The voting age is 18.

Japan

Japan, a constitutional monarchy, has an emperor with no governing power as its head of state. The prime minister, who heads the government, and his cabinet make up the executive branch. Legislative power rests with the *Diet*, a 252-seat House of

Councillors (or upper house) and the 512-seat House of Representatives (or lower house). The 47 prefectures or provinces have governors who are elected by the people. The voting age is 20.

Mexico

Mexico has a federal government with the president elected by all voters over 18 years of age. The legislature is made up of a 128-seat Senate and a 500-seat Chamber of Deputies. Although voting is compulsory, it is not enforced. Technically the 31 states of Mexico are autonomous; however, they are heavily controlled by the federal government in the areas of education, security, and national industries.

The Netherlands

The governing structure of the Netherlands is a constitutional monarchy. The Netherlands has a queen, prime minister, and Council of State. The country has a 75-seat upper house called the First Chamber and a 150-seat lower house called the Second Chamber; they are all elected by the people who are 18 or older.

New Zealand

New Zealand is a democratic parliamentary monarchy with Queen of England as head of state. The queen is represented by a governor-general. The prime minister and a 120-seat House of Representatives are elected by those 18 years of age and older.

Saudi Arabia

The Saudi Arabian political system is comprised of 14 regions called governorates. Each governorate is headed by an *emir* (governor) who answers to the king. The king, who is chief of state, rules with the Council of Ministers. The system of governance issued in 1992 changed the political structure; the new system provides for a Consultative Council of 60 appointed members who serve as advisers to the king and Council of Ministers. After the current crown prince serves, all future kings will be elected by the princes (now numbering more than 500); new crown princes will be appointed and subject to dismissal by the king. This new system will eliminate inherited rule. The Qu'ran is the official constitution.

Singapore

Singapore is a democratic republic that has a president, prime minister, and parliament. The parliament is made up of 93 members of whom 84 are elected and 9 are appointed by the president. The voting age is 21, and all citizens are required to vote in national elections.

South Korea

The Republic of South Korea elects most members of government. The State Council includes the president, the prime minister (whom the president appoints), and 15 to 30 ministry heads. The National Assembly has 273 members who serve four-year terms and are elected. The voting age is 20.

Taiwan

Taiwan is a multiparty democracy. The president, the 339-seat National Assembly, and the 225-seat Legislative Yuan are elected. The National Assembly will likely be abolished in the future. The political parties are the Nationalist Party, the Democratic Progressive Party, the New Party, and the People First Party. The voting age is 20.

WORLD ECONOMICS

Companies worldwide have become increasingly affected by economic, political, and competitive pressures from companies in other countries. Although it is well known that the automobile, steel, textile, and electronic industries face worldwide competition, it may not be as well known that many small- and medium-sized firms also have to compete in world markets (Nath, 1988).

The United States maintained a substantial technological lead after World War II during the 1950s, 1960s, and the beginning of the 1970s. Today this competitive edge is gone, and the macroeconomy of the world affects the performance of U.S. industry. Many U.S. industries were not prepared for this change in the macroeconomy, and the U.S. government had to provide temporary protection for industries and negotiate with foreign firms to limit their exports to the United States. In addition, the Department of Justice relaxed antitrust rules, thus allowing more joint ventures. When a particular industry is caught in the growing complexity of global economics, many smaller firms, regions, and communities may face adverse economic times. Although U.S. companies are facing intensive foreign competition, the groundwork has been laid to increase productivity, reduce capacity requirements, and increase flexibility, making the United States able to compete in the long run.

Although the United States had a Trade om Goods deficit of $496.5 billion in 2003, direct foreign investment in the United States that year was $29.8 billion, down from $64.30 billion (*U.S. Trade in Goods,* 2004). During the 1980s and 1990s, the inflow of foreign funds was due to high interest rates in the United States, the value of the dollar, stock prices of U.S. firms, and the formation of joint ventures. The influx of foreign investments has made it difficult to distinguish a U.S. firm from a foreign firm. Many companies now have no allegiance to a given nation but are truly multinational firms in their thinking and actions. The actions multinational firms take are in the best interest of their corporation rather than the best interest of their originating country. If a corporation can manufacture a product cheaper in another country, it will do so by closing the current plant and opening a new plant in another country. Many product lines are produced almost entirely outside the United States today, including televisions, camcorders, electronic components, tires, and clothing. Some firms have had to move abroad to compete with the imports. With wages being very high in the United States compared to many other locations in the world, firms could no longer entice United States citizens to buy their U.S.-produced products.

The multinational firm also has to deal with a very complex political environment. A successful domestic firm learns and operates within the existing political situation. A firm that moves into the international environment must learn how to manage and predict politics in other nations. The multinational firm deals successfully with many diverse and conflicting political environments. Some people are concerned that because of the size, wealth, resources, and knowledge of some multinational companies, they will become political bodies themselves. In many countries, the multinational firm exercises power that parallels the power of the country's government. For example, in the Middle East, corporations within the oil cartels exert power that equals the government's power. Some multinational managers view the world as a single marketplace, ignoring national boundaries. The multinational company may well be an agent of change in the future.

Multinational companies also must be concerned with supernationalism, international politics, and international relations of the nations in which they operate. Decrees by such organizations as the United Nations, the European Union, and NAFTA are only a few examples of **supernationalism** today. Regionalism and economic interdependency are common in international politics, and it is projected that more regional trade agreements will be formed in the near future.

Companies also have to be concerned with subnationalism and the strife and political havoc that can result. **Subnationalism** exists when a political body attempts to unite diverse people under one government. With the discarding of communism in Eastern Europe, one of the results has been that subnationals want their own countries and their own government once again.

Nationalism, supernationalism, and subnationalism are all active forces multinational companies have to consider because such factors affect the politics and the economics of the areas of the world in which they operate. Although the form and content of the "-isms" may vary from region to region, the possibility of upheaval is something multinational companies must consider. A company must analyze the political environment's positive and negative aspects before expanding into the environment. Other economic differences that may need to be considered before doing business in another nation include chronic high inflation versus low inflation, developed banking systems versus primitive systems, agricultural economy versus an industrial economy versus a technological economy, low employee productivity versus high employee productivity, favorable versus unfavorable balance of payments and currency exchange rates.

Note: CultureGrams, published by ProQuest Information and Learning, provides additional information related to conducting business in a number of countries. The four-page *CultureGram* for each country covers a variety of topics, such as greetings, visiting, eating, gestures, people, lifestyle, land and climate, history, commerce, government, economy, education, transportation, communication, health, and information for the traveler.

EDUCATIONAL SYSTEMS

The educational system of a country may be formal, informal, or a combination of the two. People in societies such as the Maoris of New Zealand and the Aleuts of Alaska still pass on a great deal of information concerning their cultural heritage by word of mouth; people in other societies, as in the United States and Canada, include most of their cultural heritage in textbooks. Other societies do some of both. However it is accomplished, every society has a way of passing on its cultural heritage. **Cultural heritage** is the body of customary beliefs, social forms, material traits, thoughts, speech, and the artistic and intellectual traditions of a society.

> There are many different and legitimate ways of thinking; we in the West value one of these ways above all others—the one we call "logic," a linear system that has been with us since Socrates. . . . We have been taught to think linearly rather than comprehensively. . . . Given our linear, step-by-step, compartmentalized way of thinking, fostered by the schools and public media, it is impossible for our leaders to consider events comprehensively. (Hall, 1976, p. 255)

Because societies are different, formal education varies between countries. The types of educational training in business also vary between and within countries and may include liberal arts, technical training, and apprenticeships. Liberal arts training includes the humanities and considers learning important in its own right. Technical business training is generally narrowly focused along specialized lines such as marketing, management, finance, economics, accounting, or management information systems. A problem with technical training is that there is very little human training and thought given to the people part of the business process. The apprenticeship program offers students practical experience and theory.

As the population of Third World nations receives training beyond the secondary level, these nations become more developed and similar in their use of technologies (Victor, 1997). One of the arguments for NAFTA is that it will help Mexico train and educate its population and will prevent foreign companies from taking advantage of an illiterate workforce. NAFTA requires that a company going into Mexico from the United States or Canada provide the same safety standards within its plants as in its home country and contribute to water treatment facilities and sewage treatment plants. The costs of such standards make the advantages of a workforce willing to work for low wages deteriorate quickly.

Accessibility to education varies from country to country. Much of Europe operates on a two-track system in which, at approximately the age of 12, children are assigned to a vocational track or a university track. The United States, Japan, and the Russian Federation, however, have open access to the educational system for all children; the importance the family places on education, the child's ability, and the quality of the child's teachers all play an important role in how far a child will go in the educational system (Victor, 1997).

How people are expected to learn may be seen as a continuum that ranges from very involved in the learning process (much interaction between teachers and students) to little involvement (no interaction between teachers and students). In the Israeli kibbutz, for example, children are expected to react spontaneously, and the classrooms are noisy. Chinese classrooms, on the other hand, are silent because of the reverence paid to knowledge, truth, and wisdom (Samovar & Porter, 2003).

The value of an education, after it is received, varies again from country to country. A description of educational systems in the United States and other selected countries is given in the following sections (*CultureGrams,* 2004). Many smaller and less developed African and Latin American countries have some of the poorest literacy rates; however, the Scandinavian countries are all 99% literate for both males and females.

United States

In the United States, education for those who are 5 to 16 years of age is compulsory and free. Although not highly competitive up to the secondary level, the U.S. educational system is somewhat competitive at the postsecondary level at such schools as Harvard, the Massachusetts Institute of Technology (MIT), and Yale, where intellectual demands may be rigorous. Because education is a state's right, competition between and within state educational systems may vary. The literacy rate in the United States is 99%. However, variations exist by region, and functional illiteracy exists in the adult population. Even though graduating from certain prestigious institutions of higher learning may help in securing initial corporate positions, what a person does on the job determines the person's career and the companies for which the person will work. University ties then become less important.

> Anybody can get into college in the United States, according to Malaysian students. Malaysians, remarking on the easy accessibility of American colleges and universities, compared U.S. schools unfavorably to those of the British who once ruled Malaysia and provided the model for their educational system. However, the Malaysians observed, "You Americans put men on the moon, so there must be something right about your system." (Althen, 2003, p. 102)

Australia

Australia has 99% literacy for males and females. Education is public and financed by federal funds. Australians have seven years of primary and five years of secondary education that are compulsory. A significant portion of the population goes on to the university to complete some higher education.

Canada

In Canada, the provinces are responsible for their educational system; however, all the provinces provide free and compulsory education for persons between the ages of 6 and 16. The literacy rate is 99%. In Newfoundland, the primary and secondary education is free but operated by different religious groups. In Quebec, the government supports school boards and directs school curricula for Catholic and Protestant schools. Although the government subsidizes a university education, students pay for tuition. About 10% of the population has university degrees, and other students may complete a two-year technical program or attend a two-year university preparatory program.

China

Although 100% of children are enrolled in the first grade, the overall literacy rate in China is 86% (the male literacy rate is 93% and female is 79%). Children attend school six days a week. The government plans to mandate school for nine years in the future. Less than 10% of the people attend college. Students have to pay their tuition or sign a contract with a state company who will sponsor them.

Hong Kong has a higher literacy rate of 94% overall (97% for males and 91% for females). Education is considered very important to success in Hong Kong, and entrance to the better secondary schools is very competitive.

England

The educational systems of England and Canada are similar. England has free and compulsory education for those between the ages of 5 and 16, and its literacy rate is 99%. The General Certificate of Secondary Education Exam is taken at age 16 to allow students to earn the General Certificate. At age 18, after earning the General Certificate of Education, they may attend one of more than 40 universities or attend one of the various professional schools. Members of England's upper class tend to go to the elite educational institutions. Although it is possible for someone in the lower classes to attend such schools, primarily those with alumni connections attend the elite educational institutions. Therefore, a person's position in society determines educational opportunities.

France

France's educational system has several unique aspects. Education is free and compulsory for those between the ages of 6 and 16. The literacy rate is 99%. The Catholic schools, partially subsidized by the state, enroll 20% of the children. Secondary school begins at age 11 and continues through age 18. Secondary education is offered by *lycées* and colleges. The *lycée* is the equivalent of a U.S. junior college. On completing secondary school, students take a comprehensive exam for one of the 60 universities. Except for marketing schools, most university training is also free in France.

The French also consider the university from which someone graduates to be very important because it determines that person's position in society. Although positions in business and government are not limited to a few institutions, alumni of the Grandes Écoles are considered more favorably. The Grandes Écoles and the alumni of the Grandes Écoles control business in France; and to be successful in business dealings in France, people must network through alumni.

Germany

In the Federal Republic of Germany's educational system, people must determine their careers early in life. Education is free from kindergarten through the university level. School begins with preschool at age 4; however, school is mandatory from age 6 to 15. Literacy overall and for males is 99% and 98% for females. People of Germany are required to choose between technical training and college training at the age of 13. The entrance exam to universities is very difficult; acceptance into the university can be gained only by passing a rigorous exam after finishing a college preparatory school.

India

In India, education is free and compulsory from 6 to 14 years of age. Girls tend to drop out of school early; in fact, only 20% graduate from secondary school and less than 10% enter higher education. India has more than 250 universities and 3,000 colleges. India's overall literacy is 58%; the literacy rate for males is 69% and 46% for females.

Iraq

The literacy rate in Iraq is 58% overall—71% for males and 45% for females. Religious education is important to the people of Iraq. Because major religious events reported in the Torah, Old Testament, New Testament, and Qu'ran happened in Iraq, Iraq is an important historical location to Judaism, Christianity, and Islam.

A verse of particular interest is the Qu'ran 9:11: "For it was written that a son of Arabia would awaken a fearsome Eagle. The wrath of the Eagle would be felt throughout the lands of Allah and lo, while some of the people trembled in despair, still more rejoiced; for the wrath of the Eagle cleansed the lands of Allah; and there was peace."

Japan

The educational system in Japan is very competitive; entrance exams to private schools and universities are rigorous. Competition is keen for acceptance to the prestigious schools because graduating from these schools usually assures the person a position in a top corporation. Japan's literacy rate is 99%. Education for persons between the ages of 6 and 15 is generally free and compulsory; after age 15, tuition must be paid. Math and science are stressed.

In Japan, education is expected to be difficult and sometimes unpleasant.

> The story goes that an elderly Japanese college professor took a student's paper, rolled it, and hit the student over the head with it yelling, "It's no good!" When asked why he had done that rather than offering the student some suggestions for improving the paper, he replied, "If I told him what to do, that would be too easy and he would forget. If I make him find it himself, he will always remember." (Dillon, 1990)

In addition, the heavy intellectual demand on the students occurs during the primary and secondary education years rather than in the college years. After high school, the students take a very competitive university entrance exam. Because the university a student graduates from determines the company for which he or she will work, the better the university, the better that person's life will be. A close allegiance (i.e., sense of loyalty) is maintained between graduating classes, employee careers, alma mater, and year of graduation.

Mexico
Education in Mexico has only recently reached the masses. Mexico has compulsory and free education for persons between the ages of 6 and 14. Although the literacy rate reported is 92% overall (94% for males and 90% for females), figures on various subcultures, such as the Amerindian, vary. Following six years of primary education and three years of secondary education, students choose either a preuniversity education or a technical education program. College entrance exams are difficult; only one-third of the students pass the exam. A university degree takes from three to seven years to complete.

The Netherlands
In the Netherlands, school is free and compulsory from 5 to 16 years of age. Primary education ends at age 12; secondary school begins with two years of basic education followed by choosing between different types of high schools from prevocational to preuniversity. Higher education is subsidized in the Netherlands. Literacy rates overall and for males and females are all 99%.

New Zealand
Education is free and compulsory from ages 5 to 16 in New Zealand. Students who attend the university study for two years after the compulsory requirements are met. A rigorous exam is administered in the fifth year for university admission. More New Zealand women meet the qualifications than men and have a higher university admission rate. New Zealand has an overall, male, and female literacy rate of 99%.

Saudi Arabia
Saudi Arabia's educational system, including university instruction, is funded by the government. In Saudi Arabia, the adult literacy rate is increasing and is currently 76% overall—for males it is 84% and for females, 68%. Children age 4 to 6 attend

kindergarten with boys and girls in the same classroom. After age six, boys and girls attend separate schools. Six years of primary school are followed by three years of intermediate school and three years of secondary school. During the second year of secondary school, the student follows either a science or a literary track. Although males and females attend the same university, they have separate classes and are given hours they can each use such common facilities as the library.

Singapore
In Singapore, school is compulsory for ages 6 to 16. At the end of primary school, students take an exit exam that places them in secondary school by ability and aptitude. Most Singaporeans graduate from a secondary school. Literacy among younger Singaporeans approaches 100%. Overall, the literacy rate is 93%–96% for males and 89% for females.

South Korea
Education is one of the virtues of Confucianism and is valued by the Korean culture. School is compulsory from ages 6 to 12. Most students complete secondary school, which is very demanding. Entering a university takes a lot of intensive training; it is very difficult to pass the entrance exam. The adult literacy rate overall is 98%–99% for males and 96% for females.

Taiwan
In Taiwan, school is free and compulsory from ages 6 to 15. Students take national exams to enter high school or senior vocational school. Entrance examinations for the university are very difficult, and students may study as long as a year before taking the exam. Many students go to universities abroad. The youth literacy rate approaches 100%. The adult literacy rate overall is 95%–98% for males and 92% for females.

Countries that do not have an entrenched formal educational infrastructure for all people tend to have two classes of people: the small, wealthy upper class and the lower class in which the majority live in poverty. The wealthy people who attend school and in many cases go to college abroad have a very different view of the world and their cultural heritage. The masses hold a strong allegiance to the cultural past. Depending on the country involved, the literacy level of the masses can vary widely. A person cannot take for granted that everyone can read, has a knowledge of mathematics, or is familiar with technology. Many times what is important in one nation may be very unimportant in another nation (Victor, 1997).

Examples of cultures that place more emphasis on informal rather than formal education include Gambia, with 48% adult literacy and no universities; Mali, with a literacy rate of 37% for males and 17% for females, their first university currently being built in Bamako; and Bangladesh, with a literacy rate of 41%. Only 3% complete three or more years at a university compared to almost 24% of U.S. citizens who complete degrees (*CultureGrams,* 2004).

MARRIAGE AND FAMILY SYSTEMS

Marriage and family systems are made up of attitudes, beliefs, and practices related to marriage and the family that are held by people in a particular culture. To survive, all societies must procreate. Because human infants must depend on adults for their basic needs, cultures have defined how the young children in their culture will be reared and who is responsible for their care. Consequently, all cultures have devised rules concerning who can marry and have set procedures to be followed when people marry and raise families. Anthropologists have researched and categorized much of this information for us (Ferraro, 2001).

Although many ways of being a family exist, people tend to consider their own background first when they consider the concept of family. In many parts of the world, the concept of family is so strong that it is of paramount importance in each person's life. This is particularly true in the Japanese, Chinese, Spanish, African, Arabic, Indian, Italian, and Turkish cultures. In some cultures, the association of the family is so strong that sharing the family wealth with outsiders or protecting outsiders is an unknown concept. In the United States and parts of Europe, work and family life are often combined; business guests are invited to the home. The Japanese, Taiwanese, and people of many Arabic nations, on the other hand, would not invite business guests to their home.

The word family has very different connotations around the world. In the United States, the definition of a family encompasses the nuclear family and the extended family. The **nuclear family** consists of the father, mother, and children; the **extended family** consists of grandparents, uncles, aunts, and cousins (Samovar & Porter, 2003).

In many countries, the family may include second-, third-, and fourth-generation relationships. Arab families may have more than a hundred close relatives, and in Mexico even godparents are considered family. Family can mean your immediate biological family, or it can mean the entire culture. In some parts of the world, the children are reared and taught communally as in parts of Israel. Each community member takes part in raising and educating each child. The family unit, as the culture views "family," will help foster individual and/or group dependency (Victor, 1997).

In Italy, the most important affiliation is to the family, which is also responsible for a large number of self-employed people and small businesses. A necessity of Italian life is an affiliation with at least one prime interest group (such as a political party or trade union) in order to live and work. The ability to be hired and work in many countries depends on your relatives. Nepotism and favoritism are considered a way of life. However, in U.S. corporations, nepotism and favoritism are viewed with disfavor because the person being hired under such circumstances is often considered unqualified or corrupt. Corporations may need to adjust their views of family relationships in multinational business relationships to be successful (Victor, 1997).

Family systems originally evolved to meet the needs of the society; subsequently, the following forms developed: **polygyny** (or **polygamy**), one man with many wives; **polyandry,** one woman with many husbands; **monogamy,** one husband and wife; and **serial monogamy,** a number of different monogamous marriages (Dodd, 1997). See Figure 2-1.

Many Arabic countries and followers of Islam practice polygyny. The Arabic countries currently have the highest birthrate in the world; however, they also have a very small population base. In the United Arab Emirates (UAE), 80% of the people who live there are not Arabian. The UAE has had to import people to fill the jobs that are available; therefore, the government encourages men to have large families and many wives. Polyandry would help reduce the birthrate and has been practiced by many of the Polynesian nations. Monogamy is practiced in North America, South America, the Orient, Europe, and parts of Africa. Serial monogamy is practiced where

FIGURE 2-1   Family Systems

people are able to remarry after divorce or the death of a spouse; the United States practices serial monogamy.

Another aspect of family is establishing who is in control or who plays the role of the authority figure. Families can be **patriarchal** (father oriented) or **matriarchal** (mother oriented) (see Figure 2-2). Inheritance rights and the naming of children help determine whether a society is matriarchal or patriarchal (Dodd, 1997).

Jewish families are matriarchal because of the Judaic code of inheritance through the mother, although the father's name is used. Christians and followers of Islam tend to be patriarchal, and the father's name is given to the children. Spanish women maintain their maiden name by hyphenating it to their married name; however, the Spanish culture is patriarchal. Many professional women in the United States are now retaining their maiden name when they marry.

A brief description of marriage and family customs in the United States and in other selected countries follows to give you an idea of how family structure and customs vary from culture to culture (*CultureGrams*, 2004).

FIGURE 2-2   Family Authority Figures

United States

Dating in the United States begins as early as age 13. Premarital sex is common, and many couples choose to live together prior to or in place of marriage. The average age for marriage is 26 for men and 24 for women. In the United States, you will find a nuclear family, which consists of either monogamous or serial monogamous parents or single-parent families. The nuclear family generally maintains a close relationship with members of the extended family. The traditional family includes a mother, father, and one or more children. However, one out of three children is born out of wedlock. Some women are choosing not to marry the father of the baby or are using sperm banks if they prefer to be solely responsible for a child. Almost half of all women work, thus affecting decisions on family size. Many older members of the extended family live in private or government institutions rather than with their immediate families, partly because of the mobility of the family and changes in living conditions.

Australia

In Australia, dating begins by age 15 and sometimes in small groups. The age to wed is 23 for women and 25 for men. Many couples are choosing to live together before or instead of marrying; however, church weddings are still common. Australian couples generally have two or three children, and extended families are not strong in Australia. Women comprise 40% of the workforce, and single-parent homes are becoming more common. Independence is valued; the elderly live in their own homes as long as they can.

Canada

The Canadian family system is similar to that of the United States in that dating begins before age 16. Many couples are choosing to live together. If they do marry, it is generally after 30 years of age. Frequently, both parents work outside the home. The average family size is two children; one-third of marriages end in divorce.

China

The family is more important than the individual to the Chinese. The elderly are highly respected and taken care of by their children. Because boys are prized as heirs to the family name, there are currently more males in China. Young people do date, but they are discouraged from getting serious until men are 22 and women are 20. If they marry before these ages, they lose government benefits. College students cannot marry until after graduation. The women maintain their maiden name; however, the children receive the father's surname.

Hong Kong couples generally wait to marry until they have job security and can live by themselves. Even if women work outside the home, they are still responsible for the home. Usually they have only one or two children. They also have one of the lowest divorce rates in the world.

England

In England, dating begins around 13 to 16 years of age. British youth typically date only one person at a time. People seem to be marrying later in life and having fewer children. The legal age to marry is 16, but most marry in their late twenties and will have one to two children. Single-parent families are becoming more common.

France

France tends to have an elitist attitude toward the family. Dating begins around age 15. In France, social class, wealth, and educational level are important when choosing a spouse. The nuclear family is common in France; however, living together before or instead of marrying is also common. The average family has only one child, with many couples choosing to have no children. Many of the French have moved away from the extended family to work or study.

Germany

The German family system includes dating that is Dutch treat (each gender pays his or her own expenses). There is no word for dating in the German language. Marriage occurs generally after the age of 20, but Germans usually believe they must have some financial security prior to marriage. Living together before marriage is not unusual. The family is generally patriarchal, and one to two children are the norm. In the former East Germany, it is common for both parents to work, although in what was West Germany, it is less common for both parents to work.

India

Dating is not customary in India. Most marriages are arranged with the consent of the bride and groom. Weddings are great feasts and ceremonies. Families still tend to be large; middle- and upper-class families provide financially for their children until they finish their education and take a position. The family is patriarchal; the elderly are revered and taken care of by their children.

Iraq

In Iraq, women are very protected; dating is rare. Marriages are arranged with the bride and groom's consent. First cousins may marry. The groom pays a dowry to the family of the bride. Weddings are great feasts and ceremonies. Families tend to be large and include the extended family in activities. Several generations often live in one household.

Japan

In Japan, the family system is different. In the past, most marriages were arranged; now, however, many of the people from Western cultures choose their own spouse. Dating begins around age 15, but the average age for marriage is 27 for men and a little younger for women. Men feel they must be financially secure before marriage, and they assume financial responsibility for the wedding. The family includes the extended family and has a strong sense of obligation and responsibility. A person's actions reflect strongly on the family as well as on the person. Although the father is the breadwinner, the mother runs the household. In the past, it has been considered improper for women to work outside the home; however, many of the younger women have chosen to have a career rather than marriage and a family. Families tend to be small with fewer than three children. Having a male heir is important in Japan as well as in most other Asian countries. The divorce rate is very low, and the marriages are monogamous.

Mexico

In the Mexican family system, dating is allowed; however, a boy often meets the girl at a prearranged place rather than picking her up at her home. Marriage follows the customary Catholic traditions. The Mexican family tends to be large by U.S. standards (more than three children), and family unity is very important. The divorce rate is low, so monogamous families are the norm. In the rural areas particularly, households include members of the extended family. Although the family is patriarchal, the mother runs the household. Family responsibilities take precedence over all other responsibilities.

The Netherlands
In the Netherlands, youth begin dating with group activities at 13 to 16 years of age. Couples often live together before marriage. Because couples pay for their own weddings, guests generally will give them money to cover the expenses. Children leave home at 18 years of age. Families are small and very close. The elderly usually live by themselves. Both parents tend to work outside the home.

New Zealand
Dating begins at 15 or 16 in New Zealand with group activities beginning at 12 years of age. Marriage comes in the late twenties, and many couples choose to live together first. The family generally has two children, and both parents work. The number of single parents is increasing. Many families are very close; however, these family ties are not as strong as they once were.

Saudi Arabia
The family system in Saudi Arabia is very different from that of the United States. Saudi Arabian marriages are arranged, although a minority of men and women are being allowed to choose their mates. Because of the separation of the genders, there is no dating. Islamic law allows a man to have four wives with the wives' permission; however, most Saudi men have only one wife. Most Saudi families live with extended families and have strong patriarchal authority but are matriarchal in the home. The family is the most important part of a Saudi's life. Women and men are separated in most aspects of life. Women do not socialize in public with men but are always accompanied by a male relative when in public. Women do not interact with men outside their family and may not drive a car or ride a bicycle.

Singapore
In Singapore, dating is discouraged until a child is 17 years of age as it is seen as interfering with school studies. Marriage comes in the late twenties. Because there are many religions, a large variety of wedding ceremonies take place. Generally couples have only one or two children. The elderly tend to live with their children or close by, and it is the responsibility of the children to take care of the parents. Because many parents both work, they tend to share the household responsibilities or hire household help.

South Korea
In South Korea, the oldest son receives the greatest respect but also has the greatest responsibilities. Family hierarchies and genealogies are very important and determine who receives more respect within the family. Because of their studies, Korean youth rarely date seriously until college or when they begin working. In the rural areas, some marriages are still arranged; however, the parties involved do know each other.

Taiwan

Family is very close in Taiwan with elderly parents often living with their children. A strong sense of unity and obligation to other family members is part of the Taiwanese culture. Dating does not begin until people start their higher education because of the concentration on education. Marriage age is generally between 27 and 30.

SOCIAL HIERARCHIES AND INTERACTION

Although human behavior is never totally controlled, society, through social order, limits its randomness. People learn through enculturation what is and is not proper social behavior. Generally, learning is introduced by the older family members to the younger family members; however, most of the social ideals arise in society in general and not in the family directly. Many times, there are family and nonfamily orientations. A good starting point to learn about another culture is from children's literature, television shows, and games that are enjoyed by the culture. The social structure of a society tends to be enduring and is shared by the members of the culture. Social values are changed very slowly when dealing with an entire society. As business becomes multinational and as people meet and deal with other ways of living, proper **social hierarchies** and **social interactions** are being tested. We either adapt or remain restricted in the cocoon of our own culture. If you are to communicate successfully in a multicultural environment, you must understand that different is simply different, not better or worse. The actions of the people of other cultures are correct for them.

The family functions at many levels within a society: they are the caregivers of the young and the old; they provide emotional support; they transmit culture; and they transmit identity. The family tells the children early in life who they are and with whom they should play. The family is part of a wider culture. As the Swedish proverb says, "Children act in the village as they have learned at home." The home is where we first learn about our culture. It is interesting that as governments change, the family unit continues to survive. The idea of family is one of the oldest and fundamental building blocks of human beings. Many cultures in the world consider the elderly the most important members of the family; these cultures include the Chinese, Japanese, Arabs, Mexicans, Malaysians, Filipinos, French, Native Americans, and African Americans (Samovar & Porter, 2004).

In examining social hierarchies and social interactions, we must consider the five sets of structures into which society can be divided: social reciprocity, group membership, intermediaries, formality, and property (Condon & Yousef, 1998).

Social reciprocity refers to the way in which formal and informal communications are handled. Someone who believes in independent social reciprocity tries to avoid commitment; under symmetrical-obligatory social reciprocity, people have an equal obligation. Under complementary-obligatory social reciprocity, people are forever indebted to others.

Group membership has two extremes: People can belong to many groups or very few groups, and there is a middle ground between the two. People belonging to many groups generally are not strongly associated with any of them and do not want to give up their personal freedom; likewise, people who belong to few groups for a long time may tend to subordinate themselves to the group. The people occupying the middle ground try to balance group affiliation and personal freedom.

The use of intermediaries in societies can tell you a great deal about the makeup of the society. **Intermediaries** are people who act as go-betweens with other people. If intermediaries are not used, society members are direct and independent. If intermediaries are always used, society members dislike confrontation and are very group oriented. In the middle, society members are sometimes direct and sometimes want someone else to intervene.

Formality is the degree of preciseness, regularity, or conformity expected within the society. Formality is particularly troublesome between cultures because even the most formal culture also has some informality and because the most informal culture has some formality. Selective formality, which is the middle ground between the two extremes, can be very different in various cultures.

The last structure is **property,** which is something that is or may be possessed. Property can be viewed as private, utilitarian, or community. U.S. Americans think of property as an extension of the self; Mexicans think of property ownership in relation to feelings and need. In the past, communist countries had community property. Native Americans also believed that land was community property. Even in private property cultures, there is common property, such as parks, land grant colleges, and hospitals. The three values of the five structures discussed are capitalism, socialism, and communism.

True equality does not exist in any country in the world because of power, wealth, and privilege, which exist in all countries. Although the United States considers equal opportunity important, the differences in children's lives make it clear that not all will grow up with an equal opportunity for wealth or position. Human beings do not choose their cultural interaction and social hierarchical foundations; they are born or adopted into them. Hierarchical divisions can be social classes, gender, ethnic groups, castes, or tribes. Although aristocracies or monarchies may not be active in many nations in the world, they still form a large network. Through this network, many members are still in positions to influence the public. Religion and legal systems are used in many cultures to enforce class distinctions.

No nation in the world treats women and men equally. The Human Development Index (HDI) was developed by the United Nations Development Program to measure individual purchasing power, health, and education for the population as a whole and for women. Table 2-1 contains the rankings of overall HDI and the Gender-Related Development Index (GDI) (*Human Development Reports*, 2004). Gender roles are learned first in the home and then in the broader culture.

Laws, rules, or religion may preserve or dictate social interaction and the social hierarchies that may evolve within a given culture. All cultures have punishments that are administered when cultural norms are violated. Although punishment is universal, the scope of punishment for the same crime may vary significantly between cultures and include fines, incarceration, or death.

When working interculturally, you may need to adjust your approach to work to match that of people in the host country. Differences exist in such areas as speed and efficiency, time, rules of work, kinesics, friendships, work-role expectations, social acceptance, the showing of respect, correct body posture, knowledge, the showing of empathy, role behavior, management interaction, and ambiguity tolerance. By taking the time to learn about the characteristics of a culture, you show people your sincerity and friendship. Management skills that consider differences among cultures will solve business problems more successfully. Friendships in many cultures are necessary before any business is ever conducted. In fact, friendship and work may be interrelated. Examples of

Country	HDI	GDI	Country	HDI	GDI
Norway	1	1	Italy	21	21
Sweden	2	2	Hong Kong	23	23
Australia	3	3	Greece	24	25
Canada	4	4	Singapore	25	28
The Netherlands	5	5	Portugal	26	24
Belgium	6	7	South Korea	28	29
Iceland	7	6	Costa Rica	45	44
United States	8	8	Mexico	53	50
Japan	9	12	Saudi Arabia	77	77
Ireland	10	14	Philippines	83	83
Switzerland	11	11	Paraguay	89	75
United Kingdom	12	9	China	94	71
Finland	13	10	Sri Lanka	96	73
Denmark	17	13	India	127	103
New Zealand	18	18	Swaziland	137	109
Germany	19	19	Kenya	148	114

TABLE 2-1 Rankings of Overall HDI and Gender-Related Development Index (GDI) in 34 Countries

social hierarchies and interactions for the United States and other selected cultures follow (*CultureGrams*, 2004; *Human Development Reports*, 2004; Samovar & Porter, 2004).

United States
In the United States, people like to believe they can rise above cultural bias and change their status; yet at the same time, many find security in the social hierarchy and social interaction patterns into which they were born. A common saying in the United States is, "The apple does not fall far from the tree." In the United States, wealth is related to social class. However, the U.S. society still admires achievement above all else. People who invent, discover, or "make it on their own" are widely admired. U.S. Americans enjoy socializing and are frank and outspoken; they will discuss most subjects except personal issues. U.S. Americans tend to be informal, belong to very few groups, do not use intermediaries, and are possessive of property.

Australia
Australians value tolerance and fairness and enjoy owning property. They dislike aggression and pompous behaviors. They are very polite people and enjoy having fun. As a culture, they are very clean and active environmentalists.

Canada
Canadians view their society as separate from the United States and do not like being considered as U.S. people living in Canada. French Canadians are very proud of the cultural heritage they maintain. Canadians in general are very proud to be Canadian, and they take special pride in their own province. Canadians are generally more formal than U.S. residents but are very friendly and kind to guests. They tend to be very social but conservative; etiquette is important to them.

China

The Chinese are a very hospitable, yet reserved, people. According to the principle of *guanxi,* friends are committed to helping each other when the need arises. Maintaining family honor and social standing is very important. Confucianism has an impact on the attitudes of the people and reinforces the biological and cultural forces that exist in China. Hong Kong also holds the Confucian standards as a way of life.

England

Tradition and customs are very important to the English. The English tend to be reserved and expect others to act accordingly. They are embarrassed by displays of emotion or excessive enthusiasm—unless it is at a cricket or *futbol* game. Owning a house with a garden is very important to the English. Politeness and humor are very important in English society; however, their sense of humor and sarcasm are very different from the United States. In a study of television advertisements, Martin, Chaney, and Moore (2003) found that companies used a local advertising style when advertising in England and used more puns and satire than they did in advertisements in Japan or Mexico.

France

The French are very hierarchical; there is a correct way to do things, and everything else would be incorrect. Success, according to the French, is measured by education, family, and finances. Friendships are not made easily, but once made, are very important.

Germany

As an individualistic culture, Germans are also a hierarchical society. Germans display a strong internal discipline and culturally have a need for order and structure. In addition, they value honesty and thriftiness. Friendships are not developed quickly, but they are considered very important.

Japan

The Japanese are very concerned with social reciprocity, which can be seen in the importance of gift giving. Gift giving signifies respect for the recipient. The peak of gift giving is at the end of each year. Formality and conformity in life, work, and family are all very important aspects of the social hierarchy of the society. The Japanese are very social and devoted to their families, employers, and superiors. Friendships are not made easily but are made for life and not taken lightly. Loyalty and seeking fulfillment through the group rather than as an individual is very important. The Japanese like to use intermediaries, particularly when trying to resolve negative situations in order to help everyone save face. Property is very important but quite expensive because so many people live in such small geographic areas.

> Japanese men have a saying: "To have the best of all worlds is to have an American house, eat Chinese food, and have a Japanese wife. To have the worst of all worlds is to have a Japanese house, eat British food, and have an American wife."

Mexico
Mexicans view social reciprocity as very important. Mexicans are good hosts and place great importance on being a good employer, a good employee, and a good friend. People of Mexico involve religion in their social interactions. Most Mexicans are Catholic and take their religion and religious celebrations very seriously. Much of their life is informal with the exception of their religion. Their attitude toward property is an aspect of their social attitude of sharing. Property is viewed in a utilitarian way as belonging to those who need it. A possessive attitude toward property is infrequent.

The Netherlands
The Dutch tend to plan and schedule rather than be spontaneous. The Dutch respect privacy, honesty, and directness. Egalitarianism is a very central part of the Dutch society. A strong need for order gives the society its hierarchical structure.

New Zealand
New Zealanders enjoy a relaxed and informal lifestyle. People of New Zealand are practical and self-reliant. They value home ownership. In addition, theirs is a multicultural and egalitarian society.

Saudi Arabia
For the people of Saudi Arabia, life moves at a slower pace than that of Western nations. Social reciprocity is very important. Although the people are very friendly and hospitable, their personal privacy is important. The social hierarchy has been maintained by formal and conservative traditions. Saudi Arabians are devoted to their extended family and to their religion. The Islamic religion is their way of life.

Singapore
In Singapore, the society is unique as it blends the traditional Asian values with Western values. Goals include a good career, a condominium, car, and money. Being able to afford material possessions is very important. Singaporeans have an ordered society that is enforced by law as well as culture.

South Korea
Confucianism permeates South Korean life. Status is determined by age, gender, education, family background, wealth, occupation, and political ideology. Social contacts determine success. South Koreans tend to be very friendly. Young people are much more materially oriented then their parents or grandparents. Genealogy and backgrounds are very important and determine how people are treated in this hierarchical society.

Taiwan
The Taiwanese are very friendly and generous. The Confucian ethics are seen throughout the society. Material possessions are important, but a good education is the most important possession. People of Taiwan are hard working and avoid criticism or frankness.

Terms

- Cultural heritage
- Cultural universals
- Economic systems
- Extended family
- Exports
- Formality
- Group membership
- Imports
- Intermediaries

- Marriage and family systems
- Matriarchal
- Monogamy
- Nuclear family
- Patriarchal
- Political systems
- Polyandry
- Polygamy
- Polygyny
- Property
- Serial monogamy
- Social hierarchies
- Social interaction
- Social reciprocity
- Subnationalism
- Supernationalism

Exercise 2.1

Instructions: Match the currencies on the right with their country on the left.

———— 1. Australia	A. dollar
———— 2. England	B. drachma
———— 3. China	C. euro
———— 4. India	D. peso
———— 5. Japan	E. pound sterling
———— 6. Mexico	F. riyal
———— 7. France	G. rupee
———— 8. South Korea	H. won
———— 9. Saudi Arabia	I. yen
————10. Germany	J. yuan

Exercise 2.2

Instructions: Circle the T for true or the F for false.

1. T   F   Most countries have similar economic systems.
2. T   F   No true universal government body exists.
3. T   F   Political systems in England and Japan are dissimilar.
4. T   F   Multinational companies are responsible only to the country in which they are based.
5. T   F   Enculturation means learning about other cultures.
6. T   F   Educational systems throughout the world vary widely.
7. T   F   The university from which a person graduates is very important in France.
8. T   F   A major family system in the United States is serial monogamy.
9. T   F   Islamic believers tend to be matriarchal.
10. T   F   Social reciprocity is relatively unimportant in Japan and Saudi Arabia.

Questions and Cases for Discussion

1. Define universal cultural systems and identify them.
2. Why do societies develop economic/political systems, and what do these systems do for the members of a society?
3. Compare the economic systems of Japan and Canada.
4. Compare the political systems of England and Mexico.
5. Discuss differences in educational systems in various cultures.
6. Explain how marriage and family systems in the United States are different from those of other cultures.

7. How important is social reciprocity in Mexico, Japan, and Saudi Arabia?
8. What are intermediaries? In which countries are intermediaries used?
9. Explain cultural variations in the way property is viewed.
10. Explain what is meant by equality in the United States. Does the term mean the same thing in other countries?

Cases

The following procedure is recommended for analyzing the cases: (a) read the case carefully paying attention to details; (b) read the questions at the end of the case; (c) reread the case, taking notes on or highlighting the details needed for answering the questions; (d) identify relevant facts, underlying assumptions, and critical issues of the case; (e) list possible answers to the questions; and (f) select the most logical response to the question. Your professor may ask that you submit answers to the case questions in writing.

Case 1

Education is offered to everyone in the United States; however, 25% of the people who enter school as five-year-olds never graduate from high school. In Japan, the high school graduation rate is 95%, and in Germany and England it is equally as high. However, in countries such as Mexico and Third World nations, many people never complete the equivalent of a high school education. The percentage of people who attend college after high school varies from country to country as described in the text.

Currently, many nations are sending a large number of students to U.S. universities, and many foreign companies are giving grants to U.S. "think tank" universities (such as MIT, Stanford, Chicago, and Harvard).

1. In light of this information, what do you see as the future role of U.S. universities in the world?
2. Is the fact that 25% of the U.S. population does not graduate from high school important in light of what is happening in other countries in the world?
3. Is the fact that so many foreign students are attending college in the United States positive or negative? What do you see as the long-term effects?

Case 2

Many Korean children and children of other nationalities have been adopted by U.S. Americans. Generally, these children were reared in homes where the parents were not of the nationality of the adopted child. Sometimes after the children become adults, they return to their native country to learn about people of their own ethnic heritage. Would language differences pose a problem? What cultural problems would they have?

Case 3

Many of the former communist countries have changed their economic and political systems. Examples are the Russian Federation, the former Czechoslovakia, and former East Germany. What cultural changes will be necessary in their educational system to have a smooth transition?

Case 4

Because more and more firms are becoming multinational and must deal with a number of monetary systems, what is the feasibility of developing one monetary system (such as the euro in Europe) to do away with exchange rates? Do multinational firms have the capability to help bring about a world currency?

Case 5

Intercultural business communication takes on many roles in the world. One that the United States is currently living in is the Iraq situation. Many U.S. businesses have signed contracts to provide services in Iraq to the Iraqi government or the U.S. military forces. The U.S. civilians who take these positions do so, for the most part, for the money because they are paid more than twice what they would be paid in the United States for the same type of work. If you chose to take one of these positions, what would you want to know, how would you prepare for the welcoming and/or the hatred you would experience, and what characteristics that you possess would be strengths or weaknesses? Do you feel that everyone who is in Iraq as a foreign worker should train an Iraqi to replace them? What are the intercultural relationship problems in this current situation?

Activities

1. Interview an Asian or a Latin American student to learn about the educational system in his or her country and the relationship between educational training and their positions in business and society. Be prepared to share your findings with the class.
2. Research the economic system of a country you would like to visit. Prepare a one-page summary for class discussion and submission to the instructor.
3. Research the marriage and family system of a country of your choice. In a one-page written summary, make comparisons with the family lifestyle in the United States.
4. Prepare a list of countries with patriarchal family systems and those with matriarchal family systems to better understand the role of women in various cultures.
5. List at least two countries that practice the following family systems: polygyny, polyandry, monogamy, and serial monogamy.

References

Althen, G. (2003). *American ways.* Yarmouth, ME: Intercultural Press.

Axtell, R. E. (1999). *Do's and taboos of humor around the world.* New York: John Wiley.

CIA Factbook. Retrieved December 6, 2004, from http://www.cia.gov/diz/publications/factbook/

Condon, J. C., & Yousef, F. (1998). *An introduction to intercultural communication.* Yarmouth, ME: Intercultural Press.

CultureGrams 2005. (2004). Lindon, UT: ProQuest Information and Learning.

Dillon, L. S. (1990, May). The occidental tourist. *Training & Development Journal,* 72–80.

Dodd, C. H. (1997). *Dynamics of intercultural communication.* New York: McGraw-Hill.

Ferraro, G. P. (2001). *The cultural dimension of international business.* Upper Saddle River, NJ: Prentice Hall.

Hall, E. (1976). *Beyond culture.* New York: Anchor Books.

Human Development Reports. Retrieved November 30, 2004, from http://hdr.undp.org/statistics/data

Martin, J. S., Chaney, L. H., & Moore, T. (2003). An assessment of the use of humor in advertising in England, Japan, and Mexico using award-winning advertisements. *The Journal of Advertising* (under review).

Nath, R. (Ed.). (1988). *Comparative management.* New York: Ballinger.

Samovar, L. A., & Porter, R. E. (2004). *Communication between cultures* (5th ed.). Belmont, CA: Wadsworth/Thomson Learning.

Samovar, L. A., & Porter, R. E. (2003). *Intercultural communication: A reader* (10th ed.). Belmont, CA: Wadsworth/Thomson Learning.

U.S. Census Bureau. (2004). Exhibit 13. *Exports, imports, and trade balances by country and area: 2003.* Retrieved December 12, 2004, from http://www.census.gov/foreign-trade/Press-Release/2003pr/final_revisions/ exh13tl.pdf

U.S. Department of Labor. Retrieved December 6, 2004, from http://stats.bls.gov/cps/home.htm

U.S. trade in goods. Retrieved November 30, 2004, from http://www.bea.doc.gov/bea/international/

Victor, D. A. (1997). *International business communication.* New York: HarperCollins.

CHAPTER

3

CONTRASTING CULTURAL VALUES

Objectives

Upon completion of this chapter, you will

- appreciate the role that values play in communicating effectively with persons from other cultures.

- understand differences in word meanings among cultures.

- learn how attribution and perception play a role in cultural values.

- appreciate attitude differences toward men and women in various cultures.

- understand how attitudes toward work and ethics vary with the culture.

- learn how religious influences impact cultural values.

- understand how individualism and collectivism play a role in cultural values.

VALUES

Values form the core of a culture. **Values** are social principles, goals, or standards accepted by persons in a culture. They establish what is proper and improper behavior as well as what is normal and abnormal behavior. Values are learned by contacts with family members, teachers, and religious leaders. What people hear, read, and watch on television influences their value systems.

People in various cultures have different attitudes toward women, ethical standards, and work. Semantic differences and attributions affect cultural values as do religious influences. Because the U.S. workplace is becoming increasingly diverse culturally, managers need to be aware of the values of all workers. Managers will understand what motivates people of different cultures and will be able to deal effectively with problem situations.

Some values held by people in the United States are not shared by people in other cultures. In his book *American Ways,* Althen (2003) identifies a number of U.S. values and assumptions, including equality, informality, individualism, directness, and attitude toward the future, time, and work.

People in the United States may claim that all persons are equal and that no person is superior to another simply because of wealth, education, or social status. In reality, subtle distinctions are made within a group to acknowledge status differences, many of which are nonverbal. Because of this belief in equality, U.S. Americans are uncomfortable with certain displays of respect, such as bowing, that are common in some cultures. Although inequalities do exist, many women hold positions of power and influence in education, government, and industry.

People in the United States also are rather informal when compared to people of other cultures. They often dress more casually. It is not unusual to see the president of the United States in jeans or jogging attire. The posture of U.S. people is often informal; assuming a slouched stance or putting feet on a desk or chair is not uncommon. Their speech is also rather informal; they often address people they hardly know by their first names.

Another quality that people in the United States value is directness. They prefer that people be open and get to the point. Such sayings as "What is the bottom line?" and "Put your cards on the table" illustrate the importance placed on directness in the United States. In some cultures, such as those found in Asia, people do not value directness. They will not reveal their emotions using the same nonverbal cues as Westerners; therefore, people in the United States have difficulty reading Asian body language (the reverse is also true). U.S. Americans generally believe that honesty and truthfulness are important unless the truth would hurt a person's feelings or unless they do not know the person well enough to be candid. They are less concerned than people in Asia with saving face.

People in the United States value time; they study time-management principles to learn how to get more work done in a day. They are concerned with punctuality for work and appointments, and they study ways of working more efficiently. The success of the fast-food industry in the United States is directly related to eating on the run rather than wasting time lingering over meals. In other parts of the world, mealtime is very leisurely. In many South American countries, businesses close for two hours in the middle of the day for a long meal and a siesta (rest), but people often work into the evening.

The importance of time to different cultures is directly related to religious dogma. The Puritans who came to the United States were very concerned with wasting time and with the future, more than the past or present. Native Americans, African Americans, Latin Americans, and Asians, however, come from a different combination of religious biases and cultural differences and are occupied with the past and present. One of the reasons Deming's theory of management was adopted in Japan before it was adopted in the United States was the amount of time it takes to formulate group decisions as opposed to individual decisions. The Japanese have always been team oriented; therefore, it was easier for Deming to sell them on his theories.

People in the United States do not place as great an emphasis on history as do people of many other cultures; they look to the future and consider change to be desirable, particularly if they are Christians. In the Asian, Arabic, and Latin cultures, the past is revered. Their future is determined by fate or, in some religions, by the Almighty. People of the Islamic faith believe that if they work very hard and pray, everything will be as Allah desires. They simply try to live in harmony with whatever changes occur, rather than seeking change, as is true in the U.S. culture. Table 3-1 contains contrasts of the priority of cultural values of U.S. Americans, Japanese, and Arabs [("1" represents the most important value); Elashmawi & Harris, 1998, p. 63].

TABLE 3-1	Priority of Cultural Values	
U.S. AMERICANS	**JAPANESE**	**ARABS**
1. Freedom	1. Belonging	1. Family security
2. Independence	2. Group harmony	2. Family harmony
3. Self-reliance	3. Collectiveness	3. Parental guidance
4. Equality	4. Age/Seniority	4. Age
5. Individualism	5. Group consensus	5. Authority
6. Competition	6. Cooperation	6. Compromise
7. Efficiency	7. Quality	7. Devotion
8. Time	8. Patience	8. Patience
9. Directness	9. Indirectness	9. Indirectness
10. Openness	10. Go-between	10. Hospitality

In the United States, companies now have to recognize the differences in values that exist in their workforces as the number of Asians, Arabs, and Latin Americans increases.

SEMANTIC DIFFERENCES

Semantics is the study of the meaning of words; it involves the way behavior is influenced by the use of words and nonverbal methods to communicate.

Words in the English language often have multiple meanings, some of which are contradictory. The word sanction, for example, may mean either to restrict a particular activity or to authorize it. Semantic differences are compounded when interacting with people of other cultures. Even when both speak the same language, a word may have a different meaning and implication in another culture.

Although England and Australia are English-speaking countries, words are often used in a different way in these countries from the way they are used in the United States. The word homely, for example, means "plain" in the United States although in England, it means friendly, warm, and comfortable. To the English, a sharp person is one who is devious and lacking in principles rather than one who is quick, smart, and clever, which is its meaning in the United States. The expression "quite good" has a different meaning to the English than to U.S. Americans. The English interpretation is "less than good," although the U.S. meaning is "very good." Australian English also holds some surprises for people in the United States. In Australia you would hear such terms as bloke for "man," lollies for "candy," and sandshoes for "sneakers."

A misunderstanding over the meaning of one word during an important meeting in World War II caused an argument between U.S. Americans and the British. The problem was caused by the British interpretation of the phrase "to table an item," which to them means to bring up the item for immediate consideration. The U.S. interpretation, on the other hand, was to shelve or postpone the subject. (Axtell, 1994)

Language problems are compounded when conducting business with persons in non-English-speaking countries. Differences in the meanings of words are often lost in translation. Sometimes a word has no real counterpart in the other language, and the translator must select a word that he or she believes is similar to the meaning intended.

> Semantic differences can be seen in the meaning of the word "stop" in the United States and in South America. A U.S. American while traveling in Bolivia observed that drivers rarely stopped at the red octagonal sign with the word *alto,* the Spanish word for "stop." A local Bolivian explained that in this country, the stop sign is more a recommendation than a traffic law.

Brand names for U.S. products have caused problems when translated into another language. For example, the Spanish translation of Ford Motor Company's Fiera truck means ugly old woman, not a very flattering name for a vehicle. U.S. firms have had to exercise greater care when introducing products in non-English-speaking countries because of marketing errors made in the past when product names and slogans were translated into another language (Axtell, 1994).

When conversing with people of other cultures, be sure your meaning is clear by avoiding slang, contractions, and idioms; by paraphrasing what the other person has said; and by speaking slowly and distinctly.

ATTRIBUTION AND PERCEPTION

Attribution, or the ability to look at social behavior from another culture's view, can cause communication problems because known experiences from your own culture are used in explaining unknown behaviors of those in another culture. **Perception,** the learned meaning of sensory images, may involve learning a new reaction to an old learned stimulus.

To lessen anxiety when communicating with someone of an unfamiliar culture, reducing uncertainty and increasing predictability about your own and the other person's behavior are important. The **uncertainty-reduction theory,** according to Gudykunst and Ting-Toomey (1988, p. 22), "involves the creation of proactive predictions and retroactive explanations about our own and others' behavior, beliefs, and attitudes." People who have high uncertainty avoidance prefer to specialize, avoid conflict, want clear instructions, and do not want competition. Some ways to reduce uncertainty about other people include observing them, trying to get information about them, and interacting with them.

Uncertainty avoidance can be used to determine whether people who have different convictions can be personal friends. People from countries with weak uncertainty avoidance are more likely to remain close friends in spite of differing opinions, although those in countries with strong uncertainty avoidance are less likely to remain friendly following open disagreements. Some key differences between weak and strong uncertainty avoidance societies in the workplace are noted in Table 3-2 (Hofstede & Hofstede, 2005).

Attribution training involves making people aware of their own cultural context and how it differs from the cultural context of the country to which they will travel. Measuring employees' attribution confidence, and then training them to be cognizant

TABLE 3-2	Uncertainty Avoidance	
Weak Uncertainty Avoidance	**Strong Uncertainty Avoidance**
Shorter employment time with employers	Longer employment time with employers
Few rules expected	Emotional need for rules
Tolerance for ambiguity	Need for precision and formalization
Top managers concerned with strategy	Top managers concerned with daily operations
Focus on decision process	Focus on decision content
Better at invention, worse at implementation	Worse at invention, better at implementation

Source: From *Cultures and Organizations* (p. 189), by G. Hofstede & G. J. Hofstede, 2005. London: McGraw-Hill Book Company.

of their personal differences with the assignment culture, is often used to prepare employees for overseas assignments. Employees are given scenarios that summarize problems they may encounter while living in another country. Participants are then asked to select the one response considered correct from the viewpoint of the native of the country being studied. With feedback from the trainer and exposure to numerous situations, participants are better able to understand cultural variations in behavior and to look at the situation from the other culture's viewpoint.

ATTITUDES TOWARD WOMEN

Attitudes are our likes (or affinities) and dislikes (or aversions) to certain people, objects, or situations. Attitudes are rooted in our behavior and in our emotions (Weaver, 1998). Sometimes our personal attitudes may differ from those of the macroculture or dominant culture. For example, a U.S. American male may have the attitude that women belong in the home and not in the workplace. The attitude of the macroculture, however, is that women may choose to work or to stay home and take care of the family.

A society's attitudes toward women are influenced by cultural roots. In some cultures, such as the United States, women are supposed to have the same rights as men. In other countries, such as Libya and Kenya, women are considered subordinate to men. In fundamental Islamic cultures, women are allowed to work only with other women.

Although women according to the Qur'an must give consent to their marriage, are given inheritance, and have equal religious rights and responsibilities with men, Qur'an verses also depict men as superior to women. However, Muslim women cover themselves for protection from those who might hurt them. The Muslim proverb demonstrates this: "A woman is like a jewel: You don't expose it to thieves." Most women of Islamic faith embrace their religious traditions just as women of other faiths embrace theirs (Samovar & Porter, 2004, p. 103).

This attitude toward a woman's role in society is carried into the workplace. In the United States, gender differences in the workplace are deemphasized. The women's rights movement has worked for such legislation as fair employment laws requiring that men and women must be given equal pay for equal work. Even though differences in pay still exist, treating men and women equally is expected in U.S. firms. The acceptance of women at higher levels is evidenced by the appointments of Sandra Day O'Connor and Ruth Bader Ginsburg to the U.S. Supreme Court and Condoleezza Rice as U.S. Secretary of State. The number of women appointees to top national- and state-level positions continues to increase. In large corporations, the number of women executives is also on the increase. Women-owned businesses are making a significant contribution. In fact, 6.5 million businesses owned by women generate more jobs than Fortune 500 firms (Aburdene & Naisbitt, 1992).

Aburdene and Naisbitt (1992), in their book *Megatrends for Women,* identified the 1990s as the decade of women in leadership positions in business. They point out that during the past two decades, women in the United States have taken two-thirds of the new jobs created and that women started new businesses at twice the rate of men. Compared to this U.S. trend, one-fifth of small businesses in France are owned by women; and one-third of small businesses in Canada are owned by women. In England, the number of self-employed women has increased three times as fast as the number of self-employed men in the past decade.

According to Axtell, Briggs, Corcoran, and Lamb (1997), attitudes towards women changed greatly during the 1990s. More companies, such as American Airlines, DuPont, and Procter & Gamble, were hiring women. More women are earning business undergraduate degrees and M.B.A.s than ever before. In certain situations, it has been found that women give a company a competitive advantage. Many times the largest hurdles for women are the misperceptions and sexist attitudes of managers in the United States rather than barriers in international business.

> Barbara Fischer, an international attorney from Minneapolis, says, "American women have an advantage over American men doing business in Japan. Japanese men's style of communicating—indirect, hesitant, ambiguous speech—is the way women have been socialized. It's what we in the United States had to unlearn, the being deferential and patient." (Axtell et al., 1997, pp. 141)

Following the collapse of communism and the rise of the Pacific Rim, a New World order is emerging with a larger number of countries following the democratic system of government. With democracy comes increased opportunities, especially for women and especially in government and politics.

Women are having a more powerful voice as they assume an increasing number of leadership positions throughout the world (Aburdene & Naisbitt, 1992). Although women are increasing the number of positions they hold in top management, the growth is slow worldwide. In the United States, women hold 5.1% of the top management positions; Australia, 1.3%; France, 2%; Germany, 3%; and the United Kingdom, 3.6%. In 1999, eight heads of state were women, and 13% of the legislators worldwide were women (Anderson, 2001). Even though women represent over half of the populations in the world, they represent only 3% of the senior management positions worldwide (Adler, 1999). U.S. women in international assignments comprised 13% to 14% of the employees on international assignment in 1998 (Varma, Stroh, & Schmitt, 2001). This is surprising because Tung (1993) found that women are successful in international assignments due to their communication styles. Female chief executives have created their own businesses or taken over family businesses unlike male chief executives (Adler, 1999).

In many countries of the world, women are just beginning to be accepted at managerial levels. Progress in the advancement of women is slow in the Middle East. In such countries as Saudi Arabia, the Islamic belief in the subordination of women has impeded the progress of working women. Women in Mexican businesses are respected, but they are expected to compete on an equal footing with men and prove their competence. Although Mexican businesses have historically been male dominated, this seems to be changing as many Mexican businesswomen are now enjoying success at managerial levels.

Women in Japan hold 6% to 8.9% of all management positions, and women are 40.6% of the workforce (Renshaw, 1999). Worthy of mention, however, is the fact that the highest-ranking person in a Japanese international agency is a woman (Aburdene & Naisbitt, 1992). Even though the 1986 equal employment law clearly bars firms from discriminating against women, no penalties are involved for companies that do not comply with the law. Japanese professional women, therefore, still face many hurdles in their climb up the corporate ladder (Rossman, 1990).

With mounting global competitiveness, companies need to examine their current attitudes and practices toward women to ensure that they are making maximum use of their resources and that selection and promotion decisions are based solely on qualifications rather than along gender lines. Fortunately, people in many other countries, including those where women are not treated as equals, are beginning to change their sexist attitudes and are less concerned with gender than performance.

INDICATIONS OF CHANGING ATTITUDES TOWARD WOMEN

Results of a 1993 survey of female readers of *Asian Business* who were asked to rate the business climate for women in 17 countries determined that Hong Kong was considered the most friendly business environment for women, followed by Singapore, the United States, and Malaysia. Other Asian countries, the Philippines, Taiwan, Thailand, China, Japan, and Indonesia, were all rated friendlier to women in business than were France and Germany. (Bosrock, 1994)

Although some women in various countries may have received their first job opportunities from family or political connections, others advanced because of professional qualifications and job competence. Major problems women in the workforce have faced, such as childcare and trying to combine a career and family, are common to all cultures. As more women are successful in managing multiple priorities and demands on their time and as they demonstrate that they are equally effective in high positions in business and politics, it will be easier for women in all cultures to advance to positions of prestige, importance, and responsibility.

"Whatever women do, they must do twice as well as men to be thought half as good. Luckily, that is not difficult" (Charlotte Whitton, late mayor of Ottawa).

WORK ATTITUDES

Attitudes toward work are culturally diverse. The term **work attitudes** refers to how people of a culture view work. **Work,** defined as mental or physical activities directed to socially productive accomplishments, in some societies is associated with economic values, status and class, and cultural values.

People in the United States value work and tend to subscribe to the **work ethic,** which means that hard work is applauded and rewarded although failure to work is viewed negatively and with disdain. U.S. Americans admire people who work hard and are motivated to achieve; they have an aversion to idleness and prefer people of action to people of ideas. This concept of the United States as a work-ethic society is sometimes referred to as the "Protestant ethic," which suggests that a person's work (or "calling") comes from God and that people demonstrate their worth to the Almighty and to themselves through their work. Proverbs such as "Blessed is he who has found his work" and "Satan finds mischief for idle hands" express the idea that in the United States, work is virtuous as well as respectable (Ferraro, 2001). Reward systems in many firms are based on an employee's achievement and willingness to work beyond a 40-hour week. U.S. senior-level executives often work 56 hours a week, far more than in many European countries. They take only 14 days of vacation a year, far fewer than in some countries in Europe, where people often close businesses for a month to go on vacation (Utroska, 1992). According to the International Labor Organization (2003), the average number of hours worked per week, per person for select countries is shown in Table 3-3.

TABLE 3-3 Working Hours per Week by Country (2002)			
Country	*Hours (avg.)*	*Country*	*Hours (avg.)*
China	47.9	Japan	42.2
India	47.3	United Kingdom	39.6
South Korea	46.2	Germany	38.7
Singapore	46.0	The Netherlands	38.5
New Zealand	44.9	France	38.2
Mexico	43.3	Switzerland	35.6
United States	42.6	Canada	31.9

This attitude toward work and responsibility to a job is ingrained from an early age in the United States. Parents teach their children about the American free enterprise system, which is based on the premise that you are the master of your own destiny, that you can be anything you want to be if you are willing to try hard enough, and that you will be rewarded for hard work. In contrast, people in the Islamic countries place great importance on the will of Allah and believe that planning for the future would conflict with religious beliefs.

To people in the United States, the job is almost an identification badge. A person's personal identity is associated with his or her occupation. Evidence of this identification with the job is shown when making introductions. People tend to include the person's occupation or job title along with the name; for example, "I'd like to present Betty Freeman, owner of the Health Hut" or "This is Jay Hunt, president of

Southern Express." Success is not only measured by the job title but by the perception of what one earns; the implication is that the high income has probably resulted from the person's willingness to work 12- and 14-hour days, seven days a week.

People in the United States are action oriented; they are often unable to relax because they feel guilty doing nothing. People from other cultures have observed that U.S. Americans even work at relaxing. Television commercials in the United States often depict an activity as leisure—activities that persons in other cultures would consider manual labor such as gardening or washing the car. When they do take vacations, U.S. Americans are inclined to plan what they will do and where they will go so that the entire time is scheduled. Even those who participate in sports for recreation seem to try to make work out of it (Althen, 2003).

> A graduate student from India recounted his first experience at being invited to the home of a U.S. graduate student. When he arrived, his U.S. friend invited him into the house where he was dressing his son while his wife was sweeping the patio. His friend then asked him to help with grilling the chicken outdoors. As the Indian student narrated the story in his intercultural communication class, he expressed surprise that his friend and his wife did all their own work. In his country, he had never swept a floor, cooked a meal, or dressed his children.

Unlike people in a number of countries, many people in the United States consider spending hours visiting a waste of time and may excuse themselves from a group because they say they need to get back to work. People in other countries view with both amazement and amusement this apparent obsession with work.

In much of Europe, attitudes toward work seem to be more relaxed. Many businesses close during the month of August when people go on vacation. Most Europeans do not work on weekends or holidays, as they believe this is time that should be spent with family or engaging in personal activities. The French, in particular, value their vacation time and prefer not to work overtime. They enjoy the longest vacations of any country in the world; French law dictates that employees receive a minimum of five weeks of vacation a year. German companies appear to be moving in this direction as well. Despite the extended free time, people of both France and Germany are very productive when they work. Australians, too, value free time; they say they work to get a vacation. Australians have the shortest working hours of any country in the world, and they enjoy taking frequent breaks throughout the day (Copeland & Griggs, 1985).

Although many people of the United States receive a two- or three-week vacation, the individual vacation time periods are staggered so that businesses will not be closed for an extended period. It is not unusual for upper-level management workers to not take all their vacation time each year. Because of these attitudes toward work, the culture of the United States is referred to as a "live to work" culture in contrast to the cultures in countries such as Mexico that are "work to live" cultures.

The attitude of Japanese men toward work is very group oriented, and it plays a major role in their lives. They work Monday through Friday; 18-hour days are not unusual. Because of the long hours, relaxation does not include working around the house. Instead, they relax by watching television, playing computer games, browsing the Internet, drinking, or joining their friends at the local bar. However, this attitude appears to be changing as they become more westernized.

ATTITUDES TOWARD ETHICS

Ethical standards are guidelines established to convey what is perceived to be correct or incorrect behavior by most people in a society. According to Ferrell and Gardiner (1991), ethical conduct "is something judged as proper or acceptable based on some standard of right and wrong" (p. 2). According to Borden (1991), being ethical means keeping your values in balance; if you compromise your values, you are being unethical. What it comes down to, according to Rabbi Dosick (2000), is that you have to determine what is right and what is wrong. Although there are sometimes penalties for doing both right and wrong, you have to be able to live with yourself and sleep at night.

Truth, according to U.S. beliefs, is an important aspect of ethical behavior. People in the United States have been taught from childhood to always tell the truth. Some parents even tell their children, "If you'll just tell me the truth, I won't punish you." Therefore, as adults, U.S. persons subscribe to the saying, "Always tell the truth; let your word be your bond, and let your honor be your word" (Dosick, 2000, p. 19).

> When Abraham Lincoln was a young boy, he was a clerk in a small dry-goods store. One day, after realizing that he had overcharged a customer, he walked two miles through the snow to return the overcharge of one penny (Dosick, 2000).

Personal ethics or moral standards may differ from societal ethics. Your own standards of what is right and wrong may be more stringent than those of your society as a whole. Problems may occur when the reverse is true, that is, when your ethical standards are lower than those considered acceptable by society. Of course, your ethical standards must meet the minimum level of behavior identified by law as acceptable. It has been found that peer reporting of unethical behavior is affected by cultural attitudes and styles of communication. Cultural unfamiliarity affects the communication of seen unethical behaviors. Culturally diverse encounters have revealed different patterns of expression, modes of behavior, value sets, attitudes, and styles of communication within the same nation. Cultural diversity includes race, gender, sexual orientation, age, religion, socio-economic backgrounds, and such. Some of the culturally diverse issues are personal, some are group, and some are corporate. Personal issues include prejudice, stereotyping, personality, values, and identity. Group issues include ethnocentrism and intergroup member conflicts, and corporate issues include acculturation, structural, informal integration, and institutional bias. It is important to understand that many levels of ethical differences exist; thus, a determination of what constitutes unethical behavior should take into consideration the cultural standards involved (King, 2000).

Although many U.S. Americans are inclined to believe that their standards of business ethics are shared by other countries, in reality, standards of business ethics are not universal. For example, the Islamic standard of ethics is based on participating in religious ceremonies, adhering to codes of sexual behavior, and honoring one's parents. This definition or interpretation of ethical standards is not shared by U.S. Americans. Another dimension of business ethics relates to what is commonly referred to as using "backdoor connections" for conducting business; using such connections is common, for example, in South Africa and Nigeria as well as in the People's

Republic of China. In fact, the Chinese use informal relationships in allocating resources and making decisions. Another ethical problem U.S. firms face when conducting business abroad is the unorthodox accounting and taxation practices used in some countries. In such countries as Brazil and Spain, keeping three sets of accounting books as a means of avoiding taxes is common. These practices violate not only the ethical standards of U.S. businesspeople but also U.S. law. Another ethical problem encountered by U.S. firms doing business in other countries is the nonsanctity of legal contracts. To U.S. businesspersons, "a card laid is a card played." To Chinese, Koreans, and Japanese, who emphasize long-term relationships, renegotiation is common. As a result, U.S. businesspersons are never sure when they have a final agreement. People of the United States also question the ethicality of certain activities such as taking a potential customer on a yachting trip or a weekend gambling outing, clearly intended to influence buying decisions (Engholm & Rowland, 1996). An increased concern for ethics has been seen in the United States because of blatant misconduct of persons in government and industry. Religious leaders have been convicted of fraud and Wall Street moguls found guilty of insider trading. Naisbitt and Aburdene (1990) foresee that all countries will have to give increased attention to values and ethics in their schools so that the next generation will be better prepared to make appropriate decisions involving ethical behavior.

Ethical standards should be addressed when conducting business with persons of other cultures, especially those whose standards of ethical behavior differ markedly from our own. Even though we carry our frame of reference and value system with us when conducting business internationally, we should also be aware that our values may differ from those of other countries. For example, in the United States, bribery and graft are illegal. In some of the Latin American countries, however, using gifts to assure success in sealing an agreement is an accepted way of conducting business. (Bribery is discussed in more detail in chapters 9 and 12.)

Religion also affects ethics. All religions are against murder, robbery, lying, and adultery. All religions also stress humility, charity, and veracity (Samovar & Porter, 2004). With these similar ethical principles, religion should be more of a unifying principle than a dividing one. However, religion is truly a way of life for many people in the world.

RELIGIOUS INFLUENCES

Religious influences have an impact on when and how business is conducted in international settings. In some cultures, such as North and South America, Australia, and Europe, lifestyle and religion are separate. In much of northern Africa and southern Asia, no distinction is made between lifestyle and religion because religion is a lifestyle. Businesspersons in these countries may seek the advice of religious leaders on business matters.

The United States has never had an official state church; religious observances rarely interfere with business. Although business is not conducted on such religious holidays as Christmas, no one feels obligated to participate in religious ceremonies or observe religious customs. Religion is a personal matter in the United States. Members of one family often hold different beliefs and belong to different denominations.

The United States subscribes to the doctrine of "separation of church and state." According to this doctrine, the government does not lend official support to any particular religion and may not interfere with a person's practicing any religion. A total of

95% of the population say they are religious. About 26% of the population is Roman Catholic; 55% is Protestant. Other Christian denominations make up about 5% of the total, while non-Christian groups also have substantial numbers in the United States (*CultureGrams*, 2004).

Some countries have officially recognized religions and participate in religious rituals that would affect business encounters. In Saudi Arabia, United Arab Emirates, Iran, and Iraq, for example, Islam is the official religion. Muslims observe the ritual of stopping work five times a day to pray. Meetings with persons in Islamic countries should be sufficiently flexible to allow for this daily ritual, which is a way of life for Muslims. Conducting business during the month of Ramadan (which varies from year to year) is not recommended because Muslims are required to fast from dawn to sunset. Because of the impact of religion on all aspects of life in Islamic countries, businesspeople should learn about religious rituals and beliefs prior to conducting business there. The majority of Chinese people practice a combination of Confucianism, Taoism, and Buddhism (Jandt, 2000).

A newly admitted patient became agitated about the arrangement of his hospital room. He kept saying that his bed should be on the opposite wall. The nurse explained that this would be impossible because the oxygen and other needed equipment had been installed on this side of the room and the wires were not long enough to reach the other side. When the nurse learned that the patient was Muslim and needed to face the east toward Mecca to say his prayers five times a day, she arranged for him to be moved to another room that met his needs. (Dresser, 1996)

When working with people in countries that practice nonliterate religions (those that lack written precepts), an understanding of the logic of their beliefs is important. Some Native Hawaiians, for example, believe in curses and spirits; this belief should be accommodated. Witchcraft is practiced in such countries as Zaire; conducting business with people of these cultures may involve changing the sales and marketing techniques that you would ordinarily use.

Religious beliefs and practices affect business in many countries. Although both the United States and Italy are primarily Christian countries, religious holidays are more numerous in Italy than in the United States. Sri Lanka, for example, has 27 holidays. Religious beliefs also affect consumption patterns; for example, Hindus do not eat beef, and Muslims and Orthodox Jews do not eat pork. When conducting business internationally, religion must be considered (Terpstra & David, 1991; Victor, 1997).

Worldwide there are 1.3 billion Muslims: 270 million in Arab nations, 400 million in the rest of the Middle East, and 6 million in the U.S., not including the Nation of Islam (excluded because they do not follow the five pillars) (Shabass, 2004). In many countries where Islam is practiced, it controls life, with all other parts of life taking a secondary role. Religion answers many questions for people such as what is life and death, how was the universe created, how did our society originate, how do we relate as individuals and members of a society, and what is our relationship to nature? Religion in many cases is the psychological welfare for individuals, helping them to understand what cannot be easily explained. Religion is responsible for many of the contrasting cultural values between people (Samovar & Porter, 2004).

INDIVIDUALISM AND COLLECTIVISM

Individualism refers to the attitude of valuing ourselves as separate individuals with responsibility for our own destinies and our own actions. Proponents of individualism believe that self-interest is an appropriate goal. **Collectivism** emphasizes common interests, conformity, cooperation, and interdependence (see Figure 3-1). Individualism and collectivism are the opposite ends of a continuum. Thus, we have to remember that some societies have factors near each end plus factors from the middle. It is impossible to put a society or an individual from a given society at one end of the continuum or the other because most people have attitudes that are associated with both ends of the continuum.

FIGURE 3-1   Individualism versus Collectivism

As we learn our culture or another culture, the cultural values are learned through shared activity or cultural practices and shared meanings or cultural interpretation. Because these components are cumulative, both within and between people in a culture, people who belong to a particular culture know how others will act. As people develop their values within a culture, they go through three tasks: relationship formation, knowledge acquisition, and autonomy/relatedness. Cultural learning evolves over a lifetime, over historical time, and over evolutionary time. The environment we are in, what society tells us is valued, and the values we develop based on cultural learning make each of us in the world unique. When someone tends toward the collectivistic or interdependent end of the continuum, they consider individual choice as less important than the group and social obligations and responsibilities to be very important. When someone leans towards the individualistic end of the spectrum, individual rights are very important; and social obligations are of primary importance. Countries that are more collectivistic include China, Japan, India, Nigeria, Cameroon, and Puerto Rico. Values that are important to these cultures include responsibility, honesty, politeness, respect for elders and family, and looking to the society for the values to embrace. Germans, European Americans, and the Dutch all embrace individualism, which includes self-maximization, independence, creativity, curiosity, assertiveness, self-esteem, and education. Cultures where people are face-to-face, in smaller communities, or are in a subsistence economy tend to value tradition, and change comes very slowly because they are more collectivistic. Examples include Iraq, Iran, Afghanistan, and many of the smaller African nations. In major cities, with extended economies, you find more individualism. Criticisms of the individualistic/collectivistic paradigm include that the paradigm is too simplistically applied to countries and all people within a country, that the paradigm does not allow for both individualistic and collectivistic values to coexist in the same culture, that some values are valued by both individualistic and collectivistic cultures, and that qualitative and quantitative variability exists within the individualistic/collectivistic paradigm (Greenfield, et al., 2003).

Hofstede originally studied the IBM Corporation in 53 countries and determined the dimensions on which countries' business cultures differed. Using statistical analysis and theoretical reasoning, Hofstede developed five dimensions, which he labeled Power Distance, Uncertainty Avoidance, Collectivism vs. Individualism, Femininity vs. Masculinity, and Long-term vs. Short-term cultures. The countries were then ranked according to their scores (Hofstede & Hofstede, 2005). This study was the first of its kind, and the data was collected in the late 1970s from 50 countries in one organization; his first book was written in 1980. Since then, many more women are working in corporations than in the 1970s, more countries are involved in international business, and cultural changes have happened during this time period; therefore, it is necessary to look at the Hofstede study data in relation to new studies that are being completed, such as the GLOBE study headed by House, Hanges, Javidan, Dorfman, and Gupta (2004).

The United States ranked first in individualism in the Hofstede study, followed by Australia, Great Britain, Canada, and the Netherlands. Countries that ranked lowest on individualism included Colombia, Venezuela, Panama, Equador, and Guatemala (Hofstede & Hofstede, 2005). People from the United States place great importance on individuality and self-reliance. Well-known phrases typically used by parents to convey this emphasis on self-reliance include "Do your own thing," "You made your bed, now lie in it," and "You'd better look out for yourself; no one else will." U.S. Americans have been conditioned from childhood to think for themselves, to express their ideas and opinions, and to make their own choices; they are taught to consider themselves as individuals who are responsible for their own actions as well as for their own destinies. Parents start training their children early in this way of thinking; they offer them choices of food, clothes, and toys and usually accommodate their preferences. When the choice does not work out, the child then experiences the results of the decision. The goal of parents is to form a self-reliant, responsible person by the age of 18. When children move out of the parents' home at that age and are completely self-supporting, parents feel successful. Children who still live with their parents past the age of 18 or 20 are viewed as immature and unable to live independently. The value U.S. Americans place on individualism, self-reliance, and independence is perceived by persons of different cultures as being self-centered with little consideration for other people (Althen, 2003). This emphasis on individuality carries over into college/university choices as well as job choices that may take children away from friends and family members. Although individualism and the value placed on the family as an important unit are often associated, evidence shows that this relationship may not always exist. Costa Ricans, for example, have individualistic tendencies but also value the extended family structure. Examining cultures within cultures is, therefore, important.

In other cultures, such as the Japanese, emphasis is placed on the group approach rather than the individual approach to all aspects of life. The Chinese and Malaysians also value the group approach and the family. Their concern with following family traditions and with respecting the opinions of their parents is perceived as a sign of weakness and indecisiveness by U.S. Americans.

The GLOBE study found individualism/collectivism to have multiple levels within the two constructs. They discovered an in-group collectivism and institutional collectivism. The institutional scale showed societal variability that was not captured by the in-group scale (House et al., 2004).

The Power Distance Index is concerned with inequality within a society and how the country distinguishes between inequalities. The inequality can be of power, wealth, status, and social position, as well as physical and intellectual differences. In the business world, it concerns whether the employee and boss prefer a dependent or independent relationship with each other. The index measures the extent to which the weaker members expect and accept the unequal distribution of power (Hofstede & Hofstede, 2005). The GLOBE study found that strong power distance was associated with male-dominated societies. In addition, they also found that where power distance was strong, it was also most disliked (House et al., 2004).

The Masculinity and Femininity Index concerns how a society views assertiveness versus modesty. It is a relative construct rather than a biological distinction being made between countries. Although the two terms are derived from what is considered important in life to the two genders (masculine includes earnings, recognition, advancement, and challenge; feminine includes manager, cooperation, living area, and employment security), the country's dimension position and equality of the genders in the workplace have no relationship to each other (Hofstede & Hofstede, 2005). The GLOBE study on the gender egalitarianism of a country is probably more appropriate for intercultural business communication because it discusses the implications for the differences in gender egalitarianism. Societies that believe men and women are suited for similar positions are more gender egalitarian than societies that believe the roles for men and women should be different. The GLOBE study found that the cultural value of gender egalitarianism affected the type of leadership dimensions of charisma, participatory, or self-protectionist. In societies where men and women are more gender egalitarian, they rate the leadership dimensions more similarly (House et al., 2004).

The Uncertainty Avoidance Index measures the threat of ambiguity and unknown situations. Does a person embrace the unknown or does he or she become anxious concerning the unknown? Countries in which people have a strong uncertainty avoidance behavior tend to have a lot of laws and rules specifying correct behaviors as opposed to the countries with weak uncertainty avoidance behavior in which people only want rules when they are absolutely necessary (Hofstede & Hofstede, 2005). In the GLOBE study, uncertainty avoidance was defined as the tendency toward orderliness, consistency, structure, and regulation. They found that uncertainty avoidance may be related to societal, economic, and organizational values such as innovation, perception of risk, per capita cash holdings, and growth. Higher uncertainty avoidance values were found where there was higher team-orientation, humane orientation, self-protective leadership, and lower participative and charismatic leadership values (House et al., 2004).

The difference in a country's orientation to long-term or short-term goals can affect business. A long-term orientation is concerned with the future, perseverance, thrift, hard work, learning, openness, accountability, and self-discipline. A short-term orientation is concerned with the bottom line, control systems, respecting tradition, preserving face, and fulfilling social obligations (Hofstede & Hofstede, 2005). The GLOBE study calls this future orientation. They found that all cultures value future orientation whether or not they practice it except for Denmark. Countries that had weak future practices aspire to having stronger future orientation. Lack of visionary leadership or government control seems to indicate weaker future orientation practices. The Hofstede and GLOBE scales showed no relationship to each other (House et al., 2004).

A brief description of selected cultural values of 10 countries with which the United States conducts most of its international business follows (Axtell et al., 1997; Bosrock, 1994, 1995a, 1995b; *CultureGrams,* 2004; Hofstede & Hofstede, 2005).

Canada

In Canada, women are accepted in business and government and are well represented. As in the United States, businesswomen feel free to invite businessmen to lunch or dinner; the one who extends the invitation usually pays. Women in Quebec are expected to dress conservatively for business meetings. The dominant religion in Canada is Catholicism, but people of British descent are mostly Protestant. Canada also has significant numbers of Muslims, Buddhists, Hindus, and Sikhs. Canada, like the United States, believes in the separation of church and state; however, religious organizations play a more visible role in politics in Canada than is seen in the United States. Canada is a work-oriented culture; both parents often work outside the home. Canada is a highly individualistic society; the country tied with the Netherlands and Hungary for fourth place in Hofstede's ranking of individualistic countries.

China

In China, the official government position is that citizens should be atheists. The Chinese constitution guarantees religious freedom with certain limitations. Many religions are practiced, including Buddhism, Taoism, Islam, and Christianity. Confucianism, a philosophy and a way of life, is practiced by the majority of the Chinese. China is a collectivistic society. Both women and men are employed in the economy. However, women generally do not have the highest positions in the economy although purportedly women are equal to men. Hofstede ranks China as 56 tied with Bangladesh, Singapore, Thailand, Vietnam, and West Africa in the ranking of individualistic countries.

Hong Kong's religious philosophies include Taoism, Confucianism, and Buddhism; only 10% of the population is Christian. Laws protect religious freedom. Both men and women are employed in the economy. The people in Hong Kong tend to be less conservative than the rest of China.

England

Although British women have made progress in the workplace, they have not fared as well as women in the United States and Canada. With the high visibility of Margaret Thatcher as Britain's first female prime minister from 1979 to 1990, anticipated gains in positions of leadership for businesswomen in England have not materialized. In

1994, British women made up 9% of the members of the House of Commons; in the United States, 11% of the House of Representatives seats and 8% of the Senate seats were held by women. According to 1992 figures, 19.5% of British barristers (lawyers) were women, although 23% of U.S. lawyers were women. England's state religion is the Church of England (Anglican Church) headed by the queen. Although it no longer has political power, the Church has had much influence on England throughout its history. Other religions represented include Roman Catholic, Protestant (Presbyterian and Methodist), and Judaism. England is a very individualistic society; it is ranked third in Hofstede's ranking of individualistic countries.

France

Although most urban French women work outside the home, few hold top business positions except in fashion, cosmetics, advertising, and art. Although many French men do not readily accept French women in business, women from other countries, especially those from Canada and the United States, are generally accepted. A businesswoman may feel free to invite a French man to lunch and pay the bill. The majority (85%) of the people of France are Roman Catholic; a small number are Protestants, Jewish, or Buddhist. France is a moderately individualistic society; the country tied with Sweden for 13th place in Hofstede's ranking of individualistic countries.

Germany

Germany is a male-dominated society; few married women work outside the home. Women have received little acceptance in positions of power and responsibility in business. German women in 1995 held less than 5% of the managerial positions and only 25% of the positions in public administration. However, this appears to be changing somewhat; the younger generation is more open to the idea of women holding higher-ranking positions. Although sex discrimination is unlawful in Germany, cases are rarely pursued. A businesswoman should feel free to invite a German businessman to dinner and pay the bill without incident.

About 34% of the German people are Protestant, and 34% are Roman Catholic. Although a number of other religions are active in Germany, almost one-fourth of the people have no official religious affiliation. In Hofstede's ranking of individualistic countries, Germany ranked 18th.

Japan

Women are highly visible in today's Japanese business world, comprising about 40% of the workforce. However, the majority hold lower-level staff positions rather than positions of power. Japanese women have made progress in the areas of government, advertising, publishing, and such technical fields as engineering. The possibility of their making significant advances to the higher levels of management in the near future is unlikely because traditionally the Japanese power structure has always been male dominated. A total of 85% of Japanese people practice a combination of Buddhism and Shinto. Only about 1% of the Japanese are Christian. Japan is not an individualistic culture; in Hofstede's ranking of individualistic societies, the country was tied with Argentina and Morocco for 33rd place. The Japanese traditionally place the welfare of the group over the welfare of the individual. They respect age and value ambition, education, hard work, loyalty, and politeness.

Mexico

The role of women in Mexican society is changing. In the past, very few women entered business and politics. Now, however, Mexican women are holding more important positions in business and politics and are visible in the professions as dentists, doctors, lawyers, and teachers. Although Mexican men control Mexican society, the women control the men. The traditional macho attitudes of Mexican men are more apparent among the lower classes than among upper-class males. Foreign businesswomen are not advised to invite Mexican businessmen to dinner because a man and woman dining alone suggests that they are romantically involved. The predominant religion (practiced by 89% of Mexicans) is Catholicism; small percentages are of Protestant and Jewish faith. Although the Catholic church has little political influence, it does play an important role in the Mexican culture. Mexico is not considered an individualistic culture; the country was ranked 46th and tied with Bulgaria and Romania in Hofstede's ranking of individualistic countries. However, Mexicans have a sense of individualism in certain areas. For example, they try very hard to distinguish themselves from other Mexicans as they are aware of how they are perceived personally. Mexicans also value the family and personal relationships.

The Netherlands

The role of women in the Netherlands is egalitarian. The Netherlands is one of the leading nations in Europe for work equality between the genders. The religions practiced in the Netherlands are Roman Catholic (31%); Protestant, which is largely Dutch Reformed (21%); Muslim (4.4%); and other religions that make up about 3% of the population. The role of religion has diminished, and there is a strong separation of church and state. Although the Dutch are known for their liberalism, it is not a topic of polite conversation. The Netherlands ranks fourth, tied with Canada and Hungary, on the individualism index of Hofstede.

South Korea

Women are not considered equal to men in South Korea; there is still a separation of female and male roles. In South Korea, 50% of the population is Christian, but Confucianism permeates the culture. Interactions are determined by a person's status and relationship to others. South Korea ranked 63rd in Hofstede's study on individualism and collectivism.

Taiwan

Although most women in Taiwan work, there is still a separation of female and male roles in this country. In Taiwan, 93% of the people practice a combination of Buddhism, Confucianism, and Taoism, and about 5% are Christians. Taiwan is 64th on Hofstede's study of individualism and collectivism. Although Taiwan is still a male-dominated society, a strong women's movement exists.

Terms

- Attitudes
- Attribution
- Attribution training
- Collectivism
- Ethical standards
- Individualism
- Perception
- Semantics
- Uncertainty-reduction theory
- Values
- Work
- Work attitudes
- Work ethic

Exercise 3.1

Instructions: Circle T for true or F for false.

1. T F Values are learned; they are not innate.
2. T F In the United States, the family is a top priority.
3. T F A characteristic valued by U.S. persons is directness.
4. T F People in Asian cultures value history.
5. T F Semantic differences between cultures that speak the same language are rare.
6. T F The word "yes" means the same in all languages.
7. T F Women in management are treated similarly in all cultures.
8. T F Japan has a well-enforced equal employment law preventing discrimination against women.
9. T F The U.S. society is considered to have a strong work ethic.
10. T F Ethical standards are culture specific.

Questions and Cases for Discussion

1. Explain how values are formed.
2. In what ways are values of persons in the United States different from those of persons in other cultures?
3. Explain how semantic differences can affect intercultural communication. Give some examples.
4. Explain what is meant by the term attribution.
5. How are attitudes toward women culturally different? In what countries are women and men treated equally in the workplace?
6. Explain the differences between work attitudes in the United States and other countries. Are your personal work attitudes typical of the U.S. culture or another culture?
7. How are attitudes toward ethics in the United States different from those in Latin America?
8. What role does religion play in conducting business in the United States and Saudi Arabia?
9. Explain individualism. Give examples of cultures that are primarily individualistic.
10. Explain collectivism. Give examples of cultures that are primarily collectivistic.

Cases

The following procedure is recommended for analyzing the cases: (a) read the case carefully paying attention to details; (b) read the questions at the end of the case; (c) reread the case, taking notes on or highlighting the details needed for answering the questions; (d) identify relevant facts, underlying assumptions, and critical issues of the case; (e) list possible answers to the questions; and (f) select the most logical response to the question. Your professor may ask that you submit answers to the case questions in writing.

Case 1

Ching Lee was transferred by his Asian firm to assume a managerial position in a large automobile production plant in the United States. In his first report to his supervisor, he expressed concern that U.S. workers were not giving him the proper respect. What behaviors by U.S. workers could have led Ching Lee to draw this conclusion?

Case 2

A U.S. firm sent its senior-level manager, Laura Green, to negotiate a contract for a chain of fast-food restaurants in Saudi Arabia. What cultural attitudes and behaviors related to gender should she expect to encounter?

Case 3

When Brandon Hunt was sent to Mexico to oversee a production facility for his company, he became concerned over what he perceived to be a lack of seriousness about work on the part of Mexican workers. Employees were frequently late for work, left early, or did not come in at all. When questioned, employees explained that they had to help members of their family with their problems. Explain the apparent differences in U.S. American and Mexican attitudes toward work.

Case 4

When Disney opened its $4.4 billion Euro Disneyland outside Paris, concerns over the park's impact on French culture were expressed. To begin with, the French dedicate Sundays only to family outings. In addition, they are unaccustomed to snacking and eat promptly at 12:30, which creates bottlenecks at parks and restaurants. Disney learned that French employees objected to providing the friendly greetings and smiles expected of all amusement park workers. They then hired multilingual employees from all over Europe because Disney's goal was to attract people from all countries of Europe. A complaint of European investors was that rigid U.S. management style did not take into account the values and customs of the people it intended to attract. For example, Europeans often bring their own lunches and do not spend money at the park's gourmet restaurants and hotels. The park initially lost money after it opened in 1992. Discuss the course of action Disney could take to accommodate the values and customs of the people it hopes to attract.

Case 5

A mission of several U.S. businesspeople visited Taiwan. After meeting with the high-level officials of the Taiwanese firm, one of the U.S. people stated that although the U.S. firm members were received with courtesy and listened intently to comments, the U.S. group members unanimously agreed that they did not have a clear understanding of the points the Taiwanese wanted to make. They also shared the impression that the atmosphere was chilly during the meeting and that the Taiwanese appeared arrogant. During the meeting, as reported in the local Taiwanese paper the next day, the Taiwanese extended their utmost courtesy, were good listeners, did not strongly push their own views, and felt the U.S. group appreciated the fact they had not been aggressive. What went wrong? How is silence being used and confused in this situation? How do the differences in individualism and collectivism affect this situation?

Activities

1. Ask one person from each of the groups listed this question: "What is your attitude toward work?" Report their responses to the class.
   a. blue-collar worker
   b. business professional
   c. educator
   d. high school student
   e. college student
2. Clip an article from the local newspaper related to ethics in business; summarize the article for class members.
3. Ask a professor or student from another culture to speak to the class on attitudes toward women in his or her culture.
4. Prepare a list of women in your state who have achieved high-ranking positions in either government or business. List the special qualifications these women possess that make them qualified for their positions. Prepare a similar list of women in high-ranking positions in another country of your choice.
5. Prepare a list of words (other than those mentioned in the chapter) that have different meanings in other areas of the United States or in other English-speaking countries.

References

Aburdene, P., & Naisbitt, J. (1992). *Megatrends for women.* New York: Fawcett Columbine.

Adler, N. J. (1999). *Global leaders. Executive excellence,* 16(12), Retrieved September 25, 2002, from Business Source Elite.

Althen, G. (2003). *American ways* (2nd ed.). Yarmouth, ME: Intercultural Press, Inc.

Anderson, P. (2001). *Women at work: Careers under glass.* CNN.com, Retrieved September 25, 2002, from http://www.cnn.com/2001/CAREER/trends/07/11/ilo.report/index.html

Axtell, R. (1994). *The do's and taboos of international trade.* New York: Wiley Inc.

Axtell, R. E., Briggs, T., Corcoran, M., & Lamb, M. B. (1997). *Do's and taboos around the world for women in business.* New York: Wiley Inc.

Borden, G. A. (1991). *Cultural orientation: An approach to understanding intercultural communication.* Upper Saddle River, NJ: Prentice Hall.

Bosrock, M. M. (1994). *Put your best foot forward: Asia.* St. Paul, MN: International Education System.

Bosrock, M. M. (1995a). *Put your best foot forward: Europe.* St. Paul, MN: International Education System.

Bosrock, M. M. (1995b). *Put your best foot forward: Mexico/Canada.* St. Paul, MN: International Education System.

Copeland, L., & Griggs, L. (1985). *Going international.* New York: A Plume Book.

CultureGrams, USA. (2004). Lindon, UT: ProQuest Information and Learning.

Dosick, W. (2000). *The business bible.* Woodstock, VT: Jewish Lights Publishing.

Dresser, N. (1996). *Multicultural manners.* New York: Wiley Inc.

Elashmawi, F., & Harris, P. R. (1998). *Multicultural management.* Butterworth-Heinemann.

Engholm, C., & Rowland, D. (1996). *International excellence.* New York: Kodansha International.

Ferraro, G. P. (2001). *The cultural dimension of international business* (4th ed.). Upper Saddle River, NJ: Prentice Hall.

Ferrell, O. C., & Gardiner, G. (1991). *In pursuit of ethics: Tough choices in the world of work.* Springfield, IL: Smith Collins.

Greenfield, P M., Keller, H., Fuligni, A., & Maynard, A. (2003). Cultural pathways through universal development. *Annual Review of Psychology, 54,* 461–490.

Gudykunst, W. B., & Ting-Toomey, S. (1988). *Culture and interpersonal communication.* Newbury Park, CA: Sage.

Hofstede, G., & Hofstede, G. J. (2005). *Cultures and organizations.* London: McGraw-Hill.

House, R. J., Hanges, P. J., Javidan, M., Dorfman, P. W., & Gupta, V. (2004). *Culture, leadership, and organizations: The GLOBE study of 62 societies.* Thousand Oaks, CA: Sage.

International Labor Organization (2003). *Yearbook of labour statistics 2003, 62nd issue.* Geneva, Switzerland: ILO Publications.

Jandt, F. E. (2000). *Intercultural communication.* Thousand Oaks, CA: Sage.

King, III, G. (2000). The implications of differences in cultural attitudes and styles of communication on peer reporting behaviour. *Cross Cultural Management— An International Journal, 7*(2), 11–17.

Naisbitt, J., & Aburdene, P. (1990). *Megatrends 2000.* New York: William Morrow.

Renshaw, J. R. (1999). *Kimono in the boardroom: The invisible evolution of Japanese women managers.* New York: Oxford University Press.

Rossman, M. L. (1990). *The international businesswoman of the 1990s.* New York: Praeger.

Samovar, L. A., & Porter, R. E. (2004). *Communication between cultures* (5th ed.). Belmont, CA: Wadsworth/Thomson Learning.

Shabass, A. (2004, July 7–8). *Content and strategies for teaching about the Arab World and Islam.* Workshop.

Terpstra, V., & David, K. (1991). *The cultural environment of international business.* Cincinnati: South-Western.

Tung, R. L. (1993). Managing cross-national and intra-national diversity. *Human Resource Management, 32*(4), 461–477.

Utroska, D. R. (1992, November). Management in Europe: More than just etiquette. *Management Review,* 21–24.

Varma, A., Stroh, L. K., & Schmitt, L. B. (2001). Women and international assignments: The impact of supervisor-subordinate relationships. *Journal of World Business, 36*(4), Retrieved September 25, 2002, from Ebscohost database.

Victor, D. A. (1997). *International business communication.* New York: Pearson Education.

Weaver, G. R. (1998). *Culture, communication, and conflict.* Needham Heights, MA: Simon & Schuster.

CHAPTER

4 | CULTURAL SHOCK

Objectives

Upon completion of this chapter, you will

- understand the nature of cultural shock and its relationship to success in overseas assignments.

- be able to identify the typical stages of cultural shock.

- learn ways to alleviate cultural shock, including careful selection of persons for overseas assignments and predeparture training.

- understand the role of cultural stress, social alienation, social class and poverty-wealth extremes, financial matters, and relationships in dealing with cultural shock.

- understand how the extent to which persons in the host culture reveal their private selves may contribute to cultural shock.

Cultural shock (commonly called culture shock) is the trauma you experience when you move into a culture different from your home culture. Cultural shock is a communication problem that involves the frustrations of not understanding the verbal and nonverbal communication of the host culture, its customs, and its value systems (Samovar & Porter, 2004). Frustrations may include lack of food, unacceptable standards of cleanliness, different bathroom facilities (see Figure 4-1), and fear for personal safety. Black, Gregersen, Mendenhall, and Stroh (1999) add another dimension to cultural shock. They suggest that the disruption of people's routines, which may range from getting up, eating breakfast, and going to work, creates a high degree of uncertainty that is very stressful. The more our routines are disrupted, the greater the level of anxiety and frustration. In addition, most people like predictability; for instance, they want the security of knowing how a hamburger at their favorite fast-food restaurant is going to taste. The English saying, "That song is best esteemed with which our ears are most acquainted," states the facts simply; we like to feel comfortable and be familiar with our surroundings. It is no surprise that cultural shock can cause so many problems with a person's comfort level. Losing our familiar signs, customs, norms, and behaviors can be very disturbing.

FIGURE 4-1   Cultural Shock Can Result from Bathrooms with Different Fixtures or Arrangements.

A woman in her mid-fifties was attending an intensive Spanish language school in Mexico and developed all the typical signs of cultural shock. She finished her five-week course and went home to find a position teaching English as a second language. Her new position was in Albania. She reported to friends that she was happy she had experienced cultural shock in a nonjob situation because when she started to feel the same things in Albania she was able to understand and work through the cultural differences. She enjoyed Albania so much she signed up for a second tour.

In a survey of 188 students from two Mid-South universities who had traveled or lived abroad, the greatest degree of cultural shock was reported in the lack of modern conveniences and standards of cleanliness. Other types of cultural shock showing statistical significance included attitudes toward women, nonverbal communication, clothing/business dress, family and marriage practices, housing, climate, educational system, financial problems, and values and ethical standards (Chaney & Martin, 1993). The absence of conveniences (such as telephones that work, running water available 24 hours a day, or buses that run on time), which are taken for granted in the United States, is an additional source of frustration. People with strong religious ties may feel spiritually adrift without a church of their faith. Without the bounty of U.S. shopping malls, supermarkets, and multiple television sets, depression may result. In addition to depression, people who experience cultural shock can become homesick, eat or drink compulsively, and even develop physical ailments. Unexplained anger and aggression toward people in the host culture are also reactions associated with cultural shock (Samovar & Porter, 2004).

On her arrival in La Paz, Bolivia, from Atlanta, Georgia, Katherine Montague asked directions to the ladies' room at the local university. On entering, she observed three males using urinals and made a hasty retreat. Her U.S. colleagues explained that all restrooms were unisex; Katherine decided to take a taxi to her hotel.

Cultural shock has received increased attention by researchers only in the past two decades. However, Jack London, in his story, "In a Far Country," which was published in 1900, stressed that a visitor to another culture should be prepared to acquire new customs and abandon old ideals. He suggested that sojourners (people who visit or reside temporarily in another country) should find pleasure in the unfamiliar because those who could not fit into the new culture would either return home or "die" of both psychological and physical ailments. London's advice is still sound more than a hundred years later (Lewis & Jungman, 1986).

Engholm (1991) has identified a special kind of cultural shock experienced by U.S. travelers—**AsiaShock.** Engholm identifies the five progressive stages of AsiaShock:

1. Frustration with the culture, which includes the language, the food, and the local customs.
2. Unwillingness to understand the rationale behind the local ways of doing things; people of the United States quickly label a cultural behavior as backward and inefficient without trying to understand the rational basis for the behavior.
3. Ethnocentricity; people of the United States often label Asians as dishonest because they seem to say one thing and do another, failing to realize that Asians consider their behavior to be face-saving rather than dishonest.
4. Racism, including the unflattering labeling of all Asians into such groups as Japs and coolies.
5. Avoidance of the culture; people of the United States tend to form their own clubs at which they commiserate about the difficulty of doing business in Asia rather than intermingling with the people of the culture.

Cultural shock can be costly to a firm because it often results in the premature return of U.S. businesspeople working overseas. Some research shows that employees sent to work in foreign countries do not fail because they lack technical or professional competence but because they lack the ability to understand and adapt to another culture's way of life. Estimates on early return of U.S. expatriate managers range from 45% to 85% (Ferraro, 1990). When companies implement measures to combat cultural shock, such as conducting training programs for sojourners, the early return rate drops to less than 2%.

> A family spent eight years in Saudi Arabia while the husband, an engineer, worked for Aramco. The youngest son had been born in Saudi Arabia. On moving back to the United States, the son, who was eight years old, went with his parents to buy a car. When the mother got in the car to drive home, the boy exclaimed, "But you can't drive a car, Mother!" He had never seen a woman drive in his entire life. Of course, his parents quickly explained that in the United States driving customs and laws are different from those in Saudi Arabia.

Some companies have used short-term stays of two to three months to determine an employee's potential for tolerating the culture. Sometimes these short-term projects are designed to prepare the person for a longer stay later. On other occasions, these brief trips are simply ways to use the talents of technical professionals who would be unwilling to go in the first place if it meant disrupting the professional advancement of a career-oriented spouse. Short trips are also cost effective as the need to move the family is reduced or eliminated. Although the degree and type of cultural shock experienced by people who travel to another country for a short stay may be similar to the shock experienced by those who plan an extended visit, the strategies for coping during the short-term visit may differ.

> Cultural shock and missing your way of life can cause you to give up free trips. A mid-level U.S. executive was in Taiwan for four weeks. The company policy was that if you were in the Far East for more than three weeks, you could take an all-expense paid trip to Hong Kong at the end of the third week. The executive chose to work through the weekend and the next week so he could finish early and go home.

Brislin (1981) identifies these five strategies used for coping with the new culture during short visits:

- **Unacceptance of the host culture**—the traveler simply behaves as he or she would in the home culture. No effort is made to learn the language or the customs of the host culture.
- **Substitution**—the traveler learns the appropriate responses or behaviors in the host culture and substitutes these responses or behaviors for the ones he or she would ordinarily use in the home culture.
- **Addition**—the person adds the behavior of the host culture when in the presence of the nationals but maintains the home culture behavior when with others of the same culture.
- **Synthesis**—this strategy integrates or combines elements of the two cultures, such as combining the dress of the United States and the Philippines.
- **Resynthesis**—the integration of ideas not found in either culture. An example of this strategy would be a U.S. traveler in China who chooses to eat neither American nor Chinese food but prefers Italian food.

STAGES OF CULTURAL SHOCK

Cultural shock generally goes through five stages: excitement or initial euphoria, crisis or disenchantment, adjustment, acceptance, and reentry. Davis and Krapels (2005) visualize cultural shock as being represented by a U-shaped curve, with the top of the left side of the curve representing the positive beginning, the crisis stage starts down the left side to the base of the U, the adjustment phase starts at the base of the curve, then acceptance moves up the right side of the curve, and reentry into the original culture is at the top of the right side of the curve.

The first stage is excitement and fascination with the new culture, which can last only a few days or several months. During this time, everything is new and different; you are fascinated with the food and the people. Sometimes this stage is referred to as the "honeymoon" stage, during which your enthusiasm for the new culture causes you to overlook minor problems, such as having to drink bottled water and the absence of central heating or air conditioning (Black et al., 1999).

During the second stage, the crisis or disenchantment period, the "honeymoon" is over; your excitement has turned to disappointment as you encounter more and more differences between your own culture and the new culture. Problems with transportation, unfamiliar foods, and people who do not speak English now seem overwhelming. The practice of bargaining over the purchase price of everything, an exercise originally found amusing, is now a constant source of irritation. Emotions of homesickness, irritation, anger, confusion, resentment, helplessness, and depression occur during the second stage. People at this stage often cope with the situation by making disparaging remarks about the culture; it is sometimes referred to as the "fight-back" technique. Others deal with this stage by leaving, either physically, emotionally, or psychologically. Those who remain may withdraw from people in the culture, refuse to learn the language, and develop coping behaviors of excessive drinking or drug use. Some individuals actually deny differences and will speak in glowing terms of the new culture. This second stage can last from a few weeks to several months.

In the third stage, the adjustment phase, you begin to accept the new culture or you return home. You try new foods and make adjustments in behavior to accommodate the shopping lines and the long waits for public transportation. You begin to see the humor in situations and realize that a change in attitude toward the host culture will make the stay abroad more rewarding.

In the fourth phase, the acceptance or adaptation phase, you feel at home in the new culture, become involved in activities of the culture, cultivate friendships among the nationals, and feel comfortable in social situations with people from the host culture. You learn the language and may adopt the new culture's style of doing things. You even learn to enjoy some customs such as afternoon tea and the midday siesta that you will miss when you return to the home country.

The final phase is reentry shock, which can be almost as traumatic as the initial adjustment to a new culture, particularly after an extended stay abroad. Many individuals are shocked at the fact that they feel the same emotional, psychological, and physical reactions they did when they entered the new culture. **Reentry shock** is experienced on returning to the home country and may follow the stages identified earlier: initial euphoria, crisis or disenchantment, adjustment, and acceptance or adaptation. You would at first be happy to be back in your own country but then become disenchanted as you realize that your friends are not really interested in hearing about your experiences abroad, your standard of living goes down, and you are unable to use such new skills as a foreign language or bargaining in the market. You then move into the adjustment stage as you become familiar with new technology and appreciate the abundance and variety of foods and clothing and the improved standards of cleanliness. You finally move into the acceptance stage when you feel comfortable with the mores of the home culture and find yourself returning to many of your earlier views and behaviors.

A former student from the United Arab Emirates called his U.S. professor to ask for information on purchasing property on the North Carolina coast. He went on to explain that he was homesick for the United States and had decided to bring his family here every summer. After spending 15 years in the United States earning his bachelor, M.B.A., and Ph.D. degrees with only occasional visits back to his home country, he was experiencing reentry shock. (He made the readjustment and did not buy the North Carolina property.)

Although reentry shock is typically shorter than the first four stages of cultural shock in a new culture, expatriates who have made a good adjustment to the host culture may go through a rather long period of adjustment, lasting six months or more, when they are confronted with the changes that have taken place in their absence. Some of these changes are work related; expatriates may feel "demoted" when they return to middle-management positions without the bonuses, perks, and professional contacts they enjoyed abroad. In other situations, changes have taken place in the home country, including politics and styles of clothing, which require readjustment. In research conducted by Chaney and Martin (1993), the four types of reentry shock experienced by college students who had traveled abroad that were statistically significant were readjusting to lifestyle, readjusting to changes in social life, readjusting to changes in standard of living, and reestablishing friendships.

Research on repatriation revealed that meeting the job expectations of the person returning to the United States was very important. Therefore, it is imperative that employers put returning expatriates into realistic positions upon their return. The feelings of alienation and isolation can cause more trauma because returnees have the expectation that they will be returning to a familiar environment (Stroh, Gregersen, & Black, 2000). Other causes of cultural dissonance for the returnee include personnel changes, new company policies and procedures, different performance evaluation methods, different benefits and compensation, and different job responsibilities (O'Sullivan, 2002).

Some reentry problems are personal in nature. Many repatriates have changed; they have acquired a broadened view of the world and have undergone changes in values and attitudes. Personal problems may include unsuccessful attempts to renew personal and professional relationships as the realization sets in that their former friends do not share their enthusiasm for their overseas experiences and accomplishments. They must then make new friends who share this common experience. Children of expatriates encounter similar readjustment problems as their former friends have made new ones and they find that the education they received abroad is sufficiently different to cause problems when returning to schools in the United States.

Because reentry shock is a natural part of cultural shock, multinational corporations must provide training for repatriates to ensure that the transition to the home culture is a favorable experience. In the absence of such training, you can do much to counteract reentry shock by sharing your feelings (not your experiences) with sympathetic family members and friends, particularly those who have lived abroad. Correspond regularly with members of the home culture; ask questions concerning changes that are taking place. Subscribe to the home newspaper to stay abreast of current events. Keep in touch with professional organizations and other groups with which you may want to affiliate. Many repatriates have found that maintaining ties with the home culture cushions the shock associated with reentry (Dodd, 1997; Dodd & Montalvo, 1987; Klopf, 2000).

ALLEVIATING CULTURAL SHOCK

Many multinational firms find that cultural shock can be alleviated by selecting employees for overseas assignments who possess certain personal and professional qualifications. Another method of easing cultural shock is to conduct training programs for employees prior to overseas deployment (Krapels, 1993). Employees who have been given feedback on how they are doing and who have been developed to their maximum potential will be more satisfied with their assignments.

Selecting Overseas Personnel

Careful selection of persons for overseas assignments is important to enhance the chances for a successful sojourn. Personal qualifications needed when working in an unfamiliar culture include adaptability, flexibility, empathy, and tolerance. Good interpersonal skills and high self-esteem are also important.

The ability to react to different and often unpredictable situations with little apparent irritation shows a tolerance for ambiguity. Ambiguities are inherent in intercultural communication; many people, situations, rules, and attitudes make little sense. A lot of confusion results from being in another culture. Maintaining a high degree of tolerance and flexibility is essential. Some companies spend a lot of time at colleges recruiting because they are looking for candidates who already have such qualifications as language proficiency and overseas experience during which time the person has learned how to adapt to another culture. Many recruiters feel that tolerance can be developed but that adaptability is difficult to develop; they prefer, therefore, to hire persons who have already acquired this trait through living abroad (Geber, 1992; McEnery & DesHarnais, 1990). Adaptability screening reduces costly turnover. Harvey (1985) suggests the use of the following questions to determine a candidate's adaptability:

- Is the person cooperative, agreeable, and sensitive to others?
- Is the candidate open to the opinions of others?
- How does the person react to new situations, and what effort does he or she make to understand and appreciate differences?
- Does the candidate understand his or her own culturally derived values?
- Is the candidate sensitive and aware of the values of other cultures?
- How does the person react to criticism?
- How well does the candidate understand the U.S. government system?
- Will the candidate be able to make and develop contacts with counterparts in the foreign culture?
- Is the candidate patient when dealing with problem situations?
- Is the candidate resilient when faced with adverse situations?

By using such questions as these, interviewers are better able to determine a candidate's suitability for the overseas assignment as well as the person's motivation for wanting to work abroad.

The ability to see the environment from the perspective of the host nationals is an indication of empathy. Bennett's concept of empathy recommends replacing the Golden Rule (do unto others as you would have them do unto you) with the **Platinum Rule** (do unto others as they would have done unto them). You can still maintain your own cultural identity but be able to interpret the new culture through the eyes of the national (Broome, 1991).

Professional qualifications include knowledge of business practices in the host culture and technical competence. Some companies consider language skills crucial. When the destination is the Far East, many companies believe some language training prior to departure is needed. When the use of English is pervasive in a country, proficiency in the host language may not be necessary. In any case, language knowledge seems to give an expatriate an extra chance of succeeding in the host culture. In addition to language knowledge, understanding the educational, political, economic, and social systems of a country is considered important (Tung, 1981).

An individual's success or failure is tied to qualities such as self-efficacy, prior international experience, age, cross-cultural fluency, interpersonal skills, flexibility, cultural sensitivity, and adaptability. **Self-efficacy** is an individual's self-image and confidence to adapt and function in a new environment. A sojourner's attitudes concerning personal safety, security, strength, and self-sufficiency correlate with a high self-efficacy. Bicultural individuals adapt better than monocultural individuals. Prior international experience is associated with a person's ability to adjust to a new culture. Bicultural people tend to be more cross-culturally fluent, culturally sensitive, and adaptable. Adaptive traits include anticipatory adjustments, psychological adjustments, and sociocultural adjustments. If what is anticipated actually happens, psychological uncertainty is reduced, so overlap between the two cultures can be very helpful in adaptation. The ability to understand new cultural behaviors, which is a personality characteristic, can reduce psychological adjustments. Sociocultural adjustments are helped if the host country people see the sojourner as a positive rather than a negative addition. Sociocultural training is very important to the success of this adaptation (Davis & Krapels, 2005).

Providing Predeparture Training for Host Country

An effective approach to cross-cultural training is to first explore how people adjust to new cultures. Learning principles that affect the success of training programs for global managers can be broken down into three steps: observing and emulating behaviors of persons in the host culture, retaining what has been learned, and experimenting with the new behavior until it becomes comfortable. For example, in the Philippines, social get-togethers are important in getting people of a company to feel comfortable together and to develop camaraderie that spills over into the workplace. These festive occasions, which often include cooking together, singing, dancing, and storytelling, serve an important function in employer/employee relations. Attending and participating are important; those who do not participate are viewed as cold and aloof. After observing such social events, U.S. managers who want to be successful in the host culture would then sponsor similar social outings to demonstrate their desire to become part of the new culture (Black, Gregersen, & Mendenhall, 1992).

Because of the reported lack of intercultural training by U.S. multinational companies, acculturation problems have affected the overall success rate of businesspersons in foreign countries. Research conducted by Krapels (1993) involving 102 international businesspersons representing 35 international Mid-South companies determined that 46% of the firms participating offered some type of predeparture training; however, only one firm had a formal training program in place. Because early return rates drop significantly when training programs are implemented, many multinational firms are now experimenting with a variety of training programs. Some companies are trying to boost tolerance of another culture by including trainees from overseas locations in their U.S.-based training programs. Other firms conduct training sessions overseas and send U.S. managers to these courses to provide training in the host culture at the same time that some exposure to the culture occurs. Still other companies incorporate cross-cultural awareness into their regular management training courses.

Advances in communication technology are now being used in intercultural training. For example, a major international firm uses global videoconferencing to train employees and their families at more than 200 sites around the world. Global educational networks with various universities are being developed to train executives who are going abroad. Computers are being used to enhance training effectiveness. Computer-aided training or learning has immense potential for multicultural education because it cuts across traditional language barriers (Harris et al., 2004). Research indicates that such instruction not only encourages one-to-one learning but can save 30% of the time of more traditional methods. Regardless of the type of training offered, companies realize that success is limited to the extent that there is no substitute for actually living in another culture.

Approaches to intercultural training may be grouped as follows:

- The **intellectual model** is also called the classroom model. Participants are given facts about the host country using a variety of instructional methods, such as lectures, group discussions, and videotapes. This model, which is used most frequently, is based on the belief that cognitive understanding is necessary for performing effectively abroad. This training method is popular in the military as well as in business and educational institutions. Reasons for the popularity of the intellectual model are that staffing is relatively easy and participants are familiar with this approach. A limitation of this approach is that the knowledge gained may not coincide with what is actually needed when a person lives abroad. In other words, the person has learned facts and generalizations about the culture that do not take into account everyday happenings that the person experiences when living in the culture. The model teaches for knowledge and is not based on experience; it does not develop problem-solving skills or flexible attitudes.

- The **area training model,** also called the simulation model, emphasizes affective goals, culture-specific content, and experiential processes. This approach is centered on the trainee rather than the trainer, requires trainee involvement in the learning process, and emphasizes problem solving rather than acquiring information. Through field trips or such simulations as Bafa, Bafa (in which participants are divided into two cultures, Alpha and Beta), trainees learn the rules of their culture and interact with members of the other culture. Critics of this approach point out that because it is a simulation, training may still be dissimilar from the actual experience abroad. In addition, those who desire to have more knowledge about the culture (the focus of the intellectual model) would consider the dissimilarity from reality a drawback of this approach.

- The **self-awareness model,** also called the human relations model, is based on the assumption that the trainee with self-understanding will adapt to the new culture better and will therefore be more effective in the overseas assignment. To accomplish desired outcomes, trainers use role play or the sensitivity or Training (T-) Group approach. The **sensitivity training,** or **T-Group,** movement, popular in the late 1960s and 1970s, has not received much attention in recent years. This approach involved training exercises in which people are told in a group setting by others why their behavior is inappropriate, such as that they are perceived as arrogant, dogmatic, or judgmental. This training approach was controversial at best. Although some may have perceived the feedback as helpful, others were uncomfortable exploring their feelings and emotions and viewed it as threatening. Some critics of this approach point out that the American T-Group is based on U.S. values of directness, openness, and equality. Further, this approach does not give participants a framework of conceptual knowledge for analyzing future situations. In addition, cultural relativity and differences in values are not addressed.

- The **cultural awareness model** emphasizes cultural insight, and like the self-awareness model, stresses affective goals and an experiential process. In this approach, participants go from recognizing their own values to contrasting their values with those of other cultures using a variety of techniques, including realistic role playing. This approach, although not as familiar to trainees as the intellectual approach, more nearly approximates interactions participants would experience in the new culture (Bennett, 1986).
- The **interaction approach** is based on participants' interacting with people in the host country, either nationals or U.S. persons who have been in the host country for an extended time (Harris, Moran, & Moran, 2004).
- The **multidimensional approach** is based on the concept that using any single training approach is not as effective as using an approach that attempts to combine cognitive, affective, and behavioral aspects of training. Critics of this approach say that integrating approaches is overly ambitious. However, advocates maintain that the integrated approach, balancing content with process, affective learning with cognitive, and culture specific with culture general, will better prepare participants for a successful overseas experience (Bennett, 1986).

Providing Feedback and Rewards

Global managers need feedback and rewards just as managers in the home culture do. The appraisal and reward system is different from the home system because people in overseas assignments have to be evaluated and rewarded in a way that takes into account the values of persons in the host culture and the expectations of the particular assignment. The evaluation criteria must be made clear. Areas typically included are leadership ability, interpersonal skills, negotiation skills, customer service, communication skills, and achievement of organizational objectives. For international managers, a key factor to be evaluated often includes profits, but in some countries, the main goal might be to build a presence in the country. In that case, making contacts and building close personal relationships with key officials in the host country are important. Another consideration in appraising overseas managers is who should do the evaluating. Many companies use a rating team headed by a senior human resources management executive. Persons who may be involved in the appraisal process include on-site superiors, peer managers, subordinates, and clients. The team leader might be expected to prepare an appraisal on the global manager every six months (Black et al., 1992).

Reward systems for global managers include special allowances for housing/utilities/furnishings, cost-of-living, hardship, education, home-leave, relocation, medical, car and driver, club memberships, and taxes. The main objective of whatever reward system is used is to attract and retain quality employees. Rewards are especially important in overseas assignments because employees need to be compensated for what they are leaving behind: favorite foods, recreation, family and friends, educational opportunities, and health care. In addition, reward systems used for global managers need to take into consideration the idea of equity—the ratio between what they contribute and what they receive. A manager in the host country who is supposed to be on the same level as the U.S. manager often sees a disparity between what the two contribute and receive; this situation can cause friction and add to feelings of inequity between expatriate managers and local managers. Managers/government employees from the same country but not the same company/government agency also can experience feelings of dissatisfaction based on equity. One spouse of a U.S. expatriate complained that her husband's firm did everything "on the cheap," including housing allowances, bonuses, and home-leave airfares (economy class only), while their friends in other companies received higher housing allowances and bonuses and flew business class (Black et al., 1992).

Developing Employees to Their Maximum Potential

In the past, insufficient attention has been given to reacclimating global managers, specifically in planning for the return of managers who have been in foreign posts for some time. As a result, many managers become dissatisfied with their positions upon their return to their U.S. firm and leave the company. In fact, an estimated 20% of managers leave the firm within a year following repatriation. When you consider the firm's investment in the success of its global managers, the importance of focusing on repatriation becomes clear. Plans for successful repatriation adjustment should begin before the manager leaves the host country; the company should make clear the reason for the new assignment, what new skills and knowledge will be learned, and how the employee will contribute to the company's development upon his or her return. In addition, human resources department personnel should begin initial preparations for the manager's return at least six months prior to repatriation by providing home-country information and contacts. Other recommendations for successful repatriation include providing appropriate compensation for transition expenses, allowing sufficient time to move and get settled before reporting to work, assisting in the location of proper housing, and showing appreciation to the entire family for their contributions to the company during their overseas assignment (Black et al., 1992).

An American expatriate made this observation on returning to his home in Dallas from an assignment in Caracas:

I was really looking forward to coming home, but now I don't feel like I belong. Before I left, I had a large corner office in my company; now I share an office with two other managers. Most people don't even know who I am. My wife isn't happy. In Caracas, our life was very social; we were invited to all the best parties. She had a cook, maid, seamstress, gardener, and nanny. Here she has no friends and no household help.

ASPECTS OF CULTURAL SHOCK

Aspects of cultural shock include cultural stress, social alienation, social class and poverty/wealth extremes, financial matters, and relationships and family considerations. In addition, differences between the extent to which persons in the host and home cultures reveal their private selves may cause acculturation problems, particularly in communication.

Cultural Stress

Entering an unfamiliar culture is stressful; in fact, transitions of any type are both psychologically and physically stressful. The stress of getting ready for the move, of unpacking and getting settled upon arrival, and of adjusting to new foods can be so stressful that people become physically ill. Problems with housing, climate, services, or communication in another language bring additional stress.

Expatriates learn to use a variety of coping skills to alleviate stress. Unfortunately, some coping behaviors are negative. Taking drugs or drinking alcohol may provide a temporary superficial relief to the stressful situation but avoids dealing with the real source of stress. Another negative coping method, using food to alleviate stress, may create weight-gain problems. Positive techniques include diversions such as taking up a hobby or learning a new skill, planning family events, sharing problems with friends and family members, and changing one's mental outlook. Physical coping mechanisms, such as exercise and meditation, are useful in alleviating stress, as are spiritual techniques such as volunteering to help others and religious worship.

Some companies have found that providing prospective expatriates with a mentor who has worked in the host country can help reduce anxiety about adjustments that may be necessary in the new culture. Providing a second mentor located in the host country can reduce stress associated with learning acceptable behavior in the new culture and help avoid serious business and social blunders.

To alleviate culture stress, prepare for the second culture by reading up on the country, studying the language, and becoming aware of customs and traditions in the culture. Maintaining a sense of humor is very important in dealing with cultural stress.

Social Alienation

An aspect of cultural shock that can have adverse effects upon the newcomer to a culture is social alienation and the feelings of loneliness associated with being isolated from friends and the home culture. Feelings of alienation may be delayed somewhat because concern over such basic matters as housing, transportation, and work may buffer these feelings initially. As the months pass, however, you may feel more isolated as you experience numerous cultural differences, such as what is considered an appropriate topic of social conversation. The concern of people in the United States with fitness, exercise, and healthful eating is not shared by persons of many cultures; such topics, therefore, are inappropriate for conversation. You also may feel uncomfortable during political discussions because persons of other cultures cannot understand the logic behind such decisions as voting for a presidential candidate who is inexperienced in the international arena rather than for a seasoned politician who is respected in the international community.

Making an effort to become familiar with the nuances of the culture and cultivating friendships with persons from the home culture as well as the host culture can alleviate feelings of alienation. Enrolling in language classes and including host nationals in social events can cushion the shock of the new culture and pave the way toward a better understanding and appreciation of the people and their culture.

Social Class and Poverty/Wealth Extremes

In many developing countries, no "middle class" exists. Social classes and extremes in poverty and wealth are readily apparent.

The mention of social class in the United States is greeted with uncertain responses because many U.S. citizens prefer to believe that no social class exists in the United States. Class distinctions do exist in the United States, but they are so complicated and subtle that visitors from other countries often miss the nuances and even the existence of a class structure. Therefore, the official propaganda of social equality is a myth. According to people in the lower stratum, class is related to the amount of money you have. People in the middle stratum acknowledge that money has something to do with it but believe that the kind of work you do and your education are almost as important. People in the top stratum believe that your tastes, values, style, and behavior indicate your class, regardless of your education, occupation, or money (Fussell, 1983). Because U.S. personnel are accustomed to perpetuating this "fable of equality," the obvious existence of social class in other societies may make U.S. Americans uncomfortable. In cultures with virtually no middle class, U.S. persons are usually forced into the upper class of the host culture and may, at least temporarily, feel ill at ease in a social role in which numerous servants are the norm and distinctions are made between acceptable and unacceptable friends.

The informality of U.S. Americans, such as greeting strangers on the street with "Hi!" and calling people they scarcely know by their first names, is a source of cultural shock for many visitors to the United States. In many cultures, starting a conversation with a stranger in a shop or on a bus is considered unacceptable; in the United States, this behavior is commonplace. Foreigners are also often shocked to discover that not all U.S. Americans are wealthy and well educated—that we have large numbers of homeless persons and people who have not graduated from high school.

The poverty of the lower class in other cultures often makes U.S. Americans so uncomfortable that they feel compelled to help but may do so in socially unacceptable ways, such as paying a gardener twice the usual rate simply because the person is poor. Mentors in the host culture can be very helpful in advising U.S. persons regarding acceptable ways of dealing with poverty/wealth extremes and with gaining an insight into the class structure of the culture.

Financial Matters

Because adapting to a new culture and reentering the home culture involves financial adjustments, companies should provide financial counseling both to expatriates and repatriates. Although the focus is a little different, the primary consideration is the same: optimum use of the financial resources available.

Financial counseling for expatriates includes such information as cost and availability of housing, banking practices (including exchange rates), use of credit cards and checks, and costs of schooling for employees with families. Because substantial salary increases are often related to an employee's willingness to relocate, these increases should be discussed in terms of real purchasing power. Expenses related to a higher standard of living that many expatriates enjoy would include hiring domestic help and investing in appropriate formal attire. Customs in purchasing, such as bargaining in the market, should be addressed as well as the additional marketing expenses, which may include paying someone to guard your car while you shop, paying someone else to carry parcels, and paying another person to find fresh eggs or meat that are available only on the black market. Buying goods in grams rather than pounds is an additional purchasing consideration. Added expenses of securing goods, such as the cost of tailor-made clothes in the absence of locally available appropriate clothing, is another appropriate topic to discuss.

By providing counseling before home-country reentry, the company is acknowledging that financial problems will occur and is demonstrating a willingness to help with these problems. One financial problem relates to the loss of buying power; on returning to the United States, the decrease can be about 30% in net disposable income. The focus of financial counseling for repatriates includes costs involved in relocating in a stateside home, accompanying adjustments to a lower salary, and the loss of perquisites. Because the loss of elite status is often difficult to accept, counseling should include the positive side of the changes, such as less money will be spent on clothes. To ease the transition financially, some companies provide a relocation pay supplement. Others grant annual leave in advance of the return to allow time for house hunting and related problems. Another expense that is receiving increased attention is the cost of providing counseling for family members, particularly children whose adolescence is delayed. Because repatriated children are usually retarded three to four years socially, counseling is often needed to help them work through this transition of readjusting to the home culture (Bird & Dunbar, 1991).

RELATIONSHIPS AND FAMILY CONSIDERATIONS

Problems with relationships, such as the failure of the spouse and other family members to adapt to the new culture, are a major factor in the early return of expatriates. Family and personal issues can be disruptive to acculturation, especially for families with children ages 3 to 5 and 14 to 16 (Harvey, 1985). The 3- to 5-year-olds often have emotional problems being uprooted from familiar surroundings; the 14- to 16-year-olds may have problems ranging from adapting socially to adjusting to a different educational system. Adolescents in particular need social continuity and often feel resentment toward their parents for uprooting them. Care must be taken to prepare children for the move by discussing openly their anxieties and fears and by providing them with information concerning expected changes in their lives. Being separated from family members and friends in the United States may cause loneliness for all involved. In addition, the spouse is experiencing his or her own problems in adjusting to an alien work environment and is unable to provide the time and emotional support needed during this difficult period of adjustment.

Two-career families in which one spouse (usually the wife) gives up a career to accompany the relocated spouse pose special adjustment problems. Job opportunities in the new culture may be nonexistent, and resentment and boredom may lead to family conflict. Adding unhappy children and an unhappy spouse to the stress of the new job in a foreign culture increases the probability of an early return to the home culture (Harvey, 1985).

Companies that provide training for employees prior to departure rarely include the family in such training. Because adjustment problems often involve the family, difficulties could be avoided in many cases by including family members in predeparture training.

PUBLIC AND PRIVATE SELF

People in various cultures differ with respect to how much of the inner self is shared with others. A method of considering a person's inner world is through the **Johari Window,** which includes "panes" that represent the self that is known and unknown to

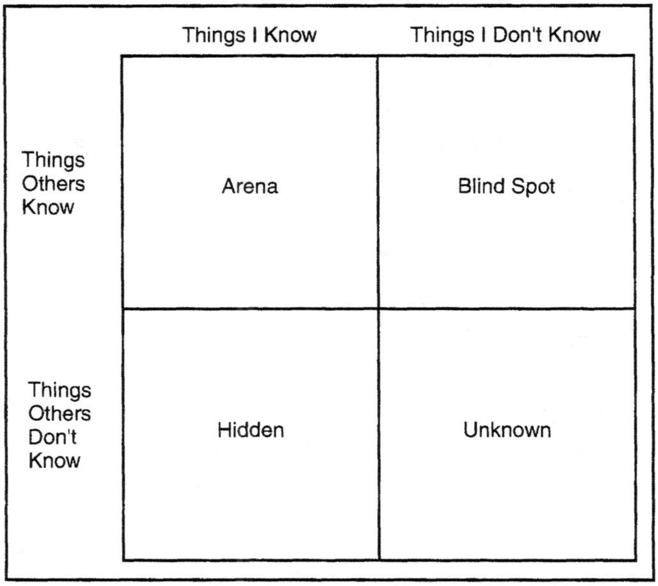

	Things I Know	Things I Don't Know
Things Others Know	Arena	Blind Spot
Things Others Don't Know	Hidden	Unknown

FIGURE 4-2   The Johari Window

Source: From *Group Processes: An Introduction to Group Dynamics* by Joseph Luft. Copyright © 1963, 1970, 1984, Palo Alto, CA: Mayfield Publishing Company. Used by permission.

a person and the self that is known and unknown to others. The Johari Window (Luft, 1984), named for its creators, Joseph and Harrington, is shown in Figure 4-2.

The first window pane is information that is shared; it includes what is known both to the person and to others. This information may be limited to a few facts that the person chooses to share, such as occupation or telephone number, or it may include numerous facts and opinions that are shared with a large audience. The second pane represents what is known to others but not to the person; it represents the person's blind area. This may include motives that others are able to discern but that the person cannot see. The third pane represents what is known to the person but is unknown to others. Information that a person chooses not to disclose to others may range from a past indiscretion to aspects of his or her family life, such as marital status. The fourth pane is that aspect of the person's inner self that is unknown both to others and to the person. This may be information that is embedded deeply in the person's subconscious to the extent that neither the person nor others know of its existence.

The major dimensions of the Johari Window (what is known to self and to others) can be translated into a person's public self and private self. The public self may include information about a person's work, family, and interests or opinions on political and social issues. In some cultures, such as the Japanese, the public self is relatively small, although the private self is relatively large. People of the United States use a style of communication that includes a larger public self with the private self being relatively small. U.S. citizens readily express their opinions and reveal their attitudes and feelings to a larger extent than do persons from the Asian cultures. U.S. Americans use a variety of communication channels, including greater verbalization and greater use of nonverbal communication, such as touch. They conceal less than the Japanese and communicate on a wide range of topics. The Japanese offer fewer opinions and feelings and have fewer physical contacts. People of the United States have less rigid boundaries between the public and private selves; they use more spontaneous forms of communication and fewer ritualized ones. Because of this larger public self, U.S. Americans are sometimes criticized by persons of other cultures as being too outgoing and friendly, too explicit, and too analytical (Barnlund, 1975).

Obstacles to effective communication may be overcome to some degree by becoming knowledgeable about the communication styles of other cultures and by compromising between the two styles. When communicating with the Japanese, for example, U.S. Americans should avoid prying questions, observe formalities and rituals, respect the use of silence, maintain harmony, and understand that evasiveness is a natural part of their communication process.

Cultural shock is a reality that must be addressed by firms doing business abroad. The subject must be openly explained and understood. By admitting the existence of cultural shock and explaining how it may affect individuals, the shock loses some of its intensity, and adapting to the new culture is less traumatic.

The length of cultural shock/reentry shock will depend on such factors as personal resiliency, the length of the assignment, and the effort you put forth prior to departure to learn about the host culture.

Terms

- Area training model
- AsiaShock
- Cultural awareness model
- Cultural shock
- Intellectual model
- Interaction approach
- Johari Window
- Multidimensional approach
- Platinum Rule
- Reentry shock
- Self-awareness model
- Self-efficacy
- Sensitivity training
- T-group

Exercise 4.1

Instructions: Circle the appropriate number to indicate the types and degree of cultural shock (either positive or negative) you experienced when entering a foreign culture.

Type of Cultural Shock	High Degree				Low Degree	None
1. Attitudes toward time	5	4	3	2	1	0
2. Attitudes toward women	5	4	3	2	1	0
3. Gestures, eye contact, and other nonverbal messages	5	4	3	2	1	0
4. Climate	5	4	3	2	1	0
5. Clothing/business dress	5	4	3	2	1	0
6. Customs, traditions, and beliefs	5	4	3	2	1	0
7. Educational system	5	4	3	2	1	0
8. Family and marriage practices	5	4	3	2	1	0
9. Financial problems	5	4	3	2	1	0

10. Food and diet	5	4	3	2	1	0
11. Housing	5	4	3	2	1	0
12. Lack of modern conveniences	5	4	3	2	1	0
13. Social class/poverty/wealth extremes	5	4	3	2	1	0
14. Social alienation (absence of people of same culture)	5	4	3	2	1	0
15. Standards of cleanliness	5	4	3	2	1	0
16. Transportation	5	4	3	2	1	0
17. Values and ethical standards	5	4	3	2	1	0
18. Work habits and practices	5	4	3	2	1	0

Exercise 4.2

Instructions: Circle T for true or F for false.

1. T F During the second stage of cultural shock, many sojourners develop such coping behaviors as drug and alcohol abuse.
2. T F Cultural shock can be alleviated by careful selection of employees for overseas assignments.
3. T F The Platinum Rule states: "Do unto others before they do unto you."
4. T F The intellectual or classroom approach to intercultural training is basically fact-oriented training.
5. T F Cultural stress can have both psychological and physical consequences.
6. T F A source of shock to foreigners is the discovery that not all U.S. citizens are well educated.
7. T F A source of cultural shock for many U.S. persons living abroad is the financial burden of the required higher standard of living.
8. T F A major factor in the early return of expatriates is family problems.
9. T F The Johari Window represents how you see the world.
10. T F Children of repatriates experience less reentry shock than do adults.

Questions and Cases for Discussion

1. Explain what is meant by the term cultural shock.
2. Identify and discuss the stages of cultural shock.
3. How can multinational firms alleviate cultural shock?
4. Identify and describe the approaches to intercultural training offered by multinational firms.
5. Identify types of cultural stress that may confront persons who are living abroad.
6. Identify positive coping skills that may be used to alleviate stress.
7. How can social class and poverty/wealth extremes be sources of cultural shock for U.S. Americans in overseas assignments?
8. What types of financial adjustments may be associated with cultural shock?
9. Explain how the Johari Window is related to cultural shock.
10. What types of reentry problems are often encountered by persons returning to the home culture? How can reentry shock be alleviated?

Cases

The following procedure is recommended for analyzing the cases: (a) read the case carefully paying attention to details; (b) read the questions at the end of the case; (c) reread the case, taking notes on or highlighting the details needed for answering the questions; (d) identify relevant facts, underlying assumptions, and critical issues of the case; (e) list possible answers to the questions; and (f) select the most logical response to the question. Your professor may ask that you submit answers to the case questions in writing.

Case 1

Larry was sent to Japan to represent his company and wanted to make a good impression on his Japanese hosts. He immediately asked them to call him by his first name and told several humorous stories intended to break the ice. He brought along gifts containing his company's logo and asked about the state of the Japanese economy. Larry got the impression that things were not going well and that he may have behaved inappropriately. What advice would you give him?

Case 2

Karl, his wife, and five-year-old son were completing a three-year assignment in Brazil and were scheduled to return to the United States in a month. Karl would return to work at the home office in Chicago. What should Karl and his family do to lessen the shock of returning to their home culture?

Case 3

Frank's company was planning to enter the Mexican market and had sent him to meet with Juan, the manager of the firm with which they planned to establish a partnership. They agreed to meet for lunch at 2 p.m. at a restaurant in Mexico City. At 2:30, Frank, thinking he had misunderstood the time or place, was leaving when he encountered Juan, who did not apologize for being late. Juan then ordered a special brandy for them and proceeded to talk about the local museums, churches, and other points of interest. Frank indicated that he did not have time to visit local sites and was anxious to discuss their proposed business partnership. When the brandy arrived, Frank declined, saying he did not drink alcoholic beverages during the day. Each time Frank tried to turn the discussion to business, Juan immediately changed the subject to other topics, including inquiring about Frank's family and personal life. At the end of the two-hour lunch, no business had been discussed. Frank returned to the United States the following day and reported to his supervisor that the Mexican firm apparently had no interest in the proposed partnership. How could Frank have better prepared himself for the cultural shock he experienced?

Case 4

Janice Davis, a marketing representative for a U.S. firm, was looking forward to her assignment in Japan because she had visited the country on one occasion. However, her anticipation quickly turned to frustration. Because all store signs were in Japanese, she didn't know where to buy even a broom. Directions and instructions for using appliances were in Japanese. How could Janice have better prepared herself for the cultural shock she experienced?

Case 5

An international team is being organized. The members of the team are from Germany, Mexico, the Netherlands, and the United States. The main language of the group is English. The German member criticized the Mexican member for not being committed to the project because the Mexican had arrived late for the first meeting. What does commitment mean to each of these cultures? As they started working on the project, they discovered that some of the members had goals that were separate from the project goals. How would task- and group-maintenance functions differ between an international team of workers and a single country? What prejudices might these members have against other members of the group? Given what you know about these four cultures from this textbook and any other cultural materials you may have, discuss the situation. Why were the members acting as they did? What would everyone need to know as a member of an international team? How would exploring each other's beliefs, norms, and values at the initial meeting of the team affect the group?

Activities

1. For persons who have traveled or lived in a foreign country for a time, discuss the degree of reentry shock experienced upon returning to the home country in the following areas:
   a. Reestablishing friendships
   b. Readjusting to lifestyle
   c. Readjusting to job
   d. Changes in social life
   e. Changes in standard of living
2. Assume that you have just been made manager of your company's plants in Egypt. Prepare a list of the types of cultural shock you would expect to encounter.
3. After a year in Kenya, you are being returned to your U.S. office. List the types of reentry shock you would expect to experience.
4. You are reviewing applications of persons in your firm who have expressed an interest in an overseas assignment. List the special qualifications you would look for in deciding which three to interview.
5. Conduct a library search to determine what training films or materials are available for predeparture intercultural training of businesspersons.

References

Barnlund, D. C. (1975). *Public and private self in Japan and the United States*. Yarmouth, ME: Intercultural Press.

Bennett, J. M. (1986). Modes of cross-cultural training: Conceptualizing cross-cultural training as education. *International*

Journal of Intercultural Relations,
10, 117–134.

Bird, A., & Dunbar, R. (1991, Spring). Getting the job done over there: Improving expatriate productivity. *National Productivity Review,* 145–156.

Black, J. S., Gregersen, H. B., & Mendenhall, M. E. (1992). *Global assignments: Successfully expatriating and repatriating international managers.* San Francisco, CA: Jossey-Bass.

Black, J. S., Gregersen, H. B., Mendenhall, M. E., & Stroh, L. K. (1999). *Globalizing people through international assignments.* Reading, MA: Addison-Wesley Publishing.

Brislin, R. W. (1981). *Cross-cultural encounters: Face-to-face interaction.* New York: Pergamon.

Broome, B. J. (1991). Building shared meaning: Implications of a relational approach to empathy for teaching intercultural communication. *Communication Education, 40*(7), 236–249.

Chaney, L. H., & Martin, J. S. (1993, October). *Cultural shock: An intercultural communication problem.* Paper presented at the annual convention of the Association for Business Communication, Montreal, Quebec, Canada.

Davis, B., & Krapels R. H. (2005). Culture shock and reverse culture shock: Developing coping skills. In S. O'Brien (Ed.), *Communication for a global society, 2005 NBEA Yearbook* (pp. 115–131). Reston, VA: National Business Education Association.

Dodd, C. H. (1997). *Dynamics of intercultural communication* (5th ed.). New York: McGraw Hill.

Dodd, C. H., & Montalvo, F. F. (Eds.). (1987). *Intercultural skills for multicultural societies.* Washington, DC: Sietar International.

Engholm, C. (1991). *When business east meets business west.* New York: Wiley.

Ferraro, G. P. (1990). *The cultural dimension of international business.* Upper Saddle River, NJ: Prentice Hall.

Fussell, P. (1983). *Class.* New York: Ballantine.

Geber, B. (1992, July). The care and breeding of global managers. *Training,* 33–37.

Harris, P. R., Moran, R. T., & Moran, S. V. (2004). *Managing cultural differences* (6th ed.). Burlington, MA: Elsevier Butterworth-Heinemann.

Harvey, M. G. (1985, Spring). The executive family: An overlooked variable in international assignments. *Columbia Journal of World Business,* 84–92.

Klopf, D. W. (2000). *Intercultural encounters* (5th ed.). Englewood, CO: Morton.

Krapels, R. H. (1993). *Predeparture intercultural communication preparation provided international business managers and professionals and perceived characteristics of intercultural training needs.* Unpublished doctoral dissertation, Memphis State University. Memphis, TN.

Lewis, T. J., & Jungman, R. E. (Eds.). (1986). *On being foreign; culture shock in short fiction.* Yarmouth, ME: Intercultural Press.

Luft, J. (1984). *Group processes: An introduction to group dynamics.* Palo Alto, CA: Mayfield Publishing Company.

McEnery, J., & DesHarnais, G. (1990, April). Culture shock. *Training and Development Journal,* 43–47.

O'Sullivan, S. L. (2002). The protean approach to managing repatriation transitions. *International Journal of Manpower, 23*(7), 597–616.

Samovar, L. A., & Porter, R. E. (2004). *Communication between cultures* (5th ed.). Belmont, CA: Wadsworth/Thomson Learning.

Stroh, L. K., Gregersen, H. B., & Black, J. S. (2000). Triumphs and tragedies: Expectations and commitments upon repatriation. *The International Journal of Human Resource Management, 11*(4), 681–697.

Tung, R. (1981, Spring). Selection and training of personnel for overseas assignments. *Columbia Journal of World Business,* 68–78.

C H A P T E R

5 | LANGUAGE

Objectives

Upon completion of this chapter, you will

- understand how language affects intercultural business communication.

- be aware of problems associated with language diversity.

- understand number usage differences that may have an impact on intercultural written communication.

- understand how language construction, thought, perceptions, and culture are linked.

- understand the limits of using a second language.

- be aware that language differences exist even when people speak the same language.

- understand the importance of accurate translation and interpretation to intercultural communication.

- understand how to use parables and proverbs as insights into the culture.

- understand the concepts of the Sapir-Whorf and Bernstein hypotheses.

Successful communication with someone from another culture involves understanding a common language. Without this shared language, communication problems may occur when a third party, the translator or interpreter, attempts to convey both the verbal and nonverbal intent of a message.

Although Chinese is the language spoken by the largest number of native speakers with English ranking second, English is considered the language of international business. However, you may fit in and be able to develop rapport if you are fluent in another person's language. Because so many variations exist in the English language (Australian English, British English, Caribbean English, Indian English, African English, and Irish English), messages are often misunderstood even when both parties speak this language with its many accents, dialects, and regional peculiarities. Unfamiliar accents may present barriers to effective communication (Gilsdorf, 2002).

People who speak English as a second language retain much of their foreign accent. Those for whom Spanish is a first language and English the second language, for example, often pronounce vowels as they are pronounced in the Spanish language. For example, "e" is pronounced as "a" and "i" is pronounced as "e." They may also pronounce certain consonants as they would in Spanish, such as "j" is pronounced as "h" ("Hoolian" for "Julian"). When the wrong syllable is accented (such as dév-eloped rather than de-véloped), understanding is difficult.

Language holds us together as groups, differentiates us into groups, and controls the way we shape concepts, how we think, how we perceive, and how we judge others. When we understand how important and complex a culture's native language is, it is easier to see why in a country such as India, English is the official language. The Indian people do, however, use more than 100 native languages or dialects for communication within their microcultures.

Women and men, at least in the United States, have different modes of discourse. Women engage in "rapport talk" and men in "report talk." Women seek connections and agreement and are more cooperative in discussions. Men tend to be more individualistic and controlling in their conversations. When women and men have conversations, the men talk and interrupt women more often and focus on their topics rather than listening to the women (Tannen, 2001). In addition, women are more personal, understanding, and sympathetic than men. They also use more verbal hedges (I feel, I think) and more qualifying terms (perhaps, possibly) than men (Samovar & Porter, 2004). Many languages are spoken differently by the men and women of the culture. For example, in Japanese, the women speak with a softer intonation than do men.

The closest concepts to common worldwide languages are numbers and music. Unlike mathematicians, businesspeople must be sensitive to the nuances of a language. This is important to assure understanding when communicating with people whose first language differs from their own or even with those whose language is the same as their own. Language is only part of communication. How the language is used in relationship to nonverbal communication and the beliefs and values of the culture is also very important.

Sociolinguistics refers to the effects of social and cultural differences upon a language. People reveal class differences by their accent, phrasing, and word usage. According to Fussell (1983), U.S. Americans with good educational backgrounds and relatively high incomes speak in a similar manner regardless of where they live in the country. People who use such terms as ain't, reckon (suppose), and afeared (afraid) are considered uneducated and/or from lower-class backgrounds.

How strongly group members feel about themselves and their membership in the group determines how members of a group talk to people in other groups. If a group views itself as a vital ethnolinguistic group (a group that views itself as culturally different from the main group and has developed its own language or dialect), they are more likely to maintain their distinctive linguistics in a multilingual setting. The more important a language is viewed, the more important the group using the language is in terms of economic, social, and language status. Because people in other cultures also reveal their class level by their accent, pronunciation, and word usage, when selecting an interpreter, be sure to determine whether the person is experienced in the regional and sociolinguistic groups with whom you are dealing.

HIGH- AND LOW-CONTEXT LANGUAGE

The concept of high- and low-context language has been researched by Hall and Hall (1990). A **high-context language** transmits very little in the explicit message; instead, the nonverbal and cultural aspects of what is not said are very important. In high-context cultures, people must read between the lines to understand the intended meaning of the message. The Japanese language and culture are examples of high-context communication. Bernstein (in Funakawa, 1997) calls the speech coding system of high-context languages restricted code. The spoken statement reflects the social relationship and the relationship's shared assumptions.

The U.S. language and culture, on the other hand, are examples of low-context communication. In a **low-context language** and culture, the message is explicit; it may be given in more than one way to ensure understanding by the receiver. In low-context languages, a person states what is expected or wanted. High-context languages tend to be indirect and nonverbal, whereas low-context languages tend to be direct and verbal. Because people of low-context cultures favor directness, they are likely to consider high-context communications as a waste of time. The speech system used in low-context cultures is elaborated code. Low-context cultures require verbal elaboration due to fewer shared assumptions (Bernstein, in Funakawa, 1997).

If there is perceived disagreement between the verbal and nonverbal message within either low- or high-context societies, the nonverbal signals are relied on versus what is actually said. However, in high-context cultures, the nonverbal signals are much more subtle and elusive to the untrained senses. An example of high-context communication is the way the Japanese indicate no. The Japanese say "yes" for no but indicate whether "yes" is yes or really no by the context, tone, time taken to answer, and facial and body expressions. This use of high-context communication can be very confusing to the uninitiated, nonsensitive intercultural businessperson. In the United States, which is a low-context society, "no" means no. Group-oriented, collectivistic cultures tend to use high-context languages; individualistic cultures tend to use low-context languages.

LANGUAGE DIVERSITY

Achieving successful communication is difficult because of the diversity of dialects and accents within a language. In the United States, more than 140 languages and dialects are currently spoken; about 11% of the population speaks a native language other than English in the home (Tsunda, 1986).

The diversity between languages and within the same language is arbitrary. Words in themselves have no meaning; meanings were assigned at some point by people in a culture. For example, the word "business" in the United States connotes how we choose to make and exchange commodities. In other languages, people assign other sounds to mean business, such as *shobai, bijinesu, shigoto, entreprise, comercio,* and *negocios.* In the English language, synonyms for business also exist, such as commerce, trade, and enterprise.

The diversity of languages causes problems both for managers and applicants for jobs. What is the correct way to assess English-language skills of job applicants?

Managers must ask themselves how important correct English-language skill is in this position. Perhaps the ability to speak and write English well is not essential to job performance; on the other hand, it may be very important. Language qualifications for each position should be assessed separately.

> Even when the language is the same as your native language, you must be careful. For example, Great Britain and Canada both speak English. However, many Canadians follow the British pronunciations and spellings. In some parts of Canada and the United States, people say the accents are nearly indistinguishable. Examples of pronunciation differences include "uh-GAIN" for "again," and "bean" for "been." And, of course, one-fifth of Canadians speak French as their primary language. (Bosrock, 1995b)

Other problems caused by language diversity include foreigners who speak their native language on the job, a practice that is not viewed favorably by the nationals. Although the main reason foreigners may use their native language is to express their ideas easily, this behavior is interpreted as an attempt to exclude nationals from the conversation and is considered extremely rude.

THE LANGUAGE OF NUMBERS

Number usage can pose special problems with written communication when communicating globally. One such problem is that decimal points are not used in the same way the world over. A number written as 34.5 in the United States is written as 34,5 in Europe. The decimal point is also used for separating thousands in Europe; for example, 8.642 in Europe is equal to 8,642 in the United States. In some countries, the decimal may be located half the distance between the top and bottom of the adjoining numbers (34·5). Another area of confusion is the difference between what constitutes a billion and a trillion. In the United States, Russia, France, Italy, Turkey, Brazil, and Greece, a billion has nine zeros (1,000,000,000) but is called a milliard in Russia, Italy, and Turkey. In Germany, Austria, the Netherlands, Hungary, Sweden, Denmark, Norway, Finland, Spain, Portugal, Serbia, Croatia, and some South American countries, a billion has 12 zeros (1,000,000,000,000), which is equal to the U.S. trillion. Although the British government announced in 1974 that all government reports and statistics would use the U.S. system for billion, you should check figures carefully in Britain (*Names of big,* 2004). Some other interesting variations from what is considered the standard way of writing numbers in the United States include the following: a one (1) may be written so that it looks like a V, sevens may be written with a slash across the middle that can be mistaken for a Y or a 4, eights may be started at the bottom loop rather than the top loop, and zeros may be crossed (Bermont, 2004).

INFORMAL AND ALTERNATIVE LANGUAGES

Informal language in the United States generally takes the form of slang, colloquialisms, acronyms, euphemisms, and jargon. Alternative languages of a coculture may take the form of cant and argot and may serve various functions. Those engaged in illegal activities may use their specialized language for concealment and to avoid arrest. Alternative languages also give certain groups a sense of identity and cohesiveness (Samovar & Porter, 2004).

Informal language comes from numerous areas, including the military, sports, computers, law, and engineering. Informal language should be used with caution in intercultural encounters because of potential miscommunication.

Slang includes idioms and other informal language. "Bottom line" and "back to square one" are examples of business slang. **Colloquialisms** are informal words or phrases often associated with certain regions of the country. Examples of colloquialisms include "y'all" (you all), "pop" (soda), and "ain't" (is/are not). **Acronyms** are words formed from the initial letters or groups of letters of words in a phrase and pronounced as one word. Examples of acronyms are RAM (random access memory), BASIC (beginner's all-purpose symbolic instruction code), Fortran (formula translation), and OSHA (Occupational Safety and Health Administration). Initial abbreviations are pronounced as separate initials, such as CEO (corporate executive officer), CAR (computer-assisted retrieval), and OJT (on-job-training). **Euphemisms** are inoffensive expressions that are used in place of offensive words or words with negative connotations. Taboo words are dealt with through euphemisms. Examples of euphemisms include "to pass or pass away" (to die), "senior citizens" (old people), "customer service department" (complaint department), and "human relations" (personnel). **Jargon** is technical terminology used within specialized groups, such as engineers, teenagers, and doctors. Examples of jargon include "on the ball" (on top of things), "oiled" (become suddenly wealthy), and "byte" (a string of binary digits) (Ferraro, 2001).

Additional business expressions include (DeVries, 1994):

- asleep at the switch: inattentive
- back off: moderate your stand or speed if driving
- blockbuster: great success
- cold turkey: abruptly, without warning
- cutthroat: harsh
- eat one's words: retract
- garbage: nonsense
- get off the ground: start successfully
- have someone's number: know the truth about someone
- kiss-off: dismissal
- miss the boat: lost opportunity
- piece of cake: something easy
- ring a bell: sound familiar
- two-bit: cheap, tacky
- red tape: many steps to completion
- bottom line: profits or loss
- ballpark figure: an estimate or amount that is close

Alternative language is generally begun by people in a subgroup of a community to differentiate themselves from the masses and determine who is a member of the "in group." Argot and cant are examples of alternative languages.

Argot is a vocabulary used by nonprofessional, noncriminal groups. Truck drivers, for example, may use the term "smoky" to refer to the highway patrol. Circus workers use the term "dip" to mean a pickpocket (Samovar & Porter, 2004).

Cant is the vocabulary of the undesirable cocultures, such as drug dealers, gangs, prostitutes, or murderers. Expressions used by people who are incarcerated include "doing a stretch" (serving a prison sentence) and "lifeboat" (a pardon). Prostitutes use the term "gorilla" to refer to a person who beats them and "outlaws" to mean prostitutes who do not have a pimp. Gangs use the term "homegirl" to refer to a girl who hangs around the gang and "claim" to mean the area gang members consider their territory (Samovar & Porter, 2004).

Some African Americans use a nonstandard form of American English sometimes referred to as **Ebonics;** for example, the word "bad" is used to mean the best. Although some people view Ebonics as a language, others see it as a dialect.

FORMS OF VERBAL INTERACTION

Forms of verbal interaction include verbal dueling, repartee conversation, rituals, and self-disclosure. **Verbal dueling** is like gamesmanship; the object is to see who can gain dominance in a friendly debate rather than who can impart needed information. The competitive conversations are generally meant in jest but are used in nonaggressive societies to release hostility. Often people who are also not familiar with verbal dueling may misunderstand the subtleties of the communication that is taking place. In the United States, urban black adolescent males have a form of insult contest called playing the dozens. The verbal dueling begins when one male insults a member of the opponent's family. The opponent can choose not to play; however, he will normally counter with an insult of his own. The verbal dueling continues until the males become bored or one is "victorious" (Ferraro, 2001). In Germany, France, and England, politics is an appropriate topic for verbal dueling. Verbal dueling may also take place when discussing sporting events, such as which team is better or which team is going to win. In the business environment, verbal dueling may occur when a group is trying to decide on a new ad campaign and members of the group are polarized as to which campaign is best. Many times when companies are interviewing candidates for positions, verbal dueling takes place over who is the best candidate for the job.

Repartee conversation is a conversation in which the parties frequently take turns speaking, usually after the first few sentences. The speakers talk only for short periods and then listen while the other person speaks briefly. Repartee is a favorite form of interaction for people of the United States; they become very irritated when someone speaks for too long. In contrast, Africans and Arabs tend to speak for extended periods.

Excellent speech is important to the French, and repartee is admired. The speaking skill is so important that for a foreigner to function effectively in France, he or she must speak French fluently (Hall & Hall, 1990).

Ritual conversation is culturally based and involves standard replies and comments for a given situation. In the United States, the interchanges are superficial; little meaning is attached to what is said. U.S. people are not actually interested in learning about others or in revealing their own emotions or personal information during such rituals as greeting others upon arriving at work. Latin Americans, on the other hand, discuss health and other personal information for extended periods during ritual conversation. Arabs in ritual conversation invoke Allah's goodwill; however, they avoid discussions of personal situations.

Self-disclosure is another form of interaction that involves telling other people about yourself so they may get to know you better. The amount of self-disclosure a person is willing to give another is culturally determined. Foreigners who need to know a person to do business with that person become very frustrated with the lack of personal information provided by people in the United States. If people in a culture feel the need to develop friendships prior to conducting business, doing business with U.S. persons can be very disconcerting because U.S. Americans are not viewed as committed to forming friendships.

LINEAR AND NONLINEAR LANGUAGE

Linear and nonlinear aspects of language involve cultural thought patterns; they indicate how people in a specific culture think and communicate (Tsunda, 1986).

Linear language is object oriented and logical with a beginning and an end. Linear languages, such as English, look at time on a continuum of present, past, and future. This view has affected communication patterns and business practices in the United States; an example of such business practices is short-range planning.

Nonlinear language is circular, tradition oriented, and subjective. Nonlinear languages, such as Chinese, look at time as cyclical and the seasons as an ever-repeating pattern. The nonlinear concepts are apparent in the long-range planning of the Chinese and Japanese and in the seasonal messages at the beginning of Japanese letters. The short term is unimportant in Asia. In the United States, for example, stockholders tend to sell their ownership in firms that are having short-term problems; Asians, on the other hand, look at the long-term position of the firm and hold on to the stock.

In intercultural business situations, people respond in a dialogue based on their linear or nonlinear orientation. In the United States, linear explanations are given as answers to *why* questions. The Japanese, however, give more details that do not need linear links. The Japanese tell *what* happened and assume the *why,* whereas U.S. people answer *why* and assume the *what.* For example, a U.S. manager might ask a Japanese worker why the production was stopped. The manager would expect a direct answer, such as, "The parts are defective." The Japanese worker would answer nonlinearly with a long, detailed explanation, including what the defects were and other related details. Miscommunication occurred because the Japanese answered with *what* was wrong instead of the *why* response expected by the U.S. manager (Tsunda, 1986).

VOCABULARY EQUIVALENCE

Because language is influenced by various aspects of a culture, exact translations for all words in one language to a second language are not possible. For example, in one language, the word "love" is used to mean love of another person, love of a pet, or love of an object, while in a second language, different words are provided to distinguish between different types of love (see Figure 5-1).

FIGURE 5-1   Vocabulary Equivalence. In the United States, the word "love" is used to mean a strong preference for an object as well as physical or emotional "love."

Many vocabulary inequivalences exist, including problems due to idiomatic equivalence, grammatical–syntactical equivalence, experiential equivalence, and conceptual equivalence (Jandt, 2004).

The English language is built on extremes, such as far and near, heavy and light, high and low, good and bad, wide and narrow, old and young, and long and short. These conceptual inequivalences can cause misunderstanding. Words may or may not exist to describe the middle area between the extremes, forcing a person speaking English to use one of the polar ends. The Portuguese language has many words in the middle area between the extremes; however, when the Portuguese is translated to English, only the extremes are available. Therefore, when the translation is read in English, it may not have a vocabulary equivalence and so will not ask or say what was said in Portuguese. The Portuguese question, *"Qual é a distancia a* New York?" becomes "How far is it to New York?" However, the Portuguese are actually asking for the location in space of New York as opposed to the far or near dichotomy of the English language (Stewart & Bennett, 1991).

The following story is an example of grammatical–syntactical equivalence. A devout Catholic, David drove south from Minnesota to celebrate the papal visit to Mexico. Overcome with emotion, David ran through the streets of Mexico City shouting "¡Viva la papa! ¡Viva la papa!" David's newfound Mexican friend, while sharing in his excitement, thought it prudent to correct David's Spanish. "The Spanish word for 'pope' is el papa," the Mexican explained. "You're shouting 'Long Live the Potato.'" (Bosrock, 1995b, p. 40)

Language misunderstandings related to vocabulary usage are numerous even between people who speak the same language.

World War II and the use of the atomic bomb may well have been the result of such a translation error. The Japanese government, in response to the ultimatum in the Potsdam Declaration, responded, "The government does not see much value in it. All we have to do is *mokusatsu* it." The Japanese had carefully chosen the word *mokusatsu* and intended it to mean "no comment." The Western translators chose one of the word's other meanings, which is "to ignore or to treat with silent contempt" (Jandt, 2004, p. 155).

Homonyms, words that sound alike but have different meanings, can be troublesome when learning a new language. The Chinese language is particularly difficult in this regard because even though the word is pronounced the same, the voice tone and pitch can change the entire meaning of a word. Within a family of languages (such as the Romance languages), words with similar spellings and sometimes very similar pronunciations may have very different or very similar meanings. Assuming a similarity could be both costly and embarrassing during intercultural communication encounters (Ferraro, 2001).

> Sound alike? Chuck Blethen of Scottsdale, Arizona, recounts his experience when ordering in Spanish at a Madrid restaurant. "I ordered *caballo*. The waiter looked at me indignantly and said, 'Sir, we don't serve horse here.' I thought I was saying *cebolla* which means onion." (Schmit, Richards, & Swingle, 1993, p. 5E)

Experiential equivalence happens when there is no word in one language because the idea or object does not exist. Ideas such as *department store, mall shopping,* or *wind surfing* are words that do not always translate well.

PARABLES AND PROVERBS

A **parable** is a story told to convey a truth or moral lesson, and a **proverb** is a saying that expresses a common truth. Parables and proverbs deal with truths simply and concretely and teach the listener a lesson.

Parables and proverbs can help you understand a culture and can help you determine whether it is a group- or individual-oriented culture. Parables and proverbs may also help you understand what is desired and undesired as well as what is considered correct or incorrect in the culture (Ferraro, 2001).

The U.S. proverb, "The squeaking wheel gets the grease," implies that the person who stands out and is the most vocal will be rewarded. The Japanese proverb, "The nail that sticks up gets knocked down," is an expression of their belief that the group is more important than the individual—the idea is that no one should stand out or be more important than anyone else.

Parables and proverbs can provide important information concerning the nature of the culture, such as whether or not it is basically an empathetic culture or an uncaring one.

Here are some other proverbs of selected cultures:

U.S. Proverbs
"The early bird gets the worm."
"Waste not, want not."
"He who holds the gold makes the rules."
"An ounce of prevention is worth a pound of cure."

Chinese Proverbs

"Man who waits for roast duck to fly into mouth must wait very, very long time."
"He who sows hemp will reap hemp; he who sows beans will reap beans."
"Man who says it cannot be done should not interrupt man doing it."
"Give a man a fish, and he will live for a day; give him a net, and he will live for a lifetime."

German Proverbs

"No one is either rich or poor who has not helped himself to be so."
"He who is afraid of doing too much always does too little."
"What's the use of running if you're not on the right road?"

Japan Proverbs

"Silence is golden."
"Still water runs deep."
"A wise man hears one and understands ten."
"A wise hawk hides his talons."

Other Proverbs

"Words do not make flour." (Italian)
"He that wishes to eat the nut does not mind cracking the shell." (Polish)
"Why kill time when one can employ it?" (French)
"Wealth which comes in at the door unjustly, goes out at the windows." (Egyptian)

CONVERSATION TABOOS

Conversation taboos are topics considered inappropriate for conversation with people in certain cultures or groups. Baldrige (1993), Braganti and Devine (1992), and Devine and Braganti (1991, 1995, 1998, 2000) discuss the culturally preferred topics of conversation as well as those that are considered taboo. Meeting another person usually involves a certain amount of "small talk" before getting down to business, so knowing what topics are considered appropriate and inappropriate is important. (Small talk as a business and social custom is discussed in more detail in chapter 9).

In the United States, the most popular topic of small talk seems to be the weather or comments on some aspect of the physical surroundings, such as the arrangement of the meeting room or some aspect of the building, such as the landscaping or the building location. Topics that are included later in the encounter include favorite restaurants, television programs, cities or countries visited, one's job, recreational interests or hobbies, and news items. Topics people in the United States have been taught to avoid discussing include religion and politics, even in family situations because they are too controversial. In the United States, family members often belong to different religions and political parties. The avoidance of such topics has caused people in other cultures to erroneously conclude that people in the United States are not intellectually capable of carrying on a conversation about anything more complex than weather and sports.

CHAPTER 5 *Language* 103

Some topics are considered too personal to discuss, such as the state of one's health or the health of family members, how much things cost, a person's salary, and personal misfortunes. People in the United States have been taught never to ask another person questions related to sensitive areas such as age, weight, height, hair color, or sexual orientation or behavior.

Topics considered inappropriate in the United States are, however, considered appropriate in other cultures. People in Germany and Iran, for example, consider discussing and arguing about politics to be completely acceptable. The state of someone's health and well-being and that of family members is an appropriate topic when people from Spanish-speaking countries meet for the first time. People from Saudi Arabia, on the other hand, would consider questions about the family inappropriate on an initial meeting.

General guidelines to follow when conversing with someone from another culture include the following (Baldrige, 1993):

- Avoid discussing politics or religion unless the other person initiates the discussion.
- Avoid highly personal questions, including "What do you do?"
- Keep the conversation positive. Avoid asking questions that would imply criticism; phrase questions so they can be answered in a positive manner.
- Avoid telling ethnic jokes because of the possibility of offending someone.

A good rule to follow is to take your cue from the other person. Let the other person initiate the discussion, particularly with culture-sensitive topics. Be a good listener and stay informed on a wide variety of topics to expand your conversational repertoire.

Table 5-1 contains some appropriate and inappropriate topics of conversation in selected countries (Braganti & Devine, 1992; Devine & Braganti, 1991, 1995, 1998, 2000).

TABLE 5-1   Appropriate and Inappropriate Conversation Topics by Country

Country	Appropriate Topics	Topics to Avoid
Austria	professions, cars, skiing, music	money, religion, divorce/separation
France	music, books, sports, theater	prices of items, person's work, income, age
Germany	travel abroad, international politics, hobbies, soccer	World War II, personal life
Great Britain	history, architecture, gardening	politics, money/prices, Falklands War
Japan	history, culture, art	World War II
Mexico	family, social concerns	politics, debt/inflation problems, border violations
Saudi Arabia	soccer, travel abroad	personal family matters, politics
South Africa	weather, beauty of the country, occupation	personal questions, political situation, ethnic differences

NATURE OF LANGUAGE

Language according to Klopf (2001), is "a series of sounds, and when these sounds are combined as symbols, they acquire meaning" (p. 160). To most people, language is the means we use to communicate with each other. However, the nature of language depends upon people involved with various aspects of language. For example, **linguists** study the phonetic aspects of language and define language by the sounds speakers produce and listeners receive. **Semanticists** study the meanings of words and where and how the words developed. **Grammarians** study how a language is governed and its grammatical forms, roots, and endings. **Novelists** believe that language is a series of words arranged to produce harmonious sounds or to have a logical effect (Klopf, 2001).

Syntactic Rules

Syntactic rules govern how words are arranged in a sentence. Different languages choose variations. English, French, and Spanish mainly follow a subject/verb/object order. Japanese and Korean use subject/object/verb. Hebrew and Welsh follow verb/subject/object. The object does not come first in any language (Klopf, 2001).

Perceptual Meanings and Verbal Styles

Different perceptual meanings are conveyed depending upon word choice. **Denotative meanings** are definition meanings, such as the name of a type of crab, the Japanese spider crab. **Connotative meanings** are the emotional meanings, such as Alaskan king crab. (The term Alaskan king crab, while it is a type of Japanese spider crab, has a more positive and appealing name.) **Figurative meanings** are descriptive meanings, such as kicking the bucket (Klopf, 2001).

Verbal styles vary across cultures as shown in Table 5-2 (Klopf, 2001).

TRANSLATION PROBLEMS

When languages are translated, the intended meaning may be lost. Although these errors may seem hilarious, they are also costly. Translation is written and does not have the advantage of nonverbal cues. You are also more likely to receive a literal translation than a literal interpretation.

Axtell (1994) identifies a number of U.S. translation problems: 1) General Motors automobile "Nova" in Spanish means "doesn't go"; 2) Pepsi-Cola's "Come Alive with Pepsi" when translated in Taiwanese is "Pepsi brings your ancestors back from the grave"; 3) Electrolux, a Swedish manufacturer, used "Nothing sucks like an Electrolux," which failed because of the negative slang meaning of "suck" in the United States; and 4) Bic pens were originally named Bich by their French manufacturer.

The word or concept may not have an exact duplicate in the other language. All languages do not have the same verb tenses, and many verbs have multiple meanings. In English, for example, the verb "get" can mean to buy, borrow, steal, rent, or retrieve. When a language is the person's second language, slang, euphemisms, and cultural thinking patterns can cause problems.

TABLE 5-2	Verbal Styles by Country
Ethnic Group	*Verbal Style*
Japanese	• They converse without responding to what the other person says. Emphasis is on nonverbal communication, so they do not listen. • They prefer less talkative persons and value silence. • They make excuses at the beginning of a conversation for what they are about to say. They do not want apologies for what was already said. • They have many different meanings for the word "yes."
Mexican	• They seem overly dramatic and emotional to U.S. persons. • They rise above and embellish facts; eloquence is admired. • They like to use diminutives, making the world smaller and more intimate. They add suffixes to words to minimize importance. • They appear to be less than truthful. Their rationale involves two types of reality: objective and interpersonal. Mexicans want to keep people happy for the moment. When asked directions, if they don't know the answer they will create directions to appear to be helpful.
Chinese	• They understate or convey meanings indirectly. They use vague terms and double negatives; even criticism is indirect. • Harmony is very important. During negotiations, the Chinese state their position in such a way that seems repetitious. They do not change their point of view without discussing it with the group. • They speak humbly and speak negatively of their supposedly meager skills and those of their subordinates and their family.
Arabian	• They encourage eloquence and "flowery" prose. They are verbose, repetitious, and shout when excited. • For dramatic effect, they punctuate remarks by pounding the table and making threatening gestures. • They view swearing, cursing, and the use of obscenities as offensive. • They like to talk about religion and politics but avoid talking about death, illness, and disasters. Emotional issues are avoided. • The first name is used immediately upon meeting but may be preceded by the title "Mr." or "Miss."
German	• In the German language, the verb often comes at the end of the sentence. In oral communication, Germans do not immediately get to the point. • Germans are honest and direct; they stick to the facts. They are low-context people; everything is spelled out. • Germans usually do not use first names unless they are close friends (of which they have few). • They do not engage in small talk; their conversations are serious on a wide variety of topics. Avoid conversations related to their private life.
U.S. American	• Some words are specific to an age group. • Men speak more and more often than women; women are more emotional and use such terms as "sweet," "darling," and "dreadful." • Racial and cocultural differences in verbal styles exist.

> Braniff Airlines promoted rendezvous lounges on its Brazilian routes. Rendezvous in Portuguese is a place to have sex.
>
> For the 1994 World Cup, both McDonald's and Coca-Cola reprinted the Saudi Arabian flag, including the verbage from the Qur'an on their paper bags and cans. Muslims were appalled that the Qur'an passage, "There is no God but Allah, and Mohammed is his Prophet," would be used to sell a product and be put on something that is thrown away.
>
> President Kennedy, giving a speech at the Berlin Wall, said *"Ich bin ein Berliner,"* which when properly translated means, "I am a jelly doughnut."
>
> One can ask a Russian who knows some English what the Russian word *drúk* means and the answer will be "friend." This is roughly true, but the precise social circumstances under which a Russian calls another person *drúk* are by no means the same as those under which we call someone a friend.
>
> Bilingual dictionaries and easy word-by-word translations are inevitably misleading; the shortcut of asking what a form means must ultimately be supplemented by active participation in the life of the community that speaks the language. This, of course, is one of the major reasons why semantic analysis is so difficult. (Hockett, 1967, p. 141)

Back translation is the concept of written work being translated to a second language and then being translated back to the first language by another person to determine if the translations are equivalent.

One type of translation assistance is **Group Decision Support System** (GDSS), a software package that allows people to communicate by computer in a meeting by using language translation software that permits participants to comment on a topic at the same time, rank order the comments, and vote on the comments in their own languages. People participate in their own language, which is translated into the other languages just as the others' communication is translated into their own languages. Words that do not translate directly are put in quotation marks to alert the reader to a possible translation problem. Pocket translators are also available to aid in learning and understanding another language.

Those who need oral interpretations or written translations in the United States can contact local universities for names of competent translators or consult the Translation Services Directory (published by the American Translators Association, http://www. translation-directory.com) or The American Association of Language Specialists in Washington, DC. Rates for on-the-spot verbal translations are charged by the hour or by the day, while written translations are charged by the word and the nature of the material being translated; they sometimes charge flat rates. They usually provide free estimates. AT&T has a Language Line Service (800-752-6096) or http://www.atanet.org to reach language professionals who interpret more than 150 languages 24 hours a day, 7 days a week.

INTERPRETER USE

An interpreter uses the oral or spoken word versus the written word. To be useful in a negotiation situation, an interpreter must be bilingual, bicultural, thoroughly familiar with the business culture of both sides, and able to use the correct meaning in all situations. They should possess a knowledge of the terminology used in your particular field and should have ethnic compatibility with members of the group for whom they will be translating (Samovar & Porter, 2004). Often, however, the interpreters supplied by the host culture are bilingual but not bicultural and understand at least some business in their own culture and perhaps a little of the other side's business culture. Their loyalty is, of course, with their employer. When an interpreter is not bicultural, his or her thoughts, feelings, and translations are formulated according to the interpreter's native language rather than the second language. When using an interpreter in international negotiations, a missed negative can turn an agreement into a disagreement. A poor translator can be the difference between the success and failure of the negotiation.

Many U.S. business travelers expect everyone to speak English and, therefore, do not feel compelled to get an interpreter. Although people may speak English as a second language, they do not think the same as U.S. businesspeople unless they are bicultural. Because of this, an interpreter can easily misinterpret the English being used by the U.S. businessperson and misstate facts when translating back to English. Unless the traveler is aware of the possibility of misinterpretation and asks additional questions, the traveler could leave with the wrong answer or conception.

When using interpreters, review with them your notes, slides, presentation, or anything else you have brought with you before the meeting. The advantage of using bicultural interpreters is that you can ask questions if you are not sure what to do next. A bicultural interpreter can also alert you to problems he or she may foresee. Interpreters should be allowed to use notes or a dictionary and be allowed sufficient time to clarify points. Try not to interrupt interpreters while they are translating. Use visuals to support presentations but allow the bicultural interpreter to check them for anything that may be offensive to the other people. Remember to avoid sarcasm or innuendoes because they are very difficult to translate. Try to state concepts in more than one way to be sure the point you are making is understood.

The following tips will help you work with interpreters (Axtell, 1994; Bosrock, 1997; Samovar & Porter, 2004):

- Get to know the interpreter in advance. Your phrasing, accent, pace, and idioms are all important to a good interpreter.
- Ask about cultural differences in nonverbal behaviors, such as eye contact, and about local customs that may affect the effectiveness of your presentation.
- Review technical terms in advance.
- Speak slowly and clearly.
- Watch the eyes; they are the key to comprehension.
- Insist that the interpreter translate in brief bursts and not wait until the end of a long statement.
- Be careful of humor and jokes; it is difficult to export U.S. humor.
- Use visual aids where possible. By combining the translator's words with visual messages, chances of effective communication are increased.
- Be especially careful with numbers; write out important numbers to ensure accurate communication.
- Confirm all important discussions in writing to avoid confusion and misunderstanding.
- Allow the interpreter to apologize for your inability to speak your counterpart's language.

- Ask your interpreter about meeting styles, small talk, and discussing major issues.
- Locate your interpreter correctly, remembering international protocol.
- Speak to your counterpart, not to the interpreter.
- Keep comments simple and direct.
- Get feedback through questions to be certain ideas are interpreted and understood correctly.
- Do not make statements you do not want your counterparts to hear, even if these points are not interpreted. Many counterparts can understand your language even if they are not speaking it.
- If the message is complex, meet with the interpreter prior to the meeting so the interpreter will have a clear understanding of what you are saying.
- Have a concluding session with the interpreters to see if they picked up all messages that will not translate.
- Be prepared to give your closing comments in the host country's language.

HOST LANGUAGE

If you choose to use the language of the country you are visiting, the **host language,** be especially cautious. Be sure to speak clearly and slowly and eliminate jargon, idioms, and slang. When in doubt, ask questions. Avoid using expressions or gestures that could be misinterpreted. Find out if the meaning in the host language is modified by cadence, tone, or gestures.

Learning a business partner's language can help you learn how the person thinks. Learning a foreign language and living in another cultural community will affect your view of life. You will begin to think from the other person's perspective and will reevaluate your own cultural heritage. To live in another country, you must develop personal relations and function effectively. To function effectively, some fluency in the language is important. Becoming competent in a foreign language is time consuming, but the process is helped by the language families. The Romance languages (Spanish, French, Portuguese, and Italian) share Latin as their source and therefore have many **cognates** or words that sound the same and have the same meaning. Be careful, however, because not all words that appear to be cognates actually are.

As mentioned earlier, significant differences exist when both people speak the same language in the same country. Those living in the Eastern United States are considered by many people in other parts of the country to be direct, rude, and to the point; Southerners are considered by many to be indirect, friendly, and more likely to skirt issues. When people speak the same language but are from different countries, additional problems are encountered. For example, the English spoken in the United States is different from the English spoken in Australia and Great Britain. The British use a very indirect style of verbalizing, while people of the United States use a more direct style.

The best advice when using the host language is to maintain a pleasant disposition and a positive attitude toward the host language; avoid making comments that could be interpreted as criticism of their language.

The language people speak, the names of the countries, and what the citizens are called can be very confusing. The following list in Table 5-3 should make references easier (Bosrock, 1995a, p. 53).

TABLE 5-3	Languages and Citizen References by Country	
Country	*People*	*Language*
• Austria	• Austrians	• German
• Belgium	• Belgians	
–Wallonia	–Walloons	–French
–Flanders	–Flemings	–Flemish/Dutch
• Canada	• Canadians	• English/French
• Denmark	• Danes	• Danish
• Finland	• Finns	• Finnish
• France	• French	• French
• Germany	• Germans	• German
• Greece	• Greeks	• Greek
• Ireland	• Irish	• English/Irish
• Italy	• Italians	• Italian
• Japan	• Japanese	• Japanese
• Luxembourg	• Luxembourgers	• Luxembourgish/French/German
• Mexico	• Mexicans	• Spanish
• The Netherlands	• Dutch/Netherlanders	• Dutch
• Norway	• Norwegians	• Norwegian
• Portugal	• Portuguese	• Portuguese
• Spain	• Spanish/Spaniards	• Spanish
• Sweden	• Swedes	• Swedish
• Switzerland	• Swiss	• French/German/Italian/Romansch
• Turkey	• Turks	• Turkish
• United Kingdom	• British	• English
–England	–British/English	–English
–Scotland	–Scots	–English/Gaelic
–Wales	–Welsh	–English/Welsh
–Northern Ireland	–Northern Irish	–English

English is spoken as a native language, a semiofficial language, or is studied in the countries listed in Table 5-4 (*U.S. News & World Report,* 1995).

THOUGHT

Thinking is universal; however, methods of classifying, categorizing, sorting, and storing information are very different.

Subjective interpretation is an interpretation placed on a message that is affected by the thought processes; it is influenced by personal judgment, state of mind, or temperament. Subjective interpretation is learned through cultural contact. We perceive what is relevant to our physical and social survival and classify, categorize, sort, and store it for future use. What is important in one culture may not be important in another.

In the United States, people tend to think in a very functional, pragmatic way; they like procedural knowledge (how to get from point A to point B). Europeans, however,

TABLE 5-4   Use of English by Country

Native English	Semiofficial English	English Studied

• North America
  –Canada, except Quebec
  –United States
• South America
  –Guyana
• Caribbean
  –Bahamas
  –Barbados
  –Grenada
  –Jamaica
  –Trinidad and Tobago
• Europe
  –Ireland
  –United Kingdom
• Pacific
  –Australia
  –New Zealand
	• Africa
	  –Botswana
	  –Cameroon
	  –Ethiopia
	  –Gambia
	  –Ghana
	  –Kenya
	  –Lesotho
	  –Liberia
	  –Malawi
	  –Mauritius
	  –Namibia
	  –Sierra Leone
	  –South Africa
	  –Sudan
	  –Swaziland
	  –Tanzania
	  –Uganda
	  –Zambia
	  –Zimbabwe
	• Asia, Pacific
	  –Bangladesh
	  –Fiji
	  –India
	  –Malaysia
	  –Myanmar (Burma)
	  –Pakistan
	  –Philippines
	  –Singapore
	  –Sri Lanka
	  –Tonga
	  –Western Samoa
	• Mideast
	  –Israel
	  –Malta
	  –Burundi–Central
		• North America
		  –Mexico
		• Central America
		• Caribbean
		  –Costa Rica
		  –Cuba
		  –Dominican Republic
		  –Honduras
		• South America
		  –Brazil
		  –Colombia
		  –Venezuela
		• Europe
		  –Austria
		  –Belgium
		  –Denmark
		  –Finland
		  –France
		  –Germany
		  –Greece
		  –Iceland
		  –Italy
		  –Luxembourg
		  –Netherlands
		  –Norway
		  –Portugal
		  –Romania
		  –Russian Federation
		  –Sweden
		  –Switzerland
		• Africa
		  –Algeria
		  –Angola
		  –Burkina Faso
		  –Central African Republic
		  –Côte d'Ivoire (Ivory Coast)
		  –Gabon
		  –Guinea
		  –Libya
		  –Madagascar
		  –Morocco
		  –Niger
		  –Senegal
		  –Togo
		  –Democratic Republic of Congo
		• Middle East
		  –Egypt
		  –Jordan
		  –Saudi Arabia
		  –Syria
		  –Turkey
		  –Yemen
		• Asia
		  –Afghanistan
		  –China
		  –Hong Kong–Indonesia
		  –Japan
		  –Nepal
		  –S. Korea
		  –Thailand

are more abstract; they like declarative knowledge, which is descriptive. The Japanese have a different way of thinking; they like to work with precedents and rules rather than abstract probability (Borden, 1991).

Thoughts and views toward nature, for example, are culturally diverse. U.S. people view nature as something to conquer; however, Native Americans and many Asians view nature as something with which to coexist. Other cultures such as the Colombian *mestizo,* consider nature to be dangerous and have a fatalistic attitude toward it and their ability to control their destiny. A culture's perception of nature can be seen in their parables and proverbs, work ethic, and religion (Condon & Yousef, 1975).

A culture's way of thinking adversely affects the culture's capability to make progress. People who worked with the Peace Corps, for example, found that introducing technology to a Third World country could not be accomplished without a change in cultural attitudes toward technology (Condon & Yousef, 1975). Initial plans for people of the Russian states following the fall of communism in 1991 were to give them stock in businesses and housing. After generations of being told what to do, however, the people had a difficult time changing their way of thinking to include taking responsibility for themselves.

In our thought processes, we make associations between color and messages. For example, in the United States, red is associated with stop, and green is associated with go. U.S. Americans associate white with purity, but in China, white is associated with death. Chapter 6 contains additional information related to messages conveyed through the use of color.

LANGUAGE AND CULTURE INTERACTION

Language can be both unifying and divisive. A common native language ties people together, yet the presence of many different native languages in a small geographic area can cause problems. Both culture and language affect each other. We have the chicken and egg dilemma—which came first, the language or the culture? The use of language/culture in creating political, social, economic, and education processes is a consequence of favoring certain ideals over others. Understanding the culture without understanding the language is difficult.

Colonialism caused many areas of the world to lose or replace their native languages with the colonial language. Because the colonies spoke the colonizers' language, the colonizers treated them from an ethnocentric view. Many areas of the world that once were colonized are now trying to regain their native language in an effort to regain their ethnic identity (Ferraro, 2001).

Because most U.S. Americans are immigrants and have learned English, their native languages have died. Although many U.S. citizens may not speak the languages of their ancestors, many of the thought patterns have been passed from generation to generation, such as how a person shows affection for male and female friends, male and female family members, spouse and children, and acquaintances. A person with a strong German background is less likely to hug any of those group members in public; however, someone of Spanish or African descent is much more likely to hug and show affection in public. Generally, when people want to continue speaking their native language, it is because they are able to express their thoughts more clearly and maintain what is culturally comfortable.

English also changes from one region of the nation to another. All these differences cause unequal power relationships to develop between people from different social and power backgrounds. Because language determines your cognition and perception, if you are removed from your linguistic environment, you no longer have the conceptual framework to explain ideas and opinions. The Sapir–Whorf hypothesis and the Bernstein hypothesis offer additional insight into language and culture interaction (Samovar & Porter, 2004; Weaver, 1998).

Sapir–Whorf Hypothesis

The main idea of the **Sapir–Whorf hypothesis,** named for Edward Sapir and Benjamin Lee Whorf, is that language functions as a way of shaping a person's experience and not just a device for reporting that experience. People adhere to the connections of their language to communicate effectively. Both structural and semantic aspects of a language are involved. The structural aspect includes phonetics and syntax. Although the syntax aspect of language is influenced by and influences perception and categorization, the semantic aspect of language deals with meaning.

The concept of linguistic determinism is often referred to as the Sapir–Whorf hypothesis because the two men figured predominately in its development. **Linguistic determinism** is the assumption that a person's view of reality stems mainly from his or her language. Even though two languages may be similar, they cannot represent the same social reality; the worlds of the people who speak the two languages are different. So although languages often do have equivalencies in other languages, the social reality cannot be fully conveyed to a person who does not speak the language.

An example of the concept of linguistic determinism is the absence of a word for "snow" in Inuit, the language of the Inuit people. The language does, however, have numerous words for types of snow, while other languages do not have the equivalent of flaky snow or crusty snow, for example. Because snow is important to the Inuit people, they need to be able to describe it precisely (Borden, 1991; Condon & Yousef, 1975; Dodd, 1997; Ferraro, 2001; Samovar & Porter, 2004).

Bernstein Hypothesis

The **Bernstein hypothesis** explains how social structure affects language and is an extension of the Sapir–Whorf hypothesis. Bernstein considers culture, subculture, social context, and social system to be part of social structure.

According to the Bernstein hypothesis, speech emerges in one of two codes— restricted or elaborated. Communication transmission channels used in the restricted code are oral, nonverbal, and paralinguistic. **Restricted codes** include highly predictable messages; they are for those who know you and what you are talking about well. These codes are similar to argot in that the communication assumes a common interest or shared experience. Because of this shared experience and identity, elaborating on the verbal message is unnecessary. You may, for example, find that your best friend sometimes finishes your sentences or knows what you are going to say before you finish speaking because of shared experiences. **Elaborated codes** are used with strangers; they involve messages that are low in predictability. You need to give explicit information to ensure that the message is understood. The verbal channel is important in elaborated codes, while restricted codes use nonverbal and paralinguistic cues (Dodd, 1997).

Terms

- Acronyms
- Argot
- Back translation
- Bernstein hypothesis
- Cant
- Cognates
- Colloquialism
- Connotative meanings
- Conversation taboos
- Denotative meanings
- Ebonics
- Elaborated codes
- Euphemisms
- Figurative meanings

- Grammarians
- Group Decision Support Systems
- High-context language
- Homonyms
- Host language
- Jargon
- Linear language
- Linguistic determinism
- Linguists
- Low-context language
- Nonlinear language
- Novelists
- Parable

- Proverb
- Repartee conversation
- Restricted codes
- Ritual conversation
- Sapir–Whorf hypothesis
- Self-disclosure
- Semanticists
- Slang
- Sociolinguistics
- Subjective interpretation
- Syntactic rules
- Verbal dueling

Exercise 5.1

Instructions: Circle T for true or F for false.

1. T F   Nonverbal aspects are very important in low-context cultures.
2. T F   The Japanese language and culture are examples of high-context communication.
3. T F   The terms "sanitation engineer" and "garbage collector" are examples of colloquialisms.
4. T F   Politics is an appropriate topic for verbal dueling in Germany.
5. T F   Repartee involves taking turns speaking.
6. T F   People of the United States provide very little self-disclosure.
7. T F   Chinese is an example of a linear language.
8. T F   Conversation taboos in Mexico include politics and border violations.
9. T F   The concept of linguistic determinism is related to the Sapir–Whorf hypothesis.
10. T F   The Bernstein hypothesis involves restricted and elaborated codes.

Questions and Cases for Discussion

1. Explain how language differentiates us as groups.
2. Teenagers and other groups develop jargon and slang. Give examples of slang or jargon used by people with whom you associate.
3. The United States is a low-context country, and Japan is a high-context country. How would the Japanese react to a flamboyant U.S. salesperson?
4. Give examples of conversation taboos in your home or group of friends.
5. Why is a bicultural/bilingual interpreter better than a monocultural/bilingual interpreter?
6. In what employee positions is knowledge of a foreign language more crucial for a company? Why?
7. Explain how ethnic groups in the United States participate in verbal dueling.
8. What does it mean to say two languages do not have vocabulary equivalence? To say the same language does not have vocabulary equivalence?
9. Explain what is meant by argot. Give examples from a culture with which you are familiar.
10. Explain the difference between restricted and elaborated codes in the Bernstein hypothesis.
11. If thinking is universal, how does culture and language affect the way different groups of humans think?

Cases

The following procedure is recommended for analyzing the cases: (a) read the case carefully paying attention to details; (b) read the questions at the end of the case; (c) reread the case, taking notes on or highlighting the details needed for answering the questions; (d) identify relevant facts, underlying assumptions, and critical issues of the case; (e) list possible answers to the questions; and (f) select the most logical response to the question. Your professor may ask that you submit answers to the case questions in writing.

Case 1

In parts of the United States, particularly in Florida where there is a large Latin American population, the suggestion has been made that Spanish should be considered the first language and English the second language and that people whose native language is Spanish should be taught in Spanish with English taught as a second language. Based on the discussion of language in this chapter, what are the advantages and disadvantages of implementing such a system? How would your argument for or against this proposed change apply to similar situations in India, Canada, or the European Union?

Case 2

A U.S. production manager, Joe Sorrells, is sent to manage a manufacturing facility in Mexico. On his arrival, his assistant production manager, Juan Lopez, suggests they go to the factory to meet the workers who have been awaiting his arrival. Joe declines Juan's offer and chooses instead to get right to work on determining why the quality and production rate of the Mexican plant are not equal to the U.S. plant. Juan stresses the importance of getting to know the workers first, but Joe lets Juan know he was sent to Mexico to straighten things out, not to form friendships with the local workers. Without further comment, Juan gets Joe the figures and records he requests. Joe made a number of changes and felt sure the plan he had prepared would improve quality and increase production. After a couple of months, no improvement has been made; Joe cannot understand why the workers seem to resist his plans. What went wrong?

Case 3

You are responsible for hiring a sales manager whose territory will include all of South America. You have narrowed your search to two people. One is a citizen of Brazil who speaks Spanish and Portuguese but very little English. The second is a U.S. citizen who speaks English and a little Spanish. Your product line necessitates that the sales manager hire two additional people in South America, run a sales office with a receptionist/secretary, live in South America, and personally call on customers in the different countries. Which of the two people would you choose? Give reasons for your choice.

Case 4

You are in a meeting in a subsidiary of a German company in the United States. The meeting has two German citizens who are living in the United States and three U.S. citizens all of whom are employees. You have been discussing the packaging of a new product, and suddenly the two Germans begin speaking in German rather than English. You wait for a couple of minutes, become irritated, and leave. Explain what is happening in this situation concerning the use of language.

Activities

1. Prepare a list of countries you have visited or countries in which you have worked. List one U.S. slang expression that has a negative meaning in each country listed.
2. Quote a parable or proverb from one of the countries listed in Activity 1 and indicate how the parable or proverb characterizes some aspect of the culture.
3. List three conversation taboos in the United States and three taboos in one of the countries identified in Activity 1.
4. Write a paragraph about language problems you have encountered when communicating with students from other cultures. Include problems with tone, enunciation, pronunciation, slang, and so on.
5. Review a journal article or a chapter in a book related to the use of interpreters. Prepare a one-page summary for submission to the instructor.
6. Because many books are translations from other languages, the Sapir–Whorf hypothesis states that these translations may not preserve the exact meaning as it was intended. This phrase paraphrased from the Bible, for example, has been translated numerous times: "It is easier for a camel to go through the eye of a needle than for a rich man to enter the kingdom of God" (Mark 10:25). (One other translation is: "The eye of the needle is a narrow doorway in an ancient wall.") Give other examples of exact translations that may make understanding a book difficult.

References

Axtell, R. E. (1994). *The do's and taboos of international trade.* New York: Wiley.

Baldrige, L. (1993). *Letitia Baldrige's new complete guide to executive manners.* New York: Rawson Associates.

Bermont, J. (2004). *How to Europe: The complete traveler's handbook.* Midland, MI: Murphy & Broad Publishing Company.

Borden, G. A. (1991). *Cultural orientation: An approach to understanding intercultural communication.* Upper Saddle River, NJ: Prentice Hall.

Bosrock, M. M. (1997). *Put your best foot forward—Asia.* St. Paul, MN: International Educational Systems.

Bosrock, M. M. (1995a). *Put your best foot forward—Europe.* St. Paul, MN: International Educational Systems.

Bosrock, M. M. (1995b). *Put your best foot forward—Mexico/Canada.* St. Paul, MN: International Educational Systems.

Braganti, N. L., & Devine, E. (1992). *European customs and manners.* New York: Meadowbrook.

Condon, J. C., & Yousef, F. S. (1975). *Introduction to intercultural communication.* New York: Macmillan Publishing Company.

Devine, E., & Braganti, N. L. (1995). *The traveler's guide to African customs and manners.* New York: St. Martin's Press.

Devine, E., & Braganti, N. (1998). *The traveler's guide to Asian customs and manners.* New York: St. Martin's Griffin.

Devine, E., & Braganti, N. (2000). *The traveler's guide to Latin American customs and manners.* New York: St. Martin's Griffin.

Devine, E., & Braganti, N. L. (1991). *The traveler's guide to Middle Eastern and North African customs and manners.* New York: St. Martin's Press.

DeVries, M. A. (1994). *Internationally yours.* Boston: Houghton Mifflin.

Dodd, C. H. (1997). *Dynamics of intercultural communication* (5th ed.). New York: McGraw Hill.

Ferraro, G. P. (2001). *The cultural dimension of international business* (4th ed.). Upper Saddle River, NJ: Prentice Hall.

Funakawa, A. (1997). *Transcultural management: A new approach for global organization.* San Francisco: Jossey-Bass.

Fussell, P. (1983). *Class.* New York: Ballantine.

Gilsdorf, J. (2002, July). Standard Englishes and world Englishes: Living with a polymorph business language. *The Journal of Business Communication, 39*(3), 365–378.

Hall, E. T., & Hall, M. R. (1990). *Understanding cultural differences.* Yarmouth, ME: Intercultural Press.

Hockett, C. (1967). *A course in modern linguistics.* New York: Macmillan.

Jandt, F. E. (2004). *An introduction to intercultural communication* (4th ed.). Thousand Oaks, CA: Sage.

Klopf, D. W. (2001). *Intercultural encounters* (5th ed.). Englewood, CO: Morton.

Names of big numbers (2004). Retrieved July 25, 2004, from http://www.sizes.com/numbers/big_numName.htm.

Samovar, L. A., & Porter, R. E. (2004). *Communication between cultures* (5th ed.). Belmont, CA: Wadsworth/Thomson Learning.

Schmit, J., Richards, R., Swingle, C. (1993, September 14). Travelers' bouts of foot-in-mouth disease. *USA Today,* 5E.

Stewart, E. C., & Bennett, M. J. (1991). *American cultural patterns.* Yarmouth, ME: Intercultural Press.

Tannen, D. (2001). *You just don't understand: Women and men in conversation.* New York: Quill.

Tsunda, Y. (1986). *Language inequality and distortion.* (p. 116). Philadelphia: John Benjamin.

U.S. News & World Report. (February 18, 1995). In F. E. Jandt, *An introduction to intercultural communication* (4th ed.). Thousand Oaks, CA: Sage.

Weaver, G. R. (1998). American identity movements. Cross cultural confrontations. In G.R. Weaver, (Ed.) *Culture, communications, and conflict.* (pp. 72–77). Needham Heights, MA: Simon & Schuster.

CHAPTER

6

ORAL AND NONVERBAL
COMMUNICATION
PATTERNS

Objectives

Upon completion of this chapter, you will

- be able to evaluate thought patterns and their relationship to intercultural business communication.

- understand how paralanguage affects successful intercultural communication.

- appreciate how attitudes toward time and use of space convey nonverbal messages in intercultural encounters.

- understand the role that eye contact, smell, color, touch, and body language play in communicating nonverbally in cultural situations.

- learn how silence is used to send nonverbal messages in various cultures.

Successful multicultural business encounters depend to a large extent on effective oral and nonverbal communication. Although much communication in the global arena is oral, the nonverbal aspects can contribute significantly to understanding and interpreting oral communication. **Nonverbal communication** refers to nonword messages such as gestures, facial expressions, interpersonal distance, touch, eye contact, smell, and silence.

Costly business blunders are often the result of a lack of knowledge of another culture's oral and nonverbal communication patterns. A knowledge of these aspects of intercultural communication is essential for conducting business in the international marketplace.

THOUGHT PATTERNS

Patterns of thought or processes of reasoning and problem solving are not the same in all cultures, but they all have an impact on oral communication.

Most people in the United States use the deductive method of reasoning to solve problems. The **deductive method** goes from broad categories or observations to specific examples to determine the facts and then the solution to the problem. The line of reasoning used by people in many other cultures, such as Asians, is typically the **inductive method.** People who use this approach start with facts or observations and go to generalizations. Thought patterns also include the pace or speed with which problems are solved or decisions made. Making quick decisions is a characteristic of an effective manager in the United States, although this behavior is viewed as impulsive by the Japanese. The slower method of problem solving is often a source of frustration for U.S. managers when conducting business with the Japanese. Thought as an aspect of language is discussed in chapter 5. Recognizing that people from other cultures may have different thought patterns is important to communicating and negotiating successfully in the global business environment.

PARALANGUAGE

Paralanguage is related to oral communication; it refers to the rate, pitch, and volume qualities of the voice that interrupt or temporarily take the place of speech and affect the meaning of a message. Paralanguage includes such vocal qualifiers as intensity (whether loud or soft); pitch (either high or low); extent (drawls and accents); vocal characterizers, such as crying and laughing; and vocal segregates, such as saying "uh" and "uh-huh." Paralanguage conveys emotions. Negative emotions of impatience, fear, and anger are easier to convey than the more positive emotions of satisfaction and admiration. An increased rate of speech could indicate anger or impatience; a decrease in rate could suggest lack of interest or a reflective attitude. An increased volume could also indicate anger; a lower volume is nonthreatening and sympathetic (Samovar & Porter, 2004).

In the United States, people usually have no difficulty distinguishing the speech of persons from specific regions of the country. Although the rate of speech and dialect may vary from region to region, they rarely cause major problems in the communication process.

Learning the nuances in speech that affect verbal messages will help when communicating with people of other cultures. Differences in volume of speech, for example, are culture specific as well as gender specific. Arabs, for example, speak loudly, feeling that this shows strength and sincerity. People from the Philippines, however, speak softly, as they believe that this is an indication of good breeding and education. Thais also speak softly, speaking loudly only when they are angry. When they first hear U.S. Americans speak, the Thais think the U.S. Americans are angry because of the loudness of their speech. Males usually speak louder and in a lower pitch than females. Differences also exist in the rate at which people speak. U.S. Americans living in the northern states usually speak faster than those in the south; Italians and Arabs speak faster than do people of the United States. People who speak slowly sometimes have difficulty understanding the speech of those who speak rapidly. Accent is also an aspect of paralanguage. Some British are able to discern a person's educational background by his or her accent. In the United States, accent has been related to hiring decisions. In one U.S. research study, standard language speakers were given more supervisory positions while persons with accents were given more semiskilled positions (Jandt, 2004; Samovar & Porter, 2004).

CHRONEMICS

Chronemics (attitudes toward time) vary from culture to culture. Two of the most important time systems that relate to international business are monochronic and polychronic time. Countries that follow **monochronic** time perform only one major activity at a time; countries that follow **polychronic** time work on several activities simultaneously.

The United States is a monochronic culture; other monochronic countries are England, Switzerland, and Germany. In monochronic cultures, time is regarded as something tangible; people use such terms as "wasting time" or "losing time." Time is seen as lineal and manageable. In monochronic cultures, it is considered rude to do two things at once, such as reading a journal in a meeting or answering the telephone while someone is in your office. Schedules and keeping appointments are consistent with values of people in monochronic cultures.

Polychronic cultures include people of Latin America and the Mediterranean as well as Arabian people. These people are well adapted to doing several things at once and do not mind interruptions. People are more important than schedules to members of polychronic cultures. The result is a lifestyle that is more unstructured than that of monochronic people (Samovar & Porter, 2004). Table 6-1 contains a summary of generalizations related to monochronic and polychronic time systems (Hall & Hall, 1990).

TABLE 6-1 Monochronic and Polychronic Time Systems	
Monochronic People	*Polychronic People*
Do one thing at a time	Do many things at once
Concentrate on the task	Are highly distractible and subject to interruptions
Take time commitments seriously and value promptness	Consider time commitments more casually; promptness based on the relationship
Are committed to the task	Are committed to people
Show respect for private property; rarely borrow or lend	Borrow and lend things often
Are accustomed to short-term relationships	Tend to build lifetime relationships

Being on time for work, business appointments and meetings, and social engagements is very important in the United States. Punctuality is considered a positive attribute that conveys the nonverbal message of being respectful of other persons. Tardiness is interpreted as rudeness, a lack of consideration for others, or a lack of interest in the job or meeting. Being late also sends the nonverbal message that you are not well organized.

The length of time someone has to wait to see another person also sends a message. In the United States, the length of the wait is associated with the person's status and importance. The person perceived as high status is seen immediately; the implied message is, "You are important; your time is just as valuable as mine." Generally in the United States, keeping a person with a business appointment waiting for 5 minutes is acceptable. Keeping a person waiting 15 minutes clearly implies that you consider yourself more important than your visitor. With a 20- to 30-minute wait, the message becomes stronger and implies contempt and/or annoyance; it also sends the message that the other person's time is not important (Fast, 1991). In time-conscious cultures, being aware of the subtextual implications associated with different lengths of waiting can be extremely important to avoid unintentionally demeaning or insulting a person with whom you want to have a business relationship.

People of Germany and Switzerland are even more time conscious than are people from the United States. In fact, northern Europeans regard tardiness as a characteristic of an undisciplined person. Scandinavians are also time conscious, with the exception of Iceland, where people are a bit more flexible regarding punctuality. A telephone call is appropriate when you are delayed (Turkington, 1999). Being on time is important to the people of Singapore and Hong Kong (except at banquets in Hong Kong—nobody arrives at the time stated on the invitation). Being punctual is also important in Malaysia and Indonesia, particularly when meeting with a person of superior status. Unlike the people in their neighboring countries, Iraqis value punctuality, so it is important to be on time for appointments in that country (Devine & Braganti, 1991). Likewise, people of India appreciate punctuality but may not be punctual themselves. Also, in Australia and New Zealand, punctuality is important for both business appointments and social events. Arriving late for meetings and appointments signifies a careless attitude toward business (Morrison, Conaway, & Borden, 1994).

In Algeria, however, punctuality is not widely regarded. In Latin American countries, the *mañana* attitude (putting off until tomorrow what does not get done today) has been a source of frustration for time-sensitive U.S. executives when conducting business with people of that culture. Because their first obligations are to family and friends, Latin Americans consider a request from a family member or friend to take precedence over a business meeting (Bosrock, 1997). People in the Arabic cultures also have a more casual attitude toward time; this attitude is related to their religious belief that God decides when things get accomplished (Engholm, 1991).

The manager of a German bank offered to host a cocktail party for the South American delegation to a bankers' conference in Hamburg. The invitation stated that cocktails were at 7 p.m., so the banker and his wife were ready to greet guests at 6:30 p.m. When no guests had arrived by 8:45 p.m., he asked his staff, "What kind of people have we invited?" The response: South Americans. (Bosrock, 1997)

In southern Europe, people are also more casual about punctuality, but position and relationship to the other party are considerations. In Spain, for example, specific but unwritten rules exist concerning who can be late and by how long in both social and business situations. The waiting also depends on whether you want something from the other person or whether they want something from you. Arriving early is not recommended, as this implies being too eager (Engholm & Rowland, 1996).

To work harmoniously with persons from other cultures, you should consider these different attitudes toward time. When conducting business with persons from cultures whose attitude toward time differs from your own, you should verify whether the meeting time is, for example, Latin American time or U.S. time.

PROXEMICS

Communicating through the use of space is known as **proxemics.** The physical distance between people when they are interacting, as well as territorial space, is strongly influenced by culture.

You should consider interpersonal space when conversing with others. Hall and Hall (1990) report that psychologists have identified four zones from which U.S. people interact: the intimate zone, the personal zone, the social zone, and the public zone. The **intimate zone,** less than 18 inches, is reserved for very close friends; it is entered by business colleagues briefly, such as when shaking hands. The **personal zone,** from 18 inches to 4 feet, is used for giving instructions to others or working closely with another person. The **social zone,** from 4 to 12 feet, is used for most business situations in which people interact more formally and impersonally, such as during a business meeting. The **public distance,** over 12 feet, is the most formal zone; therefore, fewer interactions occur because of distance.

A psychology professor at a southern university gave his students an assignment to test elevator proxemics, the use of space in such crowded places as an elevator. They reported the usual U.S. behaviors of facing the front and watching the illuminated floor indicator, assuming the Fig Leaf Position (hands/purses/briefcases hanging down in front of the body), and positioning themselves in the corners or against the elevator walls. The professor then added another assignment: students were to break the rules and get on the elevator, stand at the front facing the other occupants, and jump backward off the elevator just before the door closed. One of the elevator occupants was heard to whisper, "Call 911; we've got a real weirdo here." (Axtell, 1998)

People of the United States tend to need more space than do persons of certain cultures, such as Greeks, Latin Americans, or Arabs. When interacting with persons of these cultures, U.S. Americans back away because the person is standing too close. On the other hand, the Japanese stand farther away than do U.S. people when conversing. Negative nonverbal messages often conveyed by standing too close to a person who requires more space include being pushy or overbearing; standing too close may also be interpreted as an unwelcome sexual advance.

People also communicate through space by the arrangement of desks and chairs. When U.S. people are conversing, they generally prefer the face-to-face arrangement of chairs placed at right angles to one another. People of other cultures, such as the Chinese, prefer the side-by-side arrangement; this preference may be related to the custom of avoiding direct eye contact in that culture.

In the United States, nonverbal messages are sent by other aspects of the office environment. Private offices and offices with windows have more status than inside offices, and large offices have more status than small ones. In addition to office size, higher-ranking executives have their territory better protected than do lower-status employees; doors and secretaries are often used as barriers to access. Messages related to authority and position are also conveyed by the selection and arrangement of furniture. A large wooden desk and desk chairs with arms convey power and authority.

Placing the desk and chair in front of a window or an arrangement of pictures on the wall creates a throne-like effect that adds to the sense of power (Chaney & Lyden, 1996). Office location also conveys the presence or absence of power and status. Offices on the fourth floor have more status than offices on the first floor. The top floors of office buildings are generally occupied by the top-level executives not only in the United States but in Germany as well. However, French top-level executives occupy a position in the middle of an office area with subordinates located around them. The purpose of this arrangement is to help upper management stay informed of activities and to maintain control over the work area. The Japanese also do not consider private offices appropriate. In traditional Japanese firms, only executives of the highest rank have private offices, and they may also have desks in large work areas (Gudykunst & Ting-Toomey, 1988).

OCULESICS

Some cultures place more emphasis on **oculesics** or oculemics (gaze and eye contact) than others. People in the United States, as well as those in Canada, Great Britain, and eastern Europe, favor direct eye contact. The eye contact, however, is not steady; it is maintained for a second or two and then broken. Eye contact is considered a sign of respect and attentiveness in these countries. People who avoid eye contact may be considered insecure, untrustworthy, unfriendly, disrespectful, or inattentive.

> Students in a business communication class at a Mid-South university were asked to test the concept of gaze and eye contact in the United States by maintaining steady eye contact with a person in the car next to them when they stopped at a traffic light. Responses varied from obscene gestures to making faces to returning the gaze. Students concluded that U.S. persons are very uncomfortable with prolonged eye contact.

In other cultures, there is little direct eye contact. The Japanese direct their gaze below the chin; they are uncomfortable with maintaining direct eye contact throughout the conversation. People in China and Indonesia also lower the eyes as a sign of respect, feeling that prolonged eye contact shows bad manners. Likewise, Latin Americans and Caribbeans, as well as people in parts of Africa, show respect by avoiding direct eye contact. In some countries, such as India and Egypt, eye contact is related to position and gender. In India, eye contact is avoided between people who are on different socioeconomic levels, while in Egypt there is no eye contact between men and women who do not know each other. Germans value direct eye contact; however, their eye contact is more intense than U.S. persons are accustomed to. In fact, to a U.S. person, the prolonged stare is associated with nonverbal communication between male homosexuals who use it to signal interest in each other (Samovar & Porter, 2004). Also, in the Middle East, the eye contact is so intense that it exceeds the comfort zone for most people in the United States. Prolonged eye contact with women, however, is considered inappropriate.

Cultural variations in eye contact vary from prolonged eye contact to little eye contact as shown here.

Very direct eye contact:	Middle Easterners
	Some Latin American groups
	The French
Moderate eye contact:	Mainstream Americans
	Northern Europeans
	The British
Minimal eye contact:	East Asians
	Southeast Asians
	East Indians
	Native Americans

Very direct eye contact can be misinterpreted as hostility, aggressiveness, or intrusiveness when the intended meaning was just to appear interested. Minimal eye contact may be misinterpreted as lack of interest or understanding, dishonesty, fear, or shyness when the intended meaning was to show respect or to avoid appearing intrusive.

Barbara Walters, a television newscaster, was interviewing Mu'ammar Gadhafi and could not understand why he would not look into her eyes. She learned later that he was showing her respect by not having direct eye contact. Arabic men do not have direct eye contact with women unless they are members of their family.

The eyes can be very revealing during negotiations. The pupils of the eyes constrict or dilate in response to emotions. Well-trained negotiators watch the pupils for signs that the person is willing to make concessions (Borden, 1991).

A prolonged gaze or stare in the United States, Japan, Korea, and Thailand is considered rude. In most cultures, men do not stare at women. In France and Italy, however, men can stare at women in public. In the United States, staring at a person is considered a sign of interest and may even be interpreted as sexually suggestive.

OLFACTICS

Olfactics, or smell, as a means of nonverbal communication is important. A person's smell can have a positive or negative effect on the oral message. The way someone smells remains in our memory after the person has gone.

Most people of the United States respond negatively to what they consider bad odors, such as body odor, breath odor, or clothes that emit unpleasant aromas such as perspiration. They place great importance on personal hygiene and consider it normal for people to remove body odors by bathing or showering daily and by brushing teeth to remove mouth odors. Advertisements on U.S. American television and in newspapers and magazines for underarm deodorants, perfumes, colognes, and mouthwash emphasize the importance U.S. Americans place on personal hygiene. In a television commercial that epitomizes the fixation that U.S. Americans have concerning body odor, a young woman states, "If a guy smells, it's such a turnoff." People in the

United States are not comfortable discussing the topic, however, and generally will not tell another that his or her body odor is offensive; instead, they simply avoid being close to the person and end the discourse as quickly as possible.

Other cultures have different concepts of natural odors; they consider them as normal and think attitudes of people in the United States are unnatural. Arabs, for example, are comfortable with natural odors. Other cultures in which smell plays an important role include the Japanese and Samoans. Cultures that include little meat in the diet, such as the Chinese, say that people who consume a lot of meat, such as U.S. Americans, emit an offensive odor (Samovar & Porter, 2004).

A medical doctor from Saudi Arabia was completing an internship in a hospital in the southern United States. Problems arose when patients refused to have the Saudi doctor examine them. Interviews with patients revealed two problems: He "smelled bad," and he breathed on the patients. The doctor's orientation had apparently failed to include the incongruence between Arabic and U.S. American olfactory perceptions and practices.

To maintain harmonious intercultural business relationships, remember these diverse attitudes toward smell and, if possible, adopt the hygiene practices of the country in which you are conducting business.

HAPTICS

Haptics, or touch, refers to communicating through the use of bodily contact. When used properly, touch can create feelings of warmth and trust; when used improperly, touch can betray trust and cause annoyance (Fast, 1991). Some cultures are very comfortable with bodily contact, and others avoid it. People in the United States are taught that appropriate touch includes shaking hands but that in business situations giving hugs or other expressions of affection to supervisors and coworkers encourages familiarity that is generally considered inappropriate. Because touching may be interpreted as a form of sexual harassment, it is necessary to refrain from touching in business situations to avoid the appearance of impropriety.

Another consideration when using touch in the United States is a knowledge of the hierarchy involved. People of higher rank (the president of the company) may touch those of lower rank (office employees), but secretaries may not touch the president. Doctors may place a comforting arm around a patient, but patients may not touch doctors. Adults may touch children, but children should not touch adults unless they know them. Equals may touch each other. The general rule is that people who are older or of higher status may touch those who are younger or of lower status (Fast, 1991).

Several years ago when President Carter was mediating peace talks between Egypt and Israel, Anwar Sadat frequently placed his hand on President Carter's knee. Although this subtextual message was intended as a gesture of warm friendship, the subtler message Sadat was conveying to the world was that he was President Carter's equal. (Fast, 1991)

Axtell (1998) classified the following cultures as "touch" and "don't touch" (see Table 6-2).

TABLE 6-2 Touch and Don't Touch Cultures		
Don't Touch	*Middle Ground*	*Touch*
Japan	Australia	Latin American countries
United States	France	Italy
Canada	China	Greece
England	Ireland	Spain and Portugal
Scandinavia	India	Some Asian countries
Other Northern European countries	Middle East countries	Russian Federation

Source: Axtell, R. E. (1998). *Gestures.* Copyright © 1998 by John Wiley & Sons, Inc. Reprinted by permission of John Wiley & Sons, Inc.

In touch-oriented cultures, such as those of Italy, Greece, Spain, and Portugal, both males and females may be seen walking along the street holding hands or arm in arm. Cultural variations also exist in the extent of touching between persons of the same gender. In Mexico, Eastern Europe, and the Arab world, embracing and kissing is common, especially between friends. In Finland, however, hugs or kisses on the cheek are not appropriate in public (Samovar & Porter, 2004). In other cultures, such as in the Latin American countries, touching between men is considered acceptable (Figure 6-1).

A Mexican male will stand close to a male colleague and even hold him by the lapel or shoulder. Behavior between men in the Middle East is similar, but you should avoid touching the person with the left hand because the left hand is considered unclean and is reserved for personal hygiene. In other countries, such as in the United States, touching between men may be construed as an indication of homosexuality.

FIGURE 6-1   Touch-Oriented Culture

An additional aspect of tactile communication concerns the location of the touch. In Thailand and India, it is offensive to touch the head, as this part of the body is considered sacred. In fact, avoid touching all Asians on the head, including small children. Even placing a hand on the back of an Asian worker's chair is considered inappropriate. Although Muslims hug another person around the shoulders, in Korea young people do not touch the shoulders of their elders (Axtell, 1998). In Hong Kong, avoid initiating any type of physical contact. Tactile behavior is highly cultural; knowing when and how to touch in various cultures is important to conducting business globally.

KINESICS

Kinesics is the term used for communicating through various types of body movements, including facial expressions, gestures, posture and stance, and other mannerisms that may accompany or replace oral messages.

Facial Expressions

The face and eyes convey the most expressive types of body language. People of all cultures learn how to control facial expressions to mask emotions that are inappropriate in a specific setting, such as crying when being reprimanded or yawning when listening to a boring presentation. In some countries, such as China, people rarely show emotion. The Japanese may smile to cover a range of emotions, including anger, happiness, or sadness, although the smile to people in the United States means happiness. Asians smile or laugh softly when they are embarrassed or to conceal any discomfort. Koreans rarely smile; they perceive people who smile a great deal as shallow. The following proverb from the Korean culture illustrates the Asian attitude concerning the meaning of a smile: "The man who smiles a lot is not a real man." People of Thailand, on the other hand, smile a great deal, which may be why Thailand has been called "The Land of Smiles" (Samovar & Porter, 2004). To interpret facial expressions correctly, you should take the communication context and the culture into account.

Gestures

Gestures are another important aspect of body language. Gestures can be emblems or symbols ("V" for victory), illustrators (police officer's hand held up to stop traffic), regulators (glancing at your watch to signal that you are in a hurry), or affect displays (a person's face turns red with embarrassment).

Gestures are used to add emphasis or clarity to an oral message. Although the meaning of gestures depends on the context, following are some general guides to interpreting the meaning of gestures in the United States (Axtell, 1998):

- Interest is expressed by maintaining eye contact with the speaker, smiling, and nodding the head.
- Open-mindedness is expressed by open hands and palms turned upward.
- Nervousness is sometimes shown by fidgeting, failing to give the speaker eye contact, or jingling keys or money in your pocket.
- Suspiciousness is indicated by glancing away or touching your nose, eyes, or ears.
- Defensiveness is indicated by crossing your arms over your chest, making fisted gestures, or crossing your legs.
- Lack of interest or boredom is indicated by glancing repeatedly at your watch or staring at the ceiling or floor or out the window when the person is speaking.

Although regional differences exist, people in the United States typically use moderate gesturing. They rarely use gestures in which the elbows go above the shoulder level, as this is interpreted as being too emotional or even angry; one exception is waving hello or good-bye. Italians, Greeks, and some Latin Americans use vigorous gestures when speaking, although Chinese and Japanese people tend to keep their hands and arms close to their bodies when speaking. Most cultures have standard gestures for such daily situations as greeting someone and saying good-bye; learn and respect such gestures when conversing with persons of another culture.

Following are some additional guidelines for gesturing in various cultures (Axtell, 1998):

- The "V"-for-victory gesture (Figure 6-2), holding two fingers upright with palm and fingers faced outward, is widely used in the United States and many other countries. In England and in New Zealand, however, it has a crude connotation when used with the palm in.
- The vertical horns gesture (raised fist, index finger and little finger extended [Figure 6-3]) has a positive connotation associated with the University of Texas Longhorn football team. This gesture has an insulting connotation in Italy, but in Brazil and Venezuela it is a sign for good luck. This symbol has various meanings in U.S. subcultures, including serving as a satanic cult recognition sign signifying the devil's horns. This symbol should be used only when you are sure the other person understands its intended meaning.
- The "thumbs-up" gesture (Figure 6-4) has been widely recognized as a positive signal meaning "everything is OK" or "good going." Although well known in North America and most of Europe, in Australia and West Africa, it is seen as a rude gesture.
- The "OK" sign (Figure 6-5), with the thumb and forefinger joined to form a circle, is a positive gesture in the United States, although in Brazil it is considered obscene. The gesture has yet another meaning in Japan—it is a symbol for

FIGURE 6-2   "V"-for-Victory Gesture

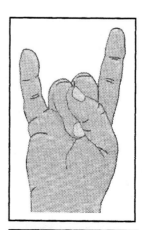

FIGURE 6-3   Vertical Horns Gesture

FIGURE 6-4   Thumbs-Up Gesture

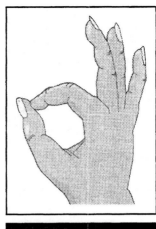

FIGURE 6-5   "OK" Gesture

money; in Belgium, it means zero. The "OK" sign should be used with great care in Tunisia; you would be saying, "I will kill you."
- The beckoning gesture (Figure 6-6), fingers upturned, palm facing the body, is used by people in the United States for summoning a waiter; it is offensive to Filipinos, as it is used to beckon animals and prostitutes. Vietnamese and Mexicans also find it offensive.
- The head nod in most countries means "yes," but in Bulgaria it means "no."

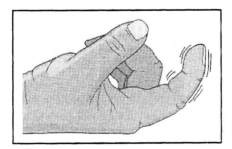

FIGURE 6-6   Beckoning Gesture

An American engineer, sent to Germany by his U.S. company that had purchased a German firm, was working side by side with a German engineer on a piece of equipment. When the American engineer made a suggestion for improving the new machine, the German engineer followed the suggestion and asked his American counterpart whether or not he had done it correctly. The American replied by giving the U.S. American "OK" gesture, making a circle with the thumb and forefinger. The German engineer put down his tools and walked away, refusing further communication with the American engineer. The U.S. American later learned from one of the supervisors the significance of this gesture to a German: "You asshole." (Axtell, 1998)

Because one culture's gestures may be misinterpreted by people in another culture, avoid using gestures when communicating in international business settings until you become knowledgeable about the meaning of such gestures.

Posture and Stance

Posture, the way someone stands, sits, or walks, can send positive or negative nonverbal messages. Posture can signal agreement or disagreement. For example, when people in a business meeting share a point of view, they are likely to mirror each other's posture. When a person disagrees with others in the group, his or her posture also disagrees with that of other group members. Posture can convey self-confidence, status, and interest. Confident people generally have a relaxed posture yet stand erect and walk with assurance. Walking with stooped shoulders and a slow, hesitating gait projects such negative messages as lack of assurance and lack of confidence. Walking rapidly and swinging the arms indicates that the person is goal oriented. A preoccupied walk, with hands clasped behind and head lowered, is thoughtful. Men who walk with hands on hips convey the message of wanting to get to their destination as quickly as possible (Fast, 1991). The posture of persons of higher status is usually more relaxed than that of their subordinates. Interest is demonstrated by leaning forward toward the person you are conversing with, while sitting back communicates a lack of interest. The posture of people in the United States tends to be casual; they sit in a relaxed manner and may slouch when they stand. This behavior in Germany is considered rude.

President Ronald Reagan was well known for using posture to convey subtextual messages. In a 1985 article in the *New York Times,* a reporter described how President Reagan's posture revealed his emotions during an interview. He said that much of the time President Reagan settled back comfortably. When the issue of Star Wars was brought up, his posture changed; he leaned forward in his chair and became totally engaged. When the talk shifted to Soviet violations, however, he placed his back straight against the chair. (Fast, 1991)

Posture when seated also varies with the culture. People in the United States often cross their legs while seated; women cross at the ankle, and men cross with ankle on the knee (Figure 6-7). Crossing the leg with ankle on the knee would be considered inappropriate by most people in the Middle East. In the Arab world, correct posture while seated is important; avoid showing the sole of your shoe or pointing your foot at someone, as the lowest part of the body is considered unclean. People from a number of countries—Turkey, India, Egypt, Saudi Arabia, Singapore, and Thailand—feel that showing the bottom of your feet is insulting, so it is important to avoid sitting so that the soles of the shoes are visible.

When communicating with persons of another culture, follow their lead; assume the posture they assume. Remember that in most cultures, standing when an older person or one of higher rank enters or leaves the room is considered a sign of respect.

An awareness of cultural differences in facial expressions, gestures, and posture is important to successful intercultural encounters. Body language can enhance the spoken message or detract from it. Even though we usually believe that actions speak

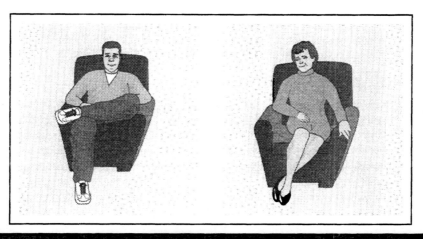

FIGURE 6-7   Sitting Postures

louder than words, in intercultural interactions what the person says may give a clearer picture of the intended message than the accompanying body language. However, if a gesture is used in the wrong context, it may be difficult for a foreigner to understand the intended message. The best advice is probably to keep gestures to a minimum when communicating with persons in other cultures; learn the words for "good" or "yes" in the local language rather than relying on gestures.

CHROMATICS

Chromatics, or color, can affect your mood, your emotions, and your impression of others. Certain colors have both negative and positive connotations. In the United States, for example, black is considered a sophisticated color, but it may also represent sadness. White is pure and peaceful, but in some cultures it is associated with mourning. Blue may represent peace and tranquility or sadness and depression, as in "I feel blue."

Color may be used to symbolize such things as patriotism. People in the United States associate red, white, and blue (the colors in the flag) with patriotism. Cultural differences associated with colors include the following (Axtell, 1998; Ricks, 1999; Scott, 2002):

- Black is the color of mourning to many Europeans and U.S. Americans, but white is worn to funerals in Japan and many other nations. Red has funereal connotations in African countries.
- In the United States, white is typically worn by brides, although in India, red or yellow is worn.
- Purple is sometimes associated with royalty, but it is the color of death in many Latin American countries.
- Red (especially red roses) is associated with romance in some cultures, including the United States. Red is not an appropriate color for wrapping gifts in Japan.

- Green is not used for wrapping packages in Egypt because green is the nationalist color (as red, white, and blue are the nationalist colors in the United States). Men should avoid wearing a green hat in China, as this signifies that their wife or sister is a prostitute.
- In many countries of the world, blue is considered a masculine color, but to people of France and the United Kingdom, red is more masculine. Blue, in Iran, is an undesirable color.
- Although people of the United States consider pink to be the most feminine color, persons in most other countries think of yellow as the most feminine color.

United Airlines unknowingly got off on the wrong foot during its initial flights from Hong Kong. To commemorate the occasion, they handed out white carnations to the passengers. When they learned that to many Asians white flowers represent bad luck and even death, they changed to red carnations. (Ricks, 1999)

Color also has an influence on foreign sales. In a study of consumers' color preferences for various countries reported by Madden, Hewett, and Roth (2000), blue was ranked as the most preferred color by people of Austria, China, and the United States (and ranked second in Brazil); other colors ranked in the top five by these four countries were white, green, black, and red. Firms who sell their products in other countries should be aware that the color used in packaging a product may influence the purchasing decisions of potential customers. For example, packaging a product in red would be appealing to customers in China but less appealing to potential buyers in South Korea because of the possible association of red with communism (Scott, 2002).

Determining cultural meanings associated with various colors is advised to ensure that nonverbal messages associated with color are positive ones.

SILENCE

Silence is a form of nonverbal communication that may be interpreted in various ways, depending on the situation, the duration of the silence, and the culture. Interpretations of silence include agreement or disagreement, lack of interest, or contempt. Silence can also mean that the person is giving the topic some thought. Silence can be used to indicate displeasure in the United States and in other cultures (Samovar & Porter, 2004).

Other aspects of silence should also be considered: the duration, appropriateness, and relationship between people who are conversing. A prolonged silence following a question could be interpreted to mean that the person does not know the answer. Silence following an inappropriate statement, such as the telling of a tasteless joke, is usually interpreted as disapproval. Silence following a conversation with someone you know well could be interpreted as dissent or disapproval (Samovar & Porter, 2004).

People of the United States are rather uncomfortable with periods of silence except with people they know well. They use fillers, such as comments on the weather, to avoid silence. In Italy, Greece, and Arabian countries, very little silence exists.

In some cultures, periods of silence are appropriate when communicating. People in east Asia consider silence an integral part of business and social discourse, not a failure to communicate. Silence in east Asia and Finland is associated with listening and learning; it protects your privacy and individualism and shows respect for the privacy and individualism of others. Silence in these cultures is viewed as restful and appropriate lulls in conversation (Lewis, 2000). The Japanese are comfortable with silence and use it as a bargaining tool when negotiating with persons from the United States. They know that U.S. Americans are not comfortable with long periods of silence and that U.S. businessperson will offer a price concession just to get the discussion going again. Learn to remain silent when negotiating with the Japanese; they like periods of silence and do not like to be hurried. People who converse with no pauses are viewed as having given little thought to what they are saying and having unfocused thinking (Axtell, 1998). Breaking the silence may also give the impression that your proposal is flawed. Japanese proverbs such as "Those who know do not speak—those who speak do not know" emphasize the value of silence over words in that culture.

An appropriate caution is to watch the behavior of the persons you are talking with and match their style. Allow pauses when speaking with Asians and avoid pauses when dealing with those from the Middle East.

Knowing cultural variations in the use of silence and other forms of nonverbal communication is helpful when conversing with persons in another culture.

A summary of guidelines related to various aspects of nonverbal communication for the 10 countries with which the United States conducts much of its international business follows.

Canada
Punctuality is important to Canadians although not to the extent that it is to people of the United States. Being on time for business functions is expected; being 15 minutes late for evening social occasions is permitted. People stand farther apart in Canada than do persons of Latin America or the Far East. The standard space between people who are conversing is 2 feet; however, French Canadians often stand closer. Little touching is seen except between relatives and good friends. However, French Canadians commonly touch while conversing. Eye contact is important when conversing with someone. Gestures are similar to those used in the United States. Because some gestures may offend people of a certain cultural group, gesturing should be kept to a minimum. Pointing with the index finger is considered rude; the entire hand should be used to motion to someone. Beckoning is done with the fingers pointing up and motioning toward one's body with the palm inward. The U.S. "thumbs-down" gesture used to indicate "no" or that something is bad is offensive in Quebec, as is slapping an open hand over a closed fist. Appropriate seated posture for men includes legs crossed at the ankles or at the knees or one ankle crossed on the other knee; appropriate seated posture for women is crossing legs at the ankle (Axtell, 1998; Bosrock, 1995).

China
Punctuality is important to the Chinese. When invited to dinner or when attending a business meeting, arriving early is recommended, as this is interpreted as a sign of respect. Touching is not common among the Chinese. They do not usually hug or kiss each other when greeting. Touch is generally limited to shaking hands. Public displays of affection, even between people who are married, are not acceptable. The Chinese tend to stand closer together than do U.S. Americans. Direct eye contact is limited, and staring is uncommon. Gesturing is somewhat limited in China. Using the open hand rather than one finger to point is important. Although many U.S. gestures are familiar to the Chinese, the "OK" sign is not widely understood. Using good posture is

important to the Chinese; feet should remain on the floor and should not be placed on chairs or desks (Axtell, 1998; Sabath, 2002; Turkington, 1999).

England
Being punctual is very important to the British. Because the people of England are polite and reserved, they respect another's personal space and do not like someone to get too close when conversing. The British do not always look at the person with whom they are conversing. Touching is avoided; avoid putting your arm around a colleague's shoulder or slapping him or her on the back. Many of the gestures used in the United States and Canada are used; however, the "V"-for-victory sign (typically with the palm out) is rude and offensive (meaning "up yours") when used with the palm inward. The accepted seated posture for men is crossing the legs at the knees rather than placing one ankle across the other knee; for women, crossing the legs at the ankle is the accepted seated posture (Axtell, 1998).

France
Punctuality is just as important in France as it is in the United States. Being on time is a sign of courtesy; however, arriving 15 minutes late for a party at someone's home is acceptable. The U.S. "OK" sign means "zero" or "worthless" to the French. Their gesture for "OK" is the "thumbs-up" sign. The "V"-for-victory sign may be done with the palm faced outward or inward; both represent "peace" or "victory." Avoid slapping a palm over a closed fist, as this gesture is considered vulgar. Another gesture used is playing an imaginary flute to indicate that someone is talking too much or to signal that you question the truth of what is being said. Because good posture and decorum are virtues in France, you should sit upright with knees together or with legs crossed at the knee or ankle. Resting your feet on tables or chairs is inappropriate. Other behaviors to be avoided include speaking loudly in public, chewing gum, and conversing with your hands in your pockets (Axtell, 1998).

Germany
Being on time for all business and social engagements is perhaps more important in Germany than in any other country in the world. Being only two to three minutes late is insulting to German managers; an explanatory call is expected if you are delayed. Gestures/behaviors considered inappropriate in Germany include talking with your hands in your pockets and chewing gum in public. Pointing the index finger to the temple and making a twisting motion is an insult to another person; the meaning is "you are crazy." Rather than crossing the fingers to wish a person good luck, Germans make a fist, folding the thumb in and pounding lightly on a surface. The gesture for waving good-bye is extending the hand upward, palm out, and waving the fingers up and down rather than side to side, which means "no." When trying to get someone's attention, such as a waiter, raise the hand, palm out, with only the index finger extended; do not wave. Posture is important; people should cross their legs with one knee over the other; feet should not be placed on furniture (Axtell, 1998; Bosrock, 1995).

Japan
Punctuality is valued. Being late to a business meeting is considered rude, but being late for social occasions is acceptable. Because the Japanese are a "do not touch" culture, avoid standing close, patting a person on the back, or any prolonged physical

contact. Prolonged eye contact should also be avoided. The U.S. "OK" gesture may signify "money" in Japan. The gesture for beckoning someone is placing an arm out, palm down, and making a scratching motion with the fingers. Chewing gum or yawning in public are impolite; standing with your hands in your pockets is inappropriate. Also avoid shouting or raising your voice in anger; the Japanese are a polite, gracious people and show great restraint. The correct seated posture includes having both feet on the floor and arms placed on chair armrests or in the lap. Slouching, leaning back in a tilted chair, or placing your feet on a table are inappropriate. Crossing the legs at the knees or ankles is acceptable; placing an ankle over a knee, however, is improper (Axtell, 1998; Morrison, Conaway, & Borden, 1994; Sabath, 2002).

Mexico

Punctuality is not highly regarded in Mexico; 30 minutes past the scheduled meeting time is considered punctual by Mexican standards. Foreigners, however, are expected to be on time for business meetings. For social engagements, being 30 minutes to an hour later than the time stated on the invitation is expected. Time may be stated as *la hora americana,* meaning that punctuality is expected; *la hora mexicana* implies a more relaxed time frame. People of Mexico usually stand close together while conversing and sometimes touch the other person's clothing, shoulders, or arm. Avoid the temptation to step back; this indicates that you are unfriendly. Increased touching should be viewed positively, as it usually indicates the development of a good relationship. Hand and arm gestures are often used during a conversation. Most people of Mexico are familiar with U.S. gestures; however, the "V"-for-victory sign, when made with the nose in the wedge of the "V" and mouth covered with the palm, is a very rude gesture. The U.S. gesture for "thumbs down" is vulgar in Mexico; the "thumbs-up" gesture means approval. Waving the hand from side to side with the index finger pointed up and palm facing forward means "no." Avoid standing with your hands on your hips, as this implies that you are angry. Standing with your hands in your pockets is considered rude (Axtell, 1998; Bosrock, 1995).

The Netherlands

Punctuality is very important to the Dutch; they expect punctuality at meetings and appointments. The Dutch are somewhat reserved and do not use nonverbal communication to the extent that many other European countries use it. They prefer direct eye contact and a distance of about an arm's length during conversations. They do not pat each other on the back or hug or touch each other in public, unless they are relatives or close friends. Chewing gum in public and standing with hands in pockets is considered rude. Interpreting gestures used by the Dutch should be done cautiously because some of their gestures may have a different meaning to people in other countries. For example, using the index finger to make a circular motion near the ear is a signal that the person is crazy in many countries; however, the Dutch use it to signal that a person has a telephone call. Their gesture to signal that someone is crazy is tapping the middle of the forehead (Axtell, 1998; Sabath, 1999).

South Korea

Although punctuality is important in South Korea, top-level executives may occasionally be a little late for meetings or appointments. Western businesspersons, however, are expected to be on time. Direct eye contact is appreciated, but touching on the arm or back is not. In public, people may stand close together while shopping or while riding on buses because of space limitations. Using correct posture when seated is important. Although it is preferable to sit with legs uncrossed, it is acceptable to cross the legs at the knees. Putting your feet on a chair or table is considered rude. Visitors should remember that South Koreans may laugh when embarrassed or when they are frustrated as well as when something is funny; they also cover the mouth when laughing. Using the index finger to beckon someone is impolite. Passing objects with the right hand or with both hands is customary (Axtell, 1998; Sabath, 2002).

Taiwan

Punctuality is appreciated in Taiwan, but they are more flexible regarding being on time for meetings and appointments than are U.S. persons. However, a telephone call to indicate you have been delayed is expected. Eye contact should be kept to a minimum. Displaying emotions is inappropriate; a calm demeanor should be maintained. The Taiwanese need even more personal space than do U.S. persons; they prefer a distance equal to two arms' length. Good posture is important; men sit with both feet on the floor. (Women, however, may sit with legs crossed at the ankles or knees.) Both hands are kept in the lap while sitting. Use the entire hand, rather than the index finger, when pointing. Beckoning someone is accomplished by motioning with the fingers, palm down (Axtell, 1998; Sabath, 2002).

Terms

- Chromatics
- Chronemics
- Deductive method
- Haptics
- Inductive method
- Intimate zone

- Kinesics
- Monochronic
- Nonverbal communication
- Oculesics
- Olfactics
- Paralanguage

- Personal zone
- Polychronic
- Proxemics
- Public distance
- Social zone

Exercise 6.1

Instructions: Circle T if the statement is true or F if false.

1. T F   Asians typically use the deductive method of reasoning to solve problems.
2. T F   People in the United States speak faster than Italians and Arabs.
3. T F   Latin Americans need more space than people of the United States.
4. T F   Punctuality is not widely regarded in Algeria.
5. T F   Private offices are generally reserved for top-level executives in all cultures.
6. T F   When conversing with the Japanese, it is best to keep steady eye contact throughout the dialogue.
7. T F   People of all cultures respond negatively to body and breath odor.
8. T F   More bodily contact occurs between Western men than between Arab men.
9. T F   Touching the head of a Thai is forbidden.
10. T F   Smiling is interpreted as happiness in all cultures.

Exercise 6.2

Instructions: Match the following terms with their definition.

_____ 1. Space   A. Chromatics
_____ 2. Body language   B. Chronemics
_____ 3. Smell   C. Deductive approach
_____ 4. Gaze/eye contact   D. Gestures
_____ 5. Symbols, illustrators, regulators, or affect displays   E. Haptics
_____ 6. Goes from facts to generalizations   F. Inductive approach
_____ 7. Time   G. Kinesics
_____ 8. Color   H. Oculesics
_____ 9. Volume, pitch, and rate that affects message meaning   I. Olfactics
_____10. Touch   J. Paralanguage
                                                                         K. Proxemics

Questions and Cases for Discussion

1. Explain how thought patterns and problem solving differ in the United States and other cultures.
2. Discuss differences in paralanguage of people in various cultures.
3. Explain how attitudes toward time vary from culture to culture.
4. Discuss differences in space needs of persons in the United States, Japan, Greece, and Latin America.
5. Identify cultures that favor direct eye contact and those that avoid eye contact.
6. Give examples to show how olfactics is an important aspect of intercultural nonverbal communication.
7. Identify cultures that are comfortable with bodily contact and those that avoid bodily contact. Give examples of appropriate and inappropriate bodily contact in the United States.
8. Discuss cultural differences in body language of people in the United States, Japan, China, Italy, Greece, and Latin America.
9. Explain how the use of color communicates nonverbal messages.
10. Identify cultures that are comfortable with silence and those that are not. Discuss possible meanings of silence in various situations.

Cases

The following procedure is recommended for analyzing the cases: (a) read the case carefully paying attention to details; (b) read the questions at the end of the case; (c) reread the case, taking notes on or highlighting the details needed for answering the questions; (d) identify relevant facts, underlying assumptions, and critical issues of the case; (e) list possible answers to the questions; and (f) select the most logical response to the question. Your professor may ask that you submit answers to the case questions in writing.

Case 1

Barbara works for a subsidiary of a German corporation in the United States. Her job involves ordering products from Germany and following up on the status of deliveries. Barbara does not speak, read, or write German; however, this is not a problem, as Barbara's contact Anna speaks, reads, and writes English. Normally all of Barbara's e-mails, letters, and faxes from Anna are written in English. Lately the German factory has been having difficulty, and Barbara has been sending e-mails to Anna with inquiries about the product delays. In her last e-mail, Barbara asks why the Germans cannot get their materials shipped on time. Barbara's answer comes back in German. Discuss what nonverbal communication was being conveyed in the situation and how you would change the behavior to be more positive.

Case 2

A U.S. company has sent a representative to negotiate a contract with a Japanese firm. The U.S. representative arrives at the appointed time for his meeting and is shown to the meeting room, where six representatives from the Japanese firm meet with him. During his presentation, the Japanese move their heads in an up-and-down motion; however, they say very little. The presentation was given in English, as the representative had been told the Japanese understood English. When the representative asked if there were any questions, everyone nodded politely; however, no one said a word. After a few minutes, the representative asked if they were ready to sign the contracts. One of the Japanese said, "It is very difficult for us to sign." At this point the representative said, "Should I leave the contract with you?" The Japanese said, "Yes." The U.S. representative returned to the United States expecting the Japanese to return the contract, which did not happen. Explain what the Japanese were really saying by nodding their heads and using the word "difficult."

Case 3

On his first trip to Mexico, Harry, a U.S. manager interested in negotiating a contract for his firm with a Mexican firm, was invited to a dinner party by his Mexican counterpart. The invitation indicated that cocktails would begin at 7 p.m., so Harry arrived promptly at that time. His host seemed surprised, and no one else had arrived. People began arriving about 8 p.m.; Harry knew he had read the invitation correctly but felt he had gotten off to a bad start. What advice would you have given Harry?

Case 4

Fred, the manager of a large U.S. bookstore, hired Ching Wu, a newcomer from China, as one of his clerks. In an attempt to get to know Ching Wu better, Fred invited her to join him for coffee. Throughout their conversation, he noticed that Ching Wu always looked down at the floor and never gave him eye contact. He interpreted this as a lack of respect. Discuss the nonverbal communication differences in this situation.

Activities

1. Write a paragraph describing an incident from your own experience involving oral and/or nonverbal miscommunication with someone from another culture. Suggest a plausible explanation for the miscommunication.
2. Prepare a short skit to illustrate nonverbal communication blunders that a person from the United States might make in a country of your choice.

3. Demonstrate a gesture (such as the "thumbs-up" or the U.S. "OK" sign) and ask class members to explain its meaning in a specific country.
4. Demonstrate the amount of space considered acceptable when interacting with persons in Latin America, the United States, and Egypt.
5. Demonstrate the amount of eye contact considered appropriate in the United States, Japan, and the Middle East.

References

Axtell, R. E. (1998). *Gestures.* New York: Wiley.

Borden, G. A. (1991). *Cultural orientation: An approach to understanding intercultural communication.* Upper Saddle River, NJ: Prentice Hall.

Bosrock, M. M. (1995). *Put your best foot forward: Europe.* St. Paul, MN: International Educational Systems.

Bosrock, M. M. (1997). *Put your best foot forward: South America.* St. Paul, MN: International Educational Systems.

Chaney, L. H., & Lyden, J. A. (1996, April). Impression management: The office environment. *Supervision, 57*(4), 3–5.

Devine, E., & Braganti, N. L. (1991). *The traveler's guide to Middle Eastern and North African customs and manners.* New York: St. Martin's Press.

Engholm, C. (1991). *When business east meets business west.* New York: Wiley.

Engholm, C., & Rowland, D. (1996). *International excellence.* New York: Kodansha International.

Fast, J. (1991). *Body language in the workplace.* New York: Penguin.

Gudykunst, W. B., & Ting-Toomey, S. (1988). *Culture and interpersonal communication.* Newbury Park, CA: Sage.

Hall, E. T., & Hall, M. R. (1990). *Understanding cultural differences: Germans, French, and Americans.* Yarmouth, ME: Intercultural Press.

Jandt, F. E. (2004). *An introduction to intercultural communication* (4th ed.). Thousand Oaks, CA: Sage.

Lewis, R. D. (2000). *When cultures collide: Managing successfully across cultures.* London: Nicholas Brealey.

Madden, T. J., Hewett, K., & Roth, M. S. (2000). Managing images in different cultures: A cross-national study of color meanings and preferences. *Journal of International Marketing, 8*(4), 90–107.

Morrison, T., Conaway, W. A., & Borden, G. A. (1994). *Kiss, bow, or shake hands.* Holbrook, MA: Bob Adams.

Ricks, D. A. (1999). *Blunders in international business* (3rd ed.). Malden, MA: Blackwell.

Sabath, A. M. (2002). *International business etiquette: Asia and the Pacific Rim.* New York, NY: ASJA Press.

Sabath, A. M. (1999). *International business etiquette: Europe.* Franklin Lakes, NJ: Career Press.

Samovar, L. A., & Porter, R. E. (2004). *Communication between cultures* (5th ed.). Belmont, CA: Wadsworth/Thomson Learning.

Scott, J. C. (2002, October). The colorful world of international business. *Business Education Forum, 57*(1), 40–43.

Turkington, C. (1999). *The complete idiot's guide to cultural etiquette.* Indianapolis: Alpha Books.

7 | WRITTEN COMMUNICATION PATTERNS

Objectives

Upon completion of this chapter, you will

■ know the guidelines for writing international messages in English.

■ be familiar with letter formats commonly used by U.S. business firms and how they differ from formats used in other countries.

■ understand how facsimiles are commonly used for communicating between U.S. firms and those in other countries.

■ understand how writing tone and style vary from culture to culture.

■ understand cultural differences in other types of written communication such as the résumé and related job-search documents.

Many U.S. companies correspond with foreign corporations; it is important, therefore, to be aware of differences in the format, tone, and style of written communication. Research results show that 97% of outgoing international correspondence is sent in English with about 1% each in Spanish, French, and German. Percentages for incoming international messages are similar: 96% are in English with the remaining 4% divided between French, German, and Spanish (Green & Scott, 1992). Because English is used for most international written messages, making these messages as clear as possible is important. Understanding the business communication practices of the culture you are writing to will help you to communicate effectively.

INTERNATIONAL ENGLISH

International English is English for businesspeople who either deal with other cultures whose native language is not English or for whom English may be a second language; it is limited to the 3,000 to 4,000 most common English words. An excellent reference is P. H. Collin, M. Lowi, and C. Weiland's *Beginner's Dictionary of American English Usage* (2002). In order to use international English, three cultural factors are important: an understanding of business communication in the other culture, an idea of how business communication is taught in the other culture, and a knowledge that content errors are more difficult than language errors for people in another culture to discern.

Content errors are **lexical errors** and refer to errors in meaning. **Syntactic errors** are errors in the order of the words in a sentence. A native speaker of a language will discover the syntactic errors in a sentence much easier than the lexical errors.

EXAMPLES OF LEXICAL ERRORS

We baste (based) this opinion on our many years of experience.
Thank you for your patients (patience).
The device omits (emits) a high-pitched signal when it is receiving.
We realize that your office will be closed on this wholey (holy) day.
It is there (their) material.
We except (accept) the invitation to dinner.

Business communication is not necessarily taught in other countries as it is in the United States. The course may not contain any information on the theory of communication and what happens between the sender and receiver. Many of the business communication courses being taught in a country that desires to do more business with the United States are simply translation courses.

Guidelines for "internationalizing" the English language have been developed to enable both native and nonnative speakers of the language to write messages clearly to decrease the possibility of misunderstanding between people of different cultures. The following guidelines adapted from those developed by Riddle and Lanham (1984–1985) are important for situations in which both cultures speak English as well as for situations in which English may be a second language for one or both of the communicators:

- Use the 3,000 to 4,000 most common English words. Uncommon words such as "onus" for "burden" and "flux" for "continual change" should be avoided.
- Use only the most common meaning of words that have multiple meanings. Choose words that have only one meaning. The word "high" has 20 meanings; the word "expensive" has 1.
- Select action-specific verbs and words with few or similar alternate meanings. Use "cook breakfast" rather than "make breakfast"; use "take a taxi" rather than "get a taxi."
- Avoid redundancies (interoffice memorandum), sports terms (ballpark figure), and words that draw mental pictures (red tape).
- Avoid using words in other than their most common way, such as making verbs out of nouns (impacting the economy and faxing a message).
- Be aware of words with a unique meaning in some cultures; the word "check" outside the United States generally means a financial instrument and is often spelled *chéque*.

- Be aware of alternate spellings in countries that use the same language, such as theatre/theater, organisation/organization, colour/color, and judgement/judgment.
- Avoid creating or using new words; avoid slang.
- Avoid two-word verbs, such as "pick up"; instead, use "lift."
- Use the formal tone and maximum punctuation to ensure clarity; avoid the use of first names in letter salutations. If you know the other country's salutation and closing, use them. End with a closing sentence that is thoughtful.
- Conform carefully to rules of grammar; be particularly careful of misplaced modifiers, dangling participles, and incomplete sentences.
- Use more short, simple sentences than you would ordinarily use; avoid compound and compound-complex sentences.
- Clarify the meaning of words that have more than one meaning.
- Adapt the tone of the letter to the reader if the cultural background of the reader is known; for example, use unconditional apologies if that is expected in the reader's culture.
- Try to capture the flavor of the language when writing to someone whose cultural background you know. Letters to people whose native language is Spanish, for example, would contain more flowery language (full of highly ornate language) and would be longer than U.S. letters.
- Avoid acronyms (ASAP, RSVP), **emoticons** (:-o), and shorthand (U for "you" and 4 representing "for") in writing letters, faxes, or e-mail messages.
- If photocopies to other members of the organization are appropriate, be sure to send them a copy or ask who should receive copies.
- Remember that numbers are written differently in some countries; for example, 7,000 may be written 7.000 or 7000. In addition, money designations are also often written differently.

THE IMPORTANCE OF GRAMMAR

The Associated Press, London, June 19, 1999—A comma in the wrong place of a sales contract cost Lockheed Martin $70 million, the *Financial Times* reported Friday. An international contract for the U.S.-based aerospace group's C-130J Hercules had the comma misplaced by one decimal point in the equation that adjusted the sales price for changes to the inflation rate, the London-based newspaper said. In Europe, commas are used instead of periods to mark decimal points. "It was a mistake," the newspaper quoted James A. "Micky" Blackwell, president of Lockheed's aeronautics division as saying. But the customer, who Lockheed refused to name, held them to the price. "That comma cost Lockheed $70 million," said Blackwell.

WRITING TONE AND STYLE

The tone and writing style of correspondents from foreign countries are usually more formal and traditional than U.S. companies typically use. When the tone and style differ greatly from that used by the recipient, the intended positive message may be negatively received.

Authors of business communication textbooks in the United States recommend using the direct approach for beginning good-news, direct request/inquiries, and neutral messages. You should use the indirect approach for bad-news messages. The direct approach means that you begin with the good news or other pleasant ideas in the good-news message, begin with the request or inquiry in request/inquiry messages, and begin with the most important idea in neutral messages. When using the indirect approach, beginning with a buffer is recommended. A **buffer** is a paragraph that tells what the letter is about with a pleasant tone but says neither yes nor no.

Park, Dillon, and Mitchell (1998), in their research comparing U.S. and Korean business letters, concluded that both U.S. and Korean letters used direct and indirect request strategies. In both countries, the structure used for direct requests was "Please" plus the imperative (*Please let us know the shipment date*). The structure for indirect requests, however, differed. Korean letters seemed to prefer "wishful" requests (*We hope you will replace the damaged shipment*). U.S. letters avoid "wishful" requests; they call for a specific action (*Your replacing the damaged shipment will be appreciated*).

In the United States, we also teach using a "you approach" or "reader orientation"; however, in a collectivistic country, you should use an inclusive approach, such as "we" or "our," to avoid making the reader lose face or be singled out. In a collectivistic culture, it is improper for one person to be addressed because the whole team is responsible for the outcome.

Women writing to men internationally must be very careful about the tone and word choice. Women have to make an exceptionally good impression if they are to be taken seriously. Flattering statements when written to a man must be carefully worded so they cannot be interpreted as flirtatious. Compliments should be given from the company or the department rather than from the woman directly. Many countries do not consider women as serious businesspeople and would regard a woman as too assertive if she used firm and direct words. Direct words such as "expect" or "require" should be softened to "would appreciate" (DeVries, 1994).

Although Germans use the buffer occasionally, they are usually more direct with negative news. Latin Americans do not use buffers; they avoid the negative news completely, feeling it is discourteous to bring bad news. This practice of omitting buffers was confirmed in research of communication in Latin America conducted by Conaway and Wardrope (2004). Thus, U.S. Americans must be able to read between the lines of letters from Latin American businesspeople. The Japanese begin letters on a warm, personal note, which is an inappropriate way of beginning a U.S. letter. The Japanese try to present negative news in a positive manner, a quality that has sometimes caused a U.S. counterpart to feel that the person was deceitful. In research conducted by Azuma (1998) to determine Japanese strategies for writing negative messages compared to U.S. strategies, findings revealed that the three areas present in Japanese letters but absent in U.S. letters were comments about the weather or seasons, congratulations to the recipient on his or her prosperity or success, and requests for forgiveness or understanding.

The Japanese begin a letter, regardless of the type of news, with a statement about the season: "It is spring, and the cherry blossoms smile to the blue sky." Islamic people use the phrase, "God willing" (*Inshallah* in Arabic).

A way to show respect is to include common phrases of the country that help make the recipient feel comfortable. Most nations consider politeness to be a very important quality in business encounters. A compliment showing knowledge of the cultural heritage of the country is also appreciated.

> U.S. businesspeople tend to be very direct in discussing business and do not want to waste anyone's time. However, showing politeness and a little small talk is considered the proper way of doing business in most countries in the world.
> Also, what U.S. persons view as a request can appear to be boasting, obnoxious, or arrogant in another culture because of the way the request is phrased.

In the United States, ending negative messages on a positive note is important, although the French do not consider this important. Beginnings and endings of French business letters are very formal, but endings tend to be somewhat flowery: "Sir, please accept the expression of my best feelings." The French organize some types of business letters differently. They recommend apologizing for mistakes and expressing regret for any inconvenience caused. U.S. business letter writers, on the other hand, avoid apologies and simply state objectively the reason for the action taken. Endings of German letters tend to be formal (Kilpatrick, 1984; Varner, 1987, 1988).

An awareness of the differences between the format, tone, and style of written communication can go far in building goodwill between cultures. If you receive a letter in which you are addressed "Dear Prof. Dr. Judith C. Simon," you need to be able to read past the unimportant style or tone differences and look for the meaning in the letter. The overuse of politeness is very common for many cultures and should not distract U.S. readers. However, as a writer, keep these cultural differences in mind to avoid sounding harsh and insensitive to the reader.

> British writers assume less shared knowledge than Finnish writers (Lampi, 1992). Politeness strategies differ when a group of Dutch businesspeople use their native language or use English. The type and frequency of the use of politeness change when a second language is used (Geluyckens & van Rillaer, 1996).

U.S. letters tend to be shorter than letters written in other cultures. As a sign of friendship, U.S. businesspeople should change the tone of their letters when writing to businesspeople in another culture. The **parochialism** or ethnocentrism that so many U.S. people display in their writing to other cultures can easily be tempered with knowledge of the person to whom they are writing.

LETTER FORMATS

Letter formats used by other countries often differ from styles used by U.S. businesses. Some countries, such as France, still use the indented letter style with closed punctuation. Latin American countries prefer the modified block format, which features the date and closing lines beginning at the center and paragraphs beginning at the left margin (Conaway & Wardrope, 2004). The preferred styles in the United States are the block (all lines beginning at the left margin) and modified block (date and closing beginning at the center and paragraphs blocked). Writing styles use either standard punctuation (colon after the salutation and comma after the closing) or open punctuation (no punctuation after either the salutation or the closing).

The French tend to use the indented style for business letters. The French place the name of the originating city before the date (*Norvége, le 15 décembre 2——*). (Use the overstrike function, symbol function, or multinational insert function of your word processing software to type special marks used in other languages.)

The format of the inside address may vary. In the United States, the title and full name are placed on the first line, street number and name on the second line, and city, state, and ZIP code on the last line. The format used in Germany puts the title (*Herr, Frau, or Fräulein*) on the first line, full name on the second line, street name followed by the street number on the third line, and ZIP code, city, and state on the last line. Spanish-language writers also place the recipient's title (*señor, señora, señorita*) on the first line above the person's name (Conaway & Wardrope, 2004). The street number also follows the name of the street in Mexico and South America.

Although U.S. letters always place the date before the inside address, the French sometimes place the date after the inside address. In their letters, the inside address is typed on the right side with the ZIP code preceding the name of the city (74010 PARIS); in U.S. letters, the inside address is on the left. The punctuation style used in French letters differs from that used in U.S. correspondence: the salutation is followed by a comma rather than a colon or no punctuation, which is used in standard and open punctuation styles of U.S. letters. The complimentary close is rather formal in French business letters; the writer's title precedes the writer's name. Care should be taken to format the inside address and the envelope address exactly as it is shown on the incoming correspondence.

Guidelines for addressing the envelope if you do not have an address to copy are as follows:

Mr./Mrs./Ms./ or appropriate title plus first, then last name
Street number followed by street name
ZIP code information placed sometimes before and sometimes after the city

The country name typed in full capital letters (whether the country and city are at the beginning or at the end of the address determined by the collectivistic or individualistic nature of the society)

Examples:

Herr Hans-Dieter Duden	JAPAN, Tokyo	Mr. John R. Smith
Bosch Gmbh	Hachioji-shi	2350 Walnut Grove
1600 Bretton Due	47-25 Nanyodai	Memphis, TN 38152
GERMANY	Nakamura Yoko	USA

Dates are written differently also. Although people in the United States would use "January 5, 2——," in many other countries, the date would be written as "5th of January 2——" or "5 January 2——." Numerals should not be used for both the month and the day as it is difficult to know which numeral is the day and which is the month.

U.S. business letters are single-spaced, but in many other countries, they may be either single-spaced or double-spaced. In U.S. letters, the name of the writer is typed four lines below the complimentary close with the title placed on the next line. In German letters, the company name is placed below the complimentary close; the writer signs the letter, but the writer's name and position are not typed in the signature block. In Japan and China, the surname is always placed before the given name (such as Smith Jack rather than Jack Smith).

Depending on how international the Japanese, Chinese, or Far Eastern businessperson is, he or she may switch the names to make you comfortable.

Example: Wu Chei will change his name to Chei Wu (surname last) to please you.

Salutations and closings are more formal in many other countries. Salutations for German letters are the English equivalent of Very Honored Mrs. Jones and in Latin American countries, My Esteemed Dr. Green. Complimentary closings are often the English equivalent of Very respectfully yours (Kilpatrick, 1984; Varner, 1987, 1988).

DIPLOMATIC TITLES

Written Forms of Address and Salutations

Title and Address Form	Salutation
AMBASSADOR	
His/Her Excellency (name)	Excellency: (or)
The Ambassador of (country)	Dear Mr./Madame Ambassador:
CHARGÉ D'AFFAIRES	
The Honorable (name)	Dear Sir/Madame:
Chargé d'Affaires of (country)	Minister:
The Honorable (name)	Dear Sir/Madame:
The Minister of (country)	Dear Mr./Madame Minister:
CONSUL GENERAL	
The Honorable (name)	Dear Mr./Ms. (name):
Consul General of (country)	
CONSUL	
The Honorable (name)	Dear Mr./Ms. (name):
Consul of (country)	

Source: Bosrock, 1995, p. 54.

Samples of Japanese, French, Spanish, and Chinese letters that have been translated into English from the native language are shown in Figures 7-1 through 7-4. Samples of a British and a U.S. letter are shown in Figures 7-5 and 7-6.

FIGURE 7-1   Japanese Letter

AZ409
April 7, 2 ---

Showa Machine Works Ltd.
Attention of Sales Department

5-1 Moriyama Maguro
Moriyamaku, Nagoya 463
Asumi Trading Co., Ltd.

President: Nobuaki Iwai

Allow us to open
with all reverence to you:

The season for cherry blossoms is here with us and everybody is beginning to feel refreshed. We sincerely congratulate you on becoming more prosperous in your business.

We have an inquiry from a foreign customer and shall be very happy to have your best price and technical literature for the item mentioned below:

Wire Drawing Machine
6 units for Taiwan

Specifications:
1. Finished sizes: 0.04 mm to 0.10 mm
2. Spooler: Single
3. Speed: Min. 1500 meters/min.
4. Type of spooler: Expanding arbor
5. Capstan: Must be covered with ceramic
6. Dimension of spool: Flange diam. 215 mm
                             Barrel diam. 163 mm
                             Bore diam. 97 mm
                             Traverse 200 mm

The above are all the information available for this inquiry. We ask you to recommend a machine that can meet these specifications.

We shall be very pleased if you will study the inquiry and let us have your reply as soon as possible. We solicit your favor.

Let us close with
great respect to you.

The Japanese have a traditional format beginning with the salutation followed by a comment about the season or weather.

EXAMPLES OF SEASONAL GREETINGS

January — I feel my body frozen as severe cold days continue.
Full scale "Winter Shogun" has arrived. (An analogy between Shogun and nature is used.)

February — Hope you are coping with the last phase of the cold season.
Cold winter still remains strong.

March — Spring has just begun on the calendar, but the cold wind reminds us winter is not over yet.
Glad to smell the soil covered by snow for a long winter.

April — Buds of cherry tree are getting large.
Spring has arrived and every field is covered by hundreds of flowers.

May — Wind blowing over the field feels like a beginning of the summer.
Flapping wind kite in the sky looks great.

June — Rice paddy fields are ready to be planted.
Continuous rain ended, and it is a beautiful day.

July — It was the hottest day of the year.
It is a season of summer festivals and people having fun.

August — Indian summer is still around this week.
Keeping a lot of summer memories in my heart.

September — Hope you are in good health with the cool weather.
The sun is still strong and casting shadow reminds me the summer season is not over.

October — It is autumn, when the sky is blue and people have an appetite.
The smell of Matsutake reminds me of fall.

November — The tree on the boulevard is bare of leaves.
All mountains are burning with crimson foliage.

December — Frost is on the ground and breath is white.
The year is almost over.

Source: M. Tsuji, personal interview, October 27, 1998.

A kind remark about a gift, kindness, or patronage will follow. Then they include the main message and close with best wishes for the receiver's health or prosperity (Haneda & Shima, 1982). Japanese who are doing business internationally are adjusting and changing the way they write. They are using a shorter seasonal greeting and writing the business message sooner. Studies show that Japanese businesspeople are using both deductive and inductive writing patterns (Kubota, 1997).

In the letter from France, notice the "we" attitude and manner of indirect apology; note also the way of explaining the situation and the format: typing the

FIGURE 7-2   French Letter

Marie Portafaix
7, Avenue Felix
75541 Paris

Mr. Pierre DESBORDE
Professor d'économie politique
IUT BB Commericial Techniques
Doyen Gosse Place
38000 GRENOBLE

MTP/GM/05.22

Paris, 25 September 2---

Sir,

We are in receipt of your letter and have given our best attention to your request.

We are unhappy to inform you, we are not able to give your proposition a favorable report.

As a matter of fact we are grateful for the interest and your support, but we must consider essential publications hereafter for the media.

We want to renew our regrets and thank you for your belief. Sir, be assured our sentiments are the best.

Public Relations Director
Marie Thérése PORTAFAIX

FIGURE 7-3   Spanish Letter

8 June 2---

Zapatería Elegánte, S.A.
May 5 Avenue
Caracas, Venezuela

Esteemed clients and friends:

Permit us to communicate to you that the fabric of the shoes of Miss Modalo that were ordered has been discontinued. Therefore much to our regret we will not be able to serve you in this situation.

We always want to fill your catalog requests, and if you find another model from the enclosed catalog that you like we would be very glad to send them.

We regret your loss and hope to be able to serve you on another occasion as you deserve.

Very cordially yours,

CIA. LATINOAMERICANA, S.A.

José Mendoza Lopez General Manager

FAL/age

Enclosure: 1 catalog

FIGURE 7-4   Letter Written in English by Chinese Writer

April 5, 2---

Prof. L. S. St. Clair
71 South Perkins Extd.
Memphis, TN 38117-3211

Dear Prof. St. Clair:

I've received your letter of Jan. 30 and your report passed on to me by Dr. Jones of CSU, Long Beach. Thank you deeply for your kindness to let me have it. I have perused it and found it very creative and enlightening, I especially admire your servant and ingenious analysis. I fully support your suggestion to establish course in intercultural business communication. Never has it been so important to globalize business communication education as it is today. It is time now to join our effort in this important area.

I made a report on the development of BC in the U.S. at a convention in Chicago last month.

You are welcome to visit China and help us with the development of business communication in China.

Sincerely,

Feng Xiang Chun
Vice President

surname in all capital letters. The date, salutation, and closing also differ from the U.S. letter.

Similarities and differences between the Spanish letter and the U.S. letter include the date, salutation, and closing.

The letter from China in Figure 7-4 is shown as it was received; notice how the syntactic errors develop when people are not writing in their native language. Also notice that the writer has used the U.S. format in deference to another culture.

As shown in Figure 7-5, the British do not use a period after Mr, Mrs, Ms, or Dr. The British are very conscious of forms of titles and addresses and expect others to use them appropriately (Janner, 1977). The British class system is becoming less rigid; how you address someone is less formal than a few years ago. However, if you do not know someone well, you need to use his or her title and surname. When

---

FIGURE 7-5　British Letter

---

23 October 2---

Mr Stevens J. Martin, Jr.
AOC Incorporated
1627 Byhalia Road
Collierville, TN 38067

Dear Mr Martin:

I have pleasure in submitting our quotation as follows:

A.　　　　Cost incurred to date.
　　1.　　　　Design. All designs presented to date and working drawings to entire booth to enable USA contractor to build.
　　　　　　1,500.00
　　2.　　　　Model. Production, packing and shipment.
　　　　　　1,100.00
B.　　　　Refurbishment of existing display.
　　　　9,425.00

I hope the above meets with your approval and should you have any queries, please do not hesitate to contact Alan Roast at Walker Roast.

It is essential that our contractors are instructed to proceed today to meet the shipping deadline. I apologise for putting pressure on this decision but time is now of the essence.

Yours sincerely,

Edward Bales

---

writing about someone in a letter, you should include after the name, the abbreviations for military and civil orders and decorations, highest degree or diploma, professional memberships, and professions. In the typed signature line, include in parentheses the title you prefer to use, such as Ms. The British are also fond of humor or sarcasm (Scott, 1998).

In the example of a U.S. letter that conveys bad news (Figure 7-6), notice the use of a buffer in the first paragraph, which does not suggest a negative message. In the second paragraph, the bad news is placed in a dependent clause to deemphasize it. The letter ends with an action close, avoiding any reference to the bad news. The letter style is blocked with standard punctuation.

FIGURE 7-6 U.S. Letter

FIGURE 7-6 U.S. Letter

September 15, 2---

Mr. Larry Green
2871 Goodlett Street
Memphis, TN 38817

Dear Mr. Green:

A beautiful driveway not only enhances the beauty of a home, but it also increases a home's value.

Although the driveway we installed at your home six years ago is no longer under warranty, we will be glad to send one of our service representatives to inspect your driveway and give you a free estimate on repairing or replacing it.

Please call 767-6334 to arrange a time for one of our representatives to evaluate the condition of your driveway.

Sincerely,

Thomas L. Johnson

pl

FACSIMILES (FAX)

Multinational businesses in the United States have found that the facsimile (fax) machine is more dependable than the mail service in many countries. However, in some countries the telephone system is also poorly managed, which means the fax machine may not be better than the mail. Poor service of both mail and phone systems occurs during the stormy seasons that a number of countries experience. In addition, many countries lack regular mail and telephone service in their remote areas. However, through telecommunication satellites and cell towers, telephone service is becoming more dependable than the mail in many locations around the globe.

The fax should be written as you would write a letter. If you are sending production schedules, budgets, or other types of written information, then a cover letter or transmittal sheet should be used so that the operator knows to whom the fax is directed, from whom the material originates, and how many total pages are included. Figure 7-7 is an example of a fax.

FIGURE 7-7	Korean Fax

To: Jim Cain, President
Cainable Vegetables

From: Wu H. Chu

I received your fax message delightly. How is your business doing? I really think that our election was better for all business in Korea. If you can make a video-tape of Ray Manner' farm, that would be great. Videotape, Blueprints together you can send me by airmail *not by ship,* regardlessly special or regular with the bill I would appreciate it very much. In designing of my vegetable farm I am take your experienced advice in good consideration. Thank you. I will look for your advices more.

ELECTRONIC MAIL (E-MAIL)

When using e-mail internationally, you should use the same writing techniques you use for a letter. However, because the format is a memorandum with TO, FROM, DATE, and SUBJECT already stated, you do not use an inside address.

Proper e-mail courtesy includes addressing the receiver by name in the opening sentence (i.e., Mr. Slovinsky, thank you for sending me the figures I requested). Avoid addressing the person by his or her first name unless permission has been granted to use the first name. You should check your e-mail inbox at least once a day and respond promptly, preferably within 24 hours. Keep messages concise and brief; most messages should be kept to a maximum of two screens. You should also devise an electronic "signature" because, unlike a letter, e-mail is not on company letterhead (Sabath, 1998).

Major cities around the world are connected by the Internet and have e-mail available. E-mail is a very convenient way to send documents, and many times the printout is clearer than when using a fax machine. Telephone lines are a problem in some countries, and the cost may be much higher than in the United States. (See chapter 8 for a discussion of e-mail etiquette.)

RÉSUMÉ AND JOB SEARCH INFORMATION

Globalization has definitely expanded the information people need to get a position in a country other than their own. Europeans have always lived with differences and adjusted as they crossed national boundaries. In the United States and other parts of the world, a person looking for a position could use the job-search method they were taught in school. The following is a description of job-search information needed to find a position in the United States, Canada, China, England, France, Germany, the Netherlands, South Korea, and Spain.

United States

U.S. hiring officials have indicated a preference for résumés that are one to two pages long. Important résumé items include personal information (name, address, and telephone number), job objective (to give the reader an idea of what type of work you want and your plans for advancement), educational background (universities attended), and work experience (current position, company name and location, job title, dates employed, responsibilities, and accomplishments). Most hiring officials prefer that you include three or four references (names of people who can verify your work experience, educational achievements, and character). Information about your family, age, religion, ethnicity, or gender should not be included, nor should you include a photograph. The résumé is accompanied by an application (cover) letter.

In the United States, good sources of job opportunities are the Sunday edition of major newspapers in cities where you are interested in working. The *Wall Street Journal* on Tuesdays has a special employment section and also produces a newspaper, *Employment Weekly,* which is a collection of all employment advertising for the previous week in all U.S. regions. In larger cities, public and private employment agencies are also adept at helping people find positions.

Canada

Canadian hiring officials prefer résumés that include information similar to that included on U.S. résumés: educational background, work experience, skills, achievements, and references. Canadian employers stress the importance of selecting keywords carefully, including use of industry jargon in describing skills and qualifications, as larger companies use résumé-scanning software. Like U.S. employers, Canadians recommend using the combination résumé, rather than the functional or chronological résumé, for job seekers who have gaps in their work history. They also emphasize the importance of writing a cover letter that is tailored to the specific company and that is free of mistakes in spelling and grammar. Additional job-search information for Canada is available at http://www.goinglobal.com/countries/canada/resume.asp.

Workopolis.com, which is offered in English and French, is Canada's largest online job site; it offers more than 30,000 jobs each day in Montreal and Toronto, as well as some other Canadian cities. Job seekers may search by location, keyword, job category, and so on. The *Toronto Star* is Canada's largest daily newspaper and has numerous job listings.

China

Résumés in China contain personal information. In addition to name and address (including e-mail), applicants include date and place of birth, gender, marital status, and children. After personal information, the job objective is listed, followed by education or employment history, depending on which is most relevant. Schools attended are listed, including dates of attendance, location, and degree(s) received. A section on Specialized Training typically follows Education. This section includes computer skills and language competencies. Employment history, including company name and location, dates of employment, and job titles, are listed as Work Experience. Duties and responsibilities are described using action verbs. Both Education and Work Experience are listed in reverse chronological order with the most recent school attended or job experience given first. References are usually omitted—the statement "References furnished on request" is usually placed at the end of the résumé. Information about careers in China (and in a number of other countries) is available at http://www.goinglobal.com.

England

The résumé for professional businesspersons in England is one to two pages in length, is typed, and generally does not have a photograph attached. The résumé contains a professional objective, name, address, phone number, professional experience, education, hobbies and other activities, and references. Military service is not listed, and family and other personal information is omitted. The résumé is sent with an application letter that is typed and formal. The letter includes reasons for wanting the position and a request for an interview.

The universities in England offer career advisory services for their graduates. Ads appear in the following journals: *The Guardian* and *The Daily Telegraph* on Thursday (Tuesday for management positions), *The Daily Telegraph* on Wednesday, the *Sunday Times* for commercial and technical positions, and the *Financial Times* on Wednesday and Thursday for finance-related positions (Tixier, 1992).

France

In France, the vita is much like the U.S. résumé. An application (cover) letter is included. The vita lists full name, address, and age, and includes telephone number, photograph, and family information. The applicant includes a job objective, education, and experience as in the U.S. résumé. In addition, information about hobbies and proficiencies in foreign languages is included.

In France, it is very difficult for someone directly from the university to get a position without experience. Connections are very important in obtaining the first position. Graduates of the *Grandes Écoles,* business, and engineering schools have an advantage over others, as graduates of these institutions are considered the intellectual elite. Age is a factor in hiring; 40 is considered old. French laws do not prevent age discrimination.

Two daily newspapers that are a good source of available positions are *Le Cosigaro* and *Le Monde.* The magazine *L'Exprés* is also a source of potential jobs (Desborde, 1993).

Germany

The Germans expect applicants to be well educated for their positions and to have experience. The résumé is a complete dossier of the candidate. A length of 20 to 30 pages is not unusual, including positions the candidate has held, photocopies of diplomas and degrees the candidate has earned, letters of recommendation from teachers, verification of previous employment, a recent photograph, and a statement of computer skills. Other information includes the names and professions of the candidate's parents; names of brothers, sisters, spouse, and children; religious affiliation; and financial obligations. In addition to the diplomas and degrees, transcripts are provided to certify all course work completed. Professional activities, including publications and personal references, are also given. A typed letter of application that is one to two pages in length accompanies the résumé. The style should be very conservative and formal.

In Germany, college students often enter into a contract with a company while in college. The two large journals where employment ads are placed are the *Frankfurter Allgemeine Zeitung* and *Suddeutsche Zeitung* (Tixier, 1992).

The Netherlands

In the Netherlands, job seekers are advised to furnish enough details on the résumé to provide an employer with sufficient information about the applicant's work experience and abilities. Providing a photo is inappropriate. Although school grades and letters of recommendation are not included on résumés, they may be requested later. During the interview, applicants may be asked personal questions, such as marital status; applicants feel free to ask questions about salary and company benefits.

Monsterboard Netherlands (Monsterboard.nl), a popular job site, provides an interactive platform. Werk.nl, available only in the Dutch language, provides job openings as well as interview advice. Additional information related to the job search is available at http://www.goinglobal.com/countries/netherlands/resume.asp.

South Korea

Job applicants in Korea are advised to use reverse chronological order when listing information related to work experience and education on the résumé. Name and address of employers, job title, and details of achievements and duties are included. Job seekers are expected to complete a standard application form typically used by Korean companies.

Job fairs are held in the COEX Convention Center several times each year; they provide job seekers an opportunity to meet with numerous representatives of South Korean mid-sized companies. Additional career information for South Korea is available at http://www.goinglobal.com/countries/korea/korea_job_resource.asp.

Spain

The résumé is a maximum of two pages in typed letter form that includes a chronology of experience, military service, and education. Including information on the family, profession of parents, clubs and associations, and a picture is not unusual. A professional objective is mentioned. Many positions are gained through personal referral rather than through school placement or advertisements. Journals that have position advertisements include *El Pais* and *La Vanguardia* (Tixier, 1992).

Books and government documents can help prevent a faux pas (a social blunder or error in etiquette). The Department of State's *Background Notes* by country, the *CultureGrams* series, the Department of Commerce's *Overseas Business Reports,* the *World Factbook,* and the *Statesman's Yearbook* are good sources for specific information on various cultures.

Terms

- Buffer
- Emoticons
- International English
- Lexical errors
- Parochialism
- Syntactic errors

Exercise 7.1

Instructions: Circle T for true or F for false.

1. T F Native speakers of a language will discover lexical errors easier than the syntactic errors.
2. T F The writing style of U.S. letters is more formal than most foreign correspondents.
3. T F The use of a buffer in bad-news messages is typical of the writing style of Latin Americans.
4. T F The Japanese try to present negative news in a positive manner.
5. T F Ending messages on a positive note is important in both French and U.S. letters.
6. T F The indented letter style for business letters is used by the French.
7. T F Salutations of German letters are more formal than in the United States.
8. T F The Japanese traditionally begin letters with comments about the season or weather.
9. T F Résumés submitted to a German firm are typically longer than those submitted to a U.S. firm.
10. T F Spanish résumés are typically in letter form.

Questions and Cases for Discussion

1. Explain how the format of business letters differs in U.S. correspondence and in Latin American countries.
2. How does the tone and writing style of Japanese letters differ from those in the United States?
3. To use international English, what cultural factors do you have to understand?
4. Explain the difference between lexical and syntactic errors.
5. Explain why people from two cultures who speak the same language may have difficulty communicating.
6. Define a buffer and how it is used.
7. Which countries expect the reader "to read between the lines" for meaning?
8. What in the German culture might explain the very long and detailed résumé that is required when job hunting in Germany?
9. What items are currently included in résumés in the United States?
10. Explain the major differences between résumés in the United States and other cultures.

Cases

The following procedure is recommended for analyzing the cases: (a) read the case carefully paying attention to details; (b) read the questions at the end of the case; (c) reread the case, taking notes on or highlighting the details needed for answering the questions; (d) identify relevant facts, underlying assumptions, and critical issues of the case; (e) list possible answers to the questions; and (f) select the most logical response to the question. Your professor may ask that you submit answers to the case questions in writing.

Case 1

You work in the personnel division of a multinational organization. You have been asked to provide a list of potential candidates for a management position in the corporation's German office. Because of their laws, you want a German national for the position. How would you go about obtaining résumés to review?

Case 2

If you are dealing with a foreign corporation in which no one speaks English as a native or second language, what may be necessary for your corporation and the foreign corporation to work together? How does a U.S. corporation react when the other corporation does not speak its language? If the corporation has the flexibility to deal with another company in which someone speaks its language versus one in which no one does, which company would receive the order?

Case 3

A U.S. executive was working with a convention booth builder in England. The English were not working on the booth and would not give a date of completion for the booth or a shipping date to the United States. For six consecutive weeks, the U.S. executive called to inquire about the state of the booth. One day, the executive called and was given the usual litany of excuses, so he gave the English an ultimatum. The next week, the English had not acted on the ultimatum, so the U.S. executive informed the company he would have a trucking company pick up and ship the booth to the United States. Twice the trucking company went to pick up the booth and was told by the English company that they were not authorized to pick up the booth. The U.S. executive finally had to hire the advertising firm in England that had originally hired the booth manufacturer to intervene and get the booth shipped. When the booth arrived in the United States, it had not been packed properly and required additional work. What cultural differences were involved in this situation? How could the executive have handled the situation differently?

Case 4

A British national was sent to the United States to work in a subsidiary. He was an engineer in a management position in charge of building a new factory for the corporation. He was initially offered intercultural training; however, he felt comfortable because both countries spoke the same language and declined the training. The British engineer later complained to the home office that he was not getting the cooperation he needed. The home office hired an intercultural trainer to go to his office to review his correspondence and sit in on some of his meetings. The intercultural trainer discovered that the U.S. employees did not understand his communications. The engineer was interjecting British humor and sarcasm in both his oral communication and his e-mail messages. The U.S. subordinates did not know when he was serious about a problem and when they were to ignore his statements. What are some examples of humor U.S. persons use with foreigners that they expect them to understand?

Activities

1. Examine the Latin or Germanic roots of simple and difficult words in the English language.
2. Take a passage from a journal or textbook in another language and compare it, in terms of sentence and paragraph length, to a passage from a journal or textbook written in English.
3. Modify a bad-news letter so it is effective for a reader who is Japanese, French, Spanish, or German.
4. Search the want ads of the local newspaper; bring to class a job announcement of a position with a multinational corporation, a position involving overseas travel, or a position located in a foreign country.
5. Prepare a résumé to be sent to a multinational company applying for an overseas assignment in a country of your choice.
6. Write a letter of application to accompany the résumé prepared in Activity 5.

7. Write a letter in English to someone who speaks English as a second language following the international English guidelines.
8. Find the errors in Figure 7-4 and explain why these particular errors may have happened.
9. Read the following two faxes and determine the reader's probable reaction. What choice of words could have been improved on? The first fax is from the U.S. corporate office to Taiwan; the second is from Taiwan to the U.S. corporate office.

TO: XYZ
ATTN: WU
FROM: BOB SMITH
DATE: SEPT. 4, 2---

RECEIVED THE HUGGER PACKAGE TODAY AND WAS VERY DISAPPOINTED. FIRST I WANT TO SAY I SUSPECT YOU MAY NOT HAVE SEEN THE PARTS BEFORE THEY WERE SENT. IT LOOKED LIKE EVERYTHING WAS JUST THROWN INTO A BOX AND A COUPLE OF THIN PIECES OF POLYFOAM LAID ON TOP. NOTHING WAS PROTECTIVE WRAPPED. THE HUGGER HOUSING IS SO BEAT UP IT LOOK LIKE SOMETHING OUT OF THE JUNK PILE.

THE HANGER BRACKETS WERE JUST THROWN INTO THE BOTTOM OF THE BOX WITH NO PROTECTION AT ALL. MOST OF THE SCREWS FOR THE TOP OF THE BALL WERE SCATTERED THROUGHOUT THE BOX AND NOT ASSEMBLED TO THE BRACKETS.

I'M AFRAID WE WILL NOT BE ABLE TO USE THE HANGER BRACKET ASSEMBLIES TO FIELD TEST THE HUGGER BECAUSE THE BALL HOLD DOWN SCREWS INTERFERE WITH THE TOP OF THE BALL. THE FIT IS SO TIGHT THAT THE BALL WILL NOT ROTATE AND CENTER IN THE SOCKET. WHAT WE REALLY NEED IS FOR THE THREE SCREWS TO CLEAR THE BALL BY APPROX. 1/32 INCH (ABOVE THE BALL) AFTER THE SCREWS HAVE BEEN ASSEMBLED TO THE BRACKET.

YOU MAY HAVE TO ADJUST THE VERTICAL LOCATION OF THE SCREW FROM THE DRAWING DIMENSION TO MAKE SURE THE SCREWS JUST CLEAR THE BALL.

PLEASE ADVISE WHEN YOU CAN SEND NEW BRACKET ASSEMBLIES SO WE CAN GET ON WITH THE TESTING. ALSO PLS HAVE YOUR PEOPLE PROTECTIVE WRAP EVERYTHING.

THANKS

BOB SMITH

TO: XYZ   DATE 9/7/2---

ATTN: MR. BOB SMITH

FROM: XYT

RE: 52″ HUGGER PARTS

At first, we have to apologize to you for not having good package of samples. With thin polyfoam for package is easily to break out when air freight. Besides say sorry to you, we will improve the protection of samples.

1. New hanger housing was made by hand. Without mold, it needs some time. Can we just make one set?
2. Hanger bracket ball—When we revised it per drawing, we found when hanger bracket is setted on ceiling plate. The fit is too tight that the ball will not rotate and center in the socket. We will ask vendor to make proper correction to improve these problem.
3. The distance above the ball and three screws needs 1/32 inch. Will also revise it.
4. Blade iron after our shaking test. It results over 60,000 times. How about your testing result?
5. After we complete correction hanger bracket and ball, will send samples to you again. We will improve our protective wrap of samples.

Best Regards,

WU

10. Have an international student write a letter for you in English but with their native language style, tone, and format. Compare the letter to the style, tone, and format of U.S. letters.

References

Azuma, S. (1998). How do Japanese say "no" in the written mode? *Academy of Managerial Communications Journal*, 2(2), 18–29.

Bosrock, M. M. (1995). *Put your best foot forward: Europe*. St. Paul, MN: International Education Systems.

Collin, P. H., Lowi, M., & Weiland, C. (2002). *Beginner's dictionary of American English usage*. Lincolnwood, IL: National Textbook Company.

Conaway, R. N., & Wardrope, W. J. (2004, December). Communication in Latin America. *Business Communication Quarterly*, 67(4), 465–474.

Desborde, R. (1993, July 23). *Personal communication*.

DeVries, M. A. (1994). *Internationally yours: Writing and communicating successfully in today's global marketplace*. Boston: Houghton Mifflin.

Green, D. J., & Scott, J. C. (1992). International business correspondence: Practices and perspectives of major U.S. companies with related implications for business education. *NABTE Review,* 19, 39–43.

Geluyckens, R., & van Rillaer, G. (1996). Face-threatening acts in international business communication: A quantitative investigation into business writing. Paper presented at the 22nd and 23rd *LAUD Symposium,* Duisburg, March 26–31.

Haneda, S., & Shima, H. (1982). Japanese communication behavior as reflected in letter writing. *Journal of Business Communication,* 19(1), 21–32.

Janner, G. (1977). *The businessman's guide to letter writing and to the law on letters* (2nd ed.). London: Business Books.

Kilpatrick, R. H. (1984). International business communication practices. *Journal of Business Communications,* 21(4), 40–42.

Kubota, R. (1997). A reevaluation of the uniqueness of Japanese written discourse. *Written Communication,* 14(4), 460–481.

Lampi, M. (1992). Rhetorical strategies in "Chairman's Statement" sections in the annual reports of Finnish and British companies: Report on a pilot study. In P. Nuolijarvi & L. Tiittula (Eds.), *Talous ja Kieli 1* [Language and Economics 1]

(pp. 127–143). Helsinki: Helsinki School of Economics and Business Administration. Helsingin kauppakorkeakoulun julkaisuja D-169.

Park, M. Y., Dillon, W. T., & Mitchell, K. L. (1998, July). Korean business letters: Strategies for effective complaints in cross-cultural communication. *The Journal of Business Communication,* 35(3), 328–345.

Riddle, D. I., & Lanham, Z. D. (1984–1985, Winter). Internationalizing written business English: 20 propositions for native English speakers. *Journal of Language for International Business,* 1, 1–11.

Sabath, A. M. (1998). *Business etiquette: 101 ways to conduct business with charm and savvy.* Franklin Lakes, NJ: Career Press.

Scott, J. C. (1998). Dear ???: Understanding British forms of address. *Business Communication Quarterly,* 61(3), 50–61.

Tixier, M. (1992). *Travailler en Europe.* Paris: Editions Liaisons.

Varner, I. I. (1987). Internationalizing business communication courses. *Bulletin of the Association for Business Communication,* 1(4), 7–11.

Varner, I. I. (1988). A comparison of American and French business correspondence. *Journal of Business Communication,* 25(4), 55–65.

8

GLOBAL ETIQUETTE

Objectives

Upon completion of this chapter, you will

- understand cultural differences in making introductions as well as customs related to business card exchange.

- understand how position and status affect cultural interaction.

- be familiar with rules of etiquette that apply to communicating by telephone and electronically with persons of other cultures.

- understand how cultural differences in dining practices may affect intercultural communication.

- be familiar with the cultural nuances of tipping.

- understand how practices of giving gifts vary from culture to culture and the role of gift giving in establishing favorable intercultural relations.

- learn the importance of travel etiquette in conveying a positive image of a person's firm and country.

When conducting business abroad or in the United States with someone of another culture, a knowledge of certain rules of business and social etiquette is important. **Etiquette** refers to manners and behavior considered acceptable in social and business situations. **Protocol** refers to customs and regulations dealing with diplomatic etiquette and courtesies expected in official dealings (such as negotiations) with persons in various cultures. Protocol during negotiations is discussed in greater detail in chapters 10 and 11.

President Clinton, during his first state dinner abroad on a visit to Korea, confused his translator and embarrassed South Korean officials when he stepped to the microphone to give his dinner speech and invited a translator to stand between himself and President Kim Young Sam. Because in South Korea it is an insult for anyone to stand between two heads of state, President Clinton had committed a serious faux pas. (Kim, 1993, p. A5)

Proper social behavior includes learning cultural variations in making introductions, exchanging business cards, recognizing position and status, communicating interculturally, dining practices, tipping etiquette, giving gifts, and traveling.

INTRODUCTIONS

Being sensitive to cultural variations when making introductions will ensure that your first encounter with a person from another country leaves a positive impression. First impressions are made only once but are remembered for a long time.

The procedure for making introductions varies from culture to culture. First names are used almost immediately by people from the United States and England, however, introductions are more formal in some other cultures. Titles are used when introducing people in Germany and Italy; they often indicate the person's profession or educational level. Germans always address each other as "Herr Guenther" or "Frau Kurr" in and out of the office, reserving first names for close friends and family.

Remember that in some cultures, such as the Chinese, the surname comes first and the given name last. Ching Lo Chang would be addressed as Mr. Ching.

President Clinton, in a meeting in Korea, addressed South Korean President Kim Young Sam's wife, Mrs. Sohn Myong-suk, as Mrs. Kim. He should have addressed her as Mrs. Sohn because in Korea, it is the custom for women to maintain their maiden name when they marry. (Kim, 1993, p. A5)

Men and women from the Latin American countries often add their mother's maiden name to their surname, so you should use the next-to-last name when addressing them. Thus, Evelyn Rodrigues Castillo would be addressed as Señorita Rodrigues. When women marry, they drop their mother's surname and add their husband's father's surname. When in doubt, ask what name is to be used. Egyptians use the title plus the first name when making introductions. In some cases, the French form of address is used for women, for example, Madame Susan. In Iraq and in India, titles such as Professor and Doctor, used with the last name, are used as part of the introduction. In African countries, such as Nigeria and Kenya, titles are used with last names until you get to know them well and they ask you to call them by their first name (Devine & Braganti, 1991, 1995, 2000). Because of such widely diverse customs in the use of titles, it is wise to research the customs of the particular culture involved.

Introductions are accompanied by a handshake, an embrace, or a bow, depending on the culture. Handshakes may vary from the soft handshake of the British to the firm handshake of U.S. persons. Hugging or embracing when being introduced is considered inappropriate in business situations in the United States but is common in many South American countries. The bow, common in China and Japan, is uncommon in many other cultures. Additional information on greeting customs, including handshakes, is included in chapter 9.

BUSINESS CARD EXCHANGE

An important aspect of business protocol is knowing the proper procedure for exchanging business cards. Because all business contacts require a business card, the admonition of a well-known credit card company, "Don't leave home without it," applies.

Although most U.S. businesspeople carry business cards, they do not always exchange them when meeting unless there is a reason to contact the person later. Rank, title, and profession are taken seriously in some cultures, so it is important to include your position and titles or degrees in addition to your company name on your card. Include foreign headquarters as appropriate as well as your fax number and perhaps e-mail address. Avoid colored type and paper. Be conservative by choosing white paper with black ink.

Presentation of the card varies with the culture. The practice in the United States of glancing at the business card and promptly putting it in the pocket is considered rude in countries like Japan. The Japanese examine the business card carefully and make some comment while accepting it. During meetings, place the business cards of others attending in front of you on the conference table to properly refer to names, ranks, and titles. Use both hands when presenting your card in Japan or South Korea; position the card so that the person can read it (Axtell, 1993; Baldrige, 1993) (see Figure 8-1).

FIGURE 8-1 Business card presentation in Japan is completed by presenting your card with both hands, positioned so that the person can read it, and bowing

An exchange of business cards is an expected part of all business introductions and most personal ones in Europe, including the Scandinavian countries. Because Scandinavians are respectful of age, include your company's date of establishment on your business cards when the company's history is a long one (Turkington, 1999). Other parts of the world in which an exchange of business cards is the norm include the Middle East, the Pacific, Asia, and the Caribbean. Australian businesspersons do not usually carry business cards; thus, when you offer them your card, you may not receive one in return. In Latin American countries, business titles are important, so be sure to include them on your business cards (Harris, Moran, & Moran, 2004). In most of the Southeast Asia, Africa, and the Middle East (with the exception of Israel), avoid presenting the card with your left hand, as the left hand is reserved for taking care of bodily functions (Axtell, 1993). In non-English speaking countries, have the information on your card printed in English on one side and in the local language on the other.

POSITION AND STATUS

Position and status may have an impact on the success of intercultural communication encounters. No standard definition of social class exists that applies to all countries because people in different cultures have their own way of identifying the classes. Some cultures believe that people should occupy their proper places and that some are entitled to more respect than others. Most people of the United States show limited respect for rank and authority, although many other cultures are very conscious of position and power.

Although the United States is not considered a nation of classes, distinctions in position and status do exist. Because class distinctions in the United States are subtle, visitors from other cultures may not be able to spot the existence of a class structure and may believe the official propaganda of social equality. Visitors to New York, Washington, DC, and other cities, however, may see both the homeless and more affluent persons in public places. Although a system of inherited titles and ranks does not exist in the United States, certain factors distinguish between the top class, the upper-middle class, the mid-middle class, and the lower-middle class. As was discussed in chapter 3, money is one factor associated with class. Further distinctions are made between those who have inherited money but are not currently employed and those who have inherited money and are employed. Style, taste, and awareness are equally important. Social class is also associated with educational opportunities and a person's occupation or profession (Fussell, 1983).

Status is associated with education in a number of cultures. Educational titles are used in introductions as a sign of respect and acknowledgment of the person's educational achievement. In Germany and Italy, executives and other professionals are proud of titles preceding their names, as they often reflect their education or profession. People with a college degree are entitled to be called Doctor (*Dottore* in Italian); the same rule applies to architects and lawyers. In Germany, the U.S. equivalent of president or managing director of a company is called *Herr Direktor;* a medical doctor, if a woman, is called *Frau Doktor;* and a female engineer is addressed as *Frau Ingenieur.* In Mexico, a lawyer is addressed as *Licenciado,* a title that is considered very important. In England, special protocol exists for addressing royalty, peers, clergy, and others. The managing director in a British firm is usually the top official and equivalent to a U.S. corporate president (U.S. corporate vice presidents do not carry much clout abroad) (Axtell, 1990). In some cultures, such as India, a very rigid class system exists with a society divided into castes. The particular caste a person belongs to is determined at birth; each **caste system** has its status, rights, and duties. Although discrimination based on caste has been outlawed, in many areas, particularly rural ones, it is still a major influence on life in India. In India's rigid caste system, interaction between members of different castes is often limited, as in the case of India's untouchables (Samovar & Porter, 2002).

Cultural differences also exist concerning the status of women in a society. Women in some cultures play a less prominent role in business than do men. In South Korea, women are considered inferior to men and thus have lower social status. Women, even those with college degrees, are rarely employed as executives; they usually hold jobs as teachers or secretaries. Social and economic inequality between men and women is also apparent in China, Malaysia, and Singapore; men are clearly the ones in positions of authority (Turkington, 1999). The Arabs are becoming more accustomed to women executives, and they are beginning to accept women executives from other countries. U.S. women doing business with the Arabs should understand this difference in cultural attitude and should make a special effort to conduct themselves appropriately, including dressing very modestly. In some Middle Eastern countries, men may refuse to work with women; women executives in Latin America may not receive the same respect given to men executives. Women in the United States are being given increased opportunities for business travel, management positions in overseas operations, and transfers to overseas assignments. The progress U.S. women have made in the workplace is viewed by many as setting a precedent for other countries because the United States is often a catalyst for international change.

In some cultures, such as the Chinese, people are very aware of age and hierarchy. Age is viewed as an indication of seniority. In addition to the Asian culture, the Arabian world has a great respect for age. Advanced years represent wisdom and respect. Age takes precedence over rank, but rank is still important. In the Japanese society, knowing the rank of the people with whom you come in contact is important. The middle-level manager in a large company outranks a department head from a smaller company. The higher the rank of the person you are introduced to, the lower you bow. The person of lower rank bows first and lowest. Status is also shown by who goes first when entering a room or an elevator. Those of lower rank wait for those of higher rank to precede them. If you are the foreign guest, you may be expected to enter a room ahead of others, so if you are motioned to enter the room, do so quickly. When the Chinese or Japanese enter a room, they generally enter in protocol order with the highest-ranking person entering first. They will also assume that the first member of your negotiating team to enter the room is the head of your group and has the higher rank. Sitting in rank order from highest to lowest during a meeting is helpful (Axtell, 1998; Turkington, 1999).

ELECTRONIC COMMUNICATION ETIQUETTE

Aspects of protocol related to successful intercultural communication include telephone manners and cyberspace etiquette, sometimes referred to as **netiquette** (network etiquette).

Many intercultural encounters are via the telephone. When talking on the telephone, the initial impression is formed mainly by vocal quality (70%) rather than on the words spoken (30%). Thus, opinions are formed more on how something is said and the voice tone rather than on what the person actually says (Mitchell, 2000).

Good telephone manners include answering the phone promptly (first or second ring), identifying yourself properly by giving your department and your name, and being courteous at all times, including the frequent use of "please" and "thank you." Successful telephone communication involves recognizing and avoiding behaviors that typically irritate others. Being put on hold has been identified as the single most irritating behavior. When the telephone call is to another country, being put on hold can go beyond irritation. Other negative behaviors that should be avoided include making mouth noises, not paying attention, and having a negative or rude attitude. A positive behavior appreciated by callers is "the voice with a smile." Callers also appreciate a cheerful attitude.

When voice mail is used, be brief but complete when leaving a message. Include your name, company, the date, and the time of the message. Give your phone number slowly and include a brief summary of what the call concerns.

Because more companies are communicating by e-mail, certain rules of etiquette should be observed. E-mail is more informal than a letter or memorandum and is inappropriate for conveying certain types of messages. Negative information, such as a person's failure to get a promotion, and personal information, such as announcing the birth of a baby, are not appropriate uses of e-mail. Proper "netiquette" avoids the following:

- **shouting**—typing the message in all capital letters.
- **dissing**—speaking ill of someone.
- **flaming**—sending vicious, insulting messages.
- **spamming**—mass mailings of commercial advertisements or material cross posted to numerous news groups. (Segaloff, 1998)

In addition to these suggestions, avoid the use of humor and sarcasm. Remember that cultural variations exist in what is perceived as humorous. Also avoid a tone that is even slightly critical (Miller, 2001). Additional suggestions were included in chapter 7.

Because a firm may be liable for information leaked into cyberspace, employees should be very careful about the messages they send. A good rule to follow: If you would not want your message posted on the company bulletin board, do not send it via e-mail. Pressing the Delete key after sending a message does not mean that it cannot be tracked back to you (Miller, 2001).

Care should be taken in deciding how a message should be sent. The advantages of using e-mail include low preparation, fast delivery time, personal, and convenient for the receiver. The disadvantages are lack of confidentiality and, of course, the lack of nonverbal interaction (Kenton & Valentine, 1997). Of course, not all countries use e-mail as frequently as people in the United States. In the United States, 68.8% of the population have Internet access (third highest of top 20 countries, according to Internet Penetration Statistics updated on September 30, 2004). Almost three-fourths of residents in Sweden have Internet access, followed closely by Hong Kong with 72.5%. Iceland, the Netherlands, Australia, and Canada each have about two-thirds of residents with Internet access; the United Kingdom has 58.5% and Japan has 52.2%. When corresponding with international persons via e-mail, avoid addressing people by their first names. Be sure to write out the name of the month when specifying a date, include country codes for telephone numbers, and indicate which time zone is being referred to when making such statements as "I will telephone you at 2 p.m. Friday."

The use of fax messages is increasing as a quick method of communication between countries. The basic guidelines for writing a fax are included in chapter 7; points of etiquette regarding their transmission follow:

- Call ahead to confirm the fax number and to alert the person that you are sending a message (in case the fax machine shares a line with a person's telephone). The message should follow within 15 minutes.
- Certain documents should not be faxed—documents of more than 10 to 15 pages, personal or confidential information, and negative news.
- Avoid using the fax when impressions are important. Résumés and proposals submitted on fax paper will not get the same attention as those submitted on good-quality, linen finish paper (Ford, 2003; Glassman, 1998).

DINING PRACTICES

Cultural dining practices vary widely. In many parts of the world, the main meal is at noon, although in the United States, the main meal is in the evening. In Mexico, lunchtime is from 2 p.m. to 4 p.m. and is the main meal of the day. However, in places near the U.S.–Mexican border, local businesses conform more to the U.S. lunchtime of noon to 2 p.m. The dinner hour also varies. In the United States, the dinner hour varies from 5 p.m. to 7 p.m., but in such countries as Spain, it may be as late as 10 p.m. In some cultures, business meals are eaten in private homes, although in other cultures, they are usually eaten at restaurants. When entertaining visitors from other countries, be considerate and ask them whether they prefer the main meal at noon or in the evening and take them to restaurants where they have a choice of a light or heavy meal (Devine & Braganti, 2000).

Cultural variations exist in the number of courses typically served as well as when the salad is served. A formal luncheon usually consists of two to three courses, and a formal dinner consists of three to seven courses. In some countries, including those in Latin America, even informal meals typically have numerous courses. In Italy and France, salads are often served after the main course rather than before.

Dining practices are viewed differently in various cultures. A U.S. dining practice that seems unusual to people of other cultures is the serving of a glass of iced water at most restaurants. Other countries that serve water do so without ice or serve bottled mineral water. Another dining practice that is viewed with astonishment is the habit of offering coffee at the beginning of a meal; serving coffee at the end of the meal is common in most cultures. The popularity of decaffeinated coffee in the United States has not yet spread to other countries, so visitors are often surprised by a waiter's question of "Will you have regular coffee or decaf?" Another U.S. custom that sometimes amazes people from other cultures is designating certain sections in restaurants as smoking and nonsmoking. A practice that makes little sense in other cultures is the U.S. custom of conducting business at breakfast. The French especially do not like breakfast meetings; they prefer a leisurely breakfast with time to read the paper in the morning. The French do conduct business over lunch; however, the meal may last two hours or more. Another U.S. business custom questioned by people in other cultures is the lengthy cocktail "hour" before dinner. Italians have commented that the endless rounds of cocktails before ordering a meal is exhausting and may result in discussions that make little sense (Baldrige, 1993).

The manner of eating is also diverse. The **U.S. eating style** uses the "zigzag" technique: cutting the meat with the knife held in the right hand and the fork in the left, then placing the knife on the plate, shifting the fork to the right hand, and eating. Diners using the **Continental eating style** place the fork in the left hand and knife in the right; they use the knife to push food onto the back of the fork, then move the food into the mouth with the tines of the fork down. Asians use chopsticks especially for eating rice but may use a spoon for soup. They appreciate foreigners' attempting to use chopsticks and are often willing to demonstrate correct usage. Chopsticks are placed on the chopstick rest at the conclusion of the meal (or when pausing during the meal); they should not be placed in an upright position in the rice bowl (Sabath, 2002) (see Figure 8-2).

Other cultural variations in dining also exist. Tahitian food is eaten with the fingers. In the Middle East, be prepared to eat with your fingers if your host does but

FIGURE 8-2   Cultural Variations in Eating Style

use the right hand only. In Bolivia, you are expected to clean your plate; Egyptians and Filipinos, however, consider it impolite to eat everything on your plate (Axtell, 1993; Turkington, 1999). In China, avoid taking the last item of food from the serving platter unless you want to convey to the host that you are still hungry (Turkington, 1999).

A dining practice in France that seems unusual to those in other cultures is the custom of bringing pet dogs into restaurants where the waiter takes the dog into the kitchen to be fed a treat. Dogs in most cultures are not allowed in public eating establishments. They may, however, be on the menu in such Asian countries as South Korea.

A wealthy American couple toured Asia accompanied by their pet poodle. They decided to dine one evening at a nice looking restaurant where, as it turned out, restaurant employees could speak no English. Because the tourists could not speak the local language, they ordered from the menu by pointing to certain items. They also tried to order food for their poodle. After several attempts using a type of sign language, the waiter seemed to understand. He pointed to the dog, then pointed to the kitchen. The couple, thinking this meant that the dog could eat in the kitchen but not the dining room, nodded their agreement. After a lengthy wait, the waiter proudly entered and lifted the lid of one of the serving platters to display a well-cooked poodle. (Ricks, 1999, p. 11)

Dining in Japan, especially in Japanese homes, requires sitting in a kneeling position on a *tatami* mat. Men keep their knees three or four inches apart; women keep their knees together. Being able to lower yourself to this position and rise from it gracefully requires practice. If you have frequent contact with the Japanese, practicing this art is warranted (Axtell, 1993).

TIPPING

People communicate nonverbally by their tipping practices; those who are basically miserly and those who are generous reveal these traits by their tipping behavior. Although it is difficult to establish definite rules for tipping, generally when service has been good or when service people go out of their way to do a favor, a tip is merited. If the service is very bad, you are not expected to leave a tip but should report the situation to the manager. "Insult tipping" (leaving a few coins) shows a lack of respect and is inappropriate regardless of how poor the service.

Trends in tipping appear to have changed in the past few years. Although a tip of 15% of the bill was considered to be a generous tip in fine restaurants, 20% is now closer to the norm when the service is excellent.

Traveling in the United States involves numerous situations in which tipping is expected. When traveling, have a supply of $1 and $5 bills in your pocket for tipping the cab driver, the bellhop, and other service personnel who may carry your luggage, summon a cab, or perform other services, such as delivering food or small appliances to your hotel room. Travel tipping needs to be included in anticipated travel expenses; tipping service personnel at a resort or luxury hotel may add an additional 25% to your bill.

Tipping in a nontipping culture can offend or insult the people of that culture. However, letters of thanks to people who have been especially helpful, including hotel managers, are very much appreciated. Tipping in Japan is frowned on. People in this culture consider helping you with your luggage a gesture of hospitality and would be offended if you tipped them. If a hotel employee has performed an extra service that you want to reward, place the yen in an envelope because the Japanese would consider openly receiving money as embarrassing or as "losing face." Likewise in Singapore and South Korea, tipping is not expected, although this practice seems to be changing in hotels where international businesspersons stay.

In many places, such as Europe, a service charge is added to your restaurant and hotel bill. Although you are usually not expected to leave an additional tip, the trend is to leave an extra amount, especially if the service was good. In the absence of a service charge, leave the usual 15% to 20% that you would leave in the United States. Observing cultural differences in tipping can communicate nonverbally that you have researched the country and that you consider local customs to be important (Axtell, 1993; Sabath, 1999, 2000, 2002).

GIFT GIVING

Each country has its seasons and occasions for giving gifts. Gift giving in some cultures is an art and is considered an integral part of building intercultural professional and social relationships. The careful selection and wrapping of a gift and presenting it at the proper time with panache (style) conveys to others your social sensitivity and good manners.

Business gifts in the United States are very modest in price; the rule to follow (because of tax regulations) is to limit the price to $25 or less. Business gifts are sometimes given to members of your staff on such occasions as birthdays and Christmas. In addition, secretaries are generally treated to flowers and/or lunch on Secretaries' Day. Remember that business gifts to staff members should be personal; an electric pencil sharpener is inappropriate. However, they should not be too personal—cologne or lingerie to a member of the opposite gender could be misinterpreted. A gift certificate to the person's favorite restaurant or specialty shop is in good taste. Subordinates wait for their supervisors to set the tone on gift giving. If you are new in an office, ask what tradition is usually followed in exchanging gifts. Several years ago when the office Christmas party was popular, colleagues often exchanged gifts as part of the occasion. The practice of exchanging gifts among colleagues, even token gifts (the office grab bag), seems to have been discontinued in many firms in favor of contributing the amount of money you would spend on such gifts to a local food bank or pooling the amount to give gifts of food or money to members of the custodial staff.

In the United States, gifts are opened in front of the giver. The gift is admired, and appreciation is expressed verbally. The oral expression of thanks is followed by a written note of appreciation unless the gift is small and is used as an advertisement (e.g., a paperweight with the company logo). Business gifts to the office or department, such as a basket of fruit or box of candy, are opened immediately and shared by all. (The manager's taking the gift home to share with his or her family is considered to be in poor taste.) The manager writes a note of thanks to the company that sent the gift and conveys expressions of appreciation from staff members (Samovar & Porter, 2004). Gifts are also opened in the presence of the giver in Brazil and in Belgium. In the Arabian countries, you must present a gift when others are present so it will not be interpreted as a bribe. In some countries, however, gifts are not opened in the presence of the giver. In Taiwan, Hong Kong, and Korea, you should not open a gift in front of the giver, and you should accept the gift with both hands (Bosrock, 1995, 1997a, 1997b).

Although flowers make appropriate gifts, learn cultural taboos related to color, variety, and number. Red roses are associated with romance in some cultures. In some countries, such as China, white is the color of mourning, and gladioli are often used in funeral sprays; thus, a gift of white gladioli is inappropriate in China. Although a gift of flowers in any color is considered appropriate by middle- and upper-class Brazilians, purple flowers are associated with death by the lower class. In most European countries, avoid a gift of carnations, which are for cemeteries only. Chrysanthemums are inappropriate in Belgium, Japan, and Italy; they are associated with funerals and mourning. Although flowers are not expected by a Mexican host, they are appreciated; however, avoid sending yellow, red, or white flowers as these colors have negative connotations for some Mexican people. In some cultures, the number of flowers given has a special significance (Barnum & Wolniansky, 1989). Armenians give an uneven number of flowers on happy occasions; even numbers of flowers are associated with death. For the Chinese, four is the most negative number (it sounds like their word for death), so gifts of four flowers—or four of anything else—should be avoided (Dresser, 2005). Because in Thailand and Hong Kong three is a lucky number, give gifts in threes in these countries (Bosrock, 1997a). A flower shop in the host country is the best place to get information concerning local customs about giving flowers (Sabath, 2002).

Exhibitors at a trade show could not understand why Chinese visitors were not stopping by their booth. Workers were wearing green hats and were using them as giveaways as well. They later learned that for many Chinese, green hats are associated with infidelity; the Chinese expression "He wears a green hat" indicates that a man's wife has been cheating on him. When they discarded the green hats and gave out T-shirts and coffee mugs instead, they had a number of Chinese visitors. (Dresser, 2005)

Gift giving is very much a part of conducting business in such countries as Japan. Japan's major gift giving times are *Ochugen* (July 15) and *Oseibo* (December). Companies give gifts to their customers as an expression of appreciation for past and future business. They also reward their employees at these times with large bonuses. U.S. companies that have ongoing business relationships with the Japanese should remember their associates with a gift at both of these times. Because Japan is one of the United States' largest trading partners, knowing the nuances associated with Japanese gift giving is considered an important aspect of protocol with people in that culture (Samovar & Porter, 2004).

The Japanese are a gracious people for whom gift giving seems to be an art. The wrapping of the gift and the manner of presenting it are just as important as the gift itself. Gifts are beautifully wrapped but without the ornate bows and other decorations typically used on gifts in the United States. The color of the wrapping should be consistent with the occasion: red, gold, and white for happy events; black and purple or black and white for other occasions. The Japanese do not open a gift in front of the giver, so you should avoid opening your gift in their presence. Also avoid giving a gift when someone else is present. Do not surprise your Japanese host with a gift, as it might cause the person to lose face. Let your host know ahead of time by mentioning, for example, that you have found a special commemorative coin to add to his collection. Favorite gifts with the Japanese are imported liquor, consumables of high quality, and designer-made products with such names as Gucci, Tiffany & Co., or Mark Cross. Musical tapes and CDs are also good choices. Avoid giving gifts manufactured elsewhere in Asia, as this is an insult (Baldrige, 1993; Sabath, 2002).

A Japanese-American whose firm conducted business in Japan told how he once averted a near disaster in United States–Japanese relations. His company selected and addressed 500 Christmas cards to its Japanese joint-venture partner. The cards were red (in Japan, funeral notices are red). The Japanese-American manager stopped the mail just in time. He said, "We almost sent 500 funeral cards to our Japanese partner!" (Engholm, 1991, p. 228)

These additional guidelines for gift giving in Asian countries should be observed because of the importance placed on this aspect of developing and maintaining harmonious business relationships:

- Take time to research the perfect gift; it could be related to the Asian counterpart's profession or hobby. Adding an item to a person's collection is much appreciated. Remember to buy gifts in the United States; avoid anything made in an Asian country.

- Always wrap gifts (no bows) and include an appropriate card. Although wrapping the gift in red paper (the color of luck) is appropriate, using red ink when addressing the card or writing the accompanying note is not; in China, using red ink indicates a desire to sever a relationship forever.
- Be aware of superstitions and taboos related to gifts. Avoid any gift depicting white wolves because the wolf is symbolic of cruelty and greed. Also avoid a gift of straw sandals in China.
- Recognize the significance of numbers in gift giving: Three is a lucky number in Thailand; eight and nine are lucky in Hong Kong (the word for eight sounds like "prosperity"; the word for nine is a homonym for "eternity").
- Expect a gift to be declined out of politeness at least once in some Asian countries; they will then accept. You are expected to decline once and then accept with thanks (Engholm, 1991). Because gift giving is very important in the Japanese culture, asking advice from a Japanese colleague or from someone who has lived in Japan is recommended (Axtell, 1993; Yager, 2001).

Knowing when to present the business gift is also important. In Korea, business gifts are usually given at the beginning of formal negotiations. In Germany, however, business gifts are seldom exchanged at the beginning of negotiations but may be given at their conclusion. In Latin American countries, present gifts only at the conclusion of negotiations.

Other gift-giving practices and guidelines in various cultures include the following:

- When dining in a person's home in Western Europe, present your gift when you arrive so that it does not appear to be intended as payment for the meal.
- Avoid giving gifts to the French until a personal relationship has been developed. Avoid gifts of perfume or wine; those are their specialties.
- Gifts to Germans should not be wrapped in black, brown, or white.
- Avoid gifts of a clock in the People's Republic of China, as the clock is considered a symbol of bad luck. (In Korea, however, the clock is considered good luck and is an appropriate gift.)
- A striped tie is not an appropriate gift to a British man; it may represent a British regiment other than his own.
- Avoid gifts of a knife or handkerchief to persons in Latin America. The knife is interpreted as a desire to cut off the relationship; the handkerchief is associated with tears.
- Avoid gifts of liquor or wine for an Arab. Because alcohol is illegal in Islamic cultures, the gift would be confiscated by customs.
- Because the cow is sacred in India, do not give any gifts made of cowhide.
- In Islamic countries, exercise restraint in admiring personal possessions; you will probably find yourself the recipient of the object you have admired (Axtell, 1993; Stewart, 1997).

When people of the United States select business gifts for people in other countries, they should remember that the gifts should be made in the United States, be utilitarian, and have conversational value. Good choices include things that are representative of the United States, such as Native American art or jewelry, DVDs of U.S. movies, U.S.-made sports equipment, or food that is unique to the United States, such as candy, nuts, and California wines. Avoid gag gifts; people of some other cultures do not appreciate them (Stewart, 1997).

TRAVEL ETIQUETTE

Travel etiquette begins with a pleasant, positive attitude and a sense of adventure, especially when it comes to international travel. People who approach international travel with eager anticipation—who look forward to meeting new people, seeing new places, and experiencing a new culture—seem to have more favorable experiences than those who approach travel with a sense of foreboding. In other words, people seem to get what they expect.

Because most international travel is by airplane, etiquette in this section concentrates on air travel and covers such topics as dressing and packing for the trip, behaving properly on the plane, and handling problem situations.

Travel dress is important because the people you meet, including ticket agents, will be strangers who will judge you first on your appearance. Being well dressed makes a favorable impression on others and in many cultures is associated with competency and respect. You are a representative of your company and your country; dressing professionally sends the message that you care about the impression you make on your compatriots and on persons of other cultures. Another benefit of being well dressed (wearing a suit or executive casual) when traveling is that you often get better service from airline personnel and from hotel employees on your arrival. Women may want to wear their business blouse and jacket with coordinating slacks and then carry a skirt in the carry-on luggage and change in the plane lavatory just before landing. This is especially important when a presentation is scheduled for that same day or when you are being met at the airport by a business colleague from the host country.

Christopher Patterson, an MBA graduate student at a Mid-South university, was invited for an interview in St. Louis for a much coveted managerial position with an international air transport firm. Because his usual classroom attire was a T-shirt, torn jeans, and a baseball cap worn backwards, his communication professor gave him this advice: "Dress professionally on the flight; you never know who you'll meet." He followed this advice on the flight over, felt very confident after the interview with three of the company's top-level executives, but relaxed and reverted to his classroom attire on the return trip. To his surprise, one of the three executives who had interviewed him was on the flight. The executive, with a shocked look, said, "Well, I almost didn't recognize you. You don't look like the same person we interviewed." Christopher reported to the professor on his return, "You were right; I blew it." As it turned out, he did blow it—he didn't get the job.

When packing for a trip, keep in mind that conservative business attire is usually preferred in other countries. This means dark suits for men and women, classic leather shoes, and good-quality accessories. Your luggage should also be of good quality to create a positive impression. All belongings should be packed in the luggage; carrying personal belongings in shopping bags does not convey a professional image. Checking large suitcases and limiting carry-on luggage to the size and number specified by the airline is important. Women should remember that they are responsible for their own luggage, including lifting a suitcase to the overhead bin of the airplane. Luggage with wheels is a good investment. With multiple bags, a porter or a cart may be used.

Travel etiquette also involves courteous treatment of airline personnel. When flights are late or canceled, travelers should remain calm and be polite to travel clerks who are anxious to get them to their destinations. Passengers who are courteous when they are inconvenienced often receive better treatment, including free food and lodging, than those who are rude and insensitive. Flight attendants should also be treated with respect. Although they are not tipped, flight attendants should be thanked at the end of the trip along with the captain/cocaptain.

> A passenger standing in line at an airline ticket counter listened to a person yelling and screaming at the ticket agent. After the mad, rude customer left, the passenger complimented the ticket agent on his patience, attitude, and calm demeanor. The clerk replied, "Thank you for your kind words, but don't worry; it's all right." The passenger asked, "How can it be all right?" The clerk answered, "It's all right because, you see, that man is going to Cleveland, but his luggage is going to Singapore." (Dosick, 2000, p. 50)

Proper behavior during the flight is especially important because of the close quarters. Complete strangers are forced into another person's intimate space. Therefore, airline passengers should be especially considerate of those around them and careful that their behavior does not offend anyone. Because of the limited space, passengers should refrain from wearing strong fragrances. They should respect the preferences for conversation of those seated next to them. Those who do not want to talk can take out a book or papers to work on to discourage a conversation. Putting the seat back in a reclining position when traveling coach without first asking permission of the person seated behind you is very insensitive. Because of the limited space, it is difficult for the person seated behind you to exit, to eat or drink, or to work with the seat in front of him or her in a reclining position. Passengers should also remember to stay out of the aisles as much as possible and limit their time on the telephone and in the bathroom. If they are traveling with their family, passengers should make sure that their children do not engage in such activities as kicking the seat back of the person in front of them or standing up in the seat and staring at the person behind them.

Sometimes problem situations arise because other passengers do not know or practice proper etiquette. When confronted with an incessant talker, you might say, "I would like to talk more, but I must finish this report." To the person in coach who reclines his seat, you might respond, "Would you please pull your seat forward while I am eating?" (Asking the flight attendant to make this request is also appropriate.) If you are seated next to a crying baby or a loud, obnoxious person, ask the flight attendant for another seat assignment.

A summary of rules for business and social etiquette for the 10 countries with which the United States conducts most of its international trade follows.

Canada

Social and business etiquette in Canada is similar to that of the United States, but Canadians are more conservative than people of the United States. As in the United States, shaking hands when meeting and on departure is the usual form of greeting. Most business entertaining is done in restaurants, and tipping is about the same as in the United States. Because of the strong French influence in certain parts of Canada, French cuisine is offered in many restaurants. If invited to someone's home, take flowers (but not white lilies, as they are associated with funerals) to the hostess (Axtell, 1993).

China

The Chinese bow or nod when greeting each other; when greeting Westerners, however, they usually offer a handshake. Remember that rank is important in China, so the senior person should be acknowledged first. In establishing business relationships, dining plays an important role. Business entertaining is typically conducted in restaurants at lunch or dinner. Because seating etiquette is important, waiting for your Chinese host to indicate where you are to sit is recommended. Leaving a small amount on your plate is a good idea to indicate your satisfaction with the food. Although the Chinese do not tip, foreigners are expected to tip. A common practice when tipping restaurant servers or taxicab drivers is to give them a handful of change. Giving gifts is a common practice except at a first meeting. Recommended gifts (wrapped in red) are pens of high quality or a paperweight. Gifts to avoid are clocks, white flowers, and handkerchiefs because of their association with death. In addition, knives and other cutlery should be avoided as they suggest a wish to sever ties (Sabath, 2002).

England

A soft handshake accompanied by "How do you do?" is the common greeting in England. Avoid the typical U.S. greeting of "Hi" (too informal) and avoid saying "Have a nice day" when departing (the British interpret it as a command). As in the United States, first names are often used after knowing the person only a short time. When dining in England, you might want to try some of their specialties: crumpets, steak and kidney pie, or Scotch eggs, which are deep-fried hardboiled eggs with a coating of sausage and breadcrumbs. Pubs and restaurants, rather than private homes, are used for most business entertaining. If invited to dine in a British home, a flower bouquet (except for white lilies) is an appropriate gift for the hostess (Axtell, 1993; Sabath, 1999).

France

The French customarily shake hands upon greeting and when they say goodbye. In addition, people who work together shake hands when they arrive in the morning and again when they leave in the afternoon. The handshake consists of a single, quick shake. Women typically wait for a man to initiate the handshake. Women are kissed on both cheeks as part of the greeting; however, men only kiss each other on the cheeks when they are good friends or relatives. Business cards are exchanged at initial meetings; they are presented first to the person of higher rank to show respect. In France, it is customary to place wrists on the table and to use the Continental style when dining. When visiting France, be sure to try some of their special foods, which vary according to the region. These specialties range from *lamproie a la bordelaise* (eels cooked in red wine) in Bordeaux to *escargots a la bourguignonne* (snails served with garlic butter) in

Burgundy. Wine is served with both lunch and dinner. Business gifts are given only after a business relationship has been established. Appropriate gifts include flowers (except chrysanthemums, carnations, or red roses), books, CDs, or gourmet food items (Braganti & Devine, 1992; *CultureGrams,* 2004; Sabath, 1999).

Germany

When greeting people in Germany, remember to use last names and a firm handshake. Status is recognized; men allow people of higher status or older women to precede them when entering a door or elevator. When dining in a restaurant, a service charge of 10% to 15% is generally added to the check, so you do not need to leave an extra tip. Try some German specialties: beers, sausages, and potato pancakes. Eating everything on your plate is considered polite. Gifts to your German host should be simple and rather inexpensive, as Germans consider expensive gifts to be in bad taste. When invited to a German home, bring the hostess a gift of flowers (an odd number except 13 and no red roses) (Braganti & Devine, 1992; Sabath, 1999).

Japan

In Japan, the usual form of greeting is a bow rather than a handshake; however, many Japanese who regularly associate with persons of other cultures may use both a bow and a handshake. Follow the lead of your Japanese host. The exchange of business cards is common, so be sure you have a good supply. These should be printed on one side in English and the other side in Japanese. Remember to address your Japanese host by his last name; only family members and close friends use the first name. Most business entertaining is done in Japanese restaurants. Some Japanese specialties include *sake* (rice wine) and *sashimi* (sliced raw fish). Do not tip in restaurants; the waiter will return the money if you do. Although being invited to a Japanese home is not the norm, if invited, remember to remove your shoes at the entrance of the home. A box of candy, rather than flowers, is an appropriate gift for the hostess. Because social and business etiquette are very different in Japan, do a thorough study of the culture and its customs before you go (Axtell, 1993; Devine & Braganti, 1998; Sabath, 2002).

A world traveler from Switzerland describes how he temporarily lost his fondness for eating fish while dining at a lavish Tokyo restaurant. After he had sampled numerous delicacies, the pièce de résistance was served: A live fish still flopping on the platter was brought to the table; the maitre d' then delicately sliced the live fish and served it to the guests. (Axtell, 1993)

Mexico

Shaking hands is the usual greeting in Mexico, and people also shake hands when saying good-bye. When introduced to a woman, a man will bow slightly and will shake hands if the woman initiates it. Address the person by his or her last name, as first names are not used during initial encounters. Business cards are exchanged at a first meeting but remember to include the Spanish translation on your cards. Be sure to indicate your position with your company and your university degrees. Deference is shown to someone whose age, social status, or position warrants it. The altitude of

Mexico City may affect your digestion, so eat lightly and carefully. Always order bottled water as tap water is not considered safe. Although Mexicans expect you to sample the fare, they will understand if you decline dishes such as *tripe* (stomach of sheep). Unlike many European cultures, they do not expect you to eat everything on your plate. You might want to sample such national dishes as *mole poblano de guajolote* (turkey in a sauce of spices, herbs, and chocolate), *quesadillas* (folded tortillas filled with cheese), and *frijoles refritos* (mashed and fried cooked beans). If invited to a Mexican home, send flowers ahead of time; avoid marigolds (used to decorate cemeteries) and red flowers (used for casting spells). Appropriate gifts include gadgets such as an electric can opener, U.S. cigarettes, a gold cigarette lighter, a gold pen, art books, or a bottle of scotch (Devine & Braganti, 2000; Sabath, 2000).

The Netherlands

In the Netherlands, both men and women shake hands when greeting each other. Waving when greeting another person from a distance is acceptable, but shouting is considered impolite. Although men do not kiss each other as part of the greeting, women who are good friends may kiss on both cheeks. Business cards are typically exchanged at initial meetings. Because English is spoken by most Dutch businesspeople, business cards may be in English only. The Dutch expect you to clean your plate and to rest both wrists on the table while dining. Visitors will want to try some Dutch specialties, such as *erwtensoep* (a thick pea soup) and *lamstongen met rozijnensaus* (lamb's tongue with a white wine sauce). Dining in restaurants is expensive, so you might want to try the numerous alternatives that are available: snack bars, cafes, street stalls, and restaurants that sell only pancakes. When invited to your Dutch host's home, it is appropriate to bring flowers or to send them the following day. Business gifts should be given only after a relationship has been developed with your Dutch associate. Appropriate gifts include desk accessories or books (Bosrock, 1995; Braganti & Devine, 1992; *CultureGrams*, 2004; Sabath, 1999).

South Korea

In South Korea, the usual greeting between men is a bow, accompanied by a handshake. To show respect, the left hand is placed below the right forearm while shaking hands. Women do not shake hands as frequently as men. Following the handshake, business cards are exchanged between professionals during initial encounters; the cards are presented and received with both hands. Both age and social standing are taken into consideration when greeting someone. Because Koreans are proud of their cuisine, you will want to sample some of their spicy foods and such delicacies as *pulkogi* (strips of beef that are marinated and barbecued) as well as the alcoholic drink *soju*, which is frequently served with meals. Those who conduct business in South Korea should remember that meals are served and eaten, usually with periods of silence, before socializing begins. When invited to a Korean home, it is appropriate to bring a small gift, such as fruit, flowers, or candy. Business gifts, although not a necessity, are appreciated and should be made in the giver's country. Gifts should be of good quality, yet inexpensive; they are opened in private rather than in the presence of the giver (Bosrock, 1997a; *CultureGrams*, 2004; Sabath, 2002).

Taiwan

Although bowing is a common form of greeting in many Asian countries, in Taiwan it is more common to shake hands. Rank is important, so be sure to acknowledge and shake hands with the person of higher rank first. Following the handshake, business cards are exchanged. Business cards are exchanged frequently in Taiwan, so carry an ample supply with you. Not presenting your business card to your Taiwanese associates is viewed as unprofessional. Having a translation of the information on your cards printed in Mandarin on the back of the card is recommended. Business card presentation is important to the Taiwanese: The card should be presented with both hands with the card turned so the recipient can read it. Dining in Taiwan involves eating with chopsticks and a spoon. Rice is served at most meals; not finishing your rice is impolite. Numerous restaurants are available, which specialize in various types of cuisine: Cantonese, Hunan, Peking, Shanghai, Szechuan, Taiwanese, and Mongolian. On the rare occasions when you may be invited to your business associate's home, be punctual and bring a small gift. When food is served at your Taiwanese host's home, it is important to sample everything and to make positive comments about the various dishes. Business gifts are presented and received with both hands. Visitors should remember that the Taiwanese will refuse a gift initially, it should be offered until it is accepted; gifts are opened in private (Bosrock, 1997a; Devine & Braganti, 1998; *CultureGrams,* 2004; Sabath, 2002).

A helpful rule to remember in most cultures is to follow the lead of the people in the other culture. If they shake hands, so do you. Eat what they eat and when they eat. If the other person gives you a gift, be prepared to reciprocate. Researching the country before you travel is always good advice.

Terms

- Caste system
- Continental eating style
- Dissing
- Etiquette

- Flaming
- Netiquette
- Protocol
- Shouting

- Spamming
- U.S. eating style

Exercise 8.1

Instructions: Encircle T for true or F for false.

1. T F In Japan, a business card should be presented with both hands.
2. T F Throughout Latin America, the main meal of the day is in the evening.
3. T F Flaming and dissing are terms associated with "netiquette."
4. T F Introductions are more formal in Germany than in the United States.
5. T F Bolivians expect visitors to eat everything on their plate.
6. T F Tipping is more common in the United States than in China and Japan.
7. T F The practice of serving a glass of water with meals is universal.
8. T F In China, the gift of a clock is considered a symbol of good luck.
9. T F In Germany, business gifts are usually exchanged at the beginning of formal negotiations.
10. T F When selecting travel attire, the main consideration is comfort.

Questions and Cases for Discussion

1. How do introductions vary between the United States and other cultures?
2. Describe cultural variations in business card exchange.
3. Explain class distinctions in the United States and India.
4. How are gender and age related to position and status in the United States?
5. Identify some guidelines for proper telephone etiquette.
6. Explain the difference between the terms "flaming" and "shouting" in relation to netiquette.
7. What are some advantages and disadvantages of using e-mail?
8. Identify some cultural differences in dining practices.
9. Explain the difference between the U.S. and Continental eating styles.
10. What are some guidelines for tipping appropriately? How do tipping customs vary with various cultures?
11. What are some guidelines for effective business gift giving in the United States?
12. What are some cultural differences in gift-giving practices? What gifts are considered appropriate for a person from the United States to give to someone in another culture?
13. Identify some cultural taboos concerning giving flowers as gifts.
14. What are some guidelines for airline travel attire?
15. List some suggestions for proper behavior during air travel.

Cases

The following procedure is recommended for analyzing the cases: (a) read the case carefully paying attention to details; (b) read the questions at the end of the case; (c) reread the case, taking notes on or highlighting the details needed for answering the questions; (d) identify relevant facts, underlying assumptions, and critical issues of the case; (e) list possible answers to the questions; and (f) select the most logical response to the question. Your professor may ask that you submit answers to the case questions in writing.

Case 1

Mark was in charge of a negotiating team sent to Japan. On learning the importance of gift giving to a successful business relationship in this culture, prior to departure he asked his secretary to wrap these gifts: a clock with the company logo, a leather briefcase, a country ham, and a pen and pencil set marked "Made in Japan." His secretary wrapped the gifts attractively in bright red paper and with matching bows and mailed them to his Japanese hosts. What rules for appropriate gift giving in this culture have been followed? Which have been violated?

Case 2

A U.S. executive was invited to dine in the home of a Latin American businessman. The dinner invitation was for 9 p.m. The U.S. executive arrived promptly at 9 p.m. bearing a gift of an unwrapped bottle of Scotch for his host and a dozen yellow and white chrysanthemums for the businessman's wife. Discuss the appropriateness of the U.S. executive's behavior.

Case 3

Joe Anthony, a U.S. graduate student, was beginning a semester-long internship in Mexico City with an international health care products firm. After he had been there about a week, some male employees invited him out to a bar to sample the local specialty, bull's testicles. Joe had heard about this practice considered a sign of young Mexican machismo (male power). The idea did not appeal to him because something he had eaten recently had made him queasy. What are Joe's options? What are the possible implications or consequences of each option? What would you do?

Case 4

When Sara Canton boarded her flight to Barcelona in New York City, she was seated in the middle with an unkempt person who apparently had not bathed recently on one side and a crying baby on the other. The person in front of her immediately reclined his seat. Sara knew she would not be pleased making a seven-hour trip under these circumstances. What can Sara do to make the trip more bearable?

Activities

1. Practice introducing your U.S. manager to each of the following:
   a. An Italian manager, John Giovanni, with a college degree
   b. Chung Lo Wang, a manager from China
   c. Marco Comerlato Velasquez, a business associate from Brazil
   d. Thomas Edward Peacock, a British associate who has been knighted
2. Role play to show how a business card is presented to someone from Japan.
3. Review back issues of the *Wall Street Journal* or a news magazine such as *Time* and make a copy of an article related to a cultural faux pas committed by either a person from the United States when traveling abroad or someone from another culture when visiting the United States. Share your information with the class.
4. Research the dining practices of such countries as Zimbabwe, Samoa, and Tanzania; write a one-page summary identifying major differences between dining practices in the United States and these countries.
5. Research the tipping practices of a European and an Asian country of your choice and make a comparison with tipping practices in the United States. Report your findings to the class.
6. Research the gift-giving practices of one of the following countries and make a brief report to the class: Japan, Taiwan, Egypt, Argentina, or Germany. Include appropriate and inappropriate gifts and other related information, such as gift presentation and reciprocation.

References

Axtell, R. E. (1998). *Gestures: The do's and taboos of body language around the world.* New York: Wiley.

Axtell, R. E. (1993). *Do's and taboos around the world.* New York: Wiley.

Axtell, R. E. (1990). *Do's and taboos of hosting international visitors.* New York: Wiley.

Baldrige, L. (1993). *Letitia Baldrige's new complete guide to executive manners.* New York: Rawson Associates.

Barnum, C., & Wolniansky, N. (1989, April). Glitches in global gift giving. *Management Review,* 61–63.

Bosrock, M. M. (1997a). *Put your best foot forward: Asia.* St. Paul, MN: International Education Systems.

Bosrock, M. M. (1997b). *Put your best foot forward: South America.* St. Paul, MN: International Education Systems.

Bosrock, M. M. (1995). *Put your best foot forward: Europe.* St. Paul, MN: International Education Systems.

Braganti, N. L., & Devine, E. (1992). *European customs and manners.* New York: Meadowbrook.

CultureGrams. (2004). Lindon, UT: ProQuest Information and Learning Company.

Devine, E., & Braganti, N. L. (2000). *The travelers' guide to Latin American customs and manners.* New York: St. Martin's Griffin.

Devine, E., & Braganti, N. L. (1998). *The travelers' guide to Asian customs and manners.* New York: St. Martin's Griffin.

Devine, E., & Braganti, N. L. (1995). *The traveler's guide to African customs and manners.* New York: St. Martin's Griffin.

Devine, E., & Braganti, N. L. (1991). *The traveler's guide to Middle Eastern and North African customs and manners.* New York: St. Martin's Press.

Dosick, W. (2000). *The business bible.* Woodstock, UT: Jewish Lights Publishing.

Dresser, N. (2005). *Multicultural manners.* New York: Wiley.

Engholm, C. (1991). *When business east meets business west: The guide to practice and protocol in the Pacific Rim.* New York: Wiley.

Ford, C. (2003). *21st-century etiquette.* Guilford, CT: Penguin Putnam Publishing.

Fussell, P. (1983). *Class.* New York: Ballantine.

Glassman, A. (1998). *Can I FAX a thank-you note?* New York: Berkley.

Harris, P. R., Moran, R.T., & Moran, S.V. (2004). *Managing cultural differences* (6th ed.). Burlington, MA: Elsevier Butterworth-Heinemann.

Internet Penetration Rate—Top 20 countries. Internet Penetration Statistics, September 30, 2004. Internet.worldstats.com.

Kenton, S. B., & Valentine, D. (1997). *Crosstalk: Communicating in a multicultural workplace.* Upper Saddle River, NJ: Prentice Hall.

Kim, J. Y. (1993, July 11). Clinton couldn't get protocol right to save his Seoul. *The Commercial Appeal,* p. A5.

Miller, S. (2001). *E-mail etiquette.* New York: Warner Books.

Mitchell, M. (2000). *The complete idiot's guide to etiquette.* New York: Alpha Books.

Ricks, D. A. (1999). *Blunders in international business.* Cambridge, MA: Blackwell.

Sabath, A. M. (2002). *International business etiquette: Asia and the Pacific Rim.* New York: ASJA Press.

Sabath, A. M. (2000). *International business etiquette: Latin America.* Franklin Lakes, NJ: Career Press.

Sabath, A. M. (1999). *International business etiquette: Europe.* Franklin Lakes, NJ: Career Press.

Samovar, L. A., & Porter, R. E. (2004). *Communication between cultures* (5th ed.). Belmont, CA: Wadsworth.

Samovar, L. A., & Porter, R. E. (2002). *Intercultural communication: A reader* (10th ed.). Belmont, CA: Wadsworth.

Segaloff, N. (1998). *The everything etiquette book.* Holbrook, MA: Adams Media Corporation.

Stewart, M. Y. (1997). *The new etiquette.* New York: St. Martin's.

Turkington, C. (1999). *The complete idiot's guide to cultural etiquette.* Indianapolis: Alpha Books.

Yager, J. (2001). *Business protocol: How to survive & succeed in business.* New York: Wiley.

CHAPTER

9

BUSINESS AND SOCIAL CUSTOMS

Objectives

Upon completion of this chapter, you will

■ learn greeting customs as well as customary verbal expressions of persons of various countries.

■ understand the importance of a knowledge of male/female relationships and workplace equality to successful intercultural communication.

■ learn the roles that humor, superstition, and taboos play in understanding persons of other cultures.

■ understand the role that dress and appearance play in interacting with persons from other countries.

■ learn the importance of knowing about the customs associated with holidays and holy days of the country in which you are traveling or conducting business.

■ understand that office customs vary from culture to culture.

■ understand the importance of appropriate demeanor/behavior in intercultural encounters.

■ recognize that bribery is culturally relative and plays an unofficial role in doing business in many cultures.

■ recognize special food and meal customs considered typical of various cultures and how to show respect for consumption taboos of other countries.

Customs are behaviors generally expected in specific situations and are established, socially acceptable ways of behaving in given circumstances. Customs vary not only by country but also by regions or locations within a country. For example, in the United States, customs differ along north–south lines and urban–rural lines. In addition, religious backgrounds and ethnic identities account for differences in customs.

People of the United States have customary behaviors associated with certain holidays, such as eating turkey on Thanksgiving, giving gifts at Christmas, and staying up until midnight on New Year's Eve. Other customary behaviors are associated with greetings and verbal expressions, male/female relationships, dress and appearance, use of humor, belief in superstitions, and special foods and consumption taboos. Although it is impossible to identify all customs of a particular culture, certain customs are important to conducting business interculturally.

GREETING AND HANDSHAKING CUSTOMS

Customary greetings vary from culture to culture. Persons from other cultures are struck by the informality of U.S. Americans who often say "Hi!" to complete strangers. In most countries of the world, this practice is uncommon. People of the United States are often perceived as insincere when they use the standard greeting of "Hi, how are you?" which does not mean that they are actually inquiring on the state of someone's health. This outward show of friendliness is often misleading because people from the United States are actually private and slow to form friendships. The use of "Hello, I'm pleased to meet you" is preferable, as it conveys a more sincere message.

British-born journalist Henry Fairlie, in writing "Why I Love America," recalled this encounter with a four-year-old boy riding his tricycle in the suburbs shortly after his arrival in the United States:

"As I passed him, he said Hi!—just like that. No four-year-old boy had ever addressed me without an introduction before. Recovering from the culture shock, I found myself saying in return: Well—hi! He pedaled off, apparently satisfied."

Fairlie, who comes from a country where you can tell another person's class from their greeting, observed that the greeting "Hi!" is a democracy. In America, anyone can say "Hi!" to anyone else. (Fairlie, 1983)

In addition to the informal "Hi!" often used when meeting someone, persons of the United States engage in other ritualistic greeting behavior. When greeting an office colleague, one person will say, "Good morning, how are you?" The appropriate response is, "Fine, thank you. And how are you?" Some people make the mistake of forgetting that this is only a ritual and proceed to describe in detail the state of their health. Remember, the appropriate response is, "Fine, thanks."

Guenter Lensges, an exchange student from Germany, recalled his experience with ritualistic greetings when he returned to the campus apartment he shared with three U.S. students following his first day of classes.

When one of his roommates said, "Hey, man, what's going on?" he was impressed that they seemed interested in how his day had gone and proceeded to recount his experiences in his classes. Noticing the strange expressions on his roommates' faces, he asked, "Did I say something wrong?" They then explained to him, "When we say, 'Hey, man, what's going on?' we don't really want to know. You're supposed to say, 'Not much, man, and what's going on with you?'; then we'll say, 'Not much.'"

When greeting people, the handshake is customary in many countries. Egyptians, both men and women, shake hands when being introduced. Men of India shake hands with other men but not with women. In African countries, such as Nigeria and Kenya, shaking hands is customary. In Saudi Arabia, handshakes are numerous and elaborate. In Finland, handshakes are firm and are typical greeting behavior for men and women—women are customarily greeted first. Although a firm handshake is considered the norm in the United States, it may be considered impolite in some cultures. Handshakes in other cultures vary from the soft grasp of the British to the brusque grasp of Germans. A summary of how various cultures differ in their ideas of a proper handshake follows in Table 9-1.

TABLE 9-1	Handshakes by Culture
Culture	*Type of Handshake*
U.S. American	Firm
Asian	Gentle (shaking hands is unfamiliar and uncomfortable for some; the exception is the Korean, who usually has a firm handshake)
British	Soft
French	Light and quick (not offered to superiors); repeated on arrival and departure
German	Brusque and firm; repeated on arrival and departure
Latin American	Moderate grasp; repeated frequently
Middle Eastern	Gentle; repeated frequently

Source: Adapted from these books by Ann Marie Sabath: *International Business Etiquette: Asia and the Pacific Rim* (2002), *International Business Etiquette: Europe* (1999), and *International Business Etiquette: Latin America* (2000). Franklin Lakes, NJ: Career Press.

Although a kiss or hug is considered inappropriate as a form of greeting in the United States, in other countries it is customary. For example, in Saudi Arabia, the handshake is accompanied with a light kiss; even males in Saudi Arabia kiss both cheeks after a handshake. In the Russian states, the "bear hug" may follow a strong, firm handshake between good male friends; neighboring Finns, on the other hand, do not hug, kiss, or have body contact with strangers. People in Latin American countries also embrace, often accompanied by a couple of slaps on the back (Samovar & Porter, 2004) (see Figure 9-1). Egyptian women who are close friends, as well as women in some African countries, often hug or kiss each other as part of the greeting.

Asians, Northern Europeans, and most North Americans are uncomfortable with touching and hugging. People of Greece have no firm customs for greeting others; they may shake hands, embrace, and/or kiss a person at the first meeting or at every meeting. Bowing is the customary form of greeting in Japan. In China, bowing is also customary, but a handshake is also acceptable. When conducting business with people of Japan or China, the handshake is often combined with a bow so that each culture shows the other proper respect (Baldrige, 1993; Samovar & Porter, 2004) (see Figure 9-2). In India, the traditional greeting is the *Namaste,* which a person says while pressing palms together with fingers up and placing the hands below the chin; a slight bow accompanies this gesture when greeting supervisors or others to whom you want to show respect (*CultureGrams,* 2004).

FIGURE 9-1   Greetings in Latin American countries are accompanied by an embrace.

FIGURE 9-2   Greetings in Japan involve bowing at the waist.

VERBAL EXPRESSIONS

Although you are not expected to learn the language of every country with whom you may conduct business, if you plan an extended relationship with a particular culture, learning to speak the language (especially commonly used expressions) is important because you may have to communicate with persons who do not speak your language.

Make an effort to learn to say such basic expressions as "please" and "thank you," greetings, and other terms commonly used by people in the culture. Examples of such terms in French, German, and Spanish are listed in Table 9-2.

In addition to learning these expressions, knowing other verbal expressions customarily used in a culture is useful. In the United States, people often respond to

TABLE 9-2   Basic Expressions by Culture

English	*French*	*German*	*Spanish*
Good day	*Bonjour* (bawn-JHOOR)	*Guten Tag* (GOO-tun TAHK)	*Buenos días* (BWAY-nos DEE-ahs)
Good-bye	*Au revoir* (o reh-VWAHR)	*Auf Wiedersehen* (owf VEE-der-zeyn)	*Adiós* (ah-DYOS)
Please	*S'il vous plait* (seel-voo-PLEH)	*Bitte* (BIT-teh)	*Por favor* (POR fah-vor)
Thank you	*Merci* (mehr-SEE)	*Danke* (DUNK-uh)	*Gracias* (GRAH-see-ahs)
Good evening	*Bonsoir* (bawn-SWAHR)	*Guten Abend* (GOO-tun AH-bent)	*Buenas noches* (BWAY-nahs NO-chase)
Excuse me	*Excusez-moi* (ex-kyou-zay MWAH)	*Verzeihung* (fare-TSY-oong)	*Perdóneme* (per-DOH-nay-may)

someone with a one-word reply: "sure," "okay," and "nope." Although such brevity seems blunt and abrupt by foreign standards, it is simply an indication of the informality typical of U.S. persons. Some expressions are used only in certain regions of the United States. For example, people in the southern United States often say "Y'all come to see us" when bidding someone good-bye. The expected reply is "Thanks! Y'all come to see us, too." This verbal exchange should not be taken as an invitation to visit but is rather only a friendly ritual. In many other cultures and certain regions in the United States, however, such an expression is meant to be an actual invitation to visit.

Other expressions, such as "Don't mention it" and "Think nothing of it" in response to a courtesy or favor, are considered rude by persons of other cultures. These expressions, however, are consistent with the U.S. custom that people should be modest and should not brag on themselves. Some persons feel awkward when people compliment or thank them and simply do not know how to respond. When being thanked for a courtesy, a response of "You are welcome" is preferable. Other confusing verbal expressions used in the United States are "What's up?" and "How's it going?" Persons for whom English is a second language have no idea what the phrases mean. Avoid using idioms and slang when conversing with new speakers of English because they rely on the literal translation of words. For example, a newcomer to the United States did not accept a job on the "graveyard shift" because he thought he would be working in a cemetery (Dresser, 2005).

On meeting someone for the first time, U.S. persons engage in **chitchat** (small talk or light conversation). Small talk is important in getting to know another person before concentrating on business. In most cultures, starting business without light conversation is rude and insensitive. Chitchat often includes comments about the weather, the physical surroundings, the day's news, or almost anything of a nonsubstantive nature (Baldrige, 1993). People of the United States excel at small talk, as do Canadians and Australians. The British and the French are likewise masters of small talk. In the United States, small talk does not include topics related to politics, religion, personal income, or personal life. Likewise in Saudi Arabia, conversations about family members are usually inappropriate. In Latin America and Mexico, on the other hand, it is not only appropriate to inquire about the health of family members but also to have lengthy discussions about their well-being. Any inquiries about one's family in the United States is brief; for example, "How is your wife?" is answered with "Fine, thanks." Small talk seems to pose problems for people of some cultures. Germans, for example, simply do not believe in it. Swedes, usually fluent in English, have little to say in addition to talking about their jobs, which lasts 10 to 15 minutes. The Japanese are frightened by the idea of small talk, as are people of Finland, who actually buy books on the art of small talk (Lewis, 2000).

South Americans can talk incessantly for hours, despite their relatively deficient foreign language skills. Author Richard Lewis reported attending an all-Latin American cocktail party in Caracas that lasted from 7 p.m. to 1 a.m. He said, "There were 300 people present, very little to eat, nobody stopped talking, except to draw breath, for six hours flat; I do not remember a single word that was said." (Lewis, 2000)

When engaging in chitchat with someone of another culture, the best advice is probably to follow the other person's lead. If they talk about their family, talk about yours. If they initiate discussions of a political nature, continue the discourse with your own perceptions.

MALE/FEMALE RELATIONSHIPS AND WORKPLACE EQUALITY

In high-context societies such as the Arab culture, people have definite ideas on what constitutes proper behavior between males and females. In low-context cultures such as the United States, little agreement exists. Both people of the United States and visitors from other cultures have difficulty knowing how to proceed in male/female relationships in the United States because a wide range of behaviors may be observed.

A problem with understanding acceptable male/female relationships in any culture is the stereotypes that exist. For example, a stereotype of U.S. women originating primarily from U.S. television shows and movies is that they are aggressive, glamorous, and promiscuous (Axtell, Briggs, Corcoran, & Lamb, 1997). Correspondingly, U.S. American men are viewed as weak men who permit women to dominate them.

The equality of men and women in the workplace has been a sensitive issue in the United States. Although 60% of U.S. women of employment age work, they still do not receive equal pay and responsibility. Some U.S. men feel threatened by the more assertive roles many women are assuming. However, most people accept that men and women can work side by side in the workplace and that they can have a friendship that does not have a sexual component. U.S. men and women often have business colleagues of the opposite gender. These work relationships may involve business travel, and no assumption is made about any sexual involvement.

In other countries, however, treatment of men and women in the workplace differs substantially from that of the United States. In Mexico, for example, male supervisors customarily kiss their female secretaries on the cheek each morning or embrace them. Despite this custom (seen as undue familiarity by U.S. managers), problems with sexual harassment and gender discrimination are uncommon according to Mexican managers. U.S. managers interviewed, however, reported that Mexican managers do have such problems (Stephens & Greer, 1995).

In the Scandinavian countries, women and men are treated equally. Many Swedish women hold middle-management positions in business. In addition, Swedish women are found in political positions, including parliament. In Iceland, the first country to have a Woman's party, women are very evident in the workplace. In fact, 70% of women in Iceland have jobs. In Finland, women hold about 38% of positions in parliament. However, women in Finland, like U.S. women, do not earn as much as men (Turkington, 1999).

In India, women do not enjoy the same privileges as men; in addition, in Saudi Arabia, women are not considered equal to men. In Egypt, only one tenth of workers are women. Although they hold positions as doctors and secretaries, few women hold executive jobs.

Korean women have traditionally not held prominent positions in government and business. Although some progress in this area has been made, women still hold low-ranking jobs. China, too, is a male-dominated country, however, women do hold important managerial positions in business (Bosrock, 1997a).

Women in the Netherlands comprise less than one third of the work force. Women who work outside the home usually have low-paying jobs; few hold managerial positions. Likewise, in Belgium and Germany, women are more likely to be in support staff jobs rather than in managerial positions. In both countries, women seem to be making progress in assuming leadership positions as the younger generation is more accepting of women in higher-level positions (Bosrock, 1995). Brazilian women are not only accepted but are well respected in business, medicine, and education (Bosrock, 1997b).

HUMOR IN BUSINESS

As more and more companies conduct business internationally, frequent opportunities exist for businesspersons to interact in an attempt to develop a good relationship. Using humorous anecdotes is a way of breaking the ice and establishing a relaxed atmosphere prior to the start of business in international meetings.

Although humor is a universal human characteristic, what is perceived as humorous varies from culture to culture. In the United States, presentations are often started with a joke or cartoon related to the topic to be covered. In addition to the United States, most European countries use humor during business meetings. The British, especially, intertwine humor in business discussions. When humor is used in business situations with Asian audiences, on the other hand, few are amused (except for Koreans, who seem to appreciate everybody's jokes). British humor is often self-deprecating. Egyptians, too, have a good sense of humor that is self-deprecating. Visitors, however, should not join in. Although it is fine for them to laugh at themselves, others may not do so (Turkington, 1999). Asian humor finds little merit in jokes about sex, religion, or minorities; however, they will laugh out of politeness when a joke is told. They take what is said literally and do not understand U.S. American humor. Germans, too, find humor out of place during business meetings. They take business seriously and do not appreciate joking remarks during negotiations. When a presentation in Germany was begun with a cartoon deriding European cultural differences, no one laughed. As the week progressed, people started laughing both in and out of the sessions. Later the presenters learned that cartoons were not appropriate in a professional setting of strangers. At the conclusion of negotiations, however, Germans enjoy relaxing and telling jokes in local bars or restaurants (Axtell, 1999; Trompenaars & Hampden-Turner, 1998).

Is there such a thing as international humor? Yes–some humor is acceptable internationally, such as slapstick, restaurant jokes, and humorous stories about golfers. Even in international jokes, however, people have their own nuances to make the jokes/anecdotes amusing to members of their own culture. In the United States, for example, sarcasm and kidding accompany humor; in Australia, humor is barbed and provocative (Lewis, 2000). In some countries, the people enjoy making citizens of a neighboring country the butt of their jokes. Belgians, for example, like to direct humor at their neighbors the Dutch, and likewise the Dutch direct humor at the Belgians. The same is true of the British and the Irish (Axtell, 1999).

Some businesspersons with global experience recommend that jokes be avoided with people of diverse cultures; they maintain that American humor is hard to export and appreciate. Even though the intention of humor is to put your international colleagues at ease and create a more relaxed environment, there is great risk of offending someone of another culture or of telling a story that no one understands. In short, we do not all laugh at the same things (Axtell, 1999).

A New York businessman who frequently traveled to Japan on business often used a translator for his speeches. After one such speech, he learned that the Japanese interpreter's version of his opening remarks went like this:

"American businessman is beginning speech with thing called joke. I am not sure why, but all American businessmen believe it necessary to start speech with joke. (Pause) He is telling joke now, but frankly you would not understand joke so I won't translate it. He thinks I am telling you joke now. Polite thing to do when he finishes is to laugh. (Pause) He is getting close. (Pause) Now!"

The audience not only laughed appreciatively, but stood and applauded as well. Later he commented to the translator, "I've been giving speeches in this country for several years, and you are the first translator who knows how to tell a good joke." (Axtell, 1990)

SUPERSTITIONS AND TABOOS

Superstitions are beliefs that are inconsistent with the known laws of science or what a society considers to be true and rational. Examples of superstitions include a belief that special charms, omens, or rituals have supernatural powers. Superstitions that are treated rather casually in Europe and North America are taken seriously in other cultures. Although few U.S. persons consult astrologers or fortune-tellers for advice on business matters, in other cultures, spiritualists are highly regarded and may be consulted in making business decisions. When doing business with persons who take business advice from seers, it is best to respect these beliefs. In parts of Asia, for example, fortune-telling and palmistry are considered influential in the lives and business dealings of the people.

In many cultures, bad luck and even death are associated with certain numbers. People of the United States, for example, think that 13 is an unlucky number. Most U.S. American hotels do not have a 13th floor, and even a hotel number ending in 13 may be refused. Friday the 13th is perceived as an unlucky day. Many U.S. persons will not schedule important events, such as weddings or major surgery, on this day. The Chinese, who also believe that good luck or bad is associated with certain numbers, feel that four is the most negative number because it sounds like the word for death. Hotels in China, Hong Kong, and Taiwan often have no fourth floor, and some Asian airports have no Gate 4. Conversely, some numbers have positive meanings in China. For example, the number six represents happiness, and nine represents long life. The number of people in a photograph also has significance. Many Chinese believe that having an uneven number of people in a photograph will bring bad luck and that having three people in a photograph will result in dire consequences–the middle person will die (Dresser, 2005). Those who take pictures as mementos for their Chinese business friends should keep this in mind. Additional superstitions regarding numbers and gift giving (e.g., the number of flowers to give as a gift) were covered in the preceding chapter on gift-giving etiquette.

Other superstitions held by persons in some cultures include the following:

- Events on New Year's Day predict what will happen for the entire year.
- Sweeping the floor on New Year's Day may sweep away your good luck for the coming year; likewise, bathing on this day washes away your good luck.
- Performing certain rituals protects a newborn child from evil spirits.
- Attaching old shoes to the car of newlyweds ensures fertility.
- Walking under a ladder or breaking a mirror brings bad luck.
- Giving too much attention to a newborn places the child in jeopardy; the evil spirits will harm the baby if it receives a lot of attention (Dresser, 2005).

Many South Americans respect these superstitions:

- Bringing coral or shells into your home brings bad luck.
- Putting your purse on the floor results in your money running away.
- Passing salt hand to hand brings bad luck.
- Scheduling important events on Tuesday the 13th should be avoided as this is an unlucky day (Bosrock, 1997b).

Taboos are practices or verbal expressions considered by a society or culture as improper or unacceptable. Taboos often are rooted in the beliefs of the people of a specific region or culture and are passed down from generation to generation. In Arab countries, for example, it is considered taboo to ask about the health of a man's wife. In Taiwan, messages should not be written in red ink, as this has death connotations. Writing a person's name in red also has negative associations in Korea, parts of Mexico, and among some Chinese (Lewis, 2000).

An American English teacher made comments and constructive criticisms in red ink on her students' papers. Although U.S. students were accustomed to this practice, her Korean students were not. These red-inked notes sent shock waves through the families of Korean students, who associated red ink with death. When the families told the principal of this taboo, he asked all teachers to refrain from using red ink on any student's paper. (Dresser, 2005)

In Malaysia, pointing with your index finger is taboo, but you may point with the thumb. Indonesia has certain taboos related to the head. Because the head is considered a sacred part of the body, it should not be touched by someone else. The practice in the United States of patting young children on the head would be cause for great concern in Indonesia. Another taboo is placing your head in a higher position than the head of a senior person. People of the Russian Federation have numerous taboos: no whistling in the street, no coats worn indoors, and no lunches on park lawns. Taboos of the people of Madagascar are perhaps the most unusual: Pregnant women are forbidden from eating brains or sitting in doorways, women may not wash their brothers' clothes, and children are not permitted to say their father's name or make reference to any part of his body (Lewis, 2000).

DRESS AND APPEARANCE

What you wear sends a nonverbal message about you and your company. Because clothes can enhance or destroy your credibility, you should determine what attire is customary in the countries you visit. According to Axtell (1993), the general rule for business everywhere is to be "buttoned up": conservative suit and tie for men and dress or skirted suit for women.

An American television program investigated the impact of an attractive, well-groomed appearance in both social and business situations. "Well-groomed men and women were placed in identical situations with less polished participants who had neglected their appearance. Every single time, the more highly groomed individual got not only the date or the help with a flat tire but also the job offer and the higher salary." (Bixler, 1997, p. 16)

According to U.S. researchers and image consultants, people who wear suits, whether male or female, are perceived as more professional than those who wear any other type of attire. Wearing professional attire is recommended when a person wants to be taken seriously. For men, professional attire includes very dark suits in charcoal gray or navy with a white, pastel, or pinstripe long-sleeved cotton shirt; for women, a medium-range or navy blue suit with a white blouse. A second choice for women is a beige suit with a light blue blouse (Baldrige, 1993; Molloy, 1996). Fabric is also important in projecting credibility, status, and power. Fabrics of pure fibers (silk, wool, and cotton) or fabrics that have the look of pure fibers convey higher credibility and status than synthetic fibers such as polyester. The recommended suit for both men and women is 100% wool (Molloy, 1996).

Business dress in Canada, England, France, Germany, Japan, and Mexico is similar to that worn in the United States with slight variances. In Canada, people dress more conservatively and formally than people in the United States. The French are very fashion conscious as France is considered a leader in fashion. When conducting business in Europe, remember that dress is very formal; coats and ties are required for business. Jackets stay on in the office and restaurants even when the weather is hot (Braganti & Devine, 1992). Dress in Japan is also formal. Japanese women dress very conservatively and usually wear muted colors to the office. (This custom seems to be changing somewhat in larger cities, especially in companies that conduct business globally.) Care should be exercised in wearing very casual attire in public in these countries, as this practice is considered inappropriate (Devine & Braganti, 1998).

Dress standards in the U.S. workplace became increasingly casual in the 1990s as did dress standards in many European companies. However, this trend toward casual office attire in the United States appears to be over (Fenton, 2002). Companies became concerned with their corporate image, as many employees seemed to be unable to distinguish between casual and slovenly. As a result, numerous companies revoked their casual dress policies a decade after the trend started; casual attire was wreaking havoc on the workplace, and some firms felt that dressing too casually was costing their company business (Hudson, 2002). Because people, particularly those from other cultures, tend to make assumptions about another person's educational level, status, and income based on dress alone, those interested in career advancement and in careers in international business should probably dress conservatively in traditional business attire—suits for men and suits or dresses for women.

> At a Washington firm, a group of Japanese businessmen who came for a meeting on a Friday found a room full of casually dressed people. They made a hasty retreat, believing they had the wrong office (Alvarez-Correa, 1996, p. 134).

Casual attire that is even more informal than is the norm in the United States is appropriate in certain cultures. In the Philippines, men wear the *barong*—a loose, white- or cream-colored shirt with tails out and no jacket or tie. In Indonesia, *batiks* (brightly patterned shirts worn without tie or jacket) are worn (Axtell, 1993).

Although Western business dress has been widely adopted among other cultures, you might want to learn cultural distinctions in appropriate business attire. When visiting Saudi Arabia, for example, the Saudi might wear the traditional Arabic white, flowing robe and head cloth. You would not, however, attempt to dress in a similar manner. You would dress in the same manner as you would for an important meeting in your U.S. office.

Color of clothing is also a consideration because in some cultures color has strong associations. Do not wear black or solid white in Thailand because these colors have funereal connotations. Avoid wearing all white in the People's Republic of China, as white is the symbol of mourning. In the United States, black is typically worn at funerals but has no special significance in business situations.

Shoes are considered inappropriate in certain situations in various cultures. They should not be worn in Muslim mosques and Buddhist temples. Shoes should also be removed when entering most Asian homes or restaurants. Place them neatly together facing the door you entered. Following the host's lead is good advice; if the host goes without shoes, so do you. Remember that in the Arab culture, the soles of the feet should not be shown, so keep both feet on the floor or the bottoms of your feet covered.

Women who conduct business abroad should be especially careful to conform to local customs concerning appropriate attire. Women conducting business in the Arabian countries, for example, should avoid wearing slacks and should wear clothes that give good coverage, such as long-sleeved dresses and dress/skirt lengths below the knees. In Europe, women do not wear slacks to the office or to nice restaurants. Ask before you go; consult a colleague who is familiar with the culture (Axtell, 1993; Devine & Braganti, 1998, 2000; Turkington, 1999).

> Dress is an important factor in most women's careers. Research shows that when a woman dresses for success, it does not guarantee success, but if she dresses poorly or inappropriately, it almost always ensures failure (Molloy, 1996, p. xi).

CUSTOMS ASSOCIATED WITH HOLIDAYS AND HOLY DAYS

An awareness of the holidays and holy days of other cultures is important in scheduling telephone calls and business trips.

Holidays may celebrate a prominent person's birthday (Washington's Birthday) or a historic event (Independence Day) or pay homage to a group (Veterans' Day and Memorial Day). Holy days are associated with religious observances (Ramadan, Christmas, Easter, and Yom Kippur). Because business may not be conducted on some of these special days, consider this information when planning a trip abroad.

People who travel to the United States, for example, should understand that it is not customary to conduct business on Christmas Day or Thanksgiving. Business is rarely conducted on the Fourth of July when Independence Day is celebrated with fireworks, picnics, parades, and parties. Many businesses, with the exception of retail establishments, are closed on Sunday, which is the Sabbath for many religions. The Sabbath in Israel, on the other hand, is observed on Saturday, while the Arabs observe the Sabbath on Friday.

In some countries, holidays are similar to those celebrated in the United States. Some Catholic countries, such as Germany, have a carnival season (similar to New Orleans' Mardi Gras), which is not a good time for conducting business. Many countries celebrate the New Year; the nature, duration, and time of the year of the celebration may vary. In Mexico, for example, the two-week period including Christmas and New Year's Day is not a good time to conduct business, nor is the two-week period prior to Easter. Businesspeople are usually traveling with their families during this time.

The holidays observed in the United States and those observed by the 10 countries with which the United States conducts most of its international business are listed here (*CultureGrams,* 2004; Sabath, 1999, 2002).

United States	New Year's Day (January 1)
	Birthday of Martin Luther King Jr. (third Monday in January)
	Presidents' Day (third Monday in February)
	Memorial Day (last Monday in May)
	Independence Day (July 4)
	Labor Day (first Monday in September)
	Columbus Day (second Monday in October)
	Veterans' Day (November 11)
	Thanksgiving (fourth Thursday in November)
	Christmas (December 25)
Canada	New Year's Day (January 1)
	Easter Sunday and Monday*
	Labor Day (May 1)
	Victoria Day (third Monday in May)
	Canada Day (July 1)
	Thanksgiving Day (second Monday in October)
	All Saints' Day (November 1)
	Remembrance Day (November 11)
	Christmas (December 25)
	Boxing Day (December 26)
	Quebec has two additional holidays: The Carnival de Quebec (February) and St. Jean Baptiste Day (June 24)

(continued)

China	New Year's Day (January 1)
	Chinese Lunar New Year and Spring Festival*
	International Working Woman's Day (March 8)
	Labor Day (May 1)
	Youth Day (May 4)
	Children's Day (June 1)
	People's Liberation Army Day (August 1)
	National Day (October 1)
England	New Year's Day (January 1)
	Good Friday*
	May Day*
	Easter Sunday and Monday*
	Spring Bank Holiday*
	Late Summer Holiday*
	Christmas (December 25)
	Boxing Day (December 26)
France	New Year's Day (January 1)
	Mardi Gras (Shrove Tuesday)*
	Easter Sunday and Monday*
	Labor Day (May 1)
	Liberation Day (May 8)
	Ascension Day*
	Whit Monday*
	Bastille Day (July 14)
	Pentecost*
	Assumption of the Virgin Mary (August 15)
	All Saints' Day (November 1)
	World War I Armistice Day*
	Christmas (December 25)
Germany	New Year's Day (January 1)
	Good Friday*
	Easter Sunday and Monday*
	Labor Day (May 1)
	Ascension Day*
	Whit Monday*
	Day of German Unity (October 3)
	All Saints' Day (November 1)
	Day of Prayer and Repentance*
	Christmas (December 25)
Japan	New Year's Day (January 1)
	Coming of Age Day (January 15)

(continued)

	National Foundation Day (February 11)
	Vernal Equinox (March 21)
	Greenery Day (April 29)
	Constitution Day (May 3)
	Children's Day (May 5)
	Bon Festival (August 15)
	Respect for the Aged Day (September 15)
	Autumnal Equinox (September 23)
	Sports Day (October 10)
	Culture Day (November 3)
	Labor Thanksgiving Day (November 23)
	Emperor Akihito's Birthday (December 23)
Mexico	New Year's Day (January 1)
	St. Anthony's Day (January 17)
	Constitution Day (February 5)
	Carnival Week*
	Birthday of Benito Juarez (March 21)
	Easter*
	Labor Day (May 1)
	Cinco de Mayo (May 5)
	Corpus Christi*
	Assumption of the Virgin Mary (August 15)
	President's Annual Message (September 1)
	Independence Day (September 16)
	Columbus Day (October 12)
	All Saints' Day (November 1)
	All Souls' Day (November 2)
	Revolution Day (November 20)
	Day of the Virgin Guadalupe (December 12)
	Christmas (December 25)
The Netherlands	New Year's Day (January 1)
	Queen Beatrix's Birthday (April 30)
	Liberation Day (May 5)
	Christmas (December 25–26)
South Korea	The New Year (January 1–3)
	The Lunar New Year (January or February*)
	Independence Day (March 1)
	Buddha's Birthday (April or May*)
	Memorial Day (June 6)
	Constitution Day (July 17)
	Liberation Day (August 15)

(continued)

	Ch'usŏk, Harvest Moon Festival (September or October*)
	National Foundation Day (October 3)
	Christmas (December 25)
Taiwan	Founding Day (January 1)
	Chinese Lunar New Year (January or February*)
	Birthday of Confucius (September 28)
	Double Ten National Day (October 10)
	Taiwan Restoration Day (October 25)
	Constitution Day (December 25)
*Dates vary.	

In addition to their holidays, some countries have other times during which business is curtailed. Do not expect to conduct business in Europe during August, as this is considered the vacation month, and many people close their businesses during this time. In addition to the Sabbath, little business is conducted with the Arabs during Ramadan, the month-long Islamic fast. In Japan, many companies close from April 29 to May 5 to celebrate various holidays and birthdays.

OFFICE CUSTOMS AND PRACTICES

Office customs and practices include typical hours of work, lunch and break times, degree of formality, and hiring/firing.

Customarily, hours of work in U.S. offices are 9 a.m. to 5 p.m. Employees are expected to start work promptly and to stay busy even during slow periods. In other words, employees are expected to find work to do and never be idle. In many countries, on the other hand, employees feel free to read the newspaper or visit with colleagues when there is nothing pressing, especially when the supervisor is out of the office.

Office hours in other countries vary. In Iran, for example, business hours are from 9:30 a.m. to 1 p.m. and 2 to 5 p.m., Monday through Friday. In some South American countries, such as Brazil and Colombia, the workweek is 8 a.m. to 6 p.m., Monday through Friday. Some offices and stores close from noon to 2 p.m. for lunch. Peru has one of the longest workweeks in the world: 48 hours with businesses open at least six days a week (Bosrock, 1997b).

The lunch period in U.S. firms may vary from 30 minutes to an hour, and break times are usually one 15-minute period in the morning with a second 15-minute period in the afternoon. These should be kept to the time specified, as extended periods result in a reprimand because in the United States "time is money." U.S. persons, who are time- and productivity-conscious seriously question the workday customs that commonplace throughout Europe. For example, Europeans have a 1- to 1½-hour lunch break, 20-minute morning and afternoon breaks (often including beer or wine), and 15 minutes at the end of the workday for cleanup time. Thus, their nine-hour workday is, in reality, a seven-hour workday (Utroska, 1992).

Hiring and firing practices vary according to the culture. In the United States, people are hired with the understanding that retention and promotions depend on performing the job satisfactorily and on getting along with their colleagues. In other words, hiring and retention are based on job effectiveness and job performance. Although workers cannot legally be fired without cause, it is understood that no job is permanent. In Europe, on the other hand, everyone in the firm has a contract that virtually guarantees permanent employment regardless of the financial condition of the company. Likewise, in such countries as Japan, employers consider an employee's job to be permanent unless the person breaks the law or is guilty of a moral turpitude. In such socialist countries as France and England, the only grounds for job termination are criminal behavior. Employees who are dismissed receive generous severance pay by U.S. standards. Employees receive a three-months' notice at full salary and benefits while they look for a new job. Executives receive an even more generous severance package: a full year's salary plus one month's pay for each year of company service plus accumulated vacation pay (Utroska, 1992). In many Asian cultures, the company is considered an extension of the family. In the United States, workers are simply employees, and the company does not serve as an extended family. Problems sometimes arise when Japanese companies take over U.S. firms. Because Japanese managers assume their employees will be with them their entire careers, they think they are entitled to ask personal questions related to the prospective employee's home life and even make recommendations regarding the improvement of their personal appearance. They then discover that such questions and comments are illegal in the United States (Dresser, 2005).

The degree of formality found in U.S. offices varies; in major corporations, especially financial institutions and those in large cities, more formality often exists than in small companies in rural areas. Characteristics of an informal atmosphere include the use of first names at all levels, frequent small talk and joking, and, in recent years, more casual attire. This informal atmosphere does not indicate a lack of respect as would be the case in many European countries.

Another important aspect of office relationships is the appropriateness of showing emotions at work. Cultures that are primarily affective feel it acceptable to show emotions; those who are emotionally neutral control or mask their feelings. In an exercise reported by Trompenaars and Hampden-Turner (1998), participants from various cultures were asked whether they would express their feelings openly if they became upset about something at work. The highest percentage of persons who would not show their emotions openly were from Ethiopia, Japan, and Poland, although the lowest percentage of persons who would not express emotions were from Kuwait, Egypt, Spain, and Cuba. No pattern was apparent by continent; the United States was in the middle range, with 43% of persons indicating they would not show emotions at work.

CUSTOMARY DEMEANOR/BEHAVIOR

What is considered customary behavior in one culture may be unacceptable in another. **Demeanor** involves a person's conduct or deportment and is influenced by culture. Behavior in public places is culture specific. U.S. Americans speak louder in public than people of Germany, and people from Brazil or Nigeria speak louder than people of the United States. The type of public place also affects the voice volume that is considered acceptable. At sports events, it is acceptable to make more noise than inside a shopping mall or health club. Good advice to follow when in a foreign country is to observe the behavior of the nationals and avoid calling attention to yourself by speaking louder than those around you.

The following rules apply to appropriate behavior in public places in the United States:

- Keep to the right when walking in malls or on the street.
- Wait your turn when standing in line at the post office, bank, or theater.
- Give priority to the first person who arrives (rather than to people who are older or wealthier as is done in Asian cultures).
- Do not block traffic.
- Do not block someone's view at a ball game or other public event.
- Be considerate of nonsmokers.
- Treat clerks, taxi drivers, and other service personnel with courtesy and respect because in the United States the principle of equality prevails.

Courtesy is, in fact, important in most areas of the United States. The use of "please" when you are making a request is expected; "thank you" is considered appropriate when someone has granted a request or performed a service. People of all social and educational levels are accorded equal courtesy.

Another behavior that varies with the culture is the extent of touching in public places. People in the United States usually avoid situations in which they would be touching strangers in public. They avoid getting on a crowded elevator because they are uncomfortable with physical contact. If they must get on a crowded elevator, they observe "elevator etiquette," refraining from speaking, facing the front, and watching the floor indicator. One exception seems to be subway trains, where people are often too crowded to move. People in South America, on the other hand, think nothing of squeezing onto a crowded bus or elevator and pushing through a crowd.

A behavior of U.S. Americans that seems unusual to those of many other countries is doing "menial" jobs. In fact, the United States is often referred to as a "do-it-yourself" society. Regardless of wealth, position, or social standing, people of the United States are often found mowing their lawn, washing their car, or building a patio. Reasons for this custom vary; some U.S. persons point out that hiring household help or a gardener represents a loss of privacy. Others reason that they prefer to do the work themselves and use the money they would spend on service personnel for vacations, sports, and labor-saving appliances. When both adults work, home cleaning services or domestic help may be used for a limited number of hours each week. In many European and South American countries, on the other hand, numerous service people are often employed by businesspersons, government officials, and professionals. Households commonly have a cook, maid, and gardener.

BRIBERY

A custom that has undergone close scrutiny in the past few years is bribery. **Bribery** is giving or promising something, often money, to influence another person's actions. In Mexico, bribes are known as *mordida*; in Southeast Asia, *kumshaw*; and in the Middle East, *baksheesh*. Although bribery is not officially sanctioned or condoned in any country, it is unofficially a part of business in many cultures. The practice is often referred to as "greasing the palm" and is considered neither unethical nor immoral in a number of countries. In Nigeria, for example, a person must pay the customs agent in order to leave the airport; in Thailand and Indonesia, getting a driver's license involves giving a tip to an agent (Engholm & Rowland, 1996).

The United States has the most restrictive laws against bribery in the world. Companies found guilty of paying bribes to foreign officials can be fined up to $1 million, and guilty employees may be fined up to $10,000 (Engholm, 1991). Many U.S. competitors, including Italian, German, and Japanese firms, not only use bribery in international transactions but also may deduct the amount of the bribe on their taxes as a necessary business expense.

> Mike Lorelli of Pizza Hut shared this experience related to bribery in other cultures:
>   In the Middle East or Brazil, they would think you are crazy for not offering a bribe because to them there is absolutely nothing wrong with bribery. You're an oddball, but there is not a thing you can do about it. (Engholm & Rowland, 1996, p. 133)

Managers in the United States are faced with situations that are considered illegal in their country that are not only lawful but also an accepted part of doing business in other countries. They must, therefore, be aware that as business becomes globalized, different perceptions exist regarding the appropriateness of certain incentives. What is perceived as bribery is culturally relative just as a person's conscience can become "culturally conditioned." What is considered a tip (to ensure promptness) in one culture is considered illegal in another (Harris, Moran, & Moran, 2004). Although people of the United States are not legally permitted to accept bribes, many U.S. businesspersons provide favorite clients with box seats at sporting events or entertain them lavishly (Dresser, 2005). Some consider this practice a form of bribery. Additional information on bribery is presented in chapter 12.

SPECIAL FOODS AND CONSUMPTION TABOOS

Most cultures have unusual foods that are viewed with surprise or even disdain by persons in other cultures. Foods that are common in the United States that people in other cultures find unusual include corn on the cob (in some countries considered a food for animals), grits, popcorn, marshmallows, and crawfish (Axtell, 1993) (see Figure 9-3).

Foods in other cultures that concern some U.S. Americans include Japanese sushi (raw fish), shark fin soup in Hong Kong, dog meat in South Korea, and sheep's eyeballs in Saudi Arabia. In parts of Mexico, chicken soup may contain the chicken's feet; in China, you may be served duck's feet (see Figure 9-4).

> A college professor from the United States who had just arrived in La Paz, Bolivia, for a two-year teaching assignment at the local university was invited to dine with U.S. colleagues at a well-known local restaurant. She was assured that the eatery's specialty was mixed grill—a variety of meats grilled at the table. After consuming one chewy morsel, she made the mistake of asking what it was. The reply: stuffed cow's teats!

Because you are expected to eat what you are served in other countries, you may find it advisable to swallow quickly, avoid asking what it is, or pretend to eat by moving the food around so that it changes form. People who are experienced travelers also advise cutting the food into very thin slices and imagining that the unusual food, such as snake or dog meat, looks or tastes like something palatable (e.g., chicken).

> Master of five languages, Patrick Larbuisson eats sheep intestines to help grease business deals in Saudi Arabia. He swallows with a smile but is "sick like hell the next day" (Jones, 1993).

Knowing consumption taboos of the host culture is important. People in the United States, for example, do not knowingly eat horse meat, although no religious taboo is associated with this practice. South Koreans, on the other hand, consider dog meat a delicacy. Strict Muslims do not consume pork (or any animal that is a scavenger) or alcohol. Orthodox Jews eat neither pork nor shellfish. They also observe such rules as not serving meat and dairy products together and requiring that cattle or fowl be ritually slaughtered (i.e., kosher). Strict Muslims also observe ritual slaughtering. Hindus do not eat any beef because the cow is considered sacred. People from such countries as India are often vegetarians because of personal or religious beliefs (Axtell, 1993).

FIGURE 9-3   Popcorn (a), crawfish (b), and corn on the cob (c) are considered unusual U.S. foods.

FIGURE 9-4   Sheep's eyeballs (a), snake (b), and chicken soup containing the feet (c) are foods in other countries considered unusual by U.S. standards.

Because business encounters are often conducted in social settings, you should become familiar with special foods associated with the host culture as well as consumption taboos so that your lack of knowledge of cultural eating habits will not negatively affect the communication process. The following section identifies special foods and consumption practices/taboos associated with the United States and with the

10 countries with which the United States conducts most of its international business: Canada, China, England, France, Germany, Japan, Mexico, the Netherlands, South Korea, and Taiwan. To secure information about countries not specifically identified, consult such sources as *CultureGrams* published by ProQuest Information and Learning, the source used for much of the following country-specific information on food customs. The 2004 edition contains briefings on more than 182 countries.

United States

The majority of U.S. people eat the meat of animals except for certain parts of the animal, such as the feet and eyes. Most U.S. people do not feel comfortable eating something they cannot easily identify. Meats that are consumed are beef, pork, and fowl as well as fish and shellfish. Fresh vegetables and fruits are enjoyed and easily obtained year-round.

U.S. Americans are great supporters of the fast-food industry, frequenting such restaurants as McDonald's, Pizza Hut, KFC, and Taco Bell. In metropolitan areas, ethnic and international cuisine is readily available.

Canada

Although the majority of Canadian people eat many of the same foods as people in the United States, the French influence is apparent in restaurants in many parts of Canada. Canadians along the Atlantic seaboard maintain a diet of seafood, including lobster and seaweed. Canadians along the Pacific Ocean are partial to smoked salmon. Canadians in the interior eat more grain products and red meats. As in the United States, ethnic and international cuisine is readily available in the metropolitan areas.

China

Food specialties in China vary from region to region. Roast Peking duck served with thin pancakes is a famous specialty in northern China. In Canton, a specialty is *dim sum*, which is a light meal consisting of small portions of food such as steamed meat and shrimp dumplings or steamed rolls with chicken served in bamboo baskets. Stuffed bean curd is also a Cantonese specialty. In Shanghai, a typical dish is sweet-and-sour spareribs. In other parts of China, *man tou* (steamed bread) is a favorite food. Noodles, rice, potatoes, and tofu are staples in the Chinese diet. Although dairy products are not readily available, fresh fruits and vegetables are enjoyed when they are in season. Dessert usually consists of fruit; seeds and nuts are typical snack foods.

England

Although similarities exist between consumption practices of the United States and England, differences are numerous. Kippers (smoked herring) and kidneys are often served at breakfast. Another difference is the serving of tea every afternoon from 3:30 to 4:30, a tradition that might include serving small sandwiches of cucumber, watercress, and egg as well as cookies and cakes. English food tends to include a lot of meat and potatoes. Popular meats include beef, mutton, and fish. Sauces and fancy preparations are not considered necessary. Cooked vegetables are also an important part of the meal. Tea and beer are popular drinks, and mixed drinks, as in much of Europe, are served with no ice or with one ice cube.

France

People of France, who typically have only coffee and a croissant for breakfast, eat lunch around noon and their main meal about 8 p.m. Although the French have resisted foreign fast food in the past, this appears to be changing as hamburger restaurants are becoming more popular. The French are renowned for their fine wines and cuisine. Eating is an art in France, and the presentation of the meal is as important as the food. French sauces, soups, breads, and pastries have been the measure of fine cooking in the Western world since the Middle Ages (Braganti & Devine, 1992).

Germany

Germany, like England, tends to have a cuisine that is meat-and-potatoes oriented. Because many cuts of meat are tough in texture, most foods are cooked for a lengthy time or cut up and served with sauces. Foods considered unusual by U.S. standards include *eisbein* (pig's knuckle), *schavelfleish* (raw hamburger), and *hasenpfeffer* (rabbit stew). The serving of warm beer, wine, and soft drinks is common in Germany.

Japan

An example of a food a U.S. person would consider unusual is dried squid, a food that is symbolic of happiness and served at New Year's in Japan. Another unusual food is *fugu* (blowfish or glowfish), which requires special preparation, as the liver and ovaries contain a dangerous poison. The Japanese diet consists of very little meat and large quantities of rice and vegetables. Coffee has surpassed tea as the preferred drink. Food presentation is a very important part of the meal.

Mexico

Typical Mexican cuisine includes tortillas, beans, and various soups, such as *sopa de lima* (chicken and lime soup). An hors d'oeuvres that people of the United States find unusual is *chicharrón* (pork crackling served with a piquant sauce). In some parts of Mexico, a favorite dish is *pollo borracho* (chicken flavored with a tequila sauce). Other foods include *ceviche* (raw fish with onions, tomatoes, lime juice, and chiles) and *huevos motuleños* (corn tortillas with black beans, ham, fried eggs, and tomato sauce). Many foods are highly spiced; bland foods, such as breads and rice, are used to temper the hot seasonings.

The Netherlands

The Dutch are famous for their pastries. For breakfast or lunch, most Dutch people like something sweet, such as a chocolate spread on their bread or raisin rolls. Seafood is part of their diet, including eel and herring. The Dutch like French fries, but they are eaten with mayonnaise, rather than ketchup. Dutch people are well known for their breaks at 10 a.m. and 4 p.m. at which time they have coffee, usually with cream and sugar, and pastries or cookies.

South Korea

The diet of Koreans includes spicy foods, such as their pickled cabbage. They consume various types of soups and dishes that combine rice with such foods as red beans and with meats, especially chicken and beef. Fish and seafood, including squid, sea cucumbers, and octopus, are also part of the Korean diet. Barley tea is a favorite beverage.

Visitors may want to avoid dog soup and live octopus. Although alcoholic beverages are an important part of business entertaining, women should consume only nonalcoholic drinks, such as juices or sodas.

Taiwan

The Taiwanese diet includes a lot of rice. In fact, the people of Taiwan consume it at practically every meal. They also eat pork, chicken, seafood (including squid, clams, and oysters), and vegetables, all of which are typically stir-fried. Unusual foods consumed in Taiwan include jellyfish, turtle, and snake. Other favorite foods are noodles, soup, bread, and fruit. Many foods are served with sauces. Although tea is consumed between meals, beverages are usually not served with their meals, except for soy milk at breakfast. Visitors should try everything, make favorable comments about the various dishes, and leave something on the plate to indicate satisfaction with the meal.

Terms

- Bribery
- Chitchat
- Customs
- Demeanor
- Superstitions
- Taboos

Exercise 9.1

Instructions: Circle T for true or F for false.

1. T F   U.S. greetings are considered informal by persons of other cultures.
2. T F   The handshakes of U.S. persons and the British are similar.
3. T F   The cost of items is an appropriate topic for small talk in most cultures.
4. T F   People in Mexico do not waste time with small talk but get right down to business.
5. T F   A stereotype of U.S. women is that they are aggressive.
6. T F   What is perceived as humorous in the United States may not be humorous in Japan.
7. T F   When conducting business in another country, wear what the people in that country typically wear.
8. T F   In some cultures, bad luck is associated with certain numbers.
9. T F   In the United States, employees consider their jobs to be permanent.
10. T F   What is perceived as bribery is culturally relative.

Questions and Cases for Discussion

1. Explain the difference in handshaking customs of U.S. and French citizens.
2. Identify some verbal expressions used in the United States that when translated literally have little meaning and are confusing to persons for whom English is a second language.
3. Give examples of how variations in the English language exist within regions of the United States.
4. How do you say "Good day" in French, German, and Spanish?
5. Explain differences in the use of humor in business in the United States and Germany.
6. Explain how women in business are treated differently in the United States and Mexico.

7. What superstitions related to numbers are held by people of the United States and China?
8. In what countries is business dress similar to that worn in the United States?
9. Identify cultures in which business dress may be different from that worn in the United States.
10. What guidelines for business dress should women observe in cultures other than their own?
11. Describe how hiring/firing practices of the United States and Japan differ.
12. Identify some rules for appropriate behavior in public places in the United States.
13. How is a knowledge of holidays and holy days helpful when conducting business with another culture?
14. What U.S. foods do people of other cultures find unusual? What foods of other cultures do people of the United States consider unusual?
15. List some consumption taboos of people in various cultures.

Cases

The following procedure is recommended for analyzing the cases: (a) read the case carefully paying attention to details; (b) read the questions at the end of the case; (c) reread the case, taking notes on or highlighting the details needed for answering the questions; (d) identify relevant facts, underlying assumptions, and critical issues of the case; (e) list possible answers to the questions; and (f) select the most logical response to the question. Your professor may ask that you submit answers to the case questions in writing.

Case 1

Your organization is having a large party for its worldwide distributors in the United States. Because there will be people from all over the world, what would you serve for meals to avoid offending anyone?

Case 2

You have unknowingly arrived in Mexico during Carnival Week. Because people are busy partying and celebrating, they are not interested in meeting with you to discuss business. However, because you are here, they have invited you to join in their activities. Should you accept or reject their invitation?

Case 3

A Japanese businessman on his first visit to the United States was pleased to be invited to a U.S. executive's home for cocktails. He arrived promptly at 7 p.m. The host introduced him to a small group of people, and then returned to the front door to greet others who were arriving. The Japanese businessman seemed to have nothing to contribute on the seemingly mindless topics that were discussed. After a few minutes, the others in the group wandered off to join other groups, and he was left alone. Because the host did not return to introduce him to others at the party, he left and returned to his hotel. What, if any, rules of proper etiquette were breached?

Case 4

At his first meeting with Mina Van Buren, a U.S. manager, Juan Velasquez, an Argentine businessman, complimented her on her appearance and invited her out for drinks and dinner that evening. Ms. Van Buren refused, saying that she preferred to keep their relationship on a professional level. Discuss the appropriateness of Mr. Velasquez's invitation and Ms. Van Buren's response and the implications for building a solid business relationship.

Activities

1. Research appropriate business and social dress in one of the following countries: India, Israel, Thailand, or Saudi Arabia.
2. List some religious taboos associated with food consumption in a coculture of the United States or a culture of your choice.
3. Write a paragraph summarizing your experience in trying a food for the first time.
4. Practice saying the following in French, German, and Spanish: "please," "thank you," "good-bye," and "excuse me."
5. Research superstitions of a country of your choice and make an oral report to the class.

References

Alvarez-Correa, W. (1996, October). Relax, it's Friday. *The Washingtonian*, 134–137.

Axtell, R. E. (1990). *Do's and taboos of hosting international visitors.* New York: Wiley.

Axtell, R. E. (1993). *Do's and taboos around the world.* New York: Wiley.

Axtell, R. E. (1999). *Do's and taboos of humor around the world.* New York: Wiley.

Axtell, R. E., Briggs, T., Corcoran, M., & Lamb, M. E. (1997). *Do's and taboos around the world for women in business.* New York: Wiley.

Baldrige, L. (1993). *Letitia Baldrige's new complete guide to executive manners.* New York: Rawson Associates.

Bixler, S. (1997). *The new professional image.* Holbrook, MA: Adams Media Corporation.

Bosrock, M. M. (1995). *Put your best foot forward: Europe.* St. Paul, MN: International Education Systems.

Bosrock, M. M. (1997a). *Put your best foot forward: Asia.* St. Paul, MN: International Education Systems.

Bosrock, M. M. (1997b). *Put your best foot forward: South America.* St. Paul, MN: International Education Systems.

Braganti, N. L., & Devine, E. (1992). *European customs and manners.* New York: Meadowbrook.

CultureGrams. (2004). Lindon, UT: ProQuest Information and Learning.

Devine, E., & Braganti, N. L. (1998). *The travelers' guide to Asian customs and manners.* New York: St. Martin's Griffin.

Devine, E., & Braganti, N. L. (2000). *The travelers' guide to Latin American customs and manners.* New York: St. Martin's Griffin.

Dresser, N. (2005). *Multicultural manners.* New York: Wiley.

Engholm, C. (1991). *When business east meets business west.* New York: Wiley.

Engholm, C., & Rowland, D. (1996). *International excellence.* New York: Kodansha International.

Fairlie, H. (1983, July 4). Why I love America. *The New Republic*, p. 12.

Fenton, L. (2002, March 24). Casual-dress craze in the workplace is over. *The Commercial Appeal*, E8.

Harris, P. R., Moran, R. T., & Moran, S. V. (2004). *Managing cultural differences*

(6th ed.). Burlington, MA: Elsevier Butterworth-Heinemann.

Hudson, R. (2002, April 15). "Business casual" on the wane. *Seattle Post-Intelligencer,* p. E-4.

Jones, D. (1993, September 14). More business travelers going global. *USA Today,* p. 1e.

Lewis, R. D. (2000). *When cultures collide: Managing successfully across cultures.* London: Nicholas Brealey.

Molloy, J. T. (1996). *New women's dress for success.* New York: Warner.

Sabath, A. M. (1999). *International business etiquette: Europe.* Franklin Lakes, NJ: Career Press.

Sabath, A. M. (2000). *International business etiquette: Latin America.* Franklin Lakes, NJ: Career Press.

Sabath, A. M. (2002). *International business etiquette: Asia and the Pacific Rim.* Franklin Lakes, NJ: Career Press.

Samovar, L. A., & Porter, R. E. (2004). *Communication between cultures* (5th ed.). Belmont, CA: Wadsworth/Thomson Learning.

Stephens, G. K., & Greer, C. R. (1995, Summer). Doing business in Mexico: Understanding cultural differences. *Organizational Dynamics,* 24(1), 39–56.

Trompenaars, F., & Hampden-Turner, C. (1998). *Riding the waves of culture* (2nd ed.). New York: McGraw-Hill.

Turkington, C. (1999). *The complete idiot's guide to cultural etiquette.* Indianapolis: Alpha Books.

Utroska, D. R. (1992, November). Management in Europe: More than just etiquette. *Management Review,* 21–24.

10 INTERCULTURAL NEGOTIATION PROCESS

Objectives

Upon completion of this chapter, you will

- be able to define the intercultural negotiation process.

- understand the steps in the negotiation process.

- know how to avoid mistakes commonly made in intercultural negotiations.

- be knowledgeable about intercultural negotiation models.

- understand negotiation strategies, including conflict resolution, in intercultural negotiations.

- understand various trade agreements that affect intercultural negotiation.

The increasing globalization of industries has necessitated an increase in strategic alliances and hence intercultural negotiations. **Intercultural negotiation** involves discussions of common and conflicting interests between persons of different cultural backgrounds who work to reach an agreement of mutual benefit. How competent and competitive firms are both domestically and internationally and how they handle customers and vendors from other cultures will determine how successful a firm is internationally. Some of the reasons global joint ventures and strategic alliances are on the increase include economic deregulation, rapid technological changes, large capital requirements, government-supported industries, economic maturation, and improved communications.

One of the most important differences in negotiating internationally rather than domestically is culture. Negotiators find out the negotiation model that their counterparts will use and then compare and contrast it to their own. A major mistake is to stereotype a national culture. Although you can learn a lot about how people in another culture negotiate, all negotiators from a country will not be the same. The less homogeneous a country is, the larger the range of negotiator styles you will find. This chapter includes steps in the negotiation process, intercultural negotiation models, and negotiation strategies; chapter 11 then looks at some of the components mentioned in chapter 10.

STEPS IN THE NEGOTIATION PROCESS

Because negotiating with people from other cultures can be challenging, it is important to first get an overview of the negotiation process by examining the steps typically followed. These steps include site and team selection, relationship building, opening talks, discussions, and agreement.

Preparation and Site Selection

When preparing to negotiate with another culture, such variables as customs, etiquette, languages, and beliefs, in addition to product issues of price and terms, must be considered. Consulting someone who has lived in the target country or who has worked there is advisable. In addition, written materials and videos on negotiating in different countries are valuable resources.

The negotiation site is relatively unimportant to U.S. negotiators; they are comfortable negotiating in their office, over the telephone, or in another country. In some countries, however, the negotiation location is an important consideration. You may be expected to go to their country. Latin Americans and Asians, for example, expect you to go to them initially as they are more comfortable in their own territory (Leaptrott, 1996).

Team Selection

To have a successful negotiation experience, it is important to select the team members carefully. The number of people on the team; the age, gender, rank, and expertise of team members; and the personalities of potential team members are all important considerations. Whenever possible, include someone on the team who is either from the target culture or who has spent time there. Expertise in the language is also a consideration; unless a team member can speak the language, the services of an interpreter may be necessary. The number of members on the team could range from two to three typically found on U.S. and Mexican teams to four to seven on Japanese teams. Inquiring ahead of time as to the size of the opponent's team is recommended so that team sizes are balanced. Age, gender, and rank are important considerations in most Asian countries, as well as in Africa and the Middle East. Keeping the same team throughout negotiations is important for building a solid business relationship. (Additional information on team selection is included in chapter 11.)

Negotiator selection is an important aspect of conflict resolution. Negotiators should be selected for their background (technical or social), emotional makeup, values, and viewpoints. It is important to find a negotiator whose qualifications most closely fit the requirements for the negotiations that will take place. Some important areas to be considered are gender, age, political affiliation, social class, cooperativeness, authoritarianism, and risk-taking propensity. Evaluating the negotiators from the other perspective is helpful in selecting or adapting your strategy (Cohen, 1998).

Evaluating yourself as an intercultural negotiator within the constraints of the situation is important. Be sure you clearly perceive your objectives, know the facts, and have chosen your strategies and tactics carefully. Negotiation is essentially communication with an encoder and a decoder. To the extent that the encoder and decoder share the same perceptions is the degree to which their communications will be sent and received as intended. Communicating successfully with someone in your own society is often difficult; when you add different cultural concepts, different experiences, and different languages and word meanings, the possibility for miscommunication increases (Cohen, 1998).

Relationship Building

Although relationship building is relatively unimportant in the United States, in some countries, a long period of time must be spent getting acquainted with the person with whom you want to conduct business. In Argentina, as in other Latin American countries, personal relationships are very important. To conduct business with governmental representatives, you need an intermediary to even get an appointment. In fact, all Hispanic countries have agents who specialize in making contacts between local firms and foreign companies (Leaptrott, 1996). In India, small talk and tea are important aspects of the negotiation process. The sweet milky tea that is offered should be accepted after an initial refusal; refusing the refreshments offered is considered an insult (Morrison, Conaway, & Borden, 1994). In Central and Eastern Europe, building relationships prior to conducting business is also important. Introductions are a necessary part of building the relationship. Establishing a relationship is also important in the Arab countries. Because Arabs only conduct business with friends, taking time to build a friendship is a necessity. However, with the friendship comes the implicit agreement to give assistance and support when needed. Although personal relationships are necessary to conducting business in Asian countries, establishing a friendship with potential business associates is not necessary. Locating an agent to serve as an intermediary with the targeted firm is recommended (Leaptrott, 1996).

Opening Talks

In the United States, as in many cultures, opening talks begin promptly, often with a short time spent in small talk. When negotiating with Australians, expect to engage in small talk for a short time to establish rapport before getting down to business (Morrison et al., 1994). In Scandinavian countries, differences exist in what is considered customary during opening talks. People from Sweden arrive promptly, have a meeting agenda, and engage in small talk. Opening the presentation with a joke, however, is a mistake because the Swedes do not use humor during negotiations. In Finland, on the other hand, there is no small talk; they prefer to get down to business promptly (Turkington, 1999). Agendas, although viewed in a positive manner in the United States, may not be viewed as positive in some countries, such as in Latin America and the Middle East. In these countries more open interaction is preferred; agendas are viewed as a hindrance to effective negotiations. Likewise, in Japan agendas may not be used because Japanese negotiators prefer to discuss several topics at the same time. When negotiating with Asians, it is important to remember that during opening talks, they will expect your top-level executives to be present (Leaptrott, 1996).

Discussions

During discussions, it is important to keep in mind that a variety of behaviors may be seen as the norm in certain countries. In Argentina, for example, negotiators may become quite emotional, although in France, you may expect a lively discourse because they enjoy debating. Concessions during the discussions should be thought out ahead of time and handled skillfully. Your plan for concessions should take into account that in some countries, such as Mexico and the Middle East, compromise is viewed negatively. In addition, the timing and amount of the concession should vary with the country. In Australia, concessions tend to increase during negotiations, although in India, they tend to decrease. During discussions with Asians, it is wise to keep in mind that they may smile, which usually indicates lack of understanding, or they may say "Yes," which may actually mean, "Yes, I understand." In negotiations with Asians, it is sometimes advisable to move discussions to a more informal location, such as a restaurant or a golf course (Leaptrott, 1996).

Agreement

Closing the negotiations properly is very important. Delays are to be expected in such countries as India, so it is advisable to allow sufficient time for completing the deal. Likewise, when completing negotiations in India, it is wise to get both tax and legal advice prior to the final agreement (Morrison et al., 1994). Delays are also common in Asian and Latin American countries; after reaching agreement, there is typically a long wait before final approval. The final written contract is vague by U.S. standards and is viewed as a guide for future negotiations rather than as a binding agreement as is true of U.S. contracts. You may, therefore, be continuing negotiations for some time even after both sides have signed the agreement. (Leaptrott, 1996).

To be successful in distributor agreements, Axtell (1994) suggests the following points that should be covered and agreed upon to assure success.

1. Effective dates of the agreement
2. Options at the end of the agreement
3. Place of jurisdiction
4. Terms of termination before agreement ends
5. Arbitration
6. Geographic boundaries of agreement
7. Degree of exclusivity
8. Description of products being distributed
9. Agreed-on sales quotas
10. Responsibility for import duty, freight, and insurance
11. Responsibility for warehousing, inventory control, and accounting
12. Information that must be reported to the sourcing company
13. Currency to be used for payment
14. Terms of payment
15. Provisions for secrecy
16. Competitive products that can or cannot be carried
17. Responsibility for warranty and repairs
18. Responsibility for advertising, merchandising, and public relations
19. Protection of patents and trademarks
20. Responsibility associated with drop shipments and payment
21. Payment provisions of commissions and bonuses
22. Responsibility for taxes
23. Responsibility for indemnification
24. Responsibility for translation

25. Consideration of legal assignment, waivers, *force majeure*, notices, severability, and Foreign Corrupt Practices Act
26. Responsibility for setting prices

Many of these points can be handled ahead of negotiations and are controlled by lawyers during negotiations between U.S. firms. However, when you are dealing interculturally and multinationally, these points need to be addressed so that everyone understands both the letter and the intent of the contract.

When barriers develop during the negotiations, the negotiators need to be creative if the negotiations are important to their company. The negotiators must sift through the information to look for the conflict, look at the goals that underlie the demands, seek ways to reconcile the two sides, and, if agreement is not reached, decide whether to pursue the negotiations by changing the goals (Pruitt, 1998).

MISTAKES COMMONLY MADE DURING NEGOTIATIONS

Although effective negotiators are generally successful in their negotiation attempts, mistakes are sometimes made during the negotiation process that may have a negative impact on the outcome. Cellich (1997) identified the following mistakes sometimes made by negotiators:

1. Making a negative initial impression
2. Failing to listen and talking too much
3. Assuming understanding by the other culture
4. Failing to ask important questions
5. Showing discomfort with silence
6. Using unfamiliar and slang words
7. Interrupting the speaker
8. Failing to read the nonverbal cues
9. Failing to note key points
10. Making statements that are irritating or contradictory
11. Failing to prepare a list of questions for discussion
12. Being easily distracted
13. Failing to start with conditional offers
14. Failing to summarize and restate to ensure understanding
15. Hearing only what they want to hear
16. Failing to use first-class supporting materials

Skilled negotiators should avoid the preceding list of common mistakes, should emphasize areas of agreement, and should consider the long-term consequences of their agreements. A mistake sometimes made by U.S. negotiators because of the self-imposed time constraints of U.S. Americans, is making concessions prematurely. Many times, the size of the concession is larger than necessary had more time been taken. If a concession is made too soon or if a large concession is made, the opponent is not as likely to see the concession as much of a gain. The Russians and the Chinese are very good at making concessions work for them. People of the United States also look at negotiations from a legal point of view. Most cultures are not as concerned with the legal view but are concerned with having a good agreement, a shared perception, and a trust of the other side (Moran & Stripp, 1991).

INTERCULTURAL NEGOTIATION MODELS

The model you choose to use when negotiating interculturally will depend on the people with whom you are negotiating as well as your own personal biases. Research has shown that social, cultural, political, and legal issues; timing of delivery; payment; terms of payment; role of consultants; and authority to make binding decisions take up most of the negotiation time, so researching a particular company and culture could greatly reduce the time spent in negotiation (Ghauri, 1983).

People tend to negotiate interculturally as they do intraculturally unless they realize they need to adapt to another culture. The effect of culture in intercultural negotiation is one of relative, not absolute, values. The negotiations will proceed as smoothly as the abilities of all participants to be empathetic and to adapt to each other's cultural constraints. For example, the Russian negotiating tactics include a need for authority, a need to avoid risk, and a need to control. Negotiating style is not neutral; it is culturally based and somewhat subconscious. A clash of negotiating styles can lead to a breakdown in the negotiation (Cohen, 1998).

Protocol helps maintain the cultural values of a country. Therefore, businesspeople who are going to negotiate outside their own culture need to learn as much about the other culture as possible. When you understand the opposition, you can formulate a course of action more accurately and obtain your goals (Leaptrott, 1996).

> Game theory holds that protocol ensures that the rules of behavior are the same for both parties; however, if one party does not understand the rules, that party will not win in the negotiations.
>
> For example, the Japanese protocol is to never say "no." A negotiator must know and understand the many meanings of "yes" to know whether a contract is forthcoming or not. (Leaptrott, 1996)

Two main negotiating styles used currently are the problem-solving approach and the competitive approach. Interculturally, the **problem-solving approach** has been identified with the need to consider national cultural characteristic differences and/or organizational cultural differences that lead to differences in communication. The **competitive approach** is more individualistic and persuasion oriented. The competitive approach also looks at a solution that is best for the negotiator's own side versus a win-win style of negotiation. The problem-solving approach to negotiation leads to adaptation by the negotiator to the negotiator's counterpart through information exchange of needs. This is accomplished by gaining information on the opposition's people. Each of the variables are affected by the cultural protocol from which both sides come, and the more difference there is between their cultures on the protocols, it follows that more problems could exist when they are working through the negotiation variables. The more negotiators are problem-solving oriented, the more they will use the problem-solving approach to negotiation. The competency of businesspersons' intercultural communication will determine how effective they are using the problem-solving approach (Chaisrakeo & Speece, 2004).

Three other negotiation approaches have been promulgated: compromising, forcing, and legalism. **Compromising** seeks a middle ground between the two parties. Although compromising distributes the outcomes equally between the parties, it does not maximize the joint gain. **Forcing** is used to make the other party comply and is closer to the competitive approach. **Legalism** uses legal documentation to force the other partner to comply and is again closer to the competitive approach (Lin & Miller, 2003).

> A Thai working in a Swiss multinational says: "National culture always influences the style of negotiation either directly or indirectly. . . . This culture comes into our life from everywhere in our country. So there is no doubt . . . it must affect our bargaining style."
>
> In contrast, a United Kingdom worker says: "I don't see that culture will affect my bargaining style. I got bargaining skills from my working experience. I also learned it from my supervisor and my friends. Individual personality should be another factor that has an effect on negotiating style but not national culture." (Chaisrakeo & Speece, 2004, p. 274)

A person's negotiating strategy may achieve a compromise agreement or an integrative agreement. The **compromise agreement** is reached when two parties find a common ground between their individual goals that results in a lower joint benefit. For example, if one side offers to sell a product for $35 per unit and the other side offers to buy it for $25, a compromise of $30 can be reached that yields a lower joint benefit. With an **integrative agreement**, the two parties reconcile their interests to yield a high joint benefit. Negotiators should seek integrative agreements rather than compromise agreements because integrative agreements tend to be more stable and more mutually rewarding and usually benefit the broader community represented by the two parties. The five methods of reaching integrative agreements described by Pruitt (1998) are expanding the pie, nonspecific compensation, logrolling, cost cutting, and bridging. Expanding the pie involves receiving additional resources. Nonspecific compensation involves repaying the party who does not receive what he or she requests in some unrelated way. Logrolling, which may be viewed as a variant of nonspecific compensation, involves both parties, rather than only one, being compensated for making concessions requested by the other party. Each party makes concessions on low-priority issues in exchange for concessions on high-priority issues. The cost-cutting solution involves the reduction of one person's costs while the other person gets what he or she wants. Bridging involves devising a new option for situations in which neither person gets his or her initial demands (Pruitt, 1998).

> A cease-fire in the Yom Kippur War found the Egyptian Third Army surrounded by Israeli forces. A dispute arose about the control of the only road available for bringing food and medicine to this army, and the two parties appeared to be at loggerheads. After a careful analysis, the mediator, Henry

> Kissinger, concluded that Israel wanted actual control of the road while Egypt wanted only the appearance that Israel did not control it for the sake of public relations. A bridging solution was found that involved continued Israeli control but the stationing of United Nations soldiers at checkpoints on the road so that they seemed to control it. (Pruitt, 1998, p. 513)

The high or low national cultural context of a negotiator, the organizational culture, the negotiator's own cultural context, and the cultural contexts of their counterparts determine the negotiators' abilities to adapt to each other during the negotiation process. This ability of the people in an organization to integrate other cultures' views into their own cultural intelligence is paramount to an organization's being successful in negotiating in other cultures.

For a negotiation to be effective, the people must work toward an agreement. This involves the people's working to build a relationship rather than a transaction. They need to exchange information honestly and openly. The negotiators must be careful in their use of persuasion tactics. Although Western societies favor rational argument, which can be aggressive and competitive, their Eastern counterparts tend to be more polite and restrained (Thomas & Inkson, 2004).

Kozicki (1998) presents a four-stage negotiation model—investigative, presentation, bargaining, and agreement. The investigative stage includes preparation or knowledge gathering about the other side and their goals. The presentation stage is a challenge because of cultural, perceptual, environmental, and power differences. The bargaining stage depends on cultural differences and the ability to stay disciplined and controlled. The agreement stage is the point at which the negotiators finalize the deal and set the stage for a continued relationship. Often people associate negotiation with only the bargaining stage, but negotiations are much more than bargaining.

Although these four stages work well in the United States, when negotiating internationally, it may be advisable to change your strategy. According to Brett (2001), those negotiators who negotiate the high-net-value integrative and distributive deals across cultures can be described as pragmatic individualists, cooperative pragmatists, and indirect strategists. The pragmatic individualist sets high targets, searches for information, makes trade-offs, and avoids distraction concerning power. The downside of the pragmatic individualist is time because their partner may feel a long-term relationship is not being established. The cooperative pragmatist is concerned with the outcome for all parties. Many questions will be asked and answered, and power will be dealt with indirectly. Cooperative pragmatists negotiate integrative deals and realize distributive outcomes. As long as the trust is genuine between the two sides in a negotiation, there should be few problems. However, a pragmatic individual may take advantage of a cooperative pragmatist because of the cooperative's need to trust. Indirect strategists are not sure about the power situation and choose to search for information indirectly. This tends to be successful within a culture that uses the indirect strategy but a problem when negotiating with a culture that is not using the indirect strategy. The indirect strategy uses cues that may be too subtle for many cultures. It is also difficult for negotiators from indirect strategy cultures to negotiate with members from a direct strategy culture. When you have direct and indirect negotiators, the conflict will not make integrative agreements possible but will make distributive agreements possible. Because these three models are used in different cultures, successful negotiators need to learn about all three and be able to use the method that will work best with the particular culture they are negotiating with. U.S. Americans, in particular, need to be aware of their shortcomings, which are well known to many of their opponents. To people of many cultures, people in the United States always seem to be in a hurry. It is generally known that U.S. negotiators are often in a rush and may not be as completely prepared as the other side.

> A young U.S. businessman related a story about negotiating a joint venture with a Japanese company. As they negotiated, it was apparent that the Japanese company knew everything about the U.S. company—who its customers were, production capacity, sales history, financial status—and the U.S. firm had only a little data on the Japanese firm. The Japanese had expected the U.S. firm to be better prepared for their visit and took their business elsewhere.

NEGOTIATION STRATEGIES

Negotiation strategies are plans organized to achieve a desired objective. Because strategies are used to elicit desired responses, negotiations can take many forms. Predicting the opponent's response is essential to strategic planning. Intercultural negotiation strategies differ from intracultural styles for most cultures.

> Mark McCormack explained how negotiations can be win-win in his book, *What They Don't Teach You at Harvard Business School*:
> "I find it helpful to try to figure out in advance where the other person would like to end up—at what point he will do the deal and still feel like he's coming away with something. This is different from 'how far will he go?' A lot of times you can push someone to the wall, and you still reach an agreement, but his resentment will come back to haunt you in a million ways." (1984, p. 149)

Upon what are negotiation strategies based? Assuming that people act on the basis of their own best interests, the question then becomes how to determine whether this is the deal to accept, or, more broadly, how to determine the truth? Different cultures arrive at truth in negotiations in one of three ways: faith, fact, and feeling. Persons operating on faith care that your religious or political ideology matches theirs. For example, small nations that believe in self-sufficiency may reject a good deal simply because they want their own people to do the work, even though your product is clearly superior and lower priced. Thus, presenting facts to these persons is futile. Persons who believe in facts are often predictable; they give the contract to the lowest bidder. Most of the people in the world are more concerned with feelings and relationships; they believe in building a relationship over time and will not buy from someone else just because they can get a lower price (Morrison et al., 1994).

U.S. Americans tend to make fewer adjustments to their opponent's behavior, and they change their negotiation strategy less than other cultures when dealing interculturally. This tendency is partially due to the fact that U.S. persons lack sufficient motivation to change their behavior in negotiation encounters because, in the past, the world has wanted what the United States produced. The more U.S. negotiators learn about negotiation styles of other cultures, however, the more they are beginning to make adjustments.

Negotiation strategies also include the preparation details; tactics; conflict resolution and mediation; and observations, analysis, and evaluation.

Preparation

Choosing where the meeting will be held is the first consideration in making preparation. When a meeting is held on your turf, you have more power; but you also have more responsibility for seeing to your counterpart's comforts. If the meeting is held on your counterpart's turf, he or she has the power and responsibilities. When it is held at a neutral location, members of each team are responsible for their own comforts.

In addition to selecting the location and determining the cultural protocol of the location, Leaptrott (1996) points out that preparation involves gathering information about the members of the other negotiation team, defining objectives, preparing a strategic plan, gathering ideas on applying your strategies within the protocol, researching the etiquette rules of the other culture, and viewing negotiations as an obstacle course to complete in order to achieve your goal. Although it is important to be prepared for questions, it is also important to safeguard strategic information that you do not want to share.

Tactics

Tactics are maneuvers used for gaining advantage or success. Tactics can take the form of verbal, nonverbal, or situational tactics. The attributes the receiver attaches to the tactic can be so distracting that the receiver has a distorted perception of the point that is communicated. Jokes often used by people of the United States to "break the ice" are examples of such tactics. Although these work well when the negotiations are between U.S. companies, jokes generally do not translate well to other cultures. Jokes are often perceived as derogatory toward a particular person, and in group-oriented cultures, this type of humor may be considered offensive (Moran & Stripp, 1991).

In addition to jokes, other verbal tactics are promises, threats, recommendations, warnings, rewards, punishments, normative appeals, commitments, self-disclosure, questions, and commands. Nonverbal tactics include tone of voice, facial expressions, body distance, dress, gestures, silence, and symbols. Situational tactics include location, time constraints, and physical arrangements.

Distracting tactics can be detrimental to the negotiation process. Allowing insufficient time for the negotiations is typical of cultures that want to get "right to business." By doing so, the other negotiating team may feel you are uninterested in a long-term relationship; consequently, they are not interested in what your team may have to say.

Whether the climate during negotiations is supportive or defensive depends on how the cultures negotiating view each other. What one culture considers defensive, dominating, retaliatory, and threatening may be considered normal by the other culture. However, if a negotiator is perceived, rightly or wrongly, as defensive or supportive, the other team will respond according to its perceptions and not according to what was intended. Climate is a very important area to research to read your opponents correctly.

One way to avoid being defensive is to ask questions and learn what your opponent is thinking. Clarify or restate what you understand to have been said and ask if that is correct. Try to follow the other side as it explores the issues rather than always taking the leadership role. Use role reversal to understand and appreciate the other side's position.

Conflict Resolution and Mediation

Conflict resolution involves a series of questions: How do we know if there is conflict? Is the conflict increasing or decreasing? Is the time to resolve the conflict now? What are the tactics to resolve the conflict? Is the conflict irresolvable? How do you tell if there is conflict or simply a lively debate? What is often an emotional, verbal disagreement for one culture can be a display of sincerity for another culture. In many countries and cultures, courts are third-party intermediaries (Weaver, 1998).

Learning the social system and cultural values of the other negotiators will help you identify the signs of conflict or prevent the conflict from developing. Knowing whether to cultivate a personal relationship, being conscious of rank and position, understanding the thought patterns of other negotiators, and knowing how to establish trust are essential to successful conflict resolution. Because of culture differences, negotiators may focus on different aspects of the negotiations as being more important. A U.S. negotiator, for example, may focus on legal and financial agreements, although the Mexican or Japanese negotiator may emphasize personal relationships (Samovar & Porter, 2004). Communicating respect, being nonjudgmental, realizing that perceptions are personal, showing empathy, and tolerating ambiguity can help you avoid conflict and negotiate successfully (Ping, 1998).

If you have done your homework and are still having conflicts that defy resolution, you might want to turn to a third party, a mediator. Mediation is the use of a third party to settle differences between negotiating teams to bring them to common agreement. Mediation may be the fastest road to discovering the negotiation barriers. If you are dealing with members of a culture who do not like confrontation, who are afraid of losing face, or who are causing you to lose face, using a mediator may be the best path to follow (Moran & Stripp, 1991).

According to Lewicki, Barry, Saunders, and Minton (2003), a mediator can sometimes productively solve disputes. A mediator first stabilizes the setting, including greeting the participants, designating seating, identifying each person, stating the purpose of the mediation, and confirming his or her neutrality. After setting this stage, the mediator gets a commitment from the participants to proceed in a businesslike manner. The second step helps the parties communicate in an orderly fashion. The mediator decides who is to speak first and provides a rationale to the group. As each participant speaks, the mediator takes notes, actively restates the points being made, is a calming influence, and focuses on the issues. The mediator then summarizes, asking the speakers for their agreement. Next, the mediator helps the participants set priorities. The third step is to help the parties solve their disagreements. The negotiator asks everyone to list alternative possibilities for settlement and a workable alternative, increases understanding of the alternatives, and rephrases them if necessary. Finally, the fourth step involves clarifying the agreement, checking to be sure both sides are in agreement and understand the terms, establishing a time for follow-up, emphasizing that the agreement belongs to the parties and not the mediator, and congratulating the negotiators on their resolution.

The best way to avoid conflict is to prepare, plan, and respect the culture with whom you are negotiating before negotiations commence. Be sure you know and respect the customs of the other negotiator's culture and be careful of gestures, nuances in meanings, and taboos of the other culture. Avoid using jargon, idioms, or slang. Realize that even if you are using a bicultural interpreter, often equivalent concepts do not exist between different languages. Many times a picture will help with explanations; therefore, you might want to bring photographs, drawings, overhead transparencies, samples, or anything else that can help the other side understand your presentation.

For the negotiation process to proceed expeditiously, observing, analyzing, and evaluating what happens between negotiators is important.

Observations, Analysis, and Evaluation

As negotiations proceed, you need to be very observant of changes from your initial expectations, analyze the differences, and adapt your negotiation strategy accordingly. Constant evaluation of verbal, nonverbal, and group interaction is necessary to negotiate from the best position possible.

For negotiations to be successful, they must allow both parties to gain something—a win-win situation—although the parties probably will not gain equally.

Analysis involves defining the problem by separating and subjectively assessing probabilities, values, risk attitudes, time preferences, structuring and sequencing of the counterpart's choices, and the unknown (Sebenius, 1992). In addition, the people who are involved in the negotiation, their style of negotiating, the national culture, the differences in the two cultures, and the interpreters and translators need to be analyzed and evaluated. The developmental process of observing, analyzing, and evaluating is completed for each step in the negotiation process. A detailed outline of the items in the negotiation process that need to be constantly observed, analyzed, and evaluated include the following: (Brett, 2001; Casse & Deol, 1991; Moran & Stripp, 1991):

1. Physical location of the negotiations
   - managing power
   - time and opportunity management—timely actions based on opportunity analysis provide needed edge in highly competitive situations

2. Agenda or policy issues in the negotiation
   - basic concept of negotiation
   - selection of negotiators
   - role of individual aspirations
   - concern with protocol
   - significance of type of issue

3. Preliminary statement and limitation considerations
   - complexity of language—need a means to communicate clearly
   - nature of persuasive argument
   - value of time
   - appreciation of cultural differences—anticipation of their moves
   - mutual understanding

- negotiation is more art than science—be natural
- statement of anticipation for the negotiations

4. Deliberation and solution of some issues and identification of the issues of no agreement
  - bases of trust
  - risk-taking propensity
  - internal decision-making systems
  - persuasion—establish credibility
  - selling—create the need

5. Preliminaries to final negotiations
  - narrow down differences—achieve consensus
  - emphasize commonalities of interest
  - understand limitations of your counterparts—use empathy
  - systematically search for alternatives
  - use conflict management

6. Final negotiations
  - give and take necessary in bargaining process
  - win-win negotiations for generating positive feelings

7. Contract or confirmation of agreement
  - satisfactory agreement
  - including country of dispute resolution
  - importance of written documents in countries involved

8. Implementation of the agreement
  - Both written and unwritten aspects of negotiation are important

Intercultural negotiation assumes that the parties are from different cultures and may not share the same values, beliefs, needs, and thought patterns. During the interaction periods of the negotiation, the values, beliefs, needs, and thought patterns that are not shared by both groups can cause many unanticipated problems. The negotiator must become adept—through continual observation, analysis, and evaluation—at catching the problems and adapting the negotiation strategy accordingly.

TRADE AGREEMENTS

Trade agreements are the laws under which U.S. business must function when exporting. All exports are controlled by the government of the country where they are produced. General and validated are two types of trade agreement licenses. Because the general license is never actually issued, many firms do not realize they are operating under such a license. The validated license is very specific, and the Department of Commerce will assist companies with the regulations that apply. The **validated license** allows a specific exporter to export specific products to specific places. To find out more about validated licenses, obtain a copy of *Export Administration Regulations* from the Department of Commerce. Another book from the Department of Commerce that will prove useful to the overseas negotiator is *Basic Guide to*

Exporting, United States Government Subscription, http://bookstore.gpo.gov/index.html.

Free trade zones (FTZ) or **trade blocs** are zones of international commerce where foreign or domestic merchandise may enter without formal customs entry or custom duties. The North American Free Trade Agreement (NAFTA) is an expansion of the FTZ concept, as is the European Union (EU).

The NAFTA among the United States, Canada, and Mexico was ratified in 1993 (see Figure 10-1) and took effect January 1, 1994. In 2008, all import and export taxes on qualified goods between the three countries will be revoked, and all qualified materials and service will flow freely among the three countries. NAFTA deals with trade in goods, technical barriers to trade, government procurement, investment, services and related matters, intellectual property, and administrative and institutional provisions.

FIGURE 10-1   Before and After NAFTA

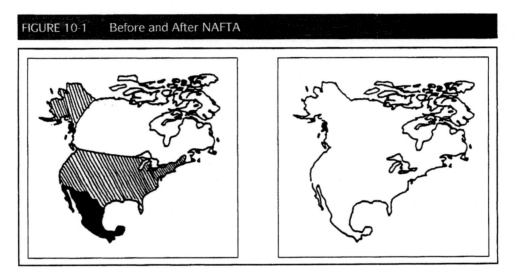

The objectives of NAFTA are the following:

1. To eliminate barriers to trade and facilitate cross-border movement of goods and services
2. To promote fair competition
3. To increase investment opportunities
4. To provide adequate and effective protection for intellectual property
5. To develop effective procedures to handle disputes
6. To expand cooperation and increase benefits to the three countries (NAFTA, 1992)

Many different products are covered by NAFTA; tariff implementation will be completed in 2006. Regional economic integration is happening all over the world. A few of the current trade blocs include the following (Trade bloc, 2004):

- **APEC**—Asia-Pacific Economic Cooperation (members include Australia, Brunei Darussalam, Canada, Chile, People's Republic of China, Hong Kong, Indonesia, Japan, Republic of Korea, Malaysia, Mexico, New Zealand, Papua

New Guinea, Peru, Philippines, Russia, Singapore, Taiwan, Thailand, United States, and Viet Nam) (http://www.apec.org/apec/member_economies.html, 2004).

- **ASEAN-AFTA**—Association of Southeast Asian Nations Free Trade Area (members include Brunei Darussalam, Indonesia, Malaysia, Philippines, Singapore, and Thailand) (http://www.aseansec.org, 2004).
- **CAFTA**—Central American Free Trade Agreement (members include United States, Guatemala, El Salvador, Honduras, Nicaragua, and Costa Rica) (http://www.pcusa.org/trade/cafta.htm, 2004).
- **CAN**—Andean Community (members include Bolivia, Colombia, Ecuador, Peru, Venezuela) (http://www.comunidadandina.org, 2004).
- **CARICOM**—Caribbean Community and Common Market (members include Antiqua and Barbuda, The Bahamas, Barbados, Belize, Dominica, Grenada, Guyana, Haiti, Mamaica, Montserrat, St. Lucia, St. Kitts and Nevis, St. Vincent and the Grenadines, Suriname, Trinidad and Tobago; associate members include Anguilla, Bermuda, British Virgin Islands, Cayman Islands, Turks and Caicos Islands) (http://www.caricom.org, 2004).
- **CEFTA**—Central European Free Trade Agreement (members include Poland, Czech Republic, Slovakia, Hungary, Slovenia, Romania, and Bulgaria) (http://www.cefta.org, 2004).
- **EAC**—East African Economic Community (members include Kenya, Uganda, and Tanzania) (http://www.africa-business.com, 2004).
- **ECCAS-CEEAC**—Economic Community of Central African States (members include Angola, Burundi, Cameroon, Central African Republic, Chad, Congo [Brazzaville], Democratic Republic of Congo, Equatorial Guinea, Gabon, Rwanda, and Sao Tome et Principe) (http://www.africa-union.org, 2004).
- **ECOWAS**—Economic Community of West African States (members include The Republic of Benin, Burkina Faso, Cabo Verde, Cote d'Ivoire, Gambia, Ghana, Guinea, Guinee Bissan, Liberia, Mali, Niger, Nigeria, Senegal, Sierra Leone, and Togolese) (http://www.sec.ecowas.int, 2004).
- **EEA**—European Economic Area (members include Afghanistan, Albania, Algeria, Andorra, Argentina, Australia, Azerbaijan, Bangladesh, Belarus, Bhutan, Bolivia, Bosnia and Herzegovina, Brazil, Brunei, Canada, Cambodia, Chile, China, Colombia, Costa Rica, Croatia, Ecuador, Egypt, El Salvador, Georgia, Guatemala, Honduras, Hong Kong, Iceland, India, Indonesia, Iran, Iraq, Israel, Japan, Jordan, Kazakhstan, Kyrgyzstan, Lao, Lebanon, Libya, Liechtenstein, Macao, Malaysia, Maldives, Mexico, Moldova, Mongolia, Morocco, Myanmar, Nepal, New Zealand, Nicaragua, Norway, Pakistan, Panama, Paraguay, People's Republic of Korea, Peru, Philippines, Republic of Macedonia, Republic of North Korea, Republic of Yugoslavia, Russia, San Marino, Singapore, Sri Lanka, Switzerland, Syria, Taiwan, Tajikistan, Thailand, Tunisia, Turkey, Turkmenistan, Ukraine, United Arab Emirates, United States, Uruguay, Uzbekistan, Venezuela, Vietnam, West Bank-Gaza Strip, and Yemen) (http://europa.eu.int/comm/external_relations/search/countries.htm, 2004).
- **EU**—European Union (members include Austria, Belgium, Cyprus (Greek part), Czech Republic, Denmark, Estonia, Finland, France, Germany, Greece,

Hungary, Ireland, Italy, Latvia, Lithuania, Luxembourg, Malta, The Netherlands, Poland, Portugal, Slovakia, Slovenia, Spain, Sweden, and The United Kingdom of Great Britain and Northern Ireland) (Evans, 2004).

- **GCC**—Gulf Cooperation Council (members include Saudi Arabia, Bahrain, Kuwait, Oman, Qatar, and United Arab Emirates) (http://www.arab.de/arabinfo/gcc.htm, 2004).
- **MERCOSUR**—Mercado Comun del Sur - Southern Zone Customs Union, (members include Argentina, Brazil, Paraguay, and Uruguay) (http://www.mercosurtc.com, 2004).
- **NAFTA**—North American Free Trade Agreement (member nations include Canada, Mexico, and the United States).
- **SAARC**—South Asian Association for Regional Cooperation (members include Bangladesh, Bhutan, India, Maldives, Nepal, Pakistan, and Sri Lanka) (http://www.saarc-sec.org/main.php, 2004).
- **SADC**—Southern African Development Community (members include Angola, Botswana, Lesotho, Malawi, Mauritius, Mozambique, Namibia, South Africa, Swaziland, Tanzania, Zambia, and Zimbabwe) (http://www.un.org/esa/earthsummit/sadc-cp.htm, 2004).
- **SAFTA**—South Asia Free Trade Agreement (members include Bhutan, India, Nepal, and Sri Lanka) (http://www.cbcglobelink.org/cbcglobelink/events/SAFTA/index.htm, 2004).

Free trade zones do not come without problems. Currently Brazil has said that a hemisphere-wide free-trade zone is in peril because the United States is pushing too hard on Brazil. The Free Trade Area of the Americas (FTAA) talks have come to a halt. Brazil is not pleased with the U.S. demand that private firms have the right to sue the Brazilian government over international investment issues; Brazil is also less than pleased with the request to tighten patent rights for U.S. pharmaceuticals (Samor, 2004). If the FTAA is implemented, it would be the most extensive trade agreement in history. It would cover 34 countries in the Americas (http://www.alca-ftaa.org/TNC_e.asp, 2004).

The EU and MERCOSUR have also allowed the deadline to pass after five years of discussion concerning their two groups' forming a new trade bloc. Agricultural concessions by the Europeans were not forthcoming at the level MERCOSUR wanted, and the member countries have added their own protection for their domestic firms. The MERCOSUR members would rather have an agreement with the EU than sign the FTAA. Trade with the United States is 20% smaller than with the EU but growing faster (The Americas, 2004). All have a lot to gain or lose in these negotiations.

The World Trade Organization (WTO) is a multinational trade agreement of which the United States is a member. WTO provisions are continually being negotiated or renegotiated. Many stalemates have occurred as countries vie to protect specific industries or commodities. The WTO deals with intellectual property, services, national treatment for services (members must treat other nations' members equal to or better than service suppliers in their own nation), market access for services, foreign investment, antidumping, subsidies, textiles, agriculture, market access, dispute settlement, and telecommunications. Small modifications to a product can change its tariff classification.

The EU is a FTZ involving 25 countries. The EU is still working out problems due, in part, to the breakdown of the communist bloc countries, but the popularity of the EU is expected to grow in the future (Evans, 2004). The number of active trade agreements between the United States and other countries for specific products is in the hundreds and grows every year.

NEGOTIATION STYLES

The following sections summarize the negotiating styles of the United States and selected countries, including the countries with which the United States conducts most of its international trade. Because individual differences exist in all cultures, it is wise to research the negotiation styles of countries with which you plan to conduct business.

United States

According to Graham and Herberger (1983), the following statements are characteristic of the U.S. style of negotiating:

- "I can handle this by myself" (to express individualism).
- "Please call me Steve" (to make people feel relaxed by being informal).
- "Pardon my French" (to excuse profanity).
- "Let's get to the point" (to speed up decisions).
- "Speak up; what do you think?" (to avoid silence).
- "Let's put our cards on the table" (to convey the expectation of honesty).
- "A deal is a deal" (to indicate an expectation that the agreement will be honored).

The space requirements in the United States have a direct bearing on negotiations. Entering the intimate space (up to 18 inches) of a person from the United States causes great discomfort. Another consideration when negotiating with people of the United States is related to their attitude toward saving face. Because people of the United States are not as concerned with saving face as people of other cultures, they may be quick with "constructive criticism" that may be a source of humiliation or discomfort for persons in other cultures.

U.S. negotiators have tended to focus on interest strategies in the past due to the valuing of individualism, egalitarianism, and polychronicity; however, this focus on interest strategies is changing (Tinsley, 2001).

Canada

Canada is a bilingual country with French as the primary language in the province of Quebec and English in the other provinces. The English spoken is closer to British English than to U.S. English. Recently, a large group of Hong Kong businesspeople immigrated to Canada during the takeover of Hong Kong by the People's Republic of China; this move has introduced another culture into the country (Harris, Moran, & Moran, 2004). Canadians appear to be open and friendly, yet they are reserved, conservative, and very formal. They are also patriotic and lawful and observe strict rules of etiquette. Canadians are not and do not like being considered to be the same as U.S. people, nor do they consider their country part of the United States. Canadians tend to be individualistic. Respect the fact that Canadians are very proud of their heritage and that they did not fight for independence from England. Otherwise, negotiation practices are similar to those in the United States.

China

China has been very ethnocentric because of its chosen isolation behind the Great Wall for some 2,300 years. Westerners have had difficulty doing business with the Chinese because they lack an understanding of the Chinese culture and the intrinsic differences between Eastern and Western mindsets. Protocol to follow during the negotiation process includes giving small, inexpensive presents. The Chinese require a high degree of interpersonal interaction and a high level of character from those with whom they do business. It is necessary to develop a relationship with the Chinese; they believe this takes time and cannot be accomplished in meeting rooms alone (Sprong, 2004).

The Chinese trust those who are in some way connected to other people they trust. Personal connections are the key to success in China. Finding a common friend to make introductions will help build such relationships quicker. However, the Chinese are some of the toughest negotiators in the world. Technical competence of the negotiators is necessary as well as a noncondescending attitude. The Chinese research their opponents thoroughly to gain competitive advantage during negotiation. Nothing is final until it is signed; they prefer to use an intermediary. The Chinese rarely use lawyers, and interpreters may have inadequate language skills and experience. Although Chinese negotiators imply that there is no compromise or third choice, in reality there is ample room for compromise (DeLozier & Chi, 2000).

England

British negotiators reflect their cultural characteristics; they are very formal and polite and place great importance on proper protocol. They are also concerned with proper etiquette. The British are not as casual or quick to make friends as are U.S. persons, nor is this considered necessary to conducting any business in England. The British can be tough and ruthless; they excel at intelligence gathering and political blackmail. Because they sometimes appear quaint and eccentric, negotiators from other cultures may underestimate their skill. As U.S. law is based on English law, understanding the meaning of a British contract is relatively easy for U.S. negotiators (Cohen, 1998; Harris et al., 2004).

France

France was the largest country in Western Europe before the reunification of Germany. Needless to say, this change has not enhanced French self-esteem. The French expect everyone to behave as they do when doing business, including speaking their language. They are very much individualists and have a sense of pride that is sometimes interpreted as supremacy. The French enjoy conversation for the sake of conversation, but they are also very pragmatic about details of the proposed agreement during negotiations. During conversations away from negotiations, keep in mind that the French consider themselves world leaders in fashion, art, literature, cuisine, and diplomacy. The French follow a type of logic referred to as "Cartesian" logic when negotiating; it is based on principles previously established and proceeds from what is known, in point-by-point fashion, until agreement is reached.

Protocol, manners, status, education, family, and individual accomplishments are keys to success when dealing with the French (Moran & Stripp, 1991). Trust has to be earned; they are impressed by results. The French prefer detailed, firm contracts.

> The difference in the U.S.–French cognitive patterns and styles can be seen in their reaction to the Richard Nixon and Bill Clinton presidential scandals. The French have a very difficult time understanding the U.S. people and why they would want to drive a president from office over a moral or ethical issue. The French view the U.S. need to be morally correct in international situations to be unnecessary.

Germany

Germany is now a unified country with the dismantling of the Berlin Wall in late 1989. In business, Germans are typically group oriented; however, as a people, they are rather individualistic. Protocol and regulations are very important. Germans prefer explicit contracts and regulations and use power in negotiations (Tinsley, 2001). Dressing conservatively during negotiations, as well as using correct posture and manners, is strongly recommended. Germans tend to use a handshake at the beginning and end of meetings. Remember to use titles when addressing members of the negotiating team and to use "please" and "thank you" freely. Because the Germans believe friendships and personal relationships can complicate negotiations, they prefer to keep a distance between themselves and the other team of negotiators.

Germans tend to be detail oriented, so having technical people as part of the negotiation team is important. Being punctual is expected. Contracts are firm guidelines to be followed exactly. Corporate decisions are made at the top but with a great deal of input from workers. Quality is important, and decisions are pondered and carefully scrutinized to be sure such quality exists in any projects they undertake. To a U.S. person, Germans may seem pessimistic because of their ability to entertain every conceivable negative point. After they accept a project, however, they give 100% to its successful implementation (Brett, 2001; Samovar & Porter, 2004; Tinsley, 2001).

India

In India, business is conducted in a formal yet relaxed manner. Bribery is common, and having connections is important. The left hand is not used in greetings and eating; it is important to request permission before smoking, entering the room, or sitting (Moran & Stripp, 1991). Building relationships is important, and an introduction is necessary. Use titles to convey respect. Knowledge of local affairs is important to people of India. Intermediaries are commonly used. Because people of India place importance on building relationships, the negotiation process can be rather long by U.S. standards. Indian management is paternalistic toward subordinates. Because of status differences, Indians generally do not use group orientations. Indians, in an effort to maintain harmony, may tell the other party what it wants to hear. People of India do not approve of displays of emotion. Negotiators must use patience and allow the Indians to take the lead in the negotiations (Moran & Stripp, 1991).

Japan

The negotiating practices of the Japanese companies are based on the keiretsu systems. A **keiretsu system** is a company group formed by the principal company and the partner companies that supply parts, equipment, financial support, or distribution of the final products. In Japan, every company in the keiretsu works to provide the customer the best product for the lowest price while maintaining an acceptable return on investment. A keiretsu group is viewed as a long-term commitment (Yonekura, 1991).

Communication is very complex with the Japanese. To avoid having someone lose face, lose the group harmony, or disappoint another person, the Japanese use very subtle and complex verbal and nonverbal cues. You need to read between the lines to interpret what has been said and to use more silence and less eye contact than is considered normal for U.S. Americans. Because the Japanese do not use "no" and have such subtle verbal and nonverbal cues, ask a number of questions to be certain you understand the intent of what is being communicated (Brett, 2001). Silence is an important Japanese nonverbal communication and should not be interrupted. Standing at the table, slouching, doodling, crossing the legs, or other informal behavior by sellers is considered disrespectful. The Japanese use status and power in negotiations as well as interest strategies and regulation arguments (Tinsley, 2001).

If a problem is found even after a written agreement is signed, the Japanese will resolve the difference through mutual agreement with the other party, as they always consider contracts flexible instruments. Because Japan has very few business lawyers by U.S. standards, the Japanese are very suspicious of a negotiating team that includes lawyers.

Latin America

Latin Americans, which include people from Mexico and Central and South America, are quite different from U.S. persons in their manner of conducting business. Because Latin Americans may have trust issues with U.S. Americans, a negotiator must be careful to maintain the self-esteem of the Latin Americans. When trust is questionable or lost, the opportunity to negotiate is probably lost as well. Relationships are important because of the need to have contacts. Bribery is common, so the local contacts can help you determine who should be approached to get the business moving. The government is very involved in business.

Latinos emphasize general principles more than problem solving. A story told by a U.S. businessman illustrates the difference in approaches. The U.S. businessman was invited by a Guatemalan to supply equipment for a cereal factory the Guatemalan was planning to open in his country. The U.S. supplier focused on the financing of the purchases, the Guatemalan's credit rating, and how the Guatemalan was going to pay the supplying company. A German contractor, who eventually received the production line order, concentrated on how the production line was going to operate and meet the Guatemalan's needs. The Germans even sent a representative of the company to live on site for the first three months of production. The U.S. interest in the financial aspects of the contract was a turnoff to the Guatemalan. (Axtell, 1994)

Negotiators are chosen on the basis of their family connections, political influence, education, and gender. Latin Americans are very individualistic in business; however, they are very group-oriented concerning family and friends. Handshaking and asking about the health and well-being of business contacts and their families are expected.

Because most agreements are consummated over lunch, suitable luncheon accommodations are important. Many meetings are held to allow a personal relationship to develop. Numerous meetings are the norm, and time is not seen as important. Latin Americans are people oriented rather than task oriented. Because body language is important and different from that in the United States, researching nonverbal aspects of communication is recommended (Harris et al., 2004).

The Netherlands
The Dutch have always been internationally oriented due to their trade dependency. They are a very open country and are very proud of their heritage and culture.

> Lawmaker Geert Wilders called for a five-year halt to non-Western immigration after the killing of Dutch filmmaker Theo van Gogh by a Muslim extremist. He stated: "We are a Dutch democratic society. We have our own norms and values. If you choose radical Islam, you can leave; and if you don't leave voluntarily, then we will send you away. This is the only message possible. The Netherlands has been too tolerant to intolerant people for too long. We should not import a retarded political Islamic society to our country. There is nothing to be ashamed of to say this." (Deutsch, 2004, p. A8)

Dutch negotiators are efficient and straightforward. However, because decisions are based on consensus, the decision-making process can be rather slow. The Dutch are tolerant and willing to listen to divergent points of view. After a decision has been made to proceed with the project, however, those involved will act quickly. Being punctual during negotiations is important; keeping promises is also important. Presentations during negotiations should include facts to back up claims. When negotiating with the Dutch, keep in mind that they admire education, humor, honesty, and modesty (Morrison et al., 1994).

Nigeria
In Nigeria, negotiation in the form of bargaining in the marketplace is practiced from childhood. Therefore, Nigerians are very skillful negotiators. Because they are an individualistic society, negotiations are viewed as a competitive process. Age is equated with wisdom and is an important criterion when selecting negotiators. Gender, cultural background, and educational credentials are also important considerations.

Developing a personal relationship is important to the success of the negotiators. Time is not particularly important; therefore, negotiations may be lengthy. An intermediary should make the initial introductions. Being well dressed is important, and conscious demonstration of courtesy and consideration is expected. A successful negotiation is completed when the parties reach a verbal understanding. Contracts are considered flexible and may be oral or written. A bribe in the form of a mobilization fee may be required to expedite business (Moran & Stripp, 1991).

Russian Federation

The Russian Federation, which is now divided into 21 autonomous republics and 49 regions, has experienced numerous political and economic changes. In 1991, the government and production facilities were decentralized. Despite these changes, some negotiation tactics may remain the same while others will probably change as various management practices are initiated. In the past, negotiation sessions with the Russians have been long with the Russians controlling the agenda. The Russians look at compromise as a weakness and try to wait out their opponents to get more concessions. The Russian negotiators tend to be very animated in their discussions. Russians seem to be concerned with age, rank, and protocol. They are addressed by their full name and tend to be somewhat formal. Like U.S. people, Russians see time as money, and friendships are not crucial to business. Russians are not concerned with equality between business partners but are concerned with maximizing their own profits. Contracts are interpreted rigidly (Elashmawi & Harris, 1998; Samovar & Porter, 2004).

South Korea

When negotiating with South Koreans, remember that getting to know each other is important before beginning business discussions. Because relationships are important, plan to take time to build a solid business relationship. Decision-making may be somewhat slow, especially by European or North American standards. Because age and status are respected by South Koreans, it is advisable to include in the negotiating team older, senior executives from your firm. Sometimes silence during negotiations indicates a lack of understanding, so it is wise to ask if additional information is needed or to simply rephrase what was previously said. The initial offer should leave room to negotiate because South Koreans typically begin with an extreme position; they are willing to compromise to assure a win-win situation. Remember that, as in other Asian countries, people are not as direct as are people from the United States; they are likely to say what they think the other person wants to hear rather than being totally candid (Morrison et al., 1994).

Taiwan

In Taiwan, trust and respect are very important in business relationships. Because relationship building is important in this country, it is wise to take time to get to know your Taiwanese counterparts. Delays are common, and the decision-making process is somewhat slower than is customary in Europe or the United States. Because both age and seniority are admired in Taiwan, it is a good idea to include on your negotiating team older, senior executives. Women are not typically included on teams, so you should mention ahead of time when you plan to include a woman on your team to allow time for your Taiwanese counterparts to become accustomed to the idea. Suggestions for negotiating with the Taiwanese include being respectful of the elderly, protecting individual dignity, and being honest, modest, and sincere. Avoid criticizing competitors, speaking loudly or with your hands, and displaying emotions (Morrison et al., 1994).

As Moran and Stripp (1991) emphasize, "Negotiating on a global scale can present tremendous opportunities" (p. 1). Corporations can expand their markets, increase their profits and productivity, and lower their costs by negotiating globally.

Terms

- Competitive approach
- Compromise agreement
- Compromising
- Forcing
- Free trade zones

- Intercultural negotiation
- Integrative agreement
- Keiretsu system
- Legalism
- Negotiation strategies

- Problem-solving approach
- Tactics
- Trade blocs
- Validated license

Exercise 10.1

Instructions: Circle T for true or F for false.

1. T F In intercultural negotiation, the meeting location is associated with power and responsibilities.
2. T F Social class is unimportant in negotiator selection.
3. T F Failing to listen and talking too much are mistakes made during negotiations.
4. T F Relationship building is important in Arab and Latin American countries.
5. T F Constantly evaluating verbal and nonverbal behaviors of negotiators is unnecessary during negotiations.
6. T F Protocol is very important when dealing with the French.
7. T F Bribery is a common part of conducting business in India.
8. T F The Japanese prefer negotiating teams rather than a single negotiator.
9. T F Gender is important when negotiating in the Latin American countries.
10. T F Russian negotiating strategies include a need to control.

Questions and Cases for Discussion

1. Give three reasons why global joint ventures and strategic alliances are increasing.
2. What are the steps in the negotiation process?
3. When analyzing a negotiation situation, what are the models to consider?
4. Explain why following the saying, "When in Rome, do as the Romans do," is appropriate to the negotiation process.
5. Are most negotiation conflicts culturally based?
6. How can you prepare for cultural shock in negotiations?
7. What is the difference between compromise and integrative agreements?
8. Regional free trade zones are becoming popular. What are the negative and positive aspects of such trade zones? How will they help or hinder global organizations?
9. Which factors would you include in developing a negotiation model when negotiating with Canadians?
10. Intercultural negotiations have many implications. Discuss how two of these implications would affect negotiations between a U.S. negotiation team and a Japanese negotiation team. Discuss how two of these implications would affect negotiations between a Japanese negotiation team and a Mexican negotiation team.

Cases

The following procedure is recommended for analyzing the cases: (a) read the case carefully paying attention to details; (b) read the questions at the end of the case; (c) reread the case, taking notes on or highlighting the details needed for answering the questions; (d) identify relevant facts, underlying assumptions, and critical issues of the case; (e) list possible answers to the questions; and (f) select the most logical response to the question. Your professor may ask that you submit answers to the case questions in writing.

Case 1

A U.S. corporation has sent four people to meet with a group from a Russian organization. As the groups have had previous negotiations and contact, the U.S. group is hoping to go home with an agreement. The first meeting lasts 12 hours and ends in a deadlock. After agreeing to meet the next day, one of the U.S. negotiators notices the Russians leaving for an evening on the town. The next morning, the meeting is a repeat of the first, except that it is cut short so that the Russian negotiators can play golf. All agree to meet the next morning. The U.S. lead negotiator asks his company for time to wait out the Russians. Three weeks later (after many repeat meetings with no concessions), the Russians begin to make concessions. What do you know of the Russian culture that could explain what happened? Did the U.S. negotiator make the right move, or would pressure have made the Russians move faster?

Case 2

A U.S. salesman is in Spain negotiating a contract with a Spanish company. He has expressed to his Spanish colleagues an interest in attending a bullfight, so they invite him to one. As the first bull is released, the salesman jokingly says, "So who's going to win? I'll put my money on the bull." The Spaniards remained silent. The salesman felt very uncomfortable during the rest of the bullfight. Explain the salesman's faux pas and the negative effects it may have on his progress. If the salesman had taken time to research bullfighting, how might he have better handled the situation?

Case 3

International negotiators must diagnose meaning, motive, and intention on the spot if they are to get the contract or sale. How does someone become nonethnocentric and "do as the Romans do" in order to get the contract? How much will previous experience help or hinder the progress of the sale? Why does the visible part of the iceberg overshadow the hidden parts of the iceberg?

Case 4

The comparison chart (Ping, 1998, p. 533) in Table 10-1 is for a U.S. person who wants to sell a Chinese person a piece of expensive equipment. As you can see, the two gentlemen are not interpreting, perceiving, or expecting the same thing. Using this list, discuss what will probably happen to these negotiations and why if the two sides do not adapt. Now look at the individual factors that must change for there to be a win-win situation for the negotiations.

TABLE 10-1	Expectations and Behaviors of U.S. Americans and Chinese			
	Person Expectations	*Expected Conversations*	*Behaviors*	*Unfulfilled Expectations*
U.S. American	Complete job; obtain contract; close deal.	Equipment; specification; price; contract terms.	Professional; technically oriented.	Disappointed and confused.
Chinese	Establish long-term relationship; obtain contract; confirm relationship built; begin working on future.	Background; introduction to company; training and services.	Hospitable; less technically oriented.	Hurt and not respected.

Case 5

The following case concerns negotiations by KE Electronics (a South Korean company) and JCP (a Japanese company) to license each other their patents. JCP and KE were discussing KE's producing plasma display products (PDP).

KE asserts that JCP has demanded excessive royalties, has asked the South Korean government to restrict imports of JCP products sold in South Korea, is considering referring the patent infringement problem to the WTO, and contends that JCP is using the legal action as a diversion-ary tactic to curb KE's growth in the PDP industry. JCP has filed a court injunction in Japan to halt the sales of PDPs produced by KE. JCP asserts that KE has violated its patents on dissipation of heat when the panels are operated and has asked Tokyo Customs to suspend imports of KE PDPs.

Describe the important points in the case, including the differences in cross-cultural negotiation components and protocols that these two companies exhibit.

Activities

1. Invite three or four businesspersons with experience in international negotiation to serve as a panel to discuss "Negotiating with the Japanese" (or another culture of your choice).
2. Prepare a negotiation profile for a person who will be negotiating with representatives of a manufacturing firm in Mexico. Include verbal and nonverbal do's and don'ts.
3. Select a book containing information on international negotiation, such as Dean Allen Foster's *Bargaining Across Borders* (1995) or Roger E. Axtell's *The Do's and Taboos of International Trade* (1994), and prepare a one-page summary of nonverbal aspects of negotiating with persons of a culture you choose.
4. Review recent issues of a business journal or newsmagazine for an article related to international negotiation to be used as a basis for class discussion.
5. Prepare a list of possible problems U.S. businesswomen might encounter when negotiating with Arabs.

References

The Americas: More jaw-jaw, MERCOSUR and the EU. (30 October, 2004). *The Economist, 373*(8399), p. 68. Retrieved November 18, 2004, Proquest.

APEC (14 December 2004). Retrieved from http://www.apec.org/apec/member_economies.html

ASEAN-AFTA (14 December 2004). Retrieved from http://www.aseansec.org

Axtell, R. E. (1994). *The do's and taboos of international trade.* New York: Wiley.

Brett, J. M. (2001). *Negotiating globally: How to negotiate deals, resolve disputes, and make decisions across cultural boundaries.* San Francisco: Jossey-Bass.

CAFTA (14 December 2004). Retrieved from http://www.pcusa.org/trade/cafta.htm

CAN (14 December 2004). Retrieved from http://www.comunidadandina.org

CARICOM (14 December 2004). Retrieved from http://www.caricom.org

CEFTA (14 December 2004). Retrieved from http://www.cefta.org

Casse, P., & Deol, S. (1991). *Managing intercultural negotiations.* Washington, DC: Sietar.

Cellich, C. (1997, July 1). Communication skills for negotiations. *International Trade Forum,* 3, 22–28.

Cohen, R. (1998). *Negotiating across cultures.* Washington, DC: United States Institute of Peace Press.

Chaisrakeo, S., & Speece, M. (2004). Culture, intercultural communication competence, and sales negotiation: A qualitative research approach. *Journal of Business & Industrial Marketing,* 19(4), 267–282. Retrieved September 6, 2004, Emerald.

DeLozier, M. W., & Chi, Y. (2000). Rules to follow for successful Chinese business relationships. In D. L. Moore & S. Fullerton (Eds.), *International business practices: Contemporary readings* (pp. 179–184). Ypsilanti, MI: Academy of Business Administration.

Deutsch, A. (2004, November 20). Dutch official takes aim at radical Islam. *The Commercial Appeal,* A8.

EAC (14 December 2004). Retrieved from http://www.africa-business.com

ECCAS-CEEAC (14 December 2004). Retrieved from http://www.africa-union.org

ECOWAS (14 December 2004). Retrieved from http://www.sec.ecowas.int

EEA (14 December 2004). Retrieved from http://europa.eu.int/comm/external_relations/search/countries.htm

Elashmawi, F., & Harris, P. (1998). *Multicultural management 2000.* Houston, TX: Butterworth-Heinemann.

Evans, R. (2004, April 30). *European Union.* Retrieved November 26, 2004, from http://userpage.chemie.fu-berlin.de/adressen/eu.html

Foster, D. A. (1995). *Bargaining across borders.* New York: McGraw-Hill.

GCC (14, December 2004). Retrieved from http://www.arab.de/arabinfo/gcc.htm

Ghauri, P. N. (1983). *Negotiating international package deals.* Doctoral dissertation, Acta Universitatis Upsaliensis Studia Oeconomiae Negotiorum.

Graham, J., & Herberger, R. (1983). Negotiators abroad—Don't shoot from the hip. *Harvard Business Review,* 61, 160–169.

Harris, P. R., Moran, R. T., & Moran, S. V. (2004). *Managing cultural differences* (6th ed.). Burlington, MA: Elsevier-Butterworth-Heineman.

Kozicki, S. (1998). *Creative negotiating.* Holbrook, MA: Adams Media Corporation.

Leaptrott, N. (1996). *Rules of the game: Global business protocol.* Cincinnati: Thomson Executive Press.

Lewicki, R. J., Barry, B., Saunders, D. M., & Minton, J. W. (2003). *Essentials of negotiation* (3rd ed.). Homewood, IL: McGraw-Hill.

Lin, X., & Miller, S. J. (2003). Negotiation approaches: Direct and indirect effect of national culture. *International Marketing Review,* 20(3), 286–303.

MERCOSUR (14 December 2004). Retrieved from http://www.mercosurtc.com/

McCormack, M. (1984). *What they don't teach you at Harvard Business School.* New York: Bantam.

Moran, R. T., & Stripp, W. G. (1991). *Dynamics of successful international business negotiations.* Houston: Gulf.

Morrison, T., Conaway, W. A., & Borden, G. A. (1994). *Kiss, bow, or shake hands.* Holbrook, MA: Adams Media Corporation.

North American Free Trade Agreement between the government of the United States of America, the government of Canada, and the government of the United Mexican States. (1992). Washington, DC: U.S. Government Printing Office.

Ping, M.D. (1998). Culture and business: Interacting effectively to achieve mutual goals. In G. R. Weaver, (Ed.), *Culture, communication, and conflict* (pp. 528–536). Needham Heights, MA: Simon & Schuster.

Pruitt, D. G. (1998). Achieving integrative agreements in negotiation. In G. R. Weaver, *Culture, communication, and conflict* (pp. 509–517). Needham Heights, MA: Simon & Schuster.

SAARC (14 December 2004). Retrieved from http://www.saarc-sec.org/main.php

SADC (14 December 2004). Retrieved from http://www.un.org/esa/earthsummit/sadc-cp.htm

SAFTA (14 December 2004) Retrieved from http://www.cbcglobelink.org/cbcglobelink/events/SAFTA/index.htm

Samor, G. (16 November 2004). Gaps between Brazil, U.S. threaten trade talks, *Wall Street Journal,* p. A22. Retrieved November 18, 2004, from ProQuest.

Samovar, L. A., & Porter, R. E. (2004). *Communication between cultures* (5th ed.). Belmont, CA: Wadsworth/Thomson Learning.

Sebenius, J. K. (1992). Negotiation analysis: A characterization and review. *Management Science, 38*(1), 18–38.

Sprong, J. W. (2004). *The truth about sourcing.* Vital Sourcing, LLC. Retrieved from http://vitalsourcing.com

Thomas, D. C., & Inkson, K. (2004). *Cultural intelligence: People skills for global business.* San Francisco: Berrett-Koehler Publishers, Inc.

Tinsley, C. H. (2001). How negotiators get to yes: Predicting the constellation of strategies used across cultures to negotiate conflict. *Journal of Applied Psychology, 86*(4), 583–593.

Trade bloc (27 October 2004). Retrieved November 21, 2004, from http://en.wikipedia.org/wiki/Trade_bloc

Turkington, C. (1999). *The complete idiot's guide to cultural etiquette.* Indianapolis, IN: Alpha Books.

Weaver, G. R. (Ed.). (1998). *Culture, communication and conflict.* Needham Heights, MA: Simon & Schuster.

Yonekura, S. (1991). *What's the "keiretsu?"* Unpublished paper, Hitotubashi University, Japan.

CHAPTER

11

INTERCULTURAL NEGOTIATION COMPONENTS

Objectives

Upon completion of this chapter, you will

■ understand the elements of cross-cultural negotiation.

■ consider stereotypes that affect intercultural negotiations.

■ take into consideration comparative negotiation styles.

■ identify characteristics of effective negotiators.

■ understand the importance of protocol in intercultural negotiations.

■ understand how group and individual orientation, face-to-face strategies, and the media affect negotiations.

■ understand how personal constructs affect negotiations.

Intercultural negotiation requires choosing the appropriate communication strategies depending upon the many individual cultural and personal characteristics the negotiators have. The greater the difference between cultures, the greater the likelihood that miscommunication could result in negative outcomes.

CROSS-CULTURAL NEGOTIATION COMPONENTS

Before negotiating with persons from another culture, you should consider the players and the situation, cultural noise, national character, power and authority, perceptions, use of interpreters and translators, gender, environment, and relationships and substantive conflicts.

The Players and the Situation

According to Fisher (1980), you should learn how the negotiators and negotiating teams were selected. Try to determine the background of the players to anticipate the counterpart's behavior. Determine the expectations of the other negotiators, their negotiating style, and the role they have played in past negotiations. Attempt to provide an environment that is free of tension and conducive to an exchange of ideas and problem resolution.

Successful companies choose the players or team members carefully. If possible, have a local person on the team handle introductions, translations, explanations of cultural differences, permits, and navigation of the laws and customs of the country. Many times it is possible to hire such an individual through a local law firm, accountant, bank, or trade organization. If the negotiations are to take place in a hierarchical society, then be sure the people on the negotiating team come from the correct levels of seniority. As Malaysians say, "match eagles with eagles." Also, if you bring management from your home country, they should be part of the negotiation process. Because many cultures consider relationships vital, changing people after negotiating a contract could be viewed very negatively. A company has to consider how the team members' negotiating experience, seniority, political affiliation, gender, ethnic ties, kinship, technical knowledge, and personal attributes will relate to the individuals with whom the team members will be negotiating (Harris, Moran, & Moran, 2004). During negotiation orientations, U.S. Americans need to learn to take advantage of the opportunity to learn more about the personalities of their opponents. U.S. Americans tend to rush through this stage or fail to note its importance. The orientation allows each side to gain valuable information about the opponents. Relationship building is important in many cultures.

In many organizations, the salespeople are responsible for the negotiations and relationship development. In an examination of cultural issues at the national, organizational, and individual levels, it was found that culture affects a salesperson's negotiating style. Salespeople with high problem-solving orientation are likely to have a problem-solving approach that is more cooperative and leads to relationship building between two organizations. Successfully communicating interculturally is easier for people with a high cultural awareness and sensitivity to changing their actions depending on the cultural environment. How supportive or bureaucratic an organization is also empowers or disempowers an individual to use the problem-solving approach effectively. A salesperson in a bureaucratic organization loses the ability to use his or her intercultural communication competency due to the rules within the organization, although an individual from a supportive organizational culture is strengthened by the organization to use his or her intercultural communication abilities (Chaisrakeo & Speece, 2004).

Cultural Noise

Cultural noise includes anything that distracts or interferes with the message being communicated. Nonverbal messages, such as body language, space, and gift giving, can impede or expedite negotiations. For example, giving an inappropriate gift or one wrapped improperly is a form of cultural noise. In addition, what a person says can result in cultural noise, such as negotiators who criticize their competitor or make disparaging comments about their competitors' products.

Other differences that can affect the negotiations include how differently both parties see items, such as the following:

- Is the issue relationship building or control based?
- Do the parties use high- or low-context communication?
- Are the parties' arguments approached emotionally or logically?
- Are the parties' goals personal or corporate?
- Is trust based on written laws or friendship?
- Are both parties low- or high-risk takers?
- How do both parties view time?
- Do the parties use an authoritative or consensual decision-making style?
- Is agreement oral or written? (Harris et al., 2004)

National Culture

Fisher (1980) maintains that "patterns of personality do exist for groups that share a common culture" (p. 37). National character affects the negotiation process a great deal. As has been mentioned in earlier chapters, people of the United States value time; punctuality is very important. To a large degree, they also believe that they determine their own fate. The people of Latin American countries, on the other hand, are less concerned with time and stoically accept their fate. While numerous other differences exist between the values of the two cultures, these two attitudes could hamper negotiations considerably regardless of the attractiveness of the terms offered. Latin Americans ethnically are also a mixture of indigenous, European, Pacific Rim, and African heritages. Ethnic identity can be very personal in different parts of the world.

In Kenya, the Maasai leaders have been negotiating without the Magadi community members concerning adding a second soda mining plant at Magadi. The Magadi community leaders say the Maasai leaders hijacked the process. It is not unusual for patronage and bribery to take place in Magadi. Workers at the Magadi Soda Company also have problems with company management concerning harsh working conditions, poor medical coverage, lack of employment opportunities, nepotism, and lack of water, education, and security (Tiampati, 2004). This is one example of national character and indigenous people having problems.

Research on the impact of national culture on negotiation outcomes has shown that U.S.-Japanese cultural differences have limited the joint gains of the negotiation partners. The researchers attributed the negotiation shortcomings on the lack of knowledge of their counterparts' national cultural priorities and the necessity of such an understanding (Brett & Okumura, 1998). Equitable governance structure, preferences for negotiation that integrate the negotiators' interests, and the dyad's collectivism to each other have all been found as important to the success of an alliance (Cai, Wilson, & Drake, 2000; Steensma, Marino, Weaver, & Dickson, 2000; Tinsley, 1998).

Studying a national culture in preparation for negotiations will give you the central tendencies of a population, but it may not give you the within-group or individual variance you may need to negotiate successfully. It also does not tell you how many cultures may exist in the individuals with whom you are negotiating. National culture is only one of the cultures we all carry inside of ourselves. Other cultures include professional, social class, ethnic, regional, gender, and organizational/corporate (Sebenius, 2002b).

Power and Authority

Power is the ability to influence others; authority is the power to give commands and make final decisions. With the ability to influence comes the responsibility of the action taken. Power can make people and companies dependent or independent. Power can be an advantage or a disadvantage, depending on how it is used, but it must be used within the bounds of moral and ethical behavior (Lewicki, Barry, Saunders, & Minton, 2003).

Negotiators use power in influence strategies. Direct influence strategies include persuasion, argument, substantiation, and threats. Indirect influence strategies include appeals for sympathy, references to personal stakes in the negotiation, and references to status. Direct power strategies are meant to help the opponent; indirect strategies are appeals to the opponent to help you. The use of direct or indirect influence strategies is different from culture to culture (Brett, 2001).

For power to be meaningful, it has to be accepted. **Authority** (associated with power) is how an alliance chooses to conduct decision-making, strategy-setting, and influence over each other. When you accept power, you are giving it the authority to exist to the extent the control is acceptable to you. The personal constructs of the receiver of the power determine the strength of the power exerted. To create a synergism between global business partners, the firms must have balanced authority. **Balanced authority** allows each partner to share the decision-making role (Bradenburger & Nalebuff, 1996). If one of the partners seeks an **authority advantage** over its partner, this is normally done by claiming to possess superior resources or a superior position in the alliance. The alliance will probably fall apart (Teegen, 1998). The incentives exist to collaborate and at the same time compete with their alliance partner both during and after negotiations (Bradenburger & Nalebuff, 1996).

The balance of authority between partners positively affects the performance of the alliance (Saxton, 1997). If each partner has authority over its areas of expertise or specialization, generally you will have a successful dyad. Many researchers have found that an unbalanced authority relationship or asymmetrical relationship are inherently unstable and tend to collapse (Anderson & Weitz, 1989; Chisholm, 1989; Lorange & Roos, 1991; Nooteboom, Berger, & Noorderhaven, 1997; Provan, 1982; Teegen & Doh, 2002).

An example of the use of power and authority might occur in a meeting between the Chinese, who do not believe in a time schedule for negotiations, and the time-conscious U.S. Americans. The Chinese have the power of time on their side and possibly could make the U.S. Americans feel pressured to make compromises. Japanese negotiators have observed that they can make U.S. negotiators agree to concessions because they can "outwait" the impatient Americans (Engholm, 1991) (see Figure 11-1).

It is only with knowledge of the relative power of those negotiating that someone can determine if a deal is possible or not, will know whether to continue to negotiate, or if it is time to accept an offer (Brett, 2001).

Perception

Perception is the process by which individuals ascribe meaning to their environment; it is strongly affected by their culture. The stress of negotiation can cause misperception,

FIGURE 11-1   The Negotiation Waiting Game

but more often it is due to the different meanings of verbal and nonverbal cues in the cultures involved. For example, U.S. Americans might "talk" with their hands to clarify or exaggerate a particular point during negotiations with a German negotiating team. The Germans may incorrectly interpret the motions as spontaneous emotional displays that they consider impolite. Likewise, if a company were to send only one person to negotiate with the Japanese, the Japanese would assume the company was not serious about negotiating an agreement (Lewicki et al., 2003).

An example of differences in perception: A group of U.S. businessmen are visiting China exploring the possibility of building a factory in China. While the Chinese are showing them sites, the U.S. people ask the level of the available water pressure. The Chinese are perplexed and ask why. The U.S. people say because they need to be sure the water pressure is sufficient to fight fires for insurance purposes. The Chinese answer that they have sufficient water pressure but want to know why the U.S. people are speaking of bad luck before they begin the project because that will assure bad luck. What one culture sees as planning and necessary, another culture may perceive differently. (Ping, 1998)

Stimuli have both a physical size and a socioenvironmental meaning that can be different for each individual within and across cultures. Our experiences determine what stimuli we are sensitive or insensitive to. Although it is obvious to the Japanese and U.S. Americans that the two cultures are very different, it may not be so obvious that U.S. citizens and Canadians also have many cultural differences. Sometimes thinking we are alike can be more dangerous than knowing we are different and being careful of our verbal and nonverbal behaviors.

Perceptions of alliance negotiation objectives, particularly uncertainty avoidance, have been found to cause problems in negotiations (Schneider & DeMeyer, 1991).

Interpreters and Translators
Language considerations when negotiating include the following:

- Language serves as a key to culture.
- Who should be at the table and conversing?
- What is the social identity of those at the table?
- Facilitated dialogue is a slow process. (D'Amico & Rubinstein, 1999)

Using interpreters and translators can affect the negotiation process both positively and negatively. On the positive side, you have more time to think about your next statement while your previous statement is being translated. Because of the time it takes to translate, you are also more careful to state the message succinctly. On the negative side, because language and culture are intertwined, translators may not convey the intended message due to the nuances of the languages involved. Additional suggestions for using interpreters and translators were given in chapter 5.

Gender
Although women have made significant strides in the U.S. business world, there are still many parts of the world where women are not welcome during business negotiations. In some countries, women are in support functions or are simply "window dressing" for the firm. Women are considered as equals at the negotiation table in the United States, Israel, England, France, Switzerland, Sweden, Norway, Denmark, and India, and are beginning to gain equality in other parts of the world.

A key challenge for Anglo businesswomen can be Latin America's very patriarchal society. Yet in a survey conducted by Wederspahn's firm, "We found that U.S. American women in management and executive roles in foreign countries can do just as well as U.S. American men. Their biggest problem was convincing their companies to give them the assignments." (Staa, 1998, p. 8)

Environment
The environment in which the negotiations take place is particularly important for intercultural negotiations. If meetings are held at the office of one of the parties, then that party has control and responsibility as host to the other party. When one of the parties is at home, they have "home court" advantage—the advantage of access to information and human resources. When negotiators are on their home territory, they are likely to be more assertive than when in the host's territory. Reasons for this include conditioning. We are taught it is rude to be impolite to someone in his or her home or office. The host negotiators may also have a feeling of superiority because the other team is coming to them (Lewicki et al., 2003). One way to avoid this competitiveness is to choose a neutral site. The neutrality of the site eliminates the psychological advantage of the home ground.

The actual room where the negotiations take place could play an important role if the room makes one of the negotiating teams feel comfortable and the other team uncomfortable. Cultural differences need to be considered when choosing the site. Details to consider include the physical arrangement of the room, the distance between people and teams, and the formal or informal atmosphere of the room.

The arrangement of the table and chairs can also make a difference. Some cultures ascribe a title to people according to the seating arrangement. Those same cultures also would expect the other team to have the same number of negotiators and negotiators of equal rank to theirs. The Japanese particularly have been surprised when the United States sends a younger person of a lower rank to meet with a top official of their company. Because the Japanese conduct side negotiations with their counterpart in the opposing company, it is necessary for everyone to know his or her counterparts. Two ways of arranging seating in a meeting to accomplish this purpose are shown in Figures 11-2 and 11-3 (Funakawa, 1997).

Relationship and Substantive Conflicts

Being able to identify the conflict in which you are involved is important. Issues form out of substantive and relationship-based differences. The substantive issues include use and control of resources. The relationship-based issues center on the long-term friendship or partnership. Negotiations should be conducted in such a way as to protect future relations.

The conflict may be seen from the point of view of both negotiators or may be seen from the point of view of only one negotiator. The conflict may involve a deadlock, behavior difference, lack of a common goal, communication problems, poor translators, misunderstandings, secrets, lack of feedback, or unfamiliar tactics. Some of these factors may be due to the negotiators' perceptions of reality and their unconscious ability to block out information that is inconsistent with their cultural beliefs. Negotiation breakdown or deadlock may be identified by the negotiators' repeating themselves using the same arguments. The negotiators may not be saying anything constructive but merely allowing the passage of time, or nonnegotiation tactics may be used to try to change the attitudes of the other side (Brett, 2001).

Jervis (1998) defines **cognitive dissonance** as follows: "Two elements are in a dissonant relation if, considering these two alone, the obverse of one element would follow from the other" (p. 452). A simpler definition is that cognitive dissonance is the psychological conflict or anxiety that results from inconsistencies between what one does and what one believes. Cognitive dissonance, logic, and reasoning differences normally due to cultural differences are often the focus of such conflicts because your perspectives are based on your cultural training, and your oppositions' perspectives are based on their cultural training. Cognitive dissonance may generate the following emotions and actions: frustration, regression, fixation, resignation, repression, projection, and aggression (Cohen, 1998). If you are aware of the possible cultural shocks before entering negotiations, it will be easier to adapt your negotiation style to accommodate both your own and others' ethnocentrism and maintain your patience while dealing with the differences. Part of negotiation is being able to discern what is going on mentally with the negotiators on the other side of the table. By studying the psychological predisposition of the other culture, you will be familiar with at least some of the variations between the two cultures. Communicating adequately is difficult when the cultural programming of the negotiators differs. Within a culture, there is normally an internal consistency to the beliefs and values of that culture. In intercultural negotiation, people need to be cognizant of not projecting their cultural thinking onto the other side. Be sure to discuss every point and not attribute motives

FIGURE 11-2   Seating Arrangement A

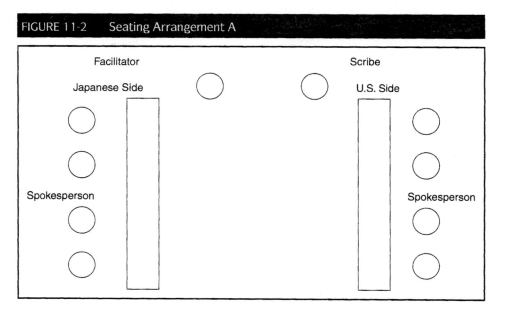

FIGURE 11-3   Seating Arrangement B

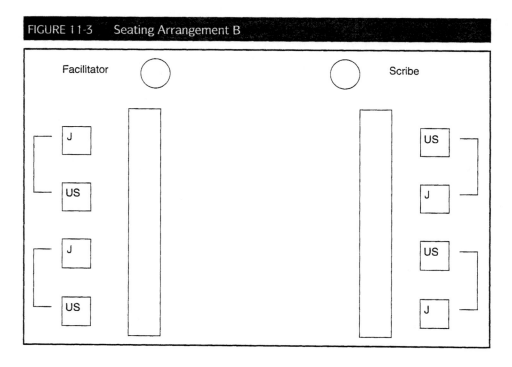

to the other side that may, in fact, be nonexistent. Cultures are different concerning how they conceptualize information, how they use information, and how they associate causes and effects.

> A sales executive who worked in Vietnam had been meeting with a potential customer to gain his business. The Vietnamese person was very difficult to convince about the advantages of the product, and it did not seem as if a contract would be signed. Later the sales executive was walking with his boss to the tennis court and ran into the potential customer. The customer knew his boss and told him to come to the customer's office the next day to sign the contract. (Verluyten, 2002)

To prepare for behavioral differences, you must train yourself to perceive the differences and adjust your reasoning accordingly. Developing "an efficient and coherent mental cross-referencing system" (Fisher, 1997, p. 22) that automatically adjusts your reactions saves time, money, and problems. Although it is not possible in the international setting, much less in our day-to-day activities, to have a built-in response to all situations, if you build a mechanism to screen, sort, code, and store differences, you are able to respond more quickly. In other words, you develop a new mindset. This new cognitive structure allows us to share a defined culture and way of acting and thinking. Because our cognitive structures are programmed to our own cultures, reprogramming is disturbing to the existing system. Our mind inherently tries to make cognitive dissonance fit our current cognitive system rather than expanding our cognitive system by recognizing the difference and developing more storage cognitively (Fisher, 1997).

Because lifestyles within cultures vary, so does the vocabulary that develops to explain the culture. When cultures are different, the words that develop are also different. The subjective meaning of the translation can be very important. The United States is a very individual-oriented society. The Japanese equivalent of the word for individual has a negative connotation because the Japanese are a group-oriented culture. Education in the United States means academic achievement and is associated with school attendance. In the Spanish-language cultures, however, education includes being polite, well bred, and sensitive as well as covering school attendance and academic achievement. The idea of "fair play" is an example of a concept that does not exist in any other language yet is used frequently in U.S. business, sports, and other aspects of life. Because fair play is a culturally bound phrase, other cultures cannot be expected to understand its meaning. Gestures, tone of voice, and cadence further complicate the translation situation (Cohen, 1998).

STEREOTYPES THAT AFFECT INTERCULTURAL NEGOTIATIONS

The way people of a culture view themselves and the way they are actually viewed by persons of other cultures often have an impact on intercultural negotiations. (A discussion of stereotypes of persons of selected cultures was included in chapter 1.) Schneider and Barsoux (2002) point out the disparities that exist between the way U.S. people think of themselves and the way they are viewed by foreigners.

U.S. Persons' Views	Foreigners' Views of U.S. Persons
• Informal, friendly, casual	• Undisciplined, too personal, familiar
• Egalitarian	• Insensitive to status
• Direct, aggressive	• Blunt, rude, oppressive
• Efficient	• Obsessed with time, opportunistic
• Goal/achievement oriented	• Promise more than they deliver
• Profit oriented	• Materialistic
• Resourceful, ingenious	• Work oriented; deals more important than people
• Individualistic, progressive	• Self-absorbed, equating the "new" with "best"
• Dynamic, find identity in work	• Driven
• Enthusiastic, prefer hard-sell	• Deceptive, fearsome
• Open	• Weak, untrustworthy

Negotiators from the United States should, therefore, take into consideration this disparity in viewpoints and make a concerted effort to change some of the negative stereotypes, such as being rude and obsessed with time, when interacting during negotiations.

COMPARATIVE NEGOTIATION STYLES

Intercultural negotiators need to be selected carefully. People who can negotiate well in their own culture may not be successful at negotiating interculturally. Intercultural negotiators need to be able to ascertain where their opposition "is coming from." The negotiator must be able to grasp the situation and be able to recognize whether the opposition's negotiators are bound by their culture or are taking on some of the opposing cultural characteristics. Being able to discern role behavior and knowing the proper deference is important in intercultural negotiations (Moran & Stripp, 1991). A brief comparison of the negotiation styles of different cultures is shown in Table 11-1 (Elashmawi & Harris, 1998; Ruch, 1989).

CHARACTERISTICS OF EFFECTIVE NEGOTIATORS

Effective negotiators are observant, patient, adaptable, and good listeners. They appreciate the humor in a situation but are careful to use humor only when appropriate. Good negotiators are mentally sharp. They think before they speak, and they are careful to speak in an agreeable, civil manner. Businesspeople who negotiate internationally know that negotiations are carried out consistently within a culture but that cultures have their own distinct negotiating styles (Simintiras & Thomas, 1998). They do their homework on the countries with which they are negotiating and become knowledgeable about their history, customs, values, and beliefs. Effective negotiators know that in many cultures history is revered, and displaying knowledge of the country's past can do much to pave the way to smooth negotiations. Good negotiators praise what is praiseworthy and refrain from criticizing anything about the negotiators or their country. They keep their promises and always negotiate in good faith (Sebenius, 2002a).

Element	U.S. Americans	Japanese	Arabians	Mexicans
Group composition	Marketing oriented	Function oriented	Committee of specialists	Friendship oriented
Number involved	2–3	4–7	4–6	2–3
Space orientation	Confrontational; competitive	Display harmonious relationship	Status	Close, friendly
Establishing rapport	Short period; direct to task	Longer period; until harmony	Long period; until trusted	Longer period; discuss family
Exchange of information	Documented; step-by-step; multimedia	Extensive; concentrate on receiving side	Less emphasis on technology, more on relationship	Less emphasis on technology, more on relationship
Persuasion tools	Time pressure; loss of saving/ making money	Maintain relationship references; intergroup connections	Go-between; hospitality	Emphasis on family and on social concerns goodwill measured in generations
Use of language	Open/direct; sense of urgency	Indirect; appreciative; cooperative	Flattery; emotional; religious	Respectful; graciousness
First offer	Fair +/−5 to 10%	+/−10 to 20%	+/−20 to 50%	Fair
Second offer	Add to package; sweeten the deal	−5%	−10%	Add incentive
Final offer	Total package	Make no further concessions	−25%	Total package
Decision-making process	Top management team	Collective	Team makes recommendation	Senior manager and secretary
Decision maker	Top management team	Middle line with team consensus	Senior manager	Senior manager
Risk taking	Calculated; personal responsibility	Low group responsibility	Religion based	Personally responsible

TABLE 11-1 Negotiation Styles of Different Cultures

Negotiators, however, cannot escape their own cultural mindsets. Even professional training cannot erase the deep-seated perceptions from childhood (Cohen, 1998). These perceptions must not be vocalized, however, because nothing is to be gained by denouncing the behavior or customs of others simply because they do not fit your cultural mindset. Because such factors as social skills, gender, age, experience in intercultural relations, and background may be important in a specific culture, considering these factors when selecting negotiators is recommended.

Noted negotiator Dr. Chester L. Karrass says, "In business, you don't get what you deserve; you get what you negotiate. Why take 'no' for an answer? Successful people don't. They get what they want by negotiating better deals for both parties" (Karrass, 1996).

IMPORTANCE OF PROTOCOL IN INTERCULTURAL NEGOTIATIONS

Protocol is important in understanding which negotiation strategy should be followed. Leaptrott (1996) gives three fundamental classifications of protocol: tribal, collective, and pluralist. Tribal involves the family unit, close relationships, and a connection to the past. Collectivism is an extension of tribal and includes larger groups, such as a town, nation, or race. The pluralist society has many different groups and combinations of groups, and individuals are free to join those they want to join. Most countries fit one of these three protocol classifications. Table 11-2 includes a comparison of the three protocol types (pp. 4–7). Parts of China, Africa, and India are examples of countries that are still basically tribal because they are agrarian societies. A person's word is more important to building a relationship than anything else in tribal cultures. Collectivistic cultures are also very concerned with relationships; examples can be found in Japan, Greece, Spain, and Indonesia. Examples of pluralist societies include the United States, Great Britain, and France.

The three styles of protocol are very different in some areas and similar in others. This makes the way the variables of policy, interaction, deliberation, and outcome are used vary, depending on the two cultures involved in the negotiation. In addition, remembering to consider the situation from the other culture's viewpoint yet maintaining your own cultural viewpoint will avoid problems in many instances.

Although all cultures share the need for honesty, courage, respect for human dignity, fairness, and love, these values can have very different meanings in different cultures (Samovar & Porter, 2004). Reality is difficult to assess when two cultures do not share the same definition of needs. If the expectations are not met and the perceptions are wrong, disastrous business consequences are usually the result (Ping, 1998).

GROUP VS. INDIVIDUAL ORIENTATION

Group orientation ideally results in a solution that is good for everyone because all points of view are supposedly considered. Negotiations with **group-oriented** negotiators are detail oriented to determine the proper solution. Your identity belongs to the group of which you are a member. The group has to reach a consensus on any and all decisions, and this probably is not done during the negotiation sessions. The individuals in the group avoid making an individual decision. Individuals who are not group oriented may feel that group-oriented negotiators appear to stall, are not interested in the negotiations, and give ambiguous statements. Group-oriented cultures tend to view contracts as flexible (Hofstede & Hofstede, 2005).

Japan is one of the most group-oriented cultures in the world, perhaps because of the number of years they were physically secluded from other cultures; however, given the number of years they have now interacted with other cultures, many Japanese have adapted very well to different negotiation strategies. Although the Japanese culture is quite different from that of the United States, Japan and the United States do have a common work ethic—both applaud hard work. Even though the original management styles were very different, as joint ventures and subsidiaries of Japanese companies become part of the U.S. economy, U.S. corporations are beginning to use some of the Japanese management concepts. Both cultures are gaining an understanding of their differences and are learning to cope. Other group-oriented cultures include the Chinese, Polynesians, Native Americans, and Africans (Hofstede & Hofstede, 2005).

TABLE 11-2	Protocol Characteristics of Tribal, Collective, and Pluralist Cultures		
Area	*Tribal*	*Collective*	*Pluralist*
Person's responsibility	Supports family and follow rules of society	Group contribution, honor, conformity	Personal growth, achievement, independence
Expectations of others	Mutual support and absolute loyalty	Humility, respect, support	Integrity, performance, competence
Interaction with others	With strangers, aloof, formal; with friends, warm, welcoming, trusting	Does not stand out, friendly yet noncommittal to strangers; loyal, firm relationship with friends	Informal, direct communication
Traits respected	Status, strength, cunning	Strength with humility, cleverness, knowledge	Creativity, personal achievement, status
Attitude toward foreigners	Cautious, defensive, formal, distrustful	Cautious, aggressive, defensive	Open, curious, nonhostile
Reason to work	Works to live	Works to live	Lives to work
Life objective	Respect of group, contribute to family	Succeeds at work, to get opponent to concede something	Success beyond goals
Definition of winning	Receiving what is asked for	Zero-sum, win-lose	Zero-sum or win-win
Business environment	Strong vertical hierarchy, leaders inaccessible, open offices for lower levels, offices for managers	Shared power, no one stands out, open offices, location important	Layered hierarchy, private spaces, best spaces for top management
Conducts business	Must control, manipulative, correspondence limited	Divided responsibilities; strategy and ritual are important; correspondence open, shared	Direct, formality with strangers, correspondence to many
Learning style	Visual, data, coaching generalized; repetition helpful	Shown, learns with others best	Detailed information, verbal text, verification
Feedback	Avoids details, not accountable, subjective feedback	Within the group, consensus a must, nothing negative	Direct, specific, objective, impersonal
Decision making	Decisions at the top; pride, emotion before objectivism	Consensus, final decisions from the top	Independent, rational process, mid-management approval
Attitude toward time, schedules, plans, and change	Linear time, process oriented, changes are okay, no detailed plans	Process oriented, no definition of length of time necessary, need for changes seen as errors	Linear time, punctual, detailed plans, change expected
Approach to problem solving	Blame assessment more important than solving problems and consequences for those who are to blame	Problems are evaded; someone loses face; conflict; no problem admitted	Addressed quickly, rationally; analyzes after the fact

This group approach assumes that the action taken is conservative and well thought out and that all options were considered in the decision (Foster, 1992).

> Aramco was losing money on one of its trucking operations in Saudi Arabia. Finally, an Arab was able to buy the franchise and set up his own system. Knowing his own people, he worked out a series of complex reinforcement schedules for each truck and driver. He even penalized them for every valve cap that was missing and rewarded drivers when nothing that was supposed to be there was missing. Oil levels in the crankcase, maintenance schedules, time schedules . . . everything was examined and recorded. The cost per ton-mile dropped to a third of what it had been under American management. (Weaver, 1998, p. 14)

Brazilians, although very gregarious, value the group over the individual, believe in saving face, and are indirect in business affairs. Brazilians also are very flexible; they feel that to be intelligent and imaginative you have to be able to adjust to new developments (Harris et al., 2004).

If you are **individually oriented,** you will be concerned with the best contract for your company and may not be concerned about whether the agreement is good for the other company. If more than one negotiator is on your team, one person will probably control the negotiations and make the final decision concerning the various issues being discussed. Usually, much individual sparring has taken place with members of the other team before the negotiation meeting. The individually oriented person tends to interpret the contract very rigidly.

The U.S. culture is probably one of the most individualistic cultures in the world. Another individualistic culture is Latin America. According to Foster (1992), a Latin negotiation is frequently an internal contest of individuals battling for position and power. Other cultures that are very individualistic include the British, French, Australians, and Canadians (Hofstede & Hofstede, 2005).

FACE-TO-FACE STRATEGIES

Face-to-face strategies are concerned with negotiating in person rather than through the mail, fax, telephone, telegraph, lawyers, or other intermediaries. People in many cultures will only negotiate on a face-to-face basis. The Japanese, in particular, do not like to make commitments over the telephone or in writing until after numerous face-to-face meetings have taken place. In many European countries, as well as in India and Japan, contracts are considered an insult to the trust of the partners. They place great importance on face-to-face encounters and oral agreements (Prosser, 1985).

Some of the face-to-face negotiators' behaviors include the following:

- **irritators**—phrases that are used repeatedly, such as "generous offer."
- **counterproposals**—immediate counterproposals made less frequently by skilled negotiators.
- **argument dilution**—using multiple arguments when one is sufficient; a technique used less by skilled negotiators.
- **reviewing the negotiation**—done more often by the more skilled negotiators. (Harris et al., 2004)

ROLE OF THE MEDIA

Representatives of the media—television, radio, and newspapers—have a unique position in creating multicultural understanding and misunderstanding. Most of the views you have of other cultures have been gained through the media window. The media have been used in various ways, including supporting and tearing down political candidates and officeholders and defining and distorting numerous messages. Media people also represent a culture and have cultural biases. The media tend to have a stereotypical view of business. Media members have generally presented other cultures through the bias of the U.S. perceptual grid.

Advertisers make up the largest group of negotiators in the world—they all compete for consumers' dollars. Advertisers use media extensively and have learned that differences in culture necessitate different delivery and content if the ad is to successfully promote a product (Prosser, 1985).

An example of media influence in the world today is the CNN (Cable News Network) broadcasts during Operation Desert Storm. The antagonists and protagonists in the battle and everyone else in the world who had access to satellite television broadcasts watched the CNN coverage. Another example of media influence is the number of teenagers worldwide who wear jeans, listen to the same music, and watch the same movies. Still more examples of world coverage were the 9/11 attacks in the United States, the war in Afghanistan against the Taliban, and Operation Iraqi Freedom.

Movies are big promoters of stereotypes. Many times, the wrong perception of a culture is gained from the subject matter presented in movies or a television series that is broadcast in foreign countries. Many of the stereotypes foreigners have of U.S. Americans (such as all carry guns) are due to movies and television series. Likewise, U.S. Americans hold views of other cultures (such as the belief that all followers of Islam do not drink alcoholic beverages) based on movie and television messages. Because perceptions of other cultures are often acquired through the media and may be brought to the negotiation table, an awareness of the role of the media is important.

PERSONAL CONSTRUCTS

Personal constructs refer to individual belief systems and attitudes. The individual belief system, attitudes, or personal constructs differ from culture to culture and often from person to person within a given culture. What you expect to happen cognitively is based on your life experiences. No two people in the world have the same set of life experiences. Cultural stereotypes are dangerous even though they provide clues to the behavior of the "average" person in the culture.

The reason "birds of a feather flock together" is such a powerful adage is because we like to spend time with those who are like us. This is one of the reasons why people say, "They're in America; they should act like Americans." The U.S. Americans who make these statements, however, do not understand they need to reciprocate and adopt certain foreign behaviors when they visit another country. Of course, without a lot of time and willingness, it is very difficult "to do as the Romans do."

The question has been raised as to whether it is possible for a person to become a "native" of another country (Brett, 2001). Perhaps not, but it is possible to learn about the culture, customs, and traditions and to be sensitive to them. People react more positively to people who shift their communication style toward the new culture; however, the other culture may become threatened if the group distinctiveness is threatened. Moderate levels of adaptation seem to improve relations, but large levels of adaptation may have negative effects. Moderate adaptation reflects respect and sensitivity toward another culture. Those who choose strong adaptation may unintentionally be perceived as having an uncomplimentary view of the new culture, a similar view held of individuals who choose not to adapt at all (Brett, 2001).

Everyone is ethnocentric to a great degree. Because losing ethnocentrism means changing, it is a very powerful construct. Resistance to change is a universal construct (Hendon, Hendon, & Herbig, 1999). Negotiations take place within the political, economic, social, and cultural systems of the countries involved; these are the environmental issues of negotiation.

The cultural systems involved in the negotiation may be similar or divergent. Negotiations take place within the context of the four Cs: common interest, conflicting interests, compromise, and criteria (Moran & Stripp, 1991).

Alfonso Lopez-Vasquez has researched Hispanic work styles brought into the Anglo workplaces. One of his main findings has been that both sides, the U.S. Americans and the Hispanics, have misconceptions and apprehensions about each other. One of the mistakes U.S. Americans have made is to treat the Hispanic workers as if there are no differences in the two cultures. To get the kind of work they want, U.S. Americans have to understand the cultural differences. (Staa, 1998)

Common interest considers that both parties in the negotiation share, have, or want something that the other party has. Without a common goal, there is no need for negotiation. Areas of **conflicting interests** include payment, distribution, profits, contractual responsibilities, and quality. **Compromise** includes areas of disagreement. Although a win-win negotiated settlement would be best for both parties, the compromises that are negotiated may not produce that result. The **criteria** include the conditions under which the negotiations take place.

Communication is plagued with misinterpretations. When perspectives, environment, the four Cs, and the negotiation situation are all considered together, the possibility of misinterpretations is magnified. When the negotiators are from different cultures, they have different mindsets or differing cognitive systems for reacting to situations. For example, ethics and ethical behavior that are always near the surface can confound negotiations if the two cultures have very different views on proper business ethics. For example, the Japanese consider a contract to be an adaptive tool rather than a rigid legal document as most U.S. Americans would interpret it. Nigerians, Mexicans, and the Chinese find that bribes placed in the proper places help business run smoothly, but such behavior is considered unethical in the United States.

During the Persian Gulf War, the soldiers from various countries were restricted to the military compounds because the Saudi Arabians were afraid that if the soldiers had contact with the Saudi civilians, it would threaten the Saudi way of life. This was the beginning of the United States' realization that everyone does not want our form of life. The Taliban and al-Qaida also are very opposed to and feel very threatened by the U.S. way of life.

The mindsets of businesspeople have developed to give stability and are mutually compatible with other businesspeople in their field in their culture. When cognitive dissonance is acknowledged due to a different culture, peace of mind is lost, and you will strive to reestablish a new peace of mind. Realizing that you are locked into your own mindsets is important. Acknowledging that the other culture's representatives are having the same mindset difficulties is crucial. When negotiating with another culture, you will find beliefs you do not share and will have cognitive dissonance. The more abstract a subject is, the more difficult it will be to view it from your counterpart's mindset (Fisher, 1997).

The following is an example of how cognitive dissonance works and how we try to make something fit into our current mindset.

In the West, we are surrounded by right angles—rooms, windows, doors, furniture, and buildings. If someone asks you what the shape of the filing cabinet across the room is, you would say rectangular. However, unless you are looking at the object directly from above or in front, you would be seeing the object from an angle, and it would not appear to have 90° angles. Because from experience you know these things have 90° angles, you know it is a rectangular object. These are preconceived cognitives that you have learned to trust. If you are placed in a room that has been devised to elude our senses because it is not built proportionally, you will try to make objects in the room fit your cognitive model. It is almost impossible for persons to visualize reality as it is, rather than how it is in their mind. (Fisher, 1997)

If friendship and trust are important, it may be necessary to plan a number of social activities. These activities are essential in building personal relationships before negotiations begin or before a solution can be reached in the negotiations. In many cultures, business is conducted with family and friends, and personal relationships are considered important for the long run. In other cultures, friendships are not important to business relationships. The following summary of negotiating strategies of the United States and other selected countries is a beginning point for anyone doing business in these countries. As was emphasized earlier, it is important to avoid stereotyping. People who have lived and worked in another culture may alter their negotiation strategies based on firsthand knowledge of strategies that have proven effective.

United States

U.S. negotiators are very focused on completing the deal. They tend to be profit oriented and direct in their negotiating strategies. Their presentations tend to be to the point. U.S. negotiators do not need a personal relationship to enter into negotiations with another party. Many U.S. persons do not even develop personal relationships with people with whom they work. They will work during meals, while playing golf, or at almost any other time. Because the U.S. is made up of many different cocultures, variations exist by ethnic group, region, gender, or age. U.S. negotiators can be very informal. U.S. negotiators respond well to facts and numbers. Many U.S. people have difficulty deciphering high-context nonverbal signals. U.S. negotiators like to bargain from a position of strength; this sometimes leads to bargains that represent a win position for them and a lose position for their opponent. U.S. negotiators tend to choose strategies that are individually oriented and many times use the media (Morrison, Conaway, & Borden, 1994). The United States is a pluralistic society (Leaptrott, 1996).

Canada

Canada has two major groups, as well as variations throughout the provinces, when it comes to negotiation strategies. The two major groups are the French province of Quebec (including parts of New Brunswick and eastern Ontario), and the remainder of Canada.

French Canadians are less open than the remainder of the Canadians and exhibit a stronger ethnocentrism than the other provinces. Canadians tend to be well informed, analytical, and prefer objective information. The French Canadians are more linear in their problem-solving process, and the English Canadians are more concerned with abstract or theoretical values in their problem-solving process. Although they are not quite as direct as U.S. negotiators, they approach negotiations with a strong sense of self-determination. Canadians are closer to the British than the United States when it comes to controlling their emotions and do not need to be friends to engage in business. Negotiators are selected for expertise and success in negotiating. However, gender, age, and social class are used to disqualify negotiators more by the French Canadians than the English Canadians. French Canadians are more concerned with protocol than are English Canadians. Promptness and wise use of time are important in Canada. Trust is also an important component in negotiations in Canada (Harris et al., 2004). Canadians choose the more individually oriented negotiation strategies. Most of Canada is considered tribal; some parts are pluralistic (Leaptrott, 1996).

China

When negotiating with the Chinese, remember that they believe in a win-win negotiation strategy that allows both sides to be winners to increase the strength of the relationship. The Chinese value a cooperative approach to negotiation rather than bargaining strategies. They actually believe that negotiators who use the win-lose approach to make a large profit at someone else's expense are "unscrupulous merchants." However, that does not mean that all Chinese negotiators are altruistic. Although concessive negotiation can be used, it is important that stability and harmony are in no way harmed by the negotiations. Both sides should be willing to make concessions to achieve and maintain a harmonious relationship. The environment is also important; a neutral site is recommended (Zhao, 2000). Because the Chinese will have many people on their negotiating team, the other side needs to match the number on the Chinese team. They should also have a seating arrangement worked out in advance—one that reflects the status and hierarchy of the team members.

Because verbal and nonverbal information is more important to the Chinese than formal, written, or legal documents, everything that is in writing also needs to be discussed. The Chinese establish that they want an agreement in broad terms and then work on the details, although the United States team wants to work from the details to an agreement. Bribery is not looked on favorably in China (Zhao, 2000). In summary, relationship building is important to the Chinese; they tend to be group oriented and prefer face-to-face negotiations. China is considered a collective culture (Leaptrott, 1996).

England

The English are very matter-of-fact about negotiations. Objective facts are listened to with interest, but emotional displays are considered improper. The English do not easily change their minds on an issue and are very analytical. They tend to understate positions during negotiations. Although they tend to be very individualistic, company policy is always followed without question. Business friendships are not necessary, and the English have no difficulty saying "no" during negotiations. Like U.S. negotiators, the English tend to be very deadline oriented (Morrison et al., 1994). They are individualistic in their negotiation strategies. England is a tribal culture (Scotland and Wales are pluralistic) (Leaptrott, 1996).

France

Before beginning negotiations with the French, it is important to have a good French-language interpreter who can decode high-context and nonverbal communication in addition to translating the language. The French expect the negotiator to have the correct social and educational background and have the authority to make decisions. If a relationship has not been developed first, it is not unusual for the French negotiator to have a certain distrust of members of the opposing team. Trust is earned. Because the French are Cartesian-logic oriented, presentations should be very complete and detailed. Negotiators need answers for many different scenarios in addition to the one they hope to sell. French negotiators do not mind if the negotiations develop into debates.

The French are indirect in their negotiating style in contrast to U.S. negotiators, who are direct and bottom-line oriented. Quality is more important than speed; the negotiations should not be rushed but should take as much time as necessary. The French do not conduct negotiations during meals; mealtimes are meant to be enjoyed (Asselin & Mastron, 2000). The French are individualistic in their negotiation strategies; they also prefer face-to-face negotiations. The French are striving toward pluralism; however, they are more tribal in the southern part of the country (Leaptrott, 1996).

Germany

Germany's strategies during negotiations are very much no-nonsense. Germans insist on permanent and stringent contracts. In the Federal Republic of Germany, the corporation, employer associations, and unions each have roles in negotiations. However, with the merging of East and West Germany, these social partnerships are changing.

The German stra'egy is to begin business immediately after introductions. Their strategy is very slow an.d methodical with no humor involved in the process. They are not impressed with "educated guesses"; it is better to acknowledge a lack of information. Although negotiating with Germans may be slow, they tend to be direct. Negotiators will know where they stand during the negotiation process (Samovar & Porter, 2004). The Germans are individualistic and also prefer face-to-face negotiations. Germany is considered a pluralistic country (Leaptrott, 1996).

Japan
In Japan, the negotiations are carried out before the transaction gets to the negotiation table. Through conversations between numerous individuals on both sides that can take place in restaurants, bars, golf courses, and offices, persuasive appeals are made. The Japanese then meet and come to a consensus before meeting with the other side at the negotiation table. The negotiation table is a ritual rather than a place to actually change offers or minds (Sebenius, 2002a). The Japanese look for a win-win situation.

For the Japanese, negotiation is a status game with people of equal levels discussing the negotiations in casual settings. The power levels between the companies can be very important. A larger corporation generally holds more relative power in the negotiations than a medium- or small-sized company. Showing commitment to a long-term relationship and being enthusiastic are very important strategies to use. The Japanese will learn everything possible about the members of the opposing negotiation team and their corporation. To negotiate successfully with the Japanese, it is important to be well prepared with data and information and to learn a great deal about them. When disputes arise, taking a break to discuss options is recommended for members of both teams. The Japanese generally do not have authority to make concessions without discussing them with their colleagues first (Nishiyama, 2000). The Japanese are very group oriented; they often use media and prefer face-to-face negotiations. Japan is a collective culture (Leaptrott, 1996).

Mexico
Connections, introductions, and relationship building are very important to doing business in Mexico. Using connections is a two-way street with favors being exchanged on both sides. While *la mordida* (a bribe) seems very unethical to U.S. negotiators, it is simply a way to get things done in Mexico. However, as salaries in Mexico increase, the practice of *la mordida* is expected to cease. Decisions tend to be made by the senior executives in all but the largest organizations rather than by committee (Hinkelman, 1994).

Mexican negotiators are selected on status, family connections, personal or political influence, and education. Protocol is very important to Mexicans; however, they are not overly concerned about time. Being on time for appointments, however, is expected. Emotional arguments are considered to be persuasive arguments. Trust is initially assumed and then proven through interpersonal actions.

Negotiating strategies are more win-win than win-lose in Mexico. Because a friendship has developed, it is expected that each side would want both parties to profit. Mexican negotiators prefer to have the issues before them well in advance of the negotiations. A neutral site should be chosen. Patience is of the utmost importance when negotiating with Mexicans. Talks will begin after social conversation has been exchanged. Bargaining in negotiations is considered part of the game by Mexicans. Using objective facts is recommended when presenting a proposal. The best proposal should not be put on the table first; leave room to bargain. Most Mexican executives view the personal commitment to be more important than the written contract (Hinkelman, 1994). Mexicans tend to be group oriented in their negotiation style and prefer face-to-face negotiations. Mexico is a tribal culture (Leaptrott, 1996).

The Netherlands
The Netherlands have been very active in trade since the 1600s. Depending on which region (north or south) people live, they will be quiet or gregarious. Overall they are honest negotiators. There is an aversion to chaos as they are very organized. They tend to be open to ideas rather than being threatened by the new phenomena. This leads to the Dutch being direct and pragmatic but not contentious. Problem solving is considered a group effort. Social status is measured by occupation, as it is in the United States, so U.S. negotiators would not see a difference. Although negotiations may move slower than in the United States because of their belief that negotiation is a team effort, after they have made a decision based on consensus, they will move very fast and will expect the same from your firm. The Netherlands is the most pluralistic of the countries (Leaptrott, 1996; Morrison et al., 1994).

South Korea
Because Koreans are rank and status conscious, you need to match the rank of the individuals who are attending the negotiations. Personal questions are not unusual and are used to help determine rank and status within your organization. Harmony is important in Korean society; however, Koreans can be direct, express emotion, and be a little aggressive during negotiations. Being overly direct, on the other hand, is not appreciated in Korea. Criticizing the competition is inappropriate. Using local foreign trading agency representatives to introduce members of your team is highly suggested. Because a relationship should be developed before doing business, it takes multiple trips to conduct any business with the Koreans. Their logical orientation is more cyclical in nature, allowing them to discuss items out of sequence. Negotiations will stress logic and the profit structure of the deal. Every Korean at the negotiations will need a counterpart from the other firm. South Korea is a collective culture (Leaptrott, 1996; Morrison et al., 1994).

Taiwan
The Taiwanese are similar to the Republic of China in their negotiations; however, they have been more active for a longer time negotiating with and manufacturing for the West. As a major exporter of textiles, electronics, machinery, metals, timber products, and high-technology items for more than three decades, they have a very modern economic system with a large middle class. They do not consider themselves part of mainland China; this fact should be remembered during negotiations. A personal relationship needs to be developed before doing business. Harmony is very important, and they never say "no." The logic used in negotiations is more cyclical than linear. Seating protocol is important; the team leader should be seated in the middle with other team members seated to the left and right in rank order. Humility, sincerity, honesty, and compatibility between counterparts are all very important. Direct criticism is

considered as very impolite. The Taiwanese believe in self-control and dislike anyone who is loud or boisterous. Reciprocity of goodwill gestures is very important. Taiwan is a collective culture (Leaptrott, 1996; Morrison et al., 1994).

Terms

- Argument dilution
- Authority
- Authority advantage
- Balanced authority
- Cognitive dissonance
- Common interest
- Compromise
- Conflicting interests
- Criteria
- Cultural noise
- Face-to-face strategies
- Group-oriented
- Individually oriented
- Irritators
- Perception
- Personal constructs
- Power
- Protocol
- Reviewing the negotiation

Exercise 11.1

Instructions: Circle T for true or F for false.

1. T F National culture is the same for all citizens within a nation.
2. T F For power to be meaningful, it should be accepted.
3. T F A woman can negotiate as well in Japan, Saudi Arabia, and France as she can in the United States.
4. T F The environment of intercultural business negotiations is unimportant.
5. T F Effective negotiators are observant, patient, adaptable, and good listeners.
6. T F Different protocols can affect negotiations.
7. T F Criteria includes changes the negotiators must make in contractual responsibilities.
8. T F U.S. Americans tend to choose strategies that are group oriented.
9. T F The Netherlands is a collectivistic culture.
10. T F If the United States were to send only one person to negotiate with the Japanese, they would assume the U.S. company was serious.

Questions and Cases for Discussion

1. Why is the selection of the players for the situation so important?
2. Explain how power and authority affect negotiations?
3. What roles do interpreters and translators play in the negotiation process?
4. Explain how gender can have an impact on successful negotiation. Identify cultures in which women are treated as equals at the negotiation table and cultures in which they are not.
5. How can the negotiation situation and environment affect the participants in the negotiation if it is held in the home country, the opponent's country, or a neutral country?
6. How do relationship and substantial conflict affect negotiations?
7. Stereotypes are how we learn about national culture. What are the advantages and limitations of stereotypes?
8. Discuss differences in negotiating with people who are group oriented versus those who are individual oriented. Give examples of cultures that are group oriented and those that are individual oriented.
9. Explain how media affect intercultural communication. Give examples of media-induced stereotypes.

10. Explain what is meant by personal constructs and how they affect the negotiation process.
11. How do conflicting interests affect negotiations?
12. Describe your strategy for negotiating with people whose culture believes that being very emotional in a negotiating setting is good, that it is not important to know facts or details, and that status is important.
13. Identify three personal constructs you hold that differentiate you from most people of the macroculture in your country and explain how these personal constructs may confuse a negotiator who has a stereotype in his or her mind about your country's culture.
14. Would it be easier for U.S. Americans to negotiate with Canadians, Mexicans, or Japanese? What support can you give for your answer?

Cases

The following procedure is recommended for analyzing the cases: (a) read the case carefully paying attention to details; (b) read the questions at the end of the case; (c) reread the case, taking notes on or highlighting the details needed for answering the questions; (d) identify relevant facts, underlying assumptions, and critical issues of the case; (e) list possible answers to the questions; and (f) select the most logical response to the question. Your professor may ask that you submit answers to the case questions in writing.

Case 1

Your instructor will separate the class into two negotiation teams. One team is from the United States; the other team is from Mexico. You are to respond from the cultural perspective of your country (either the United States or Mexico). The U.S. corporation desires to lower its cost of production and believes it can do so by manufacturing in Mexico. However, because the U.S. firm does not have experience manufacturing in Mexico, it wants to negotiate with Agua Manufacturing in Mexico. The management of Agua Manufacturing is anxious to do the production for the U.S. corporation because it has excess capacity. The negotiations will take place in Mexico so that the U.S. representatives will be able to see and evaluate the facilities. Answer the following questions from the point of view of the Mexican negotiation team and the U.S. negotiation team. You will probably need to research the cultural background of Mexico and the United States. Remember that even if you were born and reared in the United States, it is sometimes difficult to see yourself as others see you.

1. Explain the negotiation perspective, environment, and negotiation situation.
2. Where do you expect there to be common interests, conflicting interests, and compromises? What is the criteria for achievement?
3. What is your negotiation strategy? What are your tactics?
4. How important is culture in this situation?

Case 2

A U.S. American woman executive is sent to negotiate a contract with a corporation in Saudi Arabia. She dresses conservatively in a dark business suit and completes her makeup and hair as she would in the United States. She finds the Arabs to be very aloof. She is asked when her boss will be arriving and is feeling ignored. What mistakes have been made? What can be done to correct such a situation?

Case 3

Your company has chosen to use an export management company that will handle all the sales and financial transactions for your products overseas. In what way could this be an advantage, and how could it be a disadvantage? Does the size of the firm matter?

Case 4

A group of high-powered businessmen from New York City arrive in Mexico City to give a presentation. They have timed, detailed agendas; a long contract; and specific plans for a joint venture. They distribute the materials and say they are pressed for time and need to complete the meeting so they can catch their plane. The Mexicans sat very quietly during the presentation. After the presentation, the New Yorkers on their way home congratulated themselves on their success. The Mexicans, however, felt they would not be able to work with these New Yorkers. Why do the two sides view the meeting differently?

Activities

1. Write a paragraph on the role that holidays and religion might play when negotiating in Saudi Arabia.
2. Consult a book on cultural etiquette, such as Carol Turkington's, *The Complete Idiot's Guide to Cultural Etiquette* (1999), and write a one-page summary on the role that gift giving plays when negotiating with the Japanese or Chinese.
3. Consult a book on nonverbal communication, such as Roger E. Axtell's *Gestures: The Do's and Taboos of Body Language Around the World* (1998), and prepare a one-page, summary of the role that nonverbal communication plays when negotiating with persons in a South American country of your choice.
4. From recent issues of the *Wall Street Journal* or your local newspaper, find an article related to negotiations between the United States and another country. Make a short oral report summarizing the article.
5. Be prepared to discuss the role that bargaining plays when negotiating with persons in different cultures.
6. Underline unacceptable behavior in the following scenario: The ABC Corporation's negotiating team has been invited to dine with the Mexican team at a Mexican restaurant. Some of the team members do not care for Mexican food. At the restaurant, Tom is uncomfortable and very hot, so before sitting down he takes his jacket off and loosens his tie. He now feels comfortable and starts talking with two of the Mexican team members. As Juan refers to him as Dr. Ross, Tom stops him and tells him to please call him Tom. Tom asks the Mexican team leader if there is some way in which they can compromise over an issue discussed during the day. The first course is served, which is chicken soup with the chicken's feet in the dish. Tom winces as he sees the chicken's feet and pushes the bowl to the side.
7. The following is a self-assessment exercise you may take; the interpretation of the results follows.

Negotiation Skills Self-Assessment Exercise*

Please respond to this list of questions in terms of what you believe you do when interacting with others. Base your answers on your typical day-to-day activities. Be as frank as you can. For each statement, please enter on the score sheet the number corresponding to your choice of the five possible responses given below:

1. If you have never (or very rarely) observed yourself doing what is described in the statement.
2. If you have observed yourself doing what is described in the statement occasionally, but infrequently: that is, less often than most other people who are involved in similar situations.
3. If you have observed yourself doing what is described in the statement about an average amount: that is, about as often as most other people who are involved in similar situations.
4. If you have observed yourself doing what is described in the statement fairly frequently: that is, somewhat more often than most other people who are involved in similar situations.
5. If you have observed yourself doing what is described in the statement very frequently: that is, considerably more than most other people who are involved in similar situations.

Please answer each question.

1. I focus on the entire situation or problem.
2. I evaluate the facts according to a set of personal values.
3. I am relatively unemotional.
4. I think that the facts speak for themselves in most situations.
5. I enjoy working on new problems.
6. I focus on what is going on between people when interacting.
7. I tend to analyze things very carefully.
8. I am neutral when arguing.
9. I work in bursts of energy with slack periods in between.
10. I am sensitive to other people's needs and feelings.
11. I hurt people's feelings without knowing it.
12. I am good at keeping track of what has been said in a discussion.
13. I put two and two together quickly.
14. I look for common ground and compromise.
15. I use logic to solve problems.
16. I know most of the details when discussing an issue.
17. I follow my inspirations of the moment.
18. I take strong stands on matters of principle.
19. I am good at using a step-by-step approach.
20. I clarify information for others.
21. I get my facts a bit wrong.
22. I try to please people.
23. I am very systematic when making a point.
24. I relate facts to experience.
25. I am good at pinpointing essentials.
26. I enjoy harmony.
27. I weigh the pros and cons.
28. I am patient.
29. I project myself into the future.
30. I let my decisions be influenced by my personal likes and wishes.

31. I look for cause and effect.
32. I focus on what needs attention now.
33. When others become uncertain or discouraged, my enthusiasm carries them along.
34. I am sensitive to praise.
35. I make logical statements.
36. I rely on well-tested ways to solve problems.
37. I keep switching from one idea to another.
38. I offer bargains.
39. I have my ideas very well thought out.
40. I am precise in my arguments.
41. I bring others to see the exciting possibilities in a situation.
42. I appeal to emotions and feelings to reach a "fair" deal.
43. I present well-articulated arguments for the proposals I favor.
44. I do not trust inspiration.
45. I speak in a way which conveys a sense of excitement to others.
46. I communicate what I am willing to give in return for what I get.
47. I put forward proposals or suggestions which make sense even if they are unpopular.
48. I am pragmatic.
49. I am imaginative and creative in analyzing a situation.
50. I put together very well-reasoned arguments.
51. I actively solicit others' opinions and suggestions.
52. I document my statements.
53. My enthusiasm is contagious.
54. I build upon others' ideas.
55. My proposals command the attention of others.
56. I like to use the inductive method (from facts to theories).
57. I can be emotional at times.
58. I use veiled or open threats to get others to comply.
59. When I disagree with someone, I skillfully point out the flaws in the other's arguments.
60. I am low-key in my reactions.
61. In trying to persuade others, I appeal to their need for sensation and novelty.
62. I make other people feel that they have something of value to contribute.
63. I put forth ideas which are incisive.
64. I face difficulties with realism.
65. I point out the positive potential in discouraging or difficult situations.
66. I show tolerance and understanding of others' feelings.
67. I use arguments relevant to the problem at hand.
68. I am perceived as a down-to-earth person.
69. I go beyond the facts.
70. I give people credit for their ideas and contributions.
71. I like to organize and plan.
72. I am skillful at bringing up pertinent facts.
73. I have a charismatic tone.
74. When disputes arise, I search for the areas of agreement.
75. I am consistent in my reactions.
76. I quickly notice what needs attention.
77. I withdraw when the excitement is over.
78. I appeal for harmony and cooperation.
79. I am cool when negotiating.
80. I work all the way through to reach a conclusion.

Score Sheet

Enter the score you assigned each question (1, 2, 3, 4, or 5) in the space provided. (Note: The item numbers progress across the page from left to right.) When you have recorded all your scores, add them up vertically to attain four totals. Insert a "3" in any numbered space left blank.

1. _____	2. _____	3. _____	4. _____
5. _____	6. _____	7. _____	8. _____
9. _____	10. _____	11. _____	12. _____
13. _____	14. _____	15. _____	16. _____
17. _____	18. _____	19. _____	20. _____
21. _____	22. _____	23. _____	24. _____
25. _____	26. _____	27. _____	28. _____
29. _____	30. _____	31. _____	32. _____
33. _____	34. _____	35. _____	36. _____
37. _____	38. _____	39. _____	40. _____
41. _____	42. _____	43. _____	44. _____
45. _____	46. _____	47. _____	48. _____
49. _____	50. _____	51. _____	52. _____
53. _____	54. _____	55. _____	56. _____
57. _____	58. _____	59. _____	60. _____
61. _____	62. _____	63. _____	64. _____
65. _____	66. _____	67. _____	68. _____
69. _____	70. _____	71. _____	72. _____
73. _____	74. _____	75. _____	76. _____
77. _____	78. _____	79. _____	80. _____
IN: _____	NR: _____	AN: _____	FA: _____

Negotiation Style Profile

Enter your four scores on the following bar chart. Construct your profile by connecting the four data points.

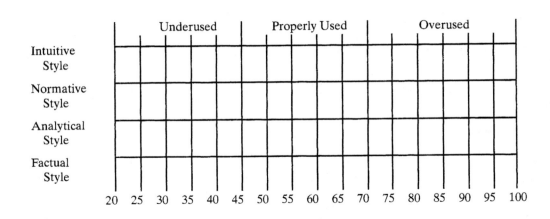

Intuitive

Basic Assumption: "Imagination can solve any problem."

Behavior: Making warm and enthusiastic statements, focusing on the entire situation or problem, pinpointing essentials, making projections, being imaginative and creative in analyzing the situation, switching from one subject to another, going beyond the facts, coming up with new ideas all the time, pushing and withdrawing from time to time, putting two and two together quickly, getting the facts a bit wrong sometimes, and being deductive.

Key Words: Principles, essential, tomorrow, creative, idea.

Normative

Basic Assumption: "Negotiating is bargaining."

Behavior: Judging, assessing, and evaluating the facts according to a set of personal values, approving and disapproving, agreeing and disagreeing, using loaded works, offering bargains, proposing rewards, incentives, appealing to feelings and emotions to reach a "fair" deal, demanding, requiring, threatening, involving power, using status, authority, correlating, looking for compromise, making effective statements, focusing on people and their reactions, judging; attention to communication; and group processes.

Key Words: Wrong, right, good, bad, like.

Analytical

Basic Assumption: "Logic leads to the right conclusions."

Behavior: Forming reasons, drawing conclusions, and applying them to the case in negotiation, arguing in favor or against one's own or others' position, directing, breaking down, dividing, analyzing each situation for cause and effect, identifying relationships of the parts, putting things into logical order, organizing, weighing the pros and cons thoroughly, making identical statements, and using linear reckoning.

Key Words: Because, then, consequently, therefore, in order to.

Factual

Basic Assumption: "The facts speak for themselves."

Behavior: Pointing out facts in neutral way, keeping track of what has been said, reminding people of their statements, knowing most of the details of the discussed issue and sharing them with others, clarifying, relating facts to experience, being low-key in their reactions, looking for proof, and documenting their statements.

Key Words: Meaning, define, explain, clarify, facts.

Guidelines for Negotiating with People Having Different Styles

1. Negotiating with someone having a factual style—
   Be precise in presenting your facts.
   Refer to the past (what has already been tried out, what has worked, what has been shown from past experiences).
   Be indicative (go from the facts to the principles).
   Know your dossier (including the details).
   Document what you say.
2. Negotiating with someone having an intuitive style—
   Focus on the situation as a whole.
   Project yourself into the future (look for opportunities).
   Tap the imagination and creativity of your partner.

Be quick in reacting (jump from one idea to another).
Build upon the reaction of the other person.
3. Negotiating with someone having an analytical style—
Use logic when arguing.
Look for causes and effects.
Analyze the relationships between the various elements of the situation or problem at stake.
Be patient.
Analyze various options with their respective pros and cons.
4. Negotiating with someone having a normative style—
Establish a sound relationship right at the outset of the negotiation.
Show your interest in what the other person is saying.
Identify his or her values and adjust to them accordingly.
Be ready to compromise.
Appeal to your partner's feelings.

*Adapted by Pierre Casse from Interactive Style Questionnaire Situation Management Systems, Inc., in *Training for the Cross-Cultural Mind,* Sietar, Washington, DC, 1981.

References

Anderson, E., & Weitz, B. (1989). Determinants of continuity in conventional industrial channel dyads. *Marketing Science, 8*(4), 310–323.

Asselin, G., & Mastron, R. (2000). *Au Contraire!* Yarmouth, ME: Intercultural Press.

Bradenburger, A. M., & Nalebuff, B. J. (1996). *Co-opetition.* New York: Doubleday.

Brett, J. M. (2001). *Negotiating globally: How to negotiate deals, resolve disputes, and make decisions across cultural boundaries.* San Francisco: Jossey-Bass.

Brett, J. M., & Okumura, T. (1998). Inter- and intracultural negotiations: U.S. and Japanese negotiators. *Academy of Management Journal, 41*(5), 495–510.

Cai, D. A., Wilson, S. R., & Drake, L. E. (2000). Culture in the context of intercultural negotiation: Individualism-collectivism and paths to integrative agreements. *Human Communication Research, 26*(4), 591–617.

Casse, P. (1981). *Training for the cross-cultural mind* (2nd ed.). Washington, DC: Sietar.

Chaisrakeo, S., & Speece, M. (2004). Culture, intercultural communication competence, and sales negotiation: A qualitative research approach. *Journal of Business & Industrial Marketing, 19*(4), 267–282. Retrieved September 6, 2004, from Emerald.

Chisholm, D. (1989). *Coordination without hierarchy.* Berkeley, CA: University of California Press.

Cohen, R. (1998). *Negotiating across cultures.* Washington, DC: United States Institute of Peace Press.

D'Amico, L. C., & Rubinstein, R. A. (1999). Cultural considerations when "setting" the negotiation table. *Negotiation Journal, 15*(4), 389–395.

Elashmawi, F., & Harris, P. (1998). *Multicultural management 2000.* Houston, TX: Butterworth-Heinemann.

Engholm, C. (1991). *When business east meets business west.* New York: Wiley.

Fisher, G. (1997). *Mindsets: The role of culture and perception in international relations.* Yarmouth, ME: Intercultural Press.

Fisher, G. (1980). *International negotiation.* Yarmouth, ME: Intercultural Press.

Foster, D. A. (1992). *Bargaining across borders.* New York: McGraw-Hill.

Funakawa, A. (1997). *Transcultural management.* San Francisco: Jossey-Bass.

Harris, P. R., Moran, R. T., & Moran, S. V. (2004). *Managing cultural differences* (6th ed.). Burlington, MA: Elsevier-Butterworth-Heineman.

Hendon, D. W., Hendon R. A., & Herbig, P. (1999). *Cross-cultural business negotiations.* Westport, CT: Praeger.

Hinkelman, E. G. (Ed.). (1994). *Mexico business: The portable encyclopedia for doing business in Mexico.* San Rafael, CA: World Trade Press.

Hofstede, G., & Hofstede G. J. (2005). *Cultures and organizations* (2nd ed.). New York: McGraw-Hill.

Jervis, R. (1998). Cognitive dissonance and international relations. In G. E. Weaver (Ed.), *Culture, communication, and conflict* (pp. 452–453). Needham Heights, MA: Simon & Schuster.

Karrass, C. L. (1996). *In business, you don't get what you deserve; you get what you negotiate.* Los Angeles: Stanford Street Press.

Leaptrott, N. (1996). *Rules of the game: Global business protocol.* Cincinnati: Thomson Executive Press.

Lewicki, R. J., Barry, B., Saunders, D. M., & Minton, J. W. (2003). *Essentials of negotiation* (3rd ed.). Homewood, IL: McGraw-Hill.

Lorange, P., & Roos, J. (1991, January/February). Why some strategic alliances succeed and others fail. *Journal of Business Strategy,* 25–30.

Moran, R. T., & Stripp, W. G. (1991). *Dynamics of successful international business negotiations.* Houston: Gulf.

Morrison, T., Conaway, W. A., & Borden, G. A. (1994). *Kiss, bow, or shake hands.* Holbrook, MA: Adams Media Corporation.

Nishiyama, K. (2000). *Doing business with Japan.* Honolulu: University of Hawaii Press.

Nooteboom, B., Berger, H., & Noorderhaven, N. G. (1997). Effects of trust and governance on relational risk. *Academy of Management Journal, 40*(2), 308–338.

Ping, M. D. (1998). Culture and business: Interacting effectively to achieve mutual goals. In G. R. Weaver (Ed.), *Culture, communication, and conflict* (pp. 528–536). Needham Heights, MA: Simon & Schuster.

Prosser, M. H. (1985). *The cultural dialogue.* Washington, DC: Sietar.

Provan, K. G. (1982). Interorganizational linkages and influence over decision making. *Academy of Management Journal, 25,* 443–451.

Ruch, W. V. (1989). *International handbook of corporate communication.* Jefferson, NC: McFarland.

Samovar, L. A., & Porter, R. E. (2004). *Communication between cultures* (5th ed.). Belmont, CA: Wadsworth/Thomson Learning.

Saxton, T. (1997). The effects of partner and relationship characteristics on alliance outcomes. *Academy of Management Journal, 40,* 443–461.

Schneider, S. C., & Barsoux, J. L. (2002). *Managing across cultures* (2nd ed.). Upper Saddle River, NJ: Prentice Hall.

Schneider, S. C., & De Meyer, A. (1991). Interpreting and responding to strategic issues: The impact of national culture. *Strategic Management Journal, 12,* 307–320.

Sebenius, J. K. (2002a). The hidden challenge of cross-border negotiations. *Harvard Business Review, 80*(3), 76–86.

Sebenius, J. K. (2002b). In practice: Caveats for cross-border negotiators. *Negotiation Journal, 18*(2), 121–133.

Simintiras, A., & Thomas, A. H. (1998). Cross-cultural sales negotiations: A literature review and research propositions. *International Marketing Review, 15*(1), 10–28.

Staa, D. (1998). No need for inter-American culture clash. *Management Review, 87*(1), 8.

Steensma, H. K., Marino, L., Weaver, K. M., & Dickson, P. H. (2000). The influence of national culture on the formation of technology alliances by entrepreneurial firms. *Academy of Management Journal, 43*(5), 951–973.

Teegen, H. J. (1998). Authority and trust in cross border partnerships: Mexican firm perspectives. *Journal of International Management, 4*(3), 223–229.

Teegen, H. J., & Doh, J. P. (2002). U.S.-Mexican alliance negotiations: Impact of culture on authority, trust, and performance. *Thunderbird International Business Review, 44*(6), 749–775.

Tiampati, M. (2004). Soda extraction threatens Magadi Maasai. *Cultural Survival Quarterly, 28*(3). Retrieved November 18, 2004, from ProQuest.

Tinsley, C. (1998). Models of conflict resolution in Japanese, German, and American cultures. *Journal of Applied Psychology, 83*(2), 316–323.

Verluyten, S. P. (2002). *Intercultural incidents and vignettes.* Distributed at the Association for Business Communication Conference, 2002.

Weaver, G. R. (Ed.). (1998). *Culture, communication, and conflict: Readings in intercultural relations.* Needham Heights, MA: Simon & Schuster.

Zhao, J. J. (2000). The Chinese approach to international business negotiation. *Journal of Business Communication, 37*(3), 209–237.

12

LAWS AFFECTING INTERNATIONAL BUSINESS AND TRAVEL

Objectives

Upon completion of this chapter, you will

■ understand the difference between home country laws and host country laws.

■ understand why a contract has a different meaning in different countries.

■ understand how ethics and laws relate.

■ know why international laws are being promulgated.

■ understand the importance of the nonwritten laws.

■ know how international travel is affected by the law.

Legal cultural research is the study of societies and how the societies develop their legal culture. The elements of legal culture include styles of legislation, court proceedings, adjudication (hearing and deciding a case), and the status, action, and acceptance by the members of the legal profession and of public officials (Blankenburg, 1988). Culture is relevant to the development of law. According to Fulop and Linstead (1999), a society's moral behavior may not be in codified law, and sometimes business activities develop before the lawmakers are able to develop laws. The current international trade agreements stress flexibility and a willingness to change, thereby showing an interest by participating countries in looking at the law from more than one country's point of view.

Understanding the law of a country allows insight into the moral and philosophical mindsets of the citizens. Laws are what a society already believes and values (Fisher, 1997). When laws or treaties are made or changed, those changes do not always represent all the people and can take time to be accepted.

Iraq is a good example of a country in change. In the fall of 2004, the International Coalition and Iraq's own military moved into Fallujah to rout out terrorists to bring peace to that part of the country in preparation for elections in January 2005. So at times it is not just the people within the country who cannot agree but insurgents from outside who want to control the outcome of the change.

The world, with 191 nations, has numerous laws that affect international business. Laws are used to regulate the flow of products entering and leaving a country. When a firm is engaged in international business, what the company representatives can legally do is controlled both by their nation and by the foreign nation with which they want to conduct business. Each nation can legally do as it wishes within its own boundaries without interference from other nations. The **Act of State Doctrine** legally protects this right.

"This market is exploding," said James Zimmerman of the San Diego law firm of Chapin, Fleming, & Winet. "I spend most of my time putting together deals between U.S. firms and foreign firms. I think this is by far the fastest growing area of the law." (Bowler, 1997, p. 1A)

HOME-COUNTRY AND HOST-COUNTRY LAWS

Business communication between persons of different national origins is governed by the laws of both countries. Because of the large number of countries and laws, a knowledge of not only your home country's laws but the host country's laws as well is important. **Home-country laws** are the laws, treaties, or acts that govern business within your country of citizenship and those governing your business with other countries. **Host-country laws** are the laws, treaties, or acts that govern business within the foreign country with which you want to conduct business.

Imports and exports are regulated in some manner by most countries. Having a lawyer who is knowledgeable of the laws of the foreign country with which you are conducting business is important, as is having a lawyer who is knowledgeable of your home country's laws and agreements with the foreign country.

There are three important legal requirements of U.S. citizens' actions during negotiations: antidiversion, antiboycott, and antitrust requirements (Axtell, 1994). The **antidiversion requirement** states that the bill of lading and the invoice must clearly display that the carrier cannot divert the shipment to a country the U.S. government considers restricted. The **antiboycott regulations** prohibit U.S. companies from participating in boycotts between two foreign countries by refusing to do business with a friendly nation to comply with a foreign boycott. Furnishing information about their business relationships to either friendly countries or blacklisted companies is also prohibited. **Antitrust laws** are designed primarily to ensure fair competition and low prices to U.S. consumers; they affect exporters in such areas as mergers and acquisitions of foreign firms, raw material procurement agreements and concessions, knowledge licenses (i.e., intellectual information), distribution channels, joint ventures for research, manufacturing, and construction.

Written Information Laws

Written information is also controlled by most nations. The United States has several laws that govern the information that can be sent to specific countries:

- The **Export Administration Act of 1985** requires federal licensing of technical information in business correspondence.
- The **Arms Export Control Act of 1968** and the **Trading with the Enemy Act of 1917** prohibit the transfer of information on military material or defense-related materials.
- The **International Emergency Economic Powers Act of 1977** governs information that is research oriented from being communicated to foreigners.

Technology Laws

The area of technology law has been very active. Mexico, Brazil, Venezuela, and the United States already have laws governing how technological knowledge may be transferred. The **World Intellectual Property Organization** (WIPO) of the United Nations promotes intellectual property rights worldwide and currently administers 22 treaties for 181 member nations (World Trade Organization, 2004). The legal area of intellectual property licensing was helped considerably by the **Berne Convention for the Protection of Literary and Artistic Works** (http://www.wipo.int/treaties/index.html), which recognizes the copyrights of all the signatory nations to the act. As of September, 2004, 157 countries are signatories to the Berne Convention. Trademarks are protected by the 34 countries that are signatories of the **Madrid Convention;** however, the United States and China are not signatories (http://www.wipo.int/treaties/index.html).

Employment Laws

Employment regulations differ between nations. Most nations have legislation governing wages, hours, union/management relations, residence visas, and work permits. Restricting foreigners as to the number and types of jobs they may hold is common; however, a great deal of variation between nations exists. Some nations require a certain ratio of nationals to foreigners, other nations require proof that no one in the nation can do the job, and other nations allow a limited time period. Questions that can be legally asked of a potential employee also vary greatly by country. In the United States, employers can ask if someone is willing to work overtime; in other countries, this is not the case.

Maquiladora Law

Mexico has a *maquiladora* program that is governed by the **Presidential Decree for the Development and Operation of the Maquiladora Industry Program, 1983.** The program allows the duty-free import of equipment, machinery, and materials to assemble parts of products that are then returned to the home country. The U.S. Tariff Code allows the final product to be brought back into the United States with only the final value added to the goods being taxed. Pacific Rim and European countries are also taking advantage of the maquiladora program. An important consideration in this program is the difference in form of law. Although Mexico borders the United States, which practices common law (except in Louisiana), Mexico practices civil law. The difference is that the civil law rather than **precedent** (interpretations of the law in previous court decisions) is considered during litigation (Jarvis, 1990).

INTERNATIONAL LAW

The **International Court of Justice,** also known as the **World Court,** is a body of the United Nations that provides a way to settle international disagreements between countries rather than corporations. There are three legal bodies in the United Nations—the United Nations Commission on International Trade Law (UNCITRAL), the **International Commission,** and the Sixth Committee of the General Assembly— that produce laws on international commerce, such as the Law of the Sea (rights of states in rules of navigation) (United Nations Commission on International Trade Law, 2004; United Nations Documentation, 2004).

The **European Union** (EU), the North American Free Trade Agreement (NAFTA), and the **World Trade Organization** (WTO) are three cross-national agreements or laws that are trying to equalize the treatment of multinational organizations. International trade agreements, such as NAFTA and the EU, have proliferated in recent years. It now appears as if the world will be divided into regional, continent, and hemisphere trade agreements, and eventually tariffs will be passé (see chapter 10). A movement by institutions concerned with international business has encouraged the development of agreements and laws that are uniformly accepted in world trade. The institutions include the **International Chamber of Commerce, Incoterms** (International Commercial Terms), **ECE Standard Conditions,** the **Hague Convention,** and the **Vienna Agreement.**

Unified laws have not produced unified judicial practices. Judges currently lack training or experience in international trade. Even in the signatory countries of an agreement, the judicial practices are not equal concerning the interpretation of the agreement. Currently, multinational corporations must be flexible and willing to learn concerning international contracts. Home-country laws frequently have nothing in common with host-country laws. Because different cultures may have divergent value conceptions, it is not surprising that they also have divergent legal conceptions. Current changes facing corporate lawyers are central and east European nations, the Russian Federation, and the EU procedural change as they either embrace free market economics or join to form new economic units with new rules.

Quasi-international laws are rules for the relationship between legal entities and states that do not have national status, such as private corporations. One such quasi-international law is sanctions. **Sanctions** prohibit U.S. companies from doing business in targeted countries.

Unocal, a U.S. oil company, was involved with the Burmese to develop the offshore natural gas that was to be sold to markets in Thailand. The U.S. government sanctioned Burma, and Unocal could not expand its business. Texaco, who was also in the area, sold its interests to a British company. The sanctions hurt U.S. corporations and benefited other foreign competitors. (Roberts, 1997)

Negotiations in international business situations play an important part in determining which laws will be followed. These negotiated contracts will eventually help define an international body of law. **Macaulay's thesis,** in fact, states that intercultural business cultures consider the development of long-term, mutually beneficial relationships more important than the contracts that lawyers so laboriously draft. Macaulay explains that business' lack of consideration of the law is due to the long-term relationships and interdependencies that develop and their importance to the organizations involved. It is to the organizations' benefit to ignore, suppress, or compromise rather than litigate; few international contracts are litigated. Macaulay (1976) cites Luhmann's thematization process as applicable to his thesis. **Thematization** is the process by which a framework for mutual communication and satisfaction is reached; this process could be related to the law, economics, power, utilitarianism, or religion.

How the parties maintain their relationship over time is called the **governance structure** (Blegvad, 1990; Macaulay, 1976). There are four types of governance structures: (1) **market governance,** which is contract based; (2) **trilateral governance,** which adds an arbitrator; (3) **bilateral governance,** which may not spell out details but has a strong recognition of a continuing economic relationship; and (4) **unified governance,** in which nothing is negotiated in advance, maximum flexibility is provided, and only one party sets terms for both parties involved. Depending on the frequency of transactions, market replaceability, the firms' tolerances for uncertainty, and the relationship of the firms, one of these governance structures covers their transactions. Consumer transactions fit the market governance structure. Trilateral governance fits transactions that involve idiosyncratic goods or services or a situation in which the establishment of the relationship is expensive. Bilateral governance is good for long-term relationships that involve uncertainty due to the mixture of goods or services that are to be included. Unified governance is appropriate for subsidiaries of a single organization (Blegvad, 1990).

The desire of organizations for long-term economic relationships that are privately governed is emerging as the preference over international laws and public governance. However, the time period that statistics have been kept is short, so this is an area that is still evolving. Modern business wants future-oriented solutions and cooperation rather than legal constraints. Time will tell if economic norms can acquire the rank of laws or if laws will have to be written to guide private governance.

CONTRACTS

In the United States, a **contract** is defined as an agreement between parties to do something that is oral, written, or implied through conduct. If a supplier ships goods to a customer that the supplier believes the buyer needs and the buyer accepts the shipment, the buyer enters into a contract with the supplier. Purchase orders that are commonly used for the written form of a contract must contain a statement such as "Confirmation of contract entered into between the buyer and seller (and date of the oral contract)." The word "contract" is important to the legal enforceability, particularly in the United States (Murray, 1992).

In the United States, an oral contract is legally enforceable if the parties admit that the contract was made even if no written contract was made. Oral contracts are also enforceable if the contract is for custom-manufactured goods and special materials have been purchased that are usable only for the custom order. An oral contract that has been partially fulfilled through shipment and acceptance of goods is also enforceable (Lewicki, Saunders, & Minton, 2003).

In Japan, a contract can also be made verbally, in writing, or by conduct but is always considered open for renegotiation. Because Japanese corporate personnel are accustomed to working within a general trading company called a *sogososha* (which are very difficult to join and look out for each other forever), when problems occur, they are discussed and resolved without legal intervention.

Before the breakup of the Soviet Union, little need existed for contracts. Goods were allocated, so that the companies had to accept what was sent to them whether or not they needed the goods. With reforms, companies now have a right to refuse unneeded allocations and can modify or cancel contracts. When the Russian Federation moved to the theory of property rights, they recognized the eventual costs to the buyer and the consumer. By allowing the companies to plan and order what they needed, central planning and binding annual production plans were eliminated. The companies now operate very much as Western companies do in that they are responsible for their operational costs, income, expenses, and profit (Kroll, 1989). The Russian Federation currently uses many of the same mechanisms United States companies use to enforce agreements, such as the courts, mediation, and negotiation; however, personal trust is still very important to Russian businesspeople (Hendley, Murrell, & Ryterman, 1999).

Because of numerous differences that exist in various countries, having legal counsel to advise you on the proper way to negotiate contracts in individual countries is recommended. Reading a book on contract law for the particular country with which you will be conducting business would also suggest questions to ask your legal counsel. Unknown foreign laws and changes in foreign laws make international investing risky.

Even in Europe not knowing the correct questions to ask can be problematic. A United States firm purchased an existing manufacturing operation in 2000 in Italy using Italian lawyers. When business slumped worldwide for their product and the pricing was further eroded by oil prices, the firm decided to sell the business in 2003. When the business did not sell, they decided to close the firm. Their lawyers worked on the process; however, they never told the U.S. firm that the Italian union at the plant could walk out before the closing was completed and that the U.S. firm would be responsible for paying their wages for a full year!

Panama Processes successfully negotiated a contract to protect its flow of dividends from a jointly owned Brazilian corporation in which Panama was the minority shareholder. After several years of compliance, Cities Service Co., the majority shareholder, decided to void the agreement and cause the jointly owned corporation to cease paying dividends. Panama filed a number of suits to protect its financial position only to discover that its contract could not be enforced due to the omission of a few normally insignificant points. These few points, normally insignificant in a domestic situation, were of pivotal importance in an international business arrangement. . . . Had Panama included even the least intrusive of these points in its original agreement, points to which Cities under the circumstances would have undoubtedly agreed, it could have enjoyed the fruits of its financial arrangements.

Basically the considerations that were omitted from the agreement between Panama and Cities were (1) in the event that relations between the parties broke down, which court of law or other tribunal would referee their dispute, and (2) which set of rules or which country's laws would be used to determine the parties' respective rights and obligations? (McCubbins, 1994, p. 95)

GLOBAL PATENTS

Global patent concerns are important for companies involved in proprietary products or methods. Previously, because it was impossible to file patents in all the nations in the world, companies tended to follow a strategy of filing for patents in key countries and regions of the world (Global patent protection, 1997). The Patent Cooperation Treaty has now been signed by 124 countries and makes protecting new products much easier in the signatory nations (http://www.wipo.int/treaties/index.html).

According to Minnesota patent attorney Philip Goldman of Fredrikson & Byron, P.A., global patent protection is important because patents are territorial in nature. "They only allow the patentee to prevent infringement that occurs within the country or region granting the patent. It is not unusual, therefore, for the owner of a process patent in one country to stand helplessly by as a competitor uses that process in another country (where the patentee has no protection) and imports the final product back into the first country to be sold." (Global patent protection, 1997, p. 23)

Currently, a corporation completes and files a patent application with the U.S. Patent Office. The initial date is significant because it begins the timetable for filing patents abroad. The limitation to file abroad is one year from the date on the U.S. application. When these patents are filed in other countries, the new patents claim priority to the date on the U.S. patent, thus prevailing over other patents and the competing rights of other inventors. This priority is made possible because of the **Patent Cooperation Treaty.** Until the patents are processed abroad, companies can expect to expend money on prosecution and maintenance of patents here and abroad. To ensure a proper foundation for protecting inventions and preserving foreign filing options, attorneys must do a lot of homework. All international patent offices do not require the same information. A company can save a lot of time and money if its patent attorney knows what the other countries require and includes those items (such as metric measurements) in advance. After the patents are granted, they need to be reassessed to be sure they are still cost-effective options.

Treaties override all other domestic laws. The U.S. Constitution, Article VI, states, "All Treaties made or which shall be made, under the Authority of the United States shall be the supreme Law of the Land; and the Judges in every State shall be bound thereby, anything in the Constitution or Laws of any State to the contrary notwithstanding." Nations do need to be cognizant of their sovereignty. They need to remember that all trade should be of mutual benefit and that treaties should be based on good science rather than on wishful thinking or bad politics (Bentacourt, 1997).

NONWRITTEN LAW

Often the interpretation of the law is very different between countries; for example, countries that communicate as high-context consider the situation more important than the letter of the law. In a high-context culture, little emphasis is given to the written word; instead, the situation determines whether to adhere to the law. The individual interpretation of the situation is more important than external rules and regulations. Oral agreements are considered binding, and written contracts are considered flexible. Japan is an example of such a high-context culture. In a low-context culture, such as the United States, what is written is expected to be followed. Laws are binding; the situation is not considered. In the United States, laws determine how people respond to each other. In view of the difference in attitudes toward the law, it is not surprising that the United States and Japan have had their share of problems trying to understand each other in negotiations. Although many agreements have been crystal clear to both sides, the enactment of the agreement generally gives rise to many problems.

Unwritten business laws are called **drawer regulations** (see Figure 12-1) in countries such as Brazil where such unwritten operational codes are used rather than laws (Rachid, 1990).

FIGURE 12-1   Drawer Regulations

Sometimes the interpretation of the law can be a problem or a solution, depending on your position. An example of such a problem occurred when the EU punished the United States for months of battling over trade matters. The EU determined that U.S. meat inspection practices were not adequate, thereby halting U.S. sales of meat to the EU. Because Canada had said its meat inspection was equivalent to that of the United States, the EU had to decide whether they should cut off Canadian imports also. The Canadian inspector offered them a way to distance Canada from the United States by saying equivalent meant "equal to or better than," thus allowing Canadian meat imports to continue.

ETHICS AND THE LAW

Because people throughout the world are culturally diverse, it is not surprising that what is considered ethical behavior in one culture may be seen as unethical in another culture. Missner (1980) cautions that when you are negotiating, it is important to understand the differences between judgments based on ethics and judgments based on concern and practicality.

Ethics judgments are based on some standard of moral behavior as to right and wrong. Practicality judgments are based on what is easiest, best, or most effective to achieve an objective. Lewicki et al. (2003) state that judgments are subjective and that the distinction between ethical or unethical is measured in degrees rather than absolutes; reasonable people disagree as to where the line is drawn between ethical and unethical acts.

In the business world, four motivations for unethical conduct exist: profit, competition, justice, and advertising (Missner, 1980). The three dimensions of negotiation ethics are means/ends, relativism/absolutism, and truth telling. The means/ends question is measured by utility. The moral value and worth of an act are judged by what is produced—the utility. The players in the negotiation game and the environment in which the negotiators are operating help determine whether the negotiators can justify being exploitative, manipulative, or devious. The relative/absolute question considers two extremes: Either everything is relative, or everything is without deviation from the rule. Although most people are somewhere between the extremes of relative and absolute, they debate which point between the two extremes is correct. Of course, it is a matter of judgment as to what particular point on the continuum is correct.

Truth telling considers whether concealing information, conscious misstatements, exaggeration, or bluffing when you are in negotiations is dishonest. Judging how honest and candid one can be in negotiations and not be vulnerable is difficult. Intercultural negotiations have the added problem of different business methods, different cultures, and different negotiation protocols. Although the decision to be "unethical" may be made to increase power and control, whether the decision was made quickly, casually, after careful evaluation, or on the basis of cultural values is important (Lewicki et al., 2003).

The U.S. government has taken a strong stance concerning bribery and the accounting practices used in international business. The **Foreign Corrupt Practices Act of 1977** requires U.S. companies to account for and report international transactions accurately and prohibits bribes that are used to gain a business advantage. Bribes can include gifts and entertainment. A gift is a bribe when your firm is receiving something in return for the gift. A U.S. firm giving a Mexican utility official money "under the table" for the Mexican's personal use to speed up the installation of an electric line to a new construction site is an example of bribery. This regulation often puts U.S. firms at a disadvantage when trying to compete with companies from cultures that have no problem with the practice of "gift giving," which U.S. persons would call a bribe. Many U.S. companies take a hard line against bribery. Bill Pomeranz, a longtime employee with Hughes Space and Communications Company, indicated that over the years Hughes had lost only two contracts by failing to pay bribes. However, Pomeranz pointed out that they are the market leader and therefore are able to offer more than any other firm, including those who would make payoffs. When asked why his company held the line on bribery, he said simply, "It's illegal. Whether it's the way somebody would want to do business or not, it's illegal—and the company has a rigid code of ethics that prohibits unlawful conduct." Many Fortune 500 companies share this company's view (Engholm & Rowland, 1996).

Because of the necessity of paying a commission in some countries to expedite business transactions, professional go-betweens are sometimes hired to ensure that the proper persons are tipped to avoid delays in approvals and delivery. People of the United States cannot, of course, be involved in paying these commissions; this responsibility would be left with the local joint-venture partner or distributor (Engholm, 1991).

The U.S. Department of Commerce's 1993 booklet *International Business Practices* (available at http://bookstore.gpo.gov/index.html) lists foreign laws by country and offers the following guidance on distributor agreements:

- Recognize that what is legal in the United States may not be legal in another country.
- Check translations for concise meanings.
- If possible, state the jurisdiction that will handle disagreements.
- Settle disagreements through an arbitrator; identify the arbitration body.
- State provisions of foreign laws that are to be waived.
- State the benefits to both parties.
- Put the agreement in writing.

Another source of information to help distributors is Export Administration Regulations; a subscription is available by going to http://bookstore.gpo.gov/index.html or http://www.access.gpo.gov/bis/ear/ear_data.html.

The **Doctrine of Sovereign Compliance** is an international legal principle that can be used as a defense in your home country for work carried out in a host country when the two countries' legal positions are different. For example, a U.S. manager working in Canada may have to trade with Cuba; however, it is illegal to do so in the United States. If prosecuted, the manager could use the Doctrine of Sovereign Compliance as a defense. The defense is necessary because U.S. citizens or corporations are held accountable to U.S. law beyond the boundaries of the country through the Trading with the Enemy Act; applying the Act beyond the U.S. border is called **extraterritoriality.**

The **Export Trading Act of 1982** allows companies that normally are not allowed to do joint ventures to develop trading companies similar to those in Britain, the Netherlands, and Japan (Axtell, 1994). As an example of this act, General Motors, Ford, and Chrysler make parts with European and Japanese car manufacturers to jointly produce and sell cars.

How different countries view legal and ethical practices is best explained by an example that Axtell (1994) has used:

A Latin businessman, commenting on the U.S. attitude toward morality in international business, once confronted me with this rather different perspective. Take the word "contraband," he said. Here in the United States, it is a very bad word. It suggests breaking the law by smuggling. However, in my country, the Spanish word is *contrabando.* It comes from the word *contrabandido,* which means literally, "against the bandits." When I was a child in the villages of my country, we were taught that the *bandidos,* the bandits, were the land and shop owners. I remember that even candy was illegally brought into our village and we were taught to favor that contraband candy because it was a way of fighting back against the *bandidos.* So, you see my culture was raised to view contraband as a good thing. That may help explain why there are differing values and differing perceptions of morality between our continents.

Intercultural business communication is affected by the laws of the countries in which companies do business and the growing body of international law. Because laws and rules develop from and are a part of cultural beliefs, values, and assumptions, interpretation and discussion of legal issues can cause communication problems between intercultural business negotiators unless they are completely prepared.

INTERNATIONAL TRAVEL AND LAW

Your **passport** is the most important document you can carry with you when traveling outside your native country. A passport is your proof of citizenship. To obtain a passport, you must have a copy of your birth certificate and two current photos, and you must apply in person the first time. In addition, you need to complete an application form that is available online. Your first passport will cost $85 if you are 16 years of age or older. Your passport is good for 10 years and currently costs $55 to renew. As a precaution, make a copy of your passport so that if the original is lost or stolen, you can give the copy to the embassy to facilitate getting a replacement. Because it takes a while for your application to be processed (passports are currently processed based on your date of departure from the United States), it is best to get a passport well before you actually need one (http://www.travel.state.gov).

Citizenship is the state of being vested with certain rights and duties as a native or naturalized member of a country. Proof of citizenship may not be clear if you were born in another country, your parents are citizens of another country, or you are a naturalized citizen of the country that you consider your home country. If the country to which you are traveling considers you a citizen of their country because it is the country of your birth or because your parents are citizens of the country, it may require you to do military service or pay income taxes.

A **visa** gives you the right to enter and stay in a country for a period of time for a specific purpose. If you are a tourist, most countries do not require a visa; however, for business purposes, a visa may be required. The country you are visiting issues the visa, and the visa may be obtained from the embassy or consulate of the country you want to visit. A **consulate** is made up of individuals sent by the government to other countries to promote the commercial interests of their home country.

All countries have **customs** agents who enforce export and import laws of the country; they have the right to search and confiscate anything you may have with you. Be sure to get a list from your embassy of items that are illegal to bring back into your home country. The host country's embassy can provide a list of restricted items. When returning home, you will be asked to declare the value of everything purchased that you are bringing home with you. Most countries have items for which they charge duties. **Duties** are an import tax. The host country's embassy can also give you immunization requirements and the verification needed for prescription drugs you may need to take. U.S. citizens should be aware that they cannot legally carry more than $10,000 out of the country without registering with U.S. customs officials before departing (Axtell, 1994).

To drive abroad, find out what type of license you may need and become familiar with the country's driving laws. If you obtain an international driver's license, it will help you learn about international driving.

PAST RULES, PRESENT PROBLEMS

- The United States taxes foreign income of nonresident citizens; many countries exempt foreign business income.
- The IRS taxes corporate income at both corporate and stockholder levels; most countries integrate the two taxes.
- U.S. foreign tax credits are complicated; other countries have simplified systems.
- The United States treats foreign subsidiary loans to a domestic parent company as a dividend; other major industrialized nations do not.
- U.S. rules for allocating and apportioning expenses between domestic and foreign income conflict with other industrial countries.
- U.S. alternative minimum tax can cause a tax on foreign income already taxed abroad.
- U.S.-based multinational corporations (MNCs) cannot take advantage of host countries' tax incentives because they are not included in treaties with developing countries.
- If other nations defined qualified residents as narrowly as the United States, our U.S.-based MNC would have trouble effectively competing in countries lacking tax treaties with the United States. (Zelade, 1996, p. 6)

To be sure you do not break the law in other countries, the following tips can be beneficial (Axtell, 1990):

1. Because of political unrest in the world, register with the U.S. embassy or consulate when you arrive in a foreign country.
2. If you have any kind of trouble, turn to the embassy or consulate for legal, medical, or financial problems.
3. The U.S. consul can visit you in jail, give you a list of attorneys, notify family, and protest any mistreatment; however, the consul cannot get you released or provide for bonds or fines.
4. Remember that you are subject to the laws of the country while you are there.
5. If you stay for a prolonged time, you must register with the local authorities. You may be requested to leave your passport overnight or to complete a data sheet.
6. Use authorized outlets for cashing checks and buying airline tickets; avoid the black market or street moneychangers that you will see in many countries.
7. Ask for permission before you photograph anything.
8. Notary publics in many countries have broader powers than in the United States.
9. Common infractions of the law include trying to take historic artifacts or antiquities out of the country, customs violations, immigration violations, drunk and disorderly conduct, and business fraud.
10. If you need to drive, obtain an international driver's license. Travel agents can assist with this. Many countries require proof of insurance while driving. Your U.S. insurance is generally not recognized in other countries.

11. Dealing in drugs is a serious offense in all countries. Penalties can be much more serious than in the United States and can include death.

12. Keep a list of credit card numbers and traveler's check numbers in a safe place in case they are lost or stolen.

13. Obtain a copy of *Safe Trip Abroad* available through http://bookstore.gpo.gov.

14. Telephone numbers/addresses that may be beneficial include the following:
    - The U.S. State Department, 2201 C Street NW, Washington, DC 20520, 202-647-4000, http://www.state.gov
    - Amnesty International USA, 5 Penn Plaza, 14th Floor, New York, NY 10001, 212-807-8400, http://www.amnestyusa.org
    - International Legal Defense Counsel, 1429 Walnut Street, Philadelphia, PA 19102, 215-977-9982

15. Your health could be a major concern. Obtain a copy of *Health Information for International Travel* by the Centers for Disease Control and Prevention at 1-888-232-3299. This offers disease and immunization advice and information on health risks for countries. International SOS Assistance (1-800-523-8930/215-244-1500) is a health provider that works through the red tape of language, insurance, travel, or anything else you may need. They can also provide travel health insurance.

COUNTRY-SPECIFIC TRAVEL TIPS

Before you travel to a foreign country, find out what documents are needed, what hotel accommodations and modes of transportation are available, what laws affect behavior (such as the legal drinking age), and other information to ensure personal safety and comfort so that your sojourn is a pleasant one. Books by Braganti and Devine (1992), Devine and Braganti (1998, 2000), and *CultureGrams* (2004) contain country-specific information that will make international travel easier. Because space does not permit an extensive examination of numerous countries, the following travel tips are limited to the top 10 countries with which the United States conducts most of its international trade.

Canada

Since the events of September 11, 2001, U.S. citizens need a passport when traveling to Canada from the United States and when coming from another country. Although visas are not required for visits of up to 180 days, U.S. citizens do need a passport as proof of citizenship.

Hotel accommodations in the large cities are comparable to those in the United States. Voltage connectors and plug adaptors are not needed for using small appliances.

Public transportation systems in Montreal and Quebec City are very good. The Montreal Metro system is one of the best subway systems in the world. The underground system includes miles of underground shopping malls; you can buy anything you want without going above ground. Because public transportation cannot accommodate the many isolated regions in the north, domestic air transportation is used to reach these areas. People who drive in Canada should remember to leave their radar detectors at home, as they are illegal in that country and will be confiscated if detected.

Additional information about traveling in Canada can be obtained from

Canadian Consulate General
1251 Avenue of the Americas
New York, NY 10020-1175
212-596-1759
http://www.canada-ny.org

Embassy of Canada
501 Pennsylvania Avenue NW
Washington, DC 20001
(202) 682-1740
http://www.canadianembassy.org

China

U.S. citizens need a passport that is good for at least six months beyond their visit period, and a visa is required. Hotel accommodations in large cities are available. Public transportation systems exist throughout the country. Beijing has a subway system, buses, and taxis. The country is tied together with a system of roads and railroads. Bicycles are the main mode of transportation with 8 million bicycles to 1.58 million cars.

More information about China can be found through

Embassy of China
2300 Connecticut Avenue, NW
Washington, DC 20008
202-328-2500
http://www.china-embassy.org

China National Tourist Office
350 Fifth Avenue, Suite 6413
New York, NY 10118
888-760-8218
http://www.cnto.org

England

A valid passport is required for travel in England. However, U.S. citizens do not need a visa for visits lasting no longer than six months. Vaccinations are not required.

If staying at a hotel, you may be asked if you would like early morning tea delivered to your room. Larger hotels may include a continental breakfast in the room price. Electrical converters and plug adapters are needed to use small U.S. appliances in England.

Public transportation includes the Underground (subway) and taxis. To drive in England, you do not need an international driver's license. Remember that people drive on the left side of the road. In rural areas, gas stations may be scarce, so fill your tank when you see a station.

The legal age for drinking in England is 18. The English police are known for being friendly and helpful; ask them for directions or assistance with travel-related problems (Braganti & Devine, 1992).

More information on traveling in England is available from

British Tourist Authority
551 Fifth Avenue, Suite 701
New York, NY 10176
800-462-2748
http://www.visitbritain.com

The British Embassy
3100 Massachusetts Avenue NW
Washington, DC 20008
202-588-7800
http://www.britainusa.com

France

To travel in France, a valid passport is required, but U.S. citizens may travel in the country without a visa for up to three months. Vaccinations are not required.

Hotels in France do not always have a bath in the room nor are they always air-conditioned. To use small appliances, such as a hair dryer, you must have a voltage converter and plug adaptor.

Public transportation in France includes the Metro (subway), buses, streetcars, taxis, and the TGV (*train á grande vitesse;* a high-speed train connecting 36 European cities). Exercise care in choosing only an "official" taxi; unauthorized taxi drivers have no meters and charge whatever they want. Driving a car in France does not require an international driver's license. Avoid honking the horn in cities because this is illegal; turning right on a red light is also not permitted.

The drinking age in France is 18. Women should exercise care when using the Metro at night because it is considered unsafe. Ask about other unsafe areas in France before exploring the locality (Braganti & Devine, 1992).

Additional information about traveling in France is available from

French Government Tourist Office
444 Madison Avenue, 16th Floor
New York, NY 10022
410-286-8310
http://us.franceguide.com

Embassy of France
4101 Reservoir Road NW
Washington, DC 20007-2185
202-944-6000
http://www.ambafrance-us.org

Germany

A valid passport is required for travel in Germany; however, U.S. citizens do not need a visa to travel in the country for up to three months. Vaccinations are not required.

If you stay at a hotel, the price of the room generally includes a continental breakfast; heat may be an extra charge. When making your reservation, inquire about bathroom facilities; some rooms do not have a bath, so you will use a communal facility. Electrical converters and plug adopters are needed to use small appliances in hotels.

Public transportation includes buses, streetcars, subways, trains, and taxis. Tickets for mass transit are purchased in advance. Because the conductor often checks your ticket during the ride, have your ticket available for inspection. An international driver's license is required for driving in Germany. Service stations in Germany are quite competitive, except on the Autobahn (freeway), so shop around for the best prices on gasoline (Braganti & Devine, 1992).

Jaywalking is illegal in Germany. Biking, hiking, or hitchhiking along the Autobahn is illegal. Because the tap water in towns along the Rhine contains dangerous chemicals, do not drink it. Always use bottled water.

More information on traveling in Germany is available from

Embassy of Germany
4645 Reservoir Road NW
Washington, DC 20007-1998
202-298-4000
http://www.germany-info.org

German National Tourist Office
122 East 42nd St
New York, NY 10168
212-661-7200
http://www.visits-to-germany.com

Japan

Although no visa is needed for visits of less than 90 days, U.S. citizens need a valid passport when traveling to Japan. Vaccinations are not required.

Numerous Western-style hotels are available in the large cities. They will probably have private baths, but you should expect some differences in accommodations. Faucets and door handles, for example, operate in the opposite direction from what is considered the norm in the United States. Toilets are often for both genders and quite different from those people of the United States are accustomed to using. Small appliances usually work in Japanese electrical outlets.

Public transportation in Japan includes trains, subways, and buses. The "bullet train," which runs between major cities, offers regular and first-class service. Taxis are available at larger hotels and in commercial districts (Braganti & Devine, 1992).

Additional information about travel in Japan is available from

Japan National Tourist Organization
One Rockefeller Plaza, Suite 1250
New York, NY 10020
212-757-5640
http://www.jnto.go.jp

Embassy of Japan
2520 Massachusetts Avenue, NW
Washington, DC 20008
202-238-6700
http://www.us.emb-japan.go.jp

Mexico

U.S. citizens may stay up to three months in Mexico with no visa but need proof of citizenship. Although no vaccinations are required, they may be advisable when traveling in certain parts of the country.

Numerous excellent hotel accommodations are available in the resort towns and in larger cities. Because many people from the United States visit Mexico and Mexicans vacation over the Christmas and Easter holidays, hotel reservations should be made well in advance for these times.

Public transportation in Mexico is varied, from the subway of Mexico City to the crowded buses. Trains are a good choice for longer distances, such as between Mexico City and Monterrey. Driving a car in many parts of Mexico is not advisable. Driving can be hazardous, especially at night, because of bicycle riders, robbers, and problems with getting help should your car break down. In addition, you need to be aware that at various checkpoints, men dressed in military or police garb may stop you, expecting money, cigarettes, or other bribes before permitting you to proceed. Failure to offer the bribe may result in lengthy delays while your car and luggage are searched (Devine & Braganti, 2000).

Additional information about traveling in Mexico is available from

Mexican Government Tourist Office
405 Park Avenue, Suite 1002
New York, NY 10022
212-755-7261
http://www.visitmexico.com

Embassy of Mexico
1911 Pennsylvania Avenue NW
Washington, DC 20006
202-728-1600
http://www.sre.gob.mx/English

The Netherlands

U.S. citizens need a passport when traveling to the Netherlands but do not need a visa when visiting for less than six months.

Hotels are very comfortable and offer good service. English is widely spoken both in hotels and in shops. The Netherlands has one of the best systems of public transportation in Europe. The network of trains is quite efficient, buses and streetcars are common, and subways are found in Amsterdam and Rotterdam. Most people own an automobile; drivers must watch for the numerous bicyclists who share the roadways and streets.

Smokers who travel to the Netherlands will need to remember that smoking in offices, trains, and various other public places has been illegal since January 2004.

Additional travel information may be obtained from

Embassy of The Netherlands
4200 Linnean Avenue NW
Washington, DC 20008
202-244-5300
http://www.netherlands-embassy.org

The Netherlands Board of Tourism for American and Canadian Tourists
355 Lexington Avenue, 19th Floor
New York, NY 10017
888-464-6552
http://www.holland.com

South Korea

U.S. citizens who visit South Korea need a passport that is valid for six months beyond their intended stay. No visa is required for visits of up to 30 days.

City transportation is handled through rail and bus connections; in urban areas, buses, taxis, and private cars are used. Transportation choices in Seoul include the subway, an express bus system, and taxis, which are inexpensive and plentiful. In February 2004, South Korea's first bullet train was tested; its speed can reach 186 miles an hour and cuts in half the travel time between Pusan and Seoul.

In addition to Western types of hotels available in South Korea, Korean-style inns called *yogwans* are popular. Although staff members do not speak English, they are helpful and make visitors feel welcome. Because practices in these inns are quite different from those in Western-style hotels (including a common washing area and the absence of a dining room), it is wise to consider these differences before making a reservation.

For more information about travel in South Korea, contact the following:

Embassy of the Republic of Korea
2320 Massachusetts Avenue NW
Washington, DC 20008
202-939-5600
http://www.koreaembassyusa.org

Korea National Tourism Organization
One Executive Drive
Suite 100
Fort Lee, NJ 07024
201-585-0909
http://www.knto.or.kr

Taiwan

U.S. citizens traveling to Taiwan need a valid passport and may stay in the country for up to 30 days without a visa.

Using public transportation or taking a taxi is recommended for city travel in Taiwan; chauffeured limousines or rental cars are available for longer trips.

Hotels should be booked well in advance when traveling during the month of October, which is their busiest month. The best hotels are equipped with meeting facilities, fitness centers, and the usual amenities found in U.S. hotels. Because most hotel employees probably will not understand spoken English, making requests in writing is recommended.

For information about traveling to Taiwan, contact the following:

Taipei Economic and Cultural Representative Office
4201 Wisconsin Avenue NW
Washington, DC 20016
202-895-1800
http://www.taipei.org

Taiwan Visitors Association
405 Lexington Avenue
37th Floor
New York, NY 10174
212-867-1632
http://www.roc-taiwan.org

When traveling in other countries, the best advice is to obey the laws of the host country and to be courteous and helpful to all you meet; remember, it is their country, so if you cannot speak positively about the country, remain silent (Axtell, 1990).

Terms

- Act of State Doctrine
- Antiboycott regulations
- Antidiversion requirement
- Antitrust laws
- Arms Export Control Act of 1968
- Berne Convention for the Protection of Literary and Artistic Works
- Bilateral governance
- Citizenship
- Consulate
- Contract
- Customs
- Doctrine of Sovereign Compliance
- Drawer regulations
- Duties
- ECE Standard Conditions
- European Union
- Export Administration Act of 1985
- Export Trading Act of 1982
- Extraterritoriality
- Foreign Corrupt Practices Act of 1977
- Governance structure
- Hague Convention
- Home-country laws
- Host-country laws
- Incoterms (International Commercial Terms)
- International Chamber of Commerce
- International Commission
- International Court of Justice (World Court)
- International Emergency Economic Powers Act of 1977
- Macaulay's thesis
- Madrid Convention
- Market governance
- Passport
- Patent Cooperation Treaty
- Precedent
- Presidential Decree for the Development and Operation of the Maquiladora Industry Program, 1983
- Quasi-international laws
- Sanctions
- Thematization
- Trading with the Enemy Act of 1917
- Trilateral governance
- Unified governance
- Vienna Agreement
- Visa
- World Intellectual Property Organization
- World Trade Organization

Exercise 12.1

Instructions: Match the following terms with their definition.

_____ 1.	Gives permission to stay in a country for a specified time and purpose	A. Bilateral governance
_____ 2.	Unwritten business laws	B. Consulate
_____ 3.	Contract relationship	C. Contract
_____ 4.	Includes an arbitrator	D. Customs
_____ 5.	Nothing negotiated in advance; one party sets terms for both	E. Drawer regulations
_____ 6.	Persons sent to other countries to promote commercial interests	F. Host-country laws
_____ 7.	Enforces export and import laws of the country	G. Macaulay's thesis
_____ 8.	Document that shows proof of citizenship	H. Market governance
_____ 9.	Agreement between parties to do something that is enforceable by law	I. Passport
_____10.	Considers long-term cultural relationship more important than written legal contract	J. Trilateral governance
		K. Unified governance
		L. Visa

Exercise 12.2

Instructions: Match the laws with their major provisions.

_____ 1.	Prohibits bribes to gain a business advantage	A. Act of State Doctrine
_____ 2.	Prohibits transfer of information on military materials	B. Berne Convention
_____ 3.	Legal right of each nation to do as it wishes within its own boundaries	C. Foreign Corrupt Practices Act
_____ 4.	Protects trademarks of countries that are signatories	D. Doctrine of Sovereign Compliance
_____ 5.	Requires federal licensing of technical information in business correspondence	E. Export Administration Act
_____ 6.	Recognizes copyrights of signatory nations	F. International Emergency Economic Powers Act
_____ 7.	Prevents research-oriented information from being communicated to foreigners	G. International Commission
_____ 8.	Affects exporters involved in mergers/acquisitions of foreign firms	H. Madrid Convention
_____ 9.	UN body involved in laws on international commerce	I. Trading with the Enemy Act
_____10.	Regulates differing legal positions of home and host country	J. U.S. Antitrust Law
		K. World Trade Organization

Questions and Cases for Discussion

1. Explain the difference between home-country and host-country laws.
2. Describe how a low-context and a high-context culture view a contract.
3. Are ethics the same around the world? Explain why or why not.
4. Explain differences among the four governance structures.
5. Why are nonwritten laws difficult to learn about before going to another country to do business?

6. Explain the importance of citizenship. Include in your answer how differences between countries in the interpretation of citizenship could affect an individual.
7. What is the difference between a passport and a visa?
8. Who governs a multinational corporation's operations?
9. Why is legal counsel important when doing business in a foreign country?
10. Which act prohibits a corporation or an individual from circumventing the Arms Export Control Act of 1968?

Cases

The following procedure is recommended for analyzing the cases: (a) read the case carefully paying attention to details; (b) read the questions at the end of the case; (c) reread the case, taking notes on or highlighting the details needed for answering the questions; (d) identify relevant facts, underlying assumptions, and critical issues of the case; (e) list possible answers to the questions; and (f) select the most logical response to the question. Your professor may ask that you submit answers to the case questions in writing.

Case 1

A famous doctor's parents emigrated from Russia in the early 1900s before he was born but eventually became naturalized citizens after all their children were born. They also changed their last name to an English-sounding name. The doctor practiced medicine during the 1950s and 1960s. The doctor spoke and wrote seven different languages and was very involved in research and education in his field of study. As the doctor became sought after for educational seminars around the world, he was invited to Russia to speak. The doctor refused to go. What are the legal, cultural, and political issues that could have caused him to reach this decision?

Case 2

Your corporation has sent you to another country to build a manufacturing facility. A representative of the government with whom you have been working informs you it will take six months to get the necessary permits to allow work to begin. You explain that you have a deadline to begin manufacturing in nine months and that three months is not sufficient time. He explains that certain people, if compensated, may be willing to help things progress at a faster pace. You must determine if it is illegal to do so. How would you respond? Explain why you have chosen your answer and whose laws you are considering.

Case 3

Aerobus, a French airplane manufacturer, and Boeing, a U.S. airplane manufacturer, have reached an agreement to jointly manufacture a new airplane to carry 600 people. Which country's laws will govern the manufacturing of the plane? Where will litigation of any disagreements take place? What form of thematization will be used? What should the governance structure be?

Case 4

A major corporation uses a great deal of a derivative from high-grade petroleum. Because of the cost of the high-grade petroleum and a decrease in the use of other derivatives that come from the cracking process, the cost of the derivative is going to increase. Substitute products are available if the cost increases sufficiently to make those products cost efficient. The purchasing agent for the corporation, without the direction of his superiors, has verbally agreed with his supplier to purchase a six-month supply of the derivative at the current cost. In the meantime, the research department has found a cheaper substitute that can be available for shipment in two months. The purchasing agent is told to purchase the substitute beginning in two months. What are the legal ramifications concerning the four extra months of the derivative that has been ordered and that the supplier has already begun to produce?

Activities

1. Bring to class a critical incident related to international law.
2. Secure forms for obtaining passports and visas for a country of your choice. How will you find out about nonwritten laws of this country before you travel there?
3. Interview students from another culture; ask them to identify at least one law in their own country that differs from that in the United States.
4. Ask a professor of international law to address the class on variations in contracts in various cultures.
5. Prepare a list of books or journal articles related to international law.
6. Using the following Web site, find out of which conventions the United States, China, Mexico, Canada, or other major trading partners with the United States are not signatories: http://lib-unique.un.org/.

References

Axtell, R. (1990). *The do's and taboos of hosting international visitors.* New York: Wiley.

Axtell, R. (1994). *The do's and taboos of international trade.* New York: Wiley.

Bentacourt, P. (1997, November 10). Tread carefully with international treaties; they override all law. *Business Journal Serving Fresno & the Central San Joaquin Valley,* (322223), 34.

Blankenburg, E. (1988). *Zum Begriff "Rechtskultur."* Paper presented at the 24th meeting of the German Sociological Association, Zurich, October 4–7.

Blegvad, B. (1990). Commercial relations, contract, and litigation in Denmark: A discussion of Macaulay's theories. *Law and Society Review,* 24(2), 397–411.

Bowler, M. (1997, July 7). Keeping up with international law. *San Diego Business Journal,* 18(27), 1A.

Braganti, N. L., & Devine, E. (1992). *European customs and manners.* New York: Meadowbrook.

CultureGrams (2004). Lindon, UT: ProQuest Information and Learning Company.

Devine, E., & Braganti, N. L. (1998). *The traveler's guide to Asian customs and manners.* New York: St. Martin's Griffin.

Devine, E., & Braganti, N. L. (2000). *The traveler's guide to Latin American customs and manners.* New York: St. Martin's Griffin.

Engholm, C. (1991). *When business east meets business west.* New York: Wiley.

Engholm, C., & Rowland, D. (1996). *International excellence.* New York: Kodansha International.

Fisher, G. (1997). *Mindsets: The role of culture and perception in international relations.* Yarmouth, ME: Intercultural Press.

Fulop, L., & Linstead, S. (Eds.). (1999). *Management: A critical text.* South Yarra, Australia: Macmillan Education.

Global patent protection can be cost-effective, achievable. (1997). *New Hampshire Business Review,* 19(9), 23.

Hendley, K., Murrell, P., & Ryterman, R. (1999). Law, relationships, and private enforcement: Transactional strategies of Russian Enterprises. *Journal of Economic Literature,* Retrieved November 8, 2004, from Google.

Jarvis, S. S. (1990). Preparing employees to work south of the border. *Personnel,* 67(6), 59–63.

Kroll, H. (1989). Property rights and the Soviet enterprise: Evidence from the law of contract. *Journal of Comparative Economics,* 13, 115–133.

Lewicki, R. J., Saunders, D. M., & Minton, J. W. (2003). *Essentials of negotiation* (3rd ed.). Homewood, IL: Irwin/McGraw-Hill Higher Education.

Macaulay, S. (1976). An empirical view of contract. *Wisconsin Law Review,* 465–482.

McCubbins, T. F. (1994). Three legal traps for small businesses engaged in international commerce. *Journal of Small Business Management,* 32(3), 95–103.

Missner, M. (1980). *Ethics of the business system.* Sherman Oaks, CA: Alfred.

Murray, J. E. (1992, March 19). What exactly is a contract? *Purchasing,* 25, 27, 29.

Rachid, R. (1990, June 15). Unwritten laws govern business in some nations. *Journal of Commerce,* 384(27250), 5A (1).

Roberts, P. C. (1997, November 24). A growing menace to free trade: U.S. sanctions. *Business Week,* 3554, 28.

United Nations Commission on International Trade Law (2004). Retrieved November 19, 2004, from http://www.uncitral.org/en-main.htm

United Nations Documentation (2004). Retrieved November 19, 2004, from http://www.un.org

United States Department of State (2004). Retrieved November 19, 2004, from http://www/travel.state.gov

World Trade Organization. (2004). Retrieved November 19, 2004, from http://www.wipo.int/treaties/index.html

Zelade, R. (1996). Past rules, present problems. *International Business: Strategies for the Global Marketplace,* 9(10), 6.

Appendix A

GLOSSARY

Acculturation is the process of becoming adapted to a new and different culture.

Acronyms are words formed from the initial letters or groups of letters and pronounced as one word.

Act of State Doctrine refers to each nation's being able to do as it wishes within its borders.

Antiboycott regulations prohibit firms or employees from refusing to do business with friendly nations.

Antidiversion requirement states that a bill of lading and an invoice must clearly display that the carrier cannot direct the shipment to a U.S.-restricted country.

Antitrust laws affect the merger or acquisition of foreign firms, raw material, licenses, and distribution channels.

Area training model is also called the simulation model; an approach to intercultural training that emphasizes affective goals, culture-specific content, and experiential processes.

Argot is a vocabulary of a particular group; it is often regional.

Argument dilution refers to using multiple arguments when one is sufficient; a technique used less by skilled negotiators.

Arms Export Control Act of 1968 prohibits transfer of military or defense-related materials.

AsiaShock is a special kind of cultural shock experienced by U.S. people when traveling to Asian countries.

Attitudes are likes (or affinities) and dislikes (or aversions) to certain people, objects, or situations.

Attribution is something seen as belonging to or representing something or someone.

Attribution training focuses on explanations of behavior from the point of view of a person in the host country.

Authority is the power to give commands and make decisions.

Authority advantage occurs when one partner in negotiations claims to possess superior resources or a superior position in the alliance.

Back translation is the concept of written translation from a first language into a second language, followed by another person's translating it back into the first language to determine if the translations are equivalent.

Backstage culture is cultural information that is concealed from outsiders.

Balanced authority allows each partner in negotiations to share the decision-making role.

Berne Convention recognizes the copyrights of all the signatory nations.

Bernstein hypothesis explains how social structure affects language; speech emerges in restricted or elaborated codes.

Bilateral governance is a strong recognition of a continuing economic relationship.

Bribery refers to giving or promising to give something, often money, to influence someone's actions.

Buffer is a paragraph used to begin a bad news letter; tells what the letter is about, is pleasant, but says neither yes nor no.

Cant is the vocabulary of the undesirable cocultures, such as drug dealers, gangs, prostitutes, and murderers.

Caste system is the rigid system of class in India. The society is divided into castes where a person is determined to belong at birth. Each caste has its status, rights, and duties.

Chitchat is small talk or light conversation.

Chromatics is the use of color to communicate nonverbally.

Chronemics is the use of time to communicate nonverbally.

Citizenship is the state of being vested with certain rights and duties as a native or naturalized member of a state or country.

Cognates are words that sound the same and have the same meaning.

Cognitive dissonance is the psychological conflict or anxiety that results from inconsistency

288

between what a person does and what a person believes.

Collectivism is the political principle of centralized social and economic control.

Colloquialism refers to informal words or phrases often associated with regions of the country.

Common interest considers that both parties in the negotiation share, have, or want something that the other party has.

Communication barriers are obstacles to effective communication.

Competitive approach looks at a solution that is best for the negotiator's own side.

Compromising is an approach to negotiation that seeks a middle ground between the two parties.

Compromise agreement is a negotiation strategy agreement reached when two parties find a common ground between their individual desires that results in a lower joint benefit.

Conflicting interests are areas of possible disagreement in negotiations, such as profits, quality, and terms of payment.

Connotative meanings are the emotional meanings of words.

Consulate is made up of individuals sent to other countries to promote commercial interests.

Continental eating style is a manner of eating in which the eater places the fork in the left hand and knife in the right, uses the knife to push food onto the back of the fork and then moves the food into the mouth with the tines of the fork down.

Contract is an agreement between parties to do something.

Conversation taboos are topics considered inappropriate for conversation with people in certain cultures or groups.

Criteria are conditions under which the negotiations take place.

Cultural awareness model includes a comparison of values and behaviors of people in the home country and the host country.

Cultural heritage includes the values, ideals, and beliefs that a person inherits from his or her culture.

Cultural intelligence is the ability to exhibit certain behaviors that are culturally tuned to the attitudes and values of others.

Cultural noise refers to anything that distracts or interferes with the message being communicated.

Cultural shock is the trauma a person experiences when he or she moves into a culture different from his or her home culture; a communication problem that involves the frustrations that accompany a lack of understanding of the verbal and nonverbal communication of the host culture, its customs, and value systems.

Cultural symbol is a word or object that represents something in the culture.

Cultural synergy occurs when people of different cultures absorb a significant number of each others' cultural differences and have a number of similarities that merge to form a stronger overriding culture.

Cultural universals are formed out of the common problems all cultures have.

Culture is the structure through which the communication is formulated and interpreted; deals with the way people live.

Customs are socially acceptable ways of behaving; also refers to enforcement of export and import laws of a country.

Deductive method refers to problem solving that goes from broad categories or observations to specific examples to determine the facts and then the solution to the problem.

Demeanor refers to a person's conduct, behavior, deportment, and facial appearance.

Denotative meanings are the explicit or direct meanings of words.

Diffusion is the process by which two cultures learn and adapt materials and adopt practices from each other.

Dissing is a term meaning to speak ill of someone.

Doctrine of Sovereign Compliance is the international legal principle used as a defense in your home country for work carried out in a host country.

Drawer regulations are unwritten laws.

Duties are import taxes.

Ebonics is a nonstandard form of English used by the U.S. African American subculture.

Economic Commission for Europe (ECE) a regional body of the UN that includes all of Europe, Canada, and the U.S.

Economic system is the way in which the physiological needs of the people are produced, distributed, and consumed.

290 *Intercultural Business Communication*

Elaborated codes are messages that are low in predictability; verbal transmission is important.

Emoticons are symbols used to convey emotions within e-mail messages.

Enculturation refers to adapting to the cultural patterns of a person's society.

Ethical standards are guidelines established to convey what is perceived to be correct or incorrect behavior by most people in a society.

Ethnocentric management occurs when a firm is located in one country and all its sales are also in the same country; does not account for cultural differences in the workforce.

Ethnocentrism is the belief that your own cultural background, including ways of analyzing problems, language, verbal communication, and nonverbal communication, is correct.

Etiquette refers to the manners and behavior considered acceptable in social and business situations.

Euphemisms are inoffensive expressions used in place of offensive words or words with negative connotations.

European Union (EU) is a free trade zone involving 25 countries: Austria, Belgium, Cyprus (Greek part), Czech Republic, Denmark, Estonia, Finland, France, Germany, Greece, Hungary, Ireland, Italy, Latvia, Lithuania, Luxembourg, Malta, the Netherlands, Poland, Portugal, Slovakia, Slovenia, Spain, Sweden, and the United Kingdom of Great Britain and Northern Ireland.

Export Administration Act of 1985 requires federal licensing of technical information in business correspondence.

Export Trading Act of 1982 permitted trading between competitors normally prohibited from association by antitrust laws.

Exports are goods sent out of the country.

Extended family consists of grandparents, uncles, aunts, and cousins.

Extraterritoriality application of laws, such as the Trading with the Enemy Act, are applied beyond the U.S. border.

Face-to-face strategies are concerned with negotiating in person.

Figurative meanings are the descriptive meanings of words.

Flaming refers to sending vicious, insulting messages via e-mail.

Forcing negotiation approach is used to make the other party comply and is closer to the competitive approach.

Foreign Corrupt Practices Act of 1977 is a law that makes bribing someone else's government a crime; applies to both parties involved.

Formality refers to the degree of preciseness, regularity, or conformity expected within the society.

Free trade zones (FTZ) are areas of international commerce where foreign or domestic merchandise may enter without formal customs entry or customs duties.

Frontstage culture refers to cultural information that you are willing to share with outsiders.

Geocentric management is a type of management that requires a common framework with enough freedom for individual locations to operate regionally to meet the cultural needs of the workers; a synergy of ideas from different countries of operation.

Globalization is the capability of a corporation to take a product and market it anywhere in the world.

Governance structure refers to how parties maintain their relationship over time.

Grammarians are people who study how a language is governed and its grammatical forms, roots, and endings.

Group Decision Support Systems (GDDS) is a business conference software package.

Group membership has two extremes: People can belong to many or to few groups. In addition, a middle area exists between the two extremes.

Group-oriented negotiators are detail oriented to determine the proper solution.

Hague Convention works toward developing agreements that are uniformly accepted in world trade.

Haptics is the use of touch to communicate nonverbally.

High-context language is communication that transmits little in the explicit message; nonverbal aspects are important.

Home-country laws are laws of the nation in which your corporation is headquartered.

Homonyms are words that sound alike and have different meanings.

Host-country laws are laws of the nation in which you are conducting business.

Host language is the native language of the country.

Imports refer to goods brought into the country.

Incoterms (International Commercial Terms) are the standard definitions of international terms of sale.

Individualism is the pursuit of individual rather than common or collective interests.

Individually oriented refers to negotiations that are concerned with the best contract for your company rather than what is good for the other company.

Inductive method is problem solving that starts with facts or observations and goes to generalizations.

Integrative agreement is a negotiation strategy in which two parties reconcile their interests to yield a high joint benefit.

Intellectual model is an approach to intercultural training, also called the classroom model, in which participants are given facts about the host country using a variety of instructional methods, such as lectures, group discussions, and videotapes.

Interaction approach refers to interaction with people in the host country, either nationals or U.S. persons who have been in the host country for some time.

Intercultural business communication refers to communication within and between businesses that involves people from more than one culture.

Intercultural communication is communication between persons of different cultures.

Intercultural negotiation is discussion between persons of different cultural backgrounds who work toward mutual agreement.

Intermediaries are people who act as go-betweens with other people.

International Chamber of Commerce is an international organization headquartered in Paris, France, that establishes a consensus on matters such as trading practices and procedures for handling trade disputes.

International Commission is a body of the United Nations that works toward laws on international commerce.

International communication is communication between nations and governments rather than individuals; quite formal and ritualized.

International Court of Justice (World Court) is a specialized body of the United Nations that provides a means of settling international disputes peacefully.

International English is a limited vocabulary for international businesses using the 3,000 to 4,000 most common English words.

International Emergency Economic Powers Act of 1977 governs information that is research oriented from being communicated to foreigners.

Interpersonal intelligence includes the ability to understand other people and their motivations.

Intimate zone is the physical distance between people in the United States, less than 18 inches; reserved for close friends.

Intracultural communication refers to communication between members of the same culture.

Intrapersonal intelligence involves an awareness of a person's own cultural style in order to make behavioral adjustments in international counterparts.

Irritators are phrases used repeatedly by negotiators, such as "generous offer."

Jargon refers to technical terminology used within specialized groups.

Johari Window is a way of looking at a person's inner world (named for its creators, Joseph and Harrington). It includes panes that represent the self that is known and unknown to a person and the self that is known and unknown to others.

Keiretsu system refers to Japanese negotiating practices in which a company group formed by the principal company and the partner companies supply parts, equipment, financial support, or distribution of the final products.

Kinesics refers to various types of body language, including facial expressions, gestures, posture and stance, and other mannerisms used to communicate or to accompany verbal messages.

Legalism uses legal documentation in negotiations to force the other partner to comply.

Lexical errors are language content errors.

Linear language has a beginning and an end; logical and object oriented.

Linguistic determinism is the assumption that a person's view of reality stems mainly from his or her language.

Linguists are people who study the phonetic aspects of language and define language by the sounds speakers produce and listeners receive.

Low-context language is communication explicitly coded and given in more than one way to be sure the receiver understands it.

Macaulay's thesis proposes that intercultural business cultures are developing that consider long-term mutually beneficial relationships more important than written contracts.

Macroculture is the larger society or culture.

Madrid Convention protects trademarks of the 34 signatory countries.

Market governance is a contract-based relationship.

Marriage and family system refers to attitudes, beliefs, and practices related to marriage and the family held by people in various cultures; importance placed on marriage and the family in a society.

Matriarchal refer to a mother-oriented family.

Melting pot is a sociocultural assimilation of people of differing backgrounds and nationalities; being or becoming the same.

Microculture is a subculture; a group of people possessing characteristic traits that distinguish them from others within the macroculture or larger culture.

Mindsets refer to a way of being that allows you to see and perceive things through your own filters.

Monochronic is a system of time that allows for performing only one major activity at a time.

Monogamy is a family system that includes one husband and one wife.

Multicultural refers to learning more than one culture and being able to move between two cultures comfortably.

Multidimensional approach is an approach to intercultural training based on the concept that using any single approach is not as effective as using an approach that attempts to combine cognitive, affective, and behavioral aspects of training.

Multinational firm is a corporation with operations and subsidiaries in many foreign countries.

Negotiation strategies are plans organized to achieve a desired working relationship.

Netiquette refers to cyberspace or network etiquette.

Networks are formed with personal ties and involve an exchange of assistance.

Nonlinear language is circular, subjective, and traditionally oriented.

Nonverbal communication includes nonword messages, such as gestures, facial expressions, interpersonal distance, touch, eye contact, smell, and silence.

Norms are culturally ingrained principles of correct and incorrect behaviors that, if broken, carry a form of overt or covert penalty.

Novelists are people who believe that language is a series of words arranged to produce harmonious sounds or to have a logical effect.

Nuclear family is a family consisting of the father, mother, and children.

Oculesics refers to the use of eye contact as a way of communicating nonverbally.

Olfactics refers to the use of smell to communicate nonverbally.

Parable is a story used to convey a truth or moral lesson.

Paralanguage refers to the linguistic elements of speech, such as pitch, loudness, quality, rate, or dialect, which interrupt or temporarily take the place of speech and affect the meaning of a message.

Parochialism is the same as ethnocentrism.

Passport is a document that shows proof of citizenship.

Patent Cooperation Treaty recognizes the patents of the 49 signatory nations.

Patriarchal refers to a father-oriented family.

Perception is awareness or comprehension through the senses.

Personal constructs are the individual belief systems and attitudes that are different for different cultures.

Personal zone refers to the physical distance between people; in the United States, from 18 inches to 4 feet; used for giving instructions to others or working closely with another person.

Platinum Rule is "do unto others as they would have done unto them."

Political system is the governing system that originates from dictatorship, inherited rights, election procedures, consensus, or conquest.

Polyandry refers to one woman with many husbands.

Polycentric management is a type of management that considers the culture of the country in which the firm is located.

Polychronic is a system of time that allows for performing several activities simultaneously.

Polygamy refers to one man with many wives.

Polygyny is a family system consisting of one man with many wives.

Power is the ability to influence others.

Precedent is the interpretation of the law in previous court decisions.

Presidential Decree for the Development and Operation of the Maquiladora Industry Program, 1983 allows duty-free import of equipment, machinery, and materials to assemble parts of products.

Problem solving approach is a negotiating style identified with the need to consider national cultural characteristic differences that lead to differences in communication.

Property is something that is or may be possessed.

Protocol refers to customs and regulations having to do with diplomatic etiquette and courtesies expected in official dealings with persons in various cultures.

Proverb is a saying that expresses a commonplace truth.

Proxemics refers to communicating through the use of space.

Public distance in the United States is the physical distance between people of about 12 to 25 feet.

Quasi-international law refers to rules between countries and specific corporations.

Reentry shock sometimes called reverse cultural shock, refers to problems with readjustment to the home culture.

Regiocentric management is a type of management that considers the region rather than the country in which the firm is located, realizing that countries can and often have many different cultural backgrounds.

Repartee conversation is a conversation in which the parties take turns speaking and talk only for short time periods.

Restricted codes include highly predictable messages; use oral, nonverbal, and paralinguistic transmission channels.

Reviewing the Negotiations is a face-to-face negotiation behavior that is done more often by more skilled negotiators.

Ritual conversation involves standard replies and comments for a given situation, with little meaning attached to what is said.

Roles include the behavioral expectations of a position within a culture and are affected by norms and rules.

Rules are formed to clarify cloudy areas of norms.

Sanctions prohibit U.S. companies from doing business in targeted countries.

Sapir-Whorf hypothesis is the belief that language functions as a way of shaping one's experiences; includes structural and semantic aspects of a language.

Self-awareness model is an approach to intercultural training also called the human relations model; it is based on the assumption that the trainee with self-understanding will understand the new culture better and will therefore be more effective in the overseas assignment.

Self-disclosure is a form of interaction that involves telling other people about yourself so they may get to know you better.

Self-efficacy is an individual's self-image and confidence to be able to adapt and function in a new environment.

Semanticists are people who study the meaning of words and where and how the words developed.

Semantics is the study of the ways behavior is influenced by the words and other symbols used to communicate.

Sensitivity training is one element used in the self-awareness approach to intercultural training; includes training exercises in which people are told in a group setting why their behavior is inappropriate.

Serial monogamy refers to a family system that includes a number of different monogamous marriages through divorce or death.

Shouting is typing a message (via e-mail) in all capital letters.

Slang refers to idioms and other informal language vocabulary.

Social hierarchy refers to the structure of a culture.

Social interaction refers to what is acceptable and unacceptable communication between people in a culture.

Social reciprocity refers to the way formal and informal obligations are handled, ranging from the belief that people are forever indebted to others to those who feel no obligation to others.

Social zone in the United States refers to physical distance between people of 4 to 12 feet; used for business situations in which people interact in a more formal, impersonal way.

Sociolinguistics refers to the effects of social and cultural differences upon a language.

Spamming refers to the cyberspace term for mass mailings of commercial advertisements or material cross-posted to numerous newsgroups.

Spatial intelligence involves the way space is used during meetings and other encounters.

Stereotypes are perceptions about certain groups of people or nationalities.

Subculture is a group of people possessing characteristic traits that set apart and distinguish it from others within a larger society (or macroculture).

Subgroups refer to groups of people possessing characteristic traits that set apart and distinguish them from others within a larger society/culture (or macroculture); groups with which the macroculture does not agree and has problems communicating.

Subjective interpretation is interpretation placed on a message that is affected by thought processes; influenced by personal judgment or temperament of a person.

Subnationalism exists when a political body attempts to unite diverse people under one government.

Supernationalism refers to extending authority over more than one nation.

Superstitions are beliefs that are inconsistent with the known laws of science or what a society considers true and rational.

Syntactic errors are errors in language meaning.

Syntactic rules govern how words are arranged in a sentence.

T-group is a group used in sensitivity training in which people are told why their behavior is inappropriate.

Taboos are practices or verbal expressions considered by a society or culture as improper or unacceptable.

Tactics are any maneuvers used for gaining advantages or success.

Thematization is the process by which a framework for mutual communication and satisfaction is reached.

Trade blocs are zones of international commerce where foreign or domestic merchandise may enter without formal customs entry or custom duties.

Trading with the Enemy Act of 1917 prohibits the transfer of information on military material or defense-related materials.

Transnational refers to corporations that cross the borders of countries in conducting their business.

Trilateral governance allows for later redetermination of terms by using an arbitrator.

Uncertainty-reduction theory refers to the creation of proactive predictions and retroactive explanations about our own behavior, beliefs, and attitudes, and those of others.

Unified governance refers to no advance negotiations; provides maximum flexibility; terms for both parties controlled by one party.

U.S. eating style is a zigzag style of eating used by people in the United States: cutting the meat with the knife held in the right hand and the fork in the left, then placing the knife on the plate, shifting the fork to the right hand, and eating.

Validated license allows a specific exporter to export specific products to specific places.

Values are beliefs and attitudes held by a culture.

Verbal dueling is a friendly type of argument or debate.

Vienna Agreement is a multilateral treaty signed by states to protect intellectual property.

Visa is written permission to enter and stay in a country for a specified time and purpose.

World culture involves the breaking down of traditional barriers among people of differing cultures, emphasizing the commonality of human needs.

Work refers to mental or physical activities directed to socially productive accomplishments.

Work attitudes are how people of a culture view work.

Work ethic refers to the attitude that work is applauded and rewarded, although failure to work is viewed negatively.

World Intellectual Property Organization (WIPO) of the United Nations promotes intellectual property rights worldwide and administers 22 treaties for 181 member nations.

World Trade Organization (WTO) is a multinational trade agreement of which the United States is a member.

Appendix B

ANSWERS TO EXERCISES

Chapter 1

Matching

1. D	2. C
3. I	4. B
5. A	6. H
7. F	8. G
9. K	10. J

Chapter 2

Matching

1. A	2. E
3. J	4. G
5. I	6. D
7. C	8. H
9. F	10. C

True/False

1. F	2. T
3. F	4. F
5. F	6. T
7. T	8. T
9. F	10. F

Chapter 3

True/False

1. T	2. F
3. T	4. T
5. F	6. F
7. F	8. F
9. T	10. T

Chapter 4

True/False

1. T	2. T
3. F	4. T
5. T	6. T
7. T	8. T
9. F	10. F

Chapter 5

True/False

1. F	2. T
3. F	4. T
5. T	6. T
7. F	8. T
9. T	10. T

Chapter 6

True/False

1. F	2. F
3. F	4. T
5. F	6. F
7. F	8. F
9. T	10. F

Matching

1. K	2. G
3. I	4. H
5. D	6. F
7. B	8. A
9. J	10. E

Chapter 7

True/False

1. F	2. F
3. F	4. T
5. F	6. T
7. T	8. T
9. T	10. T

Chapter 8

True/False

1. T	2. F
3. T	4. T
5. T	6. T
7. F	8. F
9. F	10. F

Chapter 9

True/False

1. T	2. F
3. F	4. F
5. T	6. T
7. F	8. T
9. F	10. T

Chapter 10

True/False

1. T	2. F
3. T	4. T
5. F	6. T
7. T	8. T
9. T	10. T

Chapter 11

True/False

1. F	2. T
3. F	4. F
5. T	6. T
7. F	8. F
9. F	10. F

Chapter 12

Matching

1. L	2. E
3. H	4. J
5. K	6. B
7. D	8. I
9. C	10. G

Matching

1. C	2. I
3. A	4. H
5. E	6. B
7. F	8. J
9. G	10. D

Index

Note: Entries followed by "f" denote figures; "t" tables.

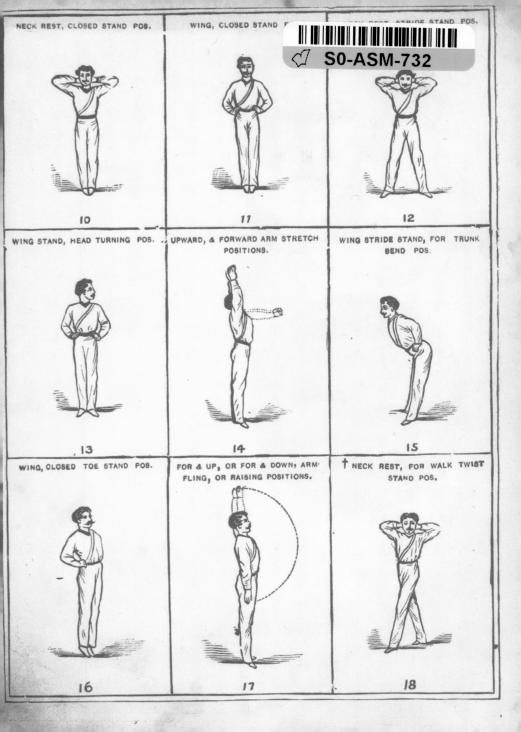

NECK REST, CLOSED STAND POS.

WING, CLOSED STAND P

NECK REST, STRIDE STAND POS.

10

11

12

WING STAND, HEAD TURNING POS.

UPWARD, & FORWARD ARM STRETCH
POSITIONS.

WING STRIDE STAND, FOR TRUNK
BEND POS.

13

14

15

WING, CLOSED TOE STAND POS.

FOR & UP, OR FOR & DOWN, ARM-
FLING, OR RAISING POSITIONS.

† NECK REST, FOR WALK TWIST
STAND POS.

16

17

18

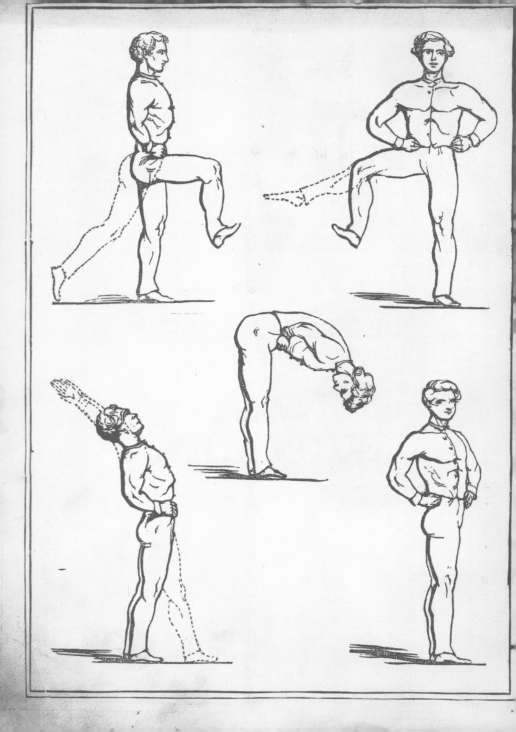

MANLY HEALTH

AND

TRAINING

To Teach the Science of a Sound and Beautiful Body

WALT
WHITMAN

Regan Arts.

NEW YORK

Regan Arts.

65 Bleecker Street
New York, NY 10012

Introduction Copyright © 2016 by Zachary Turpin

First Regan Arts hardcover edition, February 2017

Library of Congress Control Number: 2016955001

ISBN 978-1-68245-075-8

Interior design by Nancy Singer
Cover design by Richard Ljoenes

Image credits, which constitute an extension of this copyright page, appear on page 219.

Printed in the United States of America

10 9 8 7 6 5 4 3 2 1

CONTENTS

Walt Whitman

INTRODUCTION

By Zachary Turpin

Microfilm is full of surprises, the discovery of Walt Whitman's "Manly Health and Training" series being only one of them. The first time I held a spool of it, I was surprised to find that microfilm is heavy, a bit like a hockey puck—if it were made of one hundred feet of wound-up polyester. Those hundred feet are surprisingly durable; their primary purpose, after all, is to last. The pages of old books and newspapers may be more of a treat for the senses, brittle and musty and delicious, but microfilm, properly stored, will last half a millennium. And thank goodness for that, because squirreled away on microfilm are uncountably more surprises. "Surprise" just barely describes the feeling of finding "Manly Health and Training." For me, looking for the lost writings of Walt Whitman had begun almost as a joke. I'd already uncovered work by the poet Emma Lazarus, the novelist Rebecca Harding Davis, and the fantasy writer L. Frank Baum, each of whom had been very, very prolific. (Davis and Baum wrote at least a book a year.) As I looked, it slowly occurred to me that every great American writer might have written something that is now lost. But Walt Whitman? The man whose *Leaves of Grass* might be the most important book of poetry ever written in America? Whose face is, second to Abraham Lincoln's, maybe the most recognizable of the nineteenth century? Whose poems—"Song of Myself," "I Sing the Body Electric," "O Captain! My Captain!"— have so saturated our literature, songs, movies, and culture that they help define what it means to be American? No. Absolutely not. It was impossible.

I couldn't resist.

Literary research is about pursuit first, pay dirt last (if at all). The pleasure of being a researcher is in every little thing that turns up along the way, a principle that scholar Stephen Ramsay calls "the hermeneutics of screwing around." Indeed, the best treasures are always found in reading and writing. Walt Disney once said that "there is more treasure in books than in all the pirate's loot on Treasure Island," and, while I agree, when the adventure began I don't think I honestly expected to find anything in particular. Adventures often reveal themselves as such after the fact; until then, we insult them with the word "work."

The months went by slowly. As it usually happens, nothing turned up. Nothing, nothing, nothing, nothing, nothing. And then *something*, with no warning whatever. I doubt that most true discoveries are glamorous moments—this one wasn't: a hot July morning, a library basement, a cup of coffee, a loaded microfilm reader. Inside, though, I was vibrating with anticipation. These are the moments a researcher lives for. Based on a clue found in a newspaper clipping, I knew that the film I was looking at had something by Walt Whitman hidden in it, but as I scrolled, my best guess was that it would be a couple of short articles at most, a pleasant curiosity or two. Then, after a minute or so, the words I was looking for whirred into view: "Manly Health and Training." This was it—and it was, indeed, an article. (I kept scrolling.) Actually, two articles! (I kept scrolling.) No, three articles! I'd officially been wrong. (I kept scrolling.) Four articles! Long ones, at that. (More scrolling.) Five articles! Six! Seven! Eight! By the time I came to the thirteenth and final article in the series, I was in what I'm sure was a state of shock. Here was the largest cache of Whitman's work to come to light in half a century. To be the only person alive to know it existed, what amounted to a book by Walt Whitman, lost since 1858: this was more than a surprise. It was a thunderclap. Disney is right: there are untold riches in the written word—and "best of all," he adds, "you can enjoy these riches every day of your life." The book you are holding is proof that there are many more treasures out there, waiting to be found, shared, enjoyed. They may have disappeared, but as Whitman reminds us, "Nothing is ever really lost, or can be lost."

About his own disappearance, the otherwise self-confident Whitman could be surprisingly anxious, despite nearly everything he ever said in poetry. "Some day I'll die," he reminded his friend Horace Traubel, "maybe surprise you all by a sudden disappearance: then where'll my book be? That's the one thing that excites me: most authors have the same dread—the dread that something or other essential that they have written may somehow become side-tracked, lost—lost forever." And indeed, it turned out that quite a bit of his writing was lost, despite the efforts of generations of scholars to find it. He simply wrote too much. Some of his works were bound to sink from sight—with Whitman occasionally trying to scuttle them himself, anxieties be damned. His early short stories, for example, embarrassed him dreadfully: "My serious wish," he confessed in *Specimen Days and Collect* (1882), "were to have all those crude and boyish pieces quietly dropp'd in oblivion." In the end, Whitman only collected them "to avoid the annoyance of their surreptitious issue." Other early writings were less persistently annoying, and so less fortunate. Whitman's freelance journalism was particularly unfortunate in this regard. Published during the early years of *Leaves of Grass* (1855 to 1860), often anonymously or under pen names, much of it fell into near-total obscurity after the poet's death. It's taken more than a century and a half of work to recover, with plenty left to be found. Whitman himself encourages us: "Missing me one place," he

writes in *Leaves of Grass*, "search another." The most recent result of
the search is the book you hold in your hands, Walt Whitman's lost
guide to living healthily in America.

If you haven't already skipped ahead to it, you may be wondering:
what *is* "Manly Health and Training," anyway? It's a good question,
and there's more than one good answer. "Manly Health" is part guest
editorial, part self-help column, first published as a weekly serial in
the *New York Atlas* newspaper. It begins as a fairly straightforward
diet-and-exercise guide for men, but, as you will see, it gradually
becomes much more: an essay on male beauty, a chauvinistic screed,
a sports almanac, a eugenics manifesto, a description of New York
daily life, an anecdotal history of longevity, a pseudoscientific tract,
and a fitness manual for the nation. Apparently, few topics were out
of bounds for Whitman: he writes about not only diet and exercise
but also physical beauty, manly comradeship, sex and reproduction,
socialization, race, eugenics, war, climate, longevity, bathing, prize-
fighting, gymnastics, baseball, footwear, facial hair, depression, alcohol, and prostitution. At times, this book is an eyebrow raiser, not
least because it sheds more light on a period (1860–61) in which
Whitman was also writing dozens of new poems for the third edition of *Leaves of Grass*. *Manly Health and Training* also helps us understand Whitman's transition from a career journalist to one of the
premier poets of America. And it provides some much-needed information about Whitman's life at that time.

In the chronology of his life, 1858 is something of an absent
year, though from the little scholars have found, it probably wasn't a
good one. The year before, Whitman had found steady work harder
to come by, thanks to the Panic of 1857. In *Leaves of Grass*, he describes himself as a poet, a dreamer, an inspired "loafer," but in 1858,
Whitman the wage earner had to scrape by as a writer-editor for the
Brooklyn Daily Times. This is also the year when Whitman first felt

WALT WHITMAN IN 1855
(FROM THE FIRST EDITION OF *LEAVES OF GRASS*).

his health slip, when he suffered some sort of event, a "sunstroke," due to high blood pressure or overwork. One of the few things we know for sure about Whitman in 1858 is that he was seriously depressed, for reasons that can only be guessed at. It may have been lovesickness, or anxiety about his sexuality. Of the few poems scholars have dated to this year, his most celebrated—titled "Live Oak with Moss"—captures the joys and sorrows of a relationship with another man. Whomever he loved and lost, Whitman clearly felt he had no one to talk to about it: "I dare not tell it in words," he writes in "Live Oak," "not even in these songs."

Family relationships probably worsened his depression. Whitman's beloved brother Jeff was then growing closer with his sweetheart and soon-to-be wife, Martha Mitchell—leaving him less time to spend with his brother. Likewise, the death of Whitman's unpleasant father three years earlier, while liberating, may have left him aching just the same. Walter Sr. had softened toward the end, but he was nevertheless a stubborn, lifelong alcoholic. This is why in many of Whitman's early writings you will find a commitment, however superficial, to abstinence from alcohol. But by 1858, Whitman made few pretenses to teetotalism. In fact, he spent many of his nights drinking at Pfaff's beer hall in Manhattan, a popular spot for New York's young bohemians, freethinkers, and writers. Some of this was calculated. Of his uncharacteristic night-owling, Whitman scholars Ed Folsom and Kenneth Price note that he "was clearly remaking his image, going to bars more often than he had since he left New Orleans a decade earlier." His time at Pfaff's, that is, seems to have been the poet's effort at rebranding, not recovering. There, Whitman quietly greeted friends and enemies alike, and occasionally heard his *Leaves of Grass* made the butt of less-than-subtle jokes. Public reviews of the collection from this period were disheartening; an especially vicious review in the *Long-Islander*, a paper Whitman himself had founded, disposed of *Leaves of Grass* as "a repulsive and nasty book."

It's easy to see why Whitman might have questioned his calling as a poet. In "As I Ebb'd with the Ocean of Life," a poem written around this period, he expresses this anxiety:

> *I have not once had the least idea who or what I am,*
> *But that before all my insolent poems the real ME still stands*
>   *untouched, untold, altogether unreached,*
> *Withdrawn far, mocking me with mock-congratulatory signs*
>   *and bows,*
> *With peals of distant ironical laughter at every word I have*
>   *written or shall write,*
> *Striking me with insults till I fall helpless upon the sand.*

Clearly, Whitman was suffering some sort of identity crisis in 1858 and felt the need to test other outlets, social or sexual. It is during this same period that Whitman joined the Fred Gray Association, an unofficial, underground gay men's society. But beyond that, Whitman would later recall this period as a time of *conformity*, in which he drank like other writers, talked like them, even dressed like them. In a photograph from this period (see following page), we see Whitman wearing a dark, baggy suit, with pin-striped vest and pants, the kind worn by bohemian writers and dandies of the day. Little wonder that, looking at the portrait thirty years later, Whitman said, "It is me, me, unformed, undeveloped," that it "hits off phases not common in [his] photos."

In a life mostly defined by self-assurance, 1858 was an unusual time for Whitman. It was a year of self-questioning.

WALT WHITMAN IN 1859–1860.

Today, we know Whitman as one of America's greatest and most radical poets, but in 1858 he was toying with the idea of changing his profession altogether. In a letter draft dated July 28, 1857, he admits, "I have thought, for some time past, of beginning the use of

myself as a public Speaker, teacher, or lecturer." The next spring, on
his thirty-ninth birthday, Whitman expands on this in a notebook,
framing his calling as not just a personal but a national imperative:

May 31. '58

> It seems to me called for to inaugurate a revolution in American
> oratory, to change it from the excessively diffuse and impromptu
> character it has, (an ephemeral readiness, surface animation, the
> stamp of the daily newspaper, to be dismissed as soon as the next
> day's paper appears.)—and to make it the means of the grand
> modernized delivery of live modern orations, appropriate to
> America, appropriate to the world.—(May 31–2) This change is
> a serious one, and, if to be done at all cannot be done easily.—A
> great leading representative man, with perfect power, perfect con-
> fidence in his power, persevering, with repeated specimens, rang-
> ing up and down The States—such a man, above all things, would
> give it a fair start.—What are your theories?—Let us have the
> practical sample of a thing, and look upon it, and listen to it, and
> turn it about for to examine it.—
>
> Washington made free the body of America, for that was first
> in order—Now comes one who will make free the American soul.

It should probably go without saying that Whitman's "great
leading representative man" is himself. It's not all that surprising that
Whitman briefly imagined himself as the next Emerson or Webster,
the great orator of his age. His attachment to oratory began early,
when as a boy he heard the great Quaker speaker Elias Hicks deliver a
commanding sermon in Brooklyn. His love of the voice later became
a passion, when he began attending Italian opera. In his notebooks,
he wrote reminder after reminder to himself to enrich the timbre of

his voice, and expand his chest, and "restrain gesture," so that audiences would find him irresistible. By 1858, Whitman was so committed to transforming himself into a national orator that he decided privately, "Lecturing, (my own way,) [is] henceforth my employment, my means of earning my living." He even drafted programs for a lecture series, the subject being nothing less than the entire nation.

As far as anyone knows, Whitman never gave any such lectures. Besides a few early political speeches, and his reminiscences of Abraham Lincoln given later in life, his employment as a lecturer was infrequent. Skepticism of his own speaking ability may have had something to do with this. For all his excitement at the idea of lecturing on America, Whitman apparently doubted that he would get his ideas across, considering his odd notion that his words would have to be "carefully perused afterward, to be understood." (Of course, he may simply have been fishing for extra cash, since, as he adds, "I personally sell the printed copies.") Still, the reality of these lectures matters less than Whitman's *desire* to lecture. At this time in his life, he was tiring of the next-to-meaningless "stamp of the daily newspaper," as he called it, "to be dismissed as soon as the next day's paper appears." And his *Daily Times* editorials from this period are, indeed, pretty unrewarding reading. From what little we know of Whitman in 1858, he must have longed to escape this "surface animation" of journalism, to "make free the American soul"—and his own soul in the process. But, as his poetry and notebooks insist, to free the soul one must begin by freeing the body, "for that [is] first in order."

This may explain why, in 1858, Whitman drafted up a pair of ads for a newspaper series on the subject of "manly health and training." These promised a series "not only original and of a high degree of literary merit, but go[ing] into full practical details, giving that specific advice in all departments of general training for health, whose result, if faithfully followed, would be, for every man who reads it, A NOBLE AND ROBUST PHYSIQUE." Scholars have been aware of these handwritten drafts since at least 1898, but their ultimate fate has always been uncertain. Did Whitman begin a series, only to have it fall through? Or, in writing a lecture

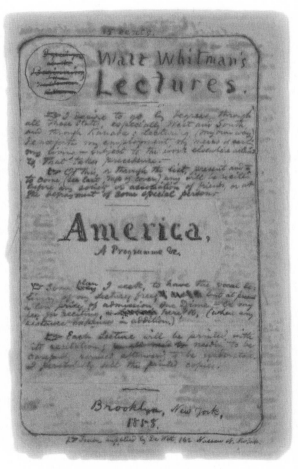

DRAFT OF AN ADVERTISEMENT FOR A
PLANNED LECTURE SERIES.

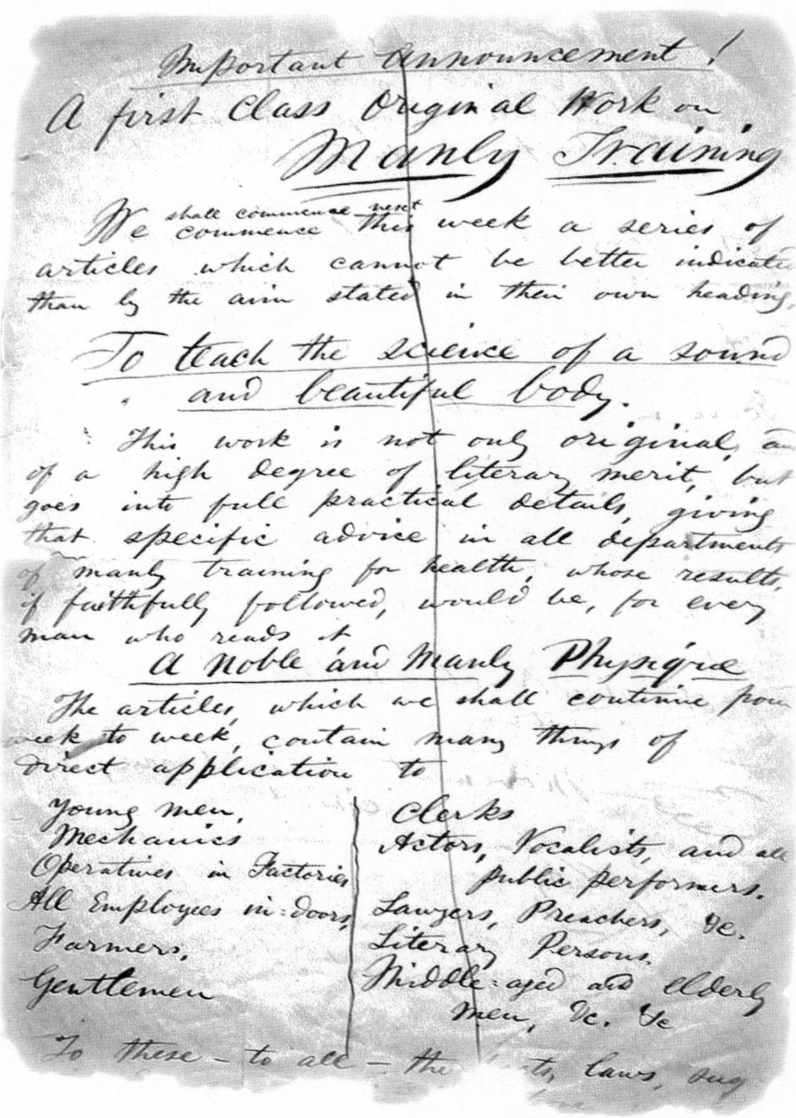

Important Announcement!

A first Class Original Work on

Manly Training

We shall commence next week a series of articles which cannot be better indicated than by the aim stated in their own heading.

To teach the science of a sound and beautiful body.

This work is not only original, and of a high degree of literary merit, but goes into full practical details, giving that specific advice in all departments of manly training for health, whose results, if faithfully followed, would be, for every man who reads it

A Noble and Manly Physique

The articles, which we shall continue from week to week, contain many things of direct application to

Young men,
Mechanics
Operatives in Factories
All Employes in-doors,
Farmers,
Gentlemen

Clerks
Actors, Vocalists, and all
public performers.
Lawyers, Preachers, &c.
Literary Persons,
Middle-aged and Elderly
men, &c. &c

To these — to all — the ?ts, laws, ?

MANUSCRIPT DRAFT FOR "MANLY HEALTH"
ANNOUNCEMENT.

on men's physiques, had he fiddled with the idea of making it into articles instead? (After all, he went so far as to draft a program for nonexistent lectures.) Without additional evidence, there has been no way to hazard a guess.

The evidence, it turns out, lay shut away in the *New York Atlas*, a weekly newspaper printed in Manhattan, now long defunct. Here is the notice that appeared in it, just once, on September 12, 1858:

ADVERTISEMENT FOR "MANLY HEALTH"
IN THE *NEW YORK ATLAS*.

The notice matches Whitman's "Manly Training" manuscript to a *T*. Without a doubt, it is his, and so is the series that follows, commencing that week in the *Atlas* under the title "Manly Health and Training, with Off-Hand Hints Toward Their Conditions." The author calls himself "Mose Velsor, of Brooklyn."

Of his many pen names, "Mose Velsor" was one of his favorites. By 1858, he'd used it numerous times, signing it to articles on everything from "the Opera" to the "b'hoys of the Bowery." (Whitman created the pseudonym by joining "Mose," a common "Bowery b'hoy" name, and "Van Velsor," his mother's maiden name.) Under the guise of "Mose," Whitman, it must be admitted, occasionally plagiarizes shamelessly; at times, "Manly Health and Training" is chockablock with outright theft from other periodicals. Of course, most installments of "Manly Health and Training" are in Whitman's own words. Only in a few of them does Whitman brazenly plagiarize. But why, in "Manly Health and Training," is Whitman so unconscientious? If nothing else, this haphazardness tells us a little bit about the circumstances behind the series.

First, it's clear that Whitman wrote hastily. His output in this period (1857–1860), between the second and third editions of *Leaves of Grass*, was already prolific, even for him. In 1857 alone, Whitman wrote close to seventy new poems. He also spent a great deal of energy trying to get out a new edition of *Leaves*, though it wasn't until three years later that any publisher would agree to it. Additionally, Whitman was editing and writing for the *Brooklyn Daily Times*, to the tune of several hundred (or even thousand) words per day, six days a week, for two straight years. Since there is no obvious break in his *Daily Times* editorials during the run of "Manly Health and Training," it's clear that he created the series in addition to his daily duties—no mean feat, considering that the series added at least three thousand words to Whitman's weekly workload. It's little wonder that no correspondence to or from Whitman exists for this period. He can hardly have had left any time, energy, or ink.

Overall, Whitman's motives for writing "Manly Health and Training" must have been at least partly financial. The first edition of *Leaves of Grass* (1855) had sold poorly; many of the copies that exist today were probably given away to friends or reviewers, rather than sold. The second edition (1856) fared even worse; it's been called, and rightly so, "Whitman's greatest publishing failure." It couldn't have helped that its publishers and retailers, Fowler and Wells, weren't poets by any measure; they specialized in books on phrenology, physiology, and self-culture for young people. Thus, "Manly Health and Training" was probably a side project, one of several freelance jobs Whitman took on during this period for extra cash. Of what interest is it today? Certainly it contributes to our understanding of a dim period in Whitman's life. But what makes this series especially important is the poet's thoughts on manhood, strength, personal health, and national character. To him, these are inseparable—but, in the end, they all relate back to the body. By Whitman's lights, the body is the most perfectible part of the American (the American man, anyway), and he is just the man to tell you how to do it. You may notice, as you read through this book, how often Whitman's suggestions sound like the diets and fitness regimens of today. Indeed, to read "Manly Health and Training" is to realize just how old the self-improvement industry is. Diets, workouts, nutritional supplements, homeopathic pills, colonics, tanning, cosmetic surgery, shape-slimming clothing, self-help books, baldness cures—almost all of these existed in Whitman's day. It's no accident that his meaty breakfasts, lunches, and dinners sound more than a little like today's Paleolithic diet, and his exercise regimen looks here and there like the weight and interval training that millions of Americans do every day. Since the time of Benjamin Franklin (who famously set himself the challenge of living "without committing any fault at any time," and spent thirteen weeks trying to do so), self-improvement has been a part of what it means to be American. "Manly Health and Training" is proof that while we have come a long, long way, we do not change as much as we think we do.

In part, the book you hold is a response to change. In Whitman's day, deep shifts were taking place in science, society, and politics. Keep in mind that Whitman wrote "Manly Health and Training" less than three years before the secession of the South, and in an atmosphere of political tension he seems to have felt that America was short on muscle, both physiologically and politically. This is probably the reason why Whitman uses the eighth installment of "Manly Health" to advocate for prizefighting. Here, he insists on "the necessity of those means that help to develope [*sic*] *a hardy, robust and combative nation* [. . .] We do not think that community able to take care of its rights, and defend them successfully against all odds, where there exist only peaceful, pious, respectable and orthodox citizens. There must be something more." That "something more" is "a race of men who could and would fight, not by rote merely, but for *the love of fight*." As an example of what he means, Whitman describes a bare-knuckle match that had just taken place in Ontario. It's unlikely that Whitman attended the match; he wouldn't travel to Canada for years. Bare-knuckle boxing was outlawed in the United States at the time, yet, in this installment, Whitman passionately argues for its reinstatement. Noting that "even Rome itself, in time, [. . .] fell a prey to outside invaders far inferior to itself," he suggests that:

> In robust training for this life, which is itself a continual fight with some form or adversary or other, the aim should be *to form that solid and adamantine fibre which will endure long and serious attacks upon it*, and come out unharmed from them, rather than the ability to perform sudden and brilliant feats, which often exhaust the powers in show, without doing any substantial good.

His example is Morrissey, who apparently endured terrible punishment in the eleven-round fight before knocking out Heenan. As Whitman would later write in "Poems of Joy" (1867), the fighter is "strong-brawn'd [. . .], towering in the arena, in perfect condition, conscious of power, thirsting to meet his opponent." But he is also gentlemanly. For Whitman, a boxer is a hero, but with a "brute" or "animal" aspect to his strength:

> Just in the way as the institution of the horse-race, and nothing less than that, brings the breed of the horse up to a far, very far, higher pitch of physical perfection than could be attained by any other means known or possible upon earth—just exactly in the same way, [. . .] it remains to be distinctly confessed that *nothing short of these fierce manly contests, in ancient and modern times, has led to the mightiest and most perfect development of the masculine frame, and proved what are the real rules consonant with its soundest physiology.* Therefore, in opposition to the views expressed by the editors of the American newspapers, (the *Atlas*, we believe, among the rest,) we say a stern word or two, not in defence of these fights only, but *in deliberate advocacy of them.*

Whitman would eventually serve as a nurse during the Civil War. He would witness things that forever changed his stance on fighting, making his argument for prizefighting, in retrospect, a bit shocking. But regardless, it is clear that in 1858 he did not feel like compromising on the subject of the American fighting spirit. Whitman does warn against the initial "splurge"—the desire to attack immediately and unthinkingly. He also notes that "the actual necessity of this kind of training, for fighting purposes, will never be the rule, but only the exception." Even so, he is adamant here that "nothing short of a prize-fight will ever bring the rules of manly health and training to that systematic perfection which they are attaining, and out of which we, among the rest, have been able to write these articles for popular use." Overall, the prizefighter is a stand-in for what Whitman thought the whole nation should be and do, with the "prize" apparently being the frontier, with all the size and strength its annexation would confer upon America:

> The nation is passing through several important physiological processes and combinations. To a great degree, it is yet getting acclimated—especially in the West, and on the Pacific coast, which latter is destined to have a huge influence on the future physique of America. [. . .] Here the air is dry and antiseptic—everything grows to a size, strength and expanse, unknown in the Northern and Eastern States. Nature is on a large scale; and here, in time to come, will be found a wonderful race of men.

Whitman's focus on the "Northern and Eastern States" and his thoughts on "race[s] of men" suggest that he may have had in mind an impending conflict: the Civil War. Political and racial tensions, as well as the threat of Southern secession, likely explain his concerns about outlasting a long and bloody conflict. Here, perhaps, is this book's deeper theme. The fitness of American democracy would, after all, soon be tested, even threatened with annihilation. The men of the Northeastern states apparently needed strengthening not only for their own health, but so that they might endure those "indescribably strong and bloody attacks, blows, and bruises" that would come in the fight for national unity. The "lesson" of such a fight, Whitman concludes, is that *"he wins who can 'best stand grief'"*—a lesson the poet would soon learn all too well.

Whitman was never quite the same after the Civil War, but he did go on to live a relatively long and happy life, dying at the age of seventy-two, an internationally recognized poet and personage, his *Leaves of Grass* having gone through six American editions. It has since gone through many, many more. But even though Whitman died nearly 125 years ago, the full recovery of his writings is far from over. Like this book, many more lost documents may exist, published or unpublished, in climate-controlled archives or, just maybe, in your very own attic. New poems, journalism, interviews, letters, and marginalia by Whitman come to light all the time. Who knows where the next manuscript, notebook, or even novel might turn up? As with "Manly Health and Training," we may find that it was just under our boot soles.

The New York Atlas.

Vol. 21, No. 17

Manly Health and Training,

September 12, 1858

With Off-Hand Hints Toward Their Conditions

By Mose Velsor

ILLUSTRATION OF MANLY STRENGTH.

To you whose eye is arrested by the above headlines, and whom we hope to make a companion to the end of our series—to every man, rich or poor, worker or idler—to all ages of life, from the beginning to the end of it—certainly nothing comes closer home, or is, without any intermission, a topic of more controlling interest, than this we are going to present, through a few articles, some plain and we hope sensible hints toward the furtherance of—*a sound and steady condition of manly health.* We will not make any apology for devoting a portion of our columns to the discussion of this subject; nor, indeed, do we think it much more than necessary to state our theme, to be quite certain that we shall have an eager and multitudinous audience.

Manly health! Is there not a kind of charm—a fascinating magic in the words? We fancy we see the look with which the phrase is met by many a young man, strong, alert, vigorous, whose mind has always felt, but never formed in words, the ambition to attain to the perfection of his bodily powers—has realized to himself that all other goods of existence would hardly be goods, in comparison with a perfect body, perfect blood—no morbid humors, no weakness, no impotency or deficiency or bad stuff in him; but all running over with animation and ardor, all marked by herculean strength, suppleness, a clear complexion, and the rich results (which follow such causes) of a laughing voice, a merry song morn and night, a sparkling eye, and an ever-happy soul!

To such a young man—to all who read these lines—let us, with rapid pen, sketch some of the requisites toward this condition of sound health we talk of—a condition, we wish it distinctly understood, far easier to attain than is generally supposed; and which, even to many of those long wrenched by bad habits or by illness, must not be despaired of, but perseveringly striven for, as, in reason, probable and almost certain yet to attain.

EFFECTS OF A SOUND BODY.

Among the signs of manly health and perfect physique, internal and external, are a clear eye, a transparent and perhaps embrowned complexion (this latter not necessarily), an upright attitude, a springy step, a sweet breath, a ringing voice and little or nothing of irritability in the temper. With your choleric man, there is apt to be something wrong in the stomach, joints or blood. In nine cases out of ten, when this is obviated the disposition comes round.

We shall speak by and by of health as being the foundation of all real manly beauty. Perhaps, too, it has more to do than is generally supposed, with the capacity of being agreeable as a companion, a social visitor, always welcome—and with the divine joys of friendship. In these particulars (and they surely include a good part of the best blessings of existence), there is that subtle virtue in a sound body, with all its functions perfect, which nothing else can make up for, and which will itself make up for many other deficiencies, as of education, refinement, and the like.

We have even sometimes fancied that there was *a wonderful medicinal effect in the mere personal presence of a man who was perfectly well!*

While, on the other hand, what can be more debilitating than to be continually surrounded by sickly people, and to have to do with them only?

REASON—OUR OBJECTS.

It is not too much to begin to demand of the young men, and indeed the masses of the people, (through conscientious writers for the press, speakers, &c.,) that, in this great matter of health and a manly form and soundness, *steady reason should assume the helm, and keep it.* We know that to many this will seem advice whose accomplishment, on anything like a general scale, is out of the question. Yet we confess we are hopeful of its success, in time. For where, we repeat, is there a man, young, old, or middle-aged, who does not mainly desire to have a perfect physique?

The object we have in view is the presentation in a collected and connected form, for popular use, of the general run of facts, rules, suggestions, &c., most desirable to be understood by those who have not yet paid any earnest attention to the subject of developing a perfect and manly physique. These, indeed, the common classes, and young men, form the immense body, the audience to whom our hints are, in the main, directed. It will, therefore, be necessary for us to go over some of the grounds that may be familiar to those of our readers who have already studied out the subject. Still it will do them also no harm to go over the same statements again. Indeed, it is probable that, of three-fourths of the young and middle-aged men, not only in this city of New York, but in every portion of the United States, one of the best goods they could do for themselves would be the careful reading, once or twice every year, during the remainder of their lives, of all these paragraphs we are now writing.

Our object is, at the same time, to be attained in our own rambling and discursive way, and our writing will be without technical terms and phrases; for we are free to confess ourselves as no physician—but one who, by observation and study, has come to view the theme of health as oftentimes able to be better treated, for popular use, by an outsider, than a medical man—for who ever knew one of the latter to write a treatise, except its main direction were to the medical fraternity more than any others?

We would have gymnasia commenced, so as gradually to form part of all the public schools of America, even from Maine to Texas, and from the northern boundary of Washington Territory to the southern point of Florida. This, no doubt, sounds extravagant to the superficial reader, but by him who has investigated the subject, and is aware how, under all circumstances, *proper training trebles the natural power, endurance, and health of the body*, it will be better understood. There is even no hunter, warrior, wild Indian, or the strongest and supplest backwoodsman of the West, but would have all his natural qualities increased far beyond what they are, by

BOY DOING GYMNASTIC EXERCISES.

judicious training. This is art, the province of which is to take natural germs or gifts, and bring them out in the fullest and best way.

A FINE ANIMAL MAN.

Do not be startled at the words, excellent reader. It is, in our
view, indispensably necessary that a man should be *a fine animal*—
sound and vigorous. This, to be candid with you, is the text and
germ of most of our remarks—which arise out of it, and seek to
promulge and explain how it can be fully accomplished. It being
the specialty of these articles, makes it necessary to consider all
that belongs to you, reader, and to your body, structure, &c., mostly
from that point of view alone. And why should we not? Almost everything else is attended to but the animal part of a man—as if that
were something to be ashamed of and repressed. Indeed, this is

avowedly the theory of many very good people, who proceed upon it in the bringing up of their children.

That such is not our theory is of course evident, or will be, in every line of these articles. We, at the same time, know with the rest that a man has a moral, affectional, and mental nature which must also be developed; but we say that, at present, the whole tendency of things is to *over*-develope [sic] those parts, while the physical is cramped and dwindled away.

Yes, reader, we teach that man must be perfect in his body first— we start with that as our premises, our foundation. We would throw into something like regular form a few principal hints and suggestions. Now this is to be done. Would that other writers, and that teachers also, would follow up in the same train of influence with ourselves—until there should be no man, especially any young man, through the length and breadth of the land, who should any longer be allowed to plead ignorance of these simple laws as a reason for his impaired constitution and loss of man's physique.

Gratified indeed should we be if we thought these hints were the means of arresting the attention of this younger part of the American people, and recalling them to a sense of that, which, once having it, is not at all difficult to restrain, but once thoroughly lost, may be mourned and sought for long afterward in vain—and even when restored must be watched over with double the former care. But yet we will not discourage any of those who having injured their health, seek to regain it. We would rather impress upon them the probability, almost certainty, under prudent management, of attaining their sound condition again.

FOR STUDENTS, CLERKS, AND THOSE IN SEDENTARY OR MENTAL EMPLOYMENTS.

Can there then be no such thing as hard study going on without detriment to health—for study is mental exercise? We have elsewhere hinted that there not only can, but that study may go on favorably to health. Only *all study, and no developed physique, is death.* Our readers must take a broad and deep view of our arguments, from our own points of observation; for we have not time to fill up the gaps, and connect one item with another as we would, if we had nothing else to do. At present, a few suggestive points must answer, and we are confident we are talking to people of intelligent minds and who know something of this subject already.

We say to the young man not only that mental development may well go on at the same time with physical development, but that indeed is the only way in which they should go on—both together, which is much to the advantage of each. If you are a student, be also a student of the body, a practiser [*sic*] of manly exercises, realizing that a broad chest, a muscular pair of arms, and two sinewy legs, will be just as much credit to you, and stand you in hand through your future life, equally with your geometry, your history, your classics, your law, medicine, or divinity. Let nothing divert you from your duty to your body. Up in the morning early! Habituate yourself to the brisk walk in the fresh air—to the exercise of pulling the oar—and to the loud declamation upon the hills, or along the shore. Such are the means by which you can seize with treble gripe upon all the puzzles and difficulties of your student life—whatever problems are presented to you in your books, or by your professors. Guard your manly power, your health and strength, from all hurts and violations—this is the most sacred charge you will ever have in your keeping.

To you, clerk, literary man, sedentary person, man of fortune, idler, the same advice. Up! The world (perhaps you now look upon it with pallid and disgusted eyes) is full of zest and beauty for you, if you approach it in the right spirit! Out in the morning! If in the city, even there you will find ample sources of amusement and interest in its myriad varieties of character and occupation—in the scenes of its awakening and adjusting itself to its daily labors—in the crowds around its ferries, and all through its main thoroughfares, and at its great depots and markets. Do not be discouraged soon. Give our advice a thorough trial—not for a few days or weeks, but for months. Early rising, early to bed, exercise, plain food, thorough and persevering continuance in gently-commenced training, the cultivation with resolute will of a cheerful temper, the society of friends and a certain number of hours spent every day in regular employment—these, we say, simple as they are, are enough to revolutionize life, and change it from a scene of gloom, feebleness, and irresolution, into *life indeed*, as becomes such a universe as this, full of all the essential means of happiness, full of well-intentioned and affectionate men and women, with the beneficent processes of nature always at work, the sun shining, the flowers blooming, the crops growing, the waters running, with all else that is wanted, only that man should be *rightly toned* to partake of the universal strength and joy. This he must do through reason, knowledge and exercise—in short, through *training*; for that is the sum of all.

The New York Atlas.

Vol. 21, No. 18

Manly Health and Training,

September 19, 1858

With Off-Hand Hints Toward Their Conditions

By Mose Velsor

CONGRESSMAN FROM NEBRASKA PLEDGING
TO ABSTAIN FROM ALCOHOL.

TO MORALISTS, REFORMERS, ETC.

It is our deeply felt conviction, the result of much observation in New York, Brooklyn, and other cities, that the only true and profitable way of reaching the morals of the young is through making them first, *healthy, clean-blooded, and vigorous specimens of men.* The wisest preacher, teacher, or philanthropist is not he who is forever dwelling on abstract qualities, off in the clouds, or that would make virtuous bloodless phantoms of our young men. That can never be; and yet we believe that, out of health and a fine physique, would arise an immensely greater development of morality and abstract good.

At present there is a mutual recoil between the pure moralist and the teacher of healthy bodily exercises and games—which recoil, in our opinion, should not exist at all. It was not so formerly. The young men of Athens, and other Greek cities, were trained in their bodily, mental, and moral developments and perfections together, and this, as we have before intimated, is the only way, indeed, in which training can be just to the whole man. We repeat, however, that the *first* requisite to a young man is that he should be well and hardy; and that from such a foundation alone, he will be more apt to become good, upright, friendly, and self-respected.

LIFE WITHOUT A SOUND BODY— WHAT IS IT GOOD FOR?

Reason seems to tell a man, not so much that death is dreadful, as that *dragging out a useless, deficient, and sickly life is dreadful.* We even think that if such a life were to be continued year after year, without probability of change, death would be preferable—would be a happy relief from it.

29

This being so, the great object of a man's exertions should be, commencing *before* he is a man, even in early youth, to lay the foundations of a sound and capable life, by forming for himself a sound and capable body. It is all in vain to say, (though practically our civilized life does say so, in many forms,) that a sick, unsound, or prematurely dying man, has a life really worth living for. And when we come to consider what vast swarms of these sick men, (or at least not-well men,) there are, the fact is one which looms up in terrible proportions!

Yes, we repeat it, there is more distress and horror in one unhappy life, made so by the want of stamina and tone, than in the mere fact of a hundred deaths. Let, then, the attention be given to making life worth the possession; let manly health and physique be oftener taught, and strenuously attended to.

ATHLETISM.

One of the objects we have in view in presenting these statements to the reader, is to help on the taste for athletic exercises and wholesome games, which seems to be sprouting up in New York, Brooklyn, and other American cities. This subject of athletism (we will coin a new word, and what seems to us a needed one) cannot be mentioned with-out the thoughts irresistibly turning back to ancient Greece, where it received its fullest attention, and, in return, aided with other means in making them the most physically and intellectually glorious nation of antiquity.

The Grecian manly games (we may mention, for the interest in them is ever fresh,) consisted of five principle exercises, running races on foot, leaping, boxing, wrestling, and throwing the discus or quoit—all of which we inherit from that ancient time and people.

Running was the exercise held in the highest estimation—and the name of the victor in it, was often identified with the Olympiad in which he had gained the triumph. It was probably prepared for by far more careful antecedents than with us; the contestants were very numerous, and the prize, an olive crown, was considered the most honorable token it lay in the power of man to attain. It is to be mentioned that the pre-examination of those who contended in these games was very strict, and that a temperate, chaste, moral, and heroic life, for a long period previously, was indispensable. (How many of our modern young men, under these tests, would have a chance of competing?)

The boxing games were dangerous and bloody, and often resulted in death. The combatants covered their fists with the cestus, which had an effect something like the "iron knuckles" of our modern sporting men, being a glove made of straps of leather, plated inside with metal. The boxers were the fiercest and roughest of the ancient athletes. They were always noticed to be more or less maimed, some with the loss of an eye, or of the teeth, or a broken nose, or frightful gashes in the face.

Leaping was performed as with us. Wrestling required great address and experience, and was a great physical art. In the arena, several matches would be going on at the same time. The wrestlers were naked, and had their bodies anointed with oil.

MOVEMENT STUDY OF TWO MEN BOXING.

TWO MEN BOXING.

There was a contest, called the Pancratium, with included all means of defence and offence [*sic*], at the option of the fighter, who was expected to do the best he could for himself, and the worst for his adversary. It was lawful to scratch, bite, gouge, kick—in short, just like a modern Arkansas rough-and-tumble of the severest kind, barring the bowie knife.

These games, in which all were interested and most of the young and middle-aged men partook, served to make a very hardy and handsome-bodied race. In such severe exercises, the Greeks not only prepared themselves for the hardships and contests of war, but for the enjoyment of life, and to acquire a happy and vigorous national temper. Nor were they, for all these rough exercises, a brutal or bloody-minded race; but, on the contrary, were friendly, tender-hearted, affectionate and benevolent.

TWO YOUNG MEN IN A PANKRATION FIGHT, DEPICTED ON A GRECIAN VASE (490–480 BC).

But the manly exercises we are describing did not comprehend the physique only. In the Olympic and other great games, there were intellectual contests also. The poets, orators and historians took part, contended for prizes, and recited their productions before the people.

There were also songs, dances, and musical instruments.

Here, too, on such occasions, the sculptors, painters and artists exhibited specimens of their skill—while the philosophers and teachers moved around, or drew groups together, to hear their arguments and disputes.

We will only add to our brief description that these great games always commenced at daybreak, and were mainly held during the forenoon—different from our modern plan of presenting amusements at night. They were also invariably held in the open air.

From them, we repeat, the Greeks become one of the healthiest, handsomest, hardiest, and happiest nations that ever lived.

MENTALITY, STUDY, &C., IN THEIR RELATIONS TO HEALTH.

We should like to say much on the various phases of this interesting topic. A high degree of mental development is generally supposed to be analagous [*sic*] to a delicate state of health. So strongly is this style of judgment fixed in the popular mind, that a person of robust physique can seldom or never obtain the credit of having a cultivated mind and a great brain. There is just this amount of truth in the popular ideas on this subject, that a man of refined mentality, and of good knowledge of physiology, will be far more liable to be injured by pernicious and unsanitary habits, than persons of low grade who have the same average strength of constitution and vigor with himself.

Any one may notice this, as it is illustrated in the low-life shanties, and in all places, both city and country, where the lowest order of the population reside. In utter defiance of all the laws of physiology, we see it arise, from the denizens of those places, some of the most splendid specimens of health and physical beauty in the world. Indeed, take the case through, it is doubtful whether the upper ranks of society, with all their superior advantages, produce as many specimens of well-built and fine-appearing men, clean-blooded and sound, as these very places where health is never thought of, and, in appearance, is constantly violated.

This fact, which is so startling at first, and seems to knock spots out of all our calculations and advice, will, when further investigated, be found to come under the simple and true theory of health, and confirm it just the same as the rest. The children of a poor family, especially in the country, and to a great extent in cities also, are never injured by those pampering luxuries and condiments that are frequently the bane of the offspring of the rich—who are often literally killed by kindness. The former, if weak and puny, are perhaps more apt to die off, leaving only the hardier shoots to buffet the storms and exposures of life. And these hardier shoots are often found to thrive

POOR FAMILY IN THE SLUMS OF NEW YORK.

all the better from such exposures and trials. Like plants left to grow where they first sprouted out of the ground, intended [sic] by the gardener, left to the nursing of the sunshine, the air, and the rains, they thrive and attain a wild and hardy beauty which the most carefully tended of their more artificial brethren seek in vain to rival. This, however, is the result of a happy combination of circumstances, all of which, as we have just said, conform to the general laws of health.

For he who is determined to reach, and experience for a continued time, the condition of perfect health, will do well to understand that caution is necessary, lest he overdo the matter. There is such a thing as taking *too minute and morbid care of the health,* and, therefore, losing it as effectually as by taking no care at all. This is a remark which will apply to those who are on the rack every hour lest something may not be exactly right with themselves or their children; and especially to those who over-protect themselves against cold, the air, and exposure.

Let it be known that a certain degree of *abandon* is necessary to the processes of perfect health and a muscular tone of the system. The fault of intellectual persons is, doubtless, not only that far too much of their general, natural fund of stimulation is diverted, year after year, from all the great organs in the trunk of the body, and concentrated in the brain, but that they think too much of health, and, perhaps, that they know too much of its laws. Of this last, it might be explained that if they only knew a little more, namely, to put their technical knowledge aside at times, and not be forever dwelling upon it, things would go on much better with them.

With all this, we have an idea, amounting to profound conviction, that the highest and palmiest state of health, ministering to a long life, and accompanied throughout by all that makes a man physically the superior animal of the earth, and crowned at last with a painless and easy death—we have an idea, we say, that all this is only attainable, (except in rare natural instances,) by a cultivated mentality, by the intellectual, by *the reasoning man.* What else, indeed, is the whole system of training for physique, but intellect applied to the bettering of the form, the blood, the strength, the life, of man?

In other and shorter terms, *true intellectual development, not overstrained and morbid, is highly favorable to long life, and a noble physique;* and what falls short of these latter aims, (if attributable to anything in the mentality of the subject,) is, that the mentality of that subject was in a vitiated condition, or, (as in these latter days is often the case,) that there was *not enough brute animal* in the man. We repeat it, strange as it may seem, this is generally the case in these extra-mental and extra-philanthropic days of ours.

That the half-way and unwholesomely developed mentality of modern times, as seen in large classes of people, literary persons, many in the professions, in sedentary employments, &c., acts injuriously upon the health, and militates against the noble form, the springy gait, the ruddy cheek and lip, and the muscular leg and arm of man, we know, full well. But, without wishing to be severe, what, critically considered, is the amount of modern mentality, except a feverish, superficial and shallow dealing with words and shams? How many of these swarms of "intellectual people," so-called, are anything but smatterers, needing yet to begin and educate themselves in nearly all real knowledge and wisdom?

TRAINING.

MAN EXERCISING.

There we print the magic word that can remedy all the troubles and accomplish all the wonders of human physique. Training! In its full sense, it involves *the entire science of manly excellence, education, beauty, and vigor*—nor is it without intimate bearings upon the moral and intellectual nature.

Human reason applied to develope [*sic*] the perfection of the body and the mind! What can there be more worthy? We are not insensible to the triumphs of the demonstrative sciences and philosophy—to the explanation of the subtleties of mind—to the accomplishment of such wonders as the Atlantic Telegraph, the great feat of the age; but for all that, we are clear in the opinion of the still greater importance of all these researches and statements directly affecting individual happiness and health—the development of *a superb race of men*, large-bodied, clean-blooded, and with all the attributes of the best material humanity. We believe this is one of the most commendable departments in which the philanthropist can exercise his time and abilities—and that literature, and the public essayist and lecturer, would do well to pay it more attention, and include it more frequently in their themes.

Development! Few understand, (you, reader, probably as little as any one,) what a fund of physical power is in them, which systematic training could bring forth, and increase to marvellous proportions.

Look at the brawny muscles attached to the arms of that young man, who, for nearly two years past, has devoted on an average two hours out of the twenty-four to rowing in a boat, swinging the dumbbells, or exercising with the Indian club. Look at the spread of his manly chest, on which also are flakes of muscle which rival those of the ox or horse.—(Start not, delicate reader! the comparison is one to be envied.)

Two years ago that same young man was puny, hollow-breasted, walking home at evening with a languid gait, and eating his meals with less than half an appetite. Training, and the simplest amount of perseverance, have altogether made a new being of him.

Training, however, it is always to be borne in mind, does not consist in mere exercise. Equally important with that are the diet, drink, habits, sleep, &c. Bathing, the breathing of good air, and certain other requisites, are also not to be overlooked. But of the details of these, we shall speak directly.

To Vocalists and public speakers, lawyers, lecturers, actors, &c., training is always to be recommended. We not only allude to habitual practising with the voice, but to great care in diet and drink. Of course, it is well understood among vocalists, that long and steady practice is the only ladder by which they can mount to success. But among the other classes we have mentioned, there is hardly ever any fit preparation for entering on their profession, as regards its physical requirements. We see, indeed, a majority of public speakers, with narrow chests, feeble lungs, diseased throats, and poor voices.

Gentle and gradual development of the vocal powers is within the reach of all; and so, by degrees, to the acquisition of a very remarkable scope of the voice. In oratory, in all ages, they who have attained the highest and most lasting fame have been those who, by slow and patient processes, have trained themselves, their voices, their movements, &c. This is *art*, which is as necessary for any great thing as the natural genius for it. Art cannot, of course, give original life, but it can shape and form it to great things, and to beautiful proportions.

Of all who have to speak, sing, or converse much, &c., the diet is important. The simplest and most natural diet is the best; and lest we be misunderstood, we specify that we do not mean a vegetarian or water-gruel diet, but one of strengthening materials, beef, lamb, &c., and that fruits, wines, and the like, are not to be excluded. But indulgence in a great variety of dishes at the same meal, and, in general terms, the absorption into the system of fat, or any indigestible substance, or the drinking of strong coffee or liquors, will be pretty sure to injure the voice.

Here, as in many things, we gain serviceable hints from the ancients, and their way in similar circumstances. Of the actors in the theatre of Bacchus, in Athens, where the tragedies of Sophocles and the other Greek poets were played, it is recorded that they observed a rigid diet, in order to give strength and clearness to their

Walt Whitman

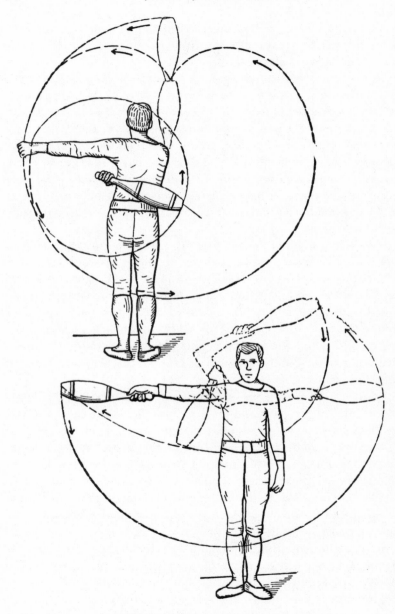

HOW TO USE INDIAN CLUBS.

CLUB-SWINGING.

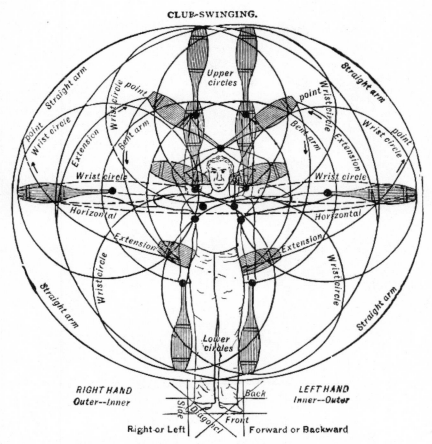

THE PRINCIPLES OF CLUB SWINGING. Fig. 1.

vocalization, and that they regularly frequented gymnasiums, in order to acquire muscular energy and pliancy of limbs.

We commend all this to our young American students for the bar, the pulpit, or any other avocation requiring oratorical power; and also to not a few of the actors and singers.

[TO BE CONTINUED]

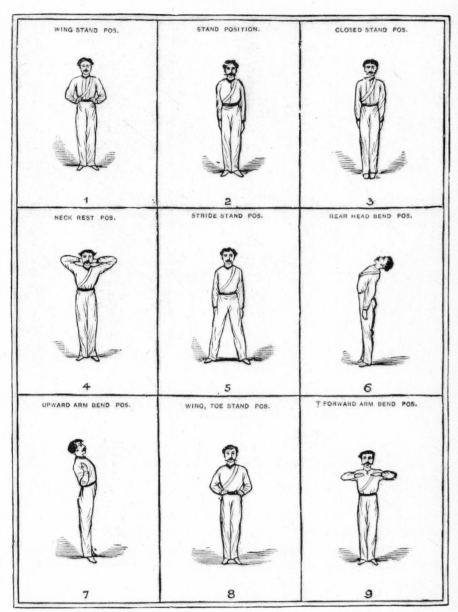

A MOVEMENT EXERCISE (SWEDISH DRILL).

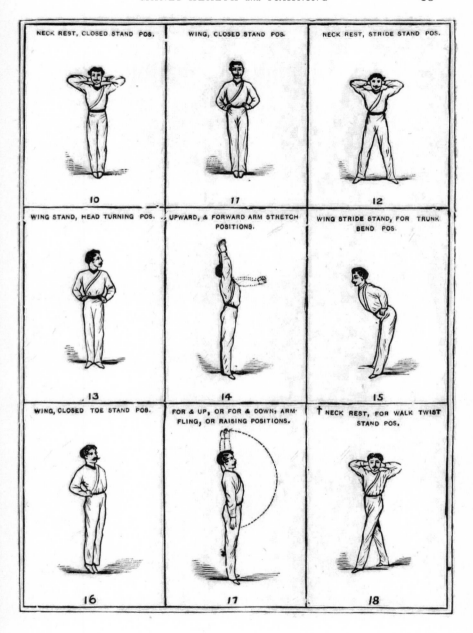

The New York Atlas.

Vol. 21, No. 19

Manly Health and Training,

September 26, 1858

With Off-Hand Hints Toward Their Conditions

By Mose Velsor

CHILDREN USING DUMB-BELLS.

[CONTINUED FROM LAST WEEK]

BRIEF SKETCH OF A DAY OF TRAINING,
FOR THE USE OF BEGINNERS.

A fine lesson may be learned from the observance and history of the operation of putting a man in perfect condition for any great feat of strength and agility, such as a prize fight, a foot race, running, or the like. The trainers will sometimes take such a man, every way in a bad state, physically, from injurious habits of eating and drinking, want of exercise, &c., his blood bad, his complexion spotted with pimples, his joints nerveless, his tone and vigor at a very low ebb, his digestion poor, his pulse flighty, his animal temperature subject to great inward changes of heat and cold—and will, after gradually inaugurating them, establish such changes in his habits as will turn that man out in a few weeks a completely renovated being, feeling well, looking well, with his muscular development carried to its ultimate degree of perfection, and all the bad humors drenched from his body.

Inquire how this wonderful change is wrought, and you will learn that it, by only a few and the most simple means, all of which lie in the reach of every man, and are not, after all, so very unpleasant in themselves, can be carried on consistently with the usual trade or employment of a mechanic, farmer, or any workingman.

In many cases, (though we do not think this quite so necessary as has been supposed—or rather, we believe the results can be attained just as well by other means,) it is usual to begin the operation of training a man by clearing out the system with medicine, an ordinary cathartic, (salts, or whatever else is

45

found to answer the purpose,) and an emetic. This puts the stomach and bowels in a fit state for the future work.

From the first, of course, the greatest care is observed in the food. At the time of taking the clearing out medicine, only a little light aliment is given; and when the medicinal effects are worked off, which will be in a day or two, the man in training, if he be of too full habit, too heavy, must be restricted to a moderate diet, including, for a while, only one substantial meal of meat a-day; the breakfast being limited to a small portion of meat, or perhaps a nearly raw egg, a slice of dry bread, and, if desired, a cup of tea, to be drank only when quite cool.

The man rises at day-break, or soon after—if in winter, rather before. In most cases the best thing he can commence the day with is a rapid wash of the whole body in cold water, using a sponge, or the hands rubbing the water over the body—and then coarse towels to rub dry with; after which, the hair gloves, the flesh-brush, or any thing handy, may be used, for friction, and to put the skin in a red glow all over. This, especially in cool weather, must all be done in a few minutes, or rather moments—not much longer than you have taken to read about it. Meanwhile, as soon as the glow is attained, the window, unless the weather is very bad, should be opened, and the door also, so that the room may become filled with good fresh air—for the play of the respiratory organs will be increased by the performances just mentioned, and it is at such times that good air tells best. Keep briskly moving all this while, however.

There is no objection, when this is through, to the man taking a crust of bread, or a piece of sea-biscuit. Then for a brisk walk, or some other exercise, of half an hour, or an hour, according to circumstances; at this, very heavy soled shoes, carrying weight, may be used—lighter at first and increased by degrees. Or if one is not inclined for a walk, the dumb-bells, or some gymnastic exercises. Whatever is done, however, ought to be in the open air; don't be afraid of that—drink it in—it won't hurt you—there is a curious virtue in it, to be found in nothing else.

This brings us to an early breakfast hour. Usually the breakfast, for a hearty man, might consist in a plate of fresh rare lean meat, without fat or gravy, a slice or chunk of bread, and, if desired, a cup of tea, which must be left till the last. If there be boiled potatoes, and one of them is desired, it may be permitted. Ham, gravy, fried potatoes, and a list too long and numerous to mention, of dishes often found on the breakfast table of boarding houses and restaurants, must be eschewed. Fortunately, there is hardly a table set but it affords *something* that will answer, at a pinch, for a meal.

The great art lies in what to avoid and what to deny one's self.

After breakfast, in the case of a man who has work to do, (for we are writing for the general public, as well as the sporting man,) he will go about his employment. One who has not, and who is devoting his attention, at the time, to the establishment of health and a manly physique, will do well to spend an hour of the forenoon (say from 10 to 11 o'clock,) in some good exercise for the arms, hands, breast, spine, shoulders, and waist; the dumb-bells, sparring, or a vigorous attack on the sand-bags, (a large bag, filled with sand, and suspended in such a position that it can be conveniently struck with the fists.) This should be done systematically, and gradually increased upon making the exertion harder and harder.

A pretty long walk may also be taken, commencing at an ordinary pace, and increasing the rapidity of the step till it takes the power of locomotion pretty well, and then keeping it up at that gait, as it can be well endured—not to the extent of fatigue, however, for it is a law of training that *a man must not exercise so hard at any time as to overdo and tire himself*; but always stop in time to avoid fatigue. We mean, of course, the sense of being fagged out, wearied, unable to do any more. We repeat the caution elsewhere given, to take everything very moderately and gently at first, and let all come on by slow degrees.

Rowing is also a good exercise during this time of day. Those engaged in this as their regular employment, (we may say, *en passant*,) ought to understand that they have one of the finest occupations in the world, for health, strength, and a fine development of form. By a tolerable attention to the laws of physiology, they could present a race of men, almost without exception for vigor, and for manly beauty.

TWO MEN ROWING.

From three quarters to half an hour before dinner, all violent exercise must cease. If the body is sweaty, as it very likely will be, it is best to strip, rub down briskly with dry cloths, and change the underclothes.

Dinner should consist of a good plate of fresh meat, (rare lean beef, broiled or roast, is best) with as few outside condiments as possible. (If thirsty during the forenoon, drink, but never before eating.) Eat according to your appetite, of one dish—always, if possible, making four or five dinners out of the week, of rare lean beef, with nothing else than a small slice of stale bread. Or, if preferred, lean mutton, cooked rare, may be eaten instead of beef, at times, for variety. No scraggly, grisly fat, or hard cooked pieces, should be eaten. Nor need the appetite be stinted—eat enough, and when you eat that, stop!

No man should be required to do any toilsome work or exercise immediately after dinner; if there be anything you know you will have to take hold of immediately, then make the dinner lighter, for it is more hurtful than is supposed, to exert one's physical powers greatly, on a hearty meal.

(We cannot resist the impulse to condemn here, what we consider the frightfully injurious dinners and dinner habits of most people who, as they would call it, "live well." Look over the bill of fare of any hotel or restaurant, or even the dinner-table of an

A LEG OF MUTTON.

ordinary boarding-house—see the incongruous dishes that, on the bills, stand in long lists, and that men devour, often three or four different kinds—soups, pastry, fat, fish, flesh, gravy, pickles, pie, pudding, coffee, water, ale, brandy—and heaven knows what else! Not one out of fifty eats a really wholesome, manly substantial dinner. All, more or less, distend the stomach, and bloat themselves with quantities of trash, to worry the digestion, thin the blood, and return, sooner or later, in lassitude, headache, constipation, or a fever, or some other attack of illness.)

The afternoon, unless it be spent in the regular work—and in most cases, unless it be a prize fight or the like, we believe that the operation of training a man for his condition may go on just as well, if he continue about his daily work. The afternoon may be spent with the same objects in view as the morning. If, during the latter, the exercises have tended to develope the chest and arms, the afternoon may be devoted more to the locomotive organs. A long walk may be taken—or a good game at leaping, or any of the games that tax the legs—straddling, standing on one leg and dipping to the ground, so as to touch the other knee, &c.

We have thus indicated the mode of filling up the hours of the day; but still more is necessary. After a moderate supper, of some digestible dish, fruit, or cold meat, or stale bread, toast, or biscuit, with perhaps a cup of tea—the evenings ought to be devoted, to some extent at least, to friendly and social recreation, (not dissipation, remember.) Friends may be visited, or some amusement, or a stroll in company—or any other means that will soothe and gratify the mind and the affections, friendship, &c.—for every man should pride himself on *having* such affections, and satisfying them, too.

Ten o'clock at night ought to find a man in bed—for that will not afford him the time requisite for rest, if he rise betimes in the morning. The bedroom must not be small and close—*that* would go far toward spoiling all other observances and cares for health. It is important that the system should be clarified, through the inspiration and respiration, with a plentiful supply of good air, during the six, seven, or eight hours that are spent in sleep. During most of the year, the window must be kept partly open for this purpose.

WHO CAN FOLLOW THESE RULES?

Such is the exclamation we fancy we hear from the reader, upon perusing what appear to him, no doubt, at first, very hard requirements. What man, among the masses who, in their various occupations, toil for their living, in city or country, can possibly conform to the strict letter of these laws of health? Have not most people enough to do to get *something* to eat, without being so very particular *what* it shall be, and how it is cooked?

We are well aware that, to those unaccustomed to consider the laws of health and a sound physique, there will appear at first something quite alarming and impracticable in these requirements. But they are really more so in appearance, and from their novelty, than anything else. So long as a man has to have something purchased for his sustenance, why may he not as well have that which is best, as that which is no good? On the score of economy, we have everything on our side—and, under what we promulge, the expenses of living would be reduced at least one third.

We know, at the same time, that men in various employments have not that chance of following out their judgment and choice in these things that would allow of their rigidly fulfilling the laws, at every point. Yet even these can come a great deal nearer the fulfillment than they now suppose. It needs mainly the knowledge and determination in a man's self—then all becomes comparatively easy, and obstacles melt away, one after another.

Besides, we are willing to admit that our exact statements with regard to diet—what must be avoided, and the few simple articles of food that, coincident with exercise, strength, digestion, &c., may be used—are to be often modified to suit cases, tastes, &c., each one for itself. We have made the statement of *a model case*; if the reader approaches the neighborhood of it, he will be doing well.

MORAL RESULTS OF TRAINING.

The results of properly chosen and well-continued courses of training are so valuable and so numerous that in mentioning them we would seem to be mentioning most of the precious treasures of character—among the rest may be specified courage, quickness of all the perceptions, full use of power, independence, fortitude, good nature, a hopeful and sunny temper, an industrious disposition, temperance in all the alimentative appetites, chastity, an aversion to artificial indulgences, easy manners without affectation, personal magnetism, and a certain silent eloquence of expression, and a general tendency to the wholesome virtues and to that moral uprightness which arises out of and is the counterpart to the physical.

For we cannot too often and too strongly promulgate the fact of the inevitable and curious conjunction, or rather resultance, of a fine manly *moral character*, out of a perfect physique. If there be those of our sporting fraternities who fail in realizing this point, it is so much loss to them and to their completeness of development, even on their own terms and for their own purposes. Why should it be so? There is truly no reason for it. The true theory and the indications are all the other way.

We are of those who believe, therefore, that a certain natural moral goodness is developed in proportion with a sound physical development—and also that a true system of training, that which aims to do justice to *the complete man* and his highest powers, (and what other system deserves the name?) will, on no account, ignore the seeds and fruits of a noble moral character.

This much we feel impelled to say, because confident are we not only that those called under the general name of the sporting fraternity, and, indeed, all who take an interest, or have a part in, physical training and manly games and exercises, would be vastly improved in their own special branches, by realizing this moral part of the theory of training, which, indeed, is its crowning glory and natural result—but we are equally sure that there exists, through all the grades and classes we have just alluded to, the very stuff and material of the kind of superior qualities we demand. They may be, doubtless are, in the crude and rough state—but they are there.

Reader, if you be one of that exclusive kind who suppose that manly actions and an honorable character belong only to one or two departments of society, and those the ones that *profess* the

greatest virtue, let us undeceive you—let us hint to you that perhaps there is equal, possibly at times even greater manliness and
heroism, in what are called less pious degrees of the social strata—
even that very sporting fraternity we spoke of.

WE DO NOT INCULCATE A MERE PASTIME.

Of exercises, games, gymnastics, &c., the reader must understand well that we inculcate the regular and appropriate practising
of them not as a frivolous pastime, or a matter of ceremony and
politeness, to be done in a genteel club way, but as *a real live thing,
a part of a robust and perfect man*. And all the rest of the habits
are to be consistent. There is no sham or make-believe about this
business of entering on the development, purification, strengthening and gracefulness of the body; but it is something to be carried
out with an earnest, conscientious, persevering soul.

We say *conscientiously*, and we mean all that is involved in the
word. The man must himself feel the importance of the objects to
be attained, and an enthusiastic, yet in a certain sense calm determination to strive for them, not for a little while merely, but for a
long while, at work or play, in company or alone, in one place or
another, and night and day. *Habit* will soon make all easy; and let us
inform you, reader, there is no small pleasure in the victory one attains, by a little sternness of will, over all deleterious gratifications
of appetite. It is as great as a general gaining an important battle.

BACKSLIDING FROM HEALTHY HABITS.

Let us be plain with you, reader. Under the impulse of studying
our articles, and awakened very strongly to the idea of health and a
strong condition, you will very likely commence carrying into practice the advice we have jotted down for your benefit. After a shorter
or longer time, it is quite certain to us there will be a relapse, however, into the old and more careless ways. A great revolution, a new
system of physical habits, cannot be inaugurated quite so easily as

you thought. Consequently, with the best intentions in the world, there is still lamentable backsliding.

But the work must not be given up for the first failure—nor even for the second, third, nor any number. It will gradually grow easier and easier, and habit will then make it followed, without thinking anything about it.

It is a great pity that about half the time spent by preachers and teachers in attention to moral and intellectual training, were not dispensed with, and bestowed on the encouragement of young men in training and perfecting their bodies. As things are, the subject is seldom mentioned in a way to arouse the lethargic, urge on the flagging, and reward those who have set a noble example.

It must be realized, throughout, that perpetual care is indispensable to health. It is just as reasonable to suppose you can squander your fortune at random, and still find it remaining at the end of many years, as that you can squander your health and have that remain. Look at those young mechanics, in Boston, New York, or Philadelphia!

Look at the many fine specimens of drivers, teamsters, firemen, lumbermen, haymen, pilots, &c.! What examples of strength,

GROUP OF HAYMEN.

THE AMERICAN FIREMAN.

beauty, and activity! What fine color in the complexion—grace in the movement—heartiness in the whole structure and appearance! Is it not lamentable that, for the want of a little knowledge and care, all these noble blessings will, probably, by degrees, be lost to them, far too prematurely? For, let us inform you, reader, if you be young, that the years of your middle age ought to be those not only of your best performances, but of your best appearance—and, if you so will it, may be. Then all has become ripe and mature; and surely the fully ripened fruit or flower is no less beautiful and welcome than any stage which precedes it.

Such are the reflections which must often arise from an observant person, at seeing the way in which American young men scatter the rich treasures of their health, to grow old before their time, and to lose, perhaps, the best and mellowest portion of life, a happy middle, and a contented old age.

TRAINING ALL THROUGH LIFE.

This carries us to another statement. He who has the idea of proficiency in any art, as music for example, will understand of what importance it is to *keep in perpetual practice*. Well, it is of just as much, or rather, it is of infinitely more importance, that he who would be a proficient in manly health and strength, should also keep in perpetual practice.

As things are, it is only on some extra occasion, as a race, a physical contest in the prize ring, &c., that men submit themselves to training. But we would have it a regular and systematic thing through life. Not only in young manhood, but in middle age, and in advanced age, also, modified to suit its appropriate requirements, should the course of training be persevered in, without intermission. We place the greatest reliance upon the forming of the habit, and therefore repeat it many times in these articles.

Neither season, place, nor circumstance should prevent the regular course of training, or as near to it as matters will allow. It is *the resolution*, the disposition, that is of the main consequence; with that, all obstacles will be overcome. The true benefits of training, indeed, lie in their permanent continuance; it is an affair for *the whole life*.

We would have exercises for all ages, without excepting any— requiring only that they should be fitted properly to each stage, modified to each individual case. There is no time of life to which the training processes do not apply, and would not improve those who use them, both for the time being and subsequently. As to the objection to any gymnastic exercises, that they are only fitted for young and robust men, and not for the feeble or old, we reply that the true and comprehensive system of gymnastics must include exercises appropriate to those very cases of weak, or very young, or more advanced persons, or else it is no complete system, and needs to be improved upon.

Yes, *training for all ages of life*, each adjusted to peculiarities, wants, and circumstances—always tenderly considering the average ability of the person, young or old, to bear fatigue, and never overtaxing or straining his powers, but letting them gradually and gently develope themselves.

One of the faults to be guarded against, in gymnastic, and indeed all the exercises of training, is the wish to get along too fast. The body is too complicated and exquisite a piece of work to be suddenly brought to bear upon, for any lasting good effects of this sort. It ought to be considered enough if the general course of exercise, health and development be started in the right direction, and kept in it, and then let the results be patiently waited for.

OVERTASKING.

We must dwell a moment specially here. Let it not be supposed that this question of exercise presents but one side, and that evil to the general health comes from not enough activity. Much is to be said also of the injury of *casually overtasking the frame*, as is done by many persons, and often at the very times of life when the injury is most fatal to the future soundness and perfection of the body— we mean youth and early manhood. This we think markedly the case in the country, among the farmers. The boys are put to hard work there too soon, and kept at it too tight. That is the reason we see (for such is the truth) fewer manly and agile forms among the young men of the country than those of the city.

Excessive toil, whether of the body or the mind, is just as hurtful to health and longevity, be it understood, as the stagnant condition of the organs which it has been the drift of our preceding remarks to guard against. We would also caution the young men against any very violent draughts upon the strength, such as an exhausting struggle or run, when the body is not prepared for it by previous training. It may have to be paid for very dearly.

Carpenters, masons, farmers, laborers, men at work on the shipping, and all at active out-door occupations, of course have a fair share of exercise already. This is so much gained. With them, however, it by no means follows but that a steady and judicious course of athletic training, from time to time, (whenever not prevented by the occasionally severe toil which makes *rest* the thing wanted,) would greatly improve their physical capacities also.

"THE LAST LOAD."

Those parts of the body should be especially attended to which are least called into use by the trade or occupation; for instance, drivers should develope the use and strength of the legs, by walking, leaping, pushing weights with the feet, &c.

Clerks, bookkeepers, literary persons, &c., need a regular, but *never too violent*, exercise of the whole of the frame, chest, arms, spine, legs and feet. They need early rising, simple food, and, almost always, would be bettered by acquiring more of an animal physique—unfashionable though it be.

Merchants, lawyers, professional people, politicians, &c., (and perhaps the American people generally,) need a little more contentment of mind—*the disposition to enjoy life and not fret, but to be happy with moderation or even a little.*

STANDARD OF HEALTH.

Take notice, as we talk, that our standard of health is not a small one, but a high one. Many of those who dash about, city and country, with an artificial glow, kept up by the excitement of company or business, and ready to collapse the moment those impulses are withdrawn, such are by no means our models of health. We speak of the real article, able to stand a great deal of buffeting and deprivation—health deeply founded, ingrained with the life, calculated to last many years, and (being encouraged by regular habits,) more to be noticed by its quiet, steady, and continued movement, than by any abrupt and striking manifestations.

It is no small thing to be perfectly well. The case is one, in our civilized and artificial forms of life, alas, how rare! It is useless to blink the unpleasant conviction that in America, all through the large cities, and even in the country, where it might be less expected, the amount of ill health, or just passable health, is enormous! Consumption, dyspepsia, rheumatism, chills and fever, and bilious attacks of one sort or another are met with in all directions. Through the streets of New York, looking at the faces of a large majority of the men you pass—even the youths. They are *not* the faces of perfect health—and yet nearly all *could be*.

PRESENT CONDITION OF THE HEALTH
OF THE MASSES.

For it is not to be denied that physical inferiority, in one form or another, is the rule rather than the exception. Seriously examined, what a condition does the health of the masses every where present. Probably one-fourth of the whole population of the world dies of consumption, or of diseases that have sprouted up from it. Thousands upon thousands suffer from some form of scrofula, and are afflicted with sores and ulcers, interior or exterior. Half the people you meet have, at times, pimples and pustules on the face and neck, indicating that health is anything but clear with them. Indeed, there are few, in any rank of life, but labor under some disorder of the blood.

Of late years, in the United States, the general illness, perhaps transcending all the rest, is dyspepsia. This is the fruitful mother of dozens of other complaints—for the regular and complete assimilation, digestion, and excretion, are the primal requisites of health. The fast living of Americans, and the general use of hot bread, grease, and strong coffee, are supposed to be the causes of this great New World complaint. But there are habits prevailing and articles of diet commonly eaten and imbibed as drink, in Germany, Holland, England, &c., far more indigestible than those just named, and yet the Dutch and English are not dyspeptic. What are the causes here?

Rheumatism is another prevalent complaint. Rare indeed, is the case of man or woman who has never felt a twinge of this distressing malady. Bilious attacks are very common in the west, and indeed in all parts of the land.

A too feverish life, mentally and physically, with too little physical calmness, and also a feeble paternity and maternity, are some of the main underlying causes of this frightful state of things. We are not disposed to grumble or overstate the evil condition of the public physique; we wish to call attention to the fact how easily most of these deficiencies might be remedied. Our theory is that America has mentality enough, but needs a far nobler physique.

THE GREAT AMERICAN EVIL—INDIGESTION.

There can be no good health, or manly and muscular vigor to the system, without thorough and regular digestion. It is doubtless here that four-fifths of the weaknesses, breakings-down, and premature deaths, of American begin. On all sides we see the proofs of this last assertion—on all sides we see results of the same. If the harm that accrues to the physical perfection of the race, here in the United States, from this one cause, were obviated for the space of time long enough to allow a single generation to grow up and advance toward maturity, we should probably see the most splendid and majestic nation of men, in their physique, that ever trod the earth!

So great a part as that, does the little matter of the right digestion of the food we eat, bear upon the most momentous of subjects—for what can be more momentous than the growth of a perfect race of

INDIGESTION.

men? All other rules and requisites may be attended to, but if the stomach be out of order, and allowed to remain so for any length of time, all will be of no avail. We are fain to alter one of the stereotyped sayings of the politicians, and say, Eternal vigilance is the price of—digestion!

In what is written so copiously on the subject of indigestion, it is customary to mention long lists of articles to be prohibited, and others to be allowed. This is perhaps well enough—except that the reader will be led very far astray if he take it for granted that the whole story is told with that. It must also be understood that indigestion, and all its brood of evils, will take birth and grow to full proportions, from other causes, just as well as from the use of articles on the list of prohibited food. Indeed, if other things make up for it sufficiently, almost any article of food may be eaten with impunity. And if certain of these prime requisites of a good condition be wanting, why all the care in selecting aliment of easy digestion will be of no avail. How healthy, for instance, are the sailors, on their diet of salt beef, sea-biscuit, and strong coffee.

We do not intend here, great as the importance of this section of our subject is, to dwell minutely or at large upon it—partly because we think that each individual requires the application of special rules to his own particular case—partly because the subject of digestion is, in effect, treated and affected by the whole tenor of our paragraphs, under almost every one of the different headings of our subject—and partly because the main thing is to impress upon him who really wishes to acquire perfect health, that *equal and thorough digestion is indispensable*; and when that impression is produced, then the most a hasty writer on the subject can do, is done. Too many rules are apt to confuse—and besides they are liable to continual exceptions.

We say to you, reader, do justice to the peculiarities of your own case, with regard to your particular wants, strength, age, trade, previous and present circumstances, &c.; always having in view the main object, regular digestion. Do not depend on medicines to place your stomach in order; that is but casting out devils through Belzebub, the prince of devils.

TWO NAVY SAILORS.

As a general thing, at a meal, if nothing very bad indeed is eaten, and if the selection of food be confined to dishes that relate to each other, and if the stomach be not deluged with liquid, it may do to follow, in reason, the demands of the taste and appetite. A few plain dishes, however, should always have the preference.

But it is perhaps apart from the body of our meals that indigestion takes its rise. We have been laying too much stress where it does not belong—like the man who denied himself a mild little glass of wine, and then ate a large dish of lobster salad, plastered over with oil and spices! If one were to be satisfied with eating his natural meals, following a natural appetite, and then stop, most of the trouble that exists would probably be avoided.

It is the afterclaps that do the mischief. Modern taste and ingenuity have contrived not a hundred, but hundreds of solid and liquid stimulants, artificial tastes, condiments—and these, in some of their various forms are partaken by all. By him who is determined to place his vigor and health above par, from *his* mouth and stomach, these must be rigidly excluded. *Simple and hearty food, and no condiments*, must be his motto. This too is the continual lesson of nature. By reason of it, we see that fine state of health which characterizes hunters, lumbermen, raftsmen, and sailors on shipboard. For in those situations the living is invariably coarse and solid, without delicacies. Of course, too, the open air and the habits of muscular exercise, must receive their due allowance. But are not exercise and the open air within the reach of us all?

In America, a great deal of the indigestion that prevails, is the result (we cannot too often recur to this,) of a cause we have elsewhere alluded to, *excessive mental action.* Those who think much, or whose business cares return upon the mind, and are brooded over and over, are often, perhaps generally, the very men whose habit it is to eat copiously of rich viands, perhaps at the hotel table, and to deluge the stomach with liquids. How can any one bear up under such inflictions, when the same person is probably the one who, week after week, and year after year, takes no systematic exercise, and does not know even what the training for health means?

Next week we shall go over the important question of when ought a man to be in his primest condition, and how long? There will, we think, be some points in this matter, that will be new to most of our readers.

[TO BE CONTINUED]

The New York Atlas.

Vol. 21, No. 2

Manly Health and Training,

October 3, 1858

With Off-Hand Hints Toward Their Conditions

By Mose Velsor

MEN WRESTLING.

(CONTINUED FROM LAST WEEK.)

WHEN OUGHT A MAN BE
IN HIS PRIMEST CONDITION,
AND HOW LONG?

Probably we shall surprise most of our readers by the answer to this question. According to the lives most of us lead, it is doubtful whether we are ever in that perfect state of health and strength that the human frame is capable of attaining, even without any special advantages—for, with most of us, all of the leading objects and aims we so eagerly pursue, bending time, energy, circumstances, every thing, to their acquisition, this matter of health, strange as it may seem, is the one which surely receives the least consistent attention.

From about the twenty-fourth to near the fiftieth or fifty-fifth year, the body, in a fair specimen of health and condition, remains nearly stationary. The liability to disease is less, and all the powers are in their best working order. This is the period when a man makes his mark, if at all. Activity is now at its fullest; indeed, the repression or non-action of it, in many cases, is the greatest misfortune that can happen to this stage of life. All the labor and employments of the earth are served with these years—without them there would be little or nothing to show for man, for governments, for industry, for science, for civilization, literature or art.

It is during some portion of this stretch of time, varied in different persons, that all the celebrated men of the world have achieved the works which have given them renown. Some have started early, and finished, it may be said, prematurely; this is the case with many of the poets, especially those of passionate imagery and tone, such as the English celebrities, Shelley, Byron,

67

68

Keats, &c. Of first-class works, however, it is doubtful whether any
have ever yet been achieved by young men. Shakespeare wrote his
best productions during the period from his thirty-seventh to his
forty-fifth year.

When we ask how long a man ought to be in prime condition, we,
of course, mean how long, allowing a favorable state of care, habits, food, &c. With these, we deliberately say that if he have a fair
natural constitution and has not ingrained his system in early life
with the germs of any incurable malady, (this last is important—
take notice young men!)—he ought to be in a h[i]gh range of health
and strength from the age of twenty-three or four years to the age
of sixty-five—a space of over forty years. We know this is not in
accordance with popular convictions on the subject; but, with great
respect and good nature, we are fain to call this popular opinion by
its true name, popular ignorance.

Take notice! however; if, *life, and its reserved fund of vitality,
are dissipated during the years from fifteen to twenty-three or
four*—if extravagant and continued drains are made on the bodily
stamina, during that period, we cannot promise any such result as
that stated in the foregoing paragraph. The years from fourteen or
fifteen to the age of twenty-four are the very ones, out of the whole
stretch of life, when there is the most danger of breaking down the
perfect tone of the body, not so much for the present, as for the
future. What is done or left undone, at that period, returns again,
after many years.

A word also to young men whose health has been injured in dissipation. Even then the case is hardly bad enough, except in rare
instances, to discourage any one who may read these lines from
adopting a serious and (if he have strength of mind sufficient) un-
shakable resolution to acquire vigor and good condition—albeit
the years between the fifteenth and twenty-fourth do present, in
their reminiscences, some of the injurious facts we have alluded to.
The human frame is full, in every case, of latent power. Though
wounded, buffeted, violated, time and again, it seems joyously to
respond to the first return of reason and natural habitudes. Indeed,

of all the amazing things about the human body, one of the most amusing is, how much it can stand, and still live on!

We dwell upon this point a little, because, of our city readers there are but few young men who, with all the recklessness of their age, have not dipped to a greater or lesser depth into the so called pleasures of city life; few, indeed, but on whom regular habits, drink, artificial diet, late hours, and other characteristic marks, now-a-days, of having spent life in one of our great cities—and of indulgences there, still more lamentable in their effects upon the future health, stamina, and long life—have not left unmistakable remains. Fortunately, however, these young men we are speaking of are the very ones who, in general, have the greatest fund of natural vigor, and are able to throw off deleterious causes.

Such reliance do we make upon the last-mentioned item, that we feel disposed to include most of that large class of young men in our cities, who have "lived too fast," in our list of peaceful and encouraging probabilities. For them too are health and a sound tone, (at least in a great degree,) if they persevere in the right means. Let it be clearly understood, however, that indulgences of perverted appetite, and violations of the laws of health, *cannot go too long*, with impunity. There *will* come a time when the turning point is reached. Our object is so to encourage the reader to realise [*sic*] what superior pleasure a good and natural state of health is, over all other gratifications, that he will bring up on the right side of that point.

Yes, nature is more tolerant and bountiful than we supposed. Long injured and insulted, she yet keeps blessings in her hands, ready to be bestowed with freedom and certainty, on the first practical signs of repentance.

To return—let it be borne in mind, especially by parents, for their offsprings' sake—let it be equally borne in mind by the youth, developing himself into early manhood—that the true plan of life involves a fine and robust condition of manhood, with every faculty of body and mind in full play and high health, from the twenty-third or fourth year, on to beyond the sixtieth.

THE SURE REWARD.

Is not all this something worth a young man's while to strive for, and lay out his plans for? We do not object to his careful and persistent regard for wealth, or for the objects of his business ambition, whatever they may be—but we say that *nothing* ought to displace the great pursuit we speak of—manly health and vigor. Even considered with reference to a far better capability of getting wealth, or of reaching the objects of ambition, health and strength are vitally important. With them, of course, not only so much more can be done, but the strain can be borne so much longer. From a money-making point of view, therefore, health is an investment that pays better than any other.

But we do not recommend the planing [*sic*] out of life by a young man, to realize this long-continued stretch of forty years of full health and strength, in order that he may make money. We recommend it for itself—*its own interest, reward, and its manliness.* For, say what we may of the pleasures of the world, and of what is heroic, it comes down to this—that there can be no first-rate heroism except in a sound body, and that there really can be no gratification or pleasure, however costly, however much vaunted or rare, or sought for, that is equal to the delicious feeling, all through middle age, and even old age, of being perfectly well.

To spring up in the morning with light feelings, and the disposition to raise the voice in some cheerful song—to feel a pleasure in going forth into the open air, and in breathing it—to sit down to your food with a keen relish for it—to pass forth, in business or occupation, among men, without distrusting them, but with a friendly feeling toward all, and finding the same feeling returned to you—to be buoyant in all your limbs and movements by the curious result of perfect digestion, (a feeling as if you could almost fly, you are so light,)—to have perfect command of your arms, legs, &c., able to strike out, if occasion demand, or to walk long distances, or to endure great labor without exhaustion—to have year after year pass on and on, and still the same calm and equable state of all the organs, and of the temper and mentality—no wrenching pains of the nerves or joints—no pangs, returning again and again, through the sensitive head, or any of its parts—no blotched and disfigured complexion—no prematurely lame and halting gait—no tremulous shaking of the hand, unable to carry a glass of water to the mouth without spilling it—no film and bleared-red about the eyes, nor bad taste in the mouth, nor tainted breath from the stomach or gums— none of that dreary, sickening, unmanly lassitude, that, to so many men, fills up and curses what ought to be the best years of their lives, without good works to show for the same—but instead of such a living death, which, (to make a terrible but true confession,) so many lead, uncomfortably realizing, through their middle age, more than the distresses and bleak impressions of death, stretched out year after year, the result of early ignorance, imprudence, and want of wholesome training—instead of that, to find life one long holiday, labor a pleasure, the body a heaven, the earth a paradise, all the commonest habits ministering to delight—and to have this continued year after year, and old age even, when it arrives, bring- ing no change to the capacity for a high state of manly enjoyment— *these* are what we would put before you, reader, as a true picture, illustrating the whole drift of our remarks, the sum of all, the best answer to the heading of the two last sections of our articles, and the main object which every youth should have, in the beginning, from the time he starts out to reason and judge for himself.

MODERN SOCIETY.—EMPLOYMENTS.

One great evil of most of the superficial advice on health and its conditions is that the writers do not consider, or have no patience with, the arbitrary lines and peculiarities of modern society, espe- cially as it operates in the cities. Granted that many of these pecu- liarities are bad, it only remains to do the best that is possible under them. And if the thing is approached in this spirit, it will generally be found that most of the essential results can be attained without the violent standing out from, or opposition to the rest, which is impossible without much offence [*sic*], and the giving up of much that conduces to prosperity, sociability and happiness.

Of the employments followed in the State of New York by the one million of grown, or nearly grown, males, 314,000 are of farming, gardening, or other agricultural pursuits; about 200,000 are laborers on various artificial works, in cities or elsewhere, (these are mostly of foreign birth); over 23,000 are sailors; 14,000 are lawyers, doctors, or ministers; 5,000 are office-holders; and 313,000 are mechanics, or engaged as operatives in some kind of manufactures—the remainder being scattered through an immense number of small, or comparatively small, occupations. In general terms it may be stated that even in the United States, new and farming-country as it is, the number of those engaged in artificial pursuits is about equal to those engaged in agriculture.

How does all this affect the general health? The question is a profound one, and the conclusions in reference to it must not be jumped at too hastily. Close investigation, and the allowance of strict candor in statements, will perhaps prove that there is a good deal of popular error as to the necessary bad effects of manufacturing and other in-door employments upon individual health. We mean simply this, that a person, with anything like a decent or average physical constitution, can follow almost any of the usual avocations to be found in our cities, and still have a fine condition of health. If the latter is wanting, it is not so much the fault of the employment as of the person himself.

Because civilization, with all its banes, and the ill health of masses, as before alluded to, has still more antidotes, if the choice were to be made between a life passed in the solitary freedom of barbarous and unartificial nature, and the highly complicated, and, in many respects, morbid life of one of our modern cities, we think the preference might deliberately and safely be given to the latter, as more likely to confer not only a greater longevity, but a greater amount of average animal happiness; and singular as it may at first appear, the chances of the latter are in favor of a higher and more robust degree of health than the former. The former, with its freedom from the artificial evils, is bereft also of the means of favoring life, and improving it, which belong to the latter.

Modern society is distinguished for much that is artificial, no doubt. It is distinguished for labor-saving machinery, the mechanical arts, and for the number of human beings engaged in regular in-door employments. Of the grown men of the United States, about two millions earn their living and spend the best part of their lives in working at some trade, or in some factory, or in commerce, mining, &c. While some of these are partially conducive to health, from being more or less hardening, a vast majority are characterized by features that, under the ignorance of physiology which prevails, must be stamped as deleterious. It remains, we say, to still do the best we can under these circumstances. Nor is the case bad, as might be judged from merely pursuing the question thus far.

Nor in the various manufactures and trades is there anything which may not, in almost all cases, be partially or wholly obviated, and the health retained under them, year after year, by proper prudence and forethought. A man, for instance, engaged in work that gave him too little exercise in the open air, should accustom himself, when not at work, to make up for that by out-door activity in some form or other—walking, or in some manly game. And this should not be occasional, but steady. Men whose occupation is partially active, but requires them to breathe close air, (as in many factories,) might retrieve the matter greatly by having well-ventilated bed rooms. This is an important matter, to which we have elsewhere devoted a special paragraph. The reader must make for himself the application of these hints in his own case.

EARLY YOUTH STAMPS THE FUTURE PHYSIQUE.

During childhood and youth much of the after-life receives its stamp and impression, for good or evil—especially the condition and power of growth of all the important functions and organs of the body. For American children it would be a great improvement if the food were more simple and digestible, instead of the hearty and seasoned dishes that are generally partaken alike by small and large. Another thing with regard to boys in the United States is, that they far too soon commence all the indulgences of men, especially tobacco, drink, &c. While the system is being formed, and before

ONE OF THE NEWS-BHOYS.

NEWSPAPER BOY IN NEW YORK.

the body has attained its growth and solidity, these ought to be forbidden indulgences.

From the age of fourteen to twenty-one or -two is a most important period, in the consideration of the health and vigor of a man with reference to the whole subsequent period of his life. Few

BOYS PLAYING AT SCHOOL.

youths consider the momentous results of all that is done, or left undone, during this part of their career. Parents, guardians, relatives, friends, are equally negligent. Otherwise, we should certainly see a far greater amount of influence directed toward this important class of persons, and their wellbeing.

We call upon those youths who read this to ponder, with all the strength and comprehension of their minds, upon what we are here trying to impress upon them—for they surely include some of the most important considerations that can be put before any human being, and come home directly to the experience of each one.

Let every youth understand that it is mainly in his power, by what he does or leaves undone, during the years we have mentioned to become a *sound, healthy and handsome man,* and remain so for many years, in full possession of his faculties and strength; or, failing in what leads to that result, to lay the sure substrata of an early decay of vigor, a loss of all buoyancy of spirit, a broken and useless middle age, and if not a premature death, an old age more miserable than death.

MANLY BEAUTY—THE TRUE AMBITION.

We would here place before our readers, especially the youth, the thought that nothing is more worthy [of] their ambition, and will surely repay the effort and resolution to follow them, than a steady pursuit of the regulations, laws, self-denials, and daily habitudes that lead to the sound condition and beautiful appearance of the body, the manly form—this wondrous and beautiful structure that never wearies the mind in contemplating its inward and outward mysteries, and in which, after all is said on other subjects, concentrates the whole interest of life, happiness, affection, dignity, and glory—around which, indeed, all history, all persons, and indeed all literature revolve, and find their sum and aggregate.

Reader! What is your ambition? We cannot, of course, tell; but one ambition, at any rate, you ought to have, and probably, while reading what we write, if never before, it will arise before you, more or less distinctly—and that is the desire and determination

WALT WHITMAN AS
A NEW YORK DANDY (1848–1854).

to put your body in a healthy and sweet-blooded condition—to be a *man*, hearty, active, muscular, handsome—yes, *handsome*—for it is not for nothing that all through the human race there is the universal desire that the body should not only be well, but look well. We would not give much for that man, young, middle-aged, or old, who was not touched by the feeling of pride or regret in his good or ill appearance. To one who has no such feeling, the electricity has gone out of that man; there is little hope for him.

Nor is there anything to be ashamed of in the ambition of a man to have a handsome physique, a fine body, clear complexion, nimble movements, and be full of manly vigor. Ashamed of! Why, we think it ought to be one of the first lessons taught to the boy, when he begins to be taught at all. It is of quite as much importance as

CARICATURE OF OBESE RESTAURANT OWNER
IN NEW YORK.

MEN WRESTLING.

any grammar, geography, or arithmetic—indeed, we should say it was of unrivalled importance. Only let it be the ambition that realizes a masculine and robust style of beauty, not the beauty of parlor elegance, of too much refinement, or of the mere fop.

There is a little popular delusion on this subject which we would like to do our part toward dispelling. It is generally considered, or rather pretended to be considered, that personal beauty is something not proper for the attention of men, but must be left for the other sex. At the same time the instinct to take a pride in manly looks, as it can never be eradicated, is always more or less operative; and it is this that, taking nature for our guide, and always using the light of good sense and manly robustness and of judgment, we would act upon. We say, encourage American youth to develope and increase their physical beauty. How, then, can this be done? Much of it is to be looked for through a diffusion of more general information upon the subtle play of causes and effects, that make

or unmake the health of the body. These often date back to early
life, to causes that operate during the period from the thirteenth or
fourteenth to the twenty-third or twenty-fourth year; and very many
of our remarks, though applying to all ages, will specially apply to
the period we have just named.

We repeat it, both for a prevalent application, and for the use of
you, reader, who may be attracted to our well-meant paragraphs,
be not afraid or ashamed definitely to make your physical beauty,
of form, face and movement, *a main point of interest you have
here in life*, at all of its periods, and whatever position of wealth
or education you may be. It is a germ, implanted by nature, that
you should make grow. And out of it will come a prolific growth
of good results, besides itself. It is a main part of that reception of
friendship, admiration and good will which all desire, and which
can always make life sweet.

[TO BE CONTINUED]

MEN'S FASHION IN THE 1850s.

The New York Atlas.

Vol. 21, No. 21

Manly Health and Training,

October 10, 1858

With Off-Hand Hints Toward Their Conditions

By Mose Velsor

MANLY PHYSIQUE.

(CONTINUED FROM LAST WEEK.)

THE MAGNETIC ATTRACTION FROM
HEALTH AND A MANLY PHYSIQUE—CAN IT BE
ATTAINED BY TRAINING?

Our theme commends itself further still. What do you suppose is the reason that some men have so much more power over the masses than other men?—such a "personality" that they can hardly appear in a crowd, or a room full of people, but their influence is felt? What is it at the bottom of the curious magnetism such men possess, and show it in house or street, in command, in the lecture-room, in the social circle, in politics, or on the field of battle? It is the subtle virtue of their physique—this just as much as intellect.

What we here affirm is proved by the fact that greater *minds* by far than any possessed by the commanding and magnetic persons we speak of, when clothed in inferior bodies, produce no effects at all, and come and go with the rest. A man of large personality, (it is not a matter of physical size—a small man may have it as well as any one,) is probably one of the most interesting studies in the world, and one of the greatest exemplifications of our theory of man's vigor. There he is, an evidence of power, of health, of tone—registering all in his port, his carriage, the atmosphere of influence that effuses out of him whenever he moves.

It is indeed our theory, (and we call upon you, reader, to mark this, for it is well worth pondering upon,) that a man of ordinary mental and physical advantages may, by training in its fullest sense, so exalt the intensity of his personal force, that virtue in him which utters itself at last through a perfect physique and a clear mind, that wherever he moves, in the private

81

circle or in the crowd, he shall attract to him attention, friendship, and respect, openly or silently—one of the noblest proofs that can be given of what *the body* is capable of effecting!

Would you succeed in anything?—ambitious projects, business, love? Then cultivate this personal force, by persistent regard to the laws of health and vigor. And remember that the best successes of life are the general resultant of all the human attributes, expressed through a fine physique. This knowledge, this practice, you, too, reader, will need. All kinds of men, herculean, obstinate, petty, profound—men of oak and men of wax—meet you at every move, crowding and jostling through the by-ways of the world. These you would confront, you would command, would you not? At least, you would not be overborne by the proudest of them, but would hold your own on equal terms. Then observe our suggestions— *train*—acquire for yourself firm fibres, a stomach clear and capable, the brain-action unabused, the stream of vital power full and voluminous, a bright eye, a strong voice, a proper degree of flesh, a transparent complexion—a fine average yet *plus* condition; and sympathy, attraction, and a heroic presence will follow. Are these trifles? Not a bit of it. They lie close to the heart of a man, and are among his secret, most cherished aspirations. With men, with women, with friends, with strangers, who is there that does not crave to be admired, to be beloved?

Is it not, indeed, worth striving for? Through a robust and clean-blooded physique, this *personal attraction is the real means that must secure any object, and, in the long run, produce effects worth having, in society, in the popular assemblage, on the boards of the stage or the concert room, on the lecturer's platform, the political hall, addressing a jury, pleading a case with a fair damsel, or in the business relations of any buying and selling.* All will succumb to it—all yield to its marvelous power.

This large potency, this subtle virtue of health and physique, we say, can be cultivated—it is hardly too much to say that it can be acquired; for we believe that, in almost every case, there are germs enough inherent in any man to work upon. But it will not be acquired except by him who perseveres and is faithful. Gluttony, sloth or inebriety must not even once be allowed to dull the perceptions, reverse the play and vigorous actions of the system—throwing the frame, and all its powers, prostrate, helpless, unable to show itself the master it would otherwise be.

This singular but sure magnetic condition, the result mainly of animal robustness, (through which the moral nature of course effuses,) is, we cannot too often repeat, the result of the health of the whole being, from top to toe—*all* must be sound, without exception—and then the stronger the tone of health, the mightier will be the stream of magnetic influence evolved. A main part doubtless lies in the department of sexuality; here a fund of vigor is a main part of a manly being, through many years; but he who exhausts himself, who commits excesses in youth, or becomes tainted in his blood, is attacked in the very citadel of manhood, and must pay the penalty through middle age, and the remaining periods of his life, as well as see the "attraction of personality" we have been speaking of depart from him.

In the department we speak of, a reserved stock of vital energy, we say, marks the *man*; and he who gives himself up, by its undue exhaustion, to lassitude and broken-down manhood, must bear the miserable consequences. The lesson is full of reflections, which we leave the reader to follow out.

Let a young man endeavor to realise of his body that, among other things, it is a machine calculated to produce force, an outpouring of subtle force, the same in moving among his fellow men as the orbs in space have in revolving through their orbits. Yes, a man, too, has his curious attraction of gravitation, and, well developed, it is one of the most amazing and delightful of natural results. This subject probably is new to you, reader, treated in this way; and yet if you will reflect a little, you will see that all history and real life in every direction abounds with illustrations of our statement.

What are most of the movements of men, all the past, whose signs we see around us, but assertions of what this human force has done—is now doing? Friendships, loves, some men well-liked wherever they go, others avoided or treated with indifference, the successful singer or actor, the orator that enchains his audience, the victory of the prize-fighter, the players of manly games, the person applauded in public, and the person whose efforts fall flat or are received with hisses of scorn or contempt—all these are just so many proofs of the powerful presence, or feeble absence, of the quality we are now treating of.

Observe the results of one day, to a man, at two different times, at a little distance from each other. He goes forth, neither feeling nor looking well; he has lived badly—his blood is bad—his joints move like those of some rusty machine, ill oiled—his eyes have red blood-shots in them—his complexion is muddied and pimpled—he is not clean, not having bathed for a long time—his stomach has been overloaded with all sorts of indigestible solids and injurious liquids. This has been going on so long that his digestion is seriously impaired—his bowels are clogged with accumulations of fearful impurity, like sewers that have been stopped—his gait is halting, and he would sit down often to rest—his appetite is morbid, seeking stimulants and spices to excess—the expression that beams from his face is anything but attractive—his breath is bad—nobody finds it a pleasure to be near him, or feels anything like delight from the magnetism of his voice, for there is no magnetism about it—he does not attract women, nor men either; and thus, going up and down, through the city, it may be, in the street, at table, wherever he moves, he is without vigor, without attraction, without pleasure, without force, without love, without independence, buoyancy, spirit or pride. Can there be a much sadder case? And is it by any means a rare one?

Now for another day—*the same man*—a little while, it may be but a few months, it need not be but a year at most, afterwards. Can this, indeed, be the result of the steady observance of a few physiological laws—the magic result of *training*? This day he rises with a merry song on his lips, and bounding strength in every muscle of his limbs. The shock of the cold-water bath in which he laves his body is delicious to him—and the friction of the brush afterward tingles finely through the skin into his blood. Food, air, the simplest drink, every motion—all these give him pleasure. His eyes are bright and sparkling, his voice melodious and strong. As he goes forth among men, he is everywhere noticed, and draws toward him good-will and even envy. His walk is springy and elastic—his complexion pure—his attitude erect, his expression full of manliness, spirit, pride and a noble self-confidence.

He has all the indescribable charm which belongs to some of the finest and most spirited animals, with flashing eyes, fine action, and unconquerable spirit, that we sometimes see in the brutes—but

ERECTITUDE.

PERFECT POSTURE.

alas! seldom see in the case of men. The full condition of power is attained by him—and the marvellous effects play invisibly out of him, wherever he moves, upon men and women in all directions.

Actors! vocalists! speakers! can you not here learn the secret of that coveted power over the public? A power as blessed to receive as it is to give.

To *all*, however, it is a great power—an art well worth the cultivation. Indeed, in the movements of common life, in the usual residence, and in company of acquaintances and friends—*there* we should say would be found its most grateful spheres of operation—for there the happiness of life, in the man, must rest.

BIRTH-INFLUENCES—BREEDING SUPERB MEN.

It is a profound reflection, deeply intertwined with our subject, that much of a man's comfort or discomfort, body and mind, depends on causes that exist and operate, in full activity, before his birth; these are the long train of hereditary causes that cannot too frequently be recurred to and dwelt upon. The laws of transmission of qualities, tendencies and forms, from parents to offspring, have always been among the most perplexing, as well as fascinating studies of the physician. The reasons of such transmission will doubtless continue to remain unexplained—the *facts* are innumerable, and run even deeper and farther backward and forward than is generally supposed. Unfortunately, however, there has never yet been found a generation that would shape its course, or give up any of its pleasures, for the greater perfection of the generation which was to follow.

While we cannot resume the past, however, in considering the health, size, looks, strength, &c., of a full-grown man—his beauty and perfection in those points, or his deficiency in them—it may be useful, for future cases, at any rate, to consider that whatever the man is, results, in a great degree, from those hereditary causes—causes that were in operation before he was born. Parentage! How great a thing it is! How the whole subject of life, of race, of temper, &c., all date back, without possibility of escape, to parentage! Yet it is not the future only that is involved—the present also comes in for consideration, as much as that.

Because the same routine of law, causes and effects, that operate to produce sound offspring, and perpetuate health, growth, vigorous maturity and long life in the same, are the identical laws, causes and effects that, by their interplay, have to do with a perfect physique in the parent. If only for the good of the latter, those laws are indispensable. They are the very ones that go to make the youth, the grown person, the middle-aged, strong and sound. So that to be in the condition of true parentage, or of preparing to be, is only another phrase for being in the true condition for yourself, and for all that makes you a true specimen of a man.

Mothers, too, it is useless to deny, are, for the main part, sadly unaware of most of the best conditions of treatment, food, &c., that lay the foundation, in early childhood and youth, for future manliness and a fine physique. So true is this, so lamentably true, that, beyond a doubt, if the mothers of the young children of this, or any other generation, were to put in practice, and carry out through the years of infancy and childhood, the simplest laws of sound physiology, and form the young into the habits thereof, we should see an entirely different and immeasurably superior race of men advancing upon the earth.

In the scope of our articles on health, we do not include the full statement of this most important and interesting part of our topic. It deserves, from every one, far more conscientious examination than is usually given to it. No considerations of morbid modesty should be allowed to stand in the way; and, indeed, are not those the immodest ones who would prohibit the enlightenment of the world, both men and women, grown and ungrown, upon what is so vital to them, and to all who come after them—prohibit it from prurient suspicions that it cannot be examined and investigated (as it certainly can be) with the noblest intentions, and in the most manly and even religious spirit?

While, therefore, it does not fall within the line of our remarks here to expatiate upon the laws of hereditary descent, and of parentage—the science, it might be called, of *breeding superb men and women*—we enjoin upon the reader to study out those laws, and what they result it. To know them is often to be forewarned with some of the most valuable knowledge it is possible for a man to have. He is able, then, to judge of much in his own case that, without which, would be dark and puzzling to him. He is also able to act understandingly toward the future.

We think proper to add, that we include women just the same as men, in the foregoing remarks.

LONG LIFE AND ITS REQUISITES.

We have always had a great curiosity, and felt an interest in cases of extreme old age. Returning from the west a couple of seasons since, we made a detour from our regular course to visit an aged woman, who numbered 103 years, and yet was in perfectly good condition, and retained her mental faculties unimpaired. This lady was Mrs. Catherine Dunn, of Nunda, in this State. She stated that she had always been very healthy and strong—altogether a pleasing and remarkable case.

One of the most noted cases of strength and faculty in old age is that of the old chaplain of the House of Representatives, at Washington, Rev. Daniel Waldo, who is between 95 and 100. He has been preaching for three quarters of a century—was a chaplain in the Revolutionary army, and was confined in the celebrated "Sugar House" prison in New York city [*sic*]. This aged man has always followed quite an active life, and has never been sick; living, for many years, on his farm near Syracuse. He keeps up with the times, too, reads all the new books, and is eager as any one to hear the latest news—quite a *young* old man.

Among the curious cases mentioned by Lord Bacon in his work on the "Prolongation of Life" are many of ancient date, among the Greeks, Asiatics, &c. Among the latter, the Esseans, a sect of Jews, are to said to have very commonly attained the age of a hundred years; it was attributed to their great temperance in diet, and to a calm habit of mind which they cultivated. As one of various specimens presented by Lord Bacon, we give the following:—Apollonius

Tyaneus exceeded a hundred years, his face betraying no such age; he was an admirable man of the heathens, reputed to have something divine in him, of the christians held for a sorcerer—in his diet Pythagorical—a great traveler, much renowned, and by some adored as a god; and lest his long life should be attributed to his vegetable diet, his grandfather before him, who did not restrict himself, lived to a hundred and thirty years.

The two next cases, quaintly related in the style of that time, are also from Lord Bacon's work: Most memorable is that of Cornarus, the Venetian, who, being in his youth of a sickly body, began first to eat and drink by measure to a certain weight, thereby to recover his health; this cure turned by use into a diet, and that diet to an extraordinarily long life, even of a hundred years and better, without any decay of his senses, and with a constant enjoying of his health. In later times, William Pestel, a Frenchman, lived to a hundred and well-nigh twenty years, the top of his beard on his upper lip being black; a man of a fancy not altogether sound, but somewhat crazed in his brain—a great traveler, mathematician, and somewhat stained with heresy.

About twelve years ago there was living in the town of Frankford, near Utica, a man by the name of Harvey, 111 years of age. He, too, had been for three-fourths of a century a preacher of the gospel. From an informant who saw him at that time, we learned that he was born in Dutchess County, N. Y., and that he distinctly remembered running about there in the woods a hundred years ago! During his life he had devoted some of his time and attention to farming, but always preached—and was doing so when we heard of him! He walked without any assistance, except that of a staff. His conversation, as well as his style of preaching, was animated—and frequently his eye brightened with the vivacity of youth. His mind appeared to be clear and sound, and his voice was strong enough to be heard through an assemblage of a thousand persons, or more. Wherever he went, multitudes flocked to hear him.

The same informant, (an amateur in the study of longevity) gives us an account of Mrs. Hannah Gough, who died in New York city in 1846, at the age of 110 years. She had always resided in New York, and had seen and conversed with every President of the United States. This case is interesting, as one of not a few that prove the city capable of conferring life as well as the country.

In cold climates, it is probable that persons are apt to live to a greater age than in tropical ones, or those toward the tropics. The climate of the Northern States, especially through New England, is favorable to longevity. We have gleaned the following from a long list of authenticated instances: A Mrs. Blake dies in Portland, Maine, in 1824, aged 112 years; Mrs. Moody died the same year, aged 111; John Gilley died in Augusta, Maine, 1813, aged 124; Morris Wheeler, in Readfield, Maine, in 1817, aged 115. Other Eastern states afford still more numerous instances, which we need not specify.

The middle states are also full of specimens of great longevity.

One of the oldest persons of whom we have any record in this or any country was Betsey Tranthram, who died in Tennessee in 1834, aged 154 years! A negro died in Pennsylvania in 1808, aged 150. While we write this, we hear accounts of an aged lady in the District of Columbia, supposed to be 150 years of age; she had had ten children previous to the commencement of the Revolutionary war.

Indeed, in all directions, in modern times just the same as any, there are plenty of instances to prove that human life may last for a century and over, and remain in pretty good condition then.

It is very much to be desired that some one should collect in a volume these cases of great longevity, and the peculiarities of them.

It being thus settled beyond a doubt that, under fair conditions, the human frame is capable of a far greater endurance than is generally supposed—that the number of persons in different parts of the earth, who have long outlived the "seventy years" allotted to man, may be numbered not by dozens merely, but by hundreds, and probably thousands—it remains to inquire into the causes that have led to such a result, and give heed to it, as a most precious lesson. Not so much that long livers have remained such a great while upon the earth, as that they must have had a good and sound life.

It will be found in all cases of these long livers, that *they did not exhaust the stamina of the frame in their adolescent years*, the years from fourteen to twenty-three or -four. During this important period of their lives, nature was left to grow strong, harden itself, and strike its roots deep—the whole system being daily prepared for all future emergencies. For it is idle to suppose of the long livers we allude to, but that they also had their ills, troubles, losses, and the various misfortunes that beset, at times, every human being in his journey through this world.

But if the body once attains its wholesome growth and solidity, without having the germs of decay infused through it while the juices of life are yet green, it can stand an immense strain upon it afterward without harm. We would impress this as the most important of the many lessons of manly development, health, and the continuance of life.

It is like a house perfect in the foundation, which then needs but the ordinary repairs, and will keep lasting an indefinite period of time. But [if] the foundation [be] shackly or insecure, it may be patched and mended forever, and still at any moment be liable to serious overthrow or damage.

REGULAR OCCUPATION.

A steady and agreeable occupation is one of the most potent adjuncts and favorers of health and long life. The idler, without object, without definite direction, is very apt to brood himself into some moral or physical fever—and one is about as bad as the other.

Disappointment, love, business troubles, and a long list of dark possibilities, are always waiting around every man; these interact, when they happen, (and none can go through life without them) in many ways upon the health. When they do happen, it is no excuse for "giving up"; if one will only persevere in the wholesome observances, and patiently wait a few days, the mind will be again at ease, and spring up with cheerful vigor again. This is one of the greatest recommendations of the training system, which, if our advice could be followed by young men, we would have never intermitted through life. It would be their best armor for all the ills that would be likely to beset them; to others baffling and overcoming, but to them obstacles easily turned aside and traveled away from.

VEGETABLE DIET.

We neither practice the vegetarian system ourselves, nor do we recommend it to others as anything like what its enthusiastic advocates claim it to be; and yet we think vegetarianism well worth a respectful mention. From the most ancient times, the system has come down to us under the most venerable authority. Nearly all of the early philosophers and saints appear to have been men who observed this diet; and, it must also be said, nearly all of them obtained a very advanced period of life. In the remarks elsewhere given on longevity, the cases mentioned, as near as can be authenticated, made use of that kind of aliment altogether, or nearly altogether. Newton, the astronomer, it is well known, in his profound and intricate discoveries, sometimes occupying his powers for weeks and months at a time, lived on vegetable food, and drank water only; thus forming a habit from which he seldom departed, and attaining to his eighty-fifth year. Boyle, the great chemist, although of extremely delicate constitution, by the simplicity and regularity of living, abstaining from animal food, and also by drinking nothing but water, preserved his useful life far beyond all expectation, dying in his sixth-sixth [*sic*] year—where most others would, in all probability, not have attained to half that age.

We recollect reading in an old book of travels a description by the traveler, of the head official of a Spanish convent of monks, an aged man, who had always lived upon vegetable food, and whose drink had been water only. He wore, says our traveler, a large garment of coarse cloth, tied at the waist with a rope, and having a hood for his head; and on his feet coarse shoes of half-tanned leather. Yet there was something in his appearance which would have enabled one to single him out at once from a whole fraternity. He had a lofty and towering form, and features of the very noblest mould. His beard descended low upon his breast, and was partly hid in the folds of his dress. The man was one who in any spot would attract attention, but as he stood there at the entrance of his convent, in addition to the effect of his apostolic garment, his complexion and his eye had a clearness that no one can conceive who is not familiar with the aspect of those who have practised a long and rigid abstinence from animal food, and from every exciting aliment. It gives a lustre, a spiritual intelligence to the countenance, that has something saint-like and divine.

This is, of course, a little enthusiastic. We have seen New England and New York vegetarians, gaunt, hard, melancholy, and unhappy looking persons, that looked like anything else than a recommendation of their doctrine—for that is the proof, after all.

(TO BE CONTINUED.)

The New York Atlas.

Vol. 21, No. 22

Manly Health and Training,

October 17, 1858

With Off-Hand Hints Toward Their Conditions

By Mose Velsor

MAN WEARING BASEBALL OUTFIT.

STUDY OF THEORIES OF HEALTH.

One of the greatest mistakes made in arbitrary theories of certain things supposed to be conducive to health, is that they forget that the true theory of health is multiform, and does not consist of one or two rules alone. The vegetarian, for instance, insists on the total salvation of the human race, if they would only abstain from animal food! This is ridiculous. Others have their hobbies—some of one kind, some of a different. But it is often to be noticed that, in the same person, habits exist that mutually contradict each other, and are parts of opposite theories.

A system of health, in order to be worth following, ought to be consistent in all its parts, and complete besides; and then followed faithfully for a long time. It is too much to expect any great immediate results; it is quite enough if they come in the course of a few months. It is also to be understood that every man's case requires something specially applicable to it.

We should recommend any one to first get a general knowledge of the subject, through what has been written upon it, without, for a while, undertaking to examine every branch minutely. It is a study, moreover, which will grow upon one, and as its illustrations lie within the daily experience of us each and all, it can be continually pursued.

EXERCISES, GAMES, AND OFF-HAND CONTRIVANCES.

The game of Base-Ball, now very generally practiced, is one of the very best of out-door exercises; the same may be said of cricket—and, in short, of all games which involve the using of the arms and legs. Rowing is a noble and manly exercise; it

95

Walt Whitman

ILLUSTRATION OF THE SPORT OF "HURLING."

developes the whole of the body. To many, the hunter's excursion, with dog and gun, will prove salutary. The fishing jaunt the same.

"Hurling" is also a noble game, and calculated, if made popular, to help with the rest in producing a noble race of men. We happened, by accident, to be present at a game of this sort, a few days since, in Brooklyn. The preliminaries being arranged (it was in a fine, large, enclosed lot,) the hurlers stripped, and with hurl-bat in hand awaited the throwing up of the ball. The latter flew high in the air amidst the silence of the crowd, which, as the ball received the first "puck," broke into a loud cheer. Once in motion, an exciting struggle commenced, in which the greatest strength, skill and activity were exhibited, which continued for nearly three hours. This was our first observation of the practical working of the game, but from what we saw of it we can recommend it as worth a high place on a list of manly exercises.

The simplest performance of hurling, however, as the name imports, is merely throwing a heavy weight, often a large stone, or a blacksmith's or stone-cutter's sledge—each person trying to outdo the rest in the distance the sledge or stone is sent. Nor do we know a better exercise than this. It should hold its place in all the programmes of work to be done.

Quoits—We wish this graceful and ancient game were more common. There is far more "science" in it than is generally supposed. In former ages, before the invention of gunpowder, when missiles were used in warfare, the lessons of this game were in vogue to give adroitness and precision in throwing objects with the arm. By a practised player, almost any mark can be hit. Boys should be encouraged to play the game. In country places it is often played with flat stones, or with horse-shoes. Most of our American cities have grounds where it is regularly played.

In truth, however, a man who is disposed to attend to the matter of strengthening and developing his muscular power, will be continually finding some means to further that object, and will do so in the simplest manner, as well as any. To toss a stone in the air from one hand and catch it in the other as you walk along, for half an hour or an hour at a stretch—to push and roll over, a similar length of time, some small rock with the foot, thus developing the strength of the

BLACKSMITH WITH SLEDGEHAMMER.

knees and the ankles and muscles of the calf—to throw forward the arms, with vigorous motion, and then extend them or lift them upward—to pummel some imaginary foe, with stroke after stroke from the doubled fists, given with a will—to place the body in position occasionally, for a moment, with all the sinews of the arms and legs strained to their utmost tension—to take very long strides rapidly forward, and then, more slowly and carefully, backward—to clap the palms of the hands on the hips and simply jump straight up, two or three minutes at a time—to stand on a hill or shore and throw stones, sometimes horizontally, sometimes perpendicularly—to spring over a fence, and then back again, and then again and again—to climb trees in the woods, or gripe [*sic*] the low branches with your hands and swing backward and forward—to run, or rapidly walk, or skip or leap along—these, and dozens more of simple contrivances, are at hand for every one—all good, all conducive to manly health, dexterity, and development, and, for many, preferable to the organized gymnasium, because they are not restricted to place or time. Nor let the reader be afraid of these because they are simple, but form the daily habit of some of them, without making himself uneasy "how it will look" to outsiders, or what they will say.

STRENGTH OF THE LEGS AND FEET.

Much, very much, ought to be said on this subject. Walking, or some form of it, is nature's great exercise—so far ahead of all others as to make them of no account in comparison. In modern times, and among all classes of people, the cheap and rapid methods of traveling almost everywhere in vogue, have certainly made a sad depreciation in the locomotive powers of the race.

Of the persistent exercise, for strengthening and developing them, of the lower legs, and of the ankles and feet, very much might also be said. No example is yet seen—not in these days, hereabout, at least—of the quality of endurance and performance by the legs—walking, running, leaping, supporting, &c. (We suppose there are some who will dissent from us; but that is our deliberate opinion.) The legs have a great deal to do with the accomplishment of the work of the other parts of the body, and give grace and impetus to it all.

It is a singular fact that what might be supposed such a simple accomplishment as *perfect and graceful walking*, is very rare—is hardly ever seen in the streets of our cities. We have plenty of teachers of dancing—yet to walk well is more desirable than the finest dancing. Perhaps some of the teachers we allude to might take a hint from the foregoing paragraph.

A DISREPUTABLE DANCE HOUSE IN NEW YORK (HARRY HILL'S).

A great deal may be done by gymnastic exercises to increase the flexibility and muscular power of the legs. The ordinary exercise of bending forward and touching the toes with the tips of the fingers, keeping the knees straight meanwhile, is a very good one, and may be kept on with, in moderation at a time, for years and years. The simple exercise of standing on one foot and lowering so as to touch the bent knee of the other leg to the ground, and then rising again on the first foot, is also a good one. On the exercise ground, a good result is obtained from having a large stone and pushing or rolling it over, first by one foot, and then by the other, as long as it can be done without fatigue.

The art of the dancing-master may also be called in play, for the development of the legs, and their graceful and supple movement. As originally intended, dancing was meant to give harmonious movements to the whole body, from the legs, by keeping time to music. In that sense, it was a beautiful art, and one of the noblest of gymnastic exercises. Modern arrangements have made it something quite different.

We would be glad to see some *manly genius* arise among the dancing teachers, who, out of such hints as we have hastily written, would assist the objects of the trainer and gymnast.

SWIMMING AND BATHING.

Many advantages are here concentrated in one—for swimming, being relieved of all the clothes, and supported in the water, allows of bringing nearly all the muscles of the body into easy and pleasant action. Persons habituated to a daily summer swim, or to the rapid wash with cold water over the whole body in the winter, are far less liable to sudden colds, inflammatory diseases, or to the suffering of chronic complaints. The skin, one of the great inlets of disease, becomes tough and thick, and the processes of life are carried on with much more vigor. Then cleanliness and enjoyment are also to be added to the merits of swimming.

Where swimming is not eligible, then bathe. The tonic and sanetary [*sic*] effects of cold water are too precious to be foregone in some of their forms. You cannot have a manly soundness, unless the pores of the skin are kept open, and encouragement given to

AN OUT-DOOR SWIMMING SCENE.

THE BAT

NEWPORT.

FULLY CLOTHED BATHING IN THE NINETEENTH CENTURY.

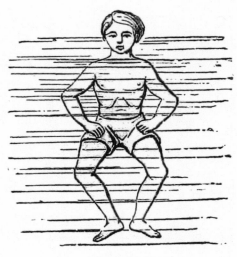

BOY SWIMMING.

the insensible perspiration, which in a *live man* is thrown off in great quantities, and the free egress of which is of the utmost importance.

Even the first shock, the reviving chill of the cold water, will soon come to be welcome. Of a hot day, how refreshing to feel the cool liquid poured over the naked body—or even dashed upon the face, head, hands and wrists. Cheap and simple as it is, there is a pleasure about it which costly enjoyments might not give.

We hear much, now-a-days, of the Water-*Cure;* but the real merit of the habitual use of water, especially swimming in it, is to *prevent* illness—in which it has a far greater scope.

Buoyed up on the liquid element, the body of the swimmer is supported by an equal pressure on every part—none of the limbs and joints are overstrained, and none relaxed. It is probably one of the most ancient of health-generating and body-perfecting exercises. The sculptors say that the ample development which the muscles, trunk, lungs, &c., obtained in the regular swimming, (in the open waters, or the large baths,) of the Greeks and Romans, gave their chests that round and full form so noticeable in their statues.

BOY DIVING INTO LAKE.

Probably the finest and best developed forms now to be found in any portion of the human race are those of the South Sea Islanders, who bathe in the sea continually, and are as much at home there as on the land; and where the diseases of civilization have not been introduced, it is rare to find among them a case of sickness, deformity, or decrepitude—and hardly a death, except from extreme old age.

In learning to swim, which should be in childhood—but at no age is it too late—the main thing is to keep going in the water, once every day in summer, in a place not deep, and in moving around, and occasionally trying to strike out a little. The art will soon come to one who does this.

Early in the morning, in summer, is a good time to swim, or take a basin-wash; the evening is also good for either. Avoid going into the water immediately after a meal; and, also, do not stay in too long—never long enough to get chilled. We do not mean by this latter the cool feeling of the first shock, after which there is a reaction, and the system soon, by the exercise, becomes all aglow—but the blue and trembling chill of exposing the naked body to a low temperature too long, especially if not accompanied by active motion of the limbs, rubbing, &c. Stop while the warmth continues, give the whole body a brisk friction and drying, and the good effects will be permanent.

It is somewhat remarkable, and equally to be regretted, that we Americans, in every part of our land, are *not* a nation of swimmers; although our coast of sea, bay, and inlet includes thousands of miles, and lakes, rivers, creeks, ponds, &c., are profusely distributed in every state and every county. To this, among other causes, is to be assigned our too frequently gaunt, bilious and non-perfect national physique. Certain it is, to our mind, that the popular commencement and intro-duction of the habit of daily swimming, which, in four-fifths of the United States, need hardly be intermitted more than from three to four months in the year, would not only be great reform in itself, but would carry with it, and cause to rise out of it, many of the other practices that complete the human form, and make it what it ought in general to be, large, clean, beautiful, and long-lived— instead of that being the marked exception, as at present.

If the reader, either a young or middle-aged man, should be induced by our remarks to commence learning to swim, or the practice of washing the body, let him (as in all new things of this sort) commence with moderation, and be satisfied to form the habit by degrees—not giving up, however, because of some little personal discomfort, or inconvenience of any kind, at first. Even in such a habit as bathing, to a novice, a good deal of resolution and perseverance is needed; but after the habit is once formed, it will almost invariably be kept up, of a man's own accord.

After washing the body, the use of dry cloths, to rub the flesh briskly, is almost always to be observed. An animated walk afterwards will come in well.

TRAINING THE VOICE.

The voice can be cultivated, strengthened and made melodious, with an ease and certainty, and to degrees of which very few people have any notion. We do not know a better exercise, either for young or middle-aged men, than practicing (at first with moderation,) in loudly reciting and declaiming in the open air, or in some large room. This should be systematic and daily; it strengthens and develops all the large organs, opens the chest, and not only gives decision and vigor to the utterance, in common life, and for all practical purposes, but has a most salutary effect on the throat, with its curious and exquisite machinery, hardening it all, and making it less liable to disease. It helps, indeed, the bodily system in many ways—gives a large inspiration and respiration, provokes the habit of electricity through the frame, plays upon the action of the stomach, and gives a dash and style to the personality of a man.

We would recommend every young man to select a few favorite poetical or other passages, of an animated description, and get in the habit of declaiming them, on all convenient occasions—especially when out upon the water, or by the sea-shore, or rambling over the hills on the country. Let him not be too timid or bashful about this, but throw himself into it with a will. Careful, however, not to overstrain his voice, or scream, for that is not the object that is aimed after. A loud, slow, firm tone, as long as it can be sustained without fatigue, and agreeably to the ear, is the test. Some voices will need to be used with great care for a long while. For in this, too, as in all physical exercises, let the learner remember, that there is plenty of time, and that it is the habit we mainly wish to form; after which the results will be sure to come in good time.

We repeat emphatically, that all persons whose life or occupation requires the frequent use of the vocal organs, and makes a fine, clear tone, and a superior pronunciation desirable, (as to what human being is it not?) may greatly aid the production of that tone and pronunciation, by exercise, by habituating themselves to open the mouth, by carefully avoiding all nasal and other unpleasant habits, and by regular attention to the health, especially in the way of simplicity of food.

NOT TOO VIOLENT EXERCISE.

Though we have once or twice alluded to the great importance of steady, daily, *moderate* exercise, as better than any extreme taxing of the bodily powers, at intervals, we think it of sufficient weight to call attention to it in a special paragraph.

The great object is to have the body in a condition of strong equilibrium—but very violent exertions defeat this end. In youth, or for young men, we may mention the evils of undue exertion, lifting immense weights, overworking in the fields of a long and hot day, being badly strained or wrenched in wrestling, or excessive and ill-timed "run" (as often happens to young firemen in our cities,) as some of the occasions when the results we deprecate are apt to take their rise.

We would over and over again caution the young reader of our articles of the often incurable effects of some of these brief but excessive outlays of strength. The fund of vigor and stamina must be used constantly, and encouraged to develope itself gently, *but never violently abused.*

In training exercises, as before remarked, begin and keep on for a few days with great moderation. "Gently does it," is the motto which must never be forgotten. The custom among some young men of trying to perform very difficult and dangerous feats should be discouraged. These are only for the professional gymnasts, who have made them the study of their lives. Nor are any of those feats worth applauding unless they are evidently performed with ease.

GYMNASTIC SCHOOLS.

It is very desirable that these should become common through our cities—some for beginners, young boys, &c., and others for grown persons, and those who have attained sufficient strength and endurance. Because the exercises for young boys should continue to be moderate, and gradually advance from the easier ones—taking particular care, in the spirit of the charge previously given, not to attempt feats of any kind merely because they are very difficult. This, indeed, in all gymnastic schools for boys, ought to be a sufficient reason to exclude any feat or exercise.

YOUNG MEN EXERCISING IN A GYMNASIUM.

OUT-DOORS.

In that word is the great antiseptic—the true medicine of humanity. We have confessed in our articles that there is no withstanding the modern requirements of life, which compel myriads of men to pass a great portion of the time employed in confined places, factories and the like; and that, this being accepted, the health and vigor of the body must be carried to a high pitch, and can be. Still, it is to be understood that, as a counterweight to the effects of confined air and employment, much, very much reliance is to be placed on inhaling the air, and in walking, or otherwise gently exercising, as much as possible out-doors. We have elsewhere mentioned the formation of the habit of walking; this is to be one of the main dependencies of the in-door employee. It does not tire, like other exercises—but, with practice, may be continued almost without limit.

Few know what virtue there is in the open air. Beyond all charms or medications, it is what renews vitality, and, as much as the nightly sleep, keeps the system from wearing out and stagnating upon itself. Naturally, we should all breathe this health-bestowing fluid; but the thousand artificial forms and necessities prevent it. We must, therefore, do the best we can—first understanding what sustenance to the blood there is in the air, even to the remedying of the evils of the great portion of our lives that we are debarred from it.

Places of training, and all for gymnastic exercises, should be in the open air—upon the turf or sand is best. Cellars and low-roofed attics are to be condemned, especially the former.

EARLY RISING.

The habit of rising early is not only of priceless value in itself, as a means toward, and concomitant of health, but is of equal importance from what the habit carries with it, apart from itself. In nature, there is no example of the bad practice of an animal, in full development of health and strength, in fine weather, lingering in its place of rest, nerveless and half dead, for hours and hours after the sun has risen. The only thing like it is the torpid condition of some animals, mostly in the Arctic and Antarctic regions, during the depth of the winter season. But civilized life, with its closed houses, its fires for warmth, and its plentiful and cheap envelopment of clothing, is protected against winters, and makes any copying of such an example unnecessary.

Summer and winter, he who intends to have his physique in good condition must rise early. This is an immutable law. It is one of the most important points of thorough training, and is to be relied on as much as anything else.

It is worth noting that the law of rising early necessitates the habit of retiring to bed in good season, which cuts off many of the dissipations most injurious in their effects upon the health. So important is this, that he who should adopt this rule alone will go a great way toward a complete reform—if reform be needed.

We will hardly reach our assertions to the extravagant length of some of the lauders of the habit of early rising—those, for instance, who hold to the celebrated maxim of Franklin, we believe, who said: "No great work can be performed, and no person can ever be good or great, without early rising." We are of those who believe that no law is without exceptions; and there may, after all, be aims, in which the health, for the time being, has to stand aside and take its chances. But, for a perfect attainment of *that* aim, namely, health and a fine physique, we may candly [*sic*] say that we do not believe it can be accomplished at all without the habit we speak of.

NIGHT-EATING.

An eccentric but wise old country physician, down in the state of Georgia, who was himself a living example of good health and unimpaired faculties, used to have a saying about people's meals, to the following purport: "Eat a good breakfast if you can, a good dinner if you will, but no supper if you please." In city life, and very largely among all classes, the spirit of the foregoing aphorism is exactly reversed; very few eating any breakfast—being without appetite for that meal, while the late hour of a fashionable dinner makes it equivalent to an evening feast. And then the habits of modern society invite to more or less indulgence of the appetite afterwards.

We allude to the custom of all modern amusements being held in the evening—parties, balls, theatres, concerts, &c. A main part of these, or an invariable accompaniment of them, are suppers, generally rich ones. Some of these are at 11, 12 or 1 o'clock at night, when numbers of people gorge themselves with hearty viands, oysters, jellies, beefsteaks, poultry, and more or less out of the hundreds of condiments, creams, and drinks.

A gentle and moderate refreshment at night is admissible enough; and, indeed, if accompanied with the convivial pleasure of friends, the cheerful song, or the excitement of company, and the wholesome stimulus of surrounding good fellowship, is every way to be commended.

But it must be borne in mind that, as a general thing, the stomach

AD FOR "THURBERS' FRUIT PRESERVES AND JELLIES."

needs rest as much as the other parts of the system—as much as the brain, the hands, or the feet. The arrangements of every individual, for his eating, ought to be so prepared, if possible, as to make his appetite always possess keenness and readiness in the morning. There is not a surer sign that things are going wrong than that which is indicated by no want or relish for food, soon after rising, or in the early part of the day.

Portions of heavy food, or large quantities of any kind, taken at evening, or any time during the night, attract an undue amount of the nervous energy to the stomach, and give an overaction to the feelings and powers, which is sure to be followed the next day by more or less bad reactionary consequences; and, if persevered in, must be a strong constitution indeed which does not break down.

Somebody has said that "we dig our graves with our teeth." There is a great deal of exaggerated statement about the evils of hearty eating, (we mean of plain food[)]—but it is very true that this habit we are complaining of, and endeavoring to guard the reader against, *habitual night-eating*, quite justifies the proverb. In this, as in all other instances, nature must be considered, and must decide before all artificial decisions. If there be those whose employments, or combinations of circumstances beyond their control, make it imperative upon them to violate the natural rules of eating, those persons must then make up for such violations by temperance, regularity and extra care in all other respects. They must choose with invariable prudence the quality of their food, simple and digestible dishes, and be as abstemious as possible. Actors and actresses, public performers, writers and printers on morning newspapers, pressmen, persons of the ferries, the city cars, and a numerous body of operatives and others, under modern arrangements, are all deeply involved in the bearings of this matter. In nearly all such and the like cases, a great and salutary improvement could be made in their comfort and health by a little prudent regard for their hours of eating and choice of aliment, and by bringing both as near to the standard of nature and simplicity as possible.

[TO BE CONTINUED]

The New York Atlas.

Vol. 21, No. 23

Manly Health and Training,

October 24, 1858

With Off-Hand Hints Toward Their Conditions

By Mose Velsor

THE BOARD OF HEALTH CLEANS OUT A "DIVE" BAR
IN NEW YORK CITY.

[CONTINUED FROM LAST WEEK.]

DRINK.

That we use far too many stimulating drinks has been too long the burden of physicians and others to make the statement anything new to our readers. But we believe, for all that, the prevailing impression has hardly been turned in the right direction.

We think that water, tea, coffee, soda, lemonade, "slops" of all sorts, have also produced, and are producing, immense injury to the health of the people—from their being used in too great quantities and at wrong times.

AD FOR "ICED LEMONADE."

115

It may sound strange that so harmless a liquid as water may require to be guarded against, but it is even so. Drenching the stomach with it just before, or during a hearty meal, plays the mischief with the digestions, and in most cases with the personal comfort. And yet it is a common practice.

We are fain to say, also, that very much of the violent crusade of modern times against brewed and distilled liquors is far from being warranted by the true theory of health, and of physiological laws, as long as those liquors are not partaken of in improper quantities and at injudicious times, disturbing the digestion. Of the two, indeed, we would rather, a little while after his dinner, a man should drink a glass of good ale or wine than one of those mixtures called "soda," or even a strong cup of hot coffee.

We mention this, not as recommending any of those drinks to whoever, young, old, or middle-aged, is in pursuit of health and a manly physique, but by comparison. The drink we recommend, and not too much of that, is water only.

By a proper choice of food, much thirst may always be avoided. For it is mostly from using great quantities of salted, and other thirst-provoking food, (also the use of tobacco,) that causes the imbibing of immense quantities of liquids used by our American men. About three-quarters of the drink is decidedly deleterious also, leaving afterward some of the various ingredients held in solution by the liquor, as a deposit in the stomach. Disguised, sweetened, &c., many a dose of semi-poison is taken in the shape of a pleasant drink.

Then of hot drinks—if you are disposed, indeed, to place your physique in perfect condition, it is probable that you must give these up entirely. In almost all cases, they are enervating, injure the action of the stomach upon the food, and produce bad effects upon the general tone of the system. Under present arrangements, at the tables of hotels, boarding-houses, and indeed everywhere, the supply of hot coffee, tea, cocoa, &c., is largely drawn upon twice a day; some drinking two cups, some three, at a meal. The result of thus deluging the stomach with liquid in large quantities, and at a high temperature, is bad, in more ways than one. Besides the injuries previously named, it really prevents the appetite from craving wholesome food at the time. This is contrary to the general supposition, but it is true. At a meal, a man must not fill himself with a quantity of hot liquid, because he has no appetite for solid aliment; it were preferable that he should eat a little of some dish that is on the table, or even a crust of dry bread, a cracker or two, or something of that kind. Be it remembered, however, that we are not disposed to be extra rigid in the matter; if one enjoys coffee or tea, one moderate cup, not hot, and taken toward the end of the meal, to moisten the articles we have just advised, need not be too strenuously prohibited. It is only that we speak with candor to those who are determined to have the condition of health we have spoken of—who realize it as a prize worth striving for, and who will not let any gratifications of the palate stand in the way.

Hot drinks, however, are so much matters of habit that it only needs a little self-denial and perseverance for a week or two, to acquire an easy way of getting along without them—of seeing them placed before you, and quietly abstaining from them yourself while you see others use them. Such things may be called trifles; but if any one wants to show his strength of mind, and ability to control himself, and prove what of *back-bone* and stamina there is in him, let him try his hand at giving supreme sway over reason, in sternly deciding to abstain from these very trifles.

Nature, it would seem, is averse to either very hot or very cold drinks or aliment. They should, in general, be as near as possible to the temperature of the body. As to the appetite for ice-water, for instance, in the hot weather, it is an artificial one; simple cool water, and not too cool, is much more wholesome.

MEDICINES—DO THEY DO ANY GOOD?

It is probable that the people of the United States use more medicines than any other equal number of persons in the world. In our cities, in all the main streets there is a drug-store to be seen every two or three blocks—and we know of some of the streets of New

A RUM CELLAR IN NEW YORK CITY'S FIVE POINTS SLUM.

York and Brooklyn, where, upon an average, there will be about three drug-stores to every four blocks! In the country towns, the same fact prevails, in proportion. We know of a small village, a little way out of New York, where an acquaintance of ours eked out a scanty living as the proprietor of a country newspaper, until the thought struck him of setting up a shop for the sale of patent medicines, and drugs generally. There he advertised in his paper, and so great was his custom, that he made quite a handsome little fortune in a few years. It is also notorious that some of the most successful speculations entered into in America are the medicine speculations—mixtures got up by some person, with greater or less degree of knowledge, and, by dint of advertising and keen business talent, sold off in enormous quantities.

These are but partial specimens of the great medicine trade—drops in the ocean. For it is quite oceanic—this dosing, and drug-

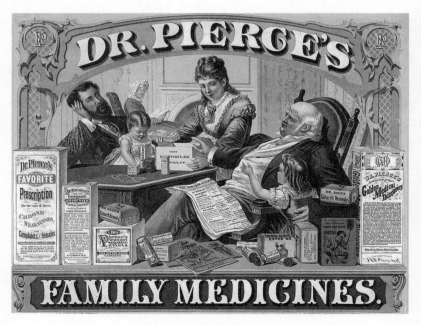

AD FOR MEDICINE.

ging, and physicing of the great American people!

Does every body, then, take medicine? Is it a regular thing with all classes, rich and poor, old and young? Perhaps not quite so bad as that; and yet the cases of those who do *not* take medicines of some kind or other, frequently during their lives, are very rare. With many it begins in early childhood and continues through life. Is it not probable that this has much to do with the deficient state of the health, vigor, digestion, and manly physique of America?

We are clear in our own mind that, in by far the vast majority of cases, these medicines do a great deal more hurt than good—that, indeed, they often lay the foundation for a permanent derangement of health, destroy comfort, and shorten life. These are severe words, but we believe them fully warranted by the facts.

It is too generally supposed, (for that is the amount of it,) that there is some magic or charm in a mysterious drug, a little vegetable or mineral compound whose nature we do not happen to know, that is going to do the wondrous work of restoring the functions of the body, when disordered, into perfect order and harmony again! And not only this, but all the diversities of age, temperament, combination, degree, &c., are overlooked, and the same drug is supposed capable of curing all the various cases under the same heading!

For there are as many varieties of disease as there are persons diseased; there are hardly any two cases alike, and cannot be. Because the degree and exact state of each person's sickness depend on combinations of circumstances that belong to him alone, and that have met together in no other instance but his. This alone makes the arbitrary use of an arbitrary medicine ridiculous. But there are other points equally important.

Really, to state the matter in plain terms, there can be very little, if any, wholesome effect produced upon almost any case of disease, probably [(]probably not one in twenty,) from the mere taking of some more or less powerful drug into the stomach, to have whatever effect it may produce upon the bowels, blood, nerves, brain, &c. The more powerful it is, the worse it is. A shock is produced, and perhaps an accelerated action—always to be paid for by a reac-

A PHARMACY AND ITS WARES.

tion, according to an eternal law of nature. We are not now speaking of marked contingencies, accidents, fits, &c., where prompt and decided means are to be adopted, and where the physician's object is to relieve the patient at once, and let the future make up for any temporary damage he may be compelled to do by those decided means, whatever they are. Our remarks, of course, have no bearing upon such cases as those: but upon the patient and sustained cure of a man laboring under some illness, the result of probably many and long-continued violations of natural laws, and of the simplest requirements of bodily condition. In such cases, (and they make up by far the main portion of the sickness of the civilized world,) it is quite certain to our mind, that any reliance upon drugs is futile. The cure must be by other means, and nature, as in all else, is to be looked to, studied, followed, and faithfully relied upon. In general terms it may be stated that the cure must be as slow as the disease was in forming.

SEXUALITY.

There is, of course, very much to be said relating to health and strength with reference to habits of sexuality, &c. It ought to be more generally understood that here concentrate what are, in many cases, the most important bearings upon manly soundness, physique, and long life.

Modern habits, in their bearings upon this particular, in all our great cities, may be concealed as far as any allusion to them in print and public discourse is concerned, but they are well known enough for our remarks to be understood and appreciated.

Through the cities, (and we don't know that we need to make an exception of country places either,) boys commence early, not only in their knowledge of licentious pleasures, but in their participation of them—increasing rapidly as they advance toward young manhood, and when they take their place in society as full grown members of it, generally with habits formed that, by their effects, stick to them through life. An appearance of decorum is preserved to the outer world; "modesty" is not shocked in parlors or in the social assemblage by any unpleasant word or allusion, but *the facts* of life, could they be exposed, would be such as to astound the whole mass, even the bad themselves.

If an investigation were candidly made, for that purpose, it would probably be found out that, through the thousands and thousands of different working-men, mechanics, employees, clerks, nearly grown apprentices, &c., in New York, and our other great cities, an immense proportion of them, probably a large majority, have had more or less unfortunate experience with syphilitic disease! This is an appaling [*sic*] fact; yet we are obliged to say we have no doubt it is a fact.

The places of resort for the classes of men and youths just mentioned are, of late years, where licentious habits are advanced

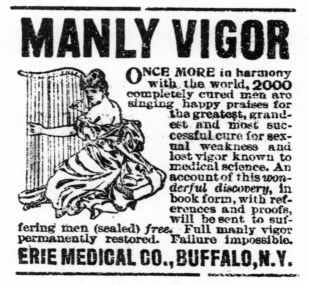

LATE 1800s ADVERTISEMENT
FOR POTENCY PILLS.

and confirmed. We are no moralist, in the usual acceptation of the term, but consider this subject solely in its reference to health and physique. And we must candidly inform the reader, especially the youth, that there is no more deadly foe to manly development than the infusion of the virus of any from [*sic*] of venereal disease, however moderate it may be, through his blood and system. It may remain lurking and lurking there for years, and appear a long while afterward, in terrible forms.

Under the present state of things, among the young and middle-aged men, it is a bitter fact that it is not considered anything alarming to be "diseased." You meet *that* everywhere, and its commonness takes off the edge of its hideousness. But it is really one of the most serious things that can happen to the body, especially in early life. Some of the best physicians assert that, after once becoming ingrained in the blood, the syphilitic taint is never afterwards thoroughly worked out of the system. They say it is analagous [*sic*] to the vaccinating matter for vareoloid; if once the smallest particle "takes," it remains in the body ever afterward.

Writers and speakers are surely too fearful of a little candid speaking upon this subject. It is considered well enough between two persons, or in a small assemblage, but indelicate where a writer is addressing a multitude. We thing [*sic*] differently. We believe that ignorance upon this subject is greatly the cause of the evil in the existing state of things; the common classes of young men do not appreciate the fearful detriment they are doing to their manly condition, vigor, and health. Neither are the facts of life, as carried on nightly in the cities, half as well understood by the public as they should be.

Upon this part of the subject we have to add that one of the greatest benefits of training, exercise, simple food, early hours, &c., is that, under them, the sexual passions are far less morbid than under a stimulated course of life. The thoughts are, by degrees, diverted from that form of pleasure, and a tone of greater coolness and evenness pervades the temper. The almost unnatural indulgence in licentiousness, of the desire for it, which previously, perhaps, characterized the man, sinks away, and a different, more wholesome and more salutary habit of feeling and practice succeeds.

BEAUTY.

What is beauty? The question is a puzzling one, and has been so in all ages. Much has been written upon it, and, like pleasure, it is supposed to vary among the different races and temperaments. Voltaire says: ask a negro of Guinea what is beautiful, and he will answer, that to him it is a black oily skin, sunken eyes, and a flat nose. The devil, (says the same author,) if you were to ask him, might tell you that the beautiful consists in a pair of horns, four claws, and a tail; while, if you consult the philosophers, they will answer you with their jargon. We give this because we would like to let our readers see what the great authors have been writing on a subject that all can realize in their own perceptions and sympathies, but that will hardly bear writing about.

As for us and our purposes, we would simply impress the fact, (without mixing ourselves up in any argument, or trying to explain reasons why,) that, as regards human beings, in an important sense, *Beauty is simply health and a sound physique.* We can hardly conceive of a man, at any age of life, who is in perfect health, and keeps his person clean and neatly attired, who has not some claims to this much-prized attribute. This may be a new doctrine to many of our readers, but the more it is examined, the more depth it will exhibit.

On the other hand, it is all in vain to pretend that there is any real beauty, or ever can be, in a *feeble or deficient man.* There is a class of writers, both in this country and Great Britain, who seem to be doing their best, in their novels, sketches, poems, &c., to present as the models for imitation and approval, a set of sickly milk-and-water men, young, middle-aged, or old, without any timber in them, very sentimental, and generally very unwell any how. We hope the young fellows who read our remarks will be on their guard against these writers and their sickly models. They are not for live, robust American men—and especially not for our youth. A very different pattern indeed is wanted to be placed before the growing generations.

The ideas of beauty allowed to prevail and take the lead are too much under the control of such sketch-writers, and of the standard of tailor's [*sic*] and milliner's [*sic*] fashion-plates, and the like. A pretty, sickly, chalk-and-pink face, either in man or woman, is not beauty. On the contrary, it should be classed with deformed things. Always, in a man, indeed, a certain dash of ugliness, rudeness, and want of prettiness, is found to set off his personal qualities—if he have otherwise perfect health.

THE SENSES.

Of course, all the senses become healthier, longer lasting in keenness, and more perfect, from the clean and buoyant state of the body which results from continued training. The eyes and sight may be mentioned as likely to be vastly improved, if they were previously ailing. Much of the bad eyesight that we notice, is simply from the fact that the whole system wants renovation, the blood being bad, from all sorts of unwholesome and injurious habits. Under good training, continued year after [*sic*], the eyes will be likely to continue good through life, however advanced it may prove.

The senses of taste and smell, also; these become dulled from all those luxurious and unwholesome habits we have cautioned the reader against, and that deteriorate the physique and manly perfection. Relieved of their evil influence, the palate and the nostrils remain clear and sound as long as the frame holds together.

Indeed, all the senses, all the functions and attributes of the body, become altogether renewed, more refined, more capable of conferring pleasure in themselves, with far more delicate susceptibilities, under the condition produced by long and faithful observance of good diet, proper exercise, and the other rules of healthy development.

THE FEET.

If a man wants personal ease, and even for health we consider it requisite too, he must pay more than the usual attention to the feet, and what is worn upon them. Besides, a great portion of the exercise necessary for health and digestion requires a far better condition of the feet than is common. Probably, in civilized life, half the men have more or less deformed feet, from the tight and wretchedly made boots generally worn.

In one of the feet there are thirty-six bones, and the same number of joints, continually playing in locomotion, and needing always a free and loose action. Yet they are always squeezed into boots not modeled from them, nor allowing the play and ease they require. For the modern boot is formed on a dandified idea of beauty, as it is understood at Paris and London, and not as it is exemplified by nature.

If you want to see the feet in their natural and beautiful proportions, you must get a view of the casts of the remains of ancient sculpture, representing the human form, doubtless from the best specimens afforded by the public games and training exercises of the Greek and Roman arenas. They exhibit what the foot is when allowed to grow up, with its free, uncramped, undeformed action. There have been no artificial coverings or compressions; and we know that the gait therefrom must have been firm and elastic. We can understand how the Macedonian phalanx, or the Roman legion, performed its long day's march. We can see the ten thousand Greeks pursuing their daily wearying course through the destroying climate of Asia, marching firmly, manfully, across the arid sand, the mountain pass, or the flinty plain. It is a truthful lesson we may learn, not for the soldier only, but for the civilian.

Probably there is no way to have good and easy boots or shoes, except to have lasts modeled exactly to the shape of the feet. This is well worth doing. Hundreds of times the cost of it are yearly spent in idle gratifications—while this, rightly looked upon, is indispensable to comfort and health.

The feet, too, must be kept well clothed with thin socks in summer, and woolen in winter—and washed daily. We may mention that one of the best remedies for continued cold feet which many people are troubled with in the winter, is bathing them frequently in cold water. If this does not succeed, add a little exercise.

Too many young men, and other men too, seriously injure their health by carelessly going with poorly protected feet, or even with improperly made boots. These last, from the distress they cause by

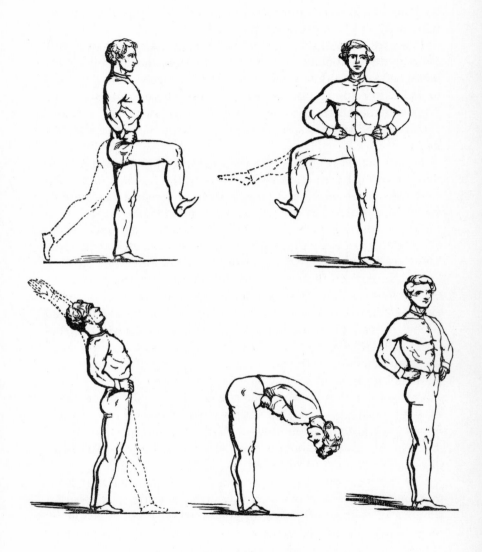

GYMNASTIC EXERCISES.

walking, indispose to exercise—which would very likely be otherwise engaged in with eagerness and pleasure. It is also to be noted, that one who makes a regular practice to bathe his feet daily, wear clean socks, and protect himself during bad weather by good boots or shoes, will hardly stop there—but will, ten chances to one, continue on until he habitually observes all the rules necessary to a clean and robust development.

The New York Atlas.

Vol. 21, No. 24

Manly Health and Training,

October 31, 1858

With Off-Hand Hints Toward Their Conditions

By Mose Velsor

BOXER JOHN C. HEENAN FIGHTING JOHN MORRISSEY IN 1858
(IN CANADA).

OUR OWN REFLECTIONS ABOUT THE LATE FIGHT— AND THE LESSON TO BE DRAWN FROM IT —WITH ONE OR TWO OTHER MATTERS.

Considering the immense prejudices of those who give the cue, we do not so much wonder at the aversion which most of the intellectual and benevolent members of the community feel toward Prize Fighting as an "institution," and which has been called forth quite loudly and generally by the late contest between Morrissey and Heenan.

At first thought, perhaps, it seems a savage and unchristian performance, for two men to go deliberately to work, to pound and batter each other, merely for the purpose of seeing who can stand the most "punishment," and do the greatest credit to his muscle, game and training. Yet (we would suggest to the reader), the question is not so abruptly decided. There are other considerations and arguments—some of them quite important. It appears, of late, as if all the indignation which might justifiably be directed towards the sins of different departments of modern life, theological, political, social, &c., were withdrawn from the rest, and turned towards the performances of the prize ring, and of those who "go in" for that amusement and branch of "science."

The vast understratum of the people, however, will continue to gratify their tastes and impulses, irrespective of the tone of polished society (so called). And it is useless to deny that, through the great masses of men who form that understratum, there is a deathless interest in these contests for physical superiority, whether expressed in a battle between two ships-of-war upon the sea, or opposing armies upon land—or, on a smaller scale, between two trained specimens of humanity in the prize ring. There is, we may also say in passing, not an argument against the combat of the prize fight, that does not equally apply to war—to all war, at least, except that for the purpose of resisting the invasion of a foreign foe.

For our own part, we believe in the necessity of those means that help to develope *a hardy, robust and combative nation,* and desire to see America in that list. We do not think that community able to take care of its rights, and defend them successfully against all odds, where there exist only peaceful, pious, respectable and orthodox citizens. There must be something more. What, for instance, did ancient Rome rise out of? How came she to be the commanding power of the world for so many centuries—the leader and master of all lands? Of course, from a plentiful infusion of just about such temper and audacity as congregated at Long Point, around the ropes that enclosed Morrissey and Heenan, the other day. And the subject nations which Rome conquered, one after another, in all directions, were conquered, in many signal cases, because they disdained the fierce encouragements to produce a race of men who could and would fight, not by rote merely, but for *the love of fight.*

Do we then, (perhaps the amazed reader asks,) openly countenance the training of men for prize-fighting? We answer, explicitly, *we do,* (of course, no one but the writer of these sketches being responsible or implicated in the opinion—it being uttered for himself alone.) It is about time to meet the floods of mawkish milk and water that are poured out upon the land, and which, if justified and put in practice, would crowd America with nothing but puny and feeble men, obedient, pious—a race, half, or perhaps wholly emasculated.

There is, of late years, an excess of philanthropy, which o'erleaps itself, and falls on the other side. We believe it would be a first-rate thing in New York, and all the other cities of the United States, if the science of fighting were made a regular branch of a young man's education—and if the exhibition of contests for physical superiority were common. Some such thing appears to be necessary, to meet the morbid weakness we have alluded to; it is, indeed, with other causes, deteriorating the race, we sometimes think. It appears to have taken possession of almost all the literary classes, and of the preachers and lecturers.

Nor are we afraid of the Americans being too combative. That is a matter which will regulate itself. There are too many varieties and competitors, North, South, East and West—and the mutual attrition of each is beneficial to all the rest. This serves to keep each individual part of it in its due place and proportion, without danger of successful aggression upon the others. But especially in the commercial and older settled states, we are free to confess we are sadly in fear of the danger of seeing that "love of fight" we have alluded to, almost extinguished.

Some such suggestions as these, at least, are certainly called for to counterbalance the tone of writing and expression which lately prevails in select society, with reference to the principle of physical combats for superiority—as if there were not something inspiriting and honorable in such a contest, as in others which involve different leading talents and powers of humanity. Is there not even a high order of heroism in the willingness and capacity to endure the most terrible blows of an opponent, and stand up under them as long as the sinews of the body answer the volition of the mind? Let others say what they will, we say *there is*—and we say, moreover, that it is a kind of heroism which we need more of in these latitudes—or rather we need the recognition of it—for we do not doubt there is plenty of the quality itself among the common people.

No amount of cultivation, intellect, or wealth, will ever make up to a community for the lack of *manly muscle, ability and pluck.* History is full of examples of intellectually developed nations, but *intellectual only,* falling a prey to others of inferior mental calibre, but of daring and overwhelming physique. Even Rome itself, in time, for such reasons, fell a prey to outside invaders far inferior to itself.

We will now proceed to draw a few inferences from the Morrissey and Heenan fight itself:

Probably the best moral to be deduced from the late fight is, that the quality of being able to endure any quantity of blows and bruises, and hold out toughly under them, is what most tells, and gives the final account of itself in a fight. This is what won the victory; while, on the other hand, we should say that, beyond question, no man who has seen only twenty-two or -three years, (Heenan's age,) is really fit for the grandest exhibition of his bodily powers. The common opinion that about that period of life affords the best show of strength and endurance, under favorable circumstances, is unquestionably an error, and a very great one. Five or six years more are required to give the human frame its *settled strength and knit*—and the friends of Heenan ought to know this fact, and inculcate it in his mind, too. If he wishes to hold out in the result, (not the beginning, mind, but *the result!*) he must avoid overtaxing his powers too soon. The hard oaken fibre of the frame does not come at his years—or during the earliest years anyhow.

BOXER JOHN C. HEENAN IN 1860.

The fight itself is, perhaps, the best illustration of what we say here, and often have said. How splendidly Heenan began it! There was, perhaps, never seen a finer show of determination, brawn, and alertness than that much-talked-of "first round," and Heenan's part in it—giving his friends undreamed-of hope, and equally discouraging to those of the opposite faction. It seemed as if there was no standing against those quick and terrible blows. But there *was*; and that made the very fact which was to bear away the palm from him who commenced so well. He began well, but *could not hold out to the last in proportion*; that spoilt all, and must ever spoil all.

The rule holds true in more cases than this of the prize fight. It runs through all that is to be said upon the subject of physical training for a man's health and vigor, and involves its most important bearings. We say, therefore, that the late fight bears a great lesson in the fierce attacks and defences of its rapid twenty-two minutes— the lesson that *he wins who can "best stand grief,"* as the sporting fraternity quaintly phrase it.

Or, in other words, in robust training for this life, which is itself a continual fight with some form of adversary or other, the aim should be *to form that solid and adamantine fibre which will endure long and serious attacks upon it*, and come out unharmed from them, rather than the ability to perform sudden and brilliant feats, which often exhaust the powers in show, without doing any substantial good. We know nothing of John Morrissey, but consider ourselves obliged to him, and his theory and tactics of fighting, for a marked example of this main element of our hints upon the general physical training of American young men.

It is for such reasons, among the rest, that we dwell upon this fight—an illustration, as it is, of such practical details of diet, exercise, abstinence, &c., as our foregoing papers would suggest for general use, as far as may be—because, of course, the actual necessity of this kind of training, for fighting purposes, will never be the rule, but only the exception. Still it is to be admitted that nothing short of a prize-fight will ever bring the rules of manly health and training to that systematic perfection which they are attaining, and out of which we, among the rest, have been able to write these articles for popular use.

Just in the way as the institution of the horse-race, and nothing less than that, brings the breed of the horse up to a far, very far, higher pitch of physical perfection than could be attained by any other means known or possible upon earth—just exactly in the same way, (after all the talk, pro and con, has been expended about it,) it remains to be distinctly confessed that *nothing short of these fierce manly contests, in ancient and modern times, has led to the mightiest and most perfect development of the masculine frame, and proved what are the real rules consonant with its soundest physiology.*

Therefore, in opposition to the views expressed by the editors of the American newspapers, (the *Atlas*, we believe, among the rest,) we say a stern word or two, not in defence of these fights only, but in *deliberate advocacy of them.* We are writing just as fast as our pen can gallop over the paper—[and] no doubt skip many of the points we should like to make, on our side of the arguments, if we had time to stop and arrange the said arguments in imposing array. At present we only throw out our views, as the Tartar shoots his arrow, passing along at full speed. But in some way, on some future occasion, we intend to resume this subject, and present our views with more preparation and effect.

By the way, the same papers that have such indignant editorials about the fight are the very ones in which we have noticed, of late, quite a good many articles bewailing the physical degeneracy of the race of men in America—statements that we are getting to have, in our cities, and on all sides, too many inferior and feeble men. Why, it is for the very reason, among the rest, that the tone of those who assume to lead in public education, public opinion, the press, &c., sounds continually in the key it does, that there is indeed too much of this same degeneracy. As we have before remarked in these off-hand sketches, the spirit of American schools, authors, &c., tends to continually develope the intellect and refinement of taste of the people, at the expense of all their bodily stoutness, muscle, and their indifference to little elegancies, niceties, and parlor and college models. We would have this met and reversed. Not that we have any objection to the colleges and the parlors—they are, of course, well enough; but they do not afford that broad and earth-deep understratum that is necessary for a nation with a resistless physique. Something a little more coarse and rank is necessary. Let the tone of public taste, instead of refusing any connivance with the vast undertow of popular sympathy with these muscular combats, and all that appertains to them, be turned to elevate and improve the said combats, and make them, it may be, far better than they are, retaining, however, the same fierce energy and combative science. We are not afraid to say, once again, that at this present writing, we are decidedly in favor of some such course as this.

As to the point of physical degeneracy here in the United States, we do not, upon the whole, make much account of it. The nation is passing through several important physiological processes and combinations. To a great degree, it is yet getting acclimated—especially in the West, and on the Pacific coast, which latter is destined to have a huge influence on the future physique of America. In its dry, wholesome, life-giving and life-preserving atmosphere, the human form, it may be, is destined to attain its grandest proportions, clearness, and longevity. We allude to California and Oregon, and indeed the immense inland stretch from Kansas down through Utah and Arizona [*sic*], to the borders of Mexico. Here the air is dry and antiseptic—everything grows to a size, strength and expanse, unknown in the Northern and Eastern States. Nature is on a large scale; and here, in time to come, will be found a wonderful race of men.

Before dismissing the subject of the late fight, we would once more specially call the attention of the reader to the astonishing power of the trained human body to endure and make light of, those indescribably strong and bloody attacks, blows, and bruises, which would be certain death to half a dozen men such as we usually see walking the streets of New York and Brooklyn. What a marvellous power this is, which enables the human body to pass off, as if in sport, such a fearful battering and pounding. We may, we say, learn a valuable lesson here, and apply it to the warding off of disease, and in the usages of every day life.

In the same train of thought, we would remark that the "sporting men" of our American cities afford quite a study, in connection with the subject of manly training. There are among them some of the finest specimens of physique, in the world. Indeed, generally they are a handsome race of men. You will see among them a number who are quite advanced in years, yet in a good state of preservation. They are generally distinguished by a certain smartness in their attire, quick movements, and by a bold, sharp, and determined expression of the countenance.

It is astonishing how much "fast life" many of these fellows go through, and come out quite unharmed. Often, we have thought, they set at defiance the ordinary rules of health and medicine, and baffle what are supposed to be the surest canons of the laws of longevity—coming out quite unscathed, and going on their ordinary course, hearty and good-looking, as if nothing had happened. But it is to be noticed, at the same time, that such specimens are of callous temperament, reckless, without any of the attributes of the finer feelings, and not disposed to stand about trifles, either of conscience or any thing else.

We have sometimes even thought, while standing among a large crowd of these sporting men, in some Broadway drinking saloon, or some such place, and quietly observing their actions and looks, that they presented about the best collection of specimens of hardy and developed physique we had anywhere seen. Their movements remind one of a fine animal. They have that clear, audacious, self-confident expression of the eye, and of the face generally, which marks some of the animals in a wild state. Notice the attitudes of them as they stand, or lean; the extended arm holding the glass of liquor, and raising it to the lips; the hat tipped down in front over the eyebrow; the "gallus" style generally. Or, see two of them square off at each other in a joking way; the limber vibration of the upper part of the body upon the waist; one foot planted forward; the movements of the arms, and the poise of the neck.

So much for the "sporting men," for they afford us a study, with the rest. And, indeed, in casting our eyes around, we feel disposed to take all the "muscle," indiscriminately, under our favor, and

WALT WHITMAN "IN SOME BROADWAY DRINKING SALOON" IN 1857
(PFAFF'S BEER CELLAR).

speak a good word for it—to counterbalance the disfavor which is so generally shown toward it.

Of course the young reader, or any reader, will have sense enough to understand that we do not pick out the life of a "sport" from all the rest, and offer it to him as a pure model for him to follow, to the rejection of the others. We express no opinion, and give no advice about it. We simply call attention to the singularly perfect physique of these men, in contradistinction to those shambling professional and genteel persons, clerks, lawyers, pious students, correct youths and middle-aged men, and the life—pale, feeble, timid,

quiet, dyspeptic, and uninteresting generally, either for the company of man or woman. And as to real viciousness, let no one suppose that it is confined to any one class of the community, or is any more to be found in those who "lead a gay life," than in those who keep demure faces, and are supposed to be lawful and orthodox— that is to say, the latter, in most cases, add hypocrisy to the natural sins of man, and to the private indulgence in the same.

[TO BE CONTINUED.]

MEN EXERCISING ON BALANCING BAR.

The New York Atlas.

Vol. 21, No. 25

Manly Health and Training,

November 7, 1858

With Off-Hand Hints Toward Their Conditions

By Mose Velsor

FRYING POT.

[CONTINUED FROM LAST WEEK]

CLIMATE—IS THIS OF OURS CONSISTENT WITH
LONGEVITY AND PERFECT HEALTH?

Much is said, (and with reason,) on the advantages of climate. The principal points of climate, in the line of latitude of New York, New England, and the Middle States, from which injury ensues to the best physical requisites of our common humanity, arise from the vast differences of temperature between a great part of the winter weather—and a great part of the summer weather—the one being often extremely hot, and the other extremely cold. Also, the sudden changes and fluctuations to which we hereabouts are liable—the same week occasionally presenting nearly all the varieties of temperature from those of the arctic regions to those on the line of the equator.

It is often argued that the human frame and organization cannot be expected to stand these amazing discords and shocks of temperature, and that it will not; consequently, if such premises be true, that a hardy, sound, large-bodied and long-lived race of men cannot flourish in such a climate—cannot stand it, for the course of permanent generations. The assertion is plausible—and yet it will not bear to be thoroughly investigated. Climate has much, very much, to do with the physique, as with all else that appertains to a nation, (its literature, laws, religion, manners, &c.;) but so marvellously can the human being adapt himself to circumstances that there is hardly any climate on the surface of the globe, but, as far as it alone is concerned, can be made to adjust itself to manly development and fine condition.

Indeed it seems as if some of the most rugged and unfavorable climates turn out the noblest specimens of men—as, in Europe, from Scandinavia descended the very best parts of the

145

elements, which served to make that composite, the English race—flowing onward to be but an element of a greater and stronger composite race still, namely, the American. From that Northern Europe, and from chilly and sterile Germania, we inherit, doubtless, we say, the toughest and most commanding part of our physique; leaving for sunnier climes to have bequeathed us what are perhaps our finer mental and sentimental attitudes. (And yet there are not a few who will contend that for the latter qualities also, the best of them, we owe, far, far back in the past, the debt of obligation to our Teutonic ancestors, many hundreds, perhaps thousands of years ago.)

In those bleak and changeable climes, too, men lived to a great age, and performed heroic deeds—no parlor gentlemen, but such as held their own in the violent combats of the open air, and upon the sea. A new age is upon us—and yet the same old qualities, and the love and admiration of them, still remain. These qualities are to exist and find their expression in new forms, conformable to modern life, usages, and tastes. Otherwise, we shall have but a nation of smirking persons, polite, dapper, correct and genteel, following the established forms, their shrunken frames concealed in costumes, because, if they were stript, their meagerness and deformity would disgust the world.

Indeed, it has sometimes appeared as if the hardiest races must necessarily flourish in rugged and stern climates; for that, among the rest, awakes them to exertion, labor, knowledge, and ingenuity, which develop the great qualities of a man. *A perfect man is the result of urged cultivation.* Nothing brings him out either so much as "a forced put." He then enters into that combat with Nature, and with circumstances, which hardens his powers, teaches him his own grandeur, and begets in him the fierce joy of combativeness and conquest.

The physique, of course, partakes largely of all this place of causes and effects. It soon learns to confront the evils that to a feeble person are so terrible—learns to find some of its highest pleasures in overcoming them. Thus, storms, the cold, exposure, the sea, perils, enemies, war—all these, and the like of these, to superior and hardier spirits, instead of giving terror, give a certain sort of grim and manly delight. They are the atmosphere most suitable to them—the aliment which suits them. A little examination, then, may perhaps show that the really superb physique of man, involving his greatest heroism, faith, and unconquerable spirit of freedom, owes its birth and breed, not to the genial climes of this earth of ours, where the air is soft and equable, and fruits and perfumes run their even round the whole year, and where man has no effort to make for the support of his existence, but is permitted to lounge an indolent holiday of life, and dream it away in the poetic enjoyments of his appetites and amours,—but to rougher and sturdier lands, where he has to fight hand-to-hand with the very earth, air, and sea. Thus truly, Mother Earth, whose sharpness is only sweetness in disguise, raises her firmer races. Ever, she seems to show, through the affairs of man, that he must be whipped and spurred into his best development. By that means, and nothing less, will he arrive at all the highest prizes and blessings of his life.

From such trains of thought and argument, we arrive at the conclusion that, allowing all which is charged against the climate of the northern portions of the United States, (and including Canada,) there is nothing to prevent our seeing there the very grandest examples of physique, strength, quickness, tone, and longevity—and these, for permanent continuance, through many an age and generation of the future. But in order to produce these effects, the public mind needs far more clearly to understand, (and act thoroughly and persistently on the understanding,) that *certain means are indispenslble [sic], for individuals, that they may resist the injurious wear and tear of a racking and variable climate.* A man must become, as we intimated in the beginning of our articles, a reasoning and reasonable being—must be willing to follow a certain course, and find his pay for the same, not in ephemeral and immediate gratifications, but those at some distance; must be willing to place *health, sound internal organs, and perfect condition, at the head of the list of the objects of his whole life, here on earth.*

The cold bath, for instance, cautiously begun, and kept up habitually morning after morning, year after year—what a toughener and hardener to this changeable climate of ours it is! In conjunction with other means, (for, be it remembered, the true theory of health is not a "one idea" theory, but involves a cluster, all hanging together,) it neutralizes the differences of the air, different weeks and seasons, and makes the body indifferent to them—thriving equally under the heats of August or in the bitter contracting air of January or December.

This simple habit, (which would occupy from five to ten minutes of your before-breakfast time,) is enough to ensure the frame, in by far the greatest number of cases, from the common and prevalent injury of colds, coughs, &c.

The modern custom of heating by stoves has much to do with the incompatibility of a large proportion of our North Americans, with the climate in which they live. Given close rooms, hot stoves and no ventilation, and you have a prolific crop of chilled bodies, whenever exposed to the otherwise bracing effects of the open air. It does not seem to be known that the best way to keep really warm in winter, (for men,) is, not to withdraw from the open air, but go out in it, and keep stirring. Habit soon settles the matter. Fifty and sixty years ago, before the introduction of cast-iron stoves, there was far more hardihood of body, and less liability to coughs, and all forms of pulmonary complaints.

Indeed, upon deliberate reflection, it would be found that many, perhaps most, of the evils which are laid to the American climate, in the northern and eastern states, are not so much to be attributed to it, as to special causes—the habits of life, the follies of dress, unwise diet, artificial overheating, and the like. This leads us to consider a special point; in the matter of diet, which, although touched upon incidentally in our foregoing articles, is of importance enough to call for its own heading.

MEAT AS THE PRINCIPAL DIET FOR THE INHABITANTS OF THE NORTHERN STATES.

In our view, if nine-tenths of all the various culinary preparations and combinations, vegetables, pastry, soups, stews, sweets, baked

"THE BEST IN THE MARKET."

AD FOR MEAT PRODUCTS.

dishes, salads, things fried in grease, and all the vast array of con-
fections, creams, pies, jellies, &c., were utterly swept aside from
the habitual eating of the people, and a simple meat diet substituted
in their place—we will be candid about it, and say in plain words,
an almost exclusive meat diet—the result would be greatly, very
greatly, in favor of that noble-bodied, pure-blooded, and superior
race we have had a leaning toward, in these articles of ours.

The effect of nearly all of these highly artificial dishes is to stim-
ulate and goad on the appetite, distend the stomach, thin the blood,
and prepare the way for some form or other of disease. They do not
harden a man in his fibre, nor make him any the better in wholesome flesh—as it is often to be noticed of such articles that the
greatest eaters of them are by no means the fattest, but often lean
and scraggly.

MEAT SOURCE: THE CHICAGO STOCKYARD.

The business of eating, in modern civilized life, is probably conducted on the most marked absence of principles, or of anything like reason or science, of aught that can be mentioned. And yet there is nothing in which there may be and ought to be more science displayed. It is here where physiology and medicine have yet to make their great foundationary beginnings—for with all the cry about medical accomplishment, in our times, it is plainly to be seen that, as far as the masses of the people are concerned, there is the same state of ignorance and darkness prevalent, that can be shown as marking any of the ages of the past.

We have been flooded in America, during the last fifteen or twenty years, with vast numbers of doctors, books, theories, publications, &c., whose general drift, with respect to diet, had been to make people live altogether on dry bread, stewed apples, or similar interesting stuff. What volumes of works have been issued from the different publishing houses, of which the foregoing is about the amount! Probably a more monstrous and enfeebling school could not be started; and yet it has undoubtedly obtained considerable foothold in the United States, especially in New England. In the latter quarter, the people are prone to be too intellectual, and to be "ashamed of the carnal body"—running very much to brains, at the expense of the brawn and muscle of their limbs. It is for this reason probably that in the eastern states the school we allude to [has] met with the greatest favor, and number the main part of their followers.

But in defiance of all that can be said in behalf of dry bread and stewed apples (good enough diet to deplete the system, at times, or in case of a fit of half sickness), we have no hesitation in publicly declaring our adherence to the motto previously inscribed—*Let the main part of the diet be meat, to the exclusion of all else.* The result of this would be that the digestive organs would have more than half the labor (agonizing labor, it often is,) withdrawn from them, and the blood relieved from an equally great amount of noxious deposit which, under the present system, is thrown into it.

This is very likely an astounding doctrine to the reader, who has perhaps been taught to believe, under the teachings of the school

"A HEALTHY SALAD?"

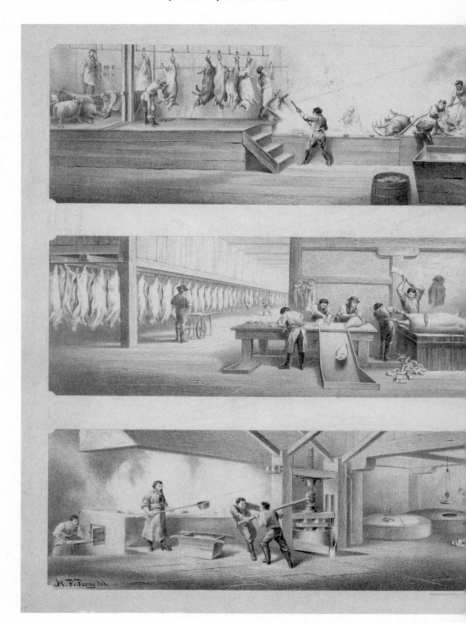

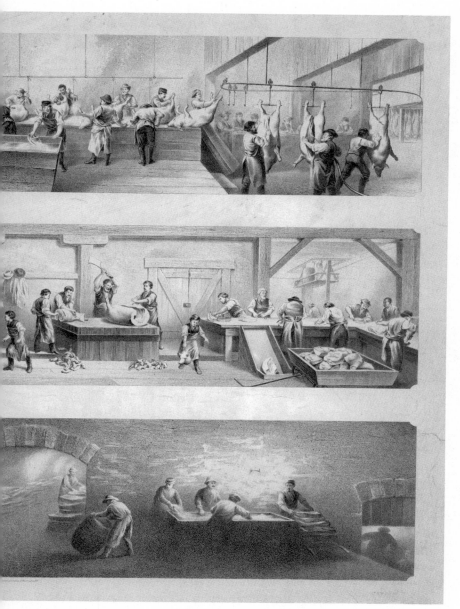

MEAT PRODUCTION IN THE NINETEENTH CENTURY.

aforesaid, that "temperance in eating" means vegetarianism, with all its weakening effects. But ours is the true doctrine, in our judgment, for all the northern and eastern states. We say less about hotter climates, because in those regions of perpetual fruits, there are other points to be considered. And it may be as well to add, that by meat diet, we do not mean the eating of meat cooked in grease and saturated therewith—or in any made dishes—but meat simply cooked, broiled, roasted, or the like. This is the natural eating of man and woman, under the first and unbiased appetites, and confirmed afterwards by the experience and the researches of reason.

"LOATHED MELANCHOLY," INDIVIDUAL AND NATIONAL— AND THE ONLY RADICAL CURE.

Brooding and all sorts of acrid thoughts, "the blues," and the varied train of depressed feelings, are among the most serious enemies of a fine physique—while the latter, in turn, possesses a marvellous power of scattering all those unpleasant visitors, and dissipating them to the winds. It is at least probable, we begin by saying, that in a vast majority of cases, melancholy of mind is the exclusive result of a disordered state of the body—a longer or shorter absence of those clarifying habits of diet, exercise, &c., which we have in previous articles jotted down for observance. If the victim of "the horrors" could but pluck up energy enough, after turning the key of his door-lock, to strip off all his clothes and gives [sic] his whole body a stinging rub-down with a flesh-brush till the skin becomes all red and aglow—then, donning his clothes again, take a long and brisk walk in the open air, expanding the chest and inhaling plentiful supplies of the health-giving element—ten to one but he would be thoroughly cured of his depression, by this alone.

Such habits, and what corresponds with them, becoming common, and especially if backed up with regular employment occupying the mind and the bodily powers for a stated portion of the day, and it were probable that the most inveterate case of melancholy would yield to those simple and harmless prescriptions.

For it is not generally realized what a wide circle of victims there is to this "ennui"—this word of France we have imported, for the English tongue hardly has any fit phrase to describe it. If one were to set out investigating the matter, it would probably be found that these victims exist in almost countless numbers, in all ranks of people in America, the working classes just the same as the rich. Not only the idler in his parlor, and without and [sic] need of occupying his time in an employment to procure his living—not only the literary man, with his overstrained mentality—or the professional person, the lawyer at his desk, the clergyman in his study, the student at his books—not these any more than the mechanic, the farmer, the carpenter, mason, boatman—and especially those of sedentary employments, the printer, shoemaker, tailor, and others at their listless work indoors—all, all are to be numbered among the habitual sufferers from the cause we have mentioned. Nor would our hints be complete without some allusion to this one of the most serious detriments to all the wholesome operations of the manly system, sapping the strength and shortening life.

What does this too prevailing melancholy in such people result from? From their bad condition of body, very generally—the reaction of the powers, often from the stimulus of drink, or other exciting causes. In those that do not drink, the stomach and nervous system are very likely out of order, after months, perhaps years, of heedless violations of natural laws—a long course of artificial living, depositing its bad dregs at last in such a way that they have effectually clogged that natural buoyancy and lightness of temperament, that nonchalance and passive [sic] and even gaiety, which seem to be at least as much the birthright of man as of any other animal. A sad and terrible price, is it not, at which even civilization and the splendid results of these improvements of arts, literature, laws, and social culture, may almost be considered to cost too much? For this same curse of sadness, in its numberless forms, is an attribute of civilized life, and must be met with those weapons which can destroy it—an infusion through civilized life of a greater degree of natural physical habits, and a stern rejection of those specious enjoyments that leave such frightful deposits afterward, that sting and fester through the middle and later years.

Nor let any one be deceived in this matter of low spirits, by the outside appearance of people as they move about in the streets, in public houses, places of amusement, &c. In public, no doubt you would judge from the show upon the surface that every one was happy, and that there was no such thing as a cloud upon the sky of the mind; all goes so well, and there is so much drinking and eating, and joking and laughing and gay music. The faces are full of color, the eyes sparkle, the voices have a ring—everybody is well dressed, and there is surely no unhappiness in these lives. A serious mistake! Many and many a silent hour, both by day and night, does every one here undergo, in which the distress of the mind equals any distress of the body, in its worst sickness or hurt. The evil we speak of, like most other human evils, is not of a kind that flaunts out and exposes itself, but is only to be detected by the powers of insight and acute observation. To those powers there is perhaps no rank of the community, and no group of men collected together, but the presence of it can be plainly seen, passive enough, but still lurking there. It shows itself in the lines of the face, cut and seamed by harrassing [*sic*] thoughts, and many an hour of discontent and nausea of life. The very classes that would be supposed to be freest from the visitations of this grim spirit—those who live a gay and reckless life, following where the animal passions lead and the appetite of gain—even those whose career is the career of prostitution, "pleasure" and play—are the very persons who give some of the most striking illustrations of its presence and effects. Some of the members of these classes (we were going to say all of them,) are subject to terrible fits of despondency and "the horrors," lasting day after day, and even, in a few instances, for weeks on the stretch—a curious study for those inquirers who indeed think that the proper study for mankind is man, with all the strange play of his interwoven warp of passions, appetites, pains and joys.

Further than this, the middle ranks of society, the sturdy body of

MELANCHOLIA.

American workingmen, even the young, afford plentiful examples of a similar sort. There seems to be something, not only in our Saxon stock, but in all the intergrafts we have here in America from the Celtic nations also, that forms the popular disposition, at times, to fits of melancholy—each individual after his or her own form special of outlet and expression. Otherwise we should be unable to account for the fact of so many of the class we have mentioned being included in the list. For that they are included we feel certain. What one of them but has his periods, (in a majority of cases frequent, and in many severe,) sombre and gloomy fits, when the whole world appears cheerless and bleak, and the best of life not worth the living? During these fits, any effort at conversation is unpleasant, and the machinery of the mind turns with a slow motion—no alertness, no spring or vivacity—incapacitated from all the talents and accomplishments that are ready enough at other times. Sometimes, in the working classes, these periods of depression become habitual, and take up the majority of the years of life—more usually in the cases of those whose occupations are sedentary, as in those, beforementioned, of tailors, shoemakers, &c.

All we are here saying is but the candid mention of a series of pregnant and positive facts, which it is impossible to deny, and which will be readily admitted by those who have looked with thinking eyes through the strata of middle society—not on the surface merely, but down in its recesses, in habits, homes, occupations, and especially during those hours when life is lived according to what itself is, inherently, and not from second-hand influences, imitation, gentility, or disguises, or, "the looks." We know very well that the subject we treat of is not often, hardly ever, indeed, mentioned in this way; but we are clear that it *ought* to be mentioned, and met, too, as every other great fact of bearings on the popular happiness or unhappiness should be. This is the only way of getting at such things, and it is all folly to cover them up or avoid them.

Through the "upper" ranks of society, it is well known, the undertone of existence is that of listlessness and low spirits—running in every vein of fashionable dawdling and occupation. The same cast appears in literature, in every volume where the imagination bears a part, giving a heavy and depressing cast to all. The novel-hero of the writers is always a gentleman who has sentimental moods— also, misfortunes and tragic adventures, placing him in all sorts of forlorn predicaments; and the same with tragedies. But we will not travel aside from our own special track.

We have dwelt at more length on this topic of "the blues," (to give it that expressive and cant name, which is common,) because we are firmly convinced that the hint we uttered at the commencement of our remarks on this branch, is possessed of the true secret of pricking and bursting the bubble—for bubble it is, even allowing all that can be said of hereditary tendency. That same tendency not only has the weakness itself, but the strength, reason, and ability to surmount it, under proper circumstances. *The observance of the laws of manly training, duly followed, can utterly rout and do away with the curse of a depressed mind, melancholy, "ennui," which now, in more than half the men of America, blights a large portion of the days of their existence.* Of this we have not the least particle of doubt—and, indeed, the thing stands to reason.

We repeat it, that it is the bad stuff stagnating in the phisical [*sic*] system, accumulated through long seasons of artificial eating, drinking, and "pleasure," (a sad mistake of a name as generally applied,) that returns in a morbid action of the mind and temper. This is the true cause at the bottom of that painful and wide-spread effect. We are not sure but the same cause is at the bottom of another still more dreadful effect—Insanity. Such was Spurzheim's deliberate opinion, if we are not mistaken in our inferences from the hints he drops in his work on that terrible malady. This celebrated and keen observer and student, after passing through all that could be found and got at, treating insanity as a "disease of the mind," seems to have learned at last that the most important points lay in another direction—physical facts and causes, including, of course, the hereditary ones. And all brooding and melancholy are the first faint tinges, of which insanity is the set color, deep and strong.

Of this aforesaid varied group of ills, then and therefore, we are firm in the conviction that the point of concentration, where, by medical men, the same as the rest, and perhaps more than the first, they are to be studied, and from which, as originally, they all spring, finally they are all to be touched there for the only effectual cure, is the point of the physical. *The body—the stomach—the blood—the nervous system—the physical brain, and what affects it for good or bad—in other words, a rational and elevated system of MANLY TRAINING*—we believe that knowledge and practice in that direction only will put to effectual flight all the phantom swarms of "loathed melancholy," so threaten-ing with their growth of worse mental derangements, now prevalent through the many classes of men here in the United States.

Have we made ourselves understood? For it is no small thing, reader, we have taken upon ourselves to treat in this section of our hints, and we have thrown out, in a rapid manner, these suggestions, in all candor, more to open the subject, and lead you to think upon it yourself, and to behold it in what we are sure is its true light, to be deliberated upon thoughtfully afterwards, than as any finished presentation of our views upon it.

There is such a deplorable ignorance everywhere, (we are more and more convinced,) of the surpassing importance of these physical considerations—these which refer to the human being, as a perfect animal, and to *the sublime science of breeding a nation of sane and cleanfleshed men.* All treatment of evils of any sort whatever, especially those evils we have just been considering, that contemplates anything less than such a science, it but patchwork and poor botching. We are, therefore, unable to apply other terms than those which end the last sentence to the usual "reforms" of the theorists of the day—as to most of the schools of the doctors, the metaphysicians, and the moralists, of which America is so rife.

When we hear the preachers preaching from their pulpits, and the lecturers from their platforms—and all the outpourings of the numerous well-intended philanthropists who flood New York with their "May anniversaries," and gatherings at the same—we see clearly enough, for our own satisfaction, that, (putting them all in a bundle together) the wisdom and application of their efforts is just precisely the wisdom of him who should attempt to medicate the superficial sores and boils on a sick body, by nothing better than surface applications, (or by praying to the sores and boils, and exhorting them to begone!) when the only cure, in the mind of a sensible person worth trial, is *the deep, interior, sane cure of the whole quality of the blood and the tissues it forms*, which make the body—a generative and altogether physical cure, involving years of time, and revolution of habits—this the vaunted reformers appear never to think of.

(CONTINUED NEXT WEEK.)

The New York Atlas.

Vol. 21, No. 28

Manly Health and Training,

November 28, 1858

With Off-Hand Hints Toward Their Conditions

By Mose Velsor

THE UNDERBELLY OF NEW YORK.

VIRILITY—PROSTITUTION.

The noblest function of mankind, the power to procreate the soundest and most perfect offspring, ought to remain to a man all through those years we have mentioned in a preceding article, as eligible, under proper training, for him to be in a high, flush condition of health, strength, beauty and happiness—namely, from the twenty-third or -fourth to at least the sixty-fifth year of his age. If, during his early years, he become diseased with any form of venereal taint—especially if that be repeated upon him again and again, as in too many cases—of course there is so much strength, and the prospect of longevity taken away; which, in the same train, deprive his system of its true procreative power. A man that exhausts himself continually among women, is not fit to be, and cannot be, the father of sound and manly children. They will be puny and scrofulous—a torment to themselves and to those who have the charge of them.

This virile power, so becoming to a man, and without which, indeed, he is not a man, seems, in modern life, to be under the curse of an insane appetite, especially among the youth of cities, which makes them think they are doing great things if they commence early with women, and keep up afterwards a huge number of intrigues and amours—having no choice about it, but sweeping at all that is female, as a fisherman sweeps fish into his net. This is one reason we see the lamentable spectacle, in New York, and other cities, of so many *old-men boys*—youths who have begun long before their time, and will never know the true feelings and attributes of that, in some respects, most glorious age, from fourteen years to twenty-one or -two—

163

but jump at once from the traits and tastes of childhood, unto all the experiences of mature age. We say this state of things is throwing a bad ingredient in the stock of the population of our cities. You see them in all directions, not without good qualities, perhaps, but in their physique feeble, small, and pale—not the large and rude-natured specimens of humanity that would seem to be called for in America. Their offspring, when in time they marry and have families, illustrate what we said in the first part of our paragraph, and, indeed, if we must be candid about it, are no credit either to their parentage or to the land.

It is related of the ancient Germans, by the Roman writers of that time, that, although in a harsh climate and with a rugged soil, they produced the finest races of men, as far as physique was concerned, then known; and also that it was the stern custom of Germania, in those primitive periods, for the young men to be so educated and trained that they had nothing to do with women till they were twenty-six or -seven years old. Our readers can ponder a while over these facts, for they are full of meaning.

There is no doubt, as things now are, among the young men of modern civilized life, in cities, that a healthy manly virility seems to be almost lost—seems to have given place to a morbid, almost insane, pursuit of women, especially of the lowest ranges of them, for the mere repetition of the sensual pleasure.

This habit, begun by a young fellow, (generally from the contagion of his companions,) and afterward formed into a regular indulgence, *that* is a case where there cannot be produced by training or any other means, a superior specimen of animal perfection, strength and beauty.

We have not read Dr. Sanger's late work, of which so much is said on the subject of female prostitution; but we dare say he has overlooked some of the most important points connected with the subject. For, great as the facts and their bearings are, with reference to the females themselves, the prostitutes, we think the most weighty of the facts, and all their bearings, out of this subject of prostitution, are those which affect men. *The effects of prostitution upon men*—there is the text for the work that should be written.

FANNY WHITE (LEFT), ANTEBELLUM NYC'S BEST-KNOWN
COURTESAN, SPEAKING TO A YOUNG COLLEAGUE.

It involves deep studies and investigations, through the popular strata of modern life—all through the masses of youth, and of men of the younger ranks, (and older ranks, too, for that matter,) in the cities,—and then radiating back again into the country regions. To us, it [*sic*] this time, and from the point of view we are now taking it is the question of physique that is affected, and of the race as a fine collection of animals—but out of that, of course, is developed all the rest, the effects upon the minds, morals, social usages, tempers, perpetuity, &c., &c., of the immense rounds of persons further affected by their causes.

One thing is very certain to any man who is at all familiar with the popular understrata of the life of our great cities—*not* that mere life upon the surface; a thin glaze of respectability and decorum which, we suppose, deceives only those who either willingly shut their eyes, or have very little power of vision anyhow.

It is, we say, quite certain that, at this very hour, *there is circulating through nearly all of the life-streams of this city, and of all great cities, a sure and increasing amount of the tainted blood of prostitution, morbid, venereal and scrofulous—and that there is probably not a street in New York where it does not now exist, and show its effects in human veins, on the human countenance, and in the birth of an enfeebled offspring.*

Those are the facts to which we would like to call passing attention, by virtue of our duty as a writer on this subject of health—and considering it, not only in the matter of the daily wholesome observances we have advised, but deeper, as an important race question, and one affected, in a most serious manner, and likely to be affected far more deeply, by the existence of the facts just treated upon.

MUSCULAR POWER AND ENDURANCE— LOCOMOTION—THE CARE OF THE FEET—DANCING.

We have before intimated that we feel inclined to doubt whether we have, hereabout, any examples of the *utmost perfection of muscular power and endurance* which man is capable of attaining to. The feats performed by the "strong men" of the shows are worthy of attention, as far as they go; but, when we have inquired into the special cases of the said "strong men," we have invariably found that each individual was the victim of habits which retarded the full development of his power. In all such cases, the power continues as a sort of monstrosity for a year or two, and the "strong man" then becomes perhaps a poor wreck, the ruins of what might have easily lasted through a long life, and been far more highly developed under a proper and sustained course of physical training.

Nothing indeed, amid the infinate [*sic*] wonders of nature, is a greater wonder than the muscular strength of certain specimens of the human body, even as things are, and have been. Many of these specimens, both in old times and new, are well authenticated. Especially in former days, when physical superiority was more generally attended to and admired than now, were there marked cases of this immense bodily energy. The relation and perusal of some of them are well calculated to provoke serviceable thoughts in the mind, and to beget a manly emulation in the same course[.]

In the Greek city of Krotona, in ancient times, one of the athletes, named Milo, accustomed himself from early years, by almost imperceptible degrees, to carry burthens of increasing weight, day after day—joining to that, of course, the other means of producing and confirming the strength and fibre of his body. He persisted in this a number of years, until at last, it is credibly reported, that in the height and strength of his vigor, he actually carried an ox four years old, and weighing upwards of a thousand pounds, for about forty yards, and then struck the animal and killed it dead with one blow of his fist! (We might offer the above—which we may say we don't think so unreasonable as some will at first sight suppose— as a special encouragement yet to Johnny Heenan, as against Morrissey. If *such things* can be done, by human training and muscular energy, even that miraculous endurance and passiveness that won the fight at Long Point, might yet be overcome.[)] This same Milo was six times crowned at the Olympian Games, for his enormous feats of strength, agility and endurance—for all those faculties went together; but the greatest of his points was strength. He was one of the disciples of Pythagoras; and to that same strength the master himself, and several others, owed their lives—for once, in school, the supports under the roof giving way, Milo uplifted the whole of the upper works, giving the philosopher and the rest time to escape, and others a chance to secure the roof from precipitate fall.

Milo was celebrated for such feats as pulling up a respectable-sized tree by the roots—and similar interesting little amusements. We would like the reader, at the same time, to take notice of what we said about this "muscle man" being a student, and doubtless a favorite one, of one of the most celebrated philosophers of antiquity—for *then* the pursuit of the means toward a superb and mighty-sinewed body was not considered anything else than appropriately joined with the most elevating and refining studies of the intellect.

Augustus Eleventh, a king of Poland, could roll up a silver plate, like a sheet of paper, and twist the strongest horse-shoe asunder. We suppose many of our readers must have seen men in the shows who could break quite large-sized stones with a blow of the fist; at any rate we have several times seen such men, and satisfied ourselves that there was no humbug in it. We may, perhaps, as well add to this casual list, a mention of some of the blows given in the Morrissey and Heenan fight—two or three of those blows are said, by old visitors to the prize-ring, here and in England, to have been the heaviest they ever saw given. They would have, without doubt, been certain death to any man not prepared for them by that condition of perfect training which the combatants had both undergone for four months before fighting.

(Four months is no time at all—better say *four years*; for when the time is small, the injurious fatigue of crowding so much into so small a space, destroys and reacts upon itself. Training ought not to be that hurried and hateful thing it is generally made, on account of these forced reasons, but rather a pleasant, acceptable, gradual, and every way welcomed season of a man's life.)

We were reading, the other day, in a book of travels in Asia, that a Hindoo runner will run not only all day long, but day after day, by the side of a European traveling on horseback—enduring the travel much better than the horse, or the rider of the horse. Habit, and a

certain agility and litheness of body, which seem to be characteristic of the Hindoo, make the endurances of these runners among
the most remarkable illustrations known of the muscular power
of the human body. Indeed, from what we have heard about them,
it would seem as if all the running and walking feats we ever have
here in America were mere child's play to what is constantly done
in India; and that even our famed performances of "walking a thousand miles in a thousand hours," are nothing at all to blow about
considering what is common off [*sic*] there.

MAN ON HORSEBACK.

So much is done by the imperceptible effects of education. A Turkish porter, for instance, will trot at a rapid pace, carrying a weight of six hundred pounds. You "muscle men" of New York! you will have to improve yourselves considerably yet, we are thinking.

Probably the best and truest average test of muscular endurance and power exists in the locomotive organs, and in their performances. *Walking is nature's great physical energy*—and, in some form or other, after all, includes the whole expression of life, the passions, and the outshowing of active beauty. Well did the old Greeks, in their highest and most refined games, concentrate their training, and the main interest and fruit of the same, to the point of producing the swiftest and longest-continued locomotion; for they knew, what it is time we should know, that *all that goes to make up the heroic physique, and its elements and powers, out of which the other kinds of perfect-bodied men branch and develope themselves—all the stuff of those elements and powers is to be found in the best runners.* In other words, there can be no grand physique, for anything, unless it stand well on its legs, and have great locomotive strength and endurance. Make a note of this, reader, and commence regular habits of walking—not forgetting other means of attention to the health, ease, and improvement of the feet, ankles, knees, and all the lower muscles.

The ease of the feet and legs, and their freedom from many of the nonsensical and hurtful environments of modern fashion, are to be insisted on, to begin with. Most of the usual fashionable boots and shoes, which neither favor comfort, nor health, nor the ease of walking, are to be discarded. In favorable weather, the shoe now specially worn by the base-ball players would be a very good improvement to be introduced for general use.

It should be carefully selected to the shape of the foot, or, better still, made from lasts modeled to the exact shape of the wearer's feet, (as all boots should be.) In a matter of such consequence as ease and pleasure of walking, these things are of serious weight, and cannot be overlooked. Of course, fashion must stand [to] one side, if we are going to enter into the spirit of the thing seriously; *no man can serve the two masters, of frivolous fashion and the*

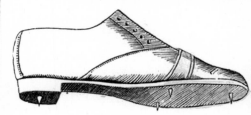

BASEBALL SHOES.

AD FOR A NEW YORK SHOE STORE.

attainment of robust health and physique, at the same time. You will have to stand out a little; but, like the first shock of entering a swimming-bath, it only needs a little determination at first, and the thing is done.

The daily bathing of the feet in cold water, we have before spoken of. This practice should never be intermitted. The feet, legs, thighs, &c., should also be subjected to the friction of a stiff bristle brush—just the same as the upper limbs. The clothing of the feet is of importance; clean cotton socks in summer, and woolen in winter, carefully selected as to the size. These are little things, but on such little things much depends—yes, even the greatest results depend. And it is, perhaps, to be noted, that many a man who is mighty careful of his *outside* apparel—his visible coat, vest, neckcloth, jewelry, &c., is habitually careless of the fixings and condition of his feet. Most of the unpleasantness from cold feet, under which many suffer, would also, by following our precepts, be obviated. In this connection, we desire to enter our protest against the use—already too prevalent, and getting more and more so—of the India-rubber shoe; it is a bad article, obstructing the perspiration, and in many ways injuring the feet. There is nothing better for this weather than good leather boots—the feet being, besides, well protected by fresh woolen stockings.

We recommend dancing, as worthy of attention, in a different manner from what use is generally made of that amusement; namely, as capable of being made a great help to develop the flexibility and strength of the hips, knees, muscles of the calf, ankles, and feet. Dancing, on true principles, would have ultimate reference to that, and would then, as an inevitable result, bring grace of movement along with it. There is no reason why, in a good gymnasium, the art of dancing should not also be included, with the intents and purposes we speak of.

[CONTINUED NEXT WEEK.]

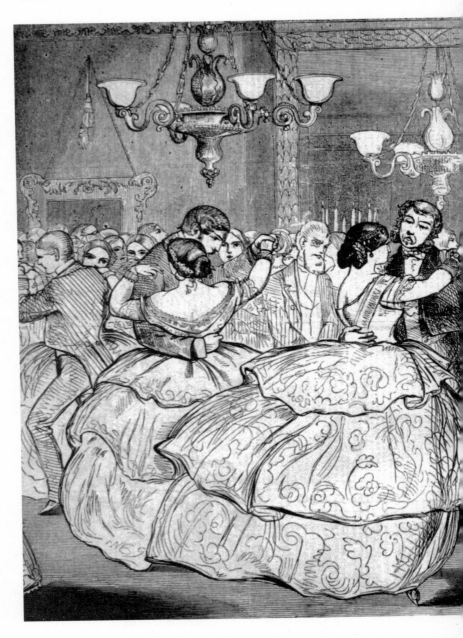

BALLROOM DANCING IN THE 1850s.

The New York Atlas.

Vol. 21, No. 30

Manly Health and Training,

December 12, 1858

With Off-Hand Hints Toward Their Conditions

By Mose Velsor

MAN ICE-SKATING.

We have before alluded to the necessity of conforming to all propositions of reform, in manly physique or anything else, as far as possible to the habits and institutions of the day—in conforming to the employments, the common hours of work, and, to some extent, even the prejudices of the people. It is therefore best for those who would follow our advice, in the matter of training, to do so without making any "blow" about it, or setting themselves up in opposition to the right of others to pursue their course also—and likewise without any special vaunts of superior judgment and wisdom. The true trainer is generally known by his quietness and serenity, and never by putting on airs; and the trained man should copy him in these respects.

Besides, after all, in modern society, especially here in America, there is such diversity of taste, and so large an infusion, (getting larger and larger every day,) of what we believe the philosophers call "individuality," that a person having any disposition to follow our rules, no matter in what situation of life he may be, or where he may live, can, in the main, do so, without serious impediment or annoyance, so long as he is quiet and self-possessed about it. In all the habitudes of diet and exercise, it is to be considered sufficient if the subject can obey them in the long run, without minding special little interruptions of a meal or so, or of a day or part of a day, which will sometimes be unavoidably forced upon him. The vigor and tone of the manly frame, (as before remarked,) are the result of the average course of life, for months, and years, and, in general, need not be seriously disturbed by a casual omission. For all this, which we say by way of consolation for the offences which must come, let the reader understand that our rules are intended to be as consistently and faithfully adhered to as possible—the omissions never without danger.

HEALTH OR DISEASE FOLLOW REGULAR LAWS.

It is too generally taken for granted that the formation and preservation of manly strength, and of all those points that conduce to longevity, are the result of accidents, hap-hazard chances, "luck." We wish distinctly to impress it upon the reader that, speaking in general terms, there is no hap-hazard or luck about the matter. In the case of brute animals, all that is necessary is to follow the natural instincts—and, in their case, health is preserved by the perpetual surroundings of the open air, and by the absence of artificial preparations of food. But man, in an artificial life, has come under the control of his reason, judgment, calculation—with frequent self-denials. We all live surrounded by these artificial circumstances—many of them unfavorable to health and condition. The important object to be gained is, to form the habit of considering these things with reference to their results on the physique—and not any longer accepting them indifferently whenever placed in the midst of them, whether injurious or no.

We repeat it, health and manly strength are under the control of regular and simple laws, and will surely follow the adoption of the means which we have jotted down in the foregoing articles. Indeed, we have often thought, without elaborate study of these laws of health, the desired result might be almost always attained by a little exercise of common sense on the part of him who realised the needlessness and evil of a weak and impure body, and the sure way of retrieving it.

BAD BLOOD.

In the shortest way of stating it the cause of disease is bad blood—often hereditary, more often from persistence in bad habits.

The object of training is, it may also be stated, to simply purify and invigorate the blood—and when that result is attained, to keep it so.

When we look over the long lists of maladies making such a terrible catalogue, with new additions every year, one is ready to be discouraged, from any attempt at renovation and the establishment of a better order of things—especially, when the doctor's books are studied, with all their formidable arrays of technical terms, (and technical nonsense we were going to add—but that is not in the innocent words, only in the narrowness and short-sight of too many who claim the name of physician.) The discouragement we allude to will be greatly obviated by discarding nineteen-twentieths of the confusing influence of mere names, and looking at this matter of health and disease in the plain bearing of general facts. After that, the particulars may be studied with as much detail as any one will.

Certain habits, be it definitely understood, invariably produce bad blood and a lowered tone of the system—if continued long enough, ending in what is generally called "a ruined constitution."

How many young men there are in New York, and all our great American cities, who, just for a transient indulgence in a few questionable "pleasures," are thus destroying the priceless treasure of their manhood, strength and virility.

There is, (to make a primitive statement of the matter,) always so much latent possibility of disease in a man's body—as [if] it were sleeping there, ready to be waked up at any time into powerful and destructive action. So long as the system is kept in good order by healthy observances, there is no trouble from these latent germs; but all forms of dissipation and violations of natural law arouse them and cause them to come rapidly forward. Then fevers, rheumatism, colds, consumption, inflammation, or some other of the scourges—generally looked upon, in the most ignorant manner, as accidental results! Of course, to one who has caught the least portion of the spirit of our theory of training, *this* error, at least, has become exploded—and he will look on all health and all illness as a play of sensible cause and effect, just as much as building a house, or pulling it down again.

THE THROAT.

From various reasons, at the present time, (gradually accumulating in strength and frequency for the last fifty years,) a very large proportion of the violations of the laws of health have concentrated in their results in *the throat*. To our mind the following are some of the leading causes: feeble and scrofulous parentage, precocious youthful indulgences and passions, a too various and too artificial diet, distilled liquors, syphilitic taint, sedentary employments, continual breathing of stale air, the use of drugs and medicines, &c., &c. More than half the diseases of the throat come from bad digestion, or no digestion, producing bad blood—in other words come from the stomach. Have *you* any one of the numerous forms of throat affection? To modify it, perhaps entirely cure it, here is your first course of remedy: discard three-quarters of the varied and unwholesome articles which you have been in the habit of eating, especially for dinner and supper. Make your principal meal, as often as possible, on a slice of beef or mutton, cooked rare, without grease—avoiding every other dish, with scrupulous self-denial. Sup lightly, drink nothing but water, and breathe as much fresh air, winter and summer, as possible.

Keep the feet well protected, and use them daily in exercise.

The beard is a great sanitary protection to the throat—for purposes of health it should always be worn, just as much as the hair of the head should be. Think what would be the result if the hair of the head should be carefully scraped off three or four times a week with the razor! Of course, the additional aches, neuralgias, colds, &c., would be immense. Well, it is just as bad with removing the natural protection of the neck; for nature indicates the necessity of that covering there, for full and sufficient reasons.

Of the throat, it may, perhaps, as well be added that its health and strength are doubtless aided by forming the habit of throwing the voice out from it, and not from the mouth only, as many do. The best Italian singers, it will be noticed, have that utterance—sending out the sound from the back of the mouth; in most of the

New England states the bad-sounding and unwholesome practice of speaking through the front of the mouth only, and through the nose as much as the mouth, is very prevalent.

We have said that the bad condition of the general health ends and shows itself, in many cases, in these throat-diseases spoken of. We are not sure but this is almost invariably the case; for we have noticed that persons with the aforesaid throat-diseases are those whose blood is bad, either clogged with the thick and morbid consequences of gluttony and inebriate habits, or else the thin and watery blood of persons whose food does not assimilate to and nourish the system. Because what is there in the throat itself, the windpipe, (trachea) or the bronchial tubes, (two continuations forking down from the trachea, and leading into the lungs[)]—what is there in these, or their ramifications, to become diseased except from bad blood? Medicines, for any of the ailments of the throat will of course be ordered by the ordinary physician, and may give temporary relief—but the only effectual medicine lies in *the entire purification and renovation of the life of the body, the blood,* after the spirit of the hints we have jotted down in our foregoing articles. It must be borne in mind also, that one of the greatest dangers of all throat-diseases is that they lead to the last and most dreaded result of all bad blood, consumption,—lungs honeycombed and consumed—the destruction of the power to vivify the blood. Much is said in books, newspapers, schools of medicines, and among the doctors, over the question, can consumption be cured? When the evil processes have gone on long enough to destroy a lung, or a great portion of the lung, it is vain to think of restoring the lost member, of course; and, in most cases, the best that can be done is to stave off the final dissolution as long as possible. But the true statement to put before the people is that which makes them realize *what causes consumption,* and all other serious diseases of the lungs, throat, and the like. It is absurd to confuse the plain popular mind with volleys of technical terms, doctor's Latin, &c.; the simple underlying truths should be set forth in common English and made to come home to the experience and understanding of every one.

Walt Whitman

VIRTUE OF OUT-DOORS, AND
A STIRRING LIFE.

What is the reason that a voyage to sea, or a journey to California, or off for months and months in a wild country, perhaps exposed to many unusual hardships and privations, half-starved, or fed on what, under ordinary circumstances, would prove unwholesome food—what is the reason, we say, that this often proves the means of re-establishing the health previously in decay, or quite given up? The actual reason of any case, necessitates a knowledge of the special particulars of that case; for there are hardly any two that are precisely alike (which proves the folly of the usual pretensions of the cure-all medicines).

Generally speaking there is that virtue in the open air, and a stirring life therein, that has more effect than any or all the prescriptions that go forth from the apothecary's shop. Hunters, raftsmen, lumbermen, and all those whose employments are away from the close life and dissipation of cities—what specimens of manly strength and beauty they frequently are! We throw out this sort of hint, in our usual rapid way, for you, reader, to cogitate upon, and draw the moral yourself.

Not that we wish to see you take to the woods or rivers—for we think you can attain all the desired results without leaving your home in the city, if you choose to stay here. But to hint that, so long as you give up your own self-control and allow yourself to be a victim to all these pestiferous little gratifications that are offered to you in the city, so long will you present a marked contrast to the noble physique of the lumberman and hunter.

Often, a complete change of scene, associations, companionship, habits, &c., is the best thing that can be done for a man's health, (and the change is perhaps beneficial to a further extent in his morals, knowledge, &c.) If you are "in a bad way" from associations, &c., wisdom and courage both indicate to you to pull up stakes and leave for a new spot—careful there to begin aright, and persevere with energy. This advice is of more necessity than might be supposed. There are thousands of young men now in New

York, and in all American cities, who go on year after year, slaves of habits they know to be bad, but pressing close and helpless upon them, because they are also the habits of their friends and intimate companions. To such, our counsel is, Up and away!

COLD WEATHER—DRESS, &C.

The winter has now set in, and some remarks appropriate to it may not be amiss. In America, where the close stove is used everywhere, much injury to health results therefrom, in consequence of the frequent and sudden changes of temperature, vibrating every hour or two between the bitter cold of the out-door air and the stifling heat of an unventilated room, warmed by a red hot coal fire. Neither the throat or lungs can stand such abrupt changes, continued month after month, and winter after winter. Neuralgia, aching joints, colds, coughs, &c., joined with inflammations and fevers, and great derangements of the stomach and bowels, are among the liabilities of health at the commencement of winter; for a change in the temperature "strikes in" where the subject has bad stuff in him, and stirs it up to action, one way or another. As to general habits, especially of diet, we can but refer the reader to our former articles, confident that they will apply to a greater or less extent to every case that can be devised. We would, however, make a few remarks upon *dress*, as appropriate for the winter. Many persons dress too much in winter for their own good—too much for the very purpose of keeping warm. Excess of clothing is really one of the most frequent causes of that tender sensitiveness to cold, which is so annoying in our climate, resulting in a morbidly sensitive skin, and thence great suffering from all those exposures to cold air, which, of course, in our climate, are almost unavoidable.

The best rule is, instead of putting on all the clothing one can stand, to dress as lightly as is consistent with comfort, at the same time affording all parts of the body their requisite protection. The most prevalent error, of course, is too little protection about the feet, and too much about the head and neck. Since shaving has come in practice, (it ought to be scouted entirely from all northern

ICE-SKATING SCENE.

countries,) and since heavy mufflers, neck-winders, shawls, &c., have got to be generally used, all sorts of head and throat distempers have multiplied a hundred fold [*sic*]. A physician of our acquaintance once informed us that he had known several cases of liability to throat-inflammation entirely cured by simply washing the neck regularly every morning, the year round, in cool water, and dispensing with all thick "comforters" in winter, with nothing but a light and loose handkerchief, leaving the throat open.

We have spoken before of the morning ablutions—we mean the cool bath for the whole body. No doubt many of our readers will start back in dismay from such a proposition [in] this weather; yet this is what we seriously mean. Not, be it well understood, for the feeble, the puny, the invalid, but for the robust, the young, and the sound only. This, cautiously begun, and by degrees formed into a habit, will so invigorate the whole surface as to make one indifferent during the day to the severest cold, and enjoy comfort in it, while others are chilly and shivering.

Then, after all is said about dress and other outside observances, we revert back to our theory of the other final understratum of warmth, health, comfort, and any other bodily perfection, viz., good blood—all sound inside. "The life-principle within," somebody has wisely observed, "is our main protection against the elements without." Yes, and against all the bodily changes, and the liabilities to disease. The quality of the blood, and the state of its circulation—if these are amiss, no care or amount of dress will keep a man warm or comfortable. They have to do with the condition of the skin, which, of course, is nothing in itself, but only a register or medium, to act between the "life principle" inside the body and the elements without.

In walking, these wintry days, we see that the men through our streets have adopted the fashion of carrying themselves with head bent downward, and arms and shoulders tightly drawn in—very much after the mode of the turtle withdrawing its head into its shell. We submit that such is not the habit a man should form for his walking style—but always go with the head erect and breast expanded—always throwing open the play of the great vital organs, inhaling the good air into the throat, lungs and stomach, and giving tone to the whole system thereby.

Another thing; hot drinks of all kinds do more hurt than good in cold weather—there is always a reaction. The morbid habit of drinking excessively, (we include tea, coffee, and water also, just the same,) is at any season pernicious to the sound state of the body, and especially so in winter. We advise the reader, if he be ambitious of that kind of a "good time" which is superior to all others, perfect bodily comfort in winter, to follow the old maxim, "keep the feet warm and the head cool," the body evenly and moderately clad, studying all our preceding articles and faithfully observing their directions—continuing on with a couple of others that are to follow, (for we are drawing nigh [*sic*] the end of our rope)—accustom himself as much as convenient to outdoor exercise—and thus, we assure him, he will, in all likelihood, pass through the winter with a degree of pleasure that will not only more than repay him for his trouble, but will give him new ideas of the capacity of bliss the simple sensation of "feeling well" is able to produce.

(CONTINUED NEXT WEEK.)

The New York Atlas.

Vol. 21, No. 31

Manly Health and Training,

December 19, 1858

With Off-Hand Hints Toward Their Conditions

By Mose Velsor

A BACK-ALLEY IN NEW YORK CITY'S FIVE POINTS SLUM.

[CONTINUED FROM LAST WEEK.]

In the course of reading one of these articles only, we must here remark, *en passant,* the student of health and a manly physique will by no means be apt to get a fair view of our positions, and of those points that have a bearing on the subject. *It is necessary that all the preceding articles of this series should be carefully read also.* We have there jotted down, as they presented themselves to our mind, most of the primary rules that are to be followed by him who would achieve a sound and clear-blooded condition of body. We have spoken of health as being the real foundation of all manly beauty, and have done our part toward dissipating the pink-and-white doll-theory of masculine good appearance. We have shown that all sickliness is fatal to beauty, and the inference follows, unavoidably, that much of the prevailing taste is morbid and unsound.

Our series is drawing to a close. This article, and one more to follow, finishes them. Disconnected as our mode of writing has been, and intended from the first to be given off-hand and just as the subjects presented themselves to our mind, we are aware that the reader who peruses one article only, will not see the drift of our writing—which we should consider an entire failure if, in a total review of it, we did not find to be compact, effective for the purpose it aims at, and comprehensive. To those of our readers who have seen only partial sections of this series, we can only repeat our charge and wish that they procure the entire series, which, if they take an interest in the subject, will amply repay them, and give them, we are sure, many new and useful items of information.

For these two concluding numbers of our series, we find we have a few more items to give, which we shall proceed to jot down in the same manner as hitherto.

The object of a correspondent, who writes to complain of

our series that "the spirit of such articles is to make an entire nation of fighting men," we think we have already answered in a preceding section. If not, we may as well confess that we do not deny the charge, but admit it. We would be quite willing to have the young men of America thoroughly trained to be able to give a good account of themselves in all contests, muscular, military, naval, and otherwise. As to the danger of belligerent habits, why for that we must take chances. We would rather see an occasional "muss," either on a small scale or a large one, than that continual and supple obedience which the opposite tack would be likely to produce.

Another correspondent (for we have had several,) objects to our statement of the time that a man ought to be in good condition, and considers it, for general purposes, quite chimerical to expect that a man, in modern times, can last, in robust tone, from his twenty-fourth or -fifth to his sixty-fifth year. Very well—our correspondent is of one opinion, and we are of another; that's the difference. We dare say a great many of the views we have expressed will find denials here and there; but what would be worth those statements that only repeat what is already so well known that it would meet a ready assent everywhere?

We do not think, indeed, upon referring to our already written articles, that we have given sufficient prominence to the subject of middle age, in all its bearings, and with reference to the flush condition of health, strength, &c., which belongs to it. We consider that the same condition and qualities, in a fitly trained man, may well be expected to advance far into the confines of what is generally termed old age. The ancients were full of the examples of this, and we see occasionally an intimation of it in modern fanciful writing.

MIDDLE AND OLD AGES.

Somebody who writes in the metaphorical style of the litterateurs of a century and a half ago, encloses some very useful wisdom in the following paragraph:

From forty to sixty a man who has properly regulated himself may be considered as in the prime of life. His matured strength of constitution renders him almost impervious to the attacks of disease, and experience has given his judgement the soundness of almost infallibility. His mind is resolute, firm and equal; all his functions are in the highest order; he assumes the mastery over business; builds up a competence on the foundation he has formed in early manhood, and passes through a period of life attended by many gratifications. Having gone a year or two past sixty, he arrives at a critical period in the road of existence; the river of death flows before him, and he remains at a stand-still. But athwart this river is a viaduct, called "The Turn of Life," which, if crossed in safety, leads to the valleys of "Old Age," round which the river winds, and then flows beyond without a boat or causeaway [*sic*] to effect its passage. The bridge is, however, constructed of fragile materials, and it depends upon how it is trodden whether it bend or break. Gout, apoplexy, and other bad characters are also in the vicinity to waylay the traveler and thrust him from the pass; but let him gird up his loins, and provide himself with a fitting staff, and he may trudge on in safety, with perfect composure.

Indeed, a very amusing and interesting volume might be written on the theme the above paragraph treats of, in the style of Bunyan's "Pilgrim's Progress." It would come home as close to the feelings and experience of people as any thing in that celebrated work— substituting the physical for the moral and spiritual, which latter Bunyan has treated with such marvelous ingenuity and power.

The periods of middle and old age are perhaps the finest, in some of the most important respects, through life. We dwell upon this the more, because we notice that too many of the tendencies of American city life so destroy the chances for this middle and old perfection, that it seems to have gone out of mind. No one seems to understand that *there is attainable a high flush condition of stamina, strength, vigor, personality, clearness and manly beauty and love-power, thoroughly sustained many years, in perfect specimens of trained health, through middle and old age, towering in its ripeness and completeness, till it rivals and fully equals the best and handsomest specimens of early manhood— and indeed transcends them!*

The mind of one familiar with antique models at once turns to the palmy ages of Greek art, and of its Roman copyists. All the grandest characters who appear in it are middle-aged or old men—and they rise into collossal [sic] proportions. No matter what the field—war, adventure, love, or what not—they are the principal figures in the foreground, or eminent above the mass.

But how can we expect specimens of perfect physique, these years, to rival the ancient ones, unless the models are more steadily presented before us? As things are, all the ambition of the young is turned in intellectual channels—to a monstrous development of the mind, and of what is called "knowledge."

TOO MUCH BRAIN ACTION AND FRETTING.

In addition to what we have already said in preceding articles, it seems necessary for us, as a counterbalance, to add a few further remarks on this part of the subject. It is indisputable that many lives are prematurely sacrificed by a too restless intellect and brain—the action thereof literally rushing a man into his grave. All through America, especially North and East, not only among the writers, lawyers, editors, preachers, &c., but through the ranks of the masses, *there is altogether too much brain action*, sapping the foundation of life, and of the enjoyment of life. The intellect is too restless. The parent bequeaths the tendency to the child—and he, when grown up, has it in increased force. Some direct it toward money-making, others to religion, and so on. It eats into the whole temperament, and produces reaction; then for fits of "the blues," and an unhappy life.

The remedy lies with the person himself. He must let up on his brain and thought-power, and form more salutary and reasonable habits—which, by-the-way, are formed astonishingly soon, if once sternly resolved upon, and the practice commenced in earnest. The homely advice to "take things easy," applies with particular force to this sort of persons. Most of the ills they labor under, and the dispensations they dread, are imaginary; at any rate, imagination distorts them, and magnifies them out of all proportion. A little calmness and coolness puts to flight three-fourths of the evils of their lives.

But the mere fact of intense mental action is itself a misfortune. We repeat again, how much it is to be regretted that, in the prevailing theories of education, the desire to make young persons prodigies of learning, statistics, science, and mental brilliancy, have gone so far in what we are clear is a very dangerous and unwholesome direction—that is, if manly health and happiness are, as they are, first to he [sic] considered in a boy's and young man's life. These hints should be more thoroughly accepted by parents and teachers, and acted upon in families and schools.

By undue action, development and concentration, the brain begets upon the system and character a high state of excitability and inflammation often resulting in later life, and sometimes in middle age, in the condition of softening of the brain. It is a terribly [sic] malady, not so much for its amount of suffering as for the pitiable condition to which it reduces the most collossal [sic] intellect. Sir Walter Scott, Daniel Webster, Dean Swift, and hundreds of persons of lesser note, are instances of the play of cause and effect resulting in this fearful disease, which has various phases, but is of one general type. Literary men, and persons in the excitement of political life, are especially liable to it, from the uncertain nature of their employment and popularity, the strain upon the brain-power, and probably also from the cares and jealousies that are forever multiplying among them, aggravated no doubt by their generally reckless habits, and irritable tempers; and besides from something inherent in the nature of their occupation, waiting upon the public. To them, too, the only salvation is in rising superior to all such petty fears and bickerings—otherwise they are at any time liable to the consequences of which we have just given the most signal examples.

And yet, as before intimated, a diseased brain, and a sadly inflamed state of the nervous system, are by no means confined to literary men. We Americans altogether, all classes, *think too much, and too morbidly,*—brood, meditate, become sickly with our own pallid fancies, allowing them to swarm upon us by night and by day. It will, of course, sound strange in the ears of many to say so, but we are fain to proclaim over and over again, in our loudest and most emphatic tones, *We are too intellectual a race.* To the brain

The physique of the Brain from a literary Life.

Take Notice

In addition to these ailments literary men are subjected, by the very nature of their pursuits, to an excitable condition of the nervous system, which often manifests itself in inordinate apprehension about small matters, and great irritability of temper. "These," says Thackrah, "mark, in common life and ordinary circumstances, the character of men who, on great occasions, manifest the noblest benevolence, courage, and coolness." This constant excitability not unfrequently leads to inflammation, and sometimes to a softening, of the brain. Dean Swift and Daniel Webster, both of whom possessed great intellects and thought profoundly, died of this affection. It is well known that the Herculean tasks assumed by Sir Walter Scott, in advanced age, led to an affection of the brain, which first dimmed and then extinguished forever the lofty intellect of this great writer, months before his body yielded to final dissolution.

Yet, notwithstanding these evils incident to to a literary life, its average duration is of a respectable length, and frequently extends to great age. This was particularly the case among the ancient philosophers, who alternated their time between abstruse studies in the closet, and conversations and speeches in the midst of their fellow-citizens in the open air and public buildings in which they were wont to assemble. Besides, their philosophy generally taught them to be placid in temper, cautious in language, abstemious in diet, and unmoved by surrounding circumstances, all of which tend to the prolongation of life. Plato died at 81; Xenocrates at 82; Thales at 89; and Democritus at 100.

Modern philosophers, whose works are not always represented by their lives, although not short-lived, fall below the age attained by the ancients. Thus, Bacon died at 64; Boyle at 65; Newton at 84; and Harvey at 88. In our own country, Rittenhouse died at 64; and Franklin at 84; and of those engaged in other literary pursuits, Noah Webster, the lexicographer, died at 85; and Dr. Thacher at 90. M. Brunard selected at random one hundred and fifty savans, one half from the Academy of Sciences, the other from the Academy of Belles Lettres, and found that their average at death was a little above 70 years.

DEFINITION ... NUMBERS.

1. AMATIVENESS, Sexual and ement—purity.
2. PHILOPROGENITIVENESS andeur.
3. ADHESIVENESS, Friendship. Copying—pattering.
4. UNION FOR LIFE, Duality in marriage.
5. INHABITIVENESS, Love of home—patriotism.
6. CONTINUITY, Completion—one thing at once.
7. COMBATIVENESS, Resistance—defence.
8. DESTRUCTIVENESS, Executiveness—force.
9. ALIMENTIVENESS, Appetite—hunger.
10. ACQUISITIVENESS, Frugality—accumulation.
11. SECRETIVENESS, Policy—management.
12. CAUTIOUSNESS, Prudence—provision.
13. APPROBATIVENESS, Honor—ambition.
14. SELF ESTEEM, Self respect and confidence.
15. FIRMNESS, Decision—perseverance.
16. CONSCIENTIOUSNESS, Justice—moral principle.
17. HOPE, Expectation—enterprise.
18. MARVELLOUSNESS, Spirituality—prescience.
19. VENERATION, Devotion—worship of God.
20. BENEVOLENCE, Kindness—goodness.
21. CONSTRUCTIVENESS, Mechanical ingenuity.

23. MIRTHFULNESS, Jocoseness—wit—fun.
24. INDIVIDUALITY, Observation—secativeness.
25. FORM, Recollection of shape.
26. SIZE, Measures by the eye.
27. WEIGHT, Balancing—muscular control.
28. COLOR, Judgment of colors.
29. ORDER, Method—system—arrangement.
30. CALCULATION, Mental arithmetic.
31. LOCALITY, Recollection of places.
32. EVENTUALITY, Memory of facts.
33. TIME, Cognizance of duration.
34. TUNE, Music—melody by ear.
35. LANGUAGE, Expression of ideas.
36. CAUSALITY, Causes applied to effects.
37. COMPARISON, Inductive reasoning.
C. HUMAN NATURE, Discernment of character
D. AGREEABLENESS, Pleasantness—suavity.

WHITMAN'S NOTES ON "THE PHYSIQUE" OF THE BRAIN.

parts of our structure we draw off much that should be devoted to the body, the muscles—neglecting what all men first require, to be fine animals. We suppose we shall excite some disdain by such remarks, but they include undoubted truths necessary to be told.

Not that calm and wholesome brain-action, tempered with regular exercise and development of the body, is meant to be called injurious. On the contrary, *that* no doubt tends to longevity, and is consistent with the best health, and is perhaps a part of it—as it is the crowning glory of a rational being, and endows the finest condition of the body with grace and beauty, otherwise lacking.

No; duly tempered mental labor is justified in the lives of its votaries in all ages. Plato lived to be 81 years of age, Diogenes 90, Democritus 100, Zeno 102, and indeed all the most celebrated philosophers and poets of ancient times seem to have been long-lived, and to have produced their most famous works in old age. In more modern times Newton attains the age of 84, Harvey that of 88, Franklin 84, Noah Webster 85, and so on. In France, a statistician, selecting at random one hundred and fifty scientific and literary men, one half from the Academy of Sciences, the other half from that of Belles Lettres, found the average age of life attained by them to be the ripe age of 70 years.

Of the ancient poets and philosophers, it is always worthy of remembrance that some of the greatest of them are as much celebrated for their physical strength and beauty as for their mental. Pythagoras, the father and master, was of large, imposing and elegantly shaped body; he often entered the arena and contended with the athletes for the prizes in running, leaping, fighting, &c., and won them too! We might ask our modern puny and dandy tribes of literary men to make a note of such facts.

CITY LIFE.

The great requisites of health being good air, proper food, and appropriate exercise, the two latter of course can be as well accomplished in the city as country—leaving the matter of pure air as the only doubtful point. And why could we not have a good atmosphere

CITY OF

NEW YORK, LITH AND

BIRDSEYE VIEW OF NEW YORK IN THE 1850s.

EAST RIVER   TOMPKINS SQUARE   BAYLEY AND MORGAN IRON WORKS   SOUTH FERRY [BROOKLYN SIDE.]   WILLIAMSBURGH   CORLEARS HOOK
              BLACKWELL ISLAND   CATHOLIC CHURCH, 2⁰ ST.   PECK SLIP FERRY.   BROOKLYN HEIGHTS
                      UNITED STATES HOTEL   FULTON FERRY.
                  HARPERS BUILDINGS
                  WALL ST. FERRY.

W YORK.

152 NASSAU STREET

NEW YORK'S BROADWAY IN 1860.

TENEMENT HOUSING IN NEW YORK CITY, OUTSIDE

. . . AND INSIDE.

in the city? The reader, accustomed to the prevailing state of things, may think this is a very unreasonable question, and yet we utter it in all seriousness. Because we think a clear and deeply based popular appreciation of the truth, with all its play of causes and effects, relating to this point, would almost certainly in the end lead to the means of having the kind of atmosphere we speak of.

The means of accomplishing this most desirable result consist of a perfect system of sewerage, in which no part or section of the city whatever shall be neglected—and in an organized plan, whose details should be overseen by the police, for gathering and carrying away daily all the garbage and refuse of the city; and these details should be joined with a rigid and perpetual sanitary inspection of every block in the city, every street, every alley, every yard. But could this be done? Of course it could be done; and the day will arrive when it *will* be done. Then the airs of our streets, instead of being reeking and pestiferous during the hot season, will not offend the most delicate nostrils.

There is, however, much in cities, it remains to be said, which is not sufficiently appreciated as offering great advantages for health. The markets, with their luxuries, afford their selection from a list of simple articles, to him who realizes the importance of attaining a fine physique, primarily through the stomach, the careful choice of his daily aliment. This is no trifling advantage, and it is one which is often deficient in the country; there the prevailing food is apt to be salt meat, vegetables, &c., which (the truth may as well be told,) are by no means the articles most favorable to produce a race of clearblooded and sound-conditioned men. The often-mentioned superiority of the country receives a great drawback on this account.

And with respect to the matter of good air, it is to be recollected that it is of serious importance only through the three or four hot months of the year. We do not intend to deprecate its vital bearings upon health, but are not willing to have the truth overstated, or made worse than it is. During the fall, winter and spring, most of our cities are as healthy as any country place. Nor let it be forgotten that a very large proportion of country places are pervaded with an atmosphere more or less bad and unwholesome. Exhalations

PRINTING HOUSE SQUARE, NEW YORK.

and vapors rise and spread around, often in neighborhoods where everything looks fair and inviting to the eye. The frame-racking and blood-thinning disease of fever and ague, which annually ruins its tens of thousands of men, is one of the results of country air.

In general terms, it may be stated that the rude forms and florid complexions of healthy specimens of country life, are to be attributed to their more natural hours, early rising, exercise, open air, and their being less under the influence of the artificial habits and overtaxed mentality which mark the life of the citizen. If citizens would only make a reasonable use of their many priceless advantages, knock off some of their artificial habits, and take daily exercise, avoiding all dissipations, they would soon show not only equally noble speci- mens of health with the country, but superior to them.

[CONCLUDED NEXT WEEK.]

The New York Atlas

Vol. 21, No. 32

Manly Health and Training,

December 26, 1858

With Off-Hand Hints Toward Their Conditions

By Mose Velsor

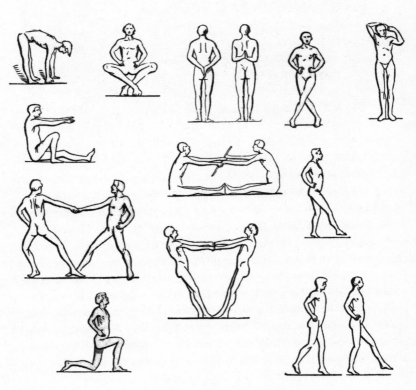

A SERIES OF EXERCISES.

CAN WE THEN HAVE AS FINE A RACE OF MEN IN MODERN ARTIFICIAL LIFE, AS IN RUDER AGES?

Are not the present races of men, through the civilized world, far less hardy and sound, less perfect as specimens of noble physique, than they were one hundred, two hundred, and three hundred years ago? We much fear that this question will have to be answered in the affirmative. We have heard it stoutly maintained that the present races *are* as physically perfect as any previous ones; but our own opinion is that the prevalence of a far more artificial life, and the occupation of such myriads of men, these times, in close factories, and all kinds of indoor work, joined with other causes, (among which may be specified the frightful adulteration of most of the grocery articles of food,) have had a deleterious effect on the general health, in comparison with what, according to all accounts, must have been presented by former times.

Is this inevitable? that is the most important question. Can we not have the principal advantages of modern civilization, with their factories, vast ranks of employees, and all the grand accompaniments of great cities, without having also a deteriorated race of men? We are clear enough that this latter is *not* the necessary result; but that, in easy accord with modern forms, with factories, the life of cities, and all the modern requirements and usages, these may be conformed to, and still, under training and physiological laws, the health kept robust, and a noble physique developed. We believe that *reason, resolution, and training, are equal to all resolutions and emergencies*. But it is necessary that working men, with the rest,

205

should understand, without softening the matter, that their best salvation depends upon their entering upon, and a persistent adherence in, a rigid course of training and habits of health. With that made general, the difference between the hardy life of old times, and our artificial forms of life, would disappear—and a fine race of men be produced.

COULD THERE BE AN ENTIRE NATION OF VIGOROUS AND BEAUTIFUL MEN?

We think it not too much to demand that not only the theories of public education, but that the municipal government, in appropriate ways, should recognize and favor *manly training*, so conducive to the public health, and to filling the land with a superior and every way better race of men. The legislative authorities have long recognized the propriety of caring for the *intellectual* development of the young; but we believe, and think we have advanced reasons to prove, not only that the physical stands first in order, and should take precedence of the other, but that the other cannot be carried on, with any degree of profit and safety, except it be combined with the training and strengthening of a fine physique, and founded upon it.

We are not prepared to say exactly in what way the recognition and support of the authorities should be bestowed. It is enough at present to broach the matter, giving a few of the reasons that have a bearing upon it—and then leaving the case to work out its consequences.

As to the schools, we have long been of opinion that no school should be established, in city or country, without its training department, its gymnasium, where health, vigor, cleanliness, activity, and the simple and broad laws of physiology, are exemplified for the young. We do not mean merely places of exercise, but of training in its full sense, with reference to the establishment of good habits of diet, self-denial, chastity, temperance, &c., or of inculcating the knowledge of them, at any rate, so that they may be generally diffused. We are encouraged to hope that these articles, among many means now at work, may help towards producing that most desirable result.

To us it is quite certain that, by right observances, *an entire nation of men may be vigorous and beautiful*—that is, that they will form the rule, and be common, while feebleness and bad looks will be the exception. What a result this would be! As it is, even with all their excesses, their dyspepsia, their abuse and overtasking of the brain, the Americans are undoubtedly the handsomest men, as a race, now upon the earth. What would they be with general sound health, and perfect physiques?

STRENGTH OF FUTURE AMERICANS.

It is a favorite theory of ours that the generations of men, in America, have yet to witness the immense perfection of physical strength that is to be attained, and to become quite general— common enough, at any rate, not to excite the remarks it now does, or serve as a wonder, a monstrosity. We have in our time seen some pretty tall specimens of strength, among the rest a Belgian, who was exhibited a few years ago in New York, named J. A. Bihin. He could lift from the ground, with his hands, eight hundred pounds, and straighten his back, when stooping, under a weight of two tons. His size, however, was the most formidable part of him. He was seven feet and a half in height; he measured fifty inches round the chest, twenty-eight inches round the thigh, and twenty-two inches round the calf of the leg—and his weight was three hundred and twenty pounds. He was no monstrosity, but was of symmetrical form throughout.

But very great strength may reside in persons of ordinary general size, and is often to be found there. Good parentage is a great thing; but training, and proper and systematic exercise, are also capable of bringing out strength to a very great degree, in those who have not inherited it.

As an illustration of the power of man's endurance, it is well known that a properly trained pedestrian can tire out a horse, (it is said any horse) on a pull sufficiently long to tax the powers of each to the utmost. In oriental countries, the performances of the Indian footmen and runners, stage after stage, day after day, are almost incredible. There seems to be no tire to the soles of their feet. They are brought up to it from their earliest youth, and so get to have unsurpassed wind and bottom. All this, too, on a simple sustenance of rice and milk, dried fruits, and the like—as, to many of them, a meat diet is unknown.

MORE ABOUT EATING AND DRINKING.

Probably the last as well [*sic*] first thing to be mentioned, and attended to, for one who considers the subject of health, and of putting himself in systematic training for its conditions, is that of diet—what he may eat and drink, and what he must avoid. Here will generally be the hardest tug of all. Everybody loves good living; and the ingenuity of modern cookery has created so many dishes to satisfy that love, that few will, at first, be willing to apply that stern check on their appetites which is necessary. It needs to be stated, however, with entire candor, that whoso wants a fine physique, continued through middle age, and carried on to old age, must fulfil this part of the conditions, or the rest will be of no avail. Most of the artificial luxuries, solid and liquid, must be cut off. Soups, pastry, fat, onions, gravies, puddings, sauces, brandy, gin, coffee, jellies, may be specified, not as by any means comprising the whole list of contraband articles, but as heading the list; nor must we forget to put in cigars and tobacco. It is useless to make a stand on these things. To the young man who sets out with the will to accomplish the end we have been placing before him, the result must reward him for his denial of these and similar gratifications.

Have greater care, very much greater care, in the choice of articles used for your food, and also in the manner of their being cooked. It is no discredit to a man, young or old, for him to show that he is jealous of his condition, and that he is determined to use the means which will preserve that condition.

What then may be eaten? If you want to know what is *best* to a hearty man, who takes plenty of exercise and fresh air, and don't want any pimples on his face or body, we will answer, (perhaps very much to your astonishment,) a simple diet of rare-cooked beef, seasoned with a little salt, and accompanied with stale bread or sea-biscuit. Mutton, if lean and tender, is also commendable.

Pork should not be eaten. Butter, pepper, catsup, oil, and most of the "dressings," must also be eschewed. Lobster and chicken salad, cabbage, cucumbers, and even potatoes, are to be turned away from. Salted meats are not to be partaken of either; and salt itself, as a seasoning, is to be used as sparingly as possible. There is quite a great popular error we will mention here, on the use of salt for food. It by no means has the merit that is generally attributed to it; but, on the contrary, if used to excess, causes a very vicious state of the blood. Salt is a mineral, and it is not solved in the juices of the body.

With early rising and "taking an airing," there will be no need of an appetite for breakfast, which, under the rules we have stated, may be pretty fully indulged in. The same as to dinner. The supper, which must not be at a late hour, we would recommend always to be light—occasionally making this meal to consist of fruit, either fresh, during the middle and latter part of the summer—and of stewed fruit during the winter and spring. As to a hearty supper of rich viands, that must be forborne on all occasions—especially by those who have to use the vocal organs in public; speakers, singers, actors, preachers, &c. For it is a well-settled fact that the voice is seriously injured by such suppers, and the "wind" (as it is called in sporting phrase,) gradually weakened and broken up. If the singer or public speaker only knew how incomparably superior his voice would become, and how steady and reliable on all occasions, under the rigid physiological habitudes we have been laying down, he would need no further persuasion from us to initiate and persevere in these rules, especially as regards diet. It is to be understood that there is an intimate analogy between many parts of the training necessary for athletic physical performances, and that necessary for a first-class vocalist.

Of the drink, the same stern system of abstinence is to be observed. Dr. Forsyth, a great training authority among "the fancy" on the other side of the Atlantic, says: "Medically speaking, as regards drink, we should say that water would be the best liquor in training. But it is never given alone in modern times, as it is thought to be a weakening diluent. The ancient athletes, however, were allowed nothing but water, or a sort of thick and sweet wine. The drink preferred by modern English trainers, for the ring, is good old malt liquor, in bottles, and as mild as possible, without any perceptible tartness or harshness, (this is for the English climate, however, not American, which is different.) Those who do not like malt liquor, particularly for breakfast, (they never have coffee or tea,) are allowed by the trainers a small quantity of wine or water. Cool tea is sometimes permitted, but this reluctantly, as it is not considered strengthening. *Hot, or even warm liquor, of any kind, is considered as enervating and weakening* to the tone of the system, and is not given—except warm gruel or beef tea, when taking physic. By the best English trainers, no spirits, (brandy, gin, &c.) are ever permitted, not even with water, at any time, or under any pretence; if used, it is always against their serious protest. No milk is allowed either, as, if creamy and rich, it is too fattening and plethoric. No drink is permitted, before meals, unless there be distressing thirst.["]

Among the English, Scotch, and Irish trainers, quite a favorite refreshment to be given their men is a "gruel," a compound of oatmeal, water and salt. This is carefully prepared, quite a large quantity, in a pitcher, and it is free to the man in training, at any hour, day or night, at exercise or between meals—with no other restriction than the man's own appetite. We have heard so much of oatmeal, and of the potent sanitary results of using it as an aliment, that we confess we are curious to see it introduced and tried in America. Would it not make a very cheap, simple, and agreeable addition to the variety of our food here? Cannot some agriculturalist or food speculator take the hint?

Among the additional rules that may be mentioned with regard to eating, are such as follow:

Make the principal part of your meal always of one dish.

Chew the food well, and do not eat fast.

Wait until you feel a good appetite before eating—even if the regular hour for a meal has arrived.

We have spoken against the use of the potato. It still remains to be said that if it agrees with you, and you are fond of it, it may be used; it is best properly boiled, at the morning meal. Do not partake of it, however, except in moderation.

Drink very sparingly at each meal; better still not at all—only between meals, when thirsty.

Any article craved by the appetite, and not of essential importance to be prohibted [*sic*], may be allowed in moderation. This permission, however, does not extend to spiritous liquors.

In general terms, avoid what disagrees with you; for there are, to every individual case, certain rules which apply to it alone. Study these, as they relate to your own case.

There are even cases where a vegetarian diet applies. Such persons have an antipathy to eat meat. Of course, to them, it follows that they must eat what their appetite will permit, and what agrees with them.

A cheerful and gay temper during and immediately after meals, is a great help to health.

Never take any violent or strained exercise immediately after a meal.

Our own opinion is, that if things could be so arranged, it would be best to make the heartiest meal in the morning, instead of the middle of the day. This, however, is contrary to modern usage, and would in most cases be inconvenient.

Use no artificial means, "bitters," or any other stimulants, to create a false appetite. If you have none, do not eat till it comes.

Finally, our repeated charge is that all spices, pepper, strong mustard, pickles, pungent preserves, bitters, tobacco, and strong liquor generally, not only injure the stomach by their excessive stimulus and fiery qualities, but the tone of the palate, the taste, by making plain and wholesome food become tasteless. To one, for instance, who is used to plastering over his beefsteak with a thick coat of pungent sauce of some kind, mustard or the like, a plain broiled steak, seasoned only with a pinch of salt, would relish poorly indeed. Yet the latter is by far the best for health; and there is no sauce like regular and daily exercise, and fresh air.

A WORD OF ENCOURAGEMENT.

What then to persons in a bad condition? After the body has been reduced by illness, and the whole organism racked and wrecked by powerful drugs, as well as prostrating disease; after the energy and endurance of youth and early manhood have passed, and one has become the slave of custom, and has, perhaps, given up the hope of health, is there still a chance remaining for such a man? Even so. We do not promise anything in the style of some of the medicine advertisements, but say that through simple and natural methods, there arises such virtue out of a few plain laws, and following a few sanitary rules, that, in due time, the result will be, in nine cases out of ten, health and comfort.

CONCLUSION.

We know very well that we have not gone over the whole field, but that much, very much, might still be mentioned, having a bearing, more or less remote, on manly training and the conditions of strength and a perfect physique. In our off-hand articles, however, we have not so much been induced by the desire to comprehend the whole subject, as to broach it to the reader, and give him a few leading hints, out of which the rest will follow; for he who once gets started, fully awakened to the precious endowment he has in his own body, beyond all other wealth that can be acquired by man, will not cease his interest in the subject, but will go on toward a greater and greater degree of inquiry, knowledge, and perfection.

One great point we would again impress on you, reader, (we have before reverted to it,) is the fact that *your own individual case doubtless has points and circumstances which more or less modify all the general laws, and perhaps call for special ones, for yourself.* This is an important consideration in all theories and statements of wealth [*sic*].

What we have given has been the general statement—the great highway of manly health, on which all may travel, and must travel; and this is indeed for all. Still there are many little by-ways and lanes leading to particular homes.

Common reason, and such knowledge as we have hastily outlined in the foregoing articles, will clear the way for you in most particulars. Occasionally the advice of an intelligent and conscientious physician may be necessary—and such men are to be found yet. But, generally speaking, the benefit of medicine, or medical advice is very much overrated. Nature's medicines are simple food, nursing, air, rest, cheerful encouragement, and the like. The art of the surgeon is certain and determined—that of the physician is vague, and affords an easy cover to ignorance and quackery. The land is too full of poisonous medicines and incompetent doctors— the less you have to do with them the better.

Our remarks, as we stated ln [*sic*] the beginning, are especially intended for young men. If read over with that attention and earnestness which we are sure they deserve, and then followed with faith and manly perseverance, we feel it not too much to say, we can promise that reliable result, the purpose of all, *a sound body and the condition of perfect health.*

In that condition your whole body and consequently your spirits too, will be elevated to a state by other persons unknown—made clear and light, inwardly and outwardly elastic—made solid, strong, and yet of rapid movement. A singular charm, better than what is called beauty, flickers out of and over your face; a transparency beams in the eyes, both in the iris and the white; you exhibit a new grace in walk, and indeed in all your movements—in the voice, which rings clearer, and has melody, perhaps, for the first time. Few are aware how much a sound condition of the whole organism of the body has to do with the voice.

Not only the looks and movement, but the *feelings*, undergo a transformation. It may almost be said that sorrows and disappointments cease: there is no more borrowing trouble. With perfect health, (and regular agreeable occupation,) there are no low spirits, and cannot be. A man realizes the old myth of the poets; he is a god walking the earth. He not only feels new powers in himself— he sees new beauties everywhere. His faculties, his eyesight, his hearing, all acquire superior capacity to give him pleasure. Indeed, merely to *move* is a pleasure; the play of the limbs in motion is enough. To breathe, to eat and drink the simplest food, outvie the most costly of previous enjoyments.

Many of those before hand [*sic*] gratifications, especially those of the palate, drink, spirits, fat grease [*sic*], coffee, strong spices, pepper, pastry, crust, mixtures, &c., are put aside voluntarily—become distasteful. The appetite is voracious enough, but it demands simple aliment. Those others were was vexations [*sic*] dreams—and now the awakening.

How happily pass the days! A blithe carol bursts from the throat to greet the opening morn. The fresh air is inhaled—exercise spreads the chest—every sinew responds to the call upon it—the whole system seems to *laugh* with glee. The occupations of the forenoon pass swiftly and cheerfully along; the dinner is eaten with such zest as only perfect health can give—and the remaining hours still continue to furnish, as they arrive, new sources of filling themselves, and affording contentment.

How sweet the evenings! The labors of the day over—whether on a farm, or in the factory, the workshop, the forge or furnace, the shipyard, or what not—*then* rest is realized indeed. For who else but such as they *can* realize it? It is a luxury almost worth being poor to enjoy. The healthy sleep—the breathing deep and regular—the unbroken and profound repose—the night as it passes soothing and renewing the whole frame. Yes, nature surely keeps her choicest blessings for the slumber of health—and nothing short of that can ever know what true sleep is.

Zachary Turpin's
Acknowledgments:

For their assistance in the preparation of this book, I would like to thank Stefan Schöberlein, Stephanie Blalock, and Ed Folsom. They deserve every credit for its elegance and accuracy, as does Aja Pollock, copy editor extraordinaire. I am also indebted to the American Antiquarian Society and the Penn State University Libraries for the materials reproduced herein; to the *Walt Whitman Quarterly Review*, where those materials first saw the light of day; to Kathryn Huck, of Regan Arts, for her patience and encouragement; and to the University of Houston English Department for its incomparable support. Finally, I dedicate this book to my wife, Markie, and my two sons, John and Henry, who make me everything I am.

PHOTO CREDITS

CLUB-SWINGING.

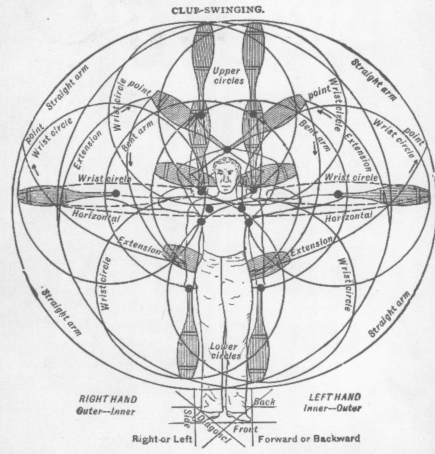

THE PRINCIPLES OF CLUB SWINGING. Fig. 1.